HUMAN
DEVOLUTION

HUMAN
DEVOLUTION

A VEDIC ALTERNATIVE
TO DARWIN'S THEORY

MICHAEL A. CREMO

**TORCHLIGHT
PUBLISHING**

Readers interested in the subject matter of this book
are invited to correspond with the author at:

Bhaktivedanta Book Publishing Inc.
3764 Watseka Avenue
Los Angeles, CA 90034
Or visit http://www.humandevolution.com

First printing 2003
Second printing 2008

Published by Bhaktivedanta Book Publishing, Inc. Science Books Division
(BBT Science Books) for the Bhaktivedanta Institute.

Exclusively distributed by Torchlight Publishing, Inc.
P. O. Box 52, Badger, CA 93603
www.torchlight.com

Library of Congress Cataloging-in-Publication Data

Cremo, Michael A., 1948–
  Human devolution : a Vedic alternative to Darwin's theory / Michael A.
Cremo.
      p. cm.
Includes bibliographical references and index.
  ISBN 978-0-89213-334-5
  1. Prehistoric peoples. 2. Human evolution. 3. Anthropology,
Prehistoric. 4. Hinduism. I. Title.

  GN741.C746 2004
  599.93'8—dc21

                    2003006505

Dedicated to

His Divine Grace
A. C. Bhaktivedanta Swami Prabhupada

*om ajnana-timirandhasya jnananjana-shalakaya
caksur unmilitam yena tasmai shri-gurave namah*

CONTENTS

INTRODUCTION

My book *Forbidden Archeology*, coauthored with Richard L. Thompson, documents archeological evidence for extreme human antiquity, consistent with the *Puranas*, the historical writings of ancient India. This evidence places a human presence so far back in time as to call into question the Darwinian account of human origins.

In his review of *Forbidden Archeology* published in *Geoarchaeology* (1994 v. 9, pp. 337–340), Kenneth Feder said, "When you attempt to deconstruct a well-accepted paradigm, it is reasonable to expect that a new paradigm be suggested in its place. The authors of *Forbidden Archeology* do not do this, and I would like to suggest a reason for their neglect here. Wishing to appear entirely scientific, the authors hoped to avoid a detailed discussion of their own beliefs."

It is not true that my coauthor and I were trying to avoid a detailed discussion of our own alternative account. Rather we were hoping to ignite just such a discussion. But some practical considerations compelled us to proceed in stages. In my introduction to *Forbidden Archeology*, I wrote: "Our research program led to results we did not anticipate, and hence a book much larger than originally envisioned." I was genuinely surprised at the massive number of cases of archeological evidence for extreme human antiquity that turned up during my eight years of historical research. *Forbidden Archeology* went to press with over nine hundred pages. "Because of this," I wrote in the introduction, "we have not been able to develop in this volume our ideas about an alternative to current theories of human origins. We are therefore planning a second volume relating our extensive research results in this area to our Vedic source material."

Human Devolution: A Vedic Alternative to Darwin's Theory is that second volume. The reasons for its late appearance have more to do with the time it takes to research and write such a book rather than any desire to avoid a detailed discussion of a Vedic alternative to Darwinism.

Nevertheless, I am not unhappy that *Human Devolution* appeared after *Forbidden Archeology* rather than along with it. Before presenting an alternative to the Darwinian concept of human origins, it is reasonable to show that one is really necessary. I have therefore welcomed the chance to introduce to scientists and other scholars the evidence in *Forbidden Archeology* before moving on to systematically presenting an alternative. After hearing the *Forbidden Archeology* presentations, many ask, "If we did not evolve from the apes, then what alternative explanation do you propose?" To them, I reply, "Do you admit a new explanation is required? If not, I have more work to do in showing that one is required. And if you do admit that a new explanation is really required, then it is not just my responsibility to come up with a new explanation. It is also your responsibility. We should all be thinking about this. Of course, I have some ideas about what the explanation should be, but you should also."

My first scientific presentation of *Forbidden Archeology's* evidence and Vedic perspective was in December of 1994 at the World Archaeological Congress in New Delhi, India. My paper "Puranic Time and the Archeological Record," delivered in the section on time and archeology chaired by Tim Murray and D. P. Agrawal, drew a large, appreciative audience. That paper was later chosen for publication in the peer reviewed conference proceedings volume *Time and Archeology,* edited by Tim Murray and published by Routledge in its One World Archaeology series in 1999 (pp. 38–48).

In March 1995, I presented my paper "The Impact of *Forbidden Archeology*" at the Kentucky State University Institute for Liberal Studies Sixth Annual Conference on Science and Culture. This paper set forth the Vedic background for my research. It also reviewed the initial scientific reactions to the publication of *Forbidden Archeology.*

In July 1996, I was invited by the Institute for the Study of Theoretical Questions of the Russian Academy of Sciences to lecture on *Forbidden Archeology* in Moscow. I then spoke about my work at a symposium organized by the Institute for Oriental Studies of the Russian Academy of Sciences. After my presentation, Indologist Evgeniya Y. Vanina commented: "I think that the statement you have made, and your paper, are very important because they touch upon ... how to look at the texts of the classical tradition as sources of information. There is a tendency among scholars to say whatever the *Vedas*—and the *Puranas,* the *Ramayana,* and the *Mahabharata*—are saying, it is all myth and concoction, and there is no positive information in it. . . . I think that such a negativist attitude toward the ancient and early medieval Indian texts as sources of information should definitely be discarded." While I was in Russia, I was also invited to give a talk on *Forbidden Archeology* to a large audience of physicists at Dubna, the science city outside Moscow. In October 1996, I spoke about the evidence in *Forbidden Archeology* at the International Conference on Revisiting Indus Sarasvati Age and Ancient India in Atlanta.

In July 1997, in Liège, Belgium, at the XXth International Congress for History of Science, I presented a detailed study of one of the cases documented in *Forbidden Archeology.* This paper, "The Later Discoveries of Boucher de Perthes at Moulin Quignon and Their Impact on the Moulin Quignon Jaw Controversy," appeared in *Proceedings of the XXth International Congress of History of Science, Vol. X., Earth Sciences, Geography, and Cartography,* edited by Goulven Laurent and published by Brepols in 2002 (pp. 39–56). In October of 1997, I presented lectures on *Forbidden Archeology* to students and faculty of archeology, anthropology, and biology at the University of Amsterdam, the Free University of Amsterdam, the University of Leiden, the University of Groningen, the University of Utrecht, and the University of Nijmegen in the Netherlands, and at the Catholic University of Louvain and University of Ghent in Belgium. In November of 1997, I lectured on *Forbidden Archeology* at universities in Hungary, including the Eötvös Loran Science University in Budapest, the University of Szeged, and the University of Eger.

In January 1999, I presented a paper titled "Forbidden Archeology of the Middle and Early Pleistocene" at the fourth World Archaeological Congress in Cape Town, South Africa. In March and April, I gave lectures on *Forbidden Archeology* at universities in England, Poland, Hungary, and the United States, including City University of London, the University of Warsaw, the University of Delaware, the University of Maryland, and Cornell University. In September 1999, I was invited to speak on *Forbidden Archeology* at the University of Oklahoma School of Geology and Geophysics, as part of the Shell Oil Colloquium Series. Also in September I presented a paper titled "Forbidden Archeology of the Paleolithic" at the European Association of Archaeologists Fifth Annual Meeting at Bournemouth in the United Kingdom. The paper was selected for inclusion in a conference proceedings volume edited by Ana C. Martins for British Archaeological Reports (forthcoming).

In March 2000, I was invited to speak on *Forbidden Archeology* in a lecture series of the Royal Institution of Great Britain, one of the world's oldest scientific societies. The lecture was given in the Royal Institution's headquarters in London. Later that year, in September, I presented a paper titled "The Discoveries of Carlos Ribeiro: A Controversial Episode in Nineteenth-Century European Archeology" at the European Association of Archaeologists Sixth Annual Meeting, in Lisbon, Portugal. In November 2000, I lectured on *Forbidden Archeology* at universities in Hungary.

In June 2001, I lectured on *Forbidden Archeology* at the Simon Fraser University in Vancouver, Canada. In September 2001, my paper "The Discoveries of Belgian Geologist Aimé Louis Rutot at Boncelles, Belgium: An Archeological Controversy from the Early Twentieth Century" was accepted for presentation at the XXIVth Congress of the International Union of Prehistoric and Protohistoric Sciences, held in September of that year in Liège, Belgium. In October 2001, I lectured on *Forbidden Archeology* at Pennsylvania State University and Cornell University. In November 2001, I lectured on *Forbidden Archeology* at the Charles University in Prague, in the Czech Republic, at the invitation of the faculty of philosophy.

In January and February 2002, I toured South India, with lectures at universities and other scientific and cultural institutions, such as the Bharatiya Vidya Bhavan in Mumbai (Bombay) and the Ana University in Chennai (Madras). In April and May 2002, I toured the Ukraine and Slovenia, speaking at universities and scientific institutions such as the Kiev Mogilanskaya Academy and the Institute of Archeology of the Ukrainian Academy of Sciences. I also spoke to archeologists in the archeology department of the Dnepropetrovsk Historical Museum. In November and December I returned to the Ukraine for another series of such talks at universities and historical museums in Odessa, Kharkov, and Lvov. As I am writing this introduction in December 2002, I am preparing a paper on the California gold mine discoveries reported by geologist Josiah D. Whitney for the fifth World Archaeological Congress, to be held in Washington, D.C., in June 2003. I am with archeologist Ana Martins of Portugal co-organizer of a section on history of archeology for the Congress.

In terms of ordinary scholarship, this modest collection of conference presentations, publications, and university lectures is not overly impressive. But given the explicit Vedic anti-evolutionary content of the papers and lectures they are, I believe, historically significant. They show that scientists and historians of science, whether or not they agree with the conclusions expressed in the presentations, now consider such presentations part of the active discourse in their disciplines. In that sense, they demonstrate that *Forbidden Archeology* accomplished one of its major purposes—sparking a discussion within the world of science about anomalous evidence for extreme human antiquity and a Vedic perspective on human origins. The presentations show that fundamentalist Darwinists within the world of science have not been as successful as they would like to be in maintaining a boundary between science and what they call religiously motivated "pseudoscience," to use their favored, and charmingly cranky, terminology. I personally do not accept the increasingly irrelevant distinctions some try to make between scientific and religious ways of knowing. I see myself as neither scientist nor religionist, but as a human being prepared to use various ways of knowing in the pursuit of truth.

Forbidden Archeology was widely reviewed in the professional journals of archeology, anthropology, and history of science. I included the complete texts of these reviews, along with related correspondence, in my book *Forbidden Archeology's Impact,* which attracted its own set of academic reviews. For example, Simon Locke wrote in *Public Understanding of Science* (1999 v. 8, no. 1, pp. 68–69), "Social constructivism, reflexivity, and all that is postmodern have inspired a variety of experiments in new literary forms to enliven the staid old world of the standard academic study.... As attempts to document the social process of knowledge production and capture some of its reflexivity, they are both consistent and courageous. So, too, Michael Cremo's book. The 'impact' the book documents is that of Cremo's earlier work, *Forbidden Archeology*. In this latest book rather than construct his own historical narrative, Cremo opts for the far more interesting strategy of directly reproducing much of the source material from which any such narrative would be constructed. The result is a multi-faceted textual kaleidoscope, in which a wide range of the many discourses surrounding contemporary science reflect and refract each other in fascinating array . . . Cremo has provided here a resource of considerable richness and value to analysts of public understanding [of science]. . . . It should also make a useful teaching resource as one of the best-documented case studies of 'science wars,' and raising a wide range of issues covering aspects of 'knowledge transfer' in a manner sure to be provocative in the classroom."

The positive or negative nature of the *Forbidden Archeology* reviews in academic journals is not as significant as the very fact that the reviews appeared at all. They represent another form of acknowledgement that the Vedic critique of the Darwinian theory of human evolution represented by *Forbidden Archeology* is a genuine part of contemporary science and scholarship. As Kenneth Feder said in his *Geoarchaeology* review (pp. 337–338), "The book itself represents something perhaps not seen before; we can fairly call it 'Krishna creationism' with no disrespect intended . . . While decidedly antievolutionary in perspective, this work is not the ordinary variety of antievolutionism in form, content, or style. In distinction to the usual brand of such writing, the authors use original sources and the book is well written. Further, the overall tone of the work is superior to that exhibited in ordinary creationist literature."

Jo Wodak and David Oldroyd published a lengthy review article about *Forbidden Archeology* in *Social Studies of Science* (1996 v. 26, pp. 192–213). In their article, titled "Vedic Creationism: A Further Twist to the Evolution Debate," they asked (p. 207), "So has *Forbidden Archeology* made any contribution at all to the literature on palaeoanthropology?" They concluded, "Our answer is a guarded 'yes', for two reasons." First, "the historical material . . . has not been scrutinized in such detail before," and, second, the book does "raise a central problematic regarding the lack of certainty in scientific 'truth' claims." They also commented (p. 198), "It must be acknowledged that *Forbidden Archeology* brings to attention many interesting issues that have not received much consideration from historians; and the authors' detailed examination of the early literature is certainly stimulating and raises questions of considerable interest, both historically and from the perspective of practitioners of SSK [sociology of scientific knowledge]. Indeed, they appear to have gone into some historical matters more deeply than any other writers of whom we have knowledge."

In the first few pages of their article (pp. 192–195), Wodak and Oldroyd gave extensive background information on: The International Society for Krishna Consciousness, of which the authors of *Forbidden Archeology* are members ("a modern variant of the Bhakti sects that have dominated Hindu religious life over the last one and a half millennia"); the teachings of the movement's founder, Bhaktivedanta Swami Prabhupada ("for Prabhupada, science gives no adequate account of the origin of the universe or of life"); the Bhaktivedanta Institute (they comment on "the boldness of its intellectual programme"); and Vedic chronology ("partial dissolutions, called *pralaya*, supposedly take place every 4.32 billion years, bringing catastrophes in which whole groups of living forms can disappear"). Wodak and Oldroyd also make many references to the *Rg Veda*, *Vedanta*, the *Puranas*, the *atma*, *yoga*, and *karma*.

In common with other reviewers, Wodak and Oldroyd drew a connection between *Forbidden Archeology* and the work of Christian creationists. "As is well known," they noted (p. 192), "Creationists try to show that humans are of recent origin, and that empirical investigations accord with human history as recorded in the Old Testament. *Forbidden Archeology* (*FA*) offers a brand of Creationism based on something quite different, namely ancient Vedic beliefs. From this starting point, instead of claiming a human history of mere millennia, *FA* argues for the existence of *Homo sapiens* way back into the Tertiary, perhaps even earlier."

In *L'Anthropologie* (1995 v.99, no. 1, p. 159), Marylène Pathou-Mathis wrote: "M. Cremo and R. Thompson have willfully written a provocative work that raises the problem of the influence of the dominant ideas of a time period on scientific research. These ideas can compel the researchers to orient their analyses according to the conceptions that are permitted by the scientific community." She concluded, "The documentary richness of this work, more historical and sociological than scientific, is not to be ignored."

And in *British Journal for the History of Science* (1995 v. 28, pp. 377 –379), Tim Murray noted in his review of *Forbidden Archeology* (p. 379): "I have no doubt that there will be some who will read this book and profit from it. Certainly it provides the historian of archaeology with a useful compendium of case studies in the history and sociology of scientific knowledge, which can be used to foster debate within archaeology about how to describe the epistemology of one's discipline." He further characterized *Forbidden Archeology* as a book that "joins others from creation science and New Age philosophy as a body of works which seek to address members of a public alienated from science, either because it has become so arcane or because it has ceased to suit some in search of meaning for their lives." Murray acknowledged that the Vedic perspective of *Forbidden Archeology* might have a role to play in the future development of archeology. He wrote in his review (p. 379) that archeology is now in a state of flux, with practitioners debating "issues which go to the conceptual core of the discipline." Murray then proposed, "Whether the *Vedas* have a role to play in this is up to the individual scientists concerned."

This openmindedness is characteristic of the reviews of *Forbidden Archeology* that appeared in respected academic and scientific journals, the only exception being a particularly vitriolic attack by Jonathan Marks in *American Journal of Physical Anthropology* (1994 v. 93, no. 1, pp. 140–141). Other than that, demands to totally exclude the Vedic perspective of *Forbidden Archeology* from the discourse of science were confined to the publications of extremist groups, such as skeptics societies (whose skepticism does not extend to the theory of evolution) and the unremittingly anticreationist National Center for Science Education in the United States (misleadingly named so as to imply some governmental connection). Also in this category is an attempted book-length debunking by Michael Brass (*The Antiquity of Man*).

Wiktor Stoczkowski, reviewing *Forbidden Archeology* in *L'Homme* (1995 v. 35, pp. 173–174), accurately noted (p. 173), "Historians of science repeat tirelessly that the Biblical version of origins was replaced in the nineteenth century by the evolution theory. In our imaginations, we substitute this simple story for the more complex reality that we are today confronted with a remarkable variety of origins accounts." Among those accounts Stoczkowski included those of the Biblical creationists. "*Forbidden Archeology*," he added, "gives us one more, dedicated to 'His Divine Grace A. C. Bhaktivedanta Swami Prabhupada' and inspired by the Vedic philosophy that disciples study in the United States at the Bhaktivedanta Institute, a branch of the International Society for Krishna Consciousness."

A favorable estimation of *Forbidden Archeology*'s Vedic roots was offered by Hillel Schwarz in *Journal of Unconventional History* (1994 v. 6, no. 1, pp. 68–76). "*Forbidden Archeology* takes the current conventions of decoding to their extreme," said Schwarz (p. 75). "The authors find modern *Homo sapiens* to be continuous contemporaries of the apelike creatures from whom evolutionary biologists usually trace human descent or bifurcation, thus confirming those Vedic sources that presume the nearly illimitable antiquity of the human race." He added (p. 76), "Despite its unhidden religious partisanship, the book deserves a reckoning in this review for its embrace of a global humanity permanently distinct from other primates." He accurately detected the book's implicit thesis, namely, that "humanity is no mere biochemical exfoliation but a work of the spirit, in touch with (and devoted to) the ancient, perfect, perfectly sufficient, unchanging wisdom of the Vedic masters."

In his book *Origin of the Human Species* (2001), published by the academic publisher Rodopi in its series on Studies in the History of Western Philosophy, Dennis Bonnette, head of the philosophy department of Niagara University, said (p. 130): "Cremo and Thompson are not evolutionary materialists or Biblical creationists. They openly state Hindu affiliation as Bhaktivedanta Institute members. Following Vedic literature, they hold that the human race is of great antiquity, hundreds of millions of years old. For this reason, many critics attack *Forbidden Archeology*, claiming its authors' belief system precludes unbiased handling of the subject matter. Such personal attacks are unjust and unfounded. Every author has a philosophical stance which might, but need not, negate objectivity. *Forbidden Archeology's* historical evidence and argumentation stand on their own merits as sociological and epistemological critiques of contemporary paleoanthropology."

As might be expected, Christian creationists have reacted favorably to *Forbidden Archeology*. Peter Line, who reviewed the abridged version of *Forbidden Archeology* in *Creation Research Society Quarterly* (1995 v. 32, p. 46), said, "This book is a must reading for anyone interested in human origins." After expressing his surprise at finding the book in a major U.S. chain store, Line noted that its "theoretical outlook is derived from the Vedic literature in India, which supports the idea that the human race is of great antiquity." Line made clear that he did not share this view: "As a recent earth creationist, I would not accept the evolutionary time scale that the authors appear to accept. However, the authors have shown that even if you accept the evolutionary view of a vast age for the earth, the theory of human evolution is not supported." *Forbidden Archeology* also got positive reactions from some Islamic and Native American authors.

Interest in a Vedic perspective on human origins and a desire to hear more explicitly about it were constant themes in the academic reviews of *Forbidden Archeology*. Kenneth Feder wrote in his *Geoarchaeology* review (pp. 339–340), "The authors are open about their membership in the Bhaktivedanta Institute, which is a branch of the International Society for Krishna Consciousness, and the book is dedicated to their 'spiritual master,' the group's founder. They make a reasonable request regarding their affiliation with this organization: 'That our theoretical outlook is derived from the Vedic literature should not disqualify it.' Fair enough, but what is their 'theoretical outlook?'" *Human Devolution* is my systematic answer to that question.

During the years I was researching and writing *Human Devolution,* I presented various parts of its argument at scientific and academic conferences. In April 1996, I presented at Toward a Science of Consciousness (a major international conference on consciousness studies held every two years at the University of Arizona in Tucson) a paper called "The City of Nine Gates: A Sophisticated Allegory for Mind/Body Dualism from the *Bhagavata Purana* of India." Elements of this paper can be found in chapter 7 of *Human Devolution.* Also in April 1996, at the Kentucky State University Institute for Liberal Studies Seventh Interdisciplinary Conference on Science and Culture, I presented a paper called "Alfred Russel Wallace and the Supernatural: A Case Study in Reenchanting Reductionistic Science's Hagiography in Light of an Alternative Cosmology." This paper served as the basis for chapter 5 of *Human Devolution.* In April 1998, I presented at the Toward a Science of Consciousness conference a paper called "Famous Scientists and the Paranormal." Material from this paper can be found in chapter 6 of *Human Devolution.* In July 2001, I presented at the XXIst International Congress for History of Science, held in Mexico City, a paper called "Paleobotanical Anomalies Bearing on the Age of the Salt Range Formation of Pakistan: A Historical Survey of an Unresolved Scientific Controversy." Chapter 3 in *Human Devolution* is based on this paper.

Having established how and why *Human Devolution* came to be written, I will now give an outline of the substance of the book. Chapter 1 of *Human Devolution* makes the point that some scientists and scholars are willing to consider alternatives to the Western scientific worldview as candidates for truth. For them, belief in such worldviews is no longer taboo. In *American Anthropologist* (1994 v. 96, no. 3), Katherine P. Ewing said (p. 572), "To rule out the possibility of belief in another's reality is to encapsulate that reality and, thus, to impose implicitly the hegemony of one's own view of the world." In *Journal of Consciousness Studies* (1994 v.

1, no. 2), William Barnard, in speaking about the world's wisdom traditions, advocated (pp. 257–258) "a scholarship that is willing and able to affirm that the metaphysical models...of these different spiritual traditions are serious contenders for truth, a scholarship that realizes that these religious worlds are not dead corpses that we can dissect and analyze at a safe distance, but rather are living, vital bodies of knowledge and practice that have the potential to change our taken-for-granted notions." I am asking that scientists and scholars approach in this spirit the Vedic perspective on human origins outlined in *Human Devolution.*

In chapter 2, I present a review of the archeological evidence for extreme human antiquity from *Forbidden Archeology.* I establish that this evidence actually exists and that it has been systematically eliminated from scientific discussion by a process of knowledge filtration. Archeological evidence that contradicts the Darwinian theory of human evolution is often rejected just for that reason. For example, in the nineteenth century, gold was discovered in California. To get it, miners dug tunnels into the sides of mountains, such as Table Mountain in Tuolumne County. Deep inside the tunnels, in deposits of early Eocene age (about 50 million years old), miners found human bones and artifacts. The discoveries were carefully documented by Dr. J. D. Whitney, the chief government geologist of California, in his book *The Auriferous Gravels of the Sierra Nevada of California,* published by Harvard University in 1880. But we do not hear very much about these discoveries today. In the *Smithsonian Institution Annual Report for 1898–1899* (p. 424), anthropologist William Holmes said, "Perhaps if Professor Whitney had fully appreciated the story of human evolution as it is understood today, he would have hesitated to announce the conclusions formulated, notwithstanding the imposing array of testimony with which he was confronted." In other words, if the facts did not fit the theory of human evolution, the facts had to be set aside, and that is exactly what happened.

Such bias continued into the twentieth century. In the 1970s, American archeologists led by Cynthia Irwin Williams discovered stone tools at Hueyatlaco, near Puebla, Mexico. The stone tools were of advanced type, made only by humans like us. A team of geologists, from the United States Geological Survey and universities in the United States, came to Hueyatlaco to date the site. Among the geologists was Virginia Steen-McIntyre. To date the site, the team used four methods—uranium series dating on butchered animal bones found along with the tools, zircon fission track dating on volcanic layers above the tools, tephra hydration dating of volcanic crystals, and standard stratigraphy. The four methods converged on an age of about 250,000 years for the site. The archeologists refused to consider this date. They could not believe that humans capable of making the Hueyatlaco artifacts existed 250,000 years ago. In defense of the dates obtained by the geologists, Virginia Steen-McIntyre wrote in a letter (March 30, 1981) to Estella Leopold, associate editor of *Quaternary Research:* "The problem as I see it is much bigger than Hueyatlaco. It concerns the manipulation of scientific thought through the suppression of 'Enigmatic Data,' data that challenges the prevailing mode of thinking. Hueyatlaco certainly does that! Not being an anthropologist, I didn't realize the full significance of our dates back in 1973, nor how deeply woven into our thought the current theory of human evolution has become. Our work at Hueyatlaco has been rejected by most archaeologists because it contradicts that theory, period." This remains true today, not only for the California gold mine discoveries and the Hueyatlaco human artifacts, but for hundreds of other discoveries documented in the scientific literature of the past 150 years.

In chapter 3, I present a case of fossil evidence showing that the current Darwinian picture of the evolution of nonhuman species is also in need of revision. Beginning in the 1940s, geologists and paleobotanists working with the Geological Survey of India explored the Salt Range Mountains in what is now Pakistan. They found deep in salt mines evidence for the existence of advanced flowering plants and insects in the early Cambrian periods, about 600 million years ago. According to standard evolutionary ideas, no land plants or animals existed at that time. Flowering plants and insects are thought to have come into existence hundreds of millions of years later. To explain the evidence some geologists proposed that there must have been a massive overthrust, by which Eocene layers, about 50 million years old, were thrust under Cambrian layers, over 550 million years old. Others pointed out that there were no geological signs of such an overthrust. According to these scientists, the layers bearing the fossils of the advanced plants and insects were found in normal position, beneath strata containing trilobites, the characteristic fossil of the Cambrian. One of these scientists, E. R. Gee, a geologist working with the Geological Survey of India, proposed a novel solution to the problem. In the proceedings of the National Academy of Sciences of India for the year 1945 (section B, v. 16, pp. xlv–xlvi), paleobotanist Birbal Sahni noted: "Quite recently, an alternative explanation has been offered by Mr. Gee. *The suggestion is that the angiosperms, gymnosperms and insects of the Saline Series may represent a highly evolved Cambrian or Precambrian flora and fauna!* In other words, it is suggested that these plants and animals made their appearance in the Salt Range area several hundred million years earlier than they did anywhere else in the world. One would scarcely have believed that such an idea would be seriously put forward by any geologist today." The controversy was left unresolved. In the 1990s, petroleum geologists, unaware of the earlier controversy, restudied the area. They determined that the salt deposits below the Cambrian deposits containing trilobites were early Cambrian or Precambrian. In other words, they found no evidence of an overthrust. The salt deposits were in a natural position below the Cambrian deposits. This supports Gee's suggestion that the plant and insect remains in the salt deposits were evidence of an advanced fauna and flora existing in the early Cambrian. This evidence contradicts not only the Darwinian concept of the evolution of humans but of other species as well.

Chapter 4 reviews evidence from genetics and developmental biology that contradicts the Darwinian theory of human evolution. The Darwinian theory of evolution is in trouble right from the start. Although the origin of life from chemicals is technically not part of the evolution theory, it has in practice become inseparably connected with it. Darwinists routinely assert that life arose from chemicals. But after decades of theorizing and experimenting, they are unable to say exactly which chemicals combined in exactly which way to form exactly which first living thing. As far as evolution itself is concerned, it has not been demonstrated in any truly scientific way. It remains an article of faith. The modern evolutionary synthesis is based on genetics. Evolutionists posit a relationship between the genotype (genetic structure) of an organism and its phenotype (physical structure). They say that changes in the genotype result in changes in the phenotype, and by natural selection the changes in phenotype conferring better fitness in a particular environment accumulate in organisms. Evolutionists claim that this process can account for the appearance of new structural features in organisms. But on the level of microbiology, these structures appear to be irreducibly complex. Scientists have not been able to specify exactly how they have come about in step by step fashion. They have not been able to tell us exactly what genetic changes resulted in what phenotypic changes to produce particular complex features of organisms. This would require the specification of intermediate stages leading up to the complex structures we observe today. In his book *Darwin's Black Box* (1996, p. 183), biochemist Michael Behe says, "In the past ten years, *Journal of Molecular Evolution* has published more than a thousand papers. . . . There were zero papers discussing detailed models for intermediates in the development of complex biomolecular structures. This is not a peculiarity of *JME*. No papers are to be found that discuss detailed models for intermediates in the development of complex biomolecular structures, whether in the *Proceedings of the National Academy of Science, Nature, Science,* the *Journal of Molecular Biology* or, to my knowledge, any science journal."

Attempts by scientists to use genetic evidence to demonstrate the time and place that anatomically modern humans have come into existence have resulted in embarrassing mistakes and contradictions. The first widely publicized reports that genetic evidence allowed scientists to say that all living humans arose from an African Eve who lived 200,000 years ago in Africa turned out to be fatally flawed. Researchers have attempted to correct the mistakes, but the results remain confused. Considering the complexities surrounding genetic data, some scientists have suggested that fossils remain the most reliable evidence for questions about human origins and antiquity. In an article in *American Anthropologist* (1993 v. 95, no. 11), David W. Frayer and his coauthors said (p. 19): "Unlike genetic data derived from living humans, fossils can be used to test predictions of theories about the past without relying on a long list of assumptions about the neutrality of genetic markers, mutational rates, or other requirements necessary to retrodict the past from current genetic variation. . . . genetic information, at best, provides a theory of how modern human origins *might have happened* if the assumptions used in interpreting the genetic data are correct." This means that the archeological evidence for extreme human antiquity documented in *Forbidden Archeology* provides a much needed check on the rampant speculations of genetic researchers. This evidence contradicts current Darwinian accounts of human origins.

Together, chapters 2, 3, and 4 of *Human Devolution* demonstrate a real need for an alternative to the current Darwinian account of human origins. The work of Sir Alfred Russel Wallace, cofounder with Darwin of the theory of evolution by natural selection, provides an introduction to the alternative explanation. Wallace, along with other British scientists, such as Sir William Crookes, a Nobel laureate in physics, conducted extensive experiments into the paranormal. These experiments and observations, reviewed in chapter 5 of *Human Devolution,* led Wallace to revise the worldview of science. Wallace concluded that the universe is populated with spirit beings. Some of the minor spirit beings, he proposed, are in contact with the human population on earth, usually through mediums. According to Wallace, the minor spirit beings, acting through mediums, were responsible for a variety of paranormal phenomena, including clairvoyance, miraculous healings, communications from the dead, apparitions, materializations of physical objects, levitations, etc. More powerful spirit beings may have played a role in the origin of species.

Wallace wrote in his autobiography (1905 v. 2, pp. 349–350): "The majority of people today have been brought up in the belief that miracles, ghosts, and the whole series of strange phenomena here described cannot exist; that they are contrary to the laws of nature; that they are the superstitions of a bygone age; and that therefore they are necessarily either impostures or delusions. There is no place in the fabric of their thought into which such facts can be fitted. When I first began this inquiry it was the same with myself. The facts did not fit into my then existing fabric of thought. All my preconceptions, all my knowledge, all my belief in the supremacy of science and of natural law were against the possibility of such phenomena. And even when, one by one, the facts were forced upon me without possibility of escape from them, still, as Sir David Brewster declared after being at first astonished by the phenomena he saw with [the medium] Mr. Home, 'spirit was the last thing I could give in to.' Every other possible solution was tried and rejected....We ask our readers not for belief, but for doubt of their own infallibility on this question; we ask for inquiry and patient experiment before hastily concluding that we are, all of us, mere dupes and idiots as regards a subject to which we have devoted our best mental faculties and powers of observation for many years." For Wallace, all this had implications for human origins. In his book *Contributions to a Theory of Natural Selection* (1870, p. 359), Wallace concluded that "a superior intelligence has guided the development of man in a definite direction, and for a special purpose, just as man guides the development of many animal and vegetable forms."

Using the work of Wallace as a starting point, I proceed in the remaining chapters of *Human Devolution* to develop a Vedic alternative to the Darwinian account of human origins. I propose that before we ask the question, "Where did human beings come from?" we should first of all ask the question, "What is a human being?" Today most scientists believe that a human being is simply a combination of the ordinary chemical elements. This assumption limits the kinds of explanations that can be offered for human origins. I propose that it is more reasonable, based on available scientific evidence, to start with the assumption that a human being is composed of three separately existing substances: matter, mind, and consciousness (or spirit). This assumption widens the circle of possible explanations.

Any scientific chain of reasoning begins with some initial assumptions that are not rigorously proved. Otherwise, one would get caught in an endless regression of proofs of assumptions, and proofs of proofs of assumptions. Initial assumptions must simply be reasonable on the basis of available evidence. In chapter 6, I show that it is reasonable, on the basis of available evidence, to posit the existence of mind and consciousness, in addition to ordinary matter, as separate elements composing the human being.

I define mind as a subtle, but nevertheless material, energy, associated with the human organism and capable of acting on ordinary matter in ways we cannot explain by our current laws of physics. Evidence for this mind element comes from scientific research into the phenomena called by some "paranormal" or "psychical." Here we are led into the hidden history of physics. Just as in archeology, there has been in physics a tremendous amount of knowledge filtration. For example, every physics student learns about the work of Pierre and Marie Curie, the husband and wife team who both received Nobel Prizes for their work in discovering radium. The account is found in practically every introductory physics textbook. What we do not read in the textbooks is that the Curies were heavily involved in psychical research. They were part of a large group of prominent European scientists, including other Nobel Prize winners, who were jointly conducting research into the paranormal in Paris early in the twentieth century. For two years, the group studied the Italian medium Eusapia Palladino (sometimes spelled Paladino, or Paladina). Historian Anna Hurwic notes in her biography of Pierre Curie (1995, p. 247), "He thought it possible to discover in spiritualism the source of an unknown energy that would reveal the secret of radioactivity. . . . He saw the séances as scientific experiments, tried to monitor the different parameters, took detailed notes of every observation. He was really intrigued by Eusapia Paladino." About some séances with Eusapia, Pierre Curie wrote to physicist Georges Gouy in a letter dated July 24, 1905: "We had at the Psychology Society a few séances with the medium Eusapia Paladina. It was very interesting, and truly those phenomena that we have witnessed seemed to us to not be some magical tricks—a table lifted four feet above the floor, movements of objects, feelings of hands that pinched you or caressed you, apparitions of light. All this in a room arranged by us, with a small number of spectators all well known and without the presence of a possible accomplice. The only possible cheating would be an extraordinary ability of the medium as a magician. But how to explain the different phenomena when we are holding her hands and legs, and the lighting of the room is sufficient to see everything going on?" On April 14, 1906, Pierre wrote to Gouy: "We are working, M. Curie and me, to precisely dose the radium by its own emanations. . . . We had a few new 'séances' with Eusapia Paladina (We already had séances with her last summer). The result is that those phenomena exist for real, and I can't doubt it any more. It is unbelievable, but it is thus, and it is impossible to negate it after the séances that we had in conditions of perfect monitoring." He concluded, "There is, according to me a completely new domain of facts and physical states of space of which we have no idea."

To me, such results, and many more like them from the hidden history of physics, suggest there is associated with the human organism a mind element that can act on ordinary matter in ways we cannot easily explain by our current physical laws. Such research continues today, although most scientists doing it are concentrating on microeffects rather than the macroeffects reported by Pierre Curie. For example, Robert Jahn, head of the engineering department at Princeton University, started to research the effects of mental attention on random number generators. A random number generator will normally generate a sequence of ones and zeros, with equal numbers of each. But Jahn, and his associates who have continued the research, found that subjects can mentally influence the random number generators to produce a statistically significant greater number of ones than zeros (or vice versa).

Evidence for a conscious self that can exist apart from mind and matter comes from medical reports of out-of-body experiences (OBEs). Dr. Michael Sabom, an American cardiologist, conducted extensive research into out-of-body experiences. He carefully interviewed heart attack patients who reported such experiences. He then compared their reports with their actual medical records. He found that a statistically significant number of the group gave correct accounts, consistent with the reports of their treatment. This is highly unusual, because according to standard medical opinion, the patients should have been completely unconscious. Could the subjects have manufactured their correct reports from their previous knowledge of heart attack treatment procedures (for example, from watching television hospital dramas)? To control for this, Sabom selected a second group of heart attack patients who did not report OBEs. He asked them to imagine the medical treatment they had undergone while unconscious. None of them was able to give a correct report, and almost all of them made major mistakes. For Sabom, the results from the control group confirmed the genuineness of the OBE reports from the first group. In his book *Recollections of Death: A Medical Investigation* (1982, p. 183), Sabom asked, "Could the mind which splits apart from the physical brain be, in essence, the 'soul,' which continues to exist after final bodily death, according to some religious doctrines?"

Sabom's results have been confirmed by further studies. For example, in February 2001, a team from the University of Southampton, in the United Kingdom, published a favorable study on OBEs in cardiac arrest patients in the journal *Resuscitation* (v. 48, pp. 149–156). The team was headed by Dr. Sam Parnia, a senior research fellow at the university. On February 16, 2001, a report published on the university's web site said that the work of Dr. Parnia "suggests consciousness and the mind may continue to exist after the brain has ceased to function and the body is clinically dead."

Past life memories also give evidence for a conscious self that can exist apart from the body. Dr. Ian Stevenson, a psychiatrist at the University of Virginia medical school, has conducted extensive research into past life memories. Stevenson, and his associates, have focused on past life memories spontaneously reported by very young children. Stevenson prefers working with children because older persons might have the motives and means to construct elaborate past life accounts. His technique is to thoroughly interview the child subjects and thus obtain as many details as possible about the reported past life. Using this information, Stevenson and his associates then attempt to identify the person the child claims to have been in the past life. In hundreds of cases, they have been successful in making such identifications.

Having established that the human organism is composed of the elements matter, mind, and consciousness (or spirit), it is natural to suppose that the cosmos is divided into regions, or levels, of matter, mind, and consciousness, each inhabited by beings adapted to life there. First, there is a region of pure consciousness. Consciousness, as we experience it, is individual and personal. This suggests that the original source of conscious selves is also individual and personal. So in addition to the individual units of consciousness existing in the realm of pure consciousness, there is also an original conscious being who is their source. When the fractional conscious selves give up their connection with their source, they are placed in lower regions of the cosmos predominated by either the subtle material energy (mind) or the gross material energy (matter). There is thus a cosmic hierarchy of conscious beings. Chapter 7 of *Human Devolution* establishes the existence of this cosmic hierarchy of beings in a cross-cultural study of cosmologies, using the Vedic cosmology of the *Shrimad Bhagavatam* as a model for comparison. The cosmologies share many features. They generally include an original God inhabiting a realm of pure consciousness, a subordinate creator god inhabiting a subtle material region of the cosmos along with many kinds of demigods and demigoddesses, an earthly realm inhabited by humans like us, and an underworld inhabited by ghosts and demons.

Chapter 8 of *Human Devolution* documents categories of observational evidence for the existence of conscious beings at various levels of the cosmic hierarchy. The first category is evidence for survival of conscious selves formerly inhabiting bodies of terrestrial humans. This evidence takes the form of communications from surviving conscious human selves, apparitions of departed humans, and possessions of living humans by spirits of departed humans. Cases where humans are possessed by beings with extraordinary powers provide evidence for superhuman creatures existing in extraterrestrial levels of the cosmic hierarchy. Marian apparitions and apparitions of angels also provide such evidence. Historical accounts of appearances of avatars provide evidence for the existence of a supreme conscious being. A final category of evidence comes from modern reports of unidentified flying objects and the "aliens" associated with them. Although the topic is very controversial, and involves a high degree of strangeness, there is a substantial quantity of credible reporting from government and military sources from several countries. The theory of purely mechanical UFOs breaks down under careful investigation, and the UFOs and aliens come to resemble beings inhabiting extraterrestrial levels of the world's traditional cosmologies.

The human devolution concept posits the action of superior intelligences in the origin of the human form and the forms of other living things. This depends on the ability of consciousness to more or less directly influence the organization of matter in living things. Chapter 9 provides evidence that such paranormal modification and production of biological forms actually occurs.

The first category of evidence comes from laboratory experiments in which human subjects are able to mentally influence the growth of micro-organisms. For example, Beverly Rubik conducted laboratory research on "volitional effects of healers on a bacterial system" while director of the Institute for Frontier Sciences at Temple University in Philadelphia, Pennsylvania. She reported the results in a paper included in her book *Life at the Edge of Science* (1996, pp. 99–117). The experiments were performed using the bacterium *Salmonella typhimurium,* a very well studied organism. The chief subject in the study was Olga Worrall, who had demonstrated positive abilities in other experiments. In one set of experiments, culture dishes of bacteria were treated with antibiotics that inhibit the growth of the bacteria. Worrall attempted to influence the bacteria in one set of culture dishes to grow. Another set of culture dishes was kept aside as a control. Compared to the control group, the group of culture dishes mentally acted upon by Worrall all showed an increase in growth. In another set of experiments, bacteria were placed on slides in a solution of phenol sufficient to immobilize but not kill them. The slides of bacteria were then o served under a microscope. In her book, Rubik (p. 108) stated, "Application of . . . phenol completely paralyzes the bacteria within 1 to 2 minutes. Worrall's treatment inhibited this effect . . . such that on the average up to 7% of the bacteria continued to swim after 12 minutes exposure to phenol compared to the control groups which were completely paralyzed in all cases."

Distance healing by prayer and other miraculous cures provide another category of evidence for paranormal modification of biological form. In a study published in the *Annals of Internal Medicine* (2000 v. 132, no. 11, pp. 903–911), John A. Astin and his coauthors found that "a growing body of evidence suggests an association between religious involvement and spirituality and positive health outcomes." In support of their conclusion, the Astin group cited over fifty credible positive reports from a variety of scientific and medical journals. Even more striking examples of paranormal modification of biological form come from the reports of the Medical Bureau at Lourdes. Since the nineteenth century, the physicians of the Medical Bureau have carefully documented a series of miraculous cures, some involving the inexplicable regeneration of damaged tissues and organs.

Psychiatrist Ian Stevenson has conducted extensive investigations into birthmarks that appear to have some relationship with wounds a person experienced in a past life. Persons who died of gunshot wounds in previous lives sometimes display on their present bodies birthmarks of appropriate size at the positions of the entry and exit wounds. This suggests that when such a person's soul and mind enter the present body, they carry with them impressions that appropriately modify the body's biological form. Some medical investigators have documented cases of "maternal impressions." These occur when a pregnant woman is exposed to a striking event that causes a strong emotional impression. Somehow the psychological impression leaves its mark on the embryo within her womb. For example, if a woman sees someone with an injured foot and then constantly remembers this, her child might be born with a malformed foot. In 1890, W. C. Dabney reviewed in *Cyclopaedia of the Diseases of Children* (1890 v. 1, pp. 191–216) sixty-nine reports published between 1853 and 1886 documenting a close correspondence between the mother's mental impression and the physical deformation in her child.

Yet another category of evidence consists of reports by prominent scientists who have witnessed mediums produce human limbs or complete human bodies. A particularly striking case was reported by Sir Alfred Russel Wallace, who, accompanied by others, saw a clergyman medium named Monk produce a complete human form. In his autobiography

(1905 v. 2, p. 330), Wallace described the event, which took place in an apartment in the Bloomsbury district of London: "It was a bright summer afternoon, and everything happened in the full light of day. After a little conversation, Monk, who was dressed in the usual clerical black, appeared to go into a trance; then stood up a few feet in front of us, and after a little while pointed to his side, saying, 'Look.' We saw there a faint white patch on his coat on the left side. This grew brighter, then seemed to flicker, and extend both upwards and downwards, till very gradually it formed a cloudy pillar extending from his shoulder to his feet and close to his body. Then he shifted himself a little sideways, the cloudy figure standing still, but appearing joined to him by a cloudy band at the height at which it had first begun to form. Then, after a few minutes more, Monk again said 'Look,' and passed his hand through the connecting band, severing it. He and the figure then moved away from each other till they were about five or six feet apart. The figure had now assumed the appearance of a thickly draped female form, with arms and hands just visible. Monk looked towards it and again said to us 'Look,' and then clapped his hands. On which the figure put out her hands, clapped them as he had done, and we all distinctly heard her clap following his, but fainter. The figure then moved slowly back to him, grew fainter and shorter, and was apparently absorbed into his body as it had grown out of it."

If the forms of humans and other living things are the result of intelligent manipulation of matter, this suggests that the universe itself may have been designed for human life and other forms of life. Chapter 10 reviews evidence for this from modern cosmology. Scientists have discovered that numbers representing fundamental physical constants and ratios of natural forces appear to be finely tuned for life to exist in our universe. Astronomer Sir Martin Rees considers six of these numbers to be especially significant. In his book *Just Six Numbers* (2000, pp. 3–4), he says, "I have highlighted these six because each plays a crucial and distinctive role in our universe, and together they determine how the universe evolves and what its internal potentialities are. . . . These six numbers constitute a 'recipe' for a universe. Moreover, the outcome is sensitive to their values: if any one of them were to be 'untuned', there would be no stars and no life." There are three main explanations for the apparent fine tuning of the physical constants and laws of nature: simple chance, many worlds, and some intelligent providential creator. Many cosmologists admit that the odds against the fine tuning are too extreme for a simple "one shot" chance to be offered as a credible scientific explanation. To avoid the conclusion of a providential designer, they have posited the existence of a practically unlimited number of universes, each with the values of fundamental constants and laws of nature adjusted in a different way. And we just happen to live in the one universe with everything adjusted correctly for the existence of human life. But these other universes have only a theoretical existence, and even if their existence could be physically demonstrated, one would further have to show that in these other universes the values of the fundamental constants and laws of nature are in fact different than those in our universe. The Vedic cosmology also speaks of many universes, but all of them are designed for life.

Chapter 11 outlines the concept of human devolution, bringing together the various lines of evidence presented in the previous chapters. We do not evolve up from matter; rather we devolve, or come down, from the level of pure consciousness. Originally, we are pure units of consciousness existing in harmonious connection with the supreme conscious being. When we give up our willing connection with that supreme conscious being, we descend to regions of the cosmos dominated by the subtle and gross material energies, mind and matter. Forgetful of our original position, we attempt to dominate and enjoy the subtle and gross material energies. For this purpose, we are provided with bodies made of the subtle and gross material energies. These bodies are vehicles for conscious selves. They are designed for existence within the realms of the subtle and gross material energies. Conscious selves who are less forgetful of their original natures receive bodies composed primarily of the subtle material energy. Those who are more forgetful receive bodies composed of both the subtle and gross material energies, with the gross material energies predominating. The original conscious being in the Vedic universe is Brahma, the first demigod. His body, manifested directly from Vishnu, is made primarily of the subtle material elements. He is tasked with manifesting bodies for the other conscious selves existing at various levels of the cosmic hierarchy. From the body of Brahma come great sages, sometimes known as his mental sons, and also the first sexually reproducing pair, Svayambhuva Manu and his consort Shatarupa. The daughters of Manu become the wives of some of the sages, and they produce generations of demigods and demigoddesses, with bodies composed primarily of the subtle material energy. These demigods and demigoddesses, by their reproductive processes, produce the forms of living things, including humans, who reside on our earth planet. In their reproductive processes, they make use of *bijas*, or mental seeds, which contain essential elements of the plans for the various bodies. The existence of DNA alone is not sufficient to explain how the forms of living things are manifested. For the most part, the genes on the DNA strand just code for the production of various proteins. How these proteins are combined in the complex forms of organisms is not specified by the DNA. The concept of a mental seed containing the developmental plan for bodies, including the human body, thus complements the existence of DNA. The human devolution concept thus has something in common with Darwinism. Like Darwinism, the human devolution concept posits a first living thing from which other living things develop by a process of reproduction with modification. But the process is intelligently guided.

I now wish to acknowledge my indebtedness to some of those who made this book possible. During the years 1984 to 1995, I worked closely with Richard L. Thompson, and *Human Devolution* owes much to the countless discussions we had during those years. Anyone desiring to understand a Vedic perspective on modern science should consult Thompson's foundational works *Mechanistic and Nonmechanistic Science, Alien Identities,* and *Mysteries of the Sacred Universe.* Since 1993 I have been fortunate to have Lori Erbs as my research assistant. With her masters degree in library science and experience as director of a science research library for an agency of the United States government, she has carried out the most complicated and demanding research requests in a prompt, thorough, professional manner. She was also responsible for preparing the *Human Devolution* manuscript for submission to my publisher. Lori was greatly assisted by Fay Fenske, the interlibrary loan specialist for the Bellingham Public Library, in Bellingham, Washington. Fay obtained many rare books and journal articles from around the world. Alister Taylor, of Torchlight Publishing, has been an understanding partner in publishing my works since 1993. I remain grateful to the international trustees of the Bhaktivedanta Book Trust for their continuing support of my research and publishing. I am especially grateful to the North American trustee Emil Beca for the various ways in which he has supported my work. For their expert help in the typesetting, proofreading, and design of this book, I thank Yamaraja Dasa, Chris Glenn, Varsana Staszak, and Mollie Thonneson. Thanks also to Gary Aleksiewicz for the index. Finally, I am grateful to Irina Martynenko and Yuri Dementyev for locating a peaceful place for me to stay in Yalta so that I could finish this introduction after a lecture tour of the Ukraine.

Michael A. Cremo
Yalta
December 14, 2002

NOTE ON ORTHOGRAPHY: In *Human Devolution* I spell Sanskrit words phonetically for ease of pronunciation by readers not familiar with the scholarly system of diacritics.

1
ASCENDED APES
OR FALLEN ANGELS?

"By next Friday evening they will all be convinced that they are monkeys," wrote Thomas Henry Huxley to his wife Henrietta (WgTdt 1972, p. 71). The year was 1860, and on June 30, Huxley would confront Samuel Wilberforce, Bishop of Oxford, in one of history's most famous debates. The topic was Charles Darwin's theory of evolution.

Samuel Wilberforce despised Darwin's theory, published the previous year in *The Origin of Species,* and he was determined to demonstrate its shortcomings. Although a bishop of the Church of England, Wilberforce knew something of science. He was a lifelong student of natural history, and he served as a vice president of the British Association for the Advancement of Science. He had also been on the governing council of the Geological Society of London, and he knew well several leading scientists of his day, such as geologist Charles Lyell, one of Darwin's chief supporters, and biologist Richard Owen, one of Darwin's chief opponents.

At the invitation of the editor of the influential *Quarterly Review,* Wilberforce had written a negative critique of *The Origin of Species.* It was not printed until after the Huxley-Wilberforce debate, but when it finally did appear, Darwin himself called it "uncommonly clever" (F. Darwin 1887, p. 324).

In his review, Wilberforce (1860) first attacked Darwin on scientific grounds. In *The Origin of Species,* Darwin had argued that living things tend to vary slightly in the course of reproduction. After giving examples from bird and animal breeding, Darwin contended that over vast periods of time, aided by natural selection, such variation could lead to the origin of new species. But Wilberforce noted that the variations obtained in breeding pigeons, dogs, and horses were not changes in the basic physical structure of these creatures, such as required for the production of new kinds of organisms. Pigeons remained pigeons, dogs remained dogs, and horses remained horses. Turning to metaphysics, Wilberforce argued that such human qualities as free will and reason were "equally and utterly

1

irreconciliable with the degrading notion of the brute origin of him who was created in the image of God."

Huxley's Triumph

On June 30, at the British Association for the Advancement of Science meeting in Oxford, Dr. J. W. Draper of New York read a paper titled "Intellectual Development of Europe Considered with Reference to the Views of Mr. Darwin." Expecting fireworks, seven hundred attentive hearers had packed the lecture hall. After Draper finished his talk, several persons offered comments. Finally, Wilberforce spoke, attacking Darwin's theory. His confident words mirrored those that would later appear in his *Quarterly Review* article on *The Origin of Species.* Attempting to draw a laugh, he wondered "if any one were willing to trace his descent through an ape as his grandfather, would he be willing to trace his descent similarly on the side of his grandmother?" (Meacham 1970, p. 216)

Huxley leaned toward one of his companions and said, "The Lord hath delivered him into my hands" (Meacham 1970, p. 216). When he was called to speak, Huxley delivered his famous retort, quoted in many books about evolution. Declaring that he felt no shame in having an ape for an ancestor, he added, "If there were an ancestor whom I should feel shame in recalling, it would rather be a *man*—a man of restless and versatile intellect—who, not content with success in his own sphere of activity, plunges into scientific questions with which he has no real acquaintance, only to obscure them by an aimless rhetoric, and distract the attention of his hearers from the real point at issue by eloquent digressions and skilled appeals to religious prejudice" (Meacham 1970, p. 216). The audience, won over by Huxley, broke into loud applause. In their opening skirmish, the apes had prevailed over the angels.

On the Side of the Angels

The angels, however, still had some highly placed advocates. On November 25, 1864, Benjamin Disraeli, then chancellor of the exchequer and soon to be prime minister, said at a speech at the Sheldon Theater in Oxford: "The question is this—Is man an ape or an angel? My Lord, I am on the side of the angels. I repudiate with indignation and abhorrence the contrary view, which is, I believe, foreign to the conscience of humanity: more than that, even in the strictest intellectual point of view, I believe the severest metaphysical analysis is opposed to such a conclusion. But what does the Church teach us? What is its interpretation of the highest nature? It teaches us that man is made in the image of his Creator—a source of inspiration and of solace from which only can flow every right principle and every Divine truth ... It is between these two contending interpretations of the nature of man [ape or angel], and their consequences, that society will have to decide" (Monypenny and Buckle 1929, p. 108). But Oxford University had already decided. Disraeli's remarks, especially the one about being on the side of the angels, met with loud disapproving laughter that today still echoes with increased volume in the halls of academia.

Disraeli's unsympathetic university audience had two components. First, there were theologians who had given up a literal reading of the Bible. Second, there were scientists who were also rejecting Biblical literalism, from the standpoint of Darwinism. They both reacted with dislike to Disraeli's talk of angels (Monypenny and Buckle 1929, pp. 104–109). Indeed, it was the unwitting alliance between these two groups that insured the relatively quick triumph of Darwinism over the Wilberforces and Disraelis of Victorian England. Within a few decades, most of the educated persons of England, and the world, whatever their religious or cultural heritages, would accept that human bodies were not direct creations of God in His image but were instead the modified bodies of apes. Disraeli's statement that he was "on the side of the angels" is often inserted, as an amusement, into books on evolution, and so is a satirical *Punch* cartoon of Disraeli dressed as an angel (Ruse 1982, p. 54).

But what exactly did Disraeli mean when he spoke of being on the side of the angels? Was this merely a metaphor, pointing to some vague involvement of God in the origin of the human species? Given the intellectual climate of his times, one is tempted to answer the question positively. For most intellectuals, God had already retreated from the visible universe, taking the role of a detached clockmaker who set a strictly material machine in motion and left it running. But a deeper study of Disraeli's writings lends support to a more literal reading of his remarks.

In *Lord George Bentinck: A Political Biography,* Disraeli (1852, pp. 495–496) spoke fondly of "the early ages of the world, when the relations of the Creator with the created were more intimate than in these days, when angels visited the earth, and God Himself even spoke with man."

Similar passages can be found in Disraeli's novels, which were fairly transparent vehicles for his own political, philosophical, and spiritual convictions. In *Tancred,* published in 1847, his visionary hero, a young Victorian aristocrat, has the following exchange with a bishop of the Church of England (Disraeli 1927, p. 76).

"'The Church represents God upon earth,' said the bishop.

"'But the Church no longer governs man,' replied Tancred.

"'There is a great spirit rising in the Church,' observed the bishop with thoughtful solemnity. . . . 'We shall soon see a bishop at Manchester.'

"'But I want to see an angel at Manchester.'

"'An angel!'

"'Why not? Why should there not be heavenly messengers, when heavenly messages are most wanted?'"

Tancred then proceeds on a spiritual quest to Jerusalem. While in Palestine, he ascends Mt. Sinai by night and is visited by an angel "vast as the surrounding hills." After identifying himself as "the angel of Arabia," the angel says, "'The relations between Jehovah and his creatures can be neither too numerous nor too near. In the increased distance between God and man have grown up all those developments that have made life mournful'" (Disraeli 1927, p. 300).

Eventually, Tancred forms a plan to revitalize Europe by first restoring the spiritual purity of Asia. "When the East has resumed its indigenous intelligence, when angels and prophets shall again mingle with humanity, the sacred quarter of the globe will recover its primeval and divine supremacy; it will act upon the modern empires, and the faint-hearted faith of Europe, which is but the shadow of a shade, will become as vigorous as befits men who are in sustained communication with the Creator" (Disraeli 1927, p. 441). Disraeli's vision of a Creator and his angels constantly interfering with the world is far less compatible with Darwinism than the vision of a Creator who keeps his angels in heaven and his hands off the world.

Given his mystical tendency, it is not surprising that Disraeli disliked materialistic evolutionary theories. *Tancred* appeared before Darwin's *The Origin of Species,* but in it Disraeli satirized Robert Chambers's *Vestiges of Creation,* which also expressed evolutionary ideas.

Before setting off to the East, Tancred developed a temporary affection for beautiful young Lady Constance, whom Tancred regarded as his spiritual guide. One evening Lady Constance spoke to him with effusive praise about a book titled, presciently, *The Revelations of Chaos* (Disraeli 1927, pp. 112–113).

"'To judge from the title, the subject is rather obscure,' said Tancred.

"'No longer so,' said Lady Constance. 'It is treated scientifically; everything is explained by geology and astronomy, and in that way. It shows you exactly how a star is formed; nothing can be so pretty! A cluster of vapour, the cream of the milky way, a sort of celestial cheese, churned into light, you must read it, 'tis charming.'

"'Nobody ever saw a star formed,' said Tancred.

"'Perhaps not. You must read the *Revelations;* it is all explained. But what is most interesting, is the way in which man has been developed. You know, all is development. The principle is perpetually going on. First, there was nothing, then there was something; then, I forget the next, I think there were shells, then fishes; then we came, let me see, did we come next? Never mind that; we came at last. And the next change there will be something very superior to us, something with wings. Ah! that's it; we were fishes, and I believe we shall be crows. But you must read it.'

"'I do not believe I ever was a fish,' said Tancred.

"'Oh, but it is all proved; you must not argue on my rapid sketch; read the book. It is impossible to contradict anything in it. You understand, it is all science; it is not like those books in which one says one thing and another the contrary, and both may be wrong. Everything is proved: by geology, you know. You see exactly how everything is made; how many worlds there have been; how long they lasted; what went before, what comes next. We are a link in the chain, as inferior animals were that preceded us: we in turn shall be inferior; all that will remain of us will be some relics in a new red sandstone. This is development. We had fins; we may have wings. . . .'

"'I was a fish, and I shall be a crow,' said Tancred to himself, when the hall door closed on him. 'What a spiritual mistress! And yesterday, for a moment, I almost dreamed of kneeling with her at the Holy Sepulchre! I must get out of this city as quickly as possible.'"

Lady Constance presents the perfect picture of someone barely hanging on to "the faint-hearted faith of Europe, which is but the shadow of a shade" (Disraeli 1927, p. 441), all too ready to be swept aside by the new prophets of evolution. The unfriendly reception Disraeli got from the dons at Sheldon Theater in Oxford is proof of that. A world in which God, angels, and miracles have retreated beyond the most distant borders of material reality was ripe for rapid conquest by Huxley and Darwin.

But while in Syria, Tancred encountered a lady whose faith was anything but insipid; indeed, she manifested a faith in things too intensely mystical for even himself. The lady was Astarte, Queen of the Ansareys. Astarte took Tancred into a secret sanctuary cut out of solid rock in an isolated ravine. There he saw an "elegant hierarchy" composed of "goddess and god, genius, and nymph, and faun" (Disraeli 1927, p. 437). Tancred thought them to be the gods of the Greeks, but Astarte called them the gods of her own people, who once ruled from ancient Antioch. The chief goddess was Astarte, her own namesake.

"'When all was over,'" said the Queen; "'when the people refused to sacrifice, and the gods, indignant quitted earth, I hope not for ever, the faithful few fled to these mountains with the sacred images, and we have cherished them'" (Disraeli 1927, pp. 437–438). She expressed a lofty hope that "'mankind will return again to those gods who made the earth beautiful and happy; and that they, in their celestial mercy, may revisit that world which, without them, has become a howling wilderness'" (Disraeli 1927, p. 438). If Disraeli's vision of an active God and angels, voiced directly by himself and indirectly through characters like Tancred, is hostile to Darwinian evolution, how much more so the vision of Astarte?

Yet Astarte's vision of a cosmos permeated with gods and goddesses once ruled Europe. These gods and goddesses were intimately involved in a temporal process of bringing into being other creatures within the universe. The universe was like a living mystical factory filled with subtle machinery, operated by subtle beings, who cooperated in the production of plants, humans, and animals. Then came Christianity. At first, Christianity simply replaced the pagan gods and goddesses with angels. But by gradually deemphasizing the role of angels, Christianity depopulated the cosmos. The visible universe became a lifeless clocklike machine that a distant creator God mysteriously built and set in motion. As far as living things were concerned, they were also machines. Mechanistic science took the final step of removing the mystery of their manufacture. They were not the instantaneous *ex nihilo* creations of the distant clockmaker, but part of a temporal material process running within the machine of the universe itself. That temporal process was evolution, guided by natural selection. In the universal scheme of life, the great clockmaker became a barely tolerated supernumerary, useful only for maintaining social order and public morality.

So man was ape, not angel. Nevertheless, there are still a great many people who take Disraeli's side of the great question. For example, on July 13, 1994, Naomi Albright, author of several books about her contacts with angels, related to me this encounter: "I had entered into a state of consciousness that I call 'living vision.' A living vision is not like something imagined. It is perfectly clear to you that you are there live and in person. In this state, an angelic being appeared before me. He said I should call him 'Lighter than Light,' as his real name would be unpronounceable by me. After identifying himself as an angel, he told me that I should accept the fact that I had been one of them, an angel, since the Beginning, but that I had come down to the human form, and had been reincarnating on this level for a long time." Experiences such as this point back to the cosmos of Disraeli, with its God and angels, its gods and goddesses, all somehow linked to human origins and destinies.

Altered States of Consciousness

Cultural anthropologists might call Albright's "living vision" and angel encounter "an altered state of consciousness (ASC)." Such ASC reports are widespread. Anthropologist E. Bourguignon (1973, p. 9) surveyed 488 world cultures and found that 90 percent of them have well-developed experiences of such altered states. These would include, for example, the experiences reported by shamans, who regularly contact spirit beings in their trances. Albright's angel-contact testimony shows, however, that ASCs are not confined to tribal peoples. Modern accounts of contacts with alien beings in connection with UFO experiences provide another example of ASCs from advanced cultures.

Many cultural anthropologists and clinical psychologists studying ASCs in non-Western cultures classify them as psychopathological—as neurotic or psychotic departures from normal consciousness, as defined by Western psychology (Price-Williams and Hughes 1994, pp. 4–5). A more charitable approach dispenses with Western psychopathological interpretations and evaluates ASCs as normal or abnormal according to the standards of the culture in which the states occur. In modern civilized societies, persons claiming to be in contact with a spirit being, and acting as if this were so, would be labeled psychotic. But in many other societies such claims and behavior would be considered normal, perhaps even prestigious. Nevertheless, most psychologists and anthropologists, although dispensing with negative descriptive language, would not normally regard a contact with an angel, spirit, or UFO entity as real, in the sense of the human subject actually contacting another existing personality. At most, those taking a Jungian point of view would say that there is contact with a real archetype from the human subconscious.

But some anthropologists are now considering a different approach. Katherine P. Ewing, a professor of cultural anthropology at Duke University, has raised the issue of positive belief as a valid stance for an anthropologist to take in relation to reports of paranormal phenomena. While engaged in researching Sufis in Pakistan, Ewing met a Sufi saint. This saint told her that he would come to her while she was sleeping. When this in fact occurred, in what Ewing took to be a dream, she felt someone touch her. The sensation was so real that, startled, she awoke sitting upright on her bed. In order to maintain her self-image as a professional anthropologist, she resisted what she called "the temptation to believe." She found herself instinctively "placing the phenomenon immediately within a psychological interpretive scheme in which dreams come only from the dreamer's internal states" (Ewing 1994, p. 574). In other words, she convinced herself that the saint had not actually come to her in the dream. But she noted, "To rule out the possibility of belief in another's reality is to encapsulate that reality and thus, to impose the hegemony of one's own view of the world" (Ewing 1994, p. 572). A better approach to experiences that challenge the worldview of Western science would be to "take them seriously and allow them to play a role in shaping what are ultimate realities we share as participants in a global human community" (Ewing 1994, p. 579).

When this step is taken, we find ourselves confronted with a wealth of empirical evidence that tends to support the worldviews of traditional cultures. When this evidence is taken into account, it would appear that human beings are not modified apes who arose on this planet by a process of physical evolution. Instead we are fallen angels, beings who came to this planet by a process of devolution from spiritual forms that preexisted in another dimension of reality.

As Lord Krishna says in the *Bhagavad Gita* (15.7), "The living entities in this conditioned world are My eternal fragmental parts. Due to conditioned life, they are struggling very hard with the six senses, which include the mind." God is an eternally conscious person, and the living entities are also eternally conscious persons. In their original state, the deathless living entities exercise their free will to act in connection with God, in the pleasure-filled realm of pure spiritual energy. Some of the living entities, however, misuse their free will to act independently of God. Attracted by the material energy, they become covered by bodies composed of mind and matter. In this state, their natural freedom is constrained by the conditions imposed upon them by their bodies, with which they struggle to enjoy the material energy, in a cycle of repeated births and deaths. It is possible, however, for such living entities to regain their deathless and blissful spiritual state.

2

FORBIDDEN ARCHEOLOGY: THE HIDDEN HISTORY OF THE HUMAN RACE

Upon hearing the proposal that human beings are devolved spirits rather than the modified descendants of extinct apelike creatures, one might ask: Has not science, using physical evidence, demonstrated beyond doubt that we did in fact evolve, by natural selection, from more anatomically primitive hominids? There is certainly a lot of talk and writing to that effect. But in the 932 pages of *Forbidden Archeology*, Richard Thompson and I documented abundant physical evidence contradicting the current evolutionary theory of human origins. *Forbidden Archeology* (also available in abridged form as *The Hidden History of the Human Race*) is thus the indispensable prelude to *Human Devolution*. In this chapter, I will summarize the essential points made in *Forbidden Archeology*. But there is no substitute for reading the entire book and seeing for oneself the massive amounts of evidence that contradict the idea that anatomically modern humans evolved within the past 6 million years from very apelike hominid ancestors. This evidence confirms that we really do require an alternative to the present theory.

William W. Howells, emeritus professor of physical anthropology at Harvard University, and one of the chief architects of the modern theory of human evolution, wrote to me on August 10, 1993: "Thank you for sending me a copy of *Forbidden Archeology*, which represents much careful effort in critically assembling published materials. I have given it a good examination.... Most of us, mistakenly or not, see human evolution as a succession of branchings from earlier to more advanced forms of primate, with man emerging rather late.... To have modern human beings ... appearing a great deal earlier, in fact at a time when even simple primates did not exist as possible ancestors, would be devastating not only to the accepted pattern. It would be devastating to the whole theory of

9

evolution." Yes, and it would demand an alternative hypothesis. Howells went on to say, "The suggested hypothesis would demand a kind of process which could not possibly be accommodated by evolutionary theory as we know it, and I should think it requires an explanation." *Human Devolution* provides the explanation Howells requested, the explanation of a process that lies outside the range of current evolutionary theory. But first, we should understand exactly why such a new hypothesis is in fact required.

Problems with Current Theory

Mainstream physical anthropologists agree among themselves that hominids, the biological group that includes today's humans and their supposed ancestors, split off from the African apes around 6 million years ago. There is, however, little agreement about the identity of the very first hominids. In the last decade of the twentieth century and the early years of the twenty-first century, physical anthropologists and archeologists uncovered fragmentary remains of a variety of new hominid species. From some of these early hominids came *Australopithecus*. There are, we are told, many species of *Australopithecus*. The earliest of these came into existence about 4 or 5 million years ago. From one of them arose *Homo habilis*, the first toolmaker. Next came *Homo erectus*, the first hominid to use fire. Then came early modern humans and the Neandertals. Finally, anatomically modern humans arrived on the scene about 100,000 years ago. It all sounds so perfectly clear when you hear a teacher say it, when you read it in a book, or when you see it in a museum display or on television. But behind the scenes, there are major ongoing disputes about each stage of this progression.

When scientists say that humans came from apes, they do not mean the modern apes we see in zoos, such as gorillas and chimpanzees. They mean the extinct dryopithecine apes of Africa. These apes, supposedly the common ancestors of both modern apes and modern humans, lived in the Miocene period, from about 5 to 20 million years ago. The human line (the hominids) and the modern ape line supposedly split off from their common dryopithecine ancestor about 6–7 million years ago. There are many species of *Dryopithecus*, however, and scientists cannot yet say exactly which of these extinct apes is our primeval ancestor. Nor can they tell us much about the very first hominids, the ones that existed before *Australopithecus*. Their fossil remains, mostly discovered after the publication of *Forbidden Archeology* in 1993, are fragmentary and subject to multiple interpretations.

Lemonick and Dorfman (2001) give a good review of the current confused state of early hominid paleontology. In 1994, researchers uncovered bones that they attributed to a creature called *Ardipithecus ramidus*, who lived in Ethiopia 4.4 million years ago. In 2001, researchers from America and Ethiopia announced the discovery of more *Ardipithecus* bones, this time 5.8 million years old. *Ardipithecus* had roughly the same size and body structure as a chimpanzee, with an important exception. The researchers found a toe bone with a humanlike structure, indicating *Ardipithecus* walked upright. But Donald Johanson, director of the Institute for Human Origins at the University of Arizona, pointed out that the toe bone was found ten miles from the other bones and was several hundred thousand years older. It was therefore not clear that the highly significant toe bone belonged to *Ardipithecus*. Perhaps it belonged to actual humans present millions of years ago in Africa? That is not impossible, because there is plenty of evidence that anatomically modern humans did exist millions of years ago in Africa and elsewhere. In any case, the *Ardipithecus* researchers proposed that the line of human origins went through the older *Ardipithecus* at 5.8 million years to the younger *Ardipithecus* at 4.4 million years to *Australopithecus afarensis* (Lucy) at 3.2 million years and then on to the first members of the genus *Homo* at around 2 million years ago.

In the year 2000 a team of French and Kenyan researchers led by Brigitte Senut and Martin Pickford uncovered some bones of a creature they called *Orrorin tugenensis,* popularly known as Millenium Man. Senut and Pickford said that *Ardipithecus* is simply an ape, with no direct place in the human lineage. They also denied that *Australopithecus afarensis* was a human ancestor. The bones of Millenium Man were 6 million years old. Senut and Pickford believed the bones showed that Millenium Man walked upright on two legs, a key human trait, but other researchers such as Meave Leakey remained unconvinced. Furthermore, Bernard Wood (Culotta 1999), of the George Washington University, questioned the whole idea that early primates with skeletal remains indicating bipedalism should automatically be considered human ancestors. Maybe they were just apes that happened to walk on two legs and had no connection with humans.

In late 2001, Meave Leakey introduced even more confusion into an already confused picture. She announced in *Nature* (Leakey et al. 2001) the discovery of a new hominid. Leakey and her colleagues found a nearly complete skull of the creature in August of 1999, near Lake Turkana, in Kenya. The creature is 3.5 million years old, roughly the same age as *Australopithecus afarensis*. Instead of identifying her find as a new member of the genus *Australopithecus,* Meave Leakey stirred up the hominid world by creating a new genus and species for it: *Kenyanthropus platyops.* The name is significant. *Anthropus* means "human" whereas *pithecus* means "ape." So Leakey was obviously putting *Kenyanthropus platyops* in the human line, implying that *Australopithecus* is nothing more than an extinct ape, unrelated to humans. Leakey suggested that *Kenyanthropus platyops* might be linked to later fossils currently attributed to *Homo rudolfensis.* Although Meave Leakey called for further research, it appeared she was positioning *Kenyanthropus platyops* so as to permanently remove the australopithecines from the line of human ancestry. My reply is that neither *Kenyanthropus* nor *Australopithecus* are human ancestors because there is evidence that anatomically modern humans existed alongside them and before them.

In short, the picture of newly discovered early hominids is quite confusing and contradictory. In all these cases, scientists are speculating about fragmentary fossil remains, seeing in them human ancestors, when they most likely are simply varieties of apes with some few features in common with modern humans. These features are, however, not necessarily signs of an evolutionary connection.

Despite the confusion surrounding *Australopithecus,* many scientists still accept this creature as a direct human ancestor. The first specimen of *Australopithecus* was discovered in 1924 by Dr. Raymond Dart in South Africa. Dart believed it was the earliest human ancestor, but most of the influential scientists of his time thought it was just a variety of ape. It was not until the late 1950s that *Australopithecus* won general acceptance as a human ancestor. But there remained important scientists who did not agree. Among these scientists were Louis Leakey, one of the most famous anthropologists of the twentieth century. Meave Leakey's interpretation of her *Kenyanthropus platyops* as the ancestor of the *Homo* line, bypassing *Australopithecus,* can be seen as continuing Louis Leakey's work.

Lord Zuckerman, a respected British zoologist, carried out many exacting statistical studies showing that *Australopithecus* was not a human ancestor. The work of Lord Zuckerman has been carried into the present by Charles E. Oxnard, now a professor of physical anthropology at the University of Western Australia. For a strong antidote to modern propaganda about the australopithecines being human ancestors, one should read his books *Uniqueness and Diversity in Human Evolution* (1975) and *The Order of Man* (1984). These books have been largely ignored by the scientific establishment, challenging as they do one of the articles of faith of human evolution studies. But they are required reading for anyone who wants to know the truth about *Australopithecus*. The anatomical studies of Oxnard place *Australopithecus* close to the gibbons and orangutans and distant from the African apes and humans. Given this set of relationships, it is difficult to see *Australopithecus* as a direct human ancestor.

Scientists who believe *Australopithecus* is a human ancestor see in its fossil bones signs of upright walking ability and other human features. But Oxnard's studies show a creature just as likely to be found swinging through the trees like a gibbon or orangutan as walking upright on the ground.

Even among scientists who do accept *Australopithecus* as a human ancestor, there is a great deal of disagreement. On one side, we have Donald Johanson, and his colleagues and supporters, who believe that the australopithecines walked upright on the ground just like modern humans. This would, according to this group, be especially true of Lucy, the specimen of *Australopithecus afarensis* that Johanson himself discovered in Ethiopia during the 1970s (Johanson and Edey 1981). But Johanson's critics, and there are many, say that the long curved fingers and toes of Lucy and her relatives, along with many other anatomical features, show that these creatures spent a lot of time in trees (Stern and Susman 1983, pp. 282–284; Susman *et al.* 1984, p 117; Marzke 1983, p. 198). Here they would be in agreement with Oxnard. Some scientists think that Johanson and his coworkers have mistakenly combined the fossils of two or three kinds of creatures into the single species *Australopithecus afarensis*.

During the 1970s, Johanson put forward the idea that Lucy was the oldest known human ancestor, and that starting with her all the other hominids could be arranged in a definite evolutionary progression. The several species could be arranged in two branches coming from the trunk of *Australopithecus afarensis*. One branch would be composed of the *Homo habilis*, *Homo erectus*, and then *Homo sapiens*. On the second branch would be the remaining australopithecines. First comes *Australopithecus africanus*, then *Australopithecus robustus*, then *Australopithecus boisei*. The trend among these is toward greater robustness. In 1985, the Black Skull, designated *Australopithecus garhi*, was discovered. This was a robust australopithecine specimen even more robust than *A. boisei*. If the Black Skull had been younger than *A. robustus* and *A. boisei*, there would have been no problem. It would have fit nicely into the progression of robust australopithecines. But instead the Black Skull was older than the oldest specimens of *A. robustus*. This completely messed up the neat little diagram drawn by Johanson.

As it stands now, there is no agreement at all about the relationships between the various species of *Australopithecus*. As physical anthropologist Pat Shipman (1986, p. 92) put it, "The best answer we can give right now is that we no longer have a very clear idea of who gave rise to whom." Shipman said that in 1986, but the situation has not changed much since then. In fact, the situation has become even more complicated with the addition of discoveries of new species of *Australopithecus* such as *Australopithecus anamensis* and *Australopithecus aethiopicus*. The confusion extends not only to the evolutionary relationships among the australopithecines but also to the relationship between *Australopithecus* and *Homo habilis*, the first member the genus to which modern humans belong. Shipman, considering all the alternatives, said, "We could assert that we have no evidence whatsoever of where *Homo* arises from and remove all members of the genus *Austra-lopithecus* from the hominid family." In other words, *Australopithecus* is not a human ancestor, which is exactly what Zuckerman and Oxnard have always said. But Shipman hesitated, noting, "I've such a visceral negative reaction to this idea that I suspect I am unable to evaluate it rationally. I was brought up on the notion that *Australopithecus* is a hominid" (Shipman 1986, p. 93).

And here is one more problem with *Australopithecus*—mainstream scientists say *Australopithecus* lived only in Africa. But other scientists have reported australopithecines from China, Indonesia, and Southeast Asia (Robinson 1953, Jian et al. 1975, Franzen 1985, and Chen 1990). If accepted, this would make a mess of most current schemes of hominid evolution, making an Asian origin for the hominids as likely as an African origin.

Up until 1987, *Homo habilis* was depicted as a marked evolutionary advance from *Australopithecus* toward the human condition. Both in the scientific literature and popular presentations, *Homo habilis* was shown as larger than its australopithecine ancestors, and with a more humanlike body, although the head still had some apelike features. In 1987, Tim White and Donald Johanson (Johanson *et al.* 1987) reported the discovery of a fairly complete *Homo habilis* skeleton at Olduvai Gorge. *Homo habilis* turned out to be a very small creature with long apelike arms, not very different from *Australopithecus* in size and body proportions. As in the case of *Australopithecus*, some researchers think that *Homo habilis* has been mistakenly put together from the fragmentary fossil bones of two or more species (Wood 1987).

The new picture of *Homo habilis* has made the supposed evolutionary transition to *Homo erectus* more problematic. In 1984, a team of scientists including Richard Leakey found an almost complete *Homo erectus* skeleton (Brown *et al.* 1985, p. 788). Up until this time, scientists had never found any limb bones that could be positively connected with a *Homo erectus* skull. Yet for decades, scientists had been making full-scale models of *Homo erectus,* as if they really knew the correct relative sizes of the head and limbs. Strikingly, the newly found skeleton was that of an adolescent youth who would have been over 6 feet tall when fully grown. Furthermore, at about 1.6 million years old, this was the oldest *Homo erectus* individual found up to that time. The OH 62 *Homo habilis* individual found by Johanson and White was only 200,000 years older, but was quite small and apelike in comparison. An evolutionary transition so great in so little time seems quite improbable, although it is accepted by evolutionists as a matter of faith. Even some evolutionists have doubts about it. The relationship between the early varieties of the genus *Homo* is further complicated by African fossils designated *Homo rudolfensis* and *Homo ergaster.*

At the more recent end of its existence, *Homo erectus* is thought by most scientists to be the direct ancestor of *Homo sapiens.* Louis Leakey (1960, pp. 210–211; 1971, pp. 25, 27), however, never accepted this. In his books, he gave many anatomical reasons why neither *Homo erectus* nor the australopithecines should be considered ancestral to modern humans. His dissenting view is rarely, if ever, mentioned in modern textbooks about human evolution.

Here is another problem. The first *Homo erectus* specimens were found by Eugene Dubois in Java in the 1890s. First he found an apelike skull. And the next year he found a femur or thighbone, about 45 feet away. Bones of many other kinds of animals were found in the same deposit. Dubois thought the skull and thighbone belonged to the same creature, which he called *Pithecanthropus erectus.* Right from the start, many scientists refused to accept that both bones belonged to the same creature. But eventually, the scientific community agreed with Dubois. Evolutionists needed a missing link connecting living humans with their extinct ape ancestors, and Dubois had given them a likely candidate.

Interestingly enough, later researchers reinterpreted the original Java *Homo erectus* fossils. In 1973, M. H. Day and T. I. Molleson determined that the femur found by Dubois is different from other *Homo erectus* femurs and is in fact indistinguishable from anatomically modern human femurs. This caused Day and Molleson (1973) to propose that the femur was not connected with the Java man skull. It thus appears that Dubois was mistaken in attributing them to the same creature. This finding is well known in professional circles, but in most textbooks and science museum displays, the Java man skull and femur are still shown as belonging together. Why? For decades, the discovery of Java man by Dubois has been practically mythologized. Apparently, scientists are hesitant to destroy the public myth they have created.

After Dubois discovered Java man, G. H. R. von Koenigswald made additional discoveries of *Homo erectus* fossils, as did other scientists. The finds look impressive in textbooks, but they are in fact of very little value because of their insecure dating. Most were found on the surface, which means they could be of almost any age, including very recent.

In 1856, some German workmen uncovered some bones in a cave high up one of the walls of the Neander valley (*Neandertal* in German). The bones were turned over to a local naturalist, and from that moment on the Neandertals have been a source of endless controversy in science. The two hottest issues are (1) the physical and cultural characteristics of the Neandertals and (2) their relationship to modern humans. Looking at the Neandertal fossils and their associated stone tools and other cultural artifacts, some scientists have characterized the Neandertals as physically bestial and culturally primitive. Others have given them more human appearance and behavior. The disagreements on this topic have been going on for about 150 years, and they have not stopped. On the relationship of the Neandertals to modern humans, the debate also remains intense. Some scientists are convinced they are our immediate ancestors, and others are convinced they are just a sidebranch that went extinct, leaving no descendants. Physical anthropologists Erik Trinkaus and Pat Shipman (1994) wrote *The Neandertals: Of Skeletons, Scientists, and Scandals*, which details in lively prose the twists and turns of the scientific debates on the Neandertals. Trinkaus and Shipman demonstrate that scientists past and present have been victims of bias and prejudice, and that they have sometimes used their positions of authority to influence the outcome of scientific debates.

One might expect that as we get closer to the present, the picture of human evolution might become somewhat clearer. Wrong. Today the heaviest disputes in human evolution studies are those concerning the most recent evolutionary event of all—the emergence of anatomically modern humans. On one side are those who say that anatomically modern humans arose once, in a single, geographically isolated part of the world, usually given as Africa. And on the other side are those who say humans arose several times in different parts of the world. This is known as the multiregional hypothesis. Complicating the picture are the Neandertals. As we have seen, some scientists would have modern humans coming directly from *Homo erectus*, with the Neandertals as a side branch that went extinct, whereas others would incorporate the Neandertals as the immediate ancestors of at least some modern humans.

In 1987, scientists (Cann et al.) announced that mitochondrial DNA studies had shown that humans had arisen from Africa about 200,000 years ago, thus disproving the multiregional hypothesis. But other scientists showed that these studies were flawed. Scientists have used other kinds of DNA studies to support their claims about human evolution. But these also have serious flaws. We shall consider this genetic evidence in depth in chapter 4.

Although Darwinist scientists present a united front to the public, proclaiming loudly that the evolution of humans from apelike ancestors is an established fact, they have not found the actual evolutionary path. But if the path has not been found, how can they assert, except as a matter of faith, that the evolution of humans from apelike ancestors actually did occur?

The Hidden History of the Human Race

Up to now, we have been looking at the problems that confront Darwinists in dealing with the evidence that is currently known and accepted by them. But in *Forbidden Archeology,* we learn that large amounts of evidence have disappeared from view by a process of knowledge filtration. Because this evidence contradicted the established evolutionary doctrines at particular times over the past 150 years, it has been eliminated from scientific discussion. This evidence shows that anatomically modern humans existed millions of years ago. If accepted, this evidence would destroy the evolutionary scenario outlined above, which has anatomically modern humans emerging about 100,000 years ago. *Australopithecus, Homo habilis, Homo erectus,* and the Neandertals would no longer be human ancestors. They would all simply be creatures that coexisted with anatomically modern humans.

Evidence for extreme human antiquity is consistent with the ancient Vedic literature of India. This literature includes a group of writings called the Puranas, or histories. The Puranas inform us that humans have existed for vast periods of cyclical time. The basic unit of this cyclical time is the day of Brahma. The day of Brahma lasts for 4,320,000,000 years. It is followed by a night of Brahma, which also lasts for 4,320,000,000 years. The days and nights of Brahma follow each other endlessly. During the days of Brahma, life, including human life, is manifest, and during the nights of Brahma, life is not manifest. According to the Vedic cosmological calendars, the current day of Brahma began about 2 billion years ago. So a Vedic archeologist might expect to find evidence that humans have existed for up to 2 billion years. The Puranas and other Vedic writings also speak of creatures with apelike bodies and humanlike intelligence. For example, the *Shrimad Bhagavatam* (9.18) tells of the monkey soldiers who assisted Lord Rama in defeating the demon Ravana. So a Vedic archeologist might also expect to find evidence for various types of ape-men coexisting with humans of our type in the distant past.

Here is an example of the kind of evidence reported in *Forbidden Archeology*. In 1979, researchers at the Laetoli, Tanzania, site in East Africa discovered footprints in volcanic ash deposits over 3.6 million years old. Mary Leakey (1979) and others said the prints were indistinguishable from those of modern humans. To these scientists, this meant only that the australopithecines of 3.6 million years ago had remarkably modern feet. But according to other scientists, such as physical anthropologist R. H. Tuttle of the University of Chicago, fossil foot bones of the known australopithecines of 3.6 million years ago show they had feet that were distinctly apelike (Tuttle 1985). Hence they were incompatible with the Laetoli prints. In an article in the March 1990 issue of *Natural History,* Tuttle (1990) confessed "we are left with somewhat of a mystery." It seems permissible, therefore, to consider a possibility neither Tuttle nor Leakey mentioned—that creatures with anatomically modern human bodies to match their anatomically modern human feet existed some 3.6 million years ago in East Africa. In *Forbidden Archeology,* I documented hundreds of other examples of this kind of evidence, grouping them in the following categories—carved bones, stone tools, human fossils, and artifacts suggestive of high levels of culture.

Carved Bones and Shells

In the decades after Darwin introduced his theory, numerous scientists discovered incised and broken animal bones and shells suggesting that tool-using humans or human precursors existed in the Pliocene (2–5 million years ago), the Miocene (5–25 million years ago), and even earlier. In analyzing cut and broken bones and shells, the discoverers carefully considered and ruled out alternative explanations—such as the action of animals or geological pressure—before concluding that humans were responsible. In some cases, stone tools were found along with the cut and broken bones or shells.

A particularly striking example in this category is a shell with a crude yet recognizably human face carved on its outer surface. Reported by geologist H. Stopes (1881) to the British Association for the Advancement of Science, this shell, from the Pliocene Red Crag formation in England, is over 2 million years old. According to standard views, humans capable of this level of artistry did not arrive in Europe until about 30,000 or 40,000 years ago. Furthermore, they supposedly did not arise in their African homeland until about 100,000 years ago.

Concerning evidence of the kind reported by Stopes, French anthropologist Armand de Quatrefages wrote in his book *Hommes Fossiles et Hommes Sauvages* (1884): "The objections made to the existence of man in the Pliocene and Miocene seem to habitually be more related to theoretical considerations than direct observation."

Eoliths: Stones of Contention

Rudimentary stone tools called eoliths ("dawn stones"), found in unexpectedly old geological contexts, inspired protracted debate in the late nineteenth and early twentieth centuries. For some, eoliths were not always easily recognizable as tools. Eoliths were not shaped into symmetrical implemental forms. Instead, an edge of a natural stone flake was chipped to make it suitable for a particular task, such as scraping, cutting, or chopping. Often, the working edge bore signs of use. Critics said eoliths were the product of natural forces, such as tumbling in stream beds. But defenders of eoliths offered convincing counterarguments, demonstrating that natural forces could not have made them.

In the late nineteenth century, Benjamin Harrison, an amateur archeologist, found eoliths on the Kent Plateau in southeastern England (Prestwich 1892). Geological evidence suggests that the eoliths were manufactured in the Middle or Late Pliocene, about 2–4 million ago. In addition to eoliths, Harrison found at various places on the Kent Plateau more advanced stone tools (paleoliths) of similar Pliocene antiquity. Having toolmaking hominids in England at that time violates all current schemes of human evolution. Among the supporters of Harrison's eoliths were Alfred Russel Wallace (E. Harrison 1928, p. 370), cofounder with Darwin of the theory of evolution by natural selection; Sir John Prestwich, (1892, p. 251) one of England's most eminent geologists; and Ray E. Lankester, a director of the British Museum (Natural History).

In the early part of the twentieth century, J. Reid Moir, a fellow of the Royal Anthropological Institute and president of the Prehistoric Society of East Anglia, found eoliths (and more advanced stone tools) in England's Red Crag formation. The tools were about 2.0–2.5 million years old. Some of Moir's tools were found in the detritus beds beneath the Red Crag and could be anywhere from 2.5 to 55 million years old.

Moir's finds won support from one of the most vocal critics of eoliths, Henri Breuil, then regarded as one of the world's preeminent authorities on stone tools. Another supporter was paleontologist Henry Fairfield Osborn, of the American Museum of Natural History in New York. And in 1923, an international commission of scientists journeyed to England to investigate Moir's principal discoveries and pronounced them genuine.

Crude Paleoliths

In the case of eoliths, chipping is confined to the working edge of a naturally broken piece of stone. But the makers of the crude paleoliths deliberately struck flakes from stone cores and then shaped them into more recognizable types of tools. In some cases, the cores themselves were shaped into tools.

Among the crude paleoliths are the early Miocene implements (about 20 million years old) found in the late nineteenth century by Carlos Ribeiro, head of the Geological Survey of Portugal. At an international conference of archeologists and anthropologists held in Lisbon, a committee of scientists investigated one of the sites where Ribeiro had found implements. One of the scientists in the party found a stone tool even more advanced than Ribeiro's better specimens. Comparable to accepted Late Pleistocene tools of the Mousterian type, it was firmly embedded in a Miocene conglomerate, in circumstances that confirmed its Miocene antiquity (Choffat 1884, p. 63).

Crude paleoliths were also found in Miocene formations at Thenay, France. S. Laing (1893, pp. 113–115), an English science writer, observed: "On the whole, the evidence for these Miocene implements seems to be very conclusive, and the objections to have hardly any other ground than the reluctance to admit the great antiquity of man." Scientists also found crude paleoliths of Miocene age at Aurillac, France. And at Boncelles, Belgium, A. Rutot uncovered an extensive collection of paleoliths of Oligocene age (25 to 38 million years old).

Advanced Paleoliths

Whereas the eoliths and crude paleoliths could be either the work of anatomically modern humans or the work of human precursors such as *Homo erectus* or *Homo habilis,* advanced paleoliths are unquestionably the work of anatomically modern humans.

Florentino Ameghino, a respected Argentine paleontologist, found advanced stone tools, signs of fire, broken mammal bones, and a human vertebra in a Pliocene formation at Monte Hermoso, Argentina. Ameghino made numerous similar discoveries in Argentina, attracting the attention of scientists around the world.

In 1912, Ales Hrdlička, of the Smithsonian Institution, published a lengthy, but not very reasonable, attack on Ameghino's work. Hrdlička asserted that all of Ameghino's finds were from recent Indian settlements. In response, Carlos Ameghino, brother of Florentino Ameghino, carried out new investigations at Miramar, on the Argentine coast south of Buenos Aires. There he found a series of stone implements, including bolas, and signs of fire in the Chapadmalalan formation, which modern geologists say is 3–5 million years old. Carlos Ameghino also found at Miramar a stone arrowhead firmly embedded in the femur of a Pliocene species of *Toxodon,* an extinct South American mammal.

Ethnographer Eric Boman disputed Carlos Ameghino's discoveries but also unintentionally helped confirm them. In 1913, Carlos Ameghino's collector, Lorenzo Parodi, found a stone implement in the Pliocene seaside *barranca* (cliff) at Miramar and left it in place. Boman was one of several scientists invited by Ameghino to witness the implement's extraction. After the implement (a bola stone) was photographed and removed, another discovery was made. "At my direction," wrote Boman (1921, p. 344), "Parodi continued to attack the *barranca* with a pick at the same point where the bola stone was discovered, when suddenly and unexpectedly, there appeared a second stone ball. . . . It is more like a grinding stone than a bola." Boman found yet another implement 200 yards away. Confounded, Boman could only hint in his written report that the implements had been planted by Parodi. In any case, Boman produced no evidence whatsoever that Parodi, a longtime employee of the Buenos Aires Museum of Natural History, had ever behaved fraudulently.

The kinds of implements found by Carlos Ameghino at Miramar (arrowheads and bolas) are usually considered the work of *Homo sapiens sapiens.* Taken at face value, the Miramar finds therefore demonstrate the presence of anatomically modern humans in South America over 3 million years ago. Interestingly enough, in 1921 M. A. Vignati discovered in the Late Pliocene Chapadmalalan formation at Miramar a fully human fossil jaw fragment.

In the early 1950s, Thomas E. Lee of the National Museum of Canada found advanced stone tools in glacial deposits at Sheguiandah, on Manitoulin Island in northern Lake Huron. Geologist John Sanford (1971) of Wayne State University argued that the oldest Sheguiandah tools were at least 65,000 years old and might be as much as 125,000 years old. For those adhering to standard views on North American prehistory, such ages were unacceptable.

Thomas E. Lee (1966, pp. 18–19) complained: "The site's discoverer [Lee] was hounded from his Civil Service position into prolonged unemployment; publication outlets were cut off; the evidence was misrepresented by several prominent authors . . . ; the tons of artifacts vanished into storage bins of the National Museum of Canada; for refusing to fire the discoverer, the Director of the National Museum, who had proposed having a monograph on the site published, was himself fired and driven into exile; official positions of prestige and power were exercised in an effort to gain control over just six Sheguiandah specimens that had not gone under cover; and the site has been turned into a tourist resort. . . . Sheguiandah would have forced embarrassing admissions that the Brahmins did not know everything. It would have forced the rewriting of almost every book in the business. It had to be killed. It was killed."

The treatment received by Lee is not an isolated case. In the early 1970s, anthropologists uncovered advanced stone tools at Hueyatlaco, Mexico. Geologist Virginia Steen-McIntyre and other members of a U. S. Geological Survey team obtained an age of about 250,000 years for the site's implement-bearing layers. This challenged not only standard views of New World anthropology but also the whole standard picture of human origins. Humans capable of making the kind of tools found at Hueyatlaco are not thought to have come into existence until around 100,000 years ago in Africa.

Virginia Steen-McIntyre experienced difficulty in getting her dating study on Hueyatlaco published. "The problem as I see it is much bigger than Hueyatlaco," she wrote to Estella Leopold, associate editor of *Quaternary Research.* "It concerns the manipulation of scientific thought through the suppression of 'Enigmatic Data,' data that challenges the prevailing mode of thinking. Hueyatlaco certainly does that! Not being an anthropologist, I didn't realize the full significance of our dates back in 1973, nor how deeply woven into our thought the current theory of human evolution has become. Our work at Hueyatlaco has been rejected by most archaeologists because it contradicts that theory, period."

This pattern of data suppression has been going on for a long time. In 1880, J. D. Whitney (1880), the state geologist of California, published a lengthy review of advanced stone tools found in California gold mines. The implements, including spear points and stone mortars and pestles, were found deep in mine shafts, underneath thick, undisturbed layers of lava, in formations ranging from 9 million to over 55 million years old. W. H. Holmes of the Smithsonian Institution, one of the most vocal critics of the California finds, wrote (1899, p. 424): "Perhaps if Professor

Whitney had fully appreciated the story of human evolution as it is understood today, he would have hesitated to announce the conclusions formulated [that humans existed in very ancient times in North America], notwithstanding the imposing array of testimony with which he was confronted." In other words, if the facts do not agree with the favored theory, then such facts, even an imposing array of them, must be discarded.

Evidence for Advanced Culture in Distant Ages

Up to this point, most of the evidence I have mentioned gives the impression that even if humans did exist in the distant past, they remained at a somewhat primitive level. But artifacts suggestive of more developed cultural and technological achievement have also been found. Not only are some of the objects decidedly more advanced than stone tools, but many also occur in geological contexts far older than we have thus far considered.

The reports of this extraordinary evidence emanate from both scientific and nonscientific sources. In some cases, the artifacts themselves, not having been preserved in standard natural history museums, are impossible to locate. But for the sake of completeness and to encourage further study I will give some examples.

In his book *Mineralogy,* Count Bournon recorded an intriguing discovery made by French workmen in the latter part of the eighteenth century. The workmen, who were quarrying limestone near Aix-en-Provence, had gone through eleven layers of limestone separated by layers of sediments. Then, in the clayey sand above the twelfth layer "they found stumps of columns and fragments of stone half wrought, and the stone was exactly similar to that of the quarry: they found moreover coins, handles of hammers, and other tools or fragments of tools in wood." The wood artifacts were petrified. These passages appeared in the *American Journal of Science and Arts* in 1820 (v. 2, pp. 145–146); today, however, it is unlikely such a report would be found in the pages of a scientific journal. Scientists simply do not take such discoveries seriously. The limestones of Aixen Provence are from the Oligocene (Pomerol 1980, pp. 172–173), which means the objects found in the limestones could be 24–36 million years old.

In 1830, letterlike shapes were discovered within a solid block of marble from a quarry near Norristown, Pennsylvania, about 12 miles northwest of Philadelphia. The marble block was taken from a depth of 60–70 feet. This was reported in the *American Journal of Science and*

Arts (v. 19, p. 361) in 1831. The marble in the quarries around Norristown is Cambro-Ordovician (Stone 1932, p. 225), or about 500–600 million years old.

In 1844, Sir David Brewster reported that a nail had been discovered firmly embedded in a block of sandstone from the Kingoodie (Mylnfield) Quarry in North Britain. Dr. A. W. Medd of the British Geological Survey wrote to my research assistant in 1985 that this sandstone is of "Lower Old Red Sandstone age" (Devonian, between 360 and 408 million years old). Brewster was a famous Scottish physicist. He was a founder of the British Association for the Advancement of Science and made important discoveries in the field of optics.

On June 22, 1844, this curious report appeared in the London *Times:* "A few days ago, as some workmen were employed in quarrying a rock close to the Tweed about a quarter of a mile below Rutherford-mill, a gold thread was discovered embedded in the stone at a depth of eight feet." Dr. A. W. Medd of the British Geological Survey wrote to my research assistant in 1985 that this stone is of Early Carboniferous age (between 320 and 360 million years old).

The following report, titled "A Relic of a Bygone Age," appeared in the magazine *Scientific American* (June 5, 1852): "A few days ago a powerful blast was made in the rock at Meeting House Hill, in Dorchester, a few rods south of Rev. Mr. Hall's meeting house. The blast threw out an immense mass of rock, some of the pieces weighing several tons, and scattered fragments in all directions. Among them was picked up a metallic vessel in two parts, rent asunder by the explosion. On putting the two parts together it formed a bell-shaped vessel. . . . On the side there are six figures of a flower, or bouquet, beautifully inlaid with pure silver, and around the lower part of the vessel a vine, or wreath, also inlaid with silver. . . . This curious and unknown vessel was blown out of the solid pudding stone, fifteen feet below the surface. . . . The matter is worthy of investigation, as there is no deception in the case." According to a recent U.S. Geological Survey map of the Boston-Dorchester area, the pudding stone, now called the Roxbury conglomerate, is of Precambrian age, over 600 million years old.

The April 1862 edition of *The Geologist* included an English translation of an intriguing report by Maximilien Melleville, the vice president of the Academic Society of Laon, France. In his report, Melleville described a round chalk ball discovered 75 meters (about 246 feet) below the surface in early Eocene lignite beds near Laon. If humans made the ball, they must have existed in France 45–55 million years ago.

Melleville (1862, p. 147) stated: "Long before this discovery, the workmen of the quarry had told me they had many times found pieces of wood changed into stone ... bearing the marks of human work. I regret greatly now not having asked to see these, but I did not hitherto believe in the possibility of such a fact."

In 1871, William E. Dubois of the Smithsonian Institution reported on several human artifacts found at deep levels in Illinois. The first object was a copper coin from Lawn Ridge, in Marshall County, Illinois. It came from a well-boring, at a depth of 114 feet (Winchell 1881, p. 170). Using the drilling record, the Illinois State Geological Survey estimated the age of the deposits at the 114-foot level. The deposits would have formed during the Yarmouthian interglacial period "sometime between 200,000 and 400,000 years ago."

The coin suggests the existence of a civilization at least 200,000 years ago in North America. Yet beings intelligent enough to make and use coins (*Homo sapiens sapiens*) are generally not thought to have lived much earlier than 100,000 years ago. According to standard views, metal coins were first used in Asia Minor during the eighth century BC.

A small human image, skillfully formed in clay, was found in 1889 at Nampa, Idaho. The figurine came from the 300-foot level of a well boring (Wright 1912, pp. 266–267). Responding to inquiries by my research assistant, the United States Geological Survey stated in a letter that the clay layer at a depth of over 300 feet is "probably of the Glenns Ferry Formation, upper Idaho Group, which is generally considered to be of Plio-Pleistocene age." The boundary between the Pliocene and the Pleistocene lies at two million years ago. Other than *Homo sapiens sapiens,* no hominid is known to have fashioned works of art like the Nampa figurine. The evidence therefore suggests that humans of the modern type were living in America around 2 million years ago, at the Plio-Pleistocene boundary.

On June 11, 1891, *The Morrisonville Times* (Illinois, U.S.A.) reported: "A curious find was brought to light by Mrs. S. W. Culp last Tuesday morning. As she was breaking a lump of coal preparatory to putting it in the scuttle, she discovered, as the lump fell apart, embedded in a circular shape a small gold chain about ten inches in length of antique and quaint workmanship." The Illinois State Geological Survey has said the coal in which the gold chain was found is 260–320 million years old. This raises the possibility that culturally advanced human beings were present in North America during that time.

The April 2, 1897 edition of the *Daily News* of Omaha, Nebraska, carried an article titled "Carved Stone Buried in a Mine," which described an object from a mine near Webster City, Iowa. The article stated: "While mining coal today in the Lehigh coal mine, at a depth of 130 feet, one of the miners came upon a piece of rock which puzzles him and he was unable to account for its presence at the bottom of the coal mine. The stone is of a dark grey color and about two feet long, one foot wide and four inches in thickness. Over the surface of the stone, which is very hard, lines are drawn at angles forming perfect diamonds. The center of each diamond is a fairly good face of an old man." The Lehigh coal is probably from the Carboniferous.

On January 10, 1949, Robert Nordling sent a photograph of an iron cup to Frank L. Marsh of Andrews University, in Berrien Springs, Michigan. Nordling wrote: "I visited a friend's museum in southern Missouri. Among his curios, he had the iron cup pictured on the enclosed snapshot" (Rusch 1971, p. 201).

At the private museum, the iron cup had been displayed along with the following affidavit, made by Frank J. Kenwood in Sulphur Springs, Arkansas, on November 27, 1948: "While I was working in the Municipal Electric Plant in Thomas, Okla. in 1912, I came upon a solid chunk of coal which was too large to use. I broke it with a sledge hammer. This iron pot fell from the center, leaving the impression or mould of the pot in the piece of coal. Jim Stall (an employee of the company) witnessed the breaking of the coal, and saw the pot fall out. I traced the source of the coal, and found that it came from the Wilburton, Oklahoma, Mines" (Rusch 1971, p. 201). According to Robert O. Fay of the Oklahoma Geological Survey, the Wilburton mine coal is about 312 million years old.

On October 8, 1922, the *American Weekly* section of the *New York Sunday American* ran a prominent feature titled "Mystery of the Petrified 'Shoe Sole'," by Dr. W. H. Ballou (1922, p. 2). Ballou wrote: "Some time ago, while he was prospecting for fossils in Nevada, John T. Reid, a distinguished mining engineer and geologist, stopped suddenly and looked down in utter bewilderment and amazement at a rock near his feet. For there, a part of the rock itself, was what seemed to be a human footprint! Closer inspection showed that it was not a mark of a naked foot, but was, apparently, a shoe sole which had been turned into stone. The forepart was missing. But there was the outline of at least two-thirds of it, and around this outline ran a well-defined sewn thread which had, it appeared, attached the welt to the sole." The Triassic rock bearing the fossil shoe sole is 213–248 million years old.

W. W. McCormick of Abilene, Texas, has a document recording his grandfather's account of a stone block wall that was found deep within a coal mine: "In the year 1928, I, Atlas Almon Mathis, was working in coal mine No. 5, located two miles north of Heavener, Oklahoma. This was a shaft mine, and they told us it was two miles deep." One evening, Mathis was blasting coal loose by explosives in "room 24" of this mine. "The next morning," said Mathis, "there were several concrete blocks laying in the room. These blocks were 12-inch cubes and were so smooth and polished on the outside that all six sides could serve as mirrors." Mathis added: "As I started to timber the room up, it caved in; and I barely escaped. When I came back after the cave-in, a solid wall of these polished blocks was left exposed. About 100 to 150 yards farther down our air core, another miner struck this same wall, or one very similar" (Steiger 1979, p. 27). The coal in the mine was probably Carboniferous, which would mean the wall was at least 286 million years old.

M. K. Jessup, an astronomer, recorded the following wall-in-coal-mine story: "It is . . . reported that James Parsons, and his two sons, exhumed a slate wall in a coal mine at Hammondville, Ohio, in 1868. It was a large, smooth wall, disclosed when a great mass of coal fell away from it, and on its surface, carved in bold relief, were several lines of hieroglyphics" (Jessup 1973, p. 65).

The foregoing sampling of discoveries indicating a relatively high level of civilization in very distant ages was compiled from reports published in the nineteenth and early twentieth centuries, but similar reports continue up to the present day. We shall now review some of them.

In 1968, William J. Meister, a draftsman and amateur trilobite collector, reported finding a shoe print in the Wheeler Shale near Antelope Springs, Utah. This shoelike indentation and its cast were revealed when Meister split open a block of shale. Clearly visible within the imprint were the remains of trilobites, extinct marine arthropods. The shale holding the print and the trilobite fossils is from the Cambrian, and would thus be 505 to 590 million years old.

Meister (1968, p. 99) described the ancient shoelike impression in an article that appeared in the *Creation Research Society Quarterly:* "The heel print was indented in the rock about an eighth of an inch more than the sole. The footprint was clearly that of the right foot because the sandal was well worn on the right side of the heel in characteristic fashion." In 1984, Richard L. Thompson visited Meister in Utah. His close inspection of the print revealed no obvious reason why it could not be accepted as genuine. The shape of the Meister print, as shown by Thompson's visual inspection and computer analysis, closely matches that of a modern shoe print.

Over the past several decades, South African miners have found hundreds of metallic spheres with up to three parallel grooves running around their equators. Roelf Marx, curator of the museum of Klerksdorp, South Africa, where some of the spheres are housed, said: "The spheres are a complete mystery. They look man-made, yet at the time in Earth's history when they came to rest in this rock no intelligent life existed. They're nothing like I have ever seen before."

My research assistant wrote to Roelf Marx for further information about the spheres. He replied in a letter dated September 12, 1984: "There is nothing scientific published about the globes, but the facts are: They are found in pyrophyllite, which is mined near the little town of Ottosdal in the Western Transvaal. This pyrophyllite is a quite soft secondary mineral. . . . formed by sedimentation about 2.8 billion years ago. On the other hand the globes, which have a fibrous structure on the inside with a shell around it, are very hard and cannot be scratched, even by steel." In the absence of a satisfactory natural explanation, the evidence is somewhat mysterious, leaving open the possibility that the South African grooved spheres—found in a mineral deposit 2.8 billion years old—were made by intelligent beings.

Extremely Old Human Fossils

As we have seen, there are lots of stone tools and other artifacts showing a human presence going back millions of years. But are there also any human fossils to further support this conclusion? The answer is yes. Of course, one should keep in mind that fossilization is a rare event. Richard Leakey once said that the key fossils related to human evolution could fit on a billiard table. And one of the comments often heard at conferences on human evolution is "we need more fossils." Given the rarity of such fossils, the examples we are about to discuss assume considerable importance.

One good example comes from the original Java *Homo erectus* discoveries of Eugene Dubois at Trinil. As we have seen, modern scientists have shown that the femur found along with the Java man skull is unlike *Homo erectus* femurs and resembles exactly modern human femurs. They have thus concluded that the femur does not belong with the skull. But what then do we make of the femur? It would appear that we have good evidence for anatomically modern humans in Java at about 800,000 years ago, which is the age previously attributed to the skull and femur. According to modern theory, anatomically modern humans did not come into existence until about 100,000 years ago.

We have also seen that *Homo habilis,* as pictured before the OH-62 discovery in 1987, is probably a composite of fossils from several species.

Donald Johanson has in fact suggested that many bones previously attributed to *Homo habilis* must now be reassigned. Among these bones is the ER 1481 femur, found at Lake Turkana, Kenya by John Harris. Richard Leakey described this femur as indistinguishable from that of a modern human being. So if it no longer belongs to *Homo habilis,* perhaps it should be assigned to an anatomically modern human living in Africa about 2 million years ago.

During the nineteenth century and early twentieth century, several discoveries of human skeletal remains were made in Middle Pleistocene formations in Europe. These discoveries include those made at Galley Hill, Moulin Quignon, Clichy, La Denise, and Ipswich. The presence of these skeletons in Middle Pleistocene strata could be attributed to recent intrusive burial, mistakes in reporting, or fraud. Nonetheless, there are reasons for thinking that the skeletons might in fact be of Middle Pleistocene age.

In 1888, workmen removing deposits at Galley Hill, near London, England, exposed a bed of chalk. One workman, Jack Allsop, informed Robert Elliott, a collector of prehistoric items, that he had discovered a human skeleton firmly embedded in these deposits about 8 feet below the surface and about 2 feet above the chalk bed (Keith 1928, pp. 250–266). Elliott stated: "We carefully looked for any signs of the section being disturbed, but failed: the stratification being unbroken." A schoolmaster named M. H. Heys also observed the bones embedded in undisturbed deposits. Heys said: "This undisturbed state of the stratum was so palpable to the workman that he said, 'The man or animal was not buried by anybody'" (Keith 1928, p. 255). Numerous stone tools were also recovered from the Galley Hill site.

According to modern opinion, the Galley Hill site belongs to the Holstein interglacial period, which occurred about 330,000 years ago. Anatomically, the Galley Hill skeleton was judged to be of the modern human type. Most scientists now think that anatomically modern humans (*Homo sapiens sapiens*) originated in Africa around 100,000 years ago. They say that *Homo sapiens sapiens* eventually entered Western Europe in the form of Cro-Magnon man approximately 30,000 or 40,000 years ago, replacing the Neandertals.

Despite the testimony by Heys and Elliott that the Galley Hill skeleton was found in undisturbed strata, K. P. Oakley and M. F. A. Montagu (1949) later concluded that the skeleton must have been recently buried in the Middle Pleistocene deposits. This is also the opinion of almost all anthropologists today.

In 1863, J. Boucher de Perthes discovered an anatomically modern human jaw in the Moulin Quignon gravel pit at Abbeville, France. He removed it from a layer of black sand and gravel 16.5 feet deep. The layer also contained stone implements of the Acheulean type (Keith 1928, p. 270). The Acheulean sites at Abbeville are about 400,000 years old. Upon hearing of the discovery of the Abbeville jaw and tools, a group of distinguished British geologists visited Abbeville and were at first favorably impressed. Later, however, it was alleged that some of the stone implements in Boucher de Perthes's collection were forgeries foisted on him by the workmen. The British scientists then began to doubt the authenticity of the jaw (Keith 1928, p. 271).

In May 1863, British geologists and archeologists met with their French counterparts in France to decide the status of the jaw. The commission jointly declared in favor of the authenticity of the jaw, despite some reservations by two of the British members. Thereafter, however, the British members continued to oppose the Moulin Quignon jaw and eventually won most scientists over to their side.

In the aftermath of the Moulin Quignon debate, Boucher des Perthes continued to maintain that his discoveries were genuine. To help prove this, he conducted several more excavations at Moulin Quignon, under very strict controls and in the presence of trained scientific observers. These excavations yielded many more anatomically modern human bones, bone fragments, and teeth. These discoveries, which received almost no attention in the English-speaking world, are significant demonstrations of a human presence in the Middle Pleistocene of Europe, over 400,000 years ago. They also tend to strengthen the case for the authenticity of the original Moulin Quignon jaw.

In 1868, Eugene Bertrand reported to the Anthropological Society of Paris that he found parts of a human skull, along with a femur, tibia, and some foot bones, in a quarry on the Avenue de Clichy. The bones were found 5.25 meters (17.3 feet) beneath the surface. Sir Arthur Keith (1928, pp. 276–277) believed the layer in which Clichy human bones were found was the same age as the one in which the Galley Hill skeleton was discovered. This would make the Clichy bones approximately 330,000 years old. The depth at which the Clichy human fossils were found (over 17 feet) argues against recent burial.

But Gabriel de Mortillet (Bertrand 1868, p. 332) said that a workman at the quarry on the Avenue de Clichy told him that he had stashed in the bottom of the pit a skeleton from the upper layers of the quarry. Even after hearing de Mortillet relate the workman's story about stashing the bones of the Clichy skeleton, a number of scientists remained convinced Bertrand's discovery was genuine. For example, Professor E. T. Hamy

(Bertrand 1868, p. 335) said: "Mr. Bertrand's discovery seems to me to be so much less debatable in that it is not the first of this kind at Avenue de Clichy. Indeed, our esteemed colleague, Mr. Reboux, found in that same locality, and almost at the same depth (4.20 meters), human bones that he has given me to study."

In his remarks to the Anthropological Society, Bertrand provided additional evidence for the great antiquity of the Clichy skeleton. He stated that he found a human ulna in the stratum containing the other bones of the Clichy human skeleton. The ulna is the larger of the two long bones of the forearm. When Bertrand tried to extract the ulna it crumbled into dust. He offered this as proof that the Clichy human skeleton must have been native to the layer in which it was found. Apparently, Bertrand reasoned that a bone as fragile as the decayed ulna could not possibly have been removed from an upper layer of the quarry and stashed by a workman in the lower layer in which Bertrand found it—it would certainly have been destroyed in the process. This indicated that the ulna belonged to the stratum in which Bertrand found it, as did the other human bones.

In 1911, J. Reid Moir discovered an anatomically modern human skeleton beneath a layer of glacial boulder clay near the town of Ipswich, in the East Anglia region of England. The skeleton was found at a depth of 1.38 meters (about 4.5 feet), in deposits as much as 400,000 years old. Moir took care to rule out the possibility of burial from a more recent level.

The discovery, however, inspired intense opposition. Sir Arthur Keith (1928, p. 299) wrote, "Under the presumption that the modern type of man is also modern in origin, a degree of high antiquity is denied to such specimens." Despite opposition, Moir initially stuck to his guns, holding that the Ipswich skeleton was genuinely old. Then suddenly he reversed himself, declaring the skeleton recent. What then happened to change his mind? He found nearby, at the same level, some advanced stone tools. He therefore concluded that the layer of boulder clay above the skeleton had been formed about 30,000 years ago from the sludgelike remnants of the original boulder clay deposit, formed hundreds of thousands of years earlier (Moir 1916, p. 109). But sophisticated stone tools turn up all over the world, in very old formations. Therefore, I cannot agree with Moir that the discovery of tools of advanced type at the same level as the Ipswich skeleton was sufficient reason to reinterpret the site stratigraphy to bring the age of the skeleton into harmony with the supposed age of the tools.

A very strong case for anatomically modern humans existing in very early times comes from Argentina. In 1896, workers excavating a dry dock in Buenos Aires found a human skull. They took it from the rudder pit at the bottom of the excavation, after breaking through a layer of a hard, limestonelike substance called *tosca*. The level at which the skull was found was 11 meters (36 feet) below the bed of the river La Plata (Hrdlička 1912, p. 318).

The workers who found the skull gave it to Mr. Junor, their supervisor. In the opinion of Argentine paleontologist Florentino Ameghino (1909, p. 108), the skull belonged to a Pliocene precursor of *Homo sapiens*. He called this precursor *Diprothomo platensis*. But according to Ales Hrdlička (1912, p. 332) of the Smithsonian Institution, the skull was just like that of modern humans.

The skull was found in what Ales Hrdlička (1912, p. 321) called "the uppermost portion of the Pre-Ensenadean stratum." According to modern geological opinion, the Pre-Ensenadan stratum should be at least 1.0–1.5 million years old. Even at 1 million years, the presence of a fully modern human skull anywhere in the world—what to speak of South America—would be unexpected.

Bailey Willis, the geologist who accompanied Hrdlička on his expedition to Argentina, offered some vague, unfounded speculations about how the skull could have arrived in the rudder pit. For his part, Hrdlička thought the fact that the skull was modern in shape was enough to rule out any great age for it. Hrdlička's prejudice is evident in the following statement (Hrdlička 1912): "The antiquity . . . of any human skeletal remains which do not present marked differences from those of modern man may be regarded, on morphologic grounds, as only insignificant geologically, not reaching in time, in all probability, beyond the modern, still unfinished, geologic formations." In other words, even if anatomically modern human bones were found in geological strata millions of years old, Hrdlička would not accept them as being that old. According to his logic, evolution is always happening, and any such bones millions of years old should, therefore, be quite different from those of modern humans. If they are not different, they are not old.

In 1913, Dr. Hans Reck, of Berlin University, found an anatomically modern human skeleton in Bed II of Olduvai Gorge. This would make the anatomically modern skeleton over 1 million years old. Aware of the possibility of intrusive burial, Reck (1914) carefully examined the sediments around the skeleton and determined that there was absolutely no sign of disturbance. Louis Leakey was initially skeptical of the discovery. However, after seeing the skeleton in a Munich museum, still embedded in its matrix of rock, and visiting the site in Africa, he changed his mind and agreed with Reck that the skeleton really belonged to Bed II. Other scientists, however, maintained their opposition. Reck and Leakey later changed their minds (L. Leakey *et al.* 1931), and agreed that the skeleton had been buried into Bed II at a later time. This turnaround is quite inexplicable, considering their earlier testimony that very close inspection had shown absolutely no sign that the skeleton had been buried in Bed II after the deposition of Bed II. During World War II, most of the skeleton was lost. After the war, a scientist did a carbon 14 test on some small fragments of bone he thought belonged to the skeleton. This test gave an age of about 17,000 years. But there are several problems with this date. First of all, it is not clear that the bone fragments he tested really belonged to Reck's skeleton. Second, even if the bone fragments did belong to Reck's skeleton, they could have been contaminated with recent carbon during the several decades they had lain exposed in the museum. This would have caused the carbon 14 test to yield a falsely young date.

In 1855, a human jaw was discovered at Foxhall, England, by workers digging in a quarry. Robert H. Collyer, an American physician then residing in London acquired the fossil. He noted that the bed from which the jaw was said to have been taken was 16 feet below the surface. The condition of the jaw, thoroughly infiltrated with iron oxide, was consistent with incorporation in this bed. The 16-foot level at Foxhall is the same from which J. Reid Moir (1924, p. 647) later recovered stone tools and signs of fire. Anything found at this level would be at least 2.5 million years old.

Aware that he was in the possession of a fossil of great significance, Collyer showed it to various English scientists, including Charles Lyell, George Busk, Richard Owen, Sir John Prestwich, and Thomas Huxley. All were skeptical of its antiquity. American paleontologist Henry Fairfield Osborn (1921, p. 568), writing in the 1920s, wondered why the above-mentioned scientists did not take the trouble to visit the site. They disbelieved, said Osborn, "probably because the shape of the jaw was not primitive."

Late in the summer of 1860, Professor Giuseppe Ragazzoni, a geologist at the Technical Institute of Brescia, traveled to Castenedolo, about 6 miles southeast of Brescia, to gather fossil shells in the Pliocene strata exposed in a pit at the base of a low hill, the Colle de Vento. There he found some human bones. Ragazzoni took the bones to the geologists A. Stoppani and G. Curioni, who said they were probably from a recent burial. Accepting their decision, Ragazzoni discarded the bones.

In December of 1879, a landowner at Castenedolo noticed some human bones in an excavation. Ragazzoni recovered the bones, which included pieces of the skull, some teeth, and parts of the backbone, ribs, arms, legs, and feet. More bones were found over the next few weeks. On February 16, a complete skeleton was discovered. Ragazzoni journeyed to the site and supervised the excavation. The skeleton, enveloped in a mass of blue green clay, turned out to be that of an anatomically modern human female.

"The complete skeleton," said Ragazzoni (1880, p. 123), "was found in the middle of the layer of blue clay.... The stratum of blue clay, which is over 1 meter [3 feet] thick, has preserved its uniform stratification, and does not show any sign of disturbance." He added, "The skeleton was very likely deposited in a kind of marine mud and not buried at a later time, for in this case one would have been able to detect traces of the overlying yellow sand and the iron-red clay called *ferretto.*"

In short, any burial would have certainly produced a noticeable mixing of different colored materials in the otherwise undisturbed blue clay layer, and Ragazzoni, a geologist, testified that there was no sign of such mixing. Also, the blue clay had its own stratification, which was intact. The same was true of the bones discovered earlier. "The fossil remains discovered on January 2 and January 25 lay at a depth of approximately 2 meters. The bones were situated at the boundary between the bank of shells and coral and the overlying blue clay. They were dispersed, as if scattered by the waves of the sea among the shells. The way they were situated allows one to entirely exclude any later mixing or disturbance of the strata" (Ragazonni 1880, p. 126). Modern geologists place the blue clays at Castenedolo in the Astian stage of the Middle Pliocene, which would give the discoveries from Castenedolo an age of about 3–4 million years.

Italian anatomist Giuseppe Sergi was convinced that the Castenedolo skeletons were the remains of humans who lived during the Pliocene period of the Tertiary. About the negative opinions of others, he said: "The tendency to reject, by reason of theoretical preconceptions, any discoveries that can demonstrate a human presence in the Tertiary is, I believe, a kind of scientific prejudice. Natural science should be stripped of this prejudice" (Sergi 1884, p. 309). This prejudice was, however, not overcome, and it persists today. Sergi wrote (1884, p. 310): "By means of a despotic scientific prejudice, call it what you will, every discovery of human remains in the Pliocene has been discredited."

But Sergi was not alone in his acceptance of Ragazzoni's discoveries at Castenedolo. Armand de Quatrefages also accepted them. Concerning the female skeleton uncovered at Castenedolo, he said in his book

Races Humaines: "There exists no serious reason for doubting the discovery of M. Ragazzoni, . . . Nothing, therefore, can be opposed to it but theoretical *a priori* objections" (Laing 1893, p. 119).

A good example of the unfair treatment given to the Castenedolo finds may be found in Professor R. A. S. Macalister's *Textbook of European Archaeology,* written in 1921. Macalister (1921, p. 183) admitted that the Castenedolo finds "whatever we may think of them, have to be treated seriously." He noted that they were "unearthed by a competent geologist, Ragazzoni . . . and examined by a competent anatomist, Sergi." Still he could not accept their Pliocene age. Faced with the uncomfortable facts, Macalister (1921, p. 183) claimed "there must be something wrong somewhere." First of all the bones were anatomically modern. "Now, if they really belonged to the stratum in which they were found," wrote Macalister (1921, p. 184), "this would imply an extraordinarily long standstill for evolution. It is much more likely that there is something amiss with the observations." Macalister (1921, p. 185) also said: "The acceptance of a Pliocene date for the Castenedolo skeletons would create so many insoluble problems that we can hardly hesitate in choosing between the alternatives of adopting or rejecting their authenticity." Here once more we find a scientist's preconceived ideas about evolution influencing him to reject skeletal evidence that would otherwise be considered of good quality.

Scientists have employed chemical and radiometric tests to deny a Pliocene age to the Castenedolo bones. Fresh bones contain a certain amount of nitrogen in their protein, and this tends to decrease with time. In a 1980 report, K. P. Oakley (1980, p. 40) found the Castenedolo bones had a nitrogen content similar to that of bones from Late Pleistocene and Holocene Italian sites and thus concluded the Castenedolo bones were recent. But the degree of nitrogen preservation in bone can vary widely from site to site, making such comparisons unreliable as age indicators. The Castenedolo bones were found in clay, a substance known to preserve nitrogen-containing bone proteins.

Bones tend to accumulate fluorine from ground water. The Castenedolo bones had a fluorine content that Oakley (1980, p. 42) considered relatively high for bones he thought were recent. Oakley explained this discrepancy by positing higher past levels of fluorine in the Castenedolo groundwater. But this was simply guesswork. The Castenedolo bones also had an unexpected high concentration of uranium, consistent with great age.

A carbon 14 test yielded an age of 958 years for some of the Castenedolo bones. But, as in the case of Galley Hill, the methods employed are now considered unreliable. And the bones themselves, which had been mouldering in a museum for almost 90 years, were very likely contaminated with recent carbon, causing the test to yield a falsely young age.

The case of Castenedolo demonstrates the shortcomings of the methodology employed by paleoanthropologists. The initial attribution of a Pliocene age to the discoveries of 1860 and 1880 appears justified. The finds were made by a trained geologist, G. Ragazzoni, who carefully observed the stratigraphy at the site. He especially searched for signs of intrusive burial, and observed none. Ragazzoni duly reported his findings to his fellow scientists in scientific journals. But because the remains were modern in morphology they came under intense negative scrutiny. As Macalister put it, there had to be something wrong.

The account of human origins now dominant in the scientific community is the product of attitudes such as Macalister's. For the last century, the idea of progressive evolution of the human type from more apelike ancestors has guided the acceptance and rejection of evidence. Evidence that contradicts the idea of human evolution is carefully screened out. Therefore, when one reads textbooks about human evolution, one may think, "Well, the idea of human evolution must be true because all the evidence supports it." But such textbook presentations are misleading, for it is the unquestioned belief that humans did in fact evolve from apelike ancestors that has determined what evidence should be included and how it should be interpreted.

We now turn our attention to another Pliocene find, made at Savona, a town on the Italian Riviera, about 30 miles west of Genoa. In the 1850s, while constructing a church, workmen discovered an anatomically modern human skeleton at the bottom of a trench 3 meters (10 feet) deep. The layer containing the skeleton was 3–4 million years old.

Arthur Issel (1868) communicated details of the Savona find to the members of the International Congress of Prehistoric Anthropology and Archeology at Paris in 1867. He declared that the Savona human "was contemporary with the strata in which he was found" (de Mortillet 1883, p. 70).

Some suggested the skeleton was buried in the place where it was found. But a report given at the International Congress of Prehistoric Anthropology and Archeology at Bologna in 1871 said: "Had it been a burial we would expect to find the upper layers mixed with the lower. The upper layers contain white quartzite sands. The result of mixing would have been the definite lightening of a closely circumscribed region of the Pliocene clay sufficient to cause some doubts in the spectators that it was genuinely ancient, as they affirmed. The biggest and smallest cavities of the human bones are filled with compacted Pliocene clay. This could only have happened when the clay was in a muddy consistency, during Pliocene times" (Deo Gratias 1873, pp. 419–420). Deo Gratias pointed out that the clay was now hard and dry. Also, the skeleton was found at a depth of 3 meters (10 feet), rather deep for a burial.

In the 1880s, Florentino Ameghino announced the discovery of flint tools and signs of intentional use of fire at Monte Hermoso in Argentina. Now we will consider the human bone found there—an atlas, the topmost bone of the spinal column. It was collected by Santiago Pozzi, an employee of the Museum of La Plata, from the Early Pliocene Montehermosan formation during the 1880s. It did not attract much notice until years later. At that time, it was still covered by the characteristic yellowish-brown loess of the Montehermosan formation, which is 3–5 million years old. After the Pliocene loess was removed, scientists carefully studied the bone. Florentino Ameghino, accepting that it was truly Pliocene, assigned the atlas to an apelike human ancestor. In his description of the bone, he identified features he thought were primitive.

But Ales Hrdlička convincingly demonstrated that the bone was actually modern in form. Like Ameghino, Hrdlička believed the human form should, as we proceed back in time, become more and more primitive. If the bone was of the fully modern human type, then no matter what layer it was found in, it had to be of recent origin. Such a bone's presence in an ancient stratum always could be, indeed had to be, explained as some kind of intrusion. But there is another possible explanation: human beings of the modern physiological type were living over 3 million years ago in Argentina. This is supported by the fact that the atlas showed signs of having been thoroughly embedded in sediments from the Montehermosan formation.

All in all, Hrdlička (1912, p. 384) felt that the Monte Hermoso atlas was worthy of being "dropped of necessity into obscurity." That is exactly what happened. Today there are many who will insist that the Monte Hermoso atlas remain in the obscurity into which it was of necessity dropped. Evidence for a fully human presence 3 million or more years ago, in Argentina of all places, is still not welcome in mainstream paleoanthropology.

In 1921, M. A. Vignati reported that a human lower jaw, with two molars, was discovered in the Late Pliocene Chapadmalalan formation at Miramar, Argentina. The jaw would thus be about 2–3 million years old. Previously, stone tools and a mammalian bone with an arrow head embedded in it had been discovered at this site. Ethnographer E. Boman, however, was skeptical. He stated: "The newspapers published bombastic articles about 'the most ancient human remains in the world.' But all who examined the molars found them to be identical to the corresponding molars of modern human beings" (Boman 1921, pp. 341–342). Boman took it for granted that the fully human nature of the Miramar jaw fragment unequivocally insured its recent date. But nothing Boman said excludes the possibility that the Miramar fossil demonstrates a fully human presence in the Pliocene of Argentina.

We have already discussed the numerous stone implements discovered in the auriferous gravels of the Sierra Nevada Mountains of California. Human bones were also found in these gravels, which range from 9 million to 55 million years old.

In February 1866, Mr. Mattison, the principal owner of the mine on Bald Hill, near Angels Creek in Calaveras County, removed a skull from a layer of gravel 130 feet below the surface. The gravel in which the skull was found was older than the Pliocene, perhaps much older. On July 16, 1866, Whitney presented to the California Academy of Sciences a report on the Calaveras skull, affirming that it was found in Pliocene strata. The skull caused a great sensation in America. According to Whitney (1880, p. 270), "The religious press in this country took the matter up . . . and were quite unanimous in declaring the Calaveras skull to be a 'hoax.'" Whitney noted that the hoax stories did not arise until after his discovery was publicized widely in newspapers.

Some of the hoax stories were propagated not by newspaper writers but by scientists such as William H. Holmes of the Smithsonian Institution. During a visit to Calaveras County, he gathered testimony suggesting the skull examined by Whitney was not a genuine Tertiary fossil. But there is a problem with the hoax hypothesis—there are many versions. Some say religious miners planted the skull to deceive the scientist Whitney. Some say the miners planted a skull to deceive another miner. Some say a genuine skull was found by Mattison and later a different skull was given to Whitney. Some say Mattison's friends from a nearby town planted the skull as a practical joke. This contradictory testimony casts doubt on the hoax idea.

Some observations supporting the hoax theory come from persons who examined the matrix of pebbles and earth in which the Calaveras skull had been discovered. Dr. F. W. Putnam of Harvard University's Peabody Museum of Natural History said the skull did not bear any trace of gravel from the mines. William J. Sinclair of the University of California also personally examined the skull and said the material attached to it was not gravel from the gold mine. He thought it was the kind of material one might find in a cave, where Indians sometimes placed bodies. On the other hand, Holmes (1899, p. 467) reported: "Dr. D. H. Dall states that while in San Francisco in 1866, he compared the material attached to the skull with portions of the gravel from the mine and that they were alike in all essentials." And W. O. Ayres (1882, p. 853), writing in the *American Naturalist*, stated: "I saw it and examined it carefully at the time when it first reached Professor Whitney's hands. It was not only incrusted with sand and gravel, but its cavities were crowded with the same material; and that material was of a peculiar sort, a sort which I had occasion to know thoroughly." It was, said Ayres, the gold-bearing gravel found in the mines, not a recent cave deposit.

Regarding the skull, Ayres noted (1882, p. 853): "It has been said that it is a modern skull which has been incrusted after a few years of interment. This assertion, however, is never made by anyone knowing the region. The gravel has not the slightest tendency toward an action of that sort. . . . the hollows of the skull were crowded with the solidified and cemented sand, in such a way as they could have been only by its being driven into them in a semi-fluid mass, a condition the gravels have never had since they were first laid down."

Whitney, in his original description of the fossil, observed that the Calaveras skull was highly fossilized. This is certainly consistent with great age; however, as Holmes pointed out, it is also true that bones can become fossilized over the course of a few hundred or thousand years. Yet geologist George Becker (1891, p. 195) reported: "I find that many good judges are fully persuaded of the authenticity of the Calaveras skull, and Messrs. Clarence King, O. C. Marsh, F. W. Putnam, and W. H. Dall have each assured me that this bone was found in place in the gravel beneath the lava." Becker added that this statement was made with the permission of the authorities named. Clarence King, as mentioned previously, was a geologist with the U. S. Geological Survey. O. C. Marsh, a paleontologist, was a pioneer dinosaur fossil hunter and served as president of the National Academy of Sciences from 1883 to 1895. But F. W. Putnam of Harvard's Peabody Museum, as we have seen, later changed his mind, saying that the matrix of the skull appeared to be a cave deposit.

It should, however, be kept in mind that the Calaveras skull was not an isolated discovery. Great numbers of stone implements were found in nearby deposits of similar age. And, as we shall see, additional human skeletal remains were also uncovered in the same region, adding credibility to the Calaveras skull. As Sir Arthur Keith (1928, p. 471) put it: "The story of the Calaveras skull . . . cannot be passed over. It is the 'bogey' which haunts the student of early man . . . taxing the powers of belief of every expert almost to the breaking point."

On January 1, 1873, the president of the Boston Society of Natural History read extracts from a letter by Dr. C. F. Winslow about a discovery of human bones at Table Mountain in Tuolumne County, California. The find was made in 1855 or 1856, and the details were communicated to Winslow by Capt. David B. Akey, who had witnessed it. The discovery took place about 10 years before J. D. Whitney first reported on the famous Calaveras skull.

Winslow (1873, pp. 257–258) gave this account of Akey's testimony: "He states that in a tunnel run into the mountain at the distance of about fifty feet from that upon which he was employed, and at the same level, a complete human skeleton was found and taken out by miners personally known to him, but whose names he does not now recollect. He did not see the bones in place, but he saw them after they were brought down from the tunnel to a neighboring cabin. . . . He thinks that the depth from the surface at which this skeleton was found was two hundred feet, and from one hundred and eighty to two hundred feet from the opening cut or face of the tunnel. The bones were in a moist condition, found among the gravel and very near the bed rock, and water was running out of the tunnel. There was a petrified pine tree, from sixty to eighty feet in length and between two and three feet in diameter at the butt, lying near this skeleton. Mr. Akey went into the tunnel with the miners, and they pointed out to him the place where the skeleton was found. He saw the tree in place and broke specimens from it." The gravel just above the bedrock, where the skeleton was found, is between 33 and 55 million years old (Slemmons 1966, p. 200). This must be the age of the skeleton unless it was introduced into the gravels at a later time, and we are not aware of any evidence indicating such an intrusion.

Dr. Winslow did not find any of the bones of the skeleton seen by Akey. But in another case, Winslow did collect some fossils, which he sent to museums in the eastern United States. A skull fragment, characterized by Dr. J. Wyman, a leading craniologist, as human (Holmes 1899, p. 456), was dispatched by Winslow to the Museum of the Natural History Society of Boston. The fossil was labeled as follows: "From a shaft in Table Mountain, 180 feet below the surface, in gold drift, among rolled stones and near mastodon debris. Overlying strata of basaltic compactness and hardness. Found July, 1857. Given to Rev. C. F. Winslow by Hon. Paul K. Hubbs, August, 1857." Another fragment, from the same skull and similarly labeled, was sent to the Museum of the Philadelphia Academy of Natural Sciences. The lava cap of Table Mountain is 9 million years old. The oldest gravels below the lava are 55 million years old. The skull fragment could thus be from 9 million to 55 million years old.

When examining a collection of stone artifacts belonging to Dr. Perez Snell, J. D. Whitney noted the presence of a human jaw. The jaw and artifacts all came from gold-bearing gravels beneath the lava cap of Tuolumne Table Mountain. The jaw measured 5.5 inches across from condyle to condyle, which is within the normal human range. Whitney (1880, p. 288) remarked that all the human fossils uncovered in the gold-mining region, including this one, were of the anatomically modern type. The gravels from which the jaw came could be anywhere from 9 to 55 million years old. Whitney also reported on other discoveries of human fossils, from deposits of similar age.

In an address to the American Association for the Advancement of Science, delivered in August, 1879, O. C. Marsh, president of the Association and one of America's foremost paleontologists, said about Tertiary man: "The proof offered on this point by Professor J. D. Whitney in his recent work (*Aurif. Gravels of Sierra Nevada*) is so strong, and his careful, conscientious method of investigation so well known, that his conclusions seem irresistible. . . . At present, the known facts indicate that the American beds containing human remains and works of man, are as old as the Pliocene of Europe. The existence of man in the Tertiary period seems now fairly established" (Southall 1882, p. 196).

More evidence for human beings in the early and middle Tertiary comes from Europe. According to Gabriel de Mortillet, M. Quiquerez reported the discovery of a skeleton at Delémont in Switzerland in ferruginous clays said to be Late Eocene. About this find, de Mortillet (1883, p. 72) simply said one should be suspicious of human skeletons found with the bones in natural connection. De Mortillet further stated that one should be cautious about a similarly complete skeleton found by Garrigou in Miocene strata at Midi de France.

It is possible, however, that these skeletons were from individuals buried during the Eocene or Miocene periods. A burial does not necessarily have to be recent. The truly frustrating thing about finds such as these is that we are not able to get more information about them. We find only a brief mention by an author bent on discrediting them. Because such finds seemed doubtful to scientists like de Mortillet, they went undocumented and uninvestigated, and were quickly forgotten. How many such finds have been made? We may never know. In contrast, finds which conform to accepted theories are thoroughly investigated, extensively reported, and safely enshrined in museums.

In December of 1862, the following brief but intriguing report appeared in a journal called *The Geologist:* "In Macoupin county, Illinois, the bones of a man were recently found on a coal-bed capped with two feet of slate rock, ninety feet below the surface of the earth. . . . The bones, when found, were covered with a crust or coating of hard glossy matter, as black as coal itself, but when scraped away left the bones white and natural." The coal in which the Macoupin County skeleton was found is at least 286 million years old and might be as much as 320 million years old.

The evidence documented in *Forbidden Archeology* demonstrates that we genuinely need an alternative to the Darwinian picture of human evolution. Even confining ourselves to physical evidence in the form of fossils and artifacts, an evolutionary picture fails to emerge. The explanation that best fits the facts is that humans like ourselves and other more or less humanlike beings have coexisted on this planet for hundreds of millions of years. This conclusion is consistent with the accounts of extreme human antiquity found in the ancient Sanskrit historical writings, which tell us that humans have been present since the beginning of the current day of Brahma. But the question remains, how did we get here in the first place? For an answer to that question, we need to look beyond stones and bones.

3

THE EXTREME ANTIQUITY
OF NONHUMAN SPECIES

In response to the evidence for extreme human antiquity presented in *Forbidden Archeology,* many have naturally asked, "Is it just our picture of human origins that is in need of revision? What about the history of other living things on earth?"

Of course, there are millions of species. Among them, I chose to first look at the fossil evidence for the antiquity of the human species because many scientists claim that the human species provides the best evidence for evolution. That effort took eight years of research, during which I studied original archeological reports of the past one hundred and fifty years in English and many other languages. When I began that effort, I did not expect that I would find as much evidence as I did for extreme human antiquity. On the basis of that experience, I cannot predict in advance what would happen if I spent several years going through the entire scientific literature on fossil discoveries relating to another species. However, some preliminary research shows that one can find in the scientific literature discoveries that challenge the Darwinian explanation for the origin of species other than the human species. In this chapter, I will give one example, based on a paper I presented at the XXIst International Congress for History of Science, which was held in July 2001 in Mexico City. The title of the paper is "Paleobotanical Anomalies Bearing on the Age of the Salt Range Form tion of Pakistan: A Historical Survey of an Unresolved Scientific Controversy." This paper presents evidence showing that flowering plants and insects existed on earth far earlier than most Darwinists now believe possible.

For well over a century the Salt Range Mountains of Pakistan have attracted the special attention of geologists. Starting in the foothills of the Himalayas in northeastern Pakistan, the mountains run about 150 miles in a westerly direction, roughly parallel to the Jhelum river until it joins the Indus. They then extend some distance beyond the Indus.

The southern edge of the eastern Salt Range Mountains drops steeply two or three thousand feet to the Jhelum River plain. In this escarpment and other locations, the Salt Range Mountains expose a series of formations ranging from the earliest Cambrian to the most recent geological periods. Such exposures are rarely encountered and are thus of great interest to geologists and other earth scientists. At the bottom of the series, beneath the Cambrian Purple Sandstone, lies the Salt Range Formation, composed of thick layers of reddish, clayey material (the Salt Marl) in which are found layers of rock salt, gypsum, shale, and dolomite. For centuries, the salt has been mined and traded widely in the northern part of the Indian subcontinent. Ever since professional geologists began studying the Salt Range Mountains in the middle part of the nineteenth century, the age of the Salt Range Formation has been a topic of extreme controversy. Some held that it was of early Cambrian antiquity, while others were certain the Salt Range Formation was far more recent. The controversy intensified in the twentieth century when scientists discovered remains of advanced plants in the Salt Range Formation.

The History of the Controversy

Scientific investigation of the Salt Range Formation began in the nineteenth century, when Pakistan was part of British India. The Cambrian age of the overlying Purple Sandstone, which contains trilobites, was generally undisputed. But there were various opinions about the age and origin of the Salt Range Formation, usually found beneath the Purple Sandstone. Questions also arose about the relative ages of the Salt Range Formation and the Kohat salt deposits, located to the north of the Salt Range Mountains.

A. B. Wynne (1878, p. 83) surveyed the Salt Range Mountains in 1869–71 and concluded that the Salt Range Formation was a normal sedimentary deposit of Paleozoic age. This view was shared by H. Warth, who had extensive knowledge of the region gathered over twenty years (Wynne 1878, p. 73). Wynne and Warth thought the Kohat salt formations were younger, perhaps Tertiary (Wynne 1875, pp. 32–37). These views were shared by W. T. Blandford (Medlicott and Blandford 1879, p. 488).

Later, C. S. Middlemiss of the Geological Survey of India (1891, p. 42) proposed that the Salt Marl was not a sedimentary formation. It was instead a secretion from an underlying layer of magma that had intruded beneath the Cambrian Purple Sandstone. R. D. Oldham (1893, p. 112), superintendent of the Geological Survey of India, came to a similar conclusion. This opened up the possiblity that the Salt Range Formation was younger than the overlying Cambrian Purple Sandstone.

The German geologist F. Noetling originally thought the Salt Range Formation was Precambrian (Zuber 1914, p. 334). But in a paper published in 1903 (Koken and Noetling, p. 35), Noetling said the Cambrian Purple Sandstone was the oldest formation in the Salt Range Mountains and assigned the underlying Salt Range Formation a much more recent age, without explicit explanation. T. H. Holland (1903, p. 26) reported that Noetling believed that the Cambrian Purple Sandstone and other overlying formations had been pushed over the Salt Range Formation by a massive overthrust. According to this idea, the Salt Range Formation was a normal sedimentary deposit, the same age as the Eocene salt deposits of the Kohat region, just north of the Salt Range Mountains. This overthrust version was accepted by Rudolf Zuber (1914).

W. Christie (1914), chemist for the Geological Survey of India, held that the Salt Range Formation was not of igneous origin, as proposed by Middlemiss. He found it to be a normal sedimentary deposit, produced by evaporation of seawater, but he did not say when this occurred.

Murray Stuart (1919) agreed with Christie that the Salt Range Formation was a normal sedimentary deposit. According to Stuart, the salt deposits in the Salt Range and Kohat regions were both of early Cambrian or Precambrian age. In the Kohat region, the salt lies directly below the far younger "nummulitic" limestones, from the Eocene. Stuart explained this by proposing originally both the Kohat and Salt Range Formation salt deposits had been covered by Paleozoic and Mesozoic layers. At Kohat, an overthrust had stripped the Paleozoic and Mesozoic layers away, and then the Eocene limestones were deposited atop the Cambrian or Precambrian Kohat salt. But in the Salt Range Mountains the Cambrian or Precambrian salt deposits remained covered with Paleozoic and Mesozoic layers.

In 1920, E. H. Pascoe, in considering all the previous reports, came up with his own conclusion. The Salt Range Formation was a normal sedimentary deposit, of Tertiary (Eocene) age, as was the Kohat salt deposit. Pascoe also believed the Purple Sandstone overlying the Salt Range Formation to be Eocene. The position of the Salt Range Formation and the Purple Sandstone below other formations of Cambrian antiquity was attributed to a massive overthrust.

Robert Van Vleck Anderson (1927) gave the first report of botanical fossil remains from the Salt Range Formation. He noted the presence of "poorly preserved impressions of leaves of a Tertiary or, at earliest, Mesozoic type." The impressions came from shale deposits at Khewra Gorge in the Salt Range. He gave samples to Dr. Ralph W. Chaney of the Carnegie Institution, who said: "This specimen clearly contains fragments of several specimens of dicotyledonous leaves. This places their age as not older than the Lower Cretaceous when the first dicots appeared. One of the leaves is very probably oak (*Quercus*) and its size and margin strongly suggest the Oligocene species *Quercus clarnensis* from western America. It is of interest to note that I found a closely related species in the Oligocene deposits of Manchuria. Your specimen is almost certainly of Tertiary age" (Anderson 1927, p. 672). From this evidence, Anderson argued for a Tertiary age for the Salt Range Formation as well as the Kohat Salt. The presence of Cambrian layers above the Salt Range Formation was attributed by him to an overthrust.

In 1928, Cyril S. Fox published a study concluding that both the Salt Range and Kohat salt deposits were early Cambrian or Precambrian. He saw no signs of an overthrust. He did not mention Anderson's discoveries.

In his presidential address to the geology section of the Eighteenth Indian Science Congress, G. Cotter (1931, p. 296) disputed Anderson's report of leaf impressions found in the Salt Range Formation. He noted that E. R. Gee had searched the same locality in January 1929 and found no new specimens. Cotter joined Gee for another search in March 1929 and also found no new specimens. Cotter noted that they found "carbonaceous markings, some of which simulated broad leaf impressions." But they were in his opinion "not plant fossils."

Anderson then sent to the Geological Survey of India office his best *Quercus* specimen. Cotter considered it "doubtful." But Pascoe (1930, p. 25) said that the specimen had perhaps been damaged by friction during transit, making it "undeterminable." Pascoe expressed a hope that the specimen had been photographed before it was shipped, but there is no record of such a photograph in Anderson's reports. Some of Anderson's specimens were sent to Professor B. Sahni at Oxford, who, according to Cotter, thought that "the specimens, if they were plants at all, were quite indeterminate."

Cotter (1931, p. 299) also made this interesting observation: "About the year 1924 a large trunk of wood of a modern type and scarcely at all decomposed was found in the salt in the upper tunnel of the Khewra mine. Dr. Dunn, who examined this wood, states that the trunk was about 2 ft. in diameter, and that there were several branches associated with it of about 3 to 4 inches in diameter. Prof. Sahni regarded this wood as modern and resembling an *Acacia* now found growing in the Salt Range."

Cotter, after considering all arguments pro and con, said he favored a pre-Cambrian age for the Salt Range Formation (1931, p. 300). But before his paper expressing this view went to press, Cotter examined occurences of nummulites, fossil foramanifera typical of the Tertiary, discovered by E. R. Gee in the salt marl at Khewra. Cotter, who had originally thought they had been washed into the Salt Range Formation from younger deposits, decided they were native to the Salt Range Formation. In a footnote added to his paper before publication, Cotter (1931, p. 300) reversed the position stated in the paper and declared the Salt Range Formation to be Tertiary. But he regarded it as intrusive, which would explain its position beneath the Cambrian Purple Sandstone. According to Cotter (1933, p. 151), the plastic salt, of Eocene age, was somehow squeezed by geological pressure and other forces into an abnormal position.

Cotter (1933, p. 150) said that the Khewra nummulites discovered by Gee "occurred in association with plant fragments." He further noted (Cotter 1933, pp. 150–151) that "plant fragments were also found by Mr. Gee in the Salt Marl at the Nila Wahan." Pascoe (1959, p. 569) cited a 1933 report that at Kalra Wahan, a sample of salt marl "yielded not only carbonised stem fragments but also several small leaves of apparently dicotyledenous type." Pascoe (1930, p. 132) also noted that Gee found a small piece of fossil wood in the reddish marls of the Salt Range Formation.

Gee (1934) gave his own opinion about the age of the Salt Range Formation, which he called "the Saline series." He concluded that both it and the Kohat salt deposits were of the same Eocene age. The Kohat salt was in its normal position, but Gee (1934, p. 461) noted that "a very regular thrust of immense dimensions must be postulated in order to explain the present position of the Saline series beneath the early Paleozoics (or pre-Cambrian)." Concerning foramanifera found by him in Salt Range Formation deposits, he admitted that they might be derived from more recent formations (Gee 1934, p. 463; Fermor 1935, p. 64). But Gee (1934, p. 463) noted, "Plant fragments, however, have been found not only in beds of doubtful age but also in beds which are regarded as being definitely *in situ* in the Saline series." He regarded this as evidence the Salt Range Formation was not Cambrian.

Some years later, B. Sahni, then a paleobotanist at the University of Lucknow, reported the existence of numerous plant microfossils in samples taken from the Salt Range Formation at the Khewra and Warcha salt mines. Previously, doubt had been cast on plant fossils from the Salt Range Formation. Critics, said Sahni (1944, p. 462), had pointed out that "in such a highly soluble and plastic substance as the Salt Marl, extraneous material might have penetrated through solution holes or have been enveloped during relatively modern earth movements."

But deep within the mines, Sahni found deposits where such objections could not apply. The salt in these places ran in layers separated by thin layers of saline earth, locally called "kallar." Sahni (1944, p. 462) noted that "the kallar lies closely interlaminated with the salt, in beds which run continuously for long distances and which, although visibly tilted, show no other visible signs of disturbance."

According to Sahni, the salt layers accumulated from evaporation of sea water in coastal lagoons, whereas the kallar represented dust and dirt blown on to the drying salt by the wind. Sahni guessed that the kallar might contain pollen and other plant microfossils. When he examined specimens, he found this to be so (Sahni 1944, p. 462): "Every single piece has yielded microfossils. . . . The great majority are undeterminable as to genus and species, being mainly shreds of angiosperm wood, but there are also gymnosperm tracheids with large round bordered pits, and at least one good, winged, six-legged insect with compound eyes." To Sahni, this meant that the Salt Range Formation must be Eocene rather than Cambrian. Sahni later found plant fragments not only in the kallar, but in associated solid rock layers composed of dolomite and shale.

Around this same time, the Geological Survey of India and an oil company sent a team of geologists to carefully study the Salt Range Formation, and on the basis of their field observations they concluded that it was in normal position below the Cambrian Purple Sandstone and was thus Cambrian in age. This conclusion was announced in a letter to *Nature* (Coates *et al.* 1945). Among the geologists signing the letter was Gee, previously an advocate of an Eocene age for the Salt Range Formation. The geologists admitted, however, that "our conclusions were arrived at despite certain difficulties, such as the occurrence of minute plant fragments of post-Cambrian age in the dolomites and oil shales, for which we have at present no clear explanation to offer." In other words, it might be possible to explain the presence of plant fragments in the soluble salt layers, but how did they get into solid rock such as dolomite and shale? This line of reasoning is based on the assumption that land plants did not come into being until the Silurian (about 400 million years ago), with advanced plants such as angiosperms not arising until the Cretaceous (about 100 million years ago).

In his presidential address to India's National Academy of Sciences in 1944, Sahni (1945) introduced numerous examples of pollen, wood fragments, and insect parts found in samples of kallar, dolomite, and shale from the Salt Range Formation. In his report, Sahni (1945, p. x) said that "stringent precautions" were taken to prevent contamination of the samples with modern organic remains. He also emphasized that samples were taken from locations where the geological evidence ruled out intrusion from younger strata.

The laboratory techniques employed by Sahni and his assistant, B. S. Trivedi, were rigorous. In a demonstration at a symposium, said Sahni (1945, p. xiv) "a piece of carbonised wood was revealed in a tiny block of dolomite . . . which had been cut and polished on all sides to show it had no pits or cracks visible even with a strong pocket lens. The block was, as usual, passed through a flame and then plunged into a jar of filtered dilute HCl."

In his own address to the National Academy of Sciences, Gee (1945, p. 293) concluded that the Salt Range Formation was a normal sedimentary deposit and in its original position below the Purple Sandstone. This meant it was Cambrian or Precambrian (Gee 1945, p. 305), while Kohat salt was Eocene. This was a change from his earlier opinion that the Salt Range Formation was Eocene (Gee 1934). He saw no compelling evidence for a massive overthrust in the region (Gee 1945, p. 305). Pascoe, formerly a supporter of the idea that the Salt Range Formation was an Eocene deposit covered by an overthrust, placed the Salt Range Formation in the Cambrian section of a new edition of his *Manual of the Geology of India* (Sahni 1947b, p. xxxi).

Gee said that foraminifera of Eocene type found by him in the Salt Range Formation were not *in situ,* as he earlier believed, but were derived from younger formations. Concerning plant fragments, Gee (1945, p. 296) noted: "Further work on the clay containing plant fragments at Katha led to the discovery of one or two small leaf impressions which were identified by Prof. B. Sahni as belonging to *Acacia,* a genus still existing in the Salt Range area, whilst in the case of the Khewra mine occurrences, the existence of an important thrust-fault nearby, running roughly parallel to the seams of rocksalt, indicated an alternative explanation for the occurrence of these plant fragments." Gee thought they might have been introduced into the salt in relatively recent times.

Concerning the Katha finds, Gee relied on the assumption that *Acacia* is quite recent, and could not possibly have existed in the Cambrian. Concerning the Khewra finds, Gee used the existence of a fault to explain the presence of advanced plants in a formation he regarded as Cambrian. But he did not explain how close the thrust fault was to the exact places where he recovered plant fragments nor whether the stratification showed any obvious signs of local disturbance. The fact that the salt was still arranged in seams, apparently unbroken, leaves open the possibility that the plant fragments were found *in situ*.

Gee (1945, p. 297) found Anderson's leaf impressions unconvincing, calling them "unidentifiable brownish markings, possibly organic." Gee (1945, p. 299) saw signs of organic deposits in the shales and dolomites of the Salt Range Formation, but characterized them as "too primitive to include resistant skeletons or woody tissues such as might be preserved."

Gee was, however, seriously troubled by the discoveries of Sahni, which were based on careful observation and laboratory work. Sahni had demonstrated the existence of advanced plant remains, including woody tissues, not only in the salt and dolomites of the Salt Range Formation but in other kinds of rock as well, such as shale. About the salt and dolomites. Gee proposed that plant fragments could have been introduced into them by "percolating water." But this explanation would not, said Gee (1945, p. 307), apply to the extremely resistant oil shales, in which Sahni had also found microfossils. Gee (1945, p. 306) noted that if Sahni, on the basis of his plant fossils, was correct in assigning an Eocene age to the Salt Range Formation, "then it will be necessary to modify our views regarding the essential characteristics of normal sedimentary and tectonic contacts." According to standard geological reasoning these indicated a Cambrian age.

At the Indian National Academy of Sciences annual meeting for 1945, the Salt Range Formation was once more a topic of extended debate. Sahni (1947a, 1947b) gave reports of additional discoveries of angiosperm and gymnosperm microfossils from the salt marl, the oil shales, and dolomites at all levels of the Salt Range Formation. Microfossils of advanced plants were also recovered from core samples from deep borings in the Khewra salt mine. Sahni (1947b, pp. xxxi–xxxvi) gave convincing evidence that the microfossils were not intrusive contaminations. Furthermore, at scientific gatherings in Great Britain, Sahni (1947b, p. xxxix) demonstrated to geologists his laboratory techniques and obtained "fragments of woody tissue" from samples of the Salt Range Formation's dolomites and oil shales.

Sahni (1947a, p. 243) added that "in a fragment of Mr. Anderson's original material several microfragments of wood have been found." This would tend to support Anderson's identification of leaf imprints in his material from Khewra Gorge. Sahni had accompanied Gee and others to Anderson's site, and had found no similar specimens. Sahni (1947b, p. xx) noted that these circumstances "do not by any means cast a doubt upon the identification of Mr. Anderson's specimen as an oak leaf." Sahni (1947b, p. xx) also noted: "As it turned out, we had been searching at the wrong place." Anderson's oak leaf imprint had come from a spot lower than that searched, and some distance away.

Concerning the advanced nature of the plant and insect microfossils found in the Salt Range Formation, Sahni (1947b, pp. xlv–xlvi) noted: "Quite recently, an alternative explanation has been offered by Mr. Gee. *The suggestion is that the angiosperms, gymnosperms and insects of the Saline Series may represent a highly evolved Cambrian or Precambrian flora and fauna!* In other words, it is suggested that these plants and animals made their appearance in the Salt Range area several hundred million years earlier than they did anywhere else in the world. One would scarcely have believed that such an idea would be seriously put forward by any geologist today."

Gee, by questioning basic evolutionary assumptions about the progression of life forms on earth, introduces another possible solution to the Salt Range Formation controversy. Up to this point, the relatively late appearance of the angiosperms, gymnosperms, and certain insects had been taken for granted. Evidence of their presence in the Salt Range Formation had to be resolved by (1) suggesting they were intrusive into the formation, which was of Cambrian age or (2) suggesting that they were native to the formation proving it was Eocene and invoking a massive overthrust to account for the formation's presence below formations generally accepted as Cambrian. Supporters of the former proposal, including Gee, were troubled, however, by the strength of Sahni's evidence for the *in situ* status of his microfossils. So Gee suggested that perhaps the Salt Range Formation is, after all, Cambrian, as the geological evidence strongly suggested, and the microfossils of angiosperms, gymnosperms, and insects were *in situ*. This could only mean that the angiosperms, gymnosperms, and insects evolved far earlier than allowed by any current evolutionary account. It was a bold proposal, but fell on deaf ears at the time.

Subsequently, evidence for angiosperms and gymnosperms was also found in other beds of Cambrian age overlying the Salt Range Formation. These included microfossils of angiosperms and gymnosperms from the Salt Pseudomorph Beds (Ghosh and Bose, 1947), gymnosperms from the Purple Sandstone (Ghosh, *et al.,* 1948), wood fragments from the Neobolus Shales (Ghosh, *et al.,* 1948), and wood fragments from the

Magnesian Sandstone (Ghosh, *et al.*, 1948).

Ghosh and Bose (1950a, p. 76) proposed two possible explanations for this evidence of advanced vascular plants in the above-mentioned formations: "1. The geologically known Cambrian beds are of post-Cambrian age. 2. The vascular plants existed in Cambrian or pre-Cambrian times." Ghosh and Bose rejected the first proposal because geologists unanimously agreed that the beds in question were in fact Cambrian. Ghosh and Bose found the second proposal more likely, even though it was "inconsistent with the prevailing concepts of plant phylogeny." They pointed out that there had been discoveries of advanced plant remains in beds of similar age in Sweden (Darrah 1937) and in the USSR (Sahni 1947b, in note following plates).

Ghosh and Bose (1947) reconfirmed the original discoveries by Sahni and his coworkers of advanced plant remains in the Salt Range Formation itself. They also obtained fragments of advanced plants from a sample of shale from the Cambrian or pre-Cambrian beds of the Vindhyans of northern India (Ghosh and Bose 1950b) and from a sample of Cambrian rock from Kashmir (Ghosh and Bose 1951a). In some cases, Ghosh and Bose (1951b, pp. 130–131; 1952) found fragments of advanced plants (conifers) in Cambrian rock samples that also contained trilobites. The samples were from the Salt Pseudomorph beds of the Salt Range and the shales of the Rainwar locality in Kashmir.

Other researchers confirmed the work of Ghosh and his associates (Jacob *et al.* 1953), finding evidence for advanced vascular plants, including gymnosperms, in Cambrian rock samples from the Salt Range and other sites in India. Jacob and his coworkers also called attention to similar Cambrian paleobotanical discoveries in Sweden, Estonia, and Russia, as reported by S. N. Naumova, A. V. Kopeliovitch, A. Reissinger, and W. C. Darrah (Jacob *et al.* 1953, p. 35).

German researchers (Schindewolf and Seilacher, 1955) took samples of rock from the Salt Range to Germany, where specialists found no evidence of plant remains. But in his discussion, Schindewolf mentioned that he personally witnessed an Indian scientist obtain plant microfossils from a Cambrian Salt Range rock sample in India. After this, active discussion of the controversy diminished. It is quite possible that this was the result of the partition of India and Pakistan. After partition, members of the Geological Survey of India may not have had such easy access to the Salt Range in the newly independent Islamic state of Pakistan.

In recent years, petroleum geologists have conducted extensive studies of the Salt Range region, with no reference or only slight reference to the debates that took place earlier in the century. Although modern geological reports acknowledge overthrusts in the Salt Range, they unanimously declare the Salt Range Formation to be Eocambrian (Yeats *et al.* 1984, Butler *et al.* 1987, Jaumé and Lillie 1988, Baker *et al.* 1988, Pennock *et al.* 1989, McDougall and Khan 1990). One paper (Butler *et al.* 1987, p. 410) mentions discoveries of wood fragments in the salt deep in the mines at Khewra. The authors propose these are intrusive, but neglect to discuss the extensive reporting by Sahni and others ruling out such an explanation for the microfossils discovered in various kinds of rock from the Salt Range Formation.

Discussion

In the early stages of the debates about the nature and age of the Salt Range Formation, fossil evidence did not play a major role. Geological considerations dominated the discussion. With the introduction of paleobotanical evidence by Sahni and others in the 1930s and 1940s, the Salt Range controversy became interesting from a paleontological perspective. Sahni, along with his coworkers and supporters, believed that microfossils of advanced plants and insects, along with a few plant macrofossils (pieces of wood and leaf imprints), indicated an Eocene age for the Salt Range formation. They explained the presence of the Salt Range Formation below undisputed Cambrian beds (the Purple Sandstone, the Neobolus beds, the Magnesian Sandstone, and the Salt Pseudomorph Beds) as the result of a massive overthrust.

Advocates of a Cambrian age for the Salt Range Formation challenged Sahni's conclusions on two fronts.

First, they argued that the plant and insect fossils must have been intrusive. But even these opponents acknowledged it would be difficult to explain how such fossils could have intruded into resistant rock such as the oil shales found in the Salt Range Formation. Overall, it seems there is fairly good evidence for the presence of microfossils and even some macrofossils in the Salt Range Formation. Sahni and his coworkers presented good arguments against possible contamination of their rock samples, either *in situ* or in the laboratory.

Second, the advocates of a Cambrian age for the Salt Range Formation argued against Sahni's hypothesis of a massive overthrust, that covered the Eocene Salt Range Formation with Cambrian formations. Opponents disputed the overthrust hypothesis, citing signs of normal contact between the Salt Range Formation and the overlying beds. Modern geological opinion partly favors Sahni. There is evidence of thrust faulting in the Salt Range. But modern geological opinion is also unanimous in assigning the Salt Range Formation to the Eocambrian.

If we stop at this point, the controversy remains unresolved. There still appears to be a conflict between the geological evidence and the paleobotanical evidence. The conflict may, however, be resolved if we adopt the approach taken by Gee, who proposed that an advanced land flora and insect fauna may have existed in the Cambrian or Precambrian. This, of course, challenges accepted views on the evolution of life on earth. But it seems to be the most reasonable way to bring all categories of evidence into harmony.

Support for the existence of advanced vascular plants (including gymnosperms and and angiosperms) in the earliest Paleozoic is supported by (1) reports by Ghosh and his coworkers of microfossils of gymnosperms and angiosperms in the Cambrian beds overlying the Salt Range Formation and in Cambrian beds elsewhere in the Indian subcontinent; (2) contemporary reports from researchers in other parts of the world giving evidence for advanced vascular plants in the Cambrian (see Leclerq 1956 for a review); (3) modern reports placing the existence of the angiosperms as far back as the Triassic (Cornet 1989, 1993). According to standard views angiosperms originated in the Cretaceous. Cornet's work places them in the Triassic, providing a step between the standard view of a Cretaceous origin for the angiosperms and Sahni's evidence showing an angiosperm presence in the Cambrian. According to standard views, the gymnosperms originated in the Devonian, and the first land plants appeared in the mid-Silurian.

Paleobotanical and geological evidence from the Salt Range in Pakistan suggests that advanced plants, including gymnosperms and angiosperms, as well as insects, existed in the early Cambrian, consistent with historical accounts in the Puranas. When considered in relation to extensive evidence for an anatomically modern human presence extending back to the same period, the evidence from the Salt Range suggests the need for a complete reevaluation of current ideas about the evolution of life on this planet. One possible outcome of this reevaluation could be the abandonment of the Darwinian evolutionary hypothesis in favor of a model for life's origin and development drawn from the Vedic and Puranic texts.

4

GENES, DESIGN, AND DESIGNER

Skeletal remains, footprints, and artifacts indicate that human beings of our type have existed for hundreds of millions of years and that we did not evolve from more primitive apelike creatures. But what about biochemical and genetic evidence? Many evolutionists assert that there is strong evidence from DNA that humans arose relatively recently, most probably between one and two hundred thousand years ago in Africa. Evolutionists also claim that one can by genetics and biochemistry trace the origin of the human species all the way back to the very beginnings of life on earth. In comparison with this genetic and te ambiguous and that the conclusions based upon it are shaky.

People often get the impression that scientists, when they talk about genetic data, are reading directly from the "book of life." But genetic data is just a series of A's, T's, G's, and C's, representing a sequence of molecules called nucleotides (adenine, thymine, guanine, and cytosine) on a DNA strand. When scientists try to turn that series of letters into statements about human origins, they use many speculative assumptions and interpretations. Anthropologist Jonathan Marks (1994, p. 61) therefore says it is a "pernicious pseudo-scientific idea that independently . . . genetic data tell a tale." Marks (1994, p. 61) says that genetics is one area of science in which "sloppy thought and work can often carry as much weight as careful thought and work," and he therefore warns that "one is forced to wonder about the epistemological foundations of any specific conclusions based on genetic data." Marks (1994, p. 59) noted that "the history of biological anthropology shows that, from the beginning of the 20th century, grossly naïve conclusions have been promoted simply on the basis that they are derived from genetics." In light of this, the fossil evidence outlined in the previous chapter retains its importance as a useful check on genetic speculations. For the following discussion, I am indebted to the works of Stephen Meyer, William Dembski, and Michael Behe, and other members of the modern intelligent design movement.

The Beginning of Life

The genetic theory of human evolution is in trouble right from the start. Technically, evolution is not about the origin of life. Instead, evolutionists study the changes in reproducing biological forms, each with a genetic system that helps determine the exact nature of the form. Changes in the genetic system result in changes in the successive generations of biological forms. But evolutionists understand that they also have to explain the origin of the first biological forms, and their genetic systems, from prebiotic chemical elements. Therefore, proposals for the natural origin of the first biological organisms have become an integral part of modern evolutionary thought.

Today, the simplest independent biological organisms are single cells, and most scientists assume that the first real living things were also single cells. Early evolutionists like Ernst Haeckel (1905, p. 111) and Thomas H. Huxley (1869, pp. 129–145) thought cells were mere blobs of protoplasm and gave relatively simple explanations for their origin. They thought chemicals like carbon dioxide, nitrogen, and oxygen would somehow spontaneously crystallize into the slimy substance of life (Haeckel 1866, pp. 179–180; 1892, pp. 411–413).

As time passed, scientists began to recognize that even simple cells are more than just blobs of protoplasm. They have a complex biochemical structure. In the twentieth century, Alexander I. Oparin, a Russian biochemist, outlined an elaborate set of chemical stages leading to the formation of the first cell. He believed that the process would take a very long time—hundreds of millions, perhaps billions of years. Oparin (1938, pp. 64–103) proposed that ammonia (a nitrogen compound), methane, hydrogen, carbon dioxide and water vapor, with ultraviolet light as an energy source, would combine with metallic elements dissolved in water. This would produce a nitrogen-rich prebiotic soup, in which simple hydrocarbon molecules would form. These would combine into amino acids, sugars, and phosphates (Oparin 1938, pp. 133–135), and these would in turn form proteins. The groups of molecules reacting together in this way would become attracted to each other and surround themselves with chemical walls, resulting in the precursors to the first cells. Oparin called them "coacervates" (Oparin 1938, pp. 148–159). These primitive cells would compete for survival, becoming more complex and stable.

Oparin's ideas remained largely theoretical until the experiments of Stanley Miller and Henry Urey. Miller and Urey proposed, as did Oparin, that the earth's early atmosphere was composed of methane, ammonia, hydrogen, and water vapor. They reproduced this atmosphere in a laboratory and then ran electric sparks through the mixture. The sparks represented lightning, which provided the energy needed to get the relatively stable chemical ingredients of the experiment to react with each other. The experimental apparatus included a flask of water, in which the tarlike residues of the experiment accumulated. When after a week the water was analyzed, it yielded, among other things, three amino acids in low concentrations (Miller 1953). Amino acids are the building blocks of proteins, which are necessary ingredients of living things.

Later experiments by other researchers produced all except one of the twenty biological amino acids. Still more experiments produced fatty acids and nucleotides, which are necessary for DNA and RNA. But the experiments did not produce another essential element of DNA and RNA, the sugars deoxyribose and ribose (Meyer 1998, p. 118). Nevertheless, many scientists believed that a viable cell could eventually arise from the chemical elements produced in the prebiotic soup.

However, this idea has several shortcomings. When geochemists analyze the sediments from the early history of the earth, they fail to find evidence of a nitrogen-rich prebiotic soup, of the kind predicted by Oparin. Other researchers have determined that the earth's early atmosphere was most probably not Oparin's mixture of water vapor and the reducing gases ammonia (a nitrogen compound), methane, and hydrogen. Instead it was a mixture of water and the neutral gases carbon dioxide and nitrogen (Walker 1977, pp. 210, 246; Kerr 1980). Some free oxygen was also included (Kerr 1980; Dimroth and Kimberley 1976). Today, scientists believe most of the oxygen in the earth's atmosphere came from photosynthesis in plants, but even before plants arose, oxygen could have been derived from the break up of H_2O molecules and from gases released into the atmosphere by volcanoes. Even small amounts of free oxygen would hamper the production of amino acids and other molecules necessary for life. The oxygen would make the required reactions more difficult, and it would also, by oxidation, break down any organic molecules that did form.

Despite these difficulties evolutionists maintain their faith that the ingredients for the bodies of the first living things could have formed spontaneously during the earth's early history. Let us now consider in a more detailed way some of their speculative ideas about how this may have happened. The ideas fall into three main categories: chance, natural selection, and self-organization.

Chance

Some evolutionists propose that chance operating on the molecular level can account for the origin of proteins, which are formed of long chains of amino acid subunits. But there are some big obstacles to such proposals. Let us consider a simple protein composed of 100 amino acid subunits. For a protein to function properly in an organism, the bonds between the amino acids must be peptide bonds. Amino acids can bond with each other in various ways, with peptide bonds occurring half the time. So the odds of getting 100 amino acids with all peptide bonds are 1 in 10^{30} (10 followed by 30 zeroes). Also each amino acid molecule has a left handed L-form (from *laevus,* the Latin word for left) and a right handed D-form (from *dexter,* the Latin word for right). The two forms are mirror images of each other, like right and left shoes, or right and left gloves. In living things, all the proteins are composed of amino acid subunits of the L form. But L and D forms of amino acids occur equally in nature. To get a chain of 100 L-form amino acids, the odds again are 1 in 10^{30}. This is equivalent to flipping a coin and getting heads one hundred times in a row. Therefore, the odds of getting a 100 amino acid chain with all peptide bonds and all L-form amino acids would be about 1 in 10^{60}, which is practically zero odds in the available time limits.

Even if all the bonds are peptide bonds and all the amino acids are L forms, that is still not enough to give us a functional protein. It is not that any combination of amino acid subunits will give us a protein that will contribute to the function of a cell. The right amino acids must be arranged in quite specific orders (Meyer 1998, p. 126). The odds of the right 100 amino acids arranging themselves in the right order are in themselves quite high—about 1 in 10^{65} (the number of atoms in our galaxy is about 10^{65}). Putting this more picturesquely, biochemist Michael Behe (1994, pp. 68–69) says that getting a sequence of 100 amino acids that functions as a protein is comparable to finding one marked grain of sand in the Sahara desert—three times in a row. If you put in the other factors (peptide binding, L-forms only) then the odds go up to 1 chance in 10^{125}. So chance does not seem to work as an explanation for the chem......ical origin of life.

To avoid this conclusion, some scientists appeal to an infinite number of universes. But they have no proof that even one additional universe exists. Neither can they tell us if stable molecules form in any of these imaginary universes (stable molecules are necessary for the kind of life we observe in this universe). We shall consider this topic in greater detail in a later chapter.

Natural Selection

Some scientists, such as Oparin (1968, pp. 146–147), have proposed that natural selection could help select among amino acid chains to produce functional proteins, thus improving the odds that these proteins could form. In other words, protein formation does not rely on pure chance. But there are two problems with this. First, this prebiotic natural selection must operate on amino acid chains that were produced randomly, and we have already seen that the odds are very heavily against getting even a simple chain of amino acids with all peptide bonds and all L forms. So it would be hard to get even the basic raw materials (amino acid chains) upon which natural selection could operate. Second, natural selection involves some kind of molecular replication system. The odds that any such replication system could form by chance are even more remote than the odds against the chance formation of several kinds of amino acid chains upon which natural selection could act. The replication system itself must be made of combinations of highly specific complex protein molecules. Proposals such as Oparin's therefore confront a major contradiction. Natural selection is supposed to produce the complex proteins, but natural selection requires a reliable molecular replication system, and all such systems known today are formed from complex and very specifically structured protein molecules. Oparin suggested that perhaps the earliest replication system did not have to be very reliable and that the system could make use of proteins that were not as specifically structured as proteins currently found in organisms. But Meyer (1998, p. 127) points out that "lack of . . . specificity produces 'error catastrophes' that efface the accuracy of self-replication and eventually render natural selection impossible."

Despite these difficulties, Richard Dawkins (1986, pp. 47–49), in his book *The Blind Watchmaker,* still proposes that chance and natural selection (represented by a simple computer algorithm) can yield biological complexity. To demonstrate that the process is workable, he programmed a computer to generate random combinations of letters and compare them to a target sequence that forms an intelligible grammatically correct sentence. Those combinations of letters that come closest to the meaningful target sequence are preserved, whereas those that depart from the target sequence are rejected. After a certain number of runs, the computer produces the target sequence. Dawkins takes this as proof that random combinations of chemicals could by natural selection gradually produce biologically functional proteins. The reasoning is, however, faulty. First, Dawkins assumes the existence of a complex computer, which we do not find in nature. Second, he assumes the presence of a target sequence. In nature there is no target sequence of amino acids that is specified in advance, and to which random sequences of amino acids can be compared. Third, the trial sequences of letters that are selected by the computer do not themselves have any linguistically functional advantage over other sequences, other than that they are one letter closer to the target sequence. For the analogy between the computer algorithm and real life to hold, each sequence of letters chosen by the computer should itself have some meaning. In real life, an amino acid sequence leading up to a complex protein with a specific function should itself have some function. If it has no function, which can be tested for fitness by natural selection, there is nothing on which natural selection can operate. Meyer (1998, p. 128) says, "In Dawkins's simulation, not a single functional English word appears until after the tenth iteration. . . . Yet to make distinctions on the basis of function among sequences that have no function whatsoever would seem quite impossible. Such determinations can only be made if considerations of proximity to possible future functions are allowed, but this requires foresight that molecules do not have." In other words, Dawkins's result can only be obtained because of the element of intelligent design embedded in the whole experiment.

Self-Organization

Some scientists have suggested that something more than chance and natural selection is involved in the linking of amino acids to form proteins. They propose that certain chemical systems have self-organizing properties or tendencies. Steinman and Cole (1967) suggested that one amino acid may be attracted to another amino acid more than it is attracted to others. There is experimental evidence that this is true. There is some differential attraction among amino acids. Steinman and Cole claimed that the ordering of amino acids they observed in their experiments matched the ordering of amino acids in ten actual proteins. But when Bradley and his coworkers (Kok et al. 1988) compared the sequences reported by Steinman and Cole to a larger sample of sequences from 250 actual proteins, they found these 250 sequences "correlate much better with random statistical probabilities than with the experimentally measured dipeptide bond frequencies of Steinman and Cole" (Bradley 1998, p. 43). Also, if the properties of the twenty biological amino acids strongly determined the bonding of protein sequences we would expect only a few kinds of proteins to form, whereas we observe that thousands form (Bradley 1998, p. 43).

Another kind of self-organization happens when disordered mol-

ecules of a substance form crystals. This is technically called "spontaneous ordering near equilibrium phase changes." The formation of crystals
is fairly easy to explain. For example, when the temperature of water is
lowered below the melting point, the tendency of water molecules to interact in a disordered way is overcome, and they link together in an ordered fashion. In this phase transition, the water molecules tend toward
a state of equilibrium, moving to the lowest potential energy, giving up
energy in the process. Imagine that there is a large depression in the
middle of a billiards table. If you tilt the table here and there, the wandering balls will naturally wind up in the depression, touching each
other and motionless. In the process energy is lost i.e. the process is exothermic. But the formation of complex biological molecules (biopolymers) is different. It is an endothermic process, meaning heat is added,
and it takes place far from thermal equilibrium. The polymers are at a
higher energy potential than their individual components. It is as if the
pool table has a hump in the middle, rather than a depression. It is a lot
more difficult to imagine all the balls winding up together on top of the
hump simply as a result of random movement, than it is to imagine them
winding up in the depression in a state of thermal equilibrium. It would
take some energy to get the balls up on to the hump and keep them
there. Bradley (1998, p. 42) says, "All living systems live energetically
well above equilibrium and require a continuous flow of energy to stay
there . . . Equilibrium is associated with death in the biosphere, making
any explanationof the origin of life that is based on equilibrium thermo-
dynamics clearly incorrect. . . . phase changes such as water freezing into
ice cubes or snowflakes is irrelevant to the processes necessary to generate biological information."

The kind of order found in crystals is repetition of simple patterns,
whereas the kind of order found in living things is highly complex and
nonrepetitive. The order found in the biochemical components of the
bodies of living things is not only highly complex, but very specific. This
specified complexity has a high information content, which allows the
biochemical components to perform specific functions that contribute
to the survival of the organism. Compare the letter sequences ABABAB
AB, RXZPRK LDMW, and THE BIG RED HOUSE. The first sequence
is ordered, but it is not complex and therefore is not informative. Crystals are like this. The second sequence is complex, but it is also not informative. But the third sequence is both complex and informative. The
sequence of letters encodes information that allows the sentence to perform a specific communication function. This property can be called "specified complexity." Biological complexity of the kind we are talking

about in proteins and other molecules in cells is specified complexity—
it is complexity that specifies a function (like protein coding ability of
DNA). Such patterns of complexity are thus different from the simple
repetitive patterns that arise in the crystallization process (Meyer 1998,
p. 134).

Prigogine proposed that self-reproducing organisms could arise
from reacting chemicals brought together in the convection currents
of thermal baths, far from thermal equilibrium. This is somewhat different from the crystal formation process, which involves phase transitions
at or near thermal equilibrium. Bradley (1998, p. 42) nevertheless concludes that although the ordered behavior of the chemicals in Prigogine's systems is more complex than that observed when the systems are
at thermal equilibrium, the order is still "more the type of order that we
see in crystals, with little resemblance to the type of complexity that is
seen in biopolymers." And whatever ordering is observed can be attributed to the complex design of the experimental apparatus. Meyer (1998,
p. 136), citing the work of Walton (1977), says, "even the self-organization
produced in Prigogine-like convection currents does not exceed the organization or information represented by the experimental apparatus
used to create the currents."

Manfred Eigen has proposed that groups of interacting chemicals called "hypercycles" could be a step toward self-reproducing organisms (Eigen and Schuster 1977, 1978a, 1978b). But John Maynard-Smith
(1979) and Freeman Dyson (1985) have exposed some flaws in this proposal. "They show, first," says Meyer (1998, p. 136), "that Eigen's hypercycles presuppose a large initial contribution in the form of a long RNA
molecule and some forty specific proteins. More significantly, they show
that because hypercycles lack an error-free mechanism of self-replication, they become susceptible to various error catastrophes that ultimately diminish, not increase, the information content of the system over
time."

Stuart Kauffman of the Sante Fe Institute has tried another approach to complexity and self-organization. He defines "life" as a closed
network of catalyzed chemical reactions that reproduce each molecule in
the network. No single molecule is engaged in self-replication. But he asserts that if you have a system of at least a million proteinlike molecules,
the odds are that each one will catalzye the formation of another molecule in the system. Therefore the system as a whole replicates. When the
system reaches a certain state, it supposedly undergoes a phase transition,
introducing a new level of complexity for the whole system. But Kauffman's concept is based purely on computer models with little relevance

to real life systems of reacting chemicals (Bradley 1998, p. 44).

First of all, Kaufmann's estimate of a million molecules is too low for each kind of molecule to catalyze the formation of another kind of molecule in the system. But even if a million kinds of molecules is enough, the odds that a particular catalyzing molecule will be near the correct chemical ingredients needed to produce another molecule are remote (Bradley 1998, p. 45).

Futhermore, Kaufmann's computer models do not adequately take into account the exothermic nature of the formation of biopolymers—the reactions require energy from the system and would quickly deplete it, leaving the system "dead." Kaufmann proposes that energy-producing reactions in the system could compensate for the energy consumed in the formation of biopolymers. But Bradley (1998, p. 45) points out that these reactions will also require that certain molecules be in the right places at the right times, in order to participate in the reactions. How all this is supposed to happen is not satisfactorily explained in Kauffman's models. Bradley (1998, p. 45) adds: "Dehydration and condensation onto substrates, his other two possible solutions to the thermodynamic problems, also further complicate the logistics of allowing all of these 1,000,000 molecules to be organized into a system in which all catalysts are rightly positioned relative to reactants to provide their catalytic function." In other words, Kauffman's system does not realistically account for getting all the molecular elements arranged in the proper places for all the needed catalytic and energy-producing reactions to take place. In a computer this may not matter, but in real life it does.

The RNA World

The biggest problem in all origin-of-life scenarios remains explaining in a detailed way the origin of the first DNA replication system found in modern cells. Trying to explain how the DNA replication system arose directly from molecular subunits has proved so difficult that scientists have given up trying. They have concluded that there must have been simpler precursors to the DNA system. Today, many scientists are concentrating their efforts on a replication system based on RNA, which plays a subordinate role in today's cellular reproduction processes. They imagine in the earth's early history an "RNA world" that existed before the DNA world. RNA is a nucleic acid, and it has the ability, under certain circumstances, to replicate itself. Proteins cannot replicate themselves without the help of enzymes that catalyze the replication process. So RNA offers a possible solution to this problem. Perhaps a system of replicating RNA molecules could eventually start catalyzing the replication of proteins, the building blocks of an organism.

The main problem with the RNA world is that scientists have not given a satisfactory explanation of how RNA could spontaneously form. Gerald Joyce and Leslie Orgel, two prominent RNA researchers, have admitted that it is difficult to see how RNA could have self-organized in the earth's early environment. The two primary subunits of RNA—nucleic acids and sugars—tend to repel each other. Joyce and Orgel (1993, p. 13) called the idea that RNA could self-organize "unrealistic in light of our current understanding of prebiotic chemistry" and spoke of "the myth of a self-replicating RNA molecule that arose de novo from a soup of random polynucleotides." They also called attention to the primary paradox of origin-of-life theories: "Without evolution it appears unlikely that a self-replicating ribozyme [RNA] could arise, but without some form of self-replication there is no way to conduct an evolutionary search for the first, primitive self-replicating ribozyme." It should also be kept in mind that RNA can self-replicate only under carefully controlled laboratory conditions not easily duplicated in the early history of the earth. Another problem is that there are many kinds of RNA molecules, and not all of them catalyze their own self-replication. Behe (1996, p. 172) observes: "The miracle that produced chemically intact RNA would not be enough. Since the vast majority of RNAs do not have useful catalytic properties, a second miraculous coincidence would be needed to get just the right chemically intact RNA."

Some researchers have expanded their search for a first nucleotide molecule capable of reproducing itself without the help of enzymes beyond RNA. But thus far all such attempts have been unsuccessful. For example, Stanley Miller and others have proposed peptide nucleic acid (PNA) as an alternative to RNA as the first self-replicating molecule. According to Miller, PNA is a more stable molecule than RNA. But in his experiments Miller has only been able to produce some components of PNA and not the molecule itself (Travis 2000b). In a study published in *Science,* Eschenmoser (1999, p. 2118) says: ". . . it has not been demonstrated that any oligonucleotide system possesses the capacity for efficient and reliable nonenyzmatic replication under potentially natural conditions." Eschenmoser, speaking of RNA or any other oligonucleotide molecule, said that "its chances for formation in an abiotic natural environment remain open to question." He admitted that although most scientists think that the formation of some kind of RNA-like oligonucleotide is a key step in the formation of life, "convincing experimental evidence that such a process can in fact occur under potentially natural conditions is still lacking."

Developmental Biology

Even if we grant the evolutionists the existence of some first simple living thing, then we have to consider how that first living thing gradually differentiated into other living things, including human beings. One source of evidence about the history of such gradual development is the fossil record. When we looked carefully into the human fossil record, we found evidence that humans have existed since the very beginnings of life. Another type of evidence can be found in developmental biology. Most animals begin life as fertilized eggs, which then become embryos, which then become infant organisms, which then become adult organisms. How this happens is the subject matter of developmental biology. Darwinists say they can find evidence for evolution in developmental biology.

Darwinists often point out that at a certain stage of its development the human embryo resembles that of a fish, and they take this as a proof of evolution. Actually, at a certain stage all vertebrate embryos resemble a fish, and thus resemble each other. Darwin himself said "the embryos of mammals, birds, fishes, and reptiles" are "closely similar." He thought the best explanation was that the adults of these species are all "the modified descendants of some ancient progenitor." He also proposed that "the embryonic or larval stages show us, more or less completely, the condition of the progenitor of the whole group in its adult state" (Darwin 1859, pp. 338, 345). In other words, the early fishlike state of the embryo in vertebrates resembles the original adult vertebrate from which all today's vertebrates supposedly came—we were all once fish. But the logic is flawed by a false estimation of the similarity of the embryos.

The process by which an embryo develops into an adult is called ontogeny, and the process of evolution by which a common ancestor supposedly develops into various descendants is called phylogeny. Many Darwinists, to greater and lesser degrees, have believed that the embryonic development of any vertebrate mirrors the evolutionary process that gave rise to it. As the German Darwinist Ernst Haeckel put it: "Ontogeny recapitulates phylogeny." To illustrate his point, Haeckel published a series of images of the embryonic development of several vertebrates, each one looking at first like a fish and then developing into its characteristic form. It was later discovered that Haeckel had doctored the images to make the early fishlike stages look more similar in his illustration than they actually were in nature. Haeckel was formally found guilty of this offense by an academic court at the University of Jena. Nevertheless, his illustration of the vertebrate embryos is still widely printed in textbooks of evolution even today.

Apart from the doctoring of the images in the classic illustration of the vertebrate embryos, there is another deception. The first images of the embryo in the illustration, the ones sharing an impressive similarity, are actually from a middle stage of embryonic development. If the illustration included the earlier stages of embryonic development, including the eggs, an entirely different impression would emerge.

The eggs, the single celled starting points of the embryos of all animals, are vastly different. The bird and reptile eggs are of very great size. Fish eggs are usually smaller, but still easily visible to human eyes. The human egg, on the other hand, is of microscopic size.

The first stage of embryonic development is cleavage, the division of the egg into cells. Each group of vertebrate animals has its own cleavage pattern, very different from the others. During the cleavage stage, the basic anterior to posterior (front to rear) direction of the body is established. Next comes the gastrula phase, during which the basic body plan of the animal is elaborated. During gastrulation, the cells begin to differentiate into the various tissues. As in the case of cleavage patterns, gastrulation patterns display a great deal of variation among the different kinds of animals. At this stage in development, the embryos therefore look quite different from each other (Nelson 1998, p. 154; Wells 1998, p. 59; Elinson 1987).

It is only in the next stage of embryonic development, the pharyngula stage, that the embryos of fish, reptiles, birds, and mammals come to temporarily resemble each other, looking somewhat like little fishes. In the pharyngula stage, all the embryos have little folds of tissue in the throat region that look like gills. In fish, they do become gills, but in other animals they form the inner ear and thyroid glands. So the embryos of humans and other mammals never have gills, nor do the embryos of birds and reptiles (Wells 1998, p. 59). After pharnygula stage, the embryos again diverge in appearance.

Considered in its entirety, the embryonic development of the vertebrates, rather than supporting evolution, tends to pose a strong challenge to it. According to evolutionists' theory, all metazoans (multicelled creatures) must have come from a common ancestor. This creature would have had a certain body plan. To change that basic body plan would require changes in the genes that control the early embryonic stages of that body plan's development. But according to evolutionary theory, the genes controlling the early stages of development should not be subject to very much change. Any such changes could cause massive disruptions in the development of the organism, causing its death or serious malformation.

That is what we see today. As Nelson (1998, p. 159) says, "All experimental evidence suggests that development, when perturbed, either shuts down, or returns via alternate and redundant pathways to its primary trajectory." Therefore, according to most evolutionary biologists, positive mutations should occur only in genes responsible for details of later phases of development of an organism.

According to evolutionary theory, we should expect the earliest phases of development in living things to be quite similar. But, as we have seen, the early developmental stages of living things are vastly different from each other (Nelson 1998, p. 154). For example, after the egg begins to divide, there are several pathways by which the embryos of different animals reach the gastrula stage. Eric Davidson (1991, p. 1), a developmental biologist, has called this variety of cleavage patterns "intellectually disturbing." It is somewhat of a mystery how all these very different patterns of early development came from some common ancestor. Richard Elinson (1987, p. 3) asked: "If early embryogenesis is conservative, how did such major changes in the earliest events of embryogenesis occur?" He calls it "a conundrum."

Some (Thomson 1988, pp. 121–122) have proposed that early changes in development are obviously possible, simply because they have obviously occurred. This is a typical example of blind faith in evolutionary doctrine. Nelson (1998, p. 158) says: "Note that this position rests entirely on the assumption of common descent. There is little if any experimental evidence that 'changes in early development are possible.' I know of only a single example of heritable changes in metazoan cleavage patterns." In other words, there is only a single experimentally verified example of a genetic change in the early development of an animal that has been passed on to its descendants. The change involves a mutation in the early development of the snail Limenaea peregra, which causes only the direction of the coiling of its shell to switch from right to left (Nelson 1998, p. 170, citing Gilbert 1991, p. 86) This is not a very significant change. It represents no new biological feature.

So today there is practically no experimental evidence that early changes in development can result in viable organisms with new features. Some scientists propose that although such changes are not possible in today's organisms, they were possible early in the history of evolution, resulting in major changes in body plans. Foote and Gould (1992, p. 1816) suggest that this proposed early period of developmental flexibility was closed off hundreds of millions of years ago at the end of the "Cambrian explosion," during which all major body plans now seen in living things supposedly emerged. After the Cambrian explosion there was "some form of genetic and developmental locking." The proof of this, say Foote and Gould, is that no new major body plans have emerged since the Cambrian. Further, they say that we do not see today that creatures with major mutations in genes that control early development survive (Foote and Gould 1992, p. 1816). But this era of early plasticity of body plans, generated by changes in early developmental stages of the embryo, is purely speculative. Scientists cannot point to any specific reason, on the biomolecular level, exactly why Cambrian creatures could survive such major mutations.

Nelson (1998, p. 168) says: "Golden ages of evolution are postulated (e.g., the Cambrian explosion), in the complete absence of any mechanistic understanding, to accommodate the demands of a philosophy of nature that holds, in the face of abundant disconfirming evidence, that complex things come into existence by undirected mutation and selection from simpler things. Yet, however unlikely they may be, these golden ages of macroevolution are preferable by neo-Darwinists to taking at face value the demonstrable limits of organismal structure and function —for those limits imply the primary discontinuity of organisms one from another." Discontinuity implies intelligent design of the separate species.

Scientists find it difficult to explain in any detailed way how these body plans (or Bauplans) came about from some common ancestor by evolutionary processes. Bruce Wallace (1984, cited in Nelson 1998, p. 160) tells of some of the problems involved in modifying a body plan: "The *Bauplan* of an organism . . . can be thought of as the arrangement of genetic switches that control the course of the embryonic and subsequent development of the individual; such control must operate properly both in time generally and sequentially in the separately differentiated tissues. Selection, both natural and artificial, that leads to morphological change and other developmental modification does so by altering the settings and triggerings of these switches . . . The extreme difficulty encountered when attempting to transform one organism into another but still functional one lies in the difficulty in resetting a number of the many controlling switches in a manner that still allows for the individual's orderly (somatic) development." It is like trying to transform a six cylinder engine into an eight cylinder engine while keeping the engine running through all the changes. Arthur (1987, cited in Nelson 1998, p. 170) says that "in the end we have to admit that we do not really know how body plans originate."

What to speak of understanding how genes can govern major changes in body plans, to produce new organisms, scientists do not yet fully understand how genes direct the development of the body plan of any particular species. R. Raff and T. Kaufman (1991, p. 336) speak of science's "currently poor understanding of the way in which genes direct the morphogenesis of even simple metazoan structures." Each human being starts as a single cell—a fertilized egg. The egg begins to divide into more cells. Each cell contains the exact same DNA, but the cells differentiate into various tissues and structures. How exactly this happens is not currently understood, even in very small multicellular organisms.

Some scientists believe that "homeotic" genes provide the answer to the specification of body plans and their development in an organism. In the late nineteenth century biologists noted that body parts of some animals sometimes grew to resemble other body parts. For example, in insects, an antenna might come to display the form of a leg (a condition called Antennapedia). Such forms were called homeotic. The prefix homeo means "like, or similar," so a homeotic leg would be a body part that resembles a leg. In the twentieth century, the gene responsible for the mutation that causes Antennapedia in fruit flies was discovered and named *Antp*. But the big question is not how a leg can grow in place of an antenna, but how such complex structures as legs and antennas came into existence in the first place—something not perfectly explained up to now by genetic researchers and developmental biologists.

Besides *Antp*, there are other homeotic genes in the fruit fly, such as *Pax-6*, related to eye development. In 1995, Walter Gehring and his colleagues mutated *Pax-6*, causing eyes to grow on the antenna and legs of fruit flies. *Pax-6* is similar in flies and mammals (humans included). Part of the gene (the DNA binding segment) is also found in worms and squids (Quiring et al. 1994). Researchers concluded that *Pax-6* was "the master control gene for eye morphogenesis" and that it is universal in multicellular animals (Halder et al. 1995, p. 1792).

But Wells (1998, pp. 56–57) points out: "If the same gene can 'determine' structures as radically different as . . . an insect's eyes and the eyes of humans and squids then that gene is not determining much of anything." He adds: "Except for telling us how an embryo directs its cells into one of several built-in developmental pathways, homeotic genes tell us nothing about how biological structures are formed."

In the case of the eye, evolutionists have to explain how this complicated biological structure arose not just once, but several times. Prominent evolutionists L. von Salvini-Palwen and Ernst Mayr (1977) say that "the earliest invertebrates, or at least those that gave rise to the more advanced phyletic lines, had no photoreceptors" and that "photoreceptors have originated independently in at least 40, but possibly up to 65 or more different phyletic lines."

The Biological Complexity of Humans

The great complexity of the organs found in the human body defies evolutionary explanation. Darwinists have not explained in any detailed way how these organs could have arisen by random genetic variations and natural selection.

The Eye

The human eye is one such organ of apparently irreducible complexity. The pupil allows light into the eye, and the lens focuses the light on the retina. The eye also has features to correct for interference between light waves of different frequencies. It is hard to see how the eye could function without all of its parts being present. Even Darwin understood that the eye and other complex structures posed a problem for his theory of evolution, which required that such structures arise over many generations, step by step. Darwin didn't give a detailed account of how this happened, but pointed to different living creatures with different kinds of eyes—some just light sensitive spots, some simple depressions with simple lenses, and others more complex. He suggested that the human eye could have arisen in stages like this. He ignored the question of how the first light sensitive spot came into being. "How a nerve comes to be sensitive to light hardly concerns us more than how life itself originated" (Darwin 1872, p. 151; Behe 1996, pp. 16–18).

Darwin's vague account of a light-sensitive spot gradually developing into the complex, cameralike human eye may have a certain superficial plausibility, but it does not constitute a scientific explanation of the eye's origin. It is simply an invitation to imagine that evolution actually took place. If one wishes to turn imagination into science, one must take into account the structure of the eye on the biomolecular level.

Devlin (1992, pp. 938–954) gives a fairly detailed biochemical description of the human vision process. Biochemist Michael Behe (1996, pp. 18–21) summarizes Devlin's explanation like this: "When light first strikes the retina a photon interacts with a molecule called 11-*cis*-retinal, which rearranges within picoseconds to *trans*-retinal. . . . The change in the shape of the retinal molecule forces a change in the shape of the protein, rhodopsin, to which the retinal is tightly bound. . . . Now called metarhodopsin II, the protein sticks to another protein, called transducin. Before bumping into metarhodopsin II, transducin had tightly bound a small molecule called GDP. But when transducin interacts with metarhodopsin II, the GDP falls off, and a molecule called GTP binds to transducin. . . . GTP-transducin-metarhodopsin II now binds to a protein called phosphodiesterase, located in the inner membrane of the cell. When attached to metarhodopsin II and its entourage, the phosphodiesterase acquires the chemical ability to 'cut' a molecule called cGMP . . . Initially there are a lot of cGMP molecules in the cell, but the phosphodiesterase lowers its concentration, just as a pulled plug lowers the water level in a bathtub. Another membrane protein that binds cGMP is called an ion channel. It acts as a gateway that regulates the number of sodium ions in the cell, while a separate protein actively pumps them out again. The dual action of the ion channel and pump keeps the level of sodium ions in the cell within a narrow range. When the amount of cGMP is reduced because of cleavage by the phosphodiesterase, the ion channel closes, causing the cellular concentration of positively charged sodium ions to be reduced. This causes an imbalance of charge across the cell membrane that, finally, causes a current to be tranmitted down the optic nerve to the brain. The result, when interpreted by the brain, is vision."

Another equally complex set of reactions restores the original chemical elements that started the process, like 11-*cis*-retinal, cGMP, and sodium ions (Behe 1996, p. 21). And this is just part of the biochemistry underlying the process of vision. Behe (1996, p. 22) stated: "Ultimately . . . *this* is the level of explanation for which biological science must aim. In order to truly understand a function, one must understand in detail every relevant step in the process. The relevant steps in biological processes occur ultimately at the molecular level, so a satisfactory explanation of a biological phenomenon—such as sight, digestion, or immunity—must include its molecular explanation." Evolutionists have not produced such an explanation.

The Vesicular Transport System

The lysosome is a compartment within the cell that disposes of damaged proteins. There are enzymes within the lysosome that dismantle the proteins. These enzymes are manufactured in ribosomes, compartments found inside another cellular compartment called the endoplasmic reticulum. As the enzymes are being manufactured in the ribosomes, they are tagged with special amino acid sequences that allow them to pass through the walls of the ribosomes into the endoplasmic reticulum. From there, they are tagged with other amino acid sequences that allow them to pass out of the endoplasmic reticulum. The enzymes make their way to the lysosome, where they bind to the surface of the lysosome. Then yet another set of signal tags allow them to enter the lysosome, where they can do their work (Behe 1998, pp. 181–182; Alberts et al. 1994, pp. 551–650). This transportation network is called the vesicular transport system.

In I-cell disease, a flaw in signal tagging disrupts the vesicular transport system. Instead of carrying the protein-degrading enzymes from the ribosomes to the lysosomes, the system carries them to the cell wall, where they are dumped outside of the cell. Meanwhile, damaged proteins flow into the lysosomes, where they are not degraded. Without the protein-degrading enzymes, the lysosomes fill up like overflowing garbage cans. To deal with this, the cell manufactures new lysosomes, which also fill up with garbage proteins. Finally, when there are too many lysosomes filled with garbage proteins, the whole cell breaks down and the person with this disease dies. This shows what happens when one part of a complex system is missing—the whole system breaks down. All the parts of the vesicular transport system have to be in place for it to work effectively.

Behe (1996, pp. 115–116) says: "Vesicular transport is a mind-boggling process, no less complex than the completely automated delivery of vaccine from a storage area to a clinic a thousand miles away. Defects in vesicular transport can have the same deadly consequences as the failure to deliver a needed vaccine to a disease-racked city. An analysis shows that vesicular transport is irreducibly complex, and so its development staunchly resists gradualistic explanations, as Darwinian evolution would have it. A search of the professional biochemical literature shows that no one has ever proposed a detailed route by which such a system could have come to be. In the face of the enormous complexity of vesicular transport, Darwinian theory is mute."

The Blood Clotting Mechanism

The human blood clotting mechanism is another puzzle for evolutionists. Behe (1996, p. 78) says: "Blood clotting is a very complex, intricately woven system consisting of scores of interdependent protein parts. The absence of, or significant defects in, any one of a number of the components causes the system to fail: blood does not clot at the proper time or at the proper place." The system is thus one of irreducible complexity, not easily explained in terms of Darwinian evolution.

The blood clotting mechanism centers around fibrinogen, a blood protein that forms the fibers that make up the clots. Normally, fibrinogen is dissolved in the blood plasma. When bleeding begins, a protein called thrombin cuts fibrinogen to make strings of a protein called fibrin. The fibrin filaments stick together, forming a network that catches blood cells, thus stopping the flow of blood from a wound (Behe 1996, p. 80). At first, the network is not very strong. It sometimes breaks, allowing the blood to flow out from the wound again. To prevent this, a protein called the fibrin stabilizing factor (FSF), creates cross links between fibrin filaments, strengthening the network (Behe 1996, p. 88).

Meanwhile, thrombin is cutting more fibrinogen into more fibrin, which forms more clots. At a certain point, the thrombin has to stop cutting fibrinogen or else so much fibrin would be produced that it would clot up the whole blood system and the person would die (Behe 1996, p. 81).

There is a complex cascade of proteins and enzymes involved in turning the blood clotting system on and off at the proper times. Thrombin originally exists as an inactive form, prothrombin. In this form, it doesn't cut fibrinogen into the fibrin filaments that make clots. So for the clotting process to start, prothrombin must be converted to thrombin. Otherwise, a person bleeds to death. And once the proper clotting is formed, thrombin has to be turned back into prothrombin. Otherwise, the clotting continues until all the blood stops flowing (Behe 1996, p. 82).

A protein called the Stuart factor is involved in the activation of prothrombin, turning it into thrombin, so that the clotting process can start. So what activates the inactive Stuart factor? There are two cascades of interactions, which begin with transformations at the wound site. Let's consider just one of them. Behe (1996, p. 84) says: "When an animal is cut, a protein called Hageman factor is then cleaved by a protein called HMK to yield activated Hageman factor. Immediately the activated Hageman factor converts another protein, called prekallikrein, to its active form, kallikrein. Kallikrein helps HMK speed up the conversion of more Hageman factor to its active form. Activated Hageman factor and HMK then together transform another protein, called PTA, to its active form. Activated PTA in turn, together with the activated form of another protein called convertin, switch a protein called Christmas factor to its active form. Finally, activated Christmas factor, together with antihemophilic factor . . . changes Stuart to its active form." The second cascade is equally complicated, and in some places merges with the first.

So now we have the activated Stuart factor. But even that is not enough to start the clotting process. Before the Stuart factor can act on prothrombin, prothrombin has to be modified by having ten of its amino acid subunits changed. After these changes, prothrombin can stick to a cell wall. Only when the prothrombin is adhering to a cell wall can it be converted (by the Stuart factor) into thrombin, which initiates clotting. The sticking of the prothrombin to the cell wall near a cut helps localize the clotting action in the exact region of the cut. But activated Stuart factor protein turns prothrombin into thrombin at a very slow rate. The organism would die before enough thrombin is produced to start any effective clotting. So another protein, called accelerin, must be present to increase the speed of the Stuart factor protein's action on prothrombin (Behe 1996, pp. 81–83).

So now the prothrombin is converted into thrombin. The thrombin cuts fibrinogen, forming fibrin, which actually forms clots. Now we can turn to the question of how to stop this clotting process once it starts. Runaway clotting would clog up the organism's blood vessels, with life threatening results. After thrombin molecules have formed, a protein called antithrombin binds to them, thus inactivating them. But antithrombin binds only when in contact with another protein called heparin, which is found in uninjured blood vessels. So this means that the antithrombin binds to the activated thrombin molecules only when they enter undamaged blood vessels, thus inactivating them and stopping the clotting. In an injured blood vessel the clotting can continue. In this way, the clotting goes on only at the site of the wound, and not in other uninjured blood vessels. Once the injured vessel is repaired the clotting will also stop there. This is accomplished by a process just as complex as the one that stops blood from clotting in uninjured blood vessels (Behe 1996 pp. 87–88).

After some time, when the wound has healed, the clot itself must be removed. A protein called plasmin cuts the fibrin network that makes up the clot. As one might guess, plasmin first exists in its unactive form, plasminogen, and must be activated at the proper time to remove the clot. Its activation, of course, involves complex interactions with other proteins (Behe 1996, p. 88).

Behe (1996, p. 86) says, "The blood-clotting system fits the definition of irreducible complexity. That is, it is a single system composed of several interacting parts that contribute to the basic function, and where the removal of any one of the parts causes the system effectively to cease functioning . . . In the absence of any one of the components, blood does not clot, and the system fails." Evolutionists have not offered any satisfactory explanation for how this complex chemical repair system, involving many unique proteins with very specific functions, came into existence.

Blood-clotting expert Russell Doolittle simply asserts that the required proteins in the system were produced by gene duplication and gene shuffling. But gene duplication just produces a duplicate of an already existing gene. Doolittle does not specify what mutations have to take place in this duplicated gene to give the protein it produces a new function useful in some evolving blood clotting system. Gene shuffling is based on the idea that each gene is made of several subsections. Sometimes in the course of reproduction the sections of genes break apart and combine back together in a new order. The reshuffled gene would produce a different protein. But the odds against getting the right subsections of genes to come together to form a new gene that would produce a protein useful in the blood-clotting cascade are astronomically high. One protein in the system, TPA, has four parts. Let us assume an animal existed at a time when the blood clotting system was just starting to form, and there was no TPA. Let us further assume that this animal had 10,000 genes. Each gene is divided into an average of three subsections. So this means 30,000 gene pieces are available for gene shuffling. The odds of getting the four parts that make up TPA to come together randomly are thus one in $30,000^4$—not very likely. But the main problem is getting all the parts together into a working system. Only such a system, which contributes to the fitness of the organism, can be acted on by natural selection. Isolated parts of a system do not really contribute to fitness, and therefore there is no natural selection possible. So, in order to explain the presence of today's human blood clotting system, evolutionists first have to show the existence of a simple blood clotting system and show step by step how changes in the genes could produce more and more effective systems that work and contribute to the fitness of an organism. That has not been done in any detailed way (Behe 1996, pp. 90–97). To escape this criticism, some scientists suggest that the parts of such a complex system could have had other functions in other systems before coming together in the system in question. But that further complicates an already complicated question. In this case, scientists would then have to show how these other systems with different functions arose in step by step fashion and how parts of these systems were co-opted for another purpose, without damaging those systems.

The DNA Replication System

When a cell divides, the DNA in the cell also has to divide and replicate itself. The DNA replication system in humans and other organisms is another system that is difficult to explain by evolutionary processes. DNA is a nucleic acid. It is composed of nucleotides. Each nucleotide is composed of two parts. The first is a carbohydrate ring (deoxyribose), and the second is a base attached to the carbohydrate ring. There are four bases: adenine (A), cytosine (C), guanine (G), and thymine (T). One base binds to each carbohydrate ring. The carbohydrate rings join to each other in a chain. At one end of the chain is a 5'OH (five prime hydroxyl) group. At the other end of the DNA chain is a 3'OH (three prime hydryoxyl) group. The sequence of base pairs in a strand of DNA is read from the 5 prime end to the 3 prime end of the strand. In cells, two strands of DNA are twisted together in a helix. The bases in the nucleotides of each strand join to each other. A always bonds with T, and G always bonds with C. The two strands are thus complementary. One of them can replicate the other. If you know the base sequence of one strand of DNA you know the base sequence of the second strand in the helix. For example, if part of the sequence of bases in one strand is TTGAC, then you know that the same part of the second strand must have the bases AACTG. So each of the two strands can serve as a template for producing the other. The end result is two new double strands of DNA, matching the parent double strand. Therefore, when a cell divides into two cells, each one winds up with a matching double strand of DNA (Behe 1998, p. 184).

For DNA to replicate, the two coiled strands of DNA have to be separated. But the two complementary strands of DNA in the parent cell are joined by a chemical bond. The replication occurs at places on the DNA strand called "origins of replication." A protein binds to the DNA at one of these places and pushes the strands apart. Then another protein called helicase moves in, and taking advantage of the opening starts pushing down the strand (like a snowplow). But once the two DNA strands are pushed apart, they want to rejoin, or if they don't rejoin, each single strand can become tangled as hydrogen bonding takes place between its different parts. To solve this problem, there is SSB, the single-strand binding protein, which coats the single strand, preventing it from tangling or rebonding with the other DNA strand. Then there is another problem. As the helicase moves forward, separating the two strands of coiled DNA, the two strands of DNA in front of the advancing helicase become knotted. To remove the knots, an enzyme called gyrase cuts, untangles, and rejoins the DNA strands (Behe 1998, p. 190).

The actual replication of a DNA strand is carried out principally by the polymerase enzyme, which binds itself to the DNA strand. The polymerase is attached to the original DNA strands by a ring of "clamp proteins." There is a complex system of proteins that loads the ring onto the DNA strand. A special kind of RNA starts the replication process by linking a few nucleotide bases together forming a short chain of DNA. The polymerase then continues adding complementary nucleotide bases to the 3 prime end of the new chain. For example, if on the original DNA strand there is a G base the polymerase adds a complementary C base to the new strand. The adding of nucleotide bases takes place at the "replication forks," the places where the two original DNA strands are pushed apart (Behe 1998, p. 188).

As a replication fork moves along one strand from the 5 prime end to the 3 prime end, the polymerase enzyme replicates this strand, called the leading strand, continuously. DNA can be replicated only in this direction, toward the 3 prime end. But the two DNA strands that make up a DNA double helix face in opposite directions. So how is the second strand replicated? While the polymerase enzyme is replicating the leading strand in the continuous manner just described, moving always toward the leading strand's 3 prime end, it simultaneously replicates the second, or lagging strand, in a discontinuous manner, adding groups of nucleotides to its new complement in the opposite direction. The process starts with a short segment of RNA, which serves as a primer. A few nucleotides are then added to this piece of RNA, going backwards towards the 3 prime end of the lagging strand. After adding these few nucleotides going backwards, the polymerase replication machinery is unclamped and moves forward and is reclamped at the new position of the replication fork, which is continually moving toward the 3 prime end of the leading strand and away from the 3 prime end of the lagging strand. The polymerase continues replicating the leading strand by adding more bases to its new complementary strand going forward and at the same time continues replicating the lagging strand by adding to its new complementary strand another set of bases going backwards. To the lagging strand's new complement, the polymerase adds another piece of RNA primer and a few more nucleotides going backward until they touch the previous set of RNA primer and nucleotides. Each set of nucleotides replicated on the lagging strand's complement is called an Okazaki fragment. To join the new Okazaki fragment to the previous one, a special enzyme has to come in and remove the RNA primer between the two fragments. Then the two Okazaki fragments have to be joined by an enzyme called DNA ligase. Then the polymerase replication machinery has to be unclamped, moved forward to the replication fork, and clamped again. The process proceeds until both the leading and lagging strands have replicated completely (Behe 1998, p. 191). There is also an elaborate proofreading system that corrects any mistakes in the replication process.

Behe (1998, p. 192) notes: "No one has ever published a paper in the professional science literature that explains in a detailed fashion how DNA replication in toto or any of its parts might have been produced in a Darwinian, step-by-step fashion." The same is true of thousands of other complex biomolecular structures and processes found in humans and other living things.

Neural Connections in the Brain

J. Travis (2000c) says, "The developing human brain . . . must make sure that its billions of nerve cells correctly establish trillions of connections among themselves." Since scientists say that all conscious functions are products of brain activity, these connections assume a lot of importance. Aside from some vague speculations about "guidance molecules," and an all abiding faith that it must have happened by evolution, scientists have offered no detailed explanation of how the connections are made. On the basis of experiments with fruit flies, scientists say they have discovered a gene that looks like it codes for 38,000 different "guidance molecules." Even if true, this creates a huge problem for evolutionists. How could one gene be responsible for so many guidance molecules? How are those 38,000 different "guidance molecules" distributed in the proper way to make the required connections among the nerve cells in the fly brain? And even assuming one could figure this out, then how would one go from there to another more complicated brain, simply by random mutations in DNA and natural selection?

The Placenta

Another problem for evolutionists is the origin of the placenta in mammals. The DNA of a fetus is a combination of DNA from both the mother and father. It is therefore different from that of the mother. The immune system of the mother should normally reject the fetus as foreign tissue. The placenta isolates the fetus from direct contact with the mother's immune system. The placenta also supplies the fetus with nutrients and expels wastes from the fetus. Harvey J. Kliman, a reproductive biologist at Yale University, says, "In many ways, the placenta is the SCUBA system for the fetus, while at the same time being the Houston Control Center guiding the mother through pregnancy." According to evolutionists, before the placental mammals came into existence, all land animals reproduced by laying eggs. In a report in *Science News,* John Travis (2000d, p. 318) says, "As with many evolutionary adaptations, the origins of the placenta remain shrouded in mystery. That hasn't kept biologists from speculating, however." But speculations are not real scientific explanations. And the real scientific explanations just are not there.

"In the past ten years," says Behe (1998, p. 183), "*Journal of Molecular Evolution* has published more than a thousand papers. . . . There were zero papers discussing detailed models for intermediates in the development of complex biomolecular structures. This is not a peculiarity of *JME*. No papers are to be found that discuss detailed models for intermediates in the development of complex biomolecular structures, whether in the *Proceedings of the National Academy of Science, Nature, Science,* the *Journal of Molecular Biology* or, to my knowledge, any science journal."

Similarity of Apes and Humans

Physical anthropologists and other scientists have tried to use genetics to clarify the supposed evolutionary relationships between humans, chimpanzees, and gorillas. Are humans closer to chimps or gorillas? Are chimps and gorillas closer to each other than either of them is to humans? Different kinds of studies yield different results. According to Marks (1994), some researchers say chromosome structure links humans and gorillas, while others say it links humans and chimps, while yet others say it links chimps and gorillas. Mitochondrial DNA evidence show that humans, chimps, and gorillas are equally close to each other. Evidence for nuclear DNA is "discordant," with the X chromosome evidence making chimps closest to gorillas and the Y chromosome evidence making chimps closest to humans. As far as skeletal evidence is concerned, the cranium links humans and chimps, but the rest of the skeleton links chimps and gorillas (Marks 1994, pp. 65–66).

In sorting out this confusing and contradictory set of conclusions, many scientists act on the belief that genetic evidence is superior to other kinds of evidence. But Marks (1994, p. 65) questions this belief: "Molecular studies bearing on problems of anthropological systematics, it seems, have often suffered from [poor] quality control, rash generalizations, belligerent conclusions, and the gratuitous assumption that if two bodies of work yield different conclusions, the genetic work is more trustworthy."

Sibley and Ahlquist (1984, p. 11) claimed to have used molecular methods (DNA hybridization) to reconstruct the phylogeny of chimps, gorillas, and humans. They said the genetic evidence showed that first chimps diverged from gorillas, and then humans diverged from chimps. But Marks (1994, p. 65) pointed out: "The conclusion here was derived by 1) moving correlated points into a regression line and recalculating their values; 2) substituting controls across experiments; and 3) making precise alterations on the basis of a variable that was not actually measured." To put it more plainly, the study by Sibley and Ahlquist was flawed by artificial manipulation of the experimental data. Marks (1994, p. 66) noted: "That these manipulations are not part of the general canon of scientific protocols, however, is not complemented by the fact that they were not mentioned in the original reports, and were discovered serendipitously by others. . . . These revelations stood to make the researchers themselves look less than honest and to make public advocates of the work look less than wise."

The study of Sibley and Ahlquist was flawed not only by these technical lapses, but also by the incorrectness of the study's fundamental assumptions. According to Marks (1994, p. 69), these assumptions were (1) that humans came from either chimps or gorillas by a two-step process (i.e. chimps from gorillas, then humans from chimps; or gorillas from chimps, and then humans from gorillas) and (2) that this process is "discernible with genetic data and theory as they currently exist." Marks (1994, p. 69) explained, "These assumptions are pernicious because . . . they misrepresent the literature. In the first place, it must be appreciated that we do not know there were in fact two sequential divergences, and not a single trifurcation." That is to say, it is quite possible that humans, chimps, and gorillas all came from an unknown common ancestor. The evidence might even be seen as consistent with creation of all three by God in nearly their present forms.

Evolutionists have for many years said that the DNA of humans and chimps is 97% identical. They have claimed that this proves an evolutionary connection between the two species. There are several things wrong with this kind of reasoning. First, of all, the claimed 97% identity was derived from crude DNA hybridization techniques (Sibley and Alhquist 1987). Researchers broke human DNA into little parts in test tubes and then observed how much of it recombined with pieces of chimp DNA. Three percent did not recombine. But no one really knows how similar humans and chimps really are on the actual genetic level. The human genome has only recently been sequenced. This sequencing merely gives the order of the roughly 3 billion nucleotide bases in the DNA molecules that make up the human genome. It is like having the sequence of letters that makes up a book in a foreign language. To read the book, you have to break the sequence of letters into words and sentences and understand their meaning. This has not happened yet with DNA. According to current understanding, ninety-seven percent of the bases in the human genome do not make up genes. They are called junk DNA. Sorting out the sequences that represent actual genes instead of junk DNA could take decades. The chimp genome has not even been sequenced, and it is not likely to be sequenced for years to come. So at the present moment there is no real basis for making any truly scientific comparison between the human genome and the chimp genome. We cannot at this point say, "Here are all the chimp genes, and here all are the human genes," and talk about how similar or different they really are in total.

We should also keep in mind that genes only specify what amino acids should be strung together to form protein molecules (or other polypeptides). In other words, the genes simply generate the molecular raw materials for the construction of bodies and body functions. It should not be surprising that the bodies of humans and chimpanzees are composed of roughly the same molecular ingredients. We exist in the same kinds of environments, and eat basically the same kinds of foods. So the similarity of genes and molecular ingredients does not rule out design. Designers of different kinds of automobiles make use of basically the same ingredients. In fact, the real problem is not the ingredients—the real problem is the arrangement of those ingredients into complex forms that work together to form a functioning machine. At a factory, the raw materials may arrive, in the form of steel, glass, rubber, plastic, etc. But the factory workers also need to shape and arrange those raw materials into an automobile. Similarly, genes may specify the formation of molecular raw materials, but it has not been shown that the genes specify exactly how those molecular raw materials are organized into the bodies of chimps or humans. Unless this can be shown, in some exact way, it is not unreasonable to attribute the similarity of chimp and human DNA, as well as the complex bodily forms of chimps and humans, to intelligent design.

The most recent research, as of the time of this writing, suggests that the human and chimpanzee genomes differ by as little as 1.5 percent (Travis 2000a). "What does that number mean? No one can say at the moment," writes John Travis in *Science News* (2000a, p. 236). With so little difference, it is hard to explain many things—such as why the human brain is twice the size of the chimpanzee brain (Travis 2000a, p. 237). So the similarity of human and chimpanzee DNA is actually seen by many evolutionists as a significant problem that needs to be explained. Frans de Waal, a primatologist at Emory University, says, "Most of us find it hard to believe we differ by only 1.5 percent from an ape. It's absolutely critical that we know what that 1.5 percent is doing" (Travis 2000a, p. 237). It appears that something more than DNA is necessary to put together the complex structures that define different species. That "something" more is arguably intelligent design.

Some scientists point out that the human chromosome 2 appears to be a combination of the chimpanzee chromosomes 12 and 13. They take this as evidence for evolution. But the fact that chromosomes may have been combined does not tell us how they were combined. It may have been part of an intelligently designed system for producing different bodily forms by systematic manipulation of the chromosomes. Other scientists point to the existence of "pseudogenes" as evidence for evolution. Pseudogenes are stretches of DNA that appear like genes, but do not function as genes. For example, the human DNA has a stretch of DNA that appears like a gene that in other animals produces vitamin C. But in humans it is not active. But the fact that a gene may have been deactivated does not tell us how it was deactivated. It could have been by the action of an intelligent designer.

African Eve

Some scientists claim that genetic evidence shows all living humans can trace their ancestry to a female who lived in Africa about 200,000 years ago. Her descendants then spread throughout the world, replacing whatever hominids existed there, without interbreeding with them. The hominids they replaced would have been Neandertals or Neandertal-like descendants of *Homo erectus*, who supposedly left Africa in a previous wave of emigration between one and two million years ago.

Evidence from Mitochondrial DNA

The above scenario is called the African Eve hypothesis, or the out-of-Africa replacement hypothesis. It was first announced in the 1980s by researchers such as Cann, Stoneking, and Vigilant, among others. Their conclusions were based on studies of mitochondrial DNA. Most of the DNA in human cells is found in the nucleus. This nuclear DNA is a combination of DNA from the mother and father. The sex cells of males and females contain half the DNA found in each parent. Thus when the father's sperm combines with the mother's egg, the fertilized egg of the offspring contains a full complement of DNA, different from that of either the father or the mother, in the nucleus. But the mother's egg cell also contains small round compartments (outside the nucleus) called mitochondria, which are involved in the cellular energy production process.

The presence of mitochondria in eukaryotic cells is a bit of a mystery. In eukaryotic cells, the DNA is found on chromosomes isolated in the cell's nucleus. In prokaryotic cells, there is no nucleus and the DNA molecules simply float in the cell's cytoplasm. Almost all of the plants and animals living today are either single eukaryotic cells or are composed of many eukaryotic cells. Only bacteria and blue-green algae are prokaryotic. Evolutionists theorize that the mitochondria in today's cells are remnants of prokaryotic cells that invaded primitive eukaryotic cells. If that were true, then this most probably happened very early in the evolutionary process, when only single celled creatures existed. This implies that the mitochondria in all living things should be quite similar. But the mitochondrial DNA in mammals "cannot generally be classified as either prokaryote-like or eukaryote-like." Furthermore: "The mammalian mt [*mitochondrial*] genetic code is different from the so-called universal genetic code . . . mammalian mitochondria are very different from other mitochondria. In yeast mitochondria, for example, not only is there a slightly different genetic code, but also the genes are widely spaced and in a different order, and in some cases they contain intervening sequences. These radical differences make it difficult to draw conclusions regarding mitochondrial evolution" (Anderson et al. 1981, p. 464). In other words, the presence of the various kinds of mitochondria in different creatures argues against an evolutionary origin.

But let us now return to the main point. In mammals, the mitochondria in the mother's egg have their own DNA. This mitochondrial DNA does not, however, combine with the DNA from the father. Therefore, all of us have in our cells mitochondria with DNA that came only from our mothers. The mitochondrial DNA in our mothers came from their mothers, and so on back into time. The African Eve researchers assume that the only changes in the mitochondrial DNA are the changes that accumulate by random mutations. By studying the rate of mutation, scientists believe they can use mitochondrial DNA as a kind of clock, relating numbers of mutations to numbers of years. And by looking at the mitochondrial DNA in different human populations in various parts of the world, scientists believe they can sort out which group is the parent group for the others.

They believe that the parent group, which must also be the oldest group, can be identified by computer programs that sort the population groups into branching tree patterns. Out of the many statistical trees that can be generated, the shortest one, the one with the least number of branchings, is called the "maximum parsimony tree," and researchers believe it to be identical to the actual historical relationships of the various population groups in the tree. The branch ("clade") forming the base of the tree (the "basal clade") is supposed to be the parent group. According to evolutionary theory, it should, in addition to being at the base of the tree, have the most variation (i.e. the most mutations) in its mitochondrial DNA, relative to the other population groups. So in this way, researchers believe they can find where and when the root population existed. But some scientists say that the clock is not very accurate and that the genetic information contained in the mitochondrial DNA in today's populations is not sufficient to tell us with certainty the geographical location of the first human population.

In one of the original African Eve reports (Cann et al. 1987), researchers analyzed the mitochondrial DNA from groups of modern humans from different regions throughout the world. They analyzed the sequence of nucleotide bases found in a particular section of the mitochondrial DNA in all of the individuals being studied. They then used a computer program to arrange the various kinds of mitochondrial DNA sequences (called haplotypes) into a tree. According to the report, the root (or basal clade) of the maximum parsimony tree of haplotypes was the African group. But Templeton (1993, p. 52) pointed out that Maddison (1991) had rerun the data and found ten thousand trees that were shorter (i.e. more parsimonious) than the "maximum parsimony tree" reported by the African Eve researchers. Many of these trees had mixed African/Asian roots. Analyzing another "African Eve" report (Vigilant et al. 1991), Templeton (1992) found 1,000 trees two steps shorter than the one put forward by those researchers, who had claimed it was a "maximum parsimony" tree. All of the thousand more parsimonious trees found by Templeton in his 1992 study had non-African basal clades (Templeton 1993, p. 53). This would be consistent with accounts found in the ancient Sanskrit writings of India, which would place the original human populations on this planet in the region between the Himalayas and the Caspian Sea.

Why such different results? Templeton (1993, p. 52), considering another African Eve report, explained: "Computer programs . . . cannot guarantee that the maximum parsimony tree will be found when dealing with such large data sets as these because the state space is too large to search exhaustively. For example, for the 147 haplotypes in Stoneking, Bhatia, and Wilson (1986), there are 1.68×10^{294} possible trees. Finding the maximum parsimony set among these many possibilities is nontrivial." The computer programs tend to pick out a tree that is maximally parsimonious only in relation to a subset of the total number of possible trees. Which subset of trees that is selected depends on the order in which data are fed into the computer. To guard against this problem, it is necessary to randomize the sequence in which the data are entered over a series of runs. When one has done this a sufficient number of times, so as to find the maximum parsimony trees for various local subsets of the data, then one can compare these trees and arrive at a conclusion. This was not done in the original African Eve studies (the computer program was run only once), and thus the conclusions are not reliable. Also, even data randomization techniques do not completely solve the problem (Templeton 1993, p. 53). So this means that it really is not possible to conclusively determine the common geographical origin of dispersed human populations from the genetic data available today.

In addition to presenting inaccurate conclusions about maximum parsimony trees with African basal clades, the African Eve researchers

(Cann et al. 1987; Vigilant et al. 1991) also made misleading statements about the level of mitochondrial DNA diversity in various populations. The African Eve researchers assumed that mutations occur at some fixed rate, and therefore the population with the most internal diversity, relative to the others, should be the oldest. Because the African populations had a higher level of internal diversity than Asian and European populations, the researchers claimed that the African populations were the oldest. But Templeton (1993, p. 56) noted that "no statistical test is presented in either paper in support of this claim." He pointed out that when proper statistical methods are applied, there is no significant degree of diversity in the mitochondrial DNA of Africans, Europeans, and Asians (Templeton 1993, p. 57). As Templeton himself put it: "The apparent greater diversity of Africans is an artifact of not using sufficient statistics for making inference about the . . .process that led to the present-day human populations. In summary, the evidence for geographical origin is ambiguous. . . . there is no statistically significant support for an African origin with any mtDNA data" (Templeton 1993, p. 57).

Now let us consider the ages for the antiquity of anatomically modern humans proposed by the original African Eve theorists. They tried to calculate the time it took for the observed mtDNA diversity in today's human populations to accumulate, based on rates of mutation. This time is called "the time to coalescence," the time at which all the mtDNA sequence diversity in present human populations coalesces into a single past mtDNA sequence, the source of the present diversity. One group of researchers (Stoneking et al. 1986) got an age of 200,000 years for Eve, within a range of 140,000 to 290,000 years, using intraspecific calculations for the molecular clock. Intraspecific means that they based calculations on rates of mutations in human populations only. Another group (Vigilant et al. 1991), using interspecific calculations, also got an age of 200,000 years for Eve, but with a range of 166,000 to 249,000 years. Interspecific means they based their calculations on assumptions about the time at which the human line separated from the chimpanzee line.

First, let us consider the report from the researchers who relied on interspecific calibration of the rate of mutation (Vigilant et al. 1991). Their calibration of the mutation rate was made using either 4 million or 6 million years as the time since the human line supposedly diverged from the chimpanzee line. These times of divergence, when used in calculations that take into account statistical uncertainty, give times of coalescence for human mtDNA of 170,000 and 256,000 years respectively (Templeton 1993, p. 58). But Gingerich (1985) estimated that the divergence between humans and chimps took place 9.2 million years ago. A rate of change based on this date, would greatly increase the time to coalescence for modern mtDNA diversity, making it as much as 554,000 years (Templeton 1993, pp. 58–59). Furthermore, Lovejoy and his coworkers (1993) pointed out that Vigilant et al. (1991) made a mathematical error (they used the wrong transition-transversion), which when corrected gives an age for Eve of at least 1.3 million years (Frayer et al. 1993, p. 40).

It is easy to see that this whole "molecular clock" business is extremely unreliable, because it is based on speculative evolutionary assumptions. It is not at all certain that humans and chimps had a common ancestor of the kind proposed by Darwinian evolutionists. And, as we have seen, even if we assume that chimps and humans did have a common ancestor, the time at which they diverged from that common ancestor is not known with certainty, thus leading to widely varying calibrations of mutation rates and widely varying age estimates for the time to coalescence of modern mitochondrial DNA diversity.

Now let's consider the conclusions of those who relied on intra-specific calculations—i.e. the rate that mutations accumulate in humans, without any reference to a supposed time of divergence between the chimpanzee and human lines. Templeton pointed out that this methodology did not take into account several "sources of error and uncertainty." For example, in actual fact, mutations don't accumulate at some steady deterministic rate. The rate of mutation is a stochastic, or probabilistic, process, with a Poisson distribution. The Poisson distribution, named after the French mathematician S. D. Poisson, is used in calculating the probabilities of occurrence of accidental events (such as spelling mistakes in printed books or mutations in DNA). "In this regard," says Templeton (1993, p. 57), "it is critical to keep in mind that the entire human species represents only one sample of the coalescent process underlying the current array of mtDNA variations. Hence, even if every human mtDNA were completely sequenced, the rate calibration were known with no error, and the molecular clock functioned exactly like an ideal Poisson process, there would still be considerable ambiguity about the time to coalescence. . . . stochasticity therefore sets an inherent limit to the accuracy of age estimates that can never be completely overcome by larger sample sizes, increased genetic resolution, or more precise rate calibration."

Stoneking and his coauthors of a 1986 study acknowledged the problem of stochasticity but did not, says Templeton, take adequate steps to account for it. Stoneking and his coauthors estimated that the divergence among the mtDNA samples in the human populations they studied amounted to between 2 and 4 percent. How long did it take for this amount of divergence to accumulate? Stoneking and his coauthors calculated it to be about 200,000 years. But Templeton found that if probabilistic effects are properly taken into account, a figure of 290,000 years is obtained. Templeton (1993, p. 58) then pointed out that "the actual calibration points in their paper indicate a fivefold range (1.8% to 9.3%), and the work of others would indicate an even broader range (1.4% to 9.3%)." These broadened rates give times to coalescence ranging from a minimum of 33,000 years to a maximum of 675,000 years.

African Eve theorists, and others, believe that mitochondrial DNA is not subject to natural selection. This is taken to mean that the only factor influencing the differences in the mitochondrial DNA sequences in different populations is the accumulation of random mutations at some fixed rate. If this is true, then the molecular clock would be running at the same speed in different populations. But if natural selection is influencing the differences in the DNA in different populations, that would mess up the clock. For example, if in one population natural selection were eliminating some of the mutations, this would make that population appear younger than it really is. If such things do happen, there would no longer be any firm basis for attaching absolute numbers of years to a particular degree of variation, nor would there be any firm basis for making relative age judgments among different populations. There is some evidence that natural selection is in fact operating in mitochondrial DNA. For example, Templeton (1993, p. 59) points out that there is a difference in the degree of variation in the protein coding and non coding regions of the mitochondrial DNA in certain populations. If the mutation rate were neutral, this should not be the case. The rate of mutation should be the same in both the coding and noncoding parts of the mitochondrial DNA. Other researchers (Frayer et al. 1993, pp. 39–40) reach similar conclusions: "All molecular clocks require evolutionary neutrality, essential for constancy in the rate of change. But continuing work on mtDNA has documented increasing evidence for selective importance in mtDNA. For example, studies by Fos et al. (1990), MacRae and Anderson (1988), Palca (1990), Wallace (1992), and others have conclusively demonstrated that mtDNA is not neutral, but under strong selection. . . . mtDNA is a poor gear to drive a molecular clock."

Frayer and his coauthors (1993, p. 40) also state: "Since random mtDNA losses result in pruning off the evidence of many past divergences, the trees constructed to link present populations are altered by unknown and unpredictable factors. Each of these unseen divergences is a genetic change that was not counted when the number of mutations was used to determine how long ago Eve lived. Since these changes are influenced by fluctuations in population size and the exact number of uncounted mutations depends on the particular details of the pruning process, unless the complete population history is known, there is no way to calibrate (and continually recalibrate) the ticking of the clock. Given the fact that each population has a separate demographic history (with respect to random loss events), this factor alone invalidates the use of mtDNA variation to 'clock' past events (Thorne and Wolpoff 1992)."

That such things happen is confirmed by the discovery of an anatomically modern human fossil from Lake Mungo, Australia, which was 62,000 years old and had mitochondrial DNA greatly different from any known from modern humans (Bower 2001). This shows that lines of mitochondrial DNA have in fact been lost, thus calling into question the accuracy of the mtDNA molecular clock.

There are other factors affecting the mtDNA diversity in today's human populations, in various regions of the world, that can throw off the accuracy of the mtDNA clock. One such factor is population size expansion. If the population increases in one region more rapidly than in another, this can cause greater diversity in that population. But the diversity is not an indication that this population is necessarily older than (and hence the source of) other populations in other regions. Also, the diversity observed in various populations can point not to population movements from one place to another, but the movement of genes through a population that is already distributed over a wide area. And this does not exhaust the possible causes of mtDNA diversity found in different human populations. Summarizing the problem, Templeton (1993, p. 59) says: "The diversity in a region does not necessarily reflect the age of the regional population but rather could reflect the age since the last favorable mutation arose in the population, the demographic history of population, size expansion, the extent of gene flow with other populations, and so on." In general, these factors contribute to underestimation of the age of the human species (Templeton 1993, p. 60).

Sophisticated statistical methods, such as "nested cladistic analysis," allow scientists to discriminate to some degree between the various possible models for the generation of mitochondrial DNA diversity in human populations (as between geographical expansion models and gene flow models). Applying nested cladistic analysis to human mitochondrial DNA variation, Templeton found no evidence of a massive migration out of Africa that replaced all other hominid populations. Templeton (1993, p. 65) said, "The failure of the cladistic geographical analysis to detect an out-of-Africa population expansion cannot be attributed to inadequate sample sizes or to low genetic resolution ... Hence, the geographical associations of mtDNA are statistically significantly incompatible with the out-of-Africa replacement hypothesis." Templeton concluded (1993, p. 70): "(1) the evidence for the geographical location of the mitochondrial common ancestor is ambiguous, (2) the time at which the mitochondrial common ancestor existed is extremely ambiguous but is likely to be considerably more than 200,000 years."

Evidence from Nuclear DNA

If, as supporters of the African Eve hypothesis claim, there was a population movement of anatomically modern humans out of their place of origin in Africa resulting in total replacement of the previous hominid populations in Europe and Asia, this should be supported not only by mitochondrial DNA evidence but also by DNA evidence from the cell's nucleus. However, in his analysis of the early African Eve reports, Templeton (1993, p. 65) said, ". . . there is no single set of assumptions that allows the mtDNA and nuclear data to be compatible with an out-of-Africa replacement hypothesis."

One group of researchers (Breguet et al. 1990) looked at variation in the B locus of the gene for the human apoprotein. According to Templeton (1993, pp. 68–69), their detailed analysis led them to conclude that "Cauca-soid populations (located from North Africa to India) were closest to the ancestral genetic stock and that worldwide genetic differentiation at this locus is best explained by westward and eastward gene flow from this geographical region and not by a sub-Saharan origin." For researchers like myself, who are operating from a perspective influenced by the ancient Sanskrit writings of India, which posit recurrent appearances of the human species (after planetary deluges) in the Himalayan region, this is quite interesting.

More recently, researchers have found yet another problem with the African origins theory. This problem involves the globin gene cluster in humans. A gene or part of a gene at a particular location on a chromosome may appear in several different forms called alleles. One individual will have one allele, and a second individual another allele. In analyzing globin alleles in various populations, authors of a recent textbook found that the observed degree of variation implied an age much greater than 200,000 years for modern human populations. Indeed, looking at another part of the globin gene cluster, the authors stated that "two alleles from a non-coding (and therefore neutral) region have apparently persisted for 3 million years." They concluded, "To date, it is unclear how the pattern found in the globin genes can be reconciled with a recent African origin of modern humans" (Page and Holmes 1998, p.

132). The globin evidence is consistent with Puranic accounts of extreme human antiquity.

Some researchers, considering the complexities surrounding genetic data, have suggested that fossils remain the most reliable evidence for questions about human origins and antiquity: "Unlike genetic data derived from living humans, fossils can be used to test predictions of theories about the past without relying on a long list of assumptions about the neutrality of genetic markers, mutational rates, or other requirements necessary to retrodict the past from current genetic variation . . . genetic information, at best, provides a theory of how modern human origins *might have happened* if the assumptions used in interpreting the genetic data are correct" (Frayer et al. 1993, p. 19). I agree that genetic evidence does not always trump archeological evidence. This means that the archeological evidence for extreme human antiquity documented in *Forbidden Archeology* provides a much needed check on the rampant speculations of genetic researchers.

So where do we stand? The whole question of human origins, analyzed from the perspective of genetic evidence, mitochondrial DNA evidence in particular, is confusing. For example, some scientists say that a small population of the genus *Homo* arose from *Australopithecus* about 2 million years ago in Africa. This population developed into *Homo erectus*, and then spread throughout Eurasia developing into Neandertals and Neandertal-like populations. About 100,000 years ago a small population of anatomically modern *Homo sapiens* emerged in Africa, and then spread around the world, replacing the earlier populations of *Homo erectus* and Neandertals, without mixing significantly with them (Vigilant et al. 1991; Stoneking et al.1986). These anatomically modern humans then developed in different regions of the world into the different races we see today. Other scientists, looking at the same genetic, archeological, and paleontological evidence, conclude that the different races of anatomically modern humans emerged simultaneously in different parts of the world, directly from the *Homo erectus* and Neandertal populations in those parts of the world (Templeton 1993). According to this idea, anatomically modern humans would have emerged in large populations over wide geographical areas, not in some small founder population confined to a small area. Another group asserts that there was a small initial population of anatomically modern humans, confined to a small geographical region. But this group holds that this population differentiated into the different racial groups we see today while still confined to this small geographical area. The racial groups then are supposed to have migrated out of this area and expanded their numbers in particular parts of the world (Rogers and Jorde 1995, p. 1). In short, there is considerable confusion about the genetic evidence and what it means.

Y Chromosome Evidence

In the foregoing discussion about mitochondrial DNA, I briefly mentioned nuclear DNA, the DNA found in the nucleus of human cells and gave a few examples. Let us now look carefully at another example of such evidence—the Y chromosome.

Human beings have 23 pairs of chromosomes in the nucleus of each cell. One of these pairs of chromosomes determines the sex of the individual. The pair of sex chromosomes in females is made up of two X chromosomes (XX). The pair of sex chromosomes in males is made up of one X chromosome and one Y chromosome (XY).

So, how is the sex of a particular individual determined? The re-pro-ductive cells (sperm and eggs) are different than the other cells in the body. Nonreproductive cells have the full complement of 23 pairs of chromosomes, for a total of 46 chromosomes. But a sperm cell or egg cell gets only half that number, just one set of 23 chromosomes instead of 23 pairs of chromosomes. When the sperm and the egg combine, the full number of chromosomes (46, or 23 pairs) is restored. When an egg is produced in a female, it will always have an X chromosome, because in the female, the pair of sex chromosomes is always XX. So when the chromosome pair XX splits to form eggs, each egg will get one X chromosome. But in the male, the pair of sex chromosomes is XY. So when the pair splits to form sperm, some of the sperm will have an X chromosome, and others will have a Y chromosome. If a sperm carrying an X chromosome combines with an egg, the fertilized egg will have an XX pair of sex chromosomes, and the egg will develop into a female child. If a sperm carrying a Y chromosome combines with an egg, the fertilized egg will have an XY pair of sex chromosomes, and the egg will develop into a male child. The Y chromosome is passed down only from father to son. Females do not carry the Y chromosome.

Certain parts of a chromosome are subject to a process called re-combination, whereby parts of one chromosome are exchanged with parts of another chromosome. But a large section of the Y chromosome is not subject to such recombination. Theoretically, the only changes that accumulate in this nonrecombining part of the Y chromosome would be random mutations. The Y chromosome is the male counterpart of the mitochondrial DNA, which is passed down only from the mother and is also supposedly not subject to variation other than random mutations. The Y chromosome can therefore be used in human origins research in just about the same way as mitochondrial DNA—as a molecular clock and geographical locator. Some researchers propose that just as there was an African Eve, there was also an African Adam, or, as some call him, a "Y-guy." As we shall see, however, the conclusions that can be drawn from Y chromosome studies are not very perfect, and therefore some researchers view "Y-guy" as "a statistical apparition generated by dubious evolutionary assumptions" (Bower 2000a).

In the May 26, 1995 issue of *Science,* Robert L. Dorit of Yale University and his coauthors published a study of the variation in the ZFY gene on the Y chromosomes of 38 humans from various parts of the world. They compared this variation with that found in chimpanzees. In converting the difference in the degree of variation into years, Dorit relied on the assumption that the human line separated from the chimp line about 5 million years ago. This led him to the conclusion that all the humans in his sample had a common ancestor who existed about 270,000 years ago. This differs from the usual age estimate of 200,000 years that comes from mitochondrial DNA studies (Adler 1995). However, a report in *Science News* (Adler 1995) pointed out that "Dorit and his coauthors acknowledge that factors other than a recent common ancestor could explain their findings" and that their conclusions relied on a lot of "background assumptions."

In the November 23, 1995 issue of *Nature,* Michael Hammer, of the University of Arizona at Tucson, published a study of Y chromosome variation in eight Africans, two Australians, three Japanese, and two Europeans. He concluded that they all had a common ancestor who lived 188,000 years ago. The geographical location of the common ancestor was not clearly defined. Hammer's study also suggested that a reanalysis of Dorit's data would give an age of 160,000 to 180,000 years for the most recent common ancestor of the individuals in the study (Ritter 1995).

In 1998, Hammer and several coauthors published a more comprehensive study of human Y chromosome variation. The time to coalescence for the observed variation was 150,000 years, and the root of the statistical tree was in the African populations. The researchers, using nested cladistic analysis methods, proposed that the Y chromosome evidence showed two migrations. One out of Africa into the Old World, and a movement back into Africa from Asia. "Thus, the previously observed high levels of Y chromosomal genetic diversity in Africa may be due in part to bidirectional population movements," said the researchers (Hammer et al. 1998, p. 427). Hammer and another set of coworkers reached similar conclusions in a 1997 study of the YAP region of the

Y chromosome (Hammer et al. 1997). The movement of Asian populations into Africa is interesting, in light of accounts from ancient Indian historical writings, which tell of the avatar Parasurama driving renegade members of the ancient Indian royal families out of India to other parts of the world, where according to some sources, they mixed with the native populations.

In the November 2000 issue of *Nature Genetics,* Peter Underhill and his coauthors said Y chromosome data suggested that the most recent common male ancestor of living humans lived in East Africa and left there for Asia between 39,000 and 89,000 years ago. By way of contrast, mitochondrial DNA evidence suggested that our common female ancestor left Africa about 143,000 years ago. Underhill simply suggested that the Y chromosome and mitochondrial DNA rates of change are different (Bower 2000a). Henry Harpending of the University of Utah in Salt Lake City thinks the Y chromosome's mutation rate is slower than Underhill and his coworkers reported. According to Harpending, this would bring Y Guy's age close to that of Mitochondrial Eve (Bower 2000a). But just as the mitochondrial DNA rate of change is really not known with certainty, the Y chromosome rate of change is also not known with certainty. In an article in *Science News,* Bower (2000a) says, "The Y chromosome segments in the new analysis exhibit much less variability than DNA regions that have been studied in other chromosomes. Low genetic variability may reflect natural selection, in this case, the spread of advantageous Y chromosome mutations after people initially migrated out of Africa, the researchers suggest. That scenario would interfere with the molecular clock, making it impossible to retrieve a reliable mutation rate from the Y chromosome, they acknowledge." And geneticist Rosalind M. Harding, of John Radcliffe Hospital in Oxford, England, says, "We don't know what selection and population structure are doing to the Y chromosome. I wouldn't make any evolutionary conclusions from [Underhill's] data" (Bower 2000a). For example, Underhill thought that Africa was the home of the most recent common ancestor of modern humans, because the African populations in his studies showed the most diversity in their Y chromosomes. But Harding points out that this diversity could have arisen not because Africa was the home of the original human population, but because Africa was more heavily populated than other parts of the world. Also, the diversity in populations outside of Africa could have been reduced by the spreading of particularly favorable genes throughout those populations. Bower says (2000a), "If the critics are right, Y guy could be history, not prehistory." In other words, humans could be millions and millions of years old, and the genetic diversity we see today could simply reflect some recent genetic events in that long history. The earlier results could simply have been erased with the passage of time.

The most recent Y chromosome studies demonstrate that firm conclusions about human origins based on this kind of evidence are still out of reach. A group of Chinese and American researchers (Ke et al. 2001) sampled 12,127 males from 163 populations from East Asia, checking the Y chromosomes for three markers (called YAP, M89, and M130). According to the researchers, three mutations of these markers (YAP+, M89T, and M130T) arose in Africa, and they can all three be traced to another African mutation, the M168T mutation, which arose in Africa between 35,000 and 89,000 years ago. The researchers found that all the East Asian males they tested had one of the three African mutations that came from the African M168T mutation. They took this to mean that populations that migrated from Africa completely replaced the original hominid populations in East Asia. Otherwise, some Y chromosomes without the three African markers should have been found.

As Ke and his coauthors (2001, p. 1152) said, "It has been shown that all the Y chromosome haplotypes found outside Africa are younger than 39,000 to 89,000 years and derived from Africa." However, they noted that "this estimation is crude and depends on several assumptions." The assumptions were not directly mentioned in their report. The authors also admitted the possibility of "selection sweep that could erase archaic Y chromosomes of modern humans in East Asia." Furthermore, they admitted that Y chromosome data is "subject to stochastic processes, e.g., genetic drift, which could also lead to the extinction of archaic lineages."

Ke and his coauthors (2001, p. 1152) acknowledged another problem, which they said "creates confusion." They observed that age estimates for a most recent common ancestor arrived at by analysis of variation in mitochondrial DNA and the Y chromosome DNA differ greatly from age estimates derived from analysis of variation in the DNA of the X chromosome and autosomes (chromosomes other than the sex-determining X and Y chromosomes). They said, "The age estimated with the use of autosome/X chromosome genes ranges from 535,000 to 1,860,000 years, much older than the mtDNA and Y chromosome" (Ke et al. 2001, p. 1152). The authors speculate that in the course of population "bottlenecks" during a supposed migration out of Africa, there may have been three or four times as many men as women, leading to the greater diversity in the autosome/X chromosome DNA.

Milford Wolpoff, a committed multiregionalist, says that it's not surprising that the Y chromosome shows an apparent African origin. Africa had the largest populations for the longest periods of time. Therefore, the African populations were responsible for the greatest number of Y chromosome lineages, which could over time have wiped out other lineages that originally existed along with the African lineages (Gibbons 2001, p. 1052). Ann Gibbons observes that it is difficult to check the reliability of the Y chromosome and mitochondrial DNA evidence. Ideally, one would want to compare this evidence with DNA evidence from many other chromosomes in the nucleus, to see if they all support the same conclusions about the age and geographical origin of anatomically modern humans. But Gibbons (2001, p. 1052) notes: "The dating of nuclear lineages is complicated because most nuclear DNA, unlike that of the mitochondria and the Y chromosome, gets scrambled when homologous chromosomes exchange their genetic material during egg and sperm formation. That makes detection of an archaic lineage so difficult that many geneticists despair they will ever be able to prove—or disprove—that replacement was complete. Says Oxford University population geneticist Rosalind Harding: 'There's no clear genetic test. We're going to have to let the fossil people answer this one.'"

Humans and Neandertals

As we have seen, one group of scientists says that modern human beings evolved from the ape man *Homo erectus* in various parts of the world, passing through a Neandertal or Neandertal-like stage. According to this view, called the multiregional hypothesis, today's Asian people came from Asian *Homo erectus,* passing through a Neandertal-like stage. Similarly, today's Europeans should be descendants of the classic Western European Neandertals.

Some scientists have compared the DNA of humans and Neandertals, seeking to clarify their evolutionary relationship. The evidence is inconclusive and subject to varying interpretations. Scientists led by Matthias Krings (1997) extracted some DNA from one of the bones of the original Neandertal specimen, discovered in Germany during the nineteenth century. The DNA was carefully analyzed to make sure it was from the bone itself, and not from modern human contamination. The DNA was mitochondrial DNA, which is passed down directly from mother to child.

Researchers compared the fragment of Neandertal mitochondrial DNA with mitochondrial DNA from 1600 modern humans from Europe, Africa, Asia, the Americas, Australia, and Oceania. The fragment of Neandertal mitochondrial DNA used in the comparison was composed of

327 nucleotide bases. Similar stretches of the modern human mitochondrial DNA samples differed from the Neandertal mitochondrial DNA sample by an average of 27 out of 327 nucleotide bases. The 1600 modern humans differed from each other by an average of 8 nucleotide bases out of 327. Chimpanzees differed from modern humans by 55 out of 327 nucleotide bases. Scientists took all this to mean that Neandertals are not closely related to modern humans. If they had been closely related to humans, the differences in nucleotide bases between humans and Neandertals should have been just slightly more than the average difference among humans—perhaps 10 or 12 nucleotide bases.

The scientists who looked at the DNA from the original Neandertal bones found it was no closer to today's Europeans than to any other group of modern humans. They took this as contrary to the theory that the modern European populations evolved from the European Neandertals. According to this line of reasoning, the Neandertal DNA evidence favors the "out of Africa" hypothesis, which says that modern humans arose only once in Africa, about 100,000 years ago, and then spread to Europe and Asia, replacing the Neandertal-type hominids without breeding with them in any significant numbers. However, the researchers said about their mitochondrial DNA evidence: "These results do not rule out the possibility that Neandertals contributed other genes to modern humans" (Krings et al. 1997, p. 27).

The group of Neandertal DNA researchers headed by Krings proposed an age for the split between the Neandertals and the line of hominids that led to modern humans. They assumed that the human and chimp lines split at four or five million years ago, a figure based on rates of mutation in mitochondrial DNA. Using this as a starting point, they estimated the human/Neandertal split took place betweeen 550,000 and 690,000 years ago. But they acknowledged the possibility of "errors of unknown magnitude" (Krings et al. 1997, p. 25). In other words, the date is speculative. Furthermore, it is based on the assumption that there is an evolutionary connection between humans, chimps, Neandertals, etc., and that the relations reflected in their DNA are also relations of biological descent. But this is simply an assumption.

After the work done by Krings and his coworkers, William Goodwin, a geneticist at the University of Glasgow in Scotland, sequenced some mitochondrial DNA from the bones of an infant Neandertal discovered in the Mezmaikaya Cave, in the northern Caucusus Mountains (Bower 2000b). The bones are thought to be 29,000 years old. Goodwin compared the mitochondrial DNA from the Caucasus Neandertal infant to the mitochondrial DNA from the original German Neandertal

(Krings et al. 1997). He found about the same amount of difference between them as between samples of mitochondrial DNA from modern humans. In other words, the two Neandertals were genetically close to each other. Furthermore, the mitochondrial DNA from the Caucasus Neandertal differed from modern humans by about the same amount as the German Neandertal, indicating that the Caucusus Neandertal, like the German one, was genetically distinct from modern humans. Goodwin said this supports the out of Africa replacement model of modern human origins. But Milford H. Wolpoff, a supporter of the multiregional modern human origins hypothesis, suggested that mitochondrial DNA from anatomically modern humans from the same time, 30,000 years ago, would differ from the mitochondrial DNA of today's modern humans by the same amount as the Neandertal DNA. This could be tested by DNA from *Homo sapiens* living at that time, 30,000 years ago.

In the June 2000 issue of *American Journal of Human Genetics,* Lutz Bachmann and his colleagues at the Field Museum, Chicago, announced the results of studies of the nuclear DNA from two Neandertals and from anatomically modern *Homo sapiens* who existed 35,000 years ago. Using the DNA hybridization technique, which shows the degree of bonding between samples, they determined that the *Homo sapiens* DNA differed from the Neandertal DNA. This tends to support the work of Krings et al. and Goodwin. But anthropologist Erik Trinkaus disagreed. He pointed out that the DNA hybridization technique gives only a very crude measure of difference. He also said that there is a lot of subjectivity in judging what amount of difference in DNA amounts to a difference in species. Trinkaus believes that humans and Neandertals interbred (implying that their DNA was similar). However, he asserted that the genetic evidence for this interbreeding may have become diluted so much as to escape detection by crude DNA hybridization techniques (Bower 2000c).

New mitochondrial DNA studies have added a new element to the debate about the relationship between modern humans and the Neandertals. A team led by Gregory J. Adcock, of the Pierre and Marie Curie University in Paris, examined mitochondrial DNA samples from anatomically modern human skeletons, ranging from 2,000 years old to 62,000 years old. The mitochondrial DNA from the oldest skeleton, from Lake Mungo, Australia, turned out to be more different from that of living humans than the mitochondrial DNA of the Neandertals mentioned above (Bower 2001). Therefore, even if Neandertal DNA is quite different from modern human DNA, this does not necessarily mean that Neandertals did not interbreed with the anatomically modern humans.

Even so, the exact nature of the relationship between modern humans and Neandertals remains an open question. Perhaps humans and Neandertals are simply varieties of the same species. Perhaps they are different species, who interbred. If we ignore evolutionary speculations, the Neandertal DNA research simply shows that modern humans and Neandertals coexisted with each other. From the available genetic evidence, it is not possible to put any definite limit on how far back in time the coexistence actually goes. This is consistent with the views presented in *Forbidden Archeology,* which posits the coexistence of anatomically modern humans and other distinct hominid types for vast periods of time.

Conclusion

Biochemical and genetic evidence is not as reliable as some would have us believe. Many researchers say that the fossil evidence is ultimately more important than the genetic evidence in answering questions about human origins and antiquity. As Frayer and his coauthors (1993, p. 19) said, "Unlike genetic data derived from living humans, fossils can be used to test predictions of theories about the past without relying on a long list of assumptions about the neutrality of genetic markers, mutational rates, or other requirements necessary to retrodict the past from current genetic variation . . . genetic information, at best, provides a theory of how modern human origins *might have happened* if the assumptions used in interpreting the genetic data are correct." Contemplating the difficulties of using genetic evidence to establish theories of human origins and antiquity, Oxford University population geneticist Rosalind Harding said, "There's no clear genetic test. We're going to have to let the fossil people answer this one" (Gibbons 2001, p. 1052). And when we do look at the fossil evidence in its entirety, we find that anatomically modern humans go so far back in time that it becomes impossible to explain their presence on this planet by current Darwinian theories of evolution. Furthermore, when we look at human origins in terms of the larger question of the origin of life on earth, we find that modern science has not been able to tell us how the first living things, with their genetic systems, came into existence.

Also, both artificial intelligence (AI) and artificial life (Alife) researchers have failed to provide convincing models of living things. Rodney Brooks, of the Artificial Intelligence Laboratory at MIT, wrote in a perceptive article in *Nature:* "Neither AI or Alife has produced artifacts that could be confused with a living organism for more than an instant. AI just does not seem as present or aware as even a simple animal and Alife cannot match the complexities of the simplest forms of life"

(Brooks 2001, p. 409). Brooks attributes the failure to something other than lack of computer power, incorrect parameters, or insufficiently complex models. He raises the possibility that "we are missing something fundamental and currently unimagined in our models." But what is that missing something? "One possibility," says Brooks (2001, p. 410), "is that some aspect of living systems is invisible to us right now. The current scientific view of things is that they are machines whose components are biomolecules. It is not completely impossible that we might discover new properties of biomolecules, or some new ingredient. . . . Let us call this the 'new stuff' hypothesis—the hypothesis that there might be some extra sort of 'stuff' in living systems outside our current scientific understanding." And what might this new stuff be? Brooks gives David Chalmers as an example of a philosopher who proposes that consciousness might be a currently unrecognized state of matter. But Brooks (2001, p. 411) goes on to say, "Other philosophers, both natural and religious, might hypothesize some more ineffable entity such as a soul or *elan vital* —the 'vital force.'" Going along with such philosophers, I would propose that both a soul (conscious self) and vital force are present in humans and other living things. This conscious self and vital force are necessary components in any explanation of living things and their origins.

5

BEYOND STONES
AND BONES:
ALFRED R. WALLACE
AND THE
SPIRIT WORLD

If, as the evidence in *Forbidden Archeology* suggests, we did not evolve from primitive apes by a process of Darwinian evolution, then where did we come from? To properly answer this question, we must first critically examine our fundamental assumptions about observable nature. If we confine ourselves to current assumptions about observable nature held by mainstream science, this limits the kinds of alternative explanations of human origins it is possible to present. Mainstream science assumes that all phenomena in observable nature are the result of the actions of ordinary matter, operating according to ordinary physical and chemical laws.

There are, I am convinced, some very good reasons why we should modify the assumptions about observable nature currently held by mainstream science. Many of these reasons can be found in a curious place —the work of one of the founders of the theory of evolution by natural selection.

In 1854, a young English naturalist named Alfred Russel Wallace journeyed to the East Indies to collect wildlife specimens. During his travels, he was intrigued by the patterns of variation among plants and animals throughout the region. In 1858, while laid up with a tropical disease, he took a couple of days to write a scientific paper explaining the origin of such variations. He then sent the paper to Charles Darwin for comments before publication. Darwin, back in England, had been working since 1844 on a book explaining the origin of species by evolution through natural selection. He was shocked to find that Wallace, a relatively unknown naturalist, was about to publish a paper outlining the whole idea. In the scientific world, priority is everything. The person who first publishes an idea or theory receives credit for it. Darwin, somewhat anxious about his priority, consulted some of his close scientific friends. On their advice, he proposed to Wallace that they co-author a paper on evolution. Wallace agreed, insuring his lasting fame, alongside Darwin, as one of the world's great scientists. Interestingly enough, Wallace, the cofounder with Darwin of the theory of evolution by natural selection, became involved in paranormal research.

Modern biology and anthropology texts often contain biographical sketches of Alfred Russel Wallace. But these idealized sketches routinely ignore Wallace's extensive research into the paranormal and his related conclusions, portraying him instead as a saint of materialism. This slanted hagiography is arguably related to the authors' cultural commitment to materialist, reductionist cosmologies.

The central feature of Wallace's paranormal research was his belief in spirits and a spirit world. On the basis of personal experiments and reliable reports from other scientists, Wallace concluded that the universe is populated with a hierarchy of spirit beings, some of whom are in contact with the human population on earth, usually through mediums. According to Wallace, the spirit beings lower in the hierarchy, acting through mediums, were responsible for a variety of paranormal phenomena, including clairvoyance, miraculous healings, communications from the dead, apparitions, materializations of physical objects, levitations, etc. More powerful spirit beings may have played a role in the process of evolution, guiding it in certain directions.

Spirits, the kind that can move matter, are the last thing today's evolutionists want to hear about. Such things threaten current evolutionary theory, which depends on philosophical naturalism—the idea that everything in nature happens according to known physical laws. Introduce nonmaterial entities and effects, and the theory of evolution loses its exclusivity as an explanation for the origin of species. Perhaps spirits were involved in the process. If so, one would have to consider "supernatural selection" in addition to natural selection.

In addition to believing in spirits, Wallace also believed that anatomically modern humans were of considerable antiquity. For example, he accepted the discoveries of J. D. Whitney, which, by modern geological reckoning, place humans in California up to 50 million years ago (Cremo and Thompson 1993, pp. 368–394, 439–458). Wallace noted that such evidence tended to be "attacked with all the weapons of doubt, accusation, and ridicule" (Wallace 1887, p. 667). Wallace suggested that "the proper way to treat evidence as to man's antiquity is to place it on record, and admit it provisionally wherever it would be held adequate in the case of other animals; not, as is too often now the case, to ignore it as unworthy of acceptance or subject its discoverers to indiscriminate accusations of being impostors or the victims of impostors" (Wallace 1887, p. 667).

Wallace encountered the same kind of opposition when he communicated to scientists the results of his spiritualistic research. Describing the reactions of the public and his scientific colleagues, Wallace wrote in his autobiography: "The majority of people today have been brought up in the belief that miracles, ghosts, and the whole series of strange phenomena here described cannot exist; that they are contrary to the laws of nature; that they are the superstitions of a bygone age; and that therefore they are necessarily either impostures or delusions. There is no place in the fabric of their thought into which such facts can be fitted. When I first began this inquiry it was the same with myself. The facts did not fit into my then existing fabric of thought. All my preconceptions, all my knowledge, all my belief in the supremacy of science and of natural law were against the possibility of such phenomena. And even when, one by one, the facts were forced upon me without possibility of escape from them, still, as Sir David Brewster declared after being at first astonished by the phenomena he saw with Mr. Home, 'spirit was the last thing I could give in to.' Every other possible solution was tried and rejected. Unknown laws of nature were found to be of no avail when there was always an unknown intelligence behind the phenomena—an intelligence that showed a human character and individuality, and an individuality which almost invariably claimed to be that of some person who had lived on earth, and who, in many cases, was able to prove his or her identity. Thus, little by little, a place was made in my fabric of thought, first for all such well-attested facts, and then, but more slowly, for the spiritualistic interpretation of them. . . . Many people think that when I and others publish accounts of such phenomena, we wish or require our readers to believe them on our testimony. But that is not the case. Neither I nor any other well-instructed spiritualist expects anything of the kind. We write not to convince, but to excite inquiry. We ask our readers not for belief, but for doubt of their own infallibility on this question; we ask for inquiry and patient experiment before hastily concluding that we are, all of us, mere dupes and idiots as regards a subject to which we have devoted our best mental faculties and powers of observation for many years" (Wallace 1905, v. 2, pp. 349–350).

Early Experiences with Mesmerism

Wallace first became interested in paranormal phenomena in 1843. Some English surgeons, including Dr. Elliotson, were then using mesmerism, an early form of hypnotism, to perform painless operations on patients. The reality of this anesthesia, although today accepted, was then a matter of extreme controversy. Wallace noted: "The greatest surgical and physiological authorities of the day declared that the patients were either impostors or persons naturally insensible to pain; the operating surgeons were accused of bribing their patients; and Dr. Elliotson was described as 'polluting the temple of science.' The Medical-Chirurgical Society opposed the reading of a paper describing an amputation during the magnetic trance, while Dr. Elliotson himself was ejected from his professorship at the University of London" (Wallace 1896, pp. *ix–x*).

At the time, Wallace was teaching school in one of the Midland counties of England. In 1844, Mr. Spencer Hall, a touring mesmerist, stopped there and gave a public demonstration. Wallace and some of his students, greatly interested, attended. Having heard from Hall that almost anyone could induce the mesmeric trance, Wallace later decided to make his own experiments. Using some of his students as subjects, he soon succeeded in mesmerizing them and produced a variety of phenomena. Some were within the range of modern medical applications of hypnotism, while some extended to the paranormal (Wallace 1896, p. *x*, pp. 126–128; 1905 v. 1, pp. 232–236).

One thing witnessed by Wallace was community of sensation. "The sympathy of sensation between my patient and myself was to me the most mysterious phenomenon I had ever witnessed," he later wrote. "I found that when I laid hold of his hand he felt, tasted, or smelt exactly the same as I did. . . . I formed a chain of several persons, at one end of which was the patient, at the other myself. And when, in perfect silence, I was pinched or pricked, he would immediately put his hand to the corresponding part of his own body, and complain of being pinched or pricked too. If I put a lump of sugar or salt in my mouth, he immediately went through the action of sucking, and soon showed by gestures and words of the most expressive nature what it was I was tasting" (Wallace 1896, pp. 127–128). During such experiments, Wallace took care to "guard against deception" (Wallace 1896, p. 126). From reports of the mesmeric experiments of other researchers, Wallace concluded that "the more remarkable phenomena, including clairvoyance both as to facts known and those unknown to the mesmeriser, have been established as absolute realities" (Wallace 1896, p. *xi*).

Despite the well-documented observations of numerous competent researchers, the scientific establishment remained hostile to mesmeric phenomena. Eventually, the production of insensibility, behavior modification, and mild delusions would be accepted under the name of hypnotism. But the more extraordinary mesmeric manifestations—such as clairvoyance and community of sensation—were never accepted. In any case, Wallace found his own experiments of lasting value: "I thus learned my first great lesson in the inquiry into these obscure fields of knowledge, never to accept the disbelief of great men, or their accusations of imposture or of imbecility, as of any great weight when opposed to the repeated observation of facts by other men admittedly sane and honest" (Wallace 1896, p. *x*).

Travels in the Tropics

From 1848 to 1862, Wallace traveled widely in the tropics, collecting wildlife specimens and filling notebooks with biological observations. While on an expedition in the Amazon region of Brazil, he saw his brother Herbert mesmerize a young Indian man in a hut. At Herbert's command, the young man's arm became rigid. Herbert restored movement to the young man's arm and then asked him to remain lying down in the hut until the brothers returned from a collecting excursion. When two hours later they came back, they found the young man still lying down, as if paralyzed, unable to rise although he had attempted it (Wallace 1905, v. 2, pp. 275–276).

When Wallace returned to England from Brazil, he did so alone, Herbert having died of a tropical disease. After a short time, Wallace set off on another expedition, this time to the East Indies. While in that region, Wallace learned of paranormal phenomena that went far beyond anything he had witnessed in his experiments with mesmerism. "During my eight years' travels in the East," he later recalled, "I heard occasionally, through the newspapers, of the strange doings of the spiritualists in America and England, some of which seemed to me too wild and outrageous to be anything but the ravings of madmen. Others, however, appeared to be so well authenticated that I could not at all understand them, but concluded, as most people do at first that such things must be either imposture or delusion" (Wallace 1905, v. 2, p. 276).

Despite his feelings of disbelief, Wallace suspended judgement. His experience with mesmerism had taught him that "there were mysteries connected with the human mind which modern science ignored because it could not explain" (Wallace 1896, p. 131). So when Wallace came back to England in 1862, he determined to look carefully into spiritualism.

First Spiritualistic Experiences

Initially, Wallace contented himself with studying reports. But in the summer of 1865, he began to directly witness spiritualistic phenomena. His first experiences took place at the home of a friend, described by Wallace as "a sceptic, a man of science, and a lawyer" (Wallace 1896, p. 132). Wallace, along with his host and members of his host's family, sat around a large, round table, upon which they placed their hands. Wallace observed inexplicable movements of the table and heard equally inexplicable sounds of rapping (Wallace 1896, pp. 132–133).

On a friend's recommendation, Wallace then visited Mrs. Marshall, a medium who gave public demonstrations of phenomena stronger than those Wallace had yet seen. Wallace paid several visits to Mrs. Marshall in London, usually in the company of a skeptical friend with a scientific background. Among the numerous physical phenomena he witnessed were levitation of a small table one foot off the ground for a period of twenty seconds, strange movements of a guitar, inexplicable sliding movements of chairs across the floor, and levitation of a chair with a woman sitting upon it. Wallace noted: "There was no room for any possible trick or deception. In each case, before we began, we turned up the tables and chairs, and saw that there was no connection between them and the floor, and we placed them where we pleased before we sat down. Several of the phenomena occurred entirely under our own hands, and quite disconnected from the 'medium'" (Wallace 1896, p. 136). At Mrs. Marshall's, Wallace also saw writing mysteriously appear on pieces of paper placed under the table and heard the spelling out by raps of intelligible messages. These messages contained names and other facts of a personal nature, not likely to have been known by the medium (Wallace 1896, pp. 137–138). Wallace himself received a message that contained his dead brother's name, the place where he died in Brazil, and the name of the last person to see him alive (Wallace 1896, p. 137).

As a result of such experiences, Wallace eventually became a convinced spiritualist. Critics suggested that Wallace was predisposed to spiritualism because of religious leanings (Wallace 1896, p. vi). But Wallace, describing his view of life at the time he encountered spiritualism, wrote: "I ought to state that for twenty-five years I had been an utter sceptic as to the existence of any preter-human or super-human intelligences, and that I never for a moment contemplated the possibility that the marvels related by Spiritualists could be literally true. If I have now changed my opinion, it is simply by the force of evidence. It is from no dread of annihilation that I have gone into this subject; it is from no inordinate longing for eternal existence that I have come to believe in facts which render this highly probable, if they do not actually prove it" (Wallace 1896, p. 132).

"The Scientific Aspect of the Supernatural"

In 1866, Wallace published in a periodical an extended explanation of spiritualism called "The Scientific Aspect of the Supernatural." The heart of the essay was a summary of scientifically documented evidence for psychical phenomena, such as spirit messages. Wallace later brought out the essay in booklet form, and sent it to many of his scientific friends and acquaintances.

Thomas Henry Huxley, who received a copy, replied: "I am neither shocked nor disposed to issue a Commission of Lunacy against you. It may all be true, for anything I know to the contrary, but really I cannot get up any interest in the subject. I never cared for gossip in my life, and disembodied gossip, such as these worthy ghosts supply their friends, is not more interesting to me than any other. As for investigating the matter—I have half a dozen investigations of infinitely greater interest to me—to which any spare time I may have will be devoted. I give it up for the same reason I abstain from chess—it's too amusing to be fair work and too hard work to be amusing" (Wallace 1905, v. 2, p. 280).

Wallace did not object to Huxley spending his time on research of his own choice, but he did protest Huxley's denigration of his work. "The objection as to 'gossip' was quite irrelevant as regards a book which had not one line of 'gossip' in it, but was wholly devoted to a summary of the evidence for facts—physical and mental—of a most extraordinary character, given on the testimony of twenty-two well-known men, mathematicians, astronomers, chemists, physiologists, lawyers, clergymen, and authors, many of world-wide reputation" (Wallace 1905, v. 2, p. 280). In his booklet, Wallace (1896, pp. 35–36) had listed them as: "Prof. A. De Morgan, mathematician and logician; Prof. Challis, astronomer; Prof. Wm. Gregory, M. D., chemist; Prof. Robert Hare, M. D., chemist; Prof. Herbert Mayo, M. D., F. R. S., physiologist; Mr. Rutter, chemist; Dr. Elliotson, physiologist; Dr. Haddock, physician; Dr. Gully, physician; Judge Edmonds, lawyer; Lord Lyndhurst, lawyer; Charles Bray, philosophical writer, Archbishop Whately, clergyman; Rev. W. Kerr, M. A., clergyman; Col. E. B. Wilbraham, military man; Sir Richard Burton, explorer, linguist, and author; Nassau E. Senior, political economist; W. M. Thackeray, author; T. A. Trollope, author; R. D. Owen, author and diplomatist; W. Howitt, author; S. C. Hall, author."

In another exchange with Huxley, Wallace pointed out that most people who daily depart this world are addicted to gossip. One should not therefore expect that their communications with earthbound friends should provide examples of the most polished discourse (Wallace 1874; in Smith 1991, pp. 90–91).

Dr. John D. Tyndall wrote to Wallace about his spiritualist publication: "I see the usual keen powers of your mind displayed in the treatment of this question. But mental power may show itself, whether its material be facts or fictions. It is not lack of logic that I see in your book, but a willingness that I deplore to accept data which are unworthy of your attention. This is frank—is it not?" (Wallace 1905, v. 2, p. 281).

Another scientist who received Wallace's pamphlet "The Scientific Aspect of the Supernatural" was A. De Morgan, professor of mathematics at University College. Already a spiritualist, De Morgan wrote a letter to Wallace, warning him to expect difficulties in demonstrating spiritualistic effects to scientists. "There is much reason to think," wrote De Morgan "that the state of mind of the inquirer has something—be it internal or external—to do with the power of the phenomena to manifest themselves. . . . Now the man of science comes to the subject in utter incredulity of the phenomena, and a wish to justify it. I think it very possible that the phenomena may be withheld. In some cases this has happened, as I have heard from good sources" (Wallace 1905, v. 2, p. 284).

Wallace nevertheless invited leading scientists and other learned persons to witness spiritualist phenomena, advising them that several sittings would be required. This seems reasonable, because most experimental work in science does require repeated trials. Dr. W. B. Carpenter and Dr. John Tyndall came for one sitting each, during which only very mild, unimpressive phenomena occurred. They refused Wallace's requests to attend more sittings (Wallace 1905, v. 2, pp. 278–279). Most scientists refused to come at all. G. H. Lewes, for example, was "too much occupied and too incredulous to give any time to the inquiry" (Wallace 1905, v. 2, p. 279).

Although Lewes refused Wallace's invitations to examine spiritualistic phenomena, he wrote to the *Pall Mall Gazette* (May 19, 1868) putting forth accusations against mediums and spiritualists. Amazingly, Lewes wrote that scientists were never allowed to investigate the phenomena. Wallace replied in a letter to the editor that this was not true. For example, Cromwell Varley, an electrical engineer, had been allowed to test the medium Daniel Dunglass Home, with results favorable to the authenticity of his paranormal phenomena. But the journal's editor refused to publish the letter (Wallace 1905, v. 2, p. 282).

Around this same time, Tyndall had called for a single test demonstration that would prove once and for all the reality or falsity of spiritualistic phenomena. Wallace replied in a letter to Tyndall that one test, even if successful, would not suffice to convince opponents. Wallace thought it better to amass reports of the numerous credible cases already on record. And to these he added, in his letter to Tyndall, one of his own experiences:

"The place was the drawing-room of a friend of mine, a brother of one of our best artists. The witnesses were his own and his brother's family, one or two of their friends, myself, and Mr. John Smith, banker, of Malton, Yorkshire, introduced by me. The medium was Miss Nichol. We sat round a pillar-table in the middle of the room, exactly under a glass chandelier. Miss Nichol sat opposite me, and my friend, Mr. Smith, sat next her. We all held our neighbour's hands, and Miss Nichol's hands were both held by Mr. Smith, a stranger to all but myself, and who had never met Miss N. before. When comfortably arranged in this manner the lights were put out, one of the party holding a box of matches ready to strike a light when asked.

"After a few minutes' conversation, during a period of silence, I heard the following sounds in rapid succession: a slight rustle, as of a lady's dress; a little tap, such as might be made by setting down a wineglass on the table; and a very slight jingling of the drops of the glass chandelier. An instant after Mr. Smith said, 'Miss Nichol is gone.' The matchholder struck a light, and on the table (which had no cloth) was Miss Nichol seated in her chair, her head just touching the chandelier. . . . Mr. Smith assured me that Miss Nichol simply glided out of his hands. No one else moved or quitted hold of their neighbour's hands. There was not more noise than I described, and no motion or even tremor of the table, although our hands were upon it. You know Miss N.'s size and probable weight, and can judge of the force and exertion required to lift her and her chair on to the exact centre of a large pillar-table, as well as the great surplus of force required to do it almost instantaneously and noiselessly, in the dark, and without pressure on the side of the table, which would have tilted it up. Will any of the known laws of nature account for this?" (Wallace 1905, v. 2, pp. 291–293).

If the facts were as Wallace reported them, it would seem that Miss Nichol herself could not have managed to place herself on the table. If all present at the table were holding hands and did not let go, it would seem that none of them could have lifted Miss Nichol in her chair. That leaves confederates as a possibility. But they should have been exposed by the struck match. Furthermore, it seems any attempt to lift Miss Nichol in complete darkness, either by persons at the table or confederates from outside the room, would have caused much more noise than reported by Wallace. One can only propose that Wallace himself gave a false report. This, however, seems unlikely.

Séances at Miss Douglas's

In 1869, Robert Chambers, author of *Vestiges of Creation*, introduced Wallace to Miss Douglas, a wealthy Scotch lady with an interest in spiritualism. Wallace attended many séances at Miss Douglas's London residence in South Audley Street. There he met many well connected spiritualists, including Darwin's relative Hensleigh Wedgwood. Among the most interesting séances were those with Mr. Haxby, a young postal employee described by Wallace as "a remarkable medium for materializations." Haxby would sit in a small room separated by curtains from a dimly lit drawing room on the first floor.

Wallace (1905 v. 2, pp. 328–329) gave this account of a typical séance with Haxby: "After a few minutes, from between the curtains would appear a tall and stately East Indian figure in white robes, a rich waistband, sandals, and large turban, snowy white and disposed with perfect elegance. Sometimes this figure would walk around the room outside the circle, would lift up a large and very heavy musical box, which he would wind up and then swing round his head with one hand. He would often come to each of us in succession, bow, and allow us to feel his hands and examine his robes. We asked him to stand against the door-post and marked his height, and on one occasion Mr. Hensleigh Wedgwood brought with him a shoe-maker's measuring-rule, and at our request, Abdullah, as he gave his name, took off a sandal, placed his foot on a chair, and allowed it to be accurately measured with the sliding-rule. After the séance Mr. Haxby removed his boot and had his foot measured by the same rule, when that of the figure was found to be full one inch and a quarter the longer, while in height it was about half a foot taller. A minute or two after Abdullah had retired into the small room, Haxby was found in a trance in his chair, while no trace of the white-robed stranger was to be seen. The door and window of the back room were securely fastened, and often secured with gummed paper, which was found intact."

The usual skeptical explanation for such manifestations is imposture by the medium or a confederate. In this case, the measurements taken rule out imposture by the medium. And the precautions taken to secure the entrances to the back room make the participation of a confederate somewhat doubtful. On the whole, circumstances point to the genuineness of the materialization.

On one occasion at Miss Douglas's, the famous Daniel Dunglass Home was the medium and Sir William Crookes, a distinguished physicist, was present. Crookes, later president of the Royal Society and recipient of the Nobel Prize for physics, was conducting his own research into spiritualistic phenomena. Wallace (1905 v. 2, p. 293) noted, however, that "his careful experiments, continued for several years, are to this day ignored or rejected by the bulk of scientific and public opinion as if they had never been made!"

At the séance attended by Wallace, Home was given an accordion. He held it with one hand, under the table around which he and the witnesses sat. Home's other hand remained on top of the table. On hearing the accordion play, Wallace went under the table to see what was happening: "The room was well lighted, and I distinctly saw Home's hand holding the instrument, which moved up and down and played a tune without any visible cause. On stating this, he said, 'Now I will take away my hand' —which he did; but the instrument went on playing, and I saw a detached hand holding it while Home's two hands were seen above the table by all present. This was one of the ordinary phenomena, and thousands of persons have witnessed it; and when we consider that Home's séances almost always took place in private homes at which he was a guest, and with people absolutely above suspicion of collusion with an impostor, and also either in the daytime or in a fully illuminated room, it will be admitted that no form of legerdemain will explain what occurred" (Wallace 1905, v. 2, pp. 286–287).

Darwin Agrees to Test a Medium

Another scientist who witnessed Home's mysterious accordion playing was Francis Galton, a cousin of Charles Darwin. At the invitation of Crookes, Galton attended three séances with Home and another medium, Kate Fox. Afterwards, in a letter dated April 19, 1872, Galton wrote enthusiastically to Darwin: "What surprises me is the perfect openness of Miss F. and Home. They let you do whatever you like within certain limits, their limits not interfering with adequate investigation. I really believe the truth of what they allege, that people who come as men of science are usually so disagreeable, opinionated and obstructive and have so little patience, that the seance rarely succeeds with them. It is curious to observe the entire absence of excitement or tension about people at a seance. Familiarity has bred contempt of the strange things witnessed. . . . Crookes, I am sure, so far as is just for me to give an opinion, is thoroughly scientific in his procedure. I am convinced that the affair is no matter of vulgar legerdemain and believe it is well worth going into, on the understanding that a first rate medium (and I hear there are only three such) puts himself at your disposal" (Pearson 1914). Darwin agreed to see Home, giving Galton a letter to send to him. But by that time Home had gone on to Russia and never returned to England (Beloff 1993, pp. 49–50). This is unfortunate. Who knows what would have happened if Darwin had actually met Home? Perhaps he would have joined Wallace in his spiritualism.

The Skeptical Sir David Brewster

Home's mediumship had long been a matter of controversy among English scientists. Home, born in Scotland, had gone to the United States as a child, returning to England in 1855. At that time, he lived in a London hotel owned by a Mr. Cox in Jermyn Street. In his autobiography, Wallace gives attention to Sir David Brewster's experiences with Home. Brewster, a noted physicist, attended a séance with Home at Cox's Hotel and another at Ealing, determined to expose any trickery. After a newspaper gave an account of what happened, Brewster wrote to the editor giving his own testimony: "It is quite true that I saw at Cox's Hotel, in company with Lord Brougham and at Ealing, in company with Mrs. Trollope, several mechanical effects which I was unable to explain. But although I could not account for all these effects, I never thought of ascribing them to spirits stalking beneath the drapery of the table; and I saw enough to satisfy myself that they could all be produced by human hands and feet, and to prove to others that some of them, at least, had such an origin" (Wallace 1905, v. 2, p. 287).

Here Brewster appears to be saying that the things he observed were produced by trickery. But a Mr. Coleman, who spoke with Brewster shortly after the séance, wrote a letter to the paper giving the following account of their conversation (Wallace 1905, v. 2, p. 288).

"Do you, Sir David, think these things were produced by trick?"

"No, certainly not," Brewster is said to have replied.

"Is it a delusion, think you?"

"No; that is out of the question."

"Then what is it?"

"I don't know; but spirit is the last thing I give in to."

Brewster replied with a letter of his own. Although he maintained his skeptical attitude, he did give some intriguing descriptions of what happened at Cox's Hotel: "When all our hands were upon the table noises were heard—rappings in abundance; and, finally, when we rose up, the table actually rose, as appeared to me, from the ground. This result I do not pretend to explain. . . . A small hand-bell to be rung by the spirits, was placed on the ground near my feet. I placed my feet round it in the form of an angle, to catch any intrusive apparatus. The bell did not ring; but when taken across to a place near Mr. Home's feet, it speedily came across, and placed its handle in my hand" (Wallace 1905, v. 2, pp. 288–289).

In his autobiography, Wallace noted that Brewster had written a letter to some of his family members shortly after the séance at Cox's Hotel. In this letter, Brewster expressed himself somewhat differently than he did in his highly skeptical newspaper letters, written half a year later. After explaining how he and Lord Brougham came to Mr. Cox's hotel to see Home, Brewster went on to say: "We four sat down at a moderately sized table, the structure of which we were invited to examine. In a short time the table shuddered, and a tremulous motion ran up all our arms; at our bidding these motions ceased and returned. The most unaccountable rappings were produced in various parts of the table, and the table actually rose from the ground when no hand was upon it. A larger table was produced, and exhibited similar movements.... A small hand-bell was then laid down with its mouth on the carpet, and after lying for some time it actually rang when nothing could have touched it. The bell was then placed on the other side, still upon the carpet, and it came over to me and placed itself in my hand. It did the same to Lord Brougham. These were the principal experiments; we could give no explanation of them, and could not conjecture how they could be produced by any kind of mechanism. Hands are sometimes seen and felt, the hand often grasps another, and melts away as it were under the grasp" (Wallace 1905, v. 2, pp. 289–290).

Wallace noted some discrepancies between this letter and Sir David's later accounts: "He told the public that he had satisfied himself that all could have been done by human hands and feet; whereas in his earlier private letter he terms them unaccountable, and says that he could not conjecture how they were done. Neither did he tell his public of the tremulous motion up his arms, while he denied that the bell rang at all, though he had before said that it actually rang, where nothing could have touched it" (Wallace 1905, v. 2, p. 290). Wallace stated that "a similar tendency has prevailed in all the scientific opponents of spiritualism" (Wallace 1905, v. 2, p. 290).

St. George Mivart and the Miracles at Lourdes

A scientist with a more favorable attitude to spiritualistic phenomena was St. George Mivart. Having become acquainted with spiritualism through talks with Wallace and by reading his booklet edition of "The Scientific Aspect of the Supernatural," Mivart decided to conduct his own investigations. In the winter of 1870, Mivart was in Naples, Italy, where Mrs. Guppy, a medium known to Wallace, resided with her husband. Wallace provided Mivart with a letter of introduction. Mivart attended three séances with Mrs. Guppy. During one séance, he received correct answers to questions he asked mentally. This greatly surprised him. At another séance, which took place in a darkened room, flowers mysteriously appeared. Mivart explained in a letter to Wallace that "the door was locked, the room searched, and all requisite precautions taken. I was not surprised, because of all I had heard from you and others; but the phenomenon was to me convincing. One such fact is as good as a hundred" (Wallace 1905, v. 2, pp. 300–301). In his letter, Mivart listed some conclusions. Among them: "I. I have encountered a power capable of removing sensible objects in a way altogether new to me. II. I have encountered an intelligence other than that of the visible assistants. III. In my séances this intelligence has shown itself capable of reading my thought" (Wallace 1905, v. 2, p. 301).

A few years later, Mivart visited Lourdes, a pilgrimage place in France where miraculous cures occurred, supposedly by the intervention of the Virgin Mary. During his stay at Lourdes, Mivart conducted a study of the cures. Wallace received from Mivart a long letter, dated April 5, 1874, about his findings. Mivart gave several case histories, gathered from French physicians, including Dr. Dozens (Wallace 1905, v. 2, pp. 302–304). Here follow two of them.

Blaisette Soupevue, a woman of fifty, had a severe eye infection lasting several years and affecting her sight. Her eyelids were turned out, lashless, and covered with fleshy growths. Doctors Dozens and Vergez pronounced the case incurable. After bathing her eyes with water from Lourdes, the woman completely recovered her sight, the growths disappeared, and her eyelashes began to grow again.

Justin Bontisharts had a child ten years old, with arms and legs much atrophied because of rickets. The child, who had never been able to walk, was near death. Dr. Dozens, who had treated the case, was present when the mother placed the child in the water at Lourdes. The child remained motionless, so much so that many bystanders thought it dead. Two days after returning home, however, the child, much to the surprise of the parents, began walking normally and continued to do so.

For more documentation of miraculous cures at Lourdes, Wallace recommended to his readers two books by Henri Lasserre, *Notre Dame de Lourdes* and *Les Episodes Miraculeux de Lourdes*. "The most remarkable feature of these cures," wrote Wallace (1905 v. 2, p. 306), "is their rapidity, often amounting to instantaneousness, which broadly marks them off from all ordinary remedial agencies."

Wallace then described some cases. "One of the most prominent of these, related by M. Lasserre, is that of Frangois Macary, a carpenter of Lavaur. He had varicose veins for thirty years; they were thick as one's finger, with enormous nodosities and frequent bleedings, producing numerous ulcers, so that it had been for many years impossible for him to walk or stand. Three physicians had declared him to be absolutely incurable. At sixty years of age he heard of the cures at Lourdes, and determined to try the waters. A bottle was sent him. Compresses with this were applied in the evening to his two legs. He slept well all night, and early next morning was quite well; his legs were smooth, and there was hardly a trace of the swollen veins, nodosities, and ulcers. The three doctors who had attended him certify to these facts" (Wallace 1905, v. 2, p. 306).

Most interesting is Wallace's explanation of the cures. The cures, according to Wallace, were not caused by the water itself but by a "a real spiritual agency," believed by those cured to be the Virgin Mary (Wallace 1905, v. 2, p. 308). The cures were, however, rare, and it was impossible to predict who would experience a cure. Wallace noted that cures were not limited to patients who were especially religious or otherwise deserving. In this respect, Wallace considered the patients to be similar to spiritualistic mediums, who were not usually paragons of virtue. Because certain patients, like mediums, were somehow sensitive, they were, regardless of other considerations, selected by spiritual entities as the conduits for psychical effects.

In many cases, cured individuals were "induced to try the Lourdes water often by a very unusual combination of circumstances" (Wallace 1905, v. 2, p. 308). To explain this Wallace suggested the following sequence of events in typical cures: (1) spiritual intelligences select particular individuals for their sensitivity to psychic intervention and possession of a normally incurable condition susceptible to paranormal healing; (2) spiritual intelligences begin the cures, unknown to the patients; (3) desiring ultimately to heighten the spiritual awareness of the patients and others, the spiritual intelligences, at critical moments in the cures, implant in the minds of the patients the idea of using Lourdes water or going to Lourdes; (4) the patients act on these implanted suggestions, experience tangible cures, and attribute them to miraculous intervention by the Virgin Mary (Wallace 1905, v. 2, pp. 308–309). According to this scheme, the spiritual intelligences would in these cases act in conformity with the religious and cultural conditioning of the patients. This is an important idea, to which we shall return in coming chapters.

Against Hume on Miracles

The cures at Lourdes, imbued with Catholic tradition, are usually called miracles, a word with religious connotations. The paranormal phenomena witnessed by Wallace at séances, although devoid of conventional religious overtones, are just as miraculous, in the sense of violating natural law, as understood by orthodox materialistic science. These phenomena might be called secular miracles. Reports of miracles, secular and religious, attained wide circulation, even in educated circles in Europe. Those who wished to dismiss such reports, which undermined the foundations of a strictly materialistic science, often did so in the name of David Hume, who a century earlier had argued in his book *An Inquiry Into Human Understanding* against the acceptance of miracles.

Hume appealed to uniform human experience in his refutation of miracles. For example, Hume observed "it is a miracle that a dead man should come to life; because that has never been observed in any age or any country." Wallace noted two flaws in this argument. First, the appeal to uniform human experience, granting the truly uniform nature of the experience, insures that no really new fact could ever be established. Second, Wallace questioned the veracity of Hume's version of uniform human experience. "Reputed miracles abound in all periods of history," wrote Wallace (1896, p. 8). And they continued up to the present, thus nullifying Hume's assumption.

Wallace (1896, p. 8) gave levitation of the human body as an instance of a miraculous event for which there is abundant human testimony: "A few well-known examples are those of St. Francis d'Assisi who was often seen by many persons to rise in the air, and the fact is testified by his secretary, who could only reach his feet. St. Theresa, a nun in a convent in Spain, was often raised into the air in the sight of all the sisterhood. Lord Orrery and Mr. Valentine Greatrak both informed Dr. Henry More and Mr. Glanvil that at Lord Conway's house at Ragley, in Ireland, a gentleman's butler, in their presence and in broad daylight, rose into the air and floated about the room above their heads. This is related by Glanvil in his Sadducismus Triumphatus. . . . So we all know that at least fifty persons of high character may be found in London who will testify that they have seen the same thing happen to Mr. Hume."

Wallace then pointed out a contradiction in the pages of Hume's own discussion of miracles. Hume had written that for testimony in favor of a miracle to be accepted, it should have the following characteristics. The testimony must be given by multiple observers. The observers should have reputations for honesty. They should be in social positions that entailed some definite material risk in the event their testimony were to be found false. As for the events themselves, they should be public, and they should take place in a civilized part of the world. Hume maintained that such satisfactory testimony was "not to be found, in all history" (Hume, cited in Wallace 1896, p. 8).

But Wallace noted that Hume then gave an account of some miraculous occurrences that fulfilled his own strict criteria. Hume told of the many extraordinary cures that took place in Paris at the tomb of the Abbé Paris, a saintly member of the Jansenists, a persecuted Catholic sect. Hume said of these events, which took place not long before he wrote his book: "The curing of the sick, giving hearing to the deaf, and sight to the blind, were everywhere talked of as the usual effects of that holy sepulchre. But what is more extraordinary, many of the miracles were immediately proved upon the spot, before judges of unquestioned integrity, attested by witnesses of credit and distinction, in a learned age, and on the most eminent theatre that is now in the world." Not only that, said Hume. The Jesuits, who thoroughly opposed the Jansenists, and desired to expose the miracles as hoaxes, were unable to do so, despite their access to the full power of church and state. Given this set of circumstances, it seems Hume should have accepted the miracle. Instead, he wrote: "Where shall we find such a number of circumstances agreeing to the corroboration of one fact? And what have we to oppose to such a cloud of witnesses, but the absolute impossibility, or miraculous nature of the events which they relate? And this, surely, in the eyes of all reasonable people, will alone be regarded as a sufficient refutation" (Wallace 1896, p. 9). Wallace faulted Hume for this blatantly self-contradictory conclusion.

Wallace then cited a particularly striking case, drawn from a book on the Parisian cures by Carré de Montgeron, and summarized in English by William Howitt in *The History of the Supernatural*: "Mademoiselle Coirin was afflicted, amongst other ailments, with a cancer in the left breast, for twelve years. The breast was destroyed by it and came away in a mass; the effluvia from the cancer was horrible, and the whole blood of the system was pronounced infected by it. Every physician pronounced the case utterly incurable, yet, by a visit to the tomb, she was perfectly cured; and, what was more astonishing, the breast and nipple were wholly restored, with the skin pure and fresh, and free from any trace of scar. This case was known to the highest people in the realm. When the miracle was denied, Mademoiselle Coirin went to Paris, was examined by the royal physician, and made a formal deposition of her cure before a public notary. . . . M. Gaulard, physician to the king, deposed officially, that, 'to restore a nipple actually destroyed, and separated from the breast, was an actual creation, because a nipple is not merely a continuity of the vessels of the breast, but a particular body, which is of distinct and peculiar organisation'" (Wallace 1896, pp. 11–12).

E. B. Tylor, one of the founders of anthropology, also offered philosophical objections to spiritualistic phenomena. Tylor called the primitive belief in a spirit world "animism." Modern spiritualism would thus represent a remnant of primitive animistic thought in civilized Europeans. Wallace countered that modern spiritualists arrived at their conclusions by careful and repeated observation. "The question is a question of facts," he wrote (Wallace 1896, p. 28). And to Wallace the facts suggested that modern spiritualism and primitive belief shared "at least a substratum of reality" and that "the uniformity of belief is due in great part to the uniformity of underlying facts" (Smith 1991, p. 83).

More Experiences

While Wallace was defending spiritualism in print, he was also gathering more experimental evidence. In 1874, he attended a series of séances with the medium Kate Cook. The sittings took place in the London apartment of Signor Randi, a painter. The medium sat in a chair, behind a curtain hung across a corner of a large reception room. Miss Cook always wore a black dress, earrings, and tightly laced boots. A few minutes after she sat behind the curtain, a female figure, wearing white robes, would sometimes come out and stand near the curtain.

Wallace (1905 v. 2, pp. 327–328) offered this description of what happened: "One after another she would beckon us to come up. We then talked together, the form in whispers; I could look closely into her face, examine the features and hair, touch her hands, and might even touch and examine her ears closely, which were not bored for earrings. The figure had bare feet, was somewhat taller than Miss Cook, and, though there was a general resemblance, was quite distinct in features, figure, and hair. After half an hour or more this figure would retire, close the curtains, and sometimes within a few seconds would say, 'Come and look.' We then opened the curtains, turned up the lamp, and Miss Cook was found in a trance, in the chair, her black dress, laced-boots, etc., in the most perfect order as when she arrived, while the full-grown white-robed figure had totally disappeared."

Wallace had a similar experience with the medium Eglington. The séance took place at a private house, in the presence of about eighteen spiritualists and people inquisitive about spiritualism. The medium was to sit behind a curtain hung across one corner of a room. The space behind the curtain was small, just large enough for the chair on which the medium was to sit. Wallace noted, "I and others examined this corner and found the walls solid and the carpet nailed down" (Wallace 1905, v. 2, p. 329). In other words, there was no concealed opening through which a confederate could enter. After Eglington arrived and sat behind the curtain, a robed male figure appeared and walked around the room, in dim light, allowing all of the witnesses to touch his robes and examine his hands and feet. Could the figure have been Eglington in disguise?

Wallace (1905 v. 2, p. 329) gave this description of what happened immediately after the sitting: "Several of the medium's friends begged him to allow himself to be searched so that the result might be published. After some difficulty he was persuaded, and four persons were appointed to make the examination. Immediately two of these led him into a bedroom, while I and a friend who had come with me closely examined the chair, floor, and walls, and were able to declare that nothing so large as a glove had been left. We then joined the other two in the bedroom, and as Eglington took off his clothes each article was passed through our hands, down to underclothing and socks, so that we could positively declare that not a single article besides his own clothes were found upon him. The result was published in the *Spiritualist* newspaper [and] certified by the names of all present."

It is true that on some occasions mediums were exposed in cheating. This should not be surprising, for even in orthodox science there is no shortage of cheating. One notable hoax was Piltdown man, which fooled the scientific world for forty years. And today the manipulation and manufacture of test results in science laboratories is fairly common. So whether we are talking about paranormal science or normal science, we cannot exclude the possibility of cheating and hoaxing. The only thing we can do is examine particular cases and make reasonable judgements about the likelihood of imposture. In the case of Wallace's experience with Eglington, a great deal of care was taken to insure against trickery. In light of this, the apparent materialization of a humanlike figure by Eglington deserves a certain degree of credibility.

The most extraordinary phenomenon witnessed by Wallace was produced by a truly remarkable medium, Mr. Monk. A nonconformist clergyman, Monk had gained a considerable reputation for his séances. In order to study him more closely and systematically, some well known spiritualists, including Hensleigh Wedgwood and Stainton Moses, rented some rooms for Monk in the Bloomsbury district of London. Wedgwood and Moses invited Wallace to come and see what Monk could do.

Wallace (1905 v. 2, p. 330) later gave this account of what happened: "It was a bright summer afternoon, and everything happened in the full light of day. After a little conversation, Monk, who was dressed in the usual clerical black, appeared to go into a trance; then stood up a few feet in front of us, and after a little while pointed to his side, saying, 'Look.'

We saw there a faint white patch on his coat on the left side. This grew brighter, then seemed to flicker, and extend both upwards and downwards, till very gradually it formed a cloudy pillar extending from his shoulder to his feet and close to his body. Then he shifted himself a little sideways, the cloudy figure standing still, but appearing joined to him by a cloudy band at the height at which it had first begun to form. Then, after a few minutes more, Monk again said 'Look,' and passed his hand through the connecting band, severing it. He and the figure then moved away from each other till they were about five or six feet apart. The figure had now assumed the appearance of a thickly draped female form, with arms and hands just visible. Monk looked towards it and again said to us 'Look,' and then clapped his hands. On which the figure put out her hands, clapped them as he had done, and we all distinctly heard her clap following his, but fainter. The figure then moved slowly back to him, grew fainter and shorter, and was apparently absorbed into his body as it had grown out of it."

Broad daylight rules out clever puppetry. That Monk was standing only a few feet from Wallace, in the middle of an ordinary room, rules out the production of the form by stage apparatus. Wedgwood told Wallace that on other occasions a tall, robed, male figure appeared alongside Monk. This figure would remain for up to half an hour, and allowed himself to be touched by Wedgwood and his colleagues, who carefully examined his body and clothes. Furthermore, the figure could exert force on material objects. Once the figure went so far as to lift a chair upon which one of the investigators was seated (Wallace 1905, v. 2, p. 331).

Exchanges with Romanes

In 1880, *Nature* published a letter from an anonymous scientist expressing an interest in carrying out experiments to verify paranormal phenomena. Wallace deduced that the scientist was George J. Romanes. He wrote to him, pointing out that several scientists had already performed such experiments but had met with "only abuse and ridicule" (Wallace 1905, v. 2, p. 310). On February 17, 1880, Romanes replied that he was aware of such scientific prejudice, but he was hopeful that further proofs would have the desired effect. He suggested that Wallace did not realize the extent to which his own work had created within the scientific community a climate favorable to the eventual acceptance of spiritualistic phenomena (Wallace 1905, v. 2, p. 311). When Romanes repeated his desire to carry out some experiments, Wallace gave him some practical advice.

Wallace paid Romanes a visit in London. Romanes told Wallace how he had become interested in spiritualism (Wallace 1905, v. 2, pp. 314–315). A relative of his—a sister or cousin—happened to be a medium. At séances with her, Romanes witnessed the communication of messages by rapping not produced by any of those present. At times, the messages contained answers to the mental questions of Romanes. Romanes was impressed, and in 1876 he had written some letters to Darwin, giving a positive account of his experiences. Wallace was later shown these letters by a friend (Wallace 1905, v. 2, p. 315).

A year or two after his visit to Romanes, Wallace (1905 v. 2, p. 330) was surprised to read in a London newspaper some remarks by Romanes very unfavorable to thought reading. Wallace did not, however, reply. But in 1890, Wallace and Romanes became involved in a controversy about evolution. In his criticism of Wallace's book *Darwinism,* published in the journal *Nineteenth Century* (May 1890, p. 831), Romanes said that in the last chapter "we encounter the Wallace of spiritualism and astrology ... the Wallace of incapacity and absurdity" (Wallace 1905, v. 2, p. 317).

Wallace replied privately in a letter dated July 18, 1890: "As to your appeal to popular scientific prejudice by referring to my belief in spiritualism and astrology (which latter I have never professed my belief in), I have something to say. In the year 1876 you wrote two letters to Darwin, detailing your experiences of spiritual phenomena. You told him that you had had mental questions answered with no paid medium present. You told him you had had a message from Mr. J. Bellew.... And you declared your belief that some non-human intelligence was then communicating with you. You also described many physical phenomena occurring in your own house with the medium Williams. You saw 'hands,' apparently human, yet not those of any one present. You saw hand-bells, etc., carried about; you saw a human head and face above the table, with mobile features and eyes. Williams was held all the time, and your brother walked round the table to prove that there was no wire or other machinery (in your own room!), yet a bell, placed on a piano some distance away, was taken up by a luminous hand and rung and carried about the room! Can you have forgotten all this? In your second letter to Darwin you expressed your conviction of the truth of these facts, and of the existence of spiritual intelligences, of mind without brain. You said these phenomena had altered your whole conceptions. Formerly you had thought there were two mental natures in Crookes and Wallace—one sane, the other lunatic! Now (you said) you belonged in the same class as they did" (Wallace 1905, v. 2, pp. 317–318). Wallace therefore thought it unfair that Romanes should have written as he did in the *Nineteenth Century* article.

In subsequent letters to Wallace, Romanes replied that his letters to Darwin were private and contained only a provisional acceptance of the phenomena he witnessed. Romanes claimed he later suspected that the medium Williams was cheating. To test this, he placed him inside a metal cage, and in this circumstance none of the usual phenomena occurred. Romanes thereupon withdrew the opinions expressed in his letters to Darwin (Wallace 1905, v. 2, pp. 319, 321).

Wallace answered that the experiment with the cage did not discredit the experiences Romanes reported in his letters (Wallace 1905, v. 2, pp. 320–321). Wallace would accept that they were fraudulent only if Romanes could explain how they were produced, under the circumstances he described. After all, the phenomena took place in Romanes's own house, with the medium held all the time, and with Romanes's brother walking around the room to make sure no wires or other tricks were being employed. Romanes admitted the events were inexplicable (Wallace 1905, v. 2, p. 322).

Wallace also pointed out that some mediums had passed the cage test: "Mr. Adshead, a gentleman of Belper, had a wire cage made, and Miss Wood sat in it in his own house, many times, and under these conditions many forms of men, women, and children, appeared in the room. A similar cage was afterwards used by the Newcastle Spiritual Evidence Society, for a year or more, and Miss Wood sat in it weekly. It was screwed up from the outside, yet all the usual phenomena of materialization occurred just the same as when no cage was used" (Wallace 1905, v. 2, pp. 322–323).

Romanes was not the only scientist to denigrate Wallace's research in spiritualism. One evening, while having tea after a lecture at the Royal Institution, Wallace found himself standing behind Dr. Ansted, who was conversing with a friend. The topic of spiritualism came up, and Dr. Ansted, unaware that Wallace was standing nearby, said, "What a strange thing it is such men as Crookes and Wallace should believe in it!" Ansted's friend laughed and said, "Oh, they are mad on that one subject" (Wallace 1905, v. 2, p. 314). The spreading of such talk is one way by which a scientific orthodoxy can maintain itself—members are subtly reminded that certain kinds of research can be damaging to one's professional reputation.

Spiritualistic Encounters in America

During the years 1886 and 1887, Wallace traveled in the United States on a scientific lecture tour. In the course of his visit, he also met many American spiritualists, such as Professor William James of Harvard, and attended several séances.

One series of séances took place at the Boston home of Mrs. Ross, a medium famous for materializations (Wallace 1905, v. 2, pp. 338–339). To make a space for the medium, a curtain was placed across the corner of a front downstairs room. The sides of this corner were an outside wall of the house and an inside wall, on the other side of which was a back room. The inside wall was occupied by a cupboard filled with china. Wallace carefully inspected the walls and floor, from within the front room, the back room, and the basement. He determined that there were no openings through which anyone could enter, other than a sliding door to the back room. This door was sealed with sticking plaster, and the witnesses secretly marked the plaster with pencil, so that if the plaster were moved they would be able to tell. The ten witnesses, including Wallace, sat in dim light in a circle in front of the curtain. The light was sufficient for Wallace to see the hands of his watch and to see the forms of everyone in the room. Under these circumstances, three figures emerged from behind the curtain—a female figure in White, Mrs. Ross dressed in black, and a male figure. When these retired, three female figures, of different heights and dressed in white, came out. These were followed by a single male figure. One of the gentleman witnesses identified him as his son. Later, a figure dressed as an American Indian came out from behind the curtain. He danced, spoke, and shook hands with some of those present, including Wallace. Finally, a female figure holding a baby appeared in front of the curtain. Wallace, on being invited by her, came up and touched the baby, and found it to be real. "Directly after the séance was over," wrote Wallace, "the gas was lighted, and I again examined the bare walls of the cabinet, the curtains, and the door, all being just as before, and affording no room or place for disposing of the baby alone, far less of the other figures" (Wallace 1905, v. 2, p. 339).

At another séance with Mrs. Ross, attended by William James, Wallace again saw eight or nine figures come out from behind the curtain. One of these was the departed niece of one of the witnesses, Mr. Brackett. Wallace noted that "Mr. Brackett has often seen her develop gradually from a cloudy mass, and almost instantly vanish away" (Wallace 1905, v. 2, p. 339).

Wallace himself saw figures known to him. "One was a beautifully draped female figure, who took my hand, looked at me smilingly, and on my appearing doubtful, said in a whisper that she had often met me at Miss Kate Cook's séances in London. She then let me feel her ears, as I had done before to prove she was not the medium. I then saw that she closely resembled the figure with whom I had often talked and joked at Signor Randi's, a fact known to no one in America. The other figure was an old gentleman with white hair and beard, and in evening-dress. He took my hand, bowed, and looked pleased, as one meeting an old friend. . . . at length I recognized the likeness to a photograph I had of my cousin Algernon Wilson, whom I had not seen since we were children, but had long corresponded with him, as he was an enthusiastic ento-mologist, living in Adelaide, where he had died not long before. . . .These two recognitions were to me very striking, because they were both so pri-vate and personal to myself, and could not possibly have been known to the medium or even to any of my friends present" (Wallace 1905, v. 2, pp. 339–340).

A few months after these events, a group of twelve men came to one of Mrs. Ross's séances with the intention of exposing the material-ized spirit forms as imposters (Wallace 1905, v. 2, p. 340). When they exe-cuted their plan, the twelve men found themselves unable to detain a sin-gle suspect (two men, one woman, two boys, and a little girl) or take a sin-gle piece of their paraphernalia. The men declared to a newspaper that the alleged imposters had entered the space behind the curtain through a sliding portion of the baseboard. Upon learning of this, some friends of Mrs. Ross brought her landlord and a carpenter to the scene, where they conducted a thorough inspection. The carpenter testified that there was no opening in the baseboard, and that none had been made and covered up. Wallace sent to the *Banner of Light* a letter stating these facts. He argued that "the utter failure of twelve men, who went for the express purpose of detecting and identifying confederates, utterly failing to do so or to secure any tangible evidence of their existence, is really a very strong proof that there were no confederates to detect" (Wallace 1905, v. 2, pp. 340–341). This is not to deny that there were cases in which medi-ums were exposed and confederates seized. But this particular case does not seem to fall in that category.

In Washington, D.C., Wallace, accompanied by a college professor, an army general, and a government official, all spiritualists, attended sé-ances with the medium P. L. O. A. Keeler (Wallace 1905, v. 2, pp. 341–345). Across one corner of the room a black curtain was stretched on a cord, five feet off the floor. In the space behind the curtain was a table, upon which rested a tambourine and a bell. Before the séance, Wallace care-fully checked the walls and floor, satisfying himself that there were no hidden entrances. He also checked the curtain, noticing it was one solid piece of cloth, with no openings. Everyone there had the chance to make similar investigations. Keeler and two guests from the audience sat in three chairs in front of the curtain. A lower curtain was then raised in front of them, up to the level of their chests. Keeler's hands were placed on those of the guest sitting next to him. Wallace (1905 v. 2, p. 343) observed: "The tambourine was rattled and played on, then a hand appeared above the curtain, and a stick was given to it which it seized. Then the tambourine was lifted high on this stick and whirled round with great rapidity, the bell being rung at the same time. All the time the medium sat quiet and impassive, and the person next him certified to his two hands being on his or hers." A pencil and notepad were then passed to the hand above the curtain. Behind the curtain, messages were written, and these were thrown over the curtain. The messages were signed with names known to certain witnesses, who found the content of the messages intelligible. Wallace himself received a message in an extraordinary way. Instead of passing the notepad over the curtain to the hand, he held it himself near the curtain. Wallace then saw a hand with a pencil come through the solid curtain and write a message to him on the pad.

On another occasion, Wallace observed a similar occurrence: "A stick was pushed out through the curtain. Two watches were handed to me through the curtain, and were claimed by the two persons who sat by the medium. The small tambourine, about ten inches in diameter, was pushed through the curtain and fell on the floor. These objects came through different parts of the curtain, but left no holes as could be seen at the time, and was proved by a close examination afterwards. More marvellous still (if that be possible), a waistcoat was handed to me over the curtain, which proved to be the medium's, though his coat was left on and his hands had been held by his companions all the time; also about a score of people were looking on all the time in a well-lighted room. These things seem impossible, but they are, nevertheless, facts" (Wallace 1905, v. 2, pp. 344–345).

In San Francisco, Wallace, along with his brother John, who lived in California, and Mr. Owen, editor of the *Golden Gate*, attended some slate writing sessions with the medium Fred Evans (Wallace 1905, v. 2, pp. 346–349). A physician, a friend of Mr. Owen, also was present. Four folding slates were cleaned with a damp sponge and then handed to the four guests for inspection. The slates were closed and placed on the table. The guests then placed their hands on the slates. When a signal was given, they opened the slates and found writing on all of them. The messages were from departed relatives of Wallace and departed spiritualists. The usual skeptical explanation is that the slates were somehow switched. But Wallace's description of the procedure appears to rule that out, as the witnesses had their own hands on the slates at critical times.

Another set of slates was set on the table. The medium marked one of these slates with a pencil. When opened, this slate was covered with writing in five colors. Wallace observed that the letters were clearly su-perimposed over the pencil marks. This appears to rule out any clever chemical means of producing the letters.

Wallace's brother had brought a new folding slate of his own. This was placed nearby on the floor for a few minutes. Wallace kept the slate in sight the entire time. When the slate was opened, a message was found written upon both sides of it. That it was a new slate, not belonging to the medium, is significant.

Wallace then asked the medium if the writing could be produced on pieces of paper placed between slates. Evans told Wallace to take six piec-es of paper from a notepad and place them between a pair of slates. Wal-lace did so. After a few minutes, the slates were opened. Wallace found portraits of five departed spiritualists and a long dead sister of his drawn in crayon on the six pieces of paper, which had rested one on top of the other between the slates. They had been placed there by Wallace himself, ruling out substitution by the medium. Given the unexpected request by Wallace, the circumstances under which the pieces of paper were placed between the slates, it is hard to see how the medium could have carried out any deception.

Wallace (1905 v. 2, pp. 348–349) noted: "The whole of the seven slates and six papers were produced so rapidly that the *séance* occupied less than an hour, and with such simple and complete openness, under the eyes of four observers, as to constitute absolutely test conditions. . . . A statement to this effect was published, with an account of the *séance*, signed by all present."

Wallace's Theory of Spiritualism: Analysis and Critique

Summarizing the conclusions he drew from his spiritual researches, Wallace (1892, p. 648) stated: "The universal teaching of modern spiritu-alism is that the world and the whole material universe exist for the pur-pose of developing spiritual beings—that death is simply a transition from material existence to the first grade of spirit-life—and that our happiness and the degree of our progress will be wholly dependent upon the use we have made of our faculties and opportunities here."

Such conclusions were drawn solely from facts that had been care-fully and repeatedly observed in nature, and they were thus entirely sci-entific, said Wallace (Wallace 1885a, p. 809). The observable facts did not, however, warrant extending spiritualist conclusions beyond certain lim-its. The verifiable facts of spiritualism were, according to Wallace, related to humans and the spirit beings nearest to earthly human existence. He therefore warned: "Speculations on the nature or origin of mind in general as well as those on the ultimate states to which human minds may attain in the infinite future, I look upon as altogether beyond the range of our faculties, and to be, therefore, utterly untrustworthy and profitless" (Wallace 1885b; in Smith 1991, p. 101). Wallace was generally content with the limited conclusions that could be drawn from the observable middle ground of human experience. He himself did, however, sometimes venture into the realm of "untrustworthy" speculation about origins and ultimate states.

Wallace found spiritualism to be a good scientific hypothesis, for it allowed him to intelligibly organize and explain many categories of evidence. For example, spiritualism allowed him to accommodate in one explanatory system the spiritlike daimon that advised Socrates, the Greek oracles, the miracles of the Old and New Testaments, the miracles of saints such as St. Bernard, St. Francis, and St. Theresa; the phenomena of witchcraft; modern Catholic miracles such as Marian apparitions; psychic powers reported in primitive peoples, and the efficacy of prayer, as well as the phenomena of modern spiritualism (Wallace 1874; in Smith 1991, pp. 87–89). All of these could be attributed to spirits acting through especially sensitive humans to produce unusual physical and mental effects.

If spirits were nonmaterial or made of "the most diffused and subtle forms of matter," (Wallace 1896, p. 44) how could they act on, or even produce, substantial material objects? Wallace observed that "all the most powerful and universal forces of nature are now referred to minute vibrations of an almost infinitely attenuated form of matter; and that, by the grandest generalisations of modern science, the most varied natural phenomena have been traced back to these recondite forces" (Wallace 1896, p. 44). Regarding the "almost infinitely attenuated form of matter," Wallace was referring to a space-filling ether. In his system, the spirit beings would act on the ether, and this subtle action would amplify through the forces of nature into action on the level of observable matter.

Wallace (1896, pp. 47–48) further proposed: "Beings of an ethereal order, if such exist, would probably possess some sense or senses . . . giving them increased insight into the constitution of the universe, and proportionately increased intelligence to guide and direct for special ends those new modes of ethereal motion with which they would in that case be able to deal. Their every faculty might be proportionate to the modes of action of the ether. They might have a power of motion as rapid as that of light or the electric current. They might have a power of vision as acute as that of our most powerful telescopes and microscopes.

They might have a sense somewhat analogous to the powers of the last triumph of science, the spectroscope, and by it be enabled to perceive instantaneously, the intimate constitution of matter under every form, whether in organised beings or in stars and nebulae. Such existences, possessed of such, to us, inconceivable powers, would not be supernatural, except in a very limited and incorrect sense of the term . . . all would still be natural."

The space-filling ether of nineteenth century physics is no longer with us. But there are modern scientific concepts that would allow Wallace's basic system to operate. According to deterministic chaos theorists, immeasurably small random perturbances of matter can rapidly propagate into large-scale effects that are not easily predictable. Scientists sometimes give the example of a Caribbean butterfly that by its wings sets off motions of air molecules. These movements might eventually amplify to steer a hurricane from open sea into the American coast. If the butterfly had flapped its wings slightly differently, the hurricane might not have hit land. According to this idea, Wallace's spirit beings might make infinitesimal adjustments on the subatomic level that would quickly propagate into observable spiritualist effects. One might also propose that they are somehow capable of manipulating the curvature of Einstein's space-time continuum. They could thus produce gravitational effects, for gravity is said to be the result of curvature in the continuum. Or one might propose that the spirit beings induce slight changes in the quantum mechanical vacuum, which in some ways resembles an ether. Of course, this approach is limiting, and rather than straining to find ways to explain spiritualist phenomena in conformity with currently accepted physical laws, it may make more sense to come up with a new theoretical system that more naturally incorporates both the normal and paranormal phenomena. Reintroducing a variety of the ether concept might be one way to do it. One could define the ether as a subtle interface between consciousness and matter.

In terms of modern discussion of the mind/body question, Wallace would be a dualist. He accepted the existence of a conscious self distinct from the physical body. Wallace noted that the bodies of organisms, from primitive to advanced, were built up from molecules, arranged in ever increasing complexity. More, however, was needed to explain consciousness. "If a material element, or a combination of a thousand material elements in a molecule, are all alike unconscious, it is impossible for us to believe, that the mere addition of one, two, or a thousand other material elements to form a more complex molecule, could in any way produce a self-conscious existence. The things are radically distinct . . . There is no escape from this dilemma,—either all matter is conscious, or conscious-ness is something distinct from matter, and in the latter case, its presence in material forms is a proof of the existence of conscious beings, outside of, and independent of, what we term matter" (Wallace 1870; in Smith 1991, p. 290).

Wallace favored the latter course, but his system has certain puz-zling features. Although a dualist, he does not appear to accept the exis-tence of individual conscious entities before their earthly embodiment. According to Wallace, there is an original spiritual mind from which mat-ter is generated. Individual spiritual minds, associated with spiritual bod-ies (souls), are only developed from and in material bodies, as they come into existence (Wallace 1885b; in Smith 1991, p. 100). After death, the in-dividual minds, as above stated, go to "the first grade of spirit life," where they experience progress or the lack of it based on their earthly hab-its. But if individual spirit souls can exist after earthly embodiment, why not before? And why is there any need at all for earthly embodiment, which is not an altogether pleasant experience? Why not skip that and go directly to the highest grade of spiritual life?

A system in which there is preexistence of spirit beings offers a solution. According to Wallace, spirit has free will, and as a result suffers or enjoys the consequences of its actions after death. So if we allow that souls exist before their material embodiment, and also possess free will, we could explain the embodiment of some of these souls by misuse of the same free will. Only those souls who misused their free will would suffer embodiment, which does seem to have some unpleasant features, such as inevitable disease and death.

Here is another problem with Wallace's system. In his works, Wal-lace details reports of varied spiritualistic phenomena, such as levitation, ap-paritions, and clairvoyance, from his own time and throughout his-tory. But he ignores reports of transmigration of souls, which occur wide-ly in almost all times and places. The reports of transmigration are just as credible as any other category of evidence he considers. The existence of this phenomenon requires, however, certain modifications in Wal-lace's system. At death, souls would pass not necessarily into the first phase of spiritual existence but perhaps into new material bodies. Ac-cording to religious systems that incorporate transmigration, such as the Vedic system, some souls, because of their strong attachment to their last embodiment, do not attain new material bodies, but remain for some time as ghosts. This actually fits in quite well with the observations of Wallace and other spiritualists, who found that the spirits they contacted often desired to communicate with living friends and relatives.

Wallace's Spiritualism and Evolution

How did Wallace incorporate his spiritualist ideas into his theory of evolution by natural selection? Specifically, how did his spiritualist ideas relate to his theory of human origins? First of all, Wallace believed that evolution was in some sense directed. Although the origin of species was in general governed by natural selection, natural selection was, in his opinion, not sufficient to account for the exact variety of species we encounter today. Some forces, the nature of which were not clearly understood, and which perhaps never could be understood, shaped the path that evolution by natural selection followed.

Stephen J. Gould, an influential modern evolutionary theorist, has proposed that if we "ran the tape" of evolution again we would not get the same result. For example, we might not get human beings. Indeed, we might "run the tape" a thousand different times and get a thousand different sets of species. In other words, there is a certain contingency rather than inevitability to the evolutionary process. There are so many variables that one cannot predict in advance the path evolution will follow. If there are so many paths, each of which is dependent on millions of accidental occurrences, great and small, then this leaves open the possibility for an original Mind to manipulate the process to get a specific result.

Given a certain initial condition and a desired end result, the Mind-directed pathway, mediated by natural selection, might contain a lot of strange features one would not expect from a Creator, but it would nevertheless be guided and intentional. For example, the panda has a thumb-like appendage that it uses to grasp bamboo shoots, its favorite food. Gould points out that the so-called thumb is not a real digit but an outgrowth from the panda's wrist. God would never have created the panda's "thumb," says Gould. Only natural selection could account for such a weird, quirky adaptation. But God and natural selection were, for Wallace, not mutually exclusive. The original Mind could have guided the path of natural selection in a certain direction to get human beings as an end result. And one of the byproducts may have been the panda, with its strange thumb.

Let us consider in more detail the source of guidance in Wallace's system of guided evolution. Anticipating Einstein, Wallace considered matter to be a transformation of force, or energy (Wallace 1870, in Smith 1991, p. 290). Force existed in two varieties: "The first consists of the primary forces of nature, such as gravitation, cohesion, repulsion, heat, electricity, etc.; the second is our own will force" (Wallace 1870, in Smith 1991, p. 290). The ancient question of free will remains an unresolved problem for most philosophers and scientists right up to the present.

Foregoing a review of the entire debate, I shall here simply reproduce the main features of Wallace's argument.

Wallace observed that many persons suggest free will is "but the result of molecular changes in the brain" (Wallace 1870, in Smith 1991, p. 291). But he countered that no one has ever proved that all force exhibited in a body can be attributed to known primary forces of nature. Accepting the existence of free will as an observed feature of human consciousness, he proposed that its exercise must involve the exertion of a force capable of setting into motion the other natural forces exhibited in organisms. In this sense, the action of natural forces in an organism could be ultimately traced to the action of will force. This led Wallace to conclude: "If, therefore, we have traced one force, however minute, to an origin in our own WILL, while we have no knowledge of any other primary cause of force, it does not seem an improbable conclusion that all force may be will-force; and thus, that the whole universe, is not merely dependent on, but actually is, the WILL of higher intelligences or of one Supreme Intelligence" (Wallace 1870; in Smith 1991, p. 291). In other words, all matter and force in the universe are transformations of the will of a Supreme Intelligence, or intelligences.

The will of higher intelligences, according to Wallace, guided the process of evolution by natural selection. Wallace stated: "A superior intelligence has guided the development of man in a definite direction, and for a special purpose, just as man guides the development of many animal and vegetable forms. The laws of evolution alone would, perhaps, never have produced a grain so well adapted to man's use as wheat and maize; such traits as the seedless banana and bread-fruit; or such animals as the Guernsey milch cow, or the London dray-horse. Yet these so closely resemble the unaided productions of nature, that we may well imagine a being who had mastered the laws of development of organic forms through past ages, refusing to believe that any new power had been concerned in their production, and scornfully rejecting the theory (as my theory will be rejected by many who agree with me on other points), that in these few cases a controlling intelligence had directed the action of the laws of variation, multiplication, and survival, for his own purposes. We know, however, that this has been done; and we must therefore admit the possibility that, if we are not the highest intelligence in the universe, some higher intelligence may have directed the process by which the human race was developed, by means of more subtle agencies than we are acquainted with (Wallace 1870, pp. 359–360; in Smith 1991, p. 289).

Wallace believed that certain physiological features of humans could not be explained by natural selection and survival of the fittest alone.

He noted that the brains of primitive peoples were as large and developed as the brains of civilized peoples. It appeared, therefore, that the primitive people had brains with capacities far in excess of those demanded by their daily lives. Wallace said "natural selection could only have endowed the savage with a brain a little superior to that of an ape" (Wallace 1869; in Smith 1991, p. 32). Concerning the human hand, Wallace said the savage "has no need for so fine an instrument, and can no more fully utilise it than he could use without instruction a complete set of joiner's tools" (Wallace 1869; in Smith 1991, p. 32). Wallace made similar arguments about the human capacity for speech. He took all of this as evidence that some intelligence had "guided the action" of the laws of evolutionary development "in definite directions and for special ends" (Wallace 1869; in Smith 1991, p. 33).

Wallace, as we have seen, believed the human race was of considerable antiquity. And interestingly enough, he thought that the current level of European civilization might not have been humankind's highest moment. "And," he added, "if we are thus led to believe that our present knowledge of nature is somewhat less complete than we have been accustomed to consider it, this is only what we might expect; for however great may have been the intellectual triumphs of the nineteenth century, we can hardly think so highly of its achievements as to imagine that, in somewhat less than twenty years, we have passed from complete ignorance to almost perfect knowledge on two such vast and complex subjects as the origin of species and the antiquity of man" (Wallace 1876; in Smith 1991, pp. 43–44). Although we must now talk of 150 years instead of twenty, what Wallace said towards the end of the nineteenth century remains true at the beginning of the twenty-first.

6

WHAT IS A HUMAN BEING? MATTER, MIND, AND CONSCIOUSNESS

The research of Sir Alfred Russel Wallace suggests that if we want to understand how human beings have come into existence, we should first of all understand what a human being is. Under the influence of materialistic assumptions about the nature of reality, most scientists have concluded that human beings are composed only of ordinary matter. This assumption limits the kinds of explanations we can offer for the origins of humanity. We are reduced to speculating about how ordinary matter organized itself into such a complex biological form. Even within this limited sphere, an exact explanation of the origin of the first life form and its subsequent development into the human form has thus far eluded science. This failure gives us the warrant to consider a different set of assumptions about the nature of the human organism, thus increasing our explanatory options.

When we consider all of the evidence available to science, we find ample justification for basing our study of human origins on the assumption that a human being, or any other living entity of our ordinary experience, is composed of not just one thing, ordinary matter, but of three things—matter, mind, and consciousness (or spirit). By mind, I mean a subtle material energy, connected with the human organism and capable of influencing ordinary matter or receiving sensory impressions in ways unexplained by the laws of science as currently accepted. Mind is not, however, conscious, although it may carry content for consciousness and may be in part instrumental for translating conscious intentions into action in the world of ordinary matter. By spirit I mean a conscious, experiencing, desiring, acting self that can exist apart from mind and matter. The assumption that humans, and other living things, are composed of matter, mind, and consciousness allows, indeed demands, new explanatory possibilities. We must explain from where these elements came, and how they combined in the human form.

Let us now review the scientific evidence favoring the assumption that a human being is composed not only of ordinary matter but also of the separate elements mind and consciousness. In the first part of this chapter, I shall include cases related to the existence of a mind element, and in the second part, I shall discuss evidence related to the existence of a conscious self apart from the subtle material mind and the gross physical body composed of ordinary matter.

PART ONE:
EVIDENCE FOR A MIND ELEMENT

In reviewing the evidence for a mind element, I have chosen to begin with contemporaries of Wallace and Darwin. This is an arbitrary decision. Because I am addressing the question of Darwinian evolution, which was formulated in the middle of the nineteenth century and developed to its mature form in the twentieth century, I thought it might be good to confine my citations of scientific evidence for a mind element to the same period of scientific development represented by Darwinism.

James Esdaile: Mesmerism in India

James Esdaile was an English physician working in Bengal in the nineteenth century, when India was under British rule. He was a pioneer in using mesmerism, now called hypnosis, as an anesthetic. Patients who got painless operations regarded Dr. Esdaile as "an incarnation of Vishnu" (Esdaile 1852, p. 166). Around this time, however, ether and chloroform came into general use, and mesmerism was no longer quite so much needed as an anesthetic. Esdaile then turned his attention to the mysterious psychical effects he had encountered in his research into mesmerism. Esdaile (1852) reported that some of his entranced and blindfolded patients could identify objects and persons not visible to them by ordinary means. In addition to his own experiments, he also included in his book similar reports by other researchers.

For example, Dr. Chalmers, a Calcutta surgeon, wanted to test the powers of a clairvoyant boy. In a room of his house, Chalmers placed two candles on a table and a banknote between them. The banknote, which until the time of the experiment had been kept locked in a drawer, had not been seen by anyone except Chalmers. In another room, the boy and some guests of Chalmers were waiting. Chalmers entered this room and asked the boy if he could see anything in any other room. The boy declared he saw two candles on a table. When asked if anything was between them, he said he saw a banknote. The boy then read accurately the four-figure serial number of the banknote and its value, twenty-five rupees. Dr. Chalmers then returned to the room and secretly substituted a ten rupee note for the twenty-five rupee note. He told the boy he had turned the twenty five rupee note over, and asked what number he saw. The boy said he saw the number ten. Chalmers returned to the room and placed a gold watch on the banknote. The boy accurately described it. Chalmers then secretly moved the watch and banknote to another room. While he was doing this, the boy announced to the guests who were with him, "He has lifted them from the table." When Chalmers came back to inform his guests of his action, he found they already knew of it (Esdaile 1852, pp. 76–78).

Esdaile possessed a remarkable ability to hypnotize people without their knowledge. For example, he described cases of silently hypnotizing blindfolded persons, inducing paralysis and insensibility in various limbs. Esdaile gave examples of entrancing unsuspecting subjects at a distance. Esdaile (1852, pp. 226–227) stated: "Mr. Grant, one of our oldest and most respected Civil servants, and now in England, has often seen me entrance patients from another room while he was taking their portraits and engaging their attention as much as possible."

Esdaile performed similar experiments with a blind man, thus ruling out any visual cues. Esdaile (1852, p. 227) reported: "I placed him on a stool without saying a word to him, and entranced him in ten minutes without touching him. I then roused him up a little, and made him a somnambulist; he walked with great difficulty, and, while doing so, said he was asleep and in his bed. He soon became unable to support himself, and fell into the trance again, in which he remained for two hours. This man became so susceptible, that by making him the object of my attention, I could entrance him in whatever occupation he was engaged, and at any distance within the hospital enclosure."

Esdaile (1852, p. 227) wrote: "It will no doubt be said by those who attempt to account for *all* the mesmeric phenomena through the influence of *suggestion, expectation,* and *imagination,* that this man became aware of my presence and intentions by smell or hearing, or by my fixed position, and altered breathing." Esdaile explained that these objections could not apply to his experiments in mesmerizing the blind man at a distance. He wrote (1852, p. 228): "My *first attempt* to influence the blind man was made by gazing at him silently over a wall, while he was engaged in the act of eating his solitary dinner, at the distance of twenty yards. He gradually ceased to eat, and in a quarter of an hour was profoundly entranced and cataleptic. This was repeated at the most untimely hours when he could not possibly know of my being in his neighbourhood; and always with like results."

Esdaile performed some interesting experiments with what he called "mesmerized water." Esdaile would "mesmerize" water by blowing into it with a tube and keeping his fingers on the surface. He performed experiments offering plain water and mesmerized water to his patients and found that the patients would go into mesmeric trance simply on drinking the mesmerized water, without being told what it was or why they were being asked to drink it (Esdaile 1846, pp. 158–164). In one set of experiments, Esdaile gave mesmerized water to patients whose sores were to be treated with nitric acid, usually quite painful. The patients felt nothing during the nitric acid treatments. These experiments were carried out over several years at six different hospitals. The patients had no idea they were being given mesmerized water. The water had been treated with tinctures of rhubarb and cardamom, along with aromatic spirit of ammonia. It was given to the patients at the same time as their normal medicine (Esdaile 1852, pp. 231–232).

Esdaile believed that the effects of mesmerism were caused by a subtle nervous fluid, which carried sense impressions to the brain and transmitted the willing powers of the brain to the bodily organs, thus producing various actions. The mesmerist could transfer this fluid from his body to that of his subject. Overloading the brain with the fluid brought about the mesmeric trance. Reducing the overload restored normal waking consciousness. Thoughts and feelings could also be transmitted by this fluid (Esdaile 1852, pp. 234–238). Esdaile apparently believed that the mind associated with the brain was endowed with a consciousness that possessed its own faculties, capable of operating without the bodily sense organs: "When we reflect that it is the *mind* that sees, smells, tastes, touches, and hears, and not the organs of sense, which are only the instruments that it uses; and that the Divine Intelligence, from whence the human mind emanates, dispenses with the use of organs, and is yet all-knowing and omnipresent, it is difficult to see why the mind of man should not, under extraordinary circumstances, occasionally partake of the same powers in a limited degree" (Esdaile 1852, p. 49). This would explain the clairvoyance displayed by some mesmerized subjects. In terms of the categories I have proposed (matter, mind, and consciousness, or soul), Esdaile is conflating mind and consciousness. But this conflation is superior to the elimination of the mind and consciousness by some modern cognitive scientists.

Alexis and Adolphe Didier: Two Extraordinary Mediums

The mediumship of Alexis and Adolphe Didier provides many examples of clairvoyance. Their remarkable abilities can perhaps be traced to their father, who would sometimes spontaneously fall into a mesmeric trance while reading the daily newspaper. At such times, he would drop the paper but would continue to read it aloud, correctly. Sometimes Alexis and Adolphe, as an amusement, would take the paper into another room, and their father would still continue to read it aloud (Dingwall 1967, pp. 159–60).

On May 17, 1847, Alexis Didier and his mesmerist Mr. Marcillet went to visit Lord Frederick Fitzclarence at the Hotel Brighton, on the Rue Rivoli in Paris. The purpose was to demonstrate the clairvoyant powers of Alexis. Also present were Lord Normanby, the English ambassador to France, and other distinguished guests. Neither Lord Frederick nor Lord Normanby believed in mesmerism. After Marcillet had sent Alexis into trance, Lord Frederick asked him to describe his country house. Alexis replied with an exact description of the house, its furnishings, and its location (Esdaile 1852, p. 80). A skeptic might propose that Alexis and Marcillet had somehow learned these details beforehand. But what are we to make of the following report by Marcillet? "Lord Normanby took up one of Lord Frederick's books, and, having stated the number of a page, Alexis read a sentence in it, though the book was not out of Lord Normanby's hands. This experiment was repeated several times, and always with the same success" (Esdaile 1852, p. 81). Before the account of these incidents was published, it was forwarded to Lord Frederick, who wrote: "I have read the statement you sent me relative to the *séance* that was held at my apartments when in Paris, in 1847, in Mesmerism. It is quite correct in every particular; indeed nothing could be much more extraordinary than the whole thing was in every respect" (Esdaile 1852, p. 82–83).

Chauncey Hare Townshend (1852) gave an account of a session with Alexis Didier in Paris, in October of 1851. The session took place at Townshend's hotel room. Alexis was first hypnotized by Marcillet, who then left the room. Townshend was left alone with Alexis. Townshend wrote: "I feel convinced there was no clue to any particular knowledge about me." To test the clairvoyance of Alexis, Townshend asked him to describe his house. Alexis answered that Townshend had two houses, one in London and another in the country. This was true. Townshend had recently acquired a place in London, and had a country home in Lausanne, Switzerland. Alexis wanted to know which house he was to describe. Townshend asked him to describe the house in the country.

"I was surprised at the accuracy of the description of my house near Lausanne," said Townshend, "particularly at the mention of *the small house on the left-hand side,* where, according to Swiss custom, dwells my landlady. It was, in fact, a marking feature of the place, not to be guessed at by a stranger, and, as such, brought much conviction to my mind." Townshend pressed Alexis for further details. Alexis said he could see water and trees around the house. This was true—the lake of Lausanne could be seen from the windows, and there were trees.

Townshend then asked Alexis to tell what he saw in the drawing room of the house. Alexis said, "You have a good many pictures on the walls. But now, this is curious—they are all modern, *except two*." Townshend asked Alexis to tell about the latter two paintings. He said, correctly, that one was of a seascape and the other of a religious subject (*sujet religieux*). Townshend said, "I really felt something of a shudder at this extreme precision. How then was I astonished when Alexis went on to describe minutely the *sujet religieux*, which was a picture I had lately bought from an Italian refugee, and which had many striking peculiarities."

About this picture, Alexis said, "There are three figures in the picture—an old man, a woman, and a child. Can the woman be the Virgin? No! She is too old! The woman has a book upon her lap, and the child *points with its finger to something in the book! There is a distaff in the corner.*" Alexis had correctly described the subject of the painting—St. Ann teaching the Virgin Mary to read. Townshend then asked Alexis, "On what is the picture painted?" Alexis answered that it was neither canvass nor metal. After some thought, he said the painting was made on stone, and that the back of the stone was rough, greyish-black, and curved. All these details were correct. The painting was made on black marble.

Alexis then gave an exact description of Townshend's house in Norfolk Street, London, a house only recently acquired. Townsend noted: "He gave an exact description of the two women-servants—one old, one young. . . . He seemed pleased to describe the young one minutely, whom he thought pretty. He made no single mistake as to the colour of eyes, or hair, etc." Alexis correctly said there was a park in front of the house, and that the furniture was of the Louis XIV style. He went on to give correct descriptions of the furnishings of different rooms, including three paintings. The first he identified as a picture with a woman and two children, a depiction of the holy family, by Raphael; the second as a painting of a stormy sea; and the third as a painting of the interior of a stable, with a grey horse lying down. All of the identifications were correct.

Townshend then decided to test Alexis's ability to read words from book pages hidden from his view. Townshend brought from another room a copy of Lamartine's *Jocelyn*. He opened the book to a certain page. With closed eyes, Alexis read some lines. He then offered to read some lines from a page not open, and asked Townshend to specify the number of pages below the open one. Townshend asked him to read something from the page eight pages below the open one. Townshend reported: "He then traced with his finger slowly along the page that was open, and read, *A dévoré d'un jet toute ma sympathie.* I counted down eight leaves from the leaf first opened, and found, exactly under where his finger had traced, the line he had read, *correct*, with the exception of a single word. He had said *déchiré* instead of *dévoré.*"

"Human incredulity began to stir in me," said Townshend, "and I really thought perhaps Alexis knew *Jocelyn* by heart. So I again went to a drawer in the next room, and brought out a large book I had also bought that day—a sort of *magazin pittoresque,* called *Les beaux Arts.* This, at least, Alexis could not know by heart. Again, the same wonder was performed. I have forgotten the exact place, which I omitted to mark as I did in *Jocelyn* (in which the pieces of paper I put to specify the marvel still remain), but I certify that Alexis read in *Les beaux Arts*, also, several words many pages below the page he had open before him. Still, to make all sure, I brought forth an English book, *The Inheritance*, Miss Ferrier's clever novel of years ago, and in this he read the name of *Gertrude*, and other words at the distance of many leaves. With regard to all the books, they were opened but once, and kept open at the place first opened, and Alexis never touched the leaves."

Alexis then asked Townshend if he had received a letter from a person in whom he was interested. He expressed a wish to reveal some things about the letter. Townshend then produced a letter he had recently received from a lady. Townshend noted, "The letter was enclosed in a perfectly opaque envelope, which Alexis (and I carefully watched him) never attempted to disturb. He held it quietly in his hand." Alexis first indicated there was inside a piece of newspaper, bearing the words "brotherhood of nations." There was in fact a newspaper clipping about a peace society enclosed with the letter. Alexis then took a pencil and wrote on the outside of the envelope the address of the lady who had written the letter. "But now—marvel of marvels!" wrote Townshend. "Alexis told me the whole history of my fair correspondent—how long I had known her, and many minute circumstances respecting herself and our acquaintance—something too about the character of her sister, and (to crown all) he wrote (still on the outside of the letter) both the Christian and family name of her father!" Alexis went on to give many details about the personal health and history of Townshend.

Dr. Elliotson, editor of *The Zoist,* appended to Townshend's account other proofs of Alexis's clairvoyance. For example, Monsieur Sabine, chief of the railway station at Le Havre came to see Alexis. Before Sabine spoke, Alexis, who was at the time in trance, said, "You come about something lost in the service to which you belong." Sabine replied, "It is true." Alexis then asked, "You are employed on the Havre Railroad?" Sabine again replied it was true. Alexis told Sabine that the missing object was a basket full of leeches (used in medical practice, for sucking blood or other fluids). Sabine replied that two baskets of leeches were missing. Alexis told Sabine that one of the baskets had been taken off the train by mistake at Rouen, and it had been placed on a large horsedrawn carriage from the station into town. A conductor found it later on the carriage, unclaimed. Alexis said: "From fear of being scolded he did not deposit it in the baggage warehouse, but hid it for some days in his stable; and while it was there you wrote to Rouen . . . about it, the reply being that it could not be found. A few days ago the conductor put it in the goods depot, near the entrance and beneath the first window on the right. You will find it if you set off to Rouen; only, on account of the length of time that has elapsed, you will find about 200 leeches dead." Sabine went to Rouen the next day and found the basket in the place indicated by Alexis, with 200 of the leeches dead.

Eric Dingwall, author of *Abnormal Hypnotic Phenomena,* gives this summary of Alexis Didier's explanation of the mechanics of his gift: "There passed within him, he wrote, something indefinable, tending to convulse both his nerves and limbs and upsetting his whole interior being. The interior vision of the spirit then became open to endless horizons and later, after this painful sensation had subsided, a feeling of well-being took its place and material obstacles became transparent, so that vision was no longer obstructed. He could without fatigue, transport himself from one side of the earth to the other; talk with Africans, walk about in China, descend Australian mines and even enter the harem of a sultan. The soul only had to wish and it was everywhere; space and time were annihilated and events of centuries became present to the interior vision, so that occurrences long past could be evoked for the purposes of description. For Alexis, lucidity, like mediumship, was not something which could be learnt: it was innate; but once there it could be developed and the power could be intensified. Belief in the soul was essential if lucidity was to be understood. The aim of somnambulism was to demonstrate the powers which primitive man enjoyed and in particular that which the soul will possess when death liberates it from the body" (Didier 1856, p. 15; in Dingwall 1967, pp. 199–200).

Adolphe Didier's abilities matched those of his brother. G. Barth (1853) described some experiences regarding Adolphe's clairvoyance in

The Zoist. Barth was engaged by two aristocratic English army officers to test Adolphe. Barth mesmerised Adolphe, who agreed to try to read unseen pages in a book. One of the officers took a book at random from a shelf, and, holding the book behind him, asked Adolphe to identify it. Adolphe correctly gave the title of the book—*Voyage en Suisse.* The officer then asked Adolphe to read the first four lines on page 27. Barth (1853, p. 409) stated: "Adolphe immediately repeated several sentences in French. On opening the book and turning to page 27, we found that Adolphe had correctly read four lines from the 27th page of a closed book . . . entirely out of all the possible range of natural vision. He then went mentally to a nobleman's residence in one of the midland counties, and described it most accurately even to the pictures and the costumes of the portraits hanging in the dining-hall."

Chauncey Hare Townshend (1853) gave the following account of Adolphe's clairvoyance. Adolphe came to Townshend's room at the Hôtel de l'Ecu at Geneva. Townshend put Adolphe into trance and then asked: "Can you see *a person* whom I know at Lausanne?" He deliberately did not tell the sex of the person. Adolphe, answered, "I shall be able; but you must first lead me to Lausanne by your thoughts." He paused and then continued, "I embark on the steamer. I go up the Lake. The vessel stops at various places. I am now opposite a small town." According to Townshend, this would have been Ouchy. Adolphe, who, according to Townshend had never been to Lausanne, continued, "I get into a boat. I land. I walk up a broad road, up hill. Now I turn to the right. Now I see a house to my right. The house stands in a sort of angle, *between two smaller roads than the one by which I first came.* It is very near the road. I go up steps to the door. I enter a not large vestibule; from this I go into a salon. There is a door open in the salon, which connects it with another room. The two rooms seem to me almost like one large apartment that stretches quite from one end of the house to the other."

"And where is the person who lives in the house?" Townshend asked. "Wait, wait," said Adolphe. "There is no one in the salon. I go up stairs. I see a woman." Townshend asked him to describe her, and Adolphe proceeded to give "a very accurate description" of Townshend's cousin. Townshend noted, "The features, the hair, way of wearing it, etc., were all correct." Adolphe then commented that the woman was wearing something funny on her head. Townshend thought he might be referring to a particular hat his cousin was accustomed to wear when she went horseback riding. But Adolphe insisted it was a "brown net." Townshend thought him mistaken. Adophe continued, exclaiming: "What an odd dress this lady wears! She has the upper and lower part of her dress quite unlike! The upper part is more like a man's—a sort of jacket; then there are skirts of quite another material." Townshend again thought him incorrect. Adolphe then said, "She goes to the window. She looks out anxiously. She is doubting about the weather: ah! she is wishing to go out on horseback. Riding horses is her current passion." Townshend noted: "Here I was indeed struck; for nothing could be more true than this assertion."

Adolphe, feeling somewhat fatigued, asked Townshend to refresh him with some mesmeric passes. He then continued speaking, "I am at a point of time *anterior* to that of which we were just now speaking. I see the same lady in another room—in another house. What I see happened *before* you left Lausanne for Geneva. She sits in a large arm-chair by the fire. *You* are sitting on another chair (*not* an arm-chair) facing her. You are telling her about your going to Geneva; you seem interested; you lean forward in your chair. I see you both perfectly!" According to Townshend, this description was correct in every detail. He especially noted that his cousin's visit to him in Lausanne was accidental: "In passing, she had seen my carriage at the door—had entered to ask where I was going, and had been seated exactly as described while I was speaking of my going to Geneva."

The séance had been witnessed by a Mr. Lawrence. After Adolphe left, Townshend and Lawrence discussed what had happened. Townshend, after telling Lawrence that most of Adolphe's statements were true, added, "I think Adolphe was wrong on some points; namely, about the being able to see from one end of the house to the other, about the brown net and the dress, possibly even about my cousin riding out at all today, for I believe it is not her day for going to the riding-school."

On returning to Lausanne, Townshend related the details of the séance to his cousin, including Adolphe's mistakes. Townshend was surprised to hear his cousin say, "But he was *not* wrong. The day you left Lausanne, I opened the door between my two rooms, to let in the warmth from the stove in the dining room, and so they have remained ever since."

"But, he was wrong about the brown net?" asked Townshend. "Not so! I was putting on a brown net to keep my hair up: I will show it you. I did not wear my wide-awake [hat] that day. Moreover, though *not* my regular day for riding, I went to take a lesson, because the days had just been changed. I also had put on only my jacket, but had my usual dress below it." Townshend asked what time this had taken place. "Between 11 and 12," replied his cousin. That was the exact time that Townshend had been with Adolphe in Geneva.

Bhaktivinoda Thakura and Bishkishin

Bhaktivinoda Thakura (1838–1914) was a prominent figure in the religious history of the Gaudiya Vaishnava sect of India. He was one of the predecessors of my own spiritual master, His Divine Grace A. C. Bhaktivedanta Swami Prabhupada. During much of his adult life, Bhaktivinoda Thakura worked with the British government of India as a magistrate. Before he adopted the honorific spiritual title Bhaktivinoda Thakura, he was known by his birth name Kedarnatha Dutt. In 1870, he was appointed deputy magistrate and collector at the holy town of Puri in the state of Orissa, working under the British commissioner, T. E. Ravenshaw. In 1872, Ravenshaw assigned Bhaktivinoda Thakura to put down a disturbance led by Bishkishin, a leader of the deviant Atibari sect (MacNaughton 1989, p. 110).

Bishkishin, a yogi who displayed some mystic powers, claimed to be an incarnation of Maha Vishnu. In the Vedic cosmology, Maha Vishnu, an expansion of the Supreme Godhead, lies in the Causal Ocean and is the source of numberless material universes, which emerge from His breathing. In essence Bishkishin was claiming to be God. To impress people, he performed many miracles indicating he possessed paranormal powers. MacNaughton, relying on a variety of biographical and autobiographical sources, wrote (1989, p. 112): "He would sit erect in front of a fire and lean into the flames for some time and then return to an erect position without injury. He could read people's minds, instantly cure diseased persons and manifest fire from his head." He also announced that soon he would, as God Himself, kill all the Europeans, thus delivering India from their control.

Bhaktivinoda Thakura went with the district superintendent, the local chief of police, and some constables to confront Bishkishin, who was staying in the jungle near the village of Sharadaipur. Bhaktivinoda Thakura, leaving the constables hiding in the jungle, went forward and found Bishkishin with a crowd of admiring people. Seeing him, Bishkishin inquired, "I know that you are a Bengali and a Magistrate. Why have you come here on this dark night?" Bhaktivinoda Thakura said, "I have come to see you." Bishkishin replied, "That being the case, please sit down and hear my teachings. I am Maha Visnu. Arising from the ocean of milk, I have come to this place, and very soon I will destroy all the Europeans, including the King of England." Bishkishin then began to reveal everything about Bhaktivinoda Thakura, including his name and his purpose in coming. MacNaughton (1989, p. 114) stated, "The *yogi*, in order to impress the Thakura with his power, then called before him many people with incurable diseases, and in a moment made them well.

One person was suffering with a spear wound. The *yogi* brought him under his control and produced some ashes which he smeared on the wound. Immediately the wounded man was well and free of pain."

After conducting further investigations in the surrounding villages, Bhaktivinoda Thakura returned later with one hundred red-turbaned police armed with rifles. Bishkishin asked, "What is the meaning of all this?" Bhaktivinoda Thakura said, "They have come to take you. It is the Governor's order that you should be brought to Puri." Bishkishin retorted, "Who is this Governor? I am king, for I am the Supreme Godhead and master of all the universes. I bow down before no one. Let us see who is able to take me away from this place!" (MacNaughton 1989, p. 115) Bhaktivinoda Thakura replied (MacNaughton 1989, p. 116), "If you do not go peacefully, we will be obliged to take you away by force." Becoming angry, Bishkishin challenged, "I order you to immediately leave this place! Let us see who has the power to take me!"

MacNaughton (1989, p. 116), relying on contemporary accounts, stated, "The yogi shook his head violently, whereupon hundreds and hundreds of fiery flames like burning snakes began to fly out of his matted locks. The yogi's eyes then became bright red and sparks of fire shot out of them. Seeing this, the police force was terrified and fell back apace." Nevertheless, Bhaktivinoda Thakura arrested Bishkishin and took him to the city of Puri on a bullock cart. In Puri, Bishkishin was placed in solitary confinement under heavy guard, day and night. He fasted completely and did not sleep at all. Eventually he was put on trial.

After the sixth day of the trial, Bishkishin threatened Bhaktivinoda Thakura (MacNaughton 1989, p. 118), "You must immediately desist from prosecuting me or everything you have will be destroyed. Go to your home now and see what disaster is taking place there!" When he returned home, Bhaktivinoda Thakura found one of his daughters had suddenly succumbed to severe fever and was falling in and out of consciousness. She later recovered, but Bhaktivinoda Thakura's wife urged him to withdraw from the case against Bishkishin, fearing further actions by the yogi. The day before trial ended, Bishkishin said to Bhaktivinoda Thakura (MacNaughton 1989, p. 119), "The final day of my judgment will be your death!" That night Bhaktivinoda Thakura felt intense pain in his chest, which continued into the morning. Finally, he felt well enough to write the final judgement, and he was carried into the courtroom on a palanquin. He found Bishkishin guilty and sentenced him to a prison term. As Bishkishin was being led out of the courtroom, the district medical officer, Dr. Walters, knowing that yogis sometimes conserve their powers in their hair, cut off his long hair. Having lost his hair, the

Bishkishin collapsed, powerless, and Bhaktivinoda Thakura's chest pains immediately disappeared. In 1873, Bishkishin took poison and died in prison.

The Society for Psychical Research

In 1876, British physicist Sir William Fletcher Barrett, later a Fellow of the Royal Society, read a paper on telepathy to the British Association for the Advancement of Science. Barrett asked that a scientific commission be formed to research such things. Many prominent British scientists dismissed the idea, but Barrett got a favorable response from the physicists Sir William Crookes and Lord Rayleigh. Joined by scholars such as Henry Sidgwick, F. W. H. Myers, and Edmund Gurney, Barrett helped found, in 1882, the Society for Psychical Research (SPR). In 1884, he became the first editor of the Society's journal. During a visit to the United States, he influenced William James and other American scholars to start the American Society for Psychical Research. By 1887 members of the English Society for Psychical Research included Gladstone (a former prime minister), Arthur Balfour (a future prime minister), eight Fellows of the Royal Society (naturalist Alfred Russel Wallace; Cambridge astronomer John Couch Adams; physicist Lord Rayleigh; physicist Oliver Lodge; A. Macalister; mathematician John Venn, inventor of the Venn diagrams; physicist Balfour Stewart; and physicist J. J. Thomson, a discoverer of the electron), two bishops, and the literary figures Alfred Lord Tennyson and John Ruskin. Lewis Carroll, author of *Alice in Wonderland,* was also a member (Gauld 1968, p. 140).

Among the members of the American SPR were many famous American astronomers, including Samuel Pierpont Langley (1834–1906), secretary of the Smithsonian Institution (NASA's Langley Research Center is named after him). Simon Newcomb (1835–1909), a Canadian American astronomer, served as president of the American SPR. He also was a United States Navy admiral and professor of mathematics at the Naval Observatory. Other astronomers who were members of the American SPR were Percival Lowell (1855–1916), Harvard professor of astronomy and founder of the Lowell Observatory in Arizona; Edward C. Pickering (1846–1919), MIT physics professor and Harvard astronomy professor; and William Henry Pickering (1858–1938).

William F. Barrett's Research

In addition to helping found the Society for Psychical Research, Sir William F. Barrett was himself a researcher. One of his earliest experiments took place in Dublin, in the late nineteenth century. Barrett attended a séance, in which the medium was the daughter of a well known photographer. He called her Miss L., and her father, Mr. L. The séance was held in light sufficient for Barrett to see everyone and everything in the room. Present were only Barrett, Miss L., and Mr. L. They sat for some time at the table. Barrett (1918, p. 44) recalled: "We all removed our hands and withdrew a short distance from the table. Whilst the hands and feet of all were clearly visible and *no one touching the table* it sidled about in an uneasy manner. It was a four-legged table, some 4 feet square and heavy. In obedience to my request, first the two legs nearest me and then the two hinder legs rose 8 or 10 inches completely off the ground and thus remained for a few moments; not a person touched the table the whole time. I withdrew my chair further, and the table then moved towards me,—Mr. and Miss L. not touching the table at all,—finally the table came up to the arm chair in which I sat and imprisoned me in my seat. When thus under my very nose the table rose repeatedly, and enabled me to be perfectly sure, by the evidence of touch, that it was quite off the ground and that no human being had any part in this or the other movements. To suppose that the table was moved by invisible and non-existent threads, worked by an imaginary accomplice, who must have floated in the air unseen, is a conjecture which sceptics are at liberty to make if they choose."

In December of 1915, Barrett was introduced by a Dr. Crawford, a lecturer on mechanical engineering at Queen's University, Belfast, to a family, which Barrett described as "highly respectable and intelligent." Crawford had been investigating psychical phenomena taking place among the family members during séances. The medium was the eldest daughter, who was seventeen years old. During the sittings for which Barrett was present, the room was lit by a gas flame in a red lantern. Describing one set of experiences, Barrett (1918, pp. 47–48) stated: "A tin trumpet which had been placed below the table now poked out its smaller end close under the top of the table near where I was sitting. I was allowed to try and catch it, but it dodged all my attempts in the most amusing way; the medium on the opposite side sat perfectly still, while at my request all held up their joined hands so that I could see no one was touching the trumpet . . . Then the table began to rise from the floor some 18 inches and remained so suspended and quite level. I was allowed to go up to the table and saw clearly that no one was touching it, a clear space separating the sitters from the table. I tried to press the table down, and though I exerted all my strength could not do so; then I climbed up on the table and sat on it, my feet off the floor, when I was swayed to and fro and finally tipped off. The table of its own accord now turned upside down, no one touching it, and I tried to lift it off the ground, but it could not be stirred; it appeared screwed down to the floor. At my request, all the sitters' clasped hands had been kept raised above their heads, and I could see that no one was touching the table;—when I desisted from trying to lift the inverted table, it righted itself, again of its own accord, no one helping it. . . . It is difficult to imagine how the cleverest conjurer with elaborate apparatus could have performed what I described."

Myers, Gurney, Podmore, and Apparitions

Frederic Myers, another founder of the Society for Psychical Research, wrote in 1900: "We must recognise that we have more in common with those who may criticise or attack our work with competent diligence than with those who may acclaim and exaggerate it without adding thereto any careful work of their own. We must experiment unweariedly; we must continue to demolish fiction as well as to accumulate truth; we must make no terms with any hollow mysticism, any half-conscious deceit" (Gauld 1968, p. 143). His attitude typified that of his colleagues, who did not fit today's stereotype of psychical researchers as sentimental incompetents.

Myers's personal research centered on the immortality of the conscious self. He gave evidence for this in his two volume study *Human Personality and Its Survival of Bodily Death* (1903). Myers (1903 v.1, p. 24) believed that once we accept the existence of extrasensory perception it naturally will follow, by a progressive chain of evidence and reasoning, that this ability "is exercised by something within us which is not generated from material elements, nor confined by mechanical limitations, but which may survive and operate uninjured in a spiritual world." In *Human Personality*, Myers therefore began his progression of evidence with psychic phenomena such as telepathy, centered in the individual consciousness. He then gave evidence of phantasmal projection—cases in which people see apparitions of living persons. He then moved to death moment apparitions, and then to apparitions or communications with the dead. For each category of phenomenon, Myers gave many well documented examples. For the purposes of the present discussion, which centers on demonstrating the existence in connection with the human organism of a mind element that can act in ways not explained by our current laws of physics, we will concentrate on his evidence for telepathy, phantasmal projections, and death moment apparitions. Evidence for apparitions of the dead and communications with the dead relate more to the existence of a conscious self apart from the body, a topic we will consider in chapter 8. Some of Myers's research into apparitions of the living was carried out with fellow SPR researchers Edmund Gurney and Frank Podmore. Their results were published in *Phantasms of the Living* (Gurney et al. 1886). Let us now consider some representative cases.

Early in the morning of November 2, 1868, in India, Mr. R. V. Boyle had a vivid dream. He was standing in the doorway of a house in Brighton, England. He saw his father-in-law, William Hack, lying on a bed, with his (Hack's) wife standing silently beside him. Boyle was certain that his father-in-law was dead. He woke up briefly. When he slipped again into sleep, he experienced the same dream. He was so struck by the clarity of the dream that he recorded it in his diary. Fifteen days later, Boyle received a telegram from England stating that his father-in-law had died on November 1 at Brighton. William Hack was 72 years old at the time of his death, but there had been no news of any danger to his health received by Boyle or his wife in India. The time of Boyle's dreams in India corresponded to the night of November 1 in England. SPR member Edmund Gurney confirmed Boyle's diary entry (Myers 1903, v.1, pp. 138–139).

On December 18, 1883, M. T. Meneer, principal of Torre College, at Torquay, England, told of an event that had taken place twenty six years before. At that time, his wife's brother, Mr. Wellington, had been living in Sarawak with Sir James Brooke, the British adventurer who became the country's ruler, or Raja. One night, Meneer's wife awoke and told him of a terrifying dream. Meneer stated, "She saw her headless brother standing at the foot of the bed with his head lying on a coffin by his side." Later that night, she had the same dream. After some time, news reached England that Mr. Wellington had been killed and decapitated during a revolt against Brooke by the Chinese in Sarawak, who apparently mistook Mr. Wellington for Brooke's son. The head alone was recovered for burial. Meneer stated, "I computed the approximate time, and found it coincided with the memorable night to which I have referred" (Myers 1903, v.1, pp. 424–425). SPR member Henry Sidgwick interviewed Meneer, who told him that his wife had no reason to suspect her brother would be in any danger (Myers 1903, v. 1, p. 425).

On a Sunday night in November 1881, Mr. S. H. B. attempted to project an image of himself into the presence of two young ladies known to him, Miss L. S. Verity, 25 years old, and Miss E. C. Verity, 11 years old. At the time of the attempt, they were sleeping in their bedroom on the second floor of a house at 22 Hogarth Road, Kensington, in London. Mr. B. was at that time living at 23 Kildare Gardens, about three miles from the house where the girls lived. Mr. B. did not mention his planned experiment to either of the young ladies. In fact, he only decided on it after he had retired on that Sunday night. At one o'clock in the morning, he made his attempt. Mr. B. noted: "On the following Thursday I went to see the ladies in question, and, in the course of conversation (without any allusion to the subject on my part), the elder one told me, that, on the previous Sunday night, she had been much terrified by perceiving me standing by her bedside, and that she screamed when the apparition advanced towards her, and awoke her little sister, who saw me also. I asked her if she was awake at the time, and she replied most decidedly in the affirmative, and upon my inquiring the time of the occurrence, she replied, about 1 o'clock in the morning. This lady, at my request, wrote down a statement of the event and signed it" (Gurney et al. 1886, v. 1, p. 105).

Here is the statement of Miss L. S. Verity, dated January 18, 1883: "On a certain Sunday evening, about twelve months since, at our house in Hogarth Road, Kensington, I distinctly saw Mr. B. in my room, about 1 o'clock. I was perfectly awake and was much terrified. I awoke my sister by screaming, and she saw the apparition herself. Three days after, when I saw Mr. B., I told him what had happened; but it was some time before I could recover from the shock I had received, and the remembrance is too vivid to be ever erased from my memory" (Gurney et al. 1886, v.1, p. 105).

One of the authors of *Phantasms of the Living* carefully interviewed the Verity sisters and learned that Miss L. S. Verity had absolutely no history of hallucinations. He also confirmed her account of the apparition from Miss E. C. Verity. Another sister, Miss A. S. Verity clearly recalled her two sisters telling her of the strange appearance of Mr. B. in their room, in evening dress, at one o'clock. The writer of the report also said of Miss L. S. Verity that "she has no love of marvels, and has a considerable dread and dislike of this particular form of marvel" (Gurney et al. 1886, v. 1, p. 105).

In February of 1850, Mrs. Georgiana Polson was attending an evening party at her home, Woolstone Lodge, in Woolstone, Berkshire, England. She went upstairs to give some instructions to her maid, regarding the duties of another household servant, a girl from Cornwall. Mrs. Polson later recalled, "As I reached the top of the stairs a lady passed me who had some time left us. She was in black silk with a muslin 'cloud' over her head and shoulders, but her silk rustled. I could just have a glance only of her face. She glided fast and noiselessly (but for the silk) past me, and was lost down two steps at the end of a long passage that led only into my private boudoir, and had no other exit. I had barely exclaimed 'Oh, Caroline,' when I felt she was a something unnatural, and rushed down to the drawing-room again, and sinking on my knees by my husband's side fainted, and it was with difficulty I was restored to myself again" (Gurney et al. 1886, v. 2, p. 178). Caroline (Mrs. Henry Gibbs) was a cousin of Mrs. Polson. She had stayed at the Polson house a few days before, and Mrs. Polson had begun writing a letter to her but had not finished it.

The next morning, Mrs. Polson learned that her Cornish maidservant had also seen the apparition. A member of the household informed Mrs. Polson that girl had seen "a lady sitting near her, in black, with white all over her head and shoulders, and her hands crossed on her bosom." The following morning, Mr. Tuffnell, a neighbor residing in Uffington, near Faringdon, came to visit. Upon hearing of the apparition, Mr. Tuffnell wrote an account in his notebook, and advised Mrs. Polson to inquire after her cousin's health. She wrote immediately to an uncle, the Reverend C. Crowley, of Hartpury, near Gloucester, and received a reply that "Caroline is very ill at Belmont and not expected to live." Mrs. Polson later learned that Caroline had in fact died "on the evening she paid me that visit." That was February 16, 1850, as mentioned in an obituary in the *Times* of London (Gurney et al. 1886, v. 1, p. 178).

Upon being interviewed by one of the authors of *Phantasms of the Living,* Mrs. Polson testified that she had not had any hallucinations before or after the apparition of Caroline. At the time of her written testimony, given in 1883, Mrs. Polson was residing at 4 Nouvelle Route de Villefranche, Nice, in France. A governess employed by Mrs. Polson at the time of the apparition testified on January 11, 1884: "Many years ago Mr. and Mrs. Polson, with the children and myself, were sitting one evening in the drawing-room at Woolstone. In the middle of the evening Mrs. Polson left the room, but soon returned; remaining silent, I looked up, and saw her drop down on the rug fainting. When she recovered, she told us she had seen Mrs. Gibbs on before her in the long passage. I recollect hearing that the little Cornish girl said she had seen that same apparition" (Gurney et al. 1886, v. 1, p. 179).

On the night of August 21, 1869, Mrs. James Cox was sitting in her bedroom in her mother's house at Devonport, England. Between the hours of eight and nine o'clock, her nephew, seven years old, came into her room, saying in a frightened voice, "Oh, auntie, I have just seen my father walking around my bed." Mrs. Cox replied, "Nonsense, you must have been dreaming." The boy replied that he had not been dreaming and refused to return to his room. Mrs. Cox placed him in her own bed, where he went to sleep while she stayed up. Mrs. Cox recalled, "Between 10 and 11, I myself retired to rest. I think about an hour afterwards, on looking towards the fireplace, I distinctly saw, to my astonishment, the form of my brother seated in a chair, and what particularly struck me was the deathly pallor of his face. (My nephew was at this time fast asleep.) I was so frightened, knowing that at this time my brother was in Hong Kong, China, that I put my head under the bed clothes. Soon after this I plainly heard his voice calling me by name; my name was repeated three times. The next time I looked, he was gone." The next morning Mrs. Cox told her mother and sister what had happened, and made some notes of the night's events. The next mail from China brought news of her brother's death. He had died August 21, 1869 in Hong Kong. A subsequent official communication from the Admiralty confirmed this. Mrs. Cox wrote her report on December 26, 1883, while at Summer Hill, Queenstown, Ireland. On February 21, 1884, Mr. James Cox responded to queries by one of the authors of *Phantasms of the Living,* confirming, on his wife's behalf, the details of the account given above. Mr. Cox was Secretary to the Naval Commander-in-Chief at Devonport. In another conversation with an author of *Phantasms of the Living,* Mrs. Cox stated that she had never experienced anything similar, before or after the apparition (Gurney et al. 1886, v. 1, pp. 235–236).

Some skeptics attributed such crisis apparitions to chance, inspiring statistical studies which tended to show that crisis apparitions were most likely not simply coincidental. William James, for example, cited studies showing that crisis apparitions occurred in the population at a rate 440 times greater than would be expected by chance (James 1897; in Murphy and Ballou 1960, pp. 35–36). This suggests that the apparitions can be attributed to some power of the mind to receive sensory impressions from distant locations, beyond the scope of ordinary perception.

Aside from researchers working with the SPR, others also documented apparition reports from the same period. The following case of an apparition of a living person is particularly interesting because of its reciprocal nature. In 1863, Mr. S. R. Wilmot was on a ship bound for the United States from Europe. He was sharing a cabin with a friend, W. J. Tait. At night, Wilmot would sleep in the lower berth, and Tait in the upper. The arrangement of the berths was unusual. The upper birth, instead of being located directly above the lower birth, was offset to the rear. One night, Wilmot, while dreaming, saw his wife, dressed in night clothes, enter the room. Wilmot recalled: "At the door she seemed to discover that I was not the only occupant of the room, hesitated a little, then advanced to my side, stooped down and kissed me and after gently caressing me for a few moments, quietly withdrew." The next morning, Tait chided his friend about having a woman come in to visit him at night. His description of what he saw, while awake, matched Wilmot's dream. When Wilmot returned home, his wife asked if he had received a visit from her the previous Tuesday. Wilmot observed such a visit would have been impossible because he had been at sea. His wife replied, "I know it, but it seemed to me that I visited you." She told her husband she had been worried about him, and had felt herself mentally going across the sea until she found the ship. She had then entered his stateroom, and noticed the unusual arrangement of the berths, with one extending back further than the other. She recalled, "A man was in the upper berth looking right at me, and for a moment I was afraid to go in, but soon I went up to the side of your berth, bent down, and kissed you and embraced you and then went away" (Griffin 1997, pp. 225–226).

About these apparition appearances, philosopher David Ray Griffin (1997, p. 211) noted, "Most people reporting them never experience another apparition in their lives; apparitions are not correlated with illness or morbidity on the part of the percipients; and telepathic apparitions are usually visual in nature (in distinction from hallucinations of the insane, which are primarily auditory)."

Sir William Crookes (Physicist)

The observations of Sir William Crookes, a Nobel laureate in physics and a president of the Royal Society, are among the most remarkable in the modern history of psychical research. Some of his observations, made along with Sir Alfred Russel Wallace, have already been noted in chapter 5. Crookes performed many experiments involving the medium Daniel Dunglass Home, who was never detected in fraud.

For one set of experiments with Home, Crookes set up a "balance apparatus." It consisted of a mahogany board (36 inches long by $9^1/_2$ inches wide by 1 inch thick) with a small portion of one end resting on the edge of a table. The rest of the board extended horizontally from the edge of the table, being supported at its other end by a spring balance, which at the board's horizontal position gave a reading of three pounds. Home, sitting in a low chair, lightly placed the tips of his fingers on the end of the board resting on the table, no more than $1^1/_2$ inches from the end of the board. Crookes noted that the other end of the board began to move slowly down and then back up, causing the pointer of the balance to move, and register changes in weight. To insure that Home was not applying any great pressure, Crookes arranged for him to put his fingers on a matchbox placed on the end of the board resting on the table. If Home did apply pressure, the box would be crushed (the box remained intact). During these tests, the balance showed additional weight of from $3^{1}/_{2}$ to 6 pounds. Once Crookes stepped on the end of the board on the table, pressing with the entire force of his whole body, and produced only $1^{1}/_{2}$ to 2 pounds of additional pressure. Also participating in this experiment was William Huggins, a prominent physicist and astronomer, and like Crookes, a Fellow of the Royal Society (Crookes 1871a; in Medhurst and Goldney 1972, pp. 28–29). Crookes then made another arrangement by which no direct muscular pressure at all was applied to the board. The medium's fingers rested in a water container placed on a separate stand just barely in contact with the board. The same results were obtained.

Crookes forwarded an account of the experiments to the Royal Society on June 15, 1871 and requested the secretaries of the Society, Professor Sharpey and Professor Stokes, to come and observe the experiments for themselves. Sharpey refused. Stokes said he would come to look at the apparatus but would not agree to meet the medium or witness experiments. Crookes replied on June 20, again inviting Stokes to witness an actual experiment. Crookes promised that the experiment would be carried out under the most careful scrutiny and that the results, positive or negative, would be published.

Stokes did not attend, but raised some questions about the previous experimental set up. Crookes replied, "It would have required a force of 74.5 lb. to have been exerted by Mr. Home to have produced the results, even if all your suppositions are granted; and, considering that he was sitting in a low, easy chair, and four pairs of sharp, suspicious eyes were watching to see that he exerted no force at all, but kept the tips of his fingers lightly on the instrument, it is sufficiently evident that an exertion of this pressure was impossible" (Crookes 1871b, in Medhurst and Goldney 1972, p. 45). Stokes suggested some of the results were caused by vibrations of vehicles passing by on the street. Crookes answered: "The upward and downward motion of the board and index was of a very slow and delicate character, occupying several seconds for each rise and fall; a tremor produced by passing vehicles is a very different thing from a steady vertical pull of from 4 to 8 lb., lasting for several seconds" (Crookes 1871b; in Medhurst and Goldney 1972, p. 46). In his letter to Stokes, Crookes added: "So many scientific men are now examining these strange phenomena (including many Fellows of the Society), that it cannot be many years before the subject will be brought before the scientific world in a way that will enforce attention" (Crookes 1871b; in Medhurst and Goldney 1972, p. 46).

Home had the ability to make an accordion play tunes while holding it by one hand, on the end opposite the keys. The immediate skeptical doubt is that he was using a trick accordion. To guard against this, Crookes purchased a new accordion, never seen or handled by Home. Another possibility was that Home was somehow using a free hand to manipulate the instrument. To guard against this, Crookes built a special cage, which was placed beneath a table. The accordion was placed inside the cage, and Home was asked to insert one hand into the cage and grasp the end of the accordion opposite the end with the keys. Under these circumstances, the accordion played as usual. Crookes (1871a) then observed: "The accordion was now again taken without any visible touch from Mr. Home's hand, which he removed from it entirely and placed upon the table, where it was taken by the person next to him, and seen, as now were both his hands, by all present. I and two of the others present saw the accordion distinctly floating about inside the cage with no visible support. This was repeated a second time, after a short interval. Mr. Home presently re-inserted his hand in the cage and again took hold of the accordion. It then commenced to play, at first, chords and runs, and afterwards a well-known sweet and plaintive melody, which it executed perfectly in a very beautiful manner. Whilst this tune was being played, I grasped Mr. Home's arm, below the elbow, and gently slid my hand down it until I touched the top of the accordion. He was not moving a muscle. His other hand was on the table, visible to all, and his feet were under the feet of those next to him" (Medhurst and Goldney 1972, p. 27).

At a sitting with Home, Crookes observed writing produced in a mysterious fashion. The sitting took place in the light, at the home of Crookes, and in the presence of friends. Crookes asked for a written message. Here is his description of what happened: "A pencil and some pieces of paper were lying on the centre of the table; presently the pencil rose on its point, and after advancing by hesitating jerks to the paper, fell down. It then rose and fell again. A third time it tried, but with no better result. After this a small wooden lath, which was lying upon the table, slid toward the pencil, and rose a few inches from the table; the pencil rose again, and propping itself against the lath, the two together made an effort to mark the paper. It fell and then a joint effort was again made. After a third trial, the lath gave it up and moved back to its place, the pencil lay as it fell across the paper, and an alphabetic message told us 'We have tried to do as you asked, but our power is exhausted'" (Crookes 1874, p. 93).

Crookes supplied these notes of another séance with Home, on May 22, 1871, attended by himself and Wallace: "The table now rose completely off the ground several times whilst the gentlemen present took a candle, and kneeling down deliberately examined the position of Mr. Home's feet and knees, and saw the three feet of the table quite off the ground. This was repeated, until each observer expressed himself satisfied that the levitation was not produced by mechanical means on the part of the medium or any one else present" (Crookes 1889; in Gauld 1968, p. 214).

Home could not only levitate objects. He himself would often float into the air. Crookes witnessed this three times and was aware of an additional one hundred recorded reports of Home's levitations. About the Home levitation events he witnessed in his own home, Crookes said: "He went to a clear part of the room, and, after standing quietly for a minute, told us he was rising. I saw him slowly rise up with a continuous gliding movement and remain about six inches off the ground for several seconds, when he slowly descended. On this occasion no one moved from their places. On another occasion I was invited to come to him, when he rose 18 inches off the ground, and I passed my hands under his feet, round him, and over his head, when he was in the air. . . . On several occasions Home and the chair on which he was sitting at the table rose off the ground. This was generally done very deliberately, and Home sometimes then tucked up his feet on the seat of the chair and held up his hands in full view of us. On such an occasion I have got down and seen and felt that all four legs were off the ground at the same time, Home's feet being on the chair. Less frequently the levitating power extended to those sitting next to him. Once my wife was thus raised off the ground in her chair" (Carrington 1931, p. 158).

The very credible reports of levitations by Home lend credence to the reports of earlier levitations reports involving Catholic saints. For example, several persons observed levitations by St. Francis of Assisi (c. 1181–1226). Around the year 1261, St. Bonaventure wrote that the radiant St. Francis was sometimes seen lifted off the ground during prayer (Thurston 1952, p. 6). In *The Little Flowers of St. Francis*, we learn that Brother Leo, a member of the Franciscan order, several times saw St. Francis "rapt in God and uplifted from the ground sometimes for the space of three cubits, sometimes of four, and sometimes even to the height of the beech-tree" (Thurston 1952, p. 5). A cubit corresponds to roughly 18 inches.

William James (Psychologist)

William James (1842–1910), one of the founders of modern psychology, was an active member of the American and English branches of the Society for Psychical Research, serving a term as the English SPR's president (1894–1896). Many other key figures in the history of psychology participated in the activities of the SPR. Freud and Jung published articles in its journal and proceedings (Gauld 1968, pp. 338–339). James had a very high opinion of the scientific quality of the publications of the SPR. He said, "Were I asked to point to a scientific journal where hard-headedness and never-sleeping suspicion of sources of error might be seen in their full bloom, I think I should have to fall back on the *Proceedings of the Society for Psychical Research*. The common run of papers, say on physiological subjects, which one finds in other professional organs, are apt to show a far lower level of critical consciousness" (James 1897; in Murphy and Ballou 1960, p. 29).

James's first major investigation into psychic phenomena involved the medium Mrs. Leonora F. Piper. She could provide information about her visitors through a spirit being named Phinuit, who spoke through her when she was in trance. Skeptics proposed she got the information from good detective work or by extracting the information from her visitors by expert psychological methods. After learning of Mrs. Piper through his mother-in-law, James went to her and began a series of experiments. During the years 1885 and 1886, James sent to Mrs. Piper twenty-five people unknown to her, under pseudonyms. Finding that Mrs. Piper was able to give information about the persons that should not have been known to her, James became convinced of the genuineness of her mediumship (Gauld 1968, pp. 251–253).

Richard Hodgson came to America in 1887 to run the American SPR. He was determined to expose Mrs. Piper. Hodgson was from Australia, and there was little chance that Mrs. Piper could know anything about his relatives. Nevertheless, in trance she was able to give information about Hodgson's family, including several deceased members. Hodgson arranged other sittings in 1888 and 1889. To guard against fraud, Hodgson hired detectives. They reported that neither Piper nor her friends or relatives were making suspicious inquiries. Nor were they receiving reports from hired agents. For more experiments, Hodgson and James then sent Mrs. Piper to England. There the researchers chose sitters randomly and introduced them to Mrs. Piper anonymously at the last moment before a sitting. Under these conditions, Mrs. Piper was able to give unexpected information about the sitters and relatives. Back in Boston, she was studied for many more years by Hodgson, who remained convinced of her abilities (Gauld 1968, pp. 254–258). James said in a report: "I am persuaded of the medium's honesty, and of the genuineness of her trance; and although at first disposed to think that the 'hits' she made were either lucky coincidences, or the result of knowledge on her part of who the sitter was and of his or her family affairs, I now believe her to be in possession of a power as yet unexplained" (James 1886–1889; in Murphy and Ballou 1960, p. 97).

But James could also be sympathetic to opposition. "I think," he said (James 1897; in Murphy and Ballou 1960, pp. 39–40), "that the sort of loathing—no milder word will do—which the very words 'psychical research' and 'psychical researcher' awaken in so many honest scientific breasts is not only natural, but in a sense praiseworthy. A man who is unable himself to conceive of any *orbit* for these mental meteors can only suppose that Messrs. Gurney, Myers, & Company's mood in dealing with them must be that of silly marveling at so many detached prodigies. And such prodigies!" Here James emphasizes that scientists need to view psychical phenomena in the context of a theoretical background that can accommodate them. James noted that most critics rejected particular psychical events because they violated their presumption that events in nature always occurred in ways not allowed by the psychical events. But James felt that "the oftener one is forced to reject an alleged sort of fact by the use of this mere presumption, the weaker does the presumption itself get to be; and one might in the course of time use up one's presumptive privileges in this way" (James 1897; in Murphy and Ballou 1960, p. 40). Specifically, James felt that the many telepathic reports from mediums like Piper "subtract presumptive force from the orthodox belief that there can be nothing in anyone's intellect that has not come in through ordinary experiences of sense" (James 1897; in Murphy and Ballou 1960, pp. 40–41).

James believed the ultimate resolution to questions about the reality of psychical phenomena would best be accomplished by "a decisive thunderbolt of fact to clear the baffling darkness." James declared, "For me the thunderbolt *has* fallen." And this thunderbolt was the Piper mediumship. "In the trances of this medium," said James, "I cannot resist the conviction that knowledge appears which she has never gained by the ordinary waking use of her eyes and ears and wits. . . . So when I turn to the rest of the evidence, ghosts and all, I cannot carry with me the irreversibly negative bias of the 'rigorously scientific' mind, with its presumption as to what the true order of nature ought to be" (James 1897; in Murphy and Ballou 1960, p. 41).

In addition to his absolute conviction in the reality of the mental phenomena of mediumship, James was open minded about the phenomena of physical mediumship, such as manifested by Home (i.e. floating accordions). For James, well documented poltergeist phenomena lent credibility to similar events experienced in the presence of mediums. In a presidential address to the Society for Psychical Research, James listed ten credible ghost and poltergeist cases, noting: "In all of these, if memory doesn't deceive me, material objects are said to have been witnessed by many persons moving through the air in broad daylight. Often the objects were multitudinous. . . . I confess that until these records, or others like them, are positively explained away, I cannot feel . . . as if the case against physical mediumship . . . were definitely closed" (James 1896; in Murphy and Ballou 1960, pp. 62–63).

On the subject of occasional cheating by mediums in the production of physical phenomena, James pointed out that "Scientific men themselves will cheat—at public lectures—rather than let experiments obey their well-known tendency towards failure" (James 1911; in Murphy and Ballou 1960, p. 312). James gave several examples of physicists who rigged machines to give the desired results in public demonstrations. James himself confessed to this kind of cheating. Once Professor Newell Martin was giving a demonstration on the physiology of a turtle's heart. A shadow image of a real turtle heart was projected onto a screen for the audience. When the nerves of the heart were stimulated, the heart was supposed to move in certain ways. At a certain point in the demonstration, the heart stopped functioning. James, who was present as an assistant, recalled: "With my forefinger . . . I found myself impulsively and automatically imitating the rhythmical movements which my colleague had prophesied the heart would undergo. . . .To this day the memory of that critical emergency has made me feel charitable towards all mediums who make phenomena come in one way when they won't come easily in another. On the principle of the S.P.R., my conduct on that one occasion ought to discredit everything I ever do, everything, for example, I may write in this article—a manifestly unjust conclusion" (James 1911; in Murphy and Ballou 1960, p. 313). Here James was objecting to the policy of the SPR of not reporting on mediums who were even once implicated in fraud.

James accepted the reality of a wide variety of facts differing from the set of facts considered by ordinary science. This is significant, because the kinds of facts accepted by science to a large extent determine its theories and laws, which establish relationships among these facts. Once science accepts certain categories of facts, and constructs theories and laws based on these facts, and further uses these theories and laws to explain and predict patterns among these facts, it becomes difficult to give serious consideration to facts that have no place in this system. James (1897, in Murphy and Ballou 1960 p. 26) said, "Phenomena unclassifiable within the system are therefore paradoxical absurdities, and must be held untrue." He called the total collection of such absurd facts "the unclassified residuum." James (1897, in Murphy and Ballou, pp. 25–27) observed: "No part of the unclassified residuum has usually been treated with a more contemptuous scientific disregard than the mass of phenomena generally called *mystical*. . . . All the while, however, the phenomena are there, lying broadcast over the surface of history. No matter where you open its pages, you find things recorded under the name of divinations, inspirations, demoniacal possessions, apparitions, trances, ecstasies, miraculous healings and productions of disease, and occult powers possessed by peculiar individuals over persons and things in their neighborhood."

James hoped that future generations of psychologists and anthropologists would carefully study these phenomena "with patience and rigor" and integrate them into a proper theoretical framework, instead of receiving them with "credulity on the one hand and dogmatic denial . . . on the other." He felt it was a "scientific scandal" that this had not yet happened (James 1897; in Murphy and Ballou 1960, p. 31). Indeed, he said, "The most urgent intellectual need which I feel at present is that science be built up again in a form in which such things may have a positive place" (James 1897; in Murphy and Ballou 1960, p. 42).

Unfortunately, it still has not happened. For this reason, James is a principal inspiration for this book, and particularly this chapter, in which I have tried to give a small indication of the actual scope and character of the unclassified residuum of observations related to the question of conscious human existence and origins. Not only much of science but much of religion has turned its back on this unclassified residuum, with unfortunate results for contemporary human consciousness. If this situation is to change, the impetus will most probably come from the world of science, a science that breaks radically with its long flirtation with materialism and once more opens its eyes to the full range of phenomena displayed to rational human inspection.

The ultimate effect of such a change would be recognition of the power of personality as an explanation for factual events. The primary characteristic of modern science is its refusal to consider personal causation of natural effects. James (1897) said, "This systematic denial on science's part of personality as a condition of events, this rigorous belief that in its own essential and innermost nature our world is a strictly impersonal world, may, conceivably . . . prove to be the very defect that our descendants will be most surprised at in our boasted science" (Murphy and Ballou 1960, p. 47). James's prediction is already coming true, and I believe it will be entirely fulfilled in the present century.

Lord Rayleigh (Physicist)

John William Strutt, third Baron Rayleigh (1842–1919), made many important contributions to physics. He studied mathematics at Cambridge, and later became interested in physics. He did most of his work at a private laboratory, which he installed on his family estate. During this time, he corresponded frequently with physicist Jame Clerk Maxwell. In 1871, he married Evelyn Balfour, sister of Arthur James Balfour, later prime minister of England. After the death of Maxwell in 1879, Rayleigh took his chair at Cambridge. He served as President of the Royal Society from 1905 to 1908, and in 1904 he received the Nobel Prize in Physics for his discovery of the element argon.

In 1919, Rayleigh became president of the Society for Psychical Research. His presidential address (Rayleigh 1919; in Lindsay 1970) gives a good summary of his own experiences and his general attitude toward the scientific investigation of the paranormal. Rayleigh began his address by noting the recent death of Sir William Crookes, a fellow Nobel laureate in physics who had also served as president of the Society for Psychical Research from 1896 to 1899. He recalled that his own interest in psychical research, awakened while a student at Cambridge, increased further when he read Crookes's "Notes of an Enquiry into the Phenomena called Spiritual during the years 1870–73." He knew of Crookes's scientific reputation, and thought that such a careful experimenter was well equipped to guard against illusions. This gave credibility to his reports of psychical phenomena.

He thought the séances with the medium Daniel Dunglas Home were particularly credible. Skeptics claimed that Crookes had been deceived, but Rayleigh said, "I found (and indeed still find) it difficult to accept what one may call the 'knave and fool theory' of these occurrences." And it therefore seemed that "one must admit the possibility of much that contrasts strongly with ordinary experience" (Lindsay 1970, p. 231).

Rayleigh, desiring to perform his own experiments, engaged a well known medium, Mrs. Jencken. He invited her to his country house, where she stayed, on a few occasions, a total of fourteen days. Rayleigh's séances with Mrs. Jencken gave some interesting results, but not as astounding as those obtained by Crookes with Home. Rayleigh explained: "Before commencing, the room was searched and the doors locked. Besides Mrs. Jencken, the sitters were usually Lady Rayleigh and myself. Sometimes a brother or a friend came. We sat close together at a small, but rather heavy, pedestal table; and when anything appeared to be doing we held Mrs. Jencken's hands, with a good attempt to control her feet also with ours; but it was impracticable to maintain this full control during all the long time occupied by the séances" (Lindsay 1970, p. 232). Rayleigh noted that paper cutters and other small objects would fly about the room. Most strikingly, lights would appear in the darkened room and drift about. "They might be imitated by phosphorus enclosed in cotton wool," said Rayleigh. "But how Mrs. Jencken could manipulate them with her hands and feet held, and it would seem with only her mouth at liberty, is a difficulty" (Lindsay 1970, p. 233).

"Another incident hard to explain," said Rayleigh (1919), "occurred at the close of a séance after we had all stood up. The table at which we had been sitting gradually tipped over until the circular top nearly touched the floor, and then slowly rose again into the normal position. Mrs. Jencken, as well as ourselves, was apparently standing quite clear of it. I have often tried since to make the table perform a similar evolution. Holding the top with both hands, I can make some, though a bad, approximation; but it was impossible that Mrs. Jencken could have worked it thus. Possibly something better could be done with the aid of an apparatus of hooks and wires; but Mrs. Jencken was a small woman, without much apparent muscular development, and the table for its size is heavy" (Lindsay 1970, p. 233). Rayleigh rejected the idea of hallucination. For one thing, all of the witnesses agreed afterwards on the movements they had observed. Rayleigh witnessed some séances with the Italian medium Eusapia Palladino, about whom we shall have much more to say. His cryptically stated conclusion was: "There is no doubt that she practised deception, but that is not the last word" (Lindsay 1970, p. 235).

Rayleigh, an accomplished experimental scientist, recognized that there was a difference between ordinary physical phenomenon and psychical phenomena, which "cannot be reproduced at pleasure and submitted to systematic experimental control" (Lindsay 1970, p. 236). But he pointed out that in the history of science there were other cases in which rare sporadic phenomena, contradicting standard scientific opinion, eventually came to be accepted as real. He gave the example of meteors. Before early nineteenth century, scientists refused to believe reports of stones falling from the sky. Rayleigh observed: "The witnesses of such an event have been treated with the disrespect usually shown to reporters of the extraordinary, and have been laughed at for their supposed delusions: this is less to be wondered at when we remember that the witnesses of a fall have usually been few in number, unaccustomed to exact observation, frightened by what they both saw and heard, and have had a common tendency towards exaggeration and superstition" (Lindsay 1970, p. 236). But eventually scientists did come to accept the reality of meteorites. Rayleigh stated, "I commend this history to the notice of those scientific men who are so sure that they understand the character of Nature's operations as to feel justified in rejecting without examination reports of occurrences which seem to conflict with ordinary experience" (Lindsay 1970, p. 237).

To his scientific contemporaries, Rayleigh said, "If my words could reach them, I would appeal to serious inquirers to give more attention to the work of this Society, conducted by experienced men and women, including several of a sceptical turn of mind, and not to indulge in hasty conclusions on the basis of reports in the less responsible newspaper press or on the careless gossip of ill-informed acquaintances. Many of our members are quite as much alive to *a priori* difficulties as any outsider can be" (Lindsay 1970, p. 239).

Pierre and Marie Curie

Marie Curie and her husband Pierre Curie are famous for their discoveries in physics, which resulted in two Nobel Prizes for Marie and one for Pierre. But their extensive research into paranormal phenomena is far less well known. In the late years of the nineteenth century, Pierre Curie was investigating the mysteries of ordinary magnetism and simultaneously became aware of the spiritualistic experiments of other European scientists, such as Charles Richet and Camille Flammarion, whose work we shall consider later in this chapter. Pierre Curie initially thought that systematic investigations into the paranormal would help him with some unanswered questions about magnetism (Hurwic 1995, p. 65). He wrote to his fiancée Marie, whom he married in 1895, "I must admit that those spiritual phenomena intensely interest me. I think that in them are questions that deal with physics" (Hurwic 1995, p. 66). Pierre Curie's notebooks from this period show he read many books on spiritualism (Hurwic 1995, p. 68).

Ten years later, Pierre Curie's interests had turned, under the influence of his wife, from magnetism to radioactivity. He again thought that spiritualism might provide some insight into some of the problems of physics, and the couple started going again to séances. Historian Anna Hurwic noted in her biography of Pierre Curie, "He thought it possible to discover in spiritualism the source of an unknown energy that would reveal the secret of radioactivity. For this reason, probably, he used the same experimental methods for studying spiritualism that he used all the time in radioactivity, especially the measure of ionization of atmospheric air in a room. . . . Curie did not go to séances as a mere spectator, and his goal certainly was not to communicate with some spirits. He saw the séances as scientific experiments, tried to monitor the different parameters, took detailed notes of every observation. He was really intrigued by Eusapia Paladino" (Hurwic 1995, p. 247).

About some séances with Eusapia, Pierre Curie wrote to physicist Georges Gouy in a letter dated July 24, 1905 (Hurwic 1995, p. 248): "We had at the Psychology Society a few séances with the medium Eusapia Paladino. It was very interesting, and truly those phenomena that we have witnessed seemed to us to not be some magical tricks—a table lifted four feet above the floor, movements of objects, feelings of hands that pinched you or caressed you, apparitions of light. All this in a room arranged by us, with a small number of spectators all well known and without the presence of a possible accomplice. Cheating would only be possible if the medium had extraordinary abilities as a magician. But how to explain the different phenomena when we are holding her hands and legs, and the lighting of the room is sufficient to see everything going on?"

Curie kept elaborate notes on the séances, which Marie also attended. About a séance on July 6, he wrote, "The table goes four feet in the air for one second, then falls down violently" (Hurwic 1995, p. 249). On April 6, 1906, he noted (Hurwic 1995, p. 250): "Table lifted up four feet . . . complete control [of Paladino] by myself. . . . lateral movements of the table without contact; excellent observation on both sides." Hurwic wrote (1995, p. 250): "We can judge to what extent he was believing in those phenomena by the fact that he thought to include them in his official research program."

On April 14, 1906, Pierre wrote to Georges Gouy: "We are working, M. Curie and me, to precisely dose the radium by its own emanations; it does not seem much work but we have been at it for many months and only now starting to get some results. We had a few new 'séances' with Eusapia Paladino (we already had séances with her last summer). The result is that those phenomena exist for real and I can't doubt it any more. It is unbelievable but it is thus, and it is impossible to negate it after the séances that we had in conditions of perfect monitoring" (Hurwic 1995, pp. 263–264). He then went on to describe how the medium had manifested bodily limbs, in addition to the other phenomena described above. Pierre Curie then told Guoy, "I would like you to witness some séances of this kind and I don't doubt that after a few good séances that you will be also convinced" (Hurwic 1995, p. 264). Like Rayleigh, Curie admitted that the phenomena could not always be reproduced, but he was hopeful that a determined program of research would yield more results. He concluded (Hurwic 1995, p. 264), "There is, according to me a completely new domain of facts and physical states of space of which we presently have no idea," Hurwic herself noted (1995, p. 263), "Coming from an experimental scientist, it is a surprising judgement."

Pierre Curie's interest in spiritualism continued to the time of his death in a road accident on April 19, 1906. Recollecting events on the day before her husband's death, Marie described a talk between French mathematician Jules Henri Poincaré and Pierre: "At one point, Eusapia was the subject of the conversation and the phenomena that she produces. Poincaré was objecting with a sceptical smile, curious of new things, while you (Pierre) were pleading the reality of the phenomena. I was looking at your face while you were talking, and once more I was admiring your nice head, your charming words, enlightened by your smile. It was the last time that I was hearing you express your ideas" (Hurwic 1995, p. 262).

Camille Flammarion (Astronomer)

Camille Flammarion (1842–1925) was a French astronomer, famous for his work on double stars and the topography of Mars. In 1861, he joined the Society for Psychologic Studies, beginning a long career of investigation into paranormal phenomena. In 1870 he was invited to submit a report to the Dialectical Society of London, which had convened a commission to study "phenomena alleged to be spiritual manifestations" (Flammarion 1909, p. 289). In his letter to the commission, Flammarion (1909, p. 302) admitted that investigations into the paranormal were complicated by fraud and the capricious nature of the phenomena. But such investigation was also hampered by those who considered such things impossible. Flammarion said that any scientific investigator free from such prejudice could assure himself of their reality. He himself had verified them through personal observation.

In the second volume of his masterpiece *Death and Its Mystery* (1922), Flammarion documented evidence for apparitions of persons living as well as on the verge of dying. Flammarion (1922, p. 37) explained: "It would seem that we are here concerned with a transmission of *images* by psychic waves between two brains harmoniously attuned, one serving as a wave-transmitter, the other as a receiver."

Flammarion (1922, p. 47) gave the following account of an apparition of a living person. The report originally appeared in English newspapers, including *The Daily News* of May 17, 1905. A member of parliament, Major Sir Carne Raschse, was stricken with influenza, and he could not come to an evening session, although he very much desired to be there to support the government on a crucial vote. Sir Gilbert Parker, a friend, was surprised to see him. Sir Gilbert said, "My gaze fell upon Sir Carne Raschse, seated near his usual place. As I knew that he had been ill, I waved to him in a friendly way, and said: 'I hope you are better.' But he gave me no sign of recognition, which greatly astonished me. His face was very pale. He was seated, his head resting, motionless, on one hand; the expression of his face was impassive and hard. For a moment I wondered what I had better do; when I again turned toward him, he had disappeared. I regretted this, and at once went to seek him, hoping to find him in the vestibule. But Raschse was not there, and no one had seen him." Sir Arthur Hayter claimed also to have seen Raschse, pointing him out to Sir Henry Bannerman. Flammarion (1922, p. 48) noted that Raschse himself "did not doubt that he had really gone in spirit to the House, for he had been extremely preoccupied with the thought of attending the session for a debate which interested him particularly."

Another example given by Flammarion (1922, p. 87) concerned an English physician, Dr. Rowland Bowstead. Once, when playing cricket, he and another player followed a ball to a hedge. On the other side, he saw his brother-in-law dressed in hunting clothes and carrying a gun. He smiled and waved to Dr. Bowstead. But his friend saw nothing. And when Bowstead looked again, he could not see his brother-in-law. Depressed, he went to his uncle's house and told him what he had seen. It was ten minutes past one. Bowstead stated: "Two days afterward I got a letter from my father, telling me of the death of my brother-in-law, which had occurred at precisely that time. His death came about in a curious way. The morning of that very day, since he was feeling fairly well, after an illness, he had declared that he was able to go hunting. Then, having taken up his gun, he had turned toward my father and had asked him if he had sent for me. My father having answered in the negative, he had flown into a rage, and had said that he would see me, in spite of everything. Suddenly he fell down as though struck by lightning, a blood-vessel in his lungs having burst. He was wearing at that time a hunting-costume and had a gun on his arm, exactly as in the apparition that had startled me."

On November 10, 1920, Monsieur Agniel, a member of the Morocco branch of the Astronomical Society of France, wrote to Flammarion about an eclipse of the sun that had occurred on that day. He added to his letter an account of a telepathic experiment. In 1906, Agniel was living in Nice. He decided to pay a surprise visit to his sister in Nimes. Because his sister liked orange blossoms, Agniel brought some with him on the train. Agniel wrote: "Alone in my compartment, I tried an experiment while the train was rushing along at full speed between

Golfe-Juan and Cannes. Concentrating my thoughts on the flowers and then closing my eyes, I sent myself, mentally, into my sister's room in Nimes, and spoke to her thus: 'I am arriving. I am coming to see you and to bring you the flowers you love.' I imagined myself at the foot of her bed, showing her my bunch of flowers, of which I formed a mental image" (Flammarion 1922, pp. 98–99). When he met his sister the next morning, she said, "It's very odd. I dreamed last night that you were coming, and that you were bringing me orange-blossoms!" (Flammarion 1922, p. 99).

In the third volume of *Death and Its Mystery*, Flammarion (1923) gave reports of apparitions that took place just before the death of the transmitting person. One such report was published in the year 1905 in the journal *Luce e Ombra*. In 1882, two Italian army officers made a pact. If one of them were about to die, he would signal this to his comrade by mentally tickling his feet. On August 5, 1888 one of the officers, Count Charles Galateri, was in bed with his wife, who suddenly said to him, "Don't tickle my feet." Galateri said he was not doing any such thing, but his wife continued to feel the tickling. Thinking it might be an insect, they got a candle and searched under the covers, but found nothing. Shortly thereafter, as they again tried to go to sleep, the Countess Galateri exclaimed, "Look! Look at the foot of the bed!" The Count saw nothing. The Countess said, "Yes, look; there's a tall young man, with a colonial helmet on his head. He's looking at you, and laughing! Oh, poor man! What a terrible wound he has in his chest! And his knee is broken! He's waving to you, with a satisfied air. He's disappearing!" The Countess told friends and relatives about the incident the next day. Over a week later, on August 14, the newspapers announced that Lt. Virgini, the Count's old friend, had died during an Italian army action in Ethiopia. He had first been wounded in the knee and then struck by a bullet in his chest (Flammarion 1923, p. 59).

Could such apparition reports be explained by chance? Flammarion (1922, p. 167) thought not: "In 'Les Hallucinations télepathiqués' Monsieur Marrillier has made, on his own account, certain calculations, from which it appears that the part played by chance is reduced . . . for visual hallucinations to $1/40,000,000,000,000$; that is to say, in forty trillion visual hallucinations there would be only one that could be explained by *chance coincidence*. Plainly, this reduces the hypothesis of chance to a number equivalent to zero."

Flammarion believed that some kind of vibration was transmitted from the dying person to a sympathetic person, whose organism converted the vibration into a perception, just as a radio receiver converts electromagnetic waves into sound. Flammarion (1922, p. 369) said: "All these observations prove that a human being does not consist only of a body that is visible, tangible, ponderable, known to every one in general, and to physicians in particular; it consists, likewise, of a psychic element that is imponderable, gifted with special, intrinsic faculties, capable of functioning apart from the physical organism and of manifesting itself at a distance with the aid of forces as to the nature of which we are still ignorant. This psychic element is not subject to the every-day restrictions of time and space." In my system, this psychic element would correspond to the mind element.

Like the Curies, Flammarion participated in extensive research with Eusapia Palladino. His first séance with her took place on July 27, 1897, in the home of the Blech family in Paris. A light-colored curtain had been stretched across one corner of the room, forming a "cabinet." Inside the cabinet were a small sofa, a guitar, and a chair, upon which had been placed a bell and music box. The cabinet had been set up at the request of Eusapia, who explained that such conditions were necessary for the effects. Flammarion would have preferred that the cabinet not be used, but noted that in every scientific experiment certain conditions may be required. "He who would seek to make photographs without a dark chamber would cloud over his plate and obtain nothing. The man who would deny the existence of electricity because he had been unable to obtain a spark in a damp atmosphere would be in error. He who would not believe in the existence of stars because we only see them at night would not be very wise" (Flammarion 1909, p. 68). Although he accepted the conditions, as requested by the medium, Flammarion (1909, p. 68) said, "In accepting these conditions, the essential point is not to be their dupe." Accordingly, Flammarion carefully examined the cabinet and the entire room, making sure that there were no concealed mechanisms, batteries, or wires in the floor or walls. Before the séance, in order to detect anything suspicious upon Eusapia, Madame Zelma Blech, whose integrity Flammarion considered beyond question, carefully undressed and dressed her.

The sitting was carried out in various conditions of lighting, ranging from full light to dim red light. Eusapia sat outside the curtain, with her back to it. A rectangular wooden table, weighing fifteen pounds, was placed in front of her. Flammarion examined the table carefully, and found nothing suspicious. Flammarion and another participant carefully controlled the hands and feet of the medium. Each held one of the medium's hands with one hand and placed a foot on one of the medium's feet. In addition, Flammarion placed his other hand upon the medium's knees. The room was fully lighted by a kerosene lamp and two candles.

Flammarion (1909, p. 70) reported, "At the end of three minutes the table begins to move, balancing itself, and rising sometimes to the right, sometimes to the left. A minute afterwards it is *lifted entirely from the floor*, to a height of about nine inches, and remains there two seconds." Several other levitations took place in this session, causing Flammarion (1909, p. 70) to conclude, "It seems that an object can be lifted, in opposition to the law of gravity, without the contact of the hands which have just been acting upon it." Then a round table a small distance away, to Flammarion's right, spontaneously moved into contact with the table that had risen into the air. Flammarion said that it appeared as if the round table was trying to climb onto the rectangular table. It then fell over. This took place in full light. The medium then signaled for less light. The two candles were put out, and the kerosene lamp was turned down somewhat, but there was still enough light for Flammarion and the other witnesses to see everything that was happening in the room. The round table, which Flammarion had set upright again, repeatedly made movements suggesting it was trying to climb onto the rectangular table. Flammarion (1909, p. 71) tried to push the table down, but it resisted. He determined that the medium was not responsible for the round table's movements.

The medium demanded less light. The kerosene lamp was turned off and a lamp of the kind used in photography dark rooms was turned on. It provided a dim red light, enough for the witnesses to see what was happening in the room. Many unusual occurrences took place, among which I consider the following to be the most significant. First of all the music box sounded behind the curtain, as if someone was turning its handle. As this was happening, the medium's hands and feet were being carefully controlled by Flammarion and another witness (de Fontenay). Eusapia moved the hand held by de Fontenay, and guiding the finger of de Fontenay, touched the finger to Flammarion's cheek and moved it in circles, as if turning the handle of the music box. When she stopped, the music box stopped playing; when she moved the finger again, the music box again played. According to Flammarion (1909, p. 72), the soundings and silences of the music box exactly matched the movements and stoppings of the finger on his cheek.

As I write this summary of what happened at the séance, I find myself desiring to leave certain things out. They seem too incredible to me, too unbelievable. But I shall resist that impulse. A small round table moved toward the table at which the party was sitting, and then it rose onto the table top. The sitters heard the guitar sounding behind the curtain and moving around. It emerged from the cabinet, floated toward the sitters, rose onto the tabletop, and then rose onto the shoulder of de Fontenay. From there it rose into the air above the sitters, emitting sounds. Flammarion (1909, p. 73) noted: "The phenomenon lasts about fifteen seconds. It can readily be seen that the guitar is floating in the air, and the reflection of the red lamp glides over its shining surface." Flammarion (1909, p. 74) also observed another striking movement of a large object: "Later, the chair within the cabinet moves out and takes up a position near Mrs. Blech. It then rises up and rests on top of Mrs. Blech's head."

After the séance at the Blech's, Flammarion held eight séances with Eusapia at his own home. Flammarion (1909, p. 85) said, "Before every séance Eusapia was undressed and dressed again in the presence of two ladies charged with seeing that she did not hide any tricking apparatus under her clothes." Arthur Levy, who came with an attitude of distrust and skepticism, gave an account of the séance of November 16, 1897. Levy examined the room, paying special attention to the cabinet, formed by hanging curtains across one corner of the room. He determined that there were no mechanisms therein and no ways to enter or leave the cabinet area except through the curtains, which were always in sight during the séance. The five sitters and the medium sat at a rectangular white table in front of the curtain. Some musical instruments were placed in the cabinet.

One of the sitters placed on the table a scale for weighing letters. Eusapia put her hands four inches from each side of the instrument and caused the scale to move. Levy noted: "Eusapia herself asked us to convince ourselves, by inspection, that she did *not* have a hair leading from one hand to the other, and with which she could fraudulently press upon the tray of the letter-weigher. This little display took place when all the lamps of the salon were fully lighted" (Flammarion 1909, p. 88).

Levy and George Mathieu controlled the hands and feet of the medium. The sitters rested their hands on the table. "In a few moments," observed Levy, "it begins to oscillate, stands on one foot, strikes the floor, rears up, wholly into the air,—sometimes twelve inches, sometimes eight inches, from the ground . . . All this in full light" (Flammarion 1909, p. 88). Eusapia asked for less light, complaining that the brightness was hurting her eyes. The lamp was moved some distance away, and was placed on the floor behind a piano. But there was still sufficient light for the sitters to see what was happening. A tambourine and violin were thrown out of the cabinet onto the table. Levy took the tambourine in his hand, and an invisible personality tried to wrest it from his grasp, cutting Levy's hand in the process. The table shook violently. An accordion was thrown from the cabinet onto the table. Levy said, "I seize it by its lower half and ask the Invisible if he can pull it out by the other end so as to make it play. The curtain comes forward, and the bellows of the accordion is methodically moved back and forth, its keys are touched, and several different notes are heard" (Flammarion 1909, p. 90). Eusapia called for the sitters to join hands with her in a chain. Eusapia then cast an inflamed look at a large sofa, which then, according to Levy, marched up to the table. Eusapia looked at the sofa "with a satanic smile" and then blew upon it, whereupon it went back to its place.

The paranormal effects continued. Levy said: "The tambourine rose almost to the height of the ceiling; the cushions took part in the sport, overturning everything on the table; M.M. [Mr. Mathieu] was thrown from his chair. This chair—a heavy dining-room chair of black walnut, with stuffed seat—rose into the air, came up on the table with a great clatter, then was pushed off. Eusapia seems shrunken together and is very much affected. We pity her. We ask her to stop. 'No, no!' she cries. She rises, we with her; the table leaves the floor, rises to a height of twenty-four inches, then comes clattering down" (Flammarion 1909, pp. 91–92). Soon thereafter, the séance, which lasted two hours, ended. Levy stated: "We took every precaution not to be the dupes of complicity, of fraud . . . And when, on looking back, doubts begin to creep into the mind, we must conclude that, given the conditions in which we were, the chicanery necessary to produce such effects would be at least as phenomenal as the effects themselves. How shall we name this mystery?" (Flammarion 1909, p. 92)

Mrs. Flammarion recorded the results of the séance held on November 19. The room was lit dimly by a night lamp set some distance from the table. Two of the sitters, Mr. Brisson and Mr. Pallotti, were controlling the medium. Mrs. Flammarion and Mrs. Brisson were sitting some yards away from the table, facing Eusapia. The curtain behind Eusapia began to move. "And what do I see?" said Mrs. Flammarion. "The little table on three feet, and leaping (apparently in high spirits) over the floor, at the height of about eight inches, while the gilded tambourine is in its turn leaping gayly at the same height above the table, and noisily tinkling its bells" (Flammarion 1909, pp. 126–127). Mrs. Flammarion drew the attention of Mrs. Brisson to this event. "And then," she wrote, "the table and the tambourine begin their carpet-dance again in perfect unison, one of them falling forcibly upon the floor and the other upon the table" (Flammarion 1909, p. 127). On November 21, Flammarion and the other sitters saw a book move through the curtain. Flammarion noted (1909, pp. 129–130): "The book went through the curtain without any opening, for the tissue of the fabric is wholly intact." Flammarion's wife, who was looking behind the curtain saw the book enter the cabinet through the curtain, while outside the cabinet, said Flammarion, the book "disappeared from the eyes of the persons who were in front, notably M. Baschet, M. Brisson, M. J. Bois, Mme. Fourton and myself. . . . Collective hallucination? But we were all in cool blood, entirely self-possessed."

In his books on psychical research, Flammarion included the results of the investigations of others. In 1891, the prominent Italian psychiatrist Cesare Lombroso, on hearing of Eusapia's phenomena, went to Naples to experience them for himself. Six sitters participated in a séance. The room was lit by candles. Lombroso and another sitter controlled Eusapia. Levitations of the table occurred. Further séances were held, giving positive results (Flammarion 1909, pp. 142–146).

Acting upon the testimony of Professor Lombroso, a commission of scientists conducted seventeen séances with Eusapia in Milan. The group included the astronomer Giovanni Schiaparelli (director of the Milan Observatory), the physicist Giuseppe Gerosa, and the Nobel laureate physiologist Dr. Charles Richet of Paris. Lombroso was present for some of the experiments. The experimenters signed a report testifying to the reality of the phenomena (Flammarion 1909, p. 151). Complete levitations of a large table were observed several times. On these occasions, the medium was carefully controlled, her hands being held by the participants sitting next to her, who also kept her feet under theirs and their knees pressed against hers, so as to detect any movement. Here are observations of table levitations from the signed report: "At the end of several minutes the table makes a side movement, rises first to the right, then to the left, and finally mounts off of its four feet straight into the air, and lies there horizontally (as if it were floating on a liquid), ordinarily at a height of from 4 to 8 inches (in exceptional cases from 24 to 27 inches); then falls back and rests on its four feet. It frequently remains in the air for several seconds, and while there also makes undulatory motions, during which the position of the feet under the table can be thoroughly examined" (Flammarion 1909, p. 154). The researchers concluded that the conditions they imposed ruled out various possible deceptions, for example hidden rods or supports that the medium might have introduced.

The joint report of the participants recorded several instances of the spontaneous movement of objects, without the touch of any person present. The report stated: "A remarkable instance occurred in the second séance, everything being *all the time in full light*. A heavy chair, weighing twenty-two pounds, which stood a yard from the table and behind the medium, came up to M. Schiaparelli, who was seated next to the medium. He rose to put it back in its place; but scarcely was he seated when the chair advanced a second time toward him" (Flammarion 1909, p. 156). The researchers also noted the movement of objects through the air. To prevent the medium from surreptitiously using her hands, they were securely tied to the hands of her controllers (Flammarion 1909, pp. 157–159). On two occasions the medium herself levitated to the top of the table, seated on her chair while her hands were being held by her controllers. In the first case, the controllers were Richet and Lombroso, who according to the report "are sure they did not assist her in this ascension." During the medium's descent from the table, the controllers were Finzi and Richet, who according to the report were "following her movements without at all assisting them" (Flammarion 1909, pp. 159–160).

Charles Richet (Physiologist)

In 1913, Charles Robert Richet, professor of physiology at the University of Paris, won the Nobel Prize in medicine and physiology for his pioneering work in immunology. His interest in the occult began with hypnotism. After seeing a stage performance, he performed his own experiments. He then became interested in clairvoyance, and published an article on the statistical validity of extrasensory perception (Richet 1884). His studies involved people correctly naming playing cards turned over by another person beyond their sight. The results were beyond those that could be expected by chance. Richet persuaded his friend, Jean Meyer, a wealthy industrialist, to establish a society for the impartial scientific investigation of psychical phenomena. It was formed in 1919 as the Institut Métapsychique. Richet believed that just as chemistry had emerged from alchemy, a new science of the mind would emerge from metapsychology. Richet summarized the results of his studies in his book *Thirty Years of Psychical Research* (1923).

According to Richet, there are two kinds of metapsychic phenomena—objective and subjective. The objective phenomena comprise physical objects moving under the influence of psychic forces. The subjective phenomena comprise purely mental manifestations, such as remote vision. Richet noted (1923, pp. 4–5): "The forces that govern presentiments, telepathy, movements of objects without contact, apparitions, and certain mechanical and luminous phenomena do not seem to be blind and unconscious forces . . . They have none of the fatality that attaches to the mechanical and chemical reactions of matter. They appear to have intellectuality, will, and *intuition*, which may not be human, but which resemble human will and intention. Intellectuality—the power of choice, intention, and decision conformably to a personal will—characterizes all metapsychic phenomena."

Richet performed experiments in telekinesis with Eusapia Palladino. He attended over one hundred of her séances (Richet 1923, p. 412). Richet (1923, p. 413) noted: "All the men of science, without exception, who experimented with her were in the end convinced that she produced genuine phenomena." He admitted that on occasion she would try to cheat, if allowed. But Richet regarded it as the responsibility of the investigators to insure that she did not cheat. In his own experiments, Richet did take such precautions. "At the moment in an experiment when a movement without contact was about to take place," wrote Richet (1923, p. 413), "Eusapia gave warning that a phenomena was coming, so that these did not occur unexpectedly. The full attention of the observers was awakened and all possible precautions could be taken at the fateful moment that no trickery should be possible. Professors of legerdemain do the exact opposite, and endeavour to distract attention at the critical moment of their tricks." Primarily, investigators took care to control Eusapia's hands and feet, to make sure that she was not using them to produce the effects observed in her presence—usually the movement of objects in the room.

In 1893 and 1894, ethologist Henryk Siemiradzki (1843–1902) and philosopher Julian Ochorowicz (1850–1917) conducted experiments with Eusapia in Rome. Richet was present for these experiments. "While Eusapia's hands were held, a hand-organ floated over the table, sounding all the while as if the handle were being turned," wrote Richet (1923, p. 416). Ochorowicz made further investigations. While Eusapia's hands and feet were carefully held and controlled, interesting psychokinetic effects were observed. Richet (1923, p. 416) wrote, "In light, dimmed, but still quite sufficient to enable the experimenters to distinguish forms, the table rose horizontally three times into the air."

The most significant of Richet's reports are about the sessions with Eusapia at his house at Ribaud Island. On this small island in the Mediterranean, Richet had a vacation home. The only other residents of the island were a lighthouse keeper and his wife. Richet invited Ochorowicz to join him. "For three months we experimented three times a week, and continually verified, fully, movements of objects without contact and other phenomena," wrote Richet (1923, pp. 416–417).

Richet then invited Frederick Myers and the physicist Oliver Lodge to join them. Richet (1923, p. 417) included in his book the following summary statement by Lodge: "A chair placed near the window, several feet distant from the medium, slid along, rose up, and struck the floor. The medium was held and no person was near the chair. I heard some notes on an accordion placed not far from us. A musical box was floated through the air and carried above our heads. The key was turned in the lock of the door, laid on the table, and again replaced in the lock; a heavy table (forty-eight pounds) was raised eight inches off the floor, the medium standing up and placing her hands lightly on one corner of the table."

The reports from Ribaud Island were upsetting to SPR member Henry Sidgwick, who wrote in a letter to James Bryce Sidgwick, on August 8, 1894: "A crisis is impending. Three chief members of our group of investigators: F. Myers, O. J. Lodge, and Richet, (Professor of Physiology in Paris) have convinced themselves of the truth of the physical phenomena of Spiritualism . . . we have read the notes taken from day to day of the experiments, and it is certainly difficult to see how the results recorded can have been produced by ordinary physical means . . . At the same time as the S.P.R. has now for some years acquired a reputation for comparative sanity and intelligence by detecting and exposing the frauds of mediums; and as Eusapia's 'phenomena' are similar [in] kind to the frauds we have exposed, it will be a rather sharp turn in our public career if our most representative men come forward as believers" (Gauld 1968, p. 230).

To check Eusapia's phenomena, Mr. and Mrs. Henry Sidgwick, along with Lodge, then went to Richet's chateau at Carqueiranne, near Toulon. There the researchers also witnessed phenomena under conditions that ruled out deception. Objects such as a melon and a small wicker table floated from behind the medium onto the table around which the researchers were seated. The researchers also felt mysterious touches and saw manifestations of hands. They also heard notes sounding on a piano, which was apparently out of reach of the medium (Gauld 1968, p. 231). But some SPR members retained doubts.

To settle the matter, Eusapia was brought to Myers's house at Cambridge. There she gave an impromptu demonstration to Myers and his wife. Myers noted that it was still light outside when the sitting took place, in the early evening of July 31, 1895. Myers stated: "Under these circumstances the table rose in the air with all feet off the ground five or six times during about ten minutes . . . On each occasion it appeared to us that no known force cd. [could] have raised & sustained the table as we in fact saw it raised & maintained" (Gauld 1968, p. 235). Altogether, Eusapia held twenty sittings at Myers's house. In attendance at least once were many prominent researchers, including Lord Rayleigh, J. J. Thomson, Francis Darwin, the Maskelynes (magicians), Richet, and Lodge. The usual phenomena were reported (Gauld 1968, p. 235).

The researchers then invited Richard Hodgson to come from America. He arrived in time for the last seven of the sittings. Hodgson, very suspicious of Eusapia, decided that she must be using trickery. To see if he could catch her he decided to relax the stringent controls. He found that on some occasions Eusapia, if allowed, would manage to get a hand free by tricking two controllers into accepting the same one. This led Hodgson and others to conclude that all the Cambridge phenomena were fraudulent (Gauld 1968, p. 238).

Other investigators objected. It was always known that Eusapia might in some cases cheat, if the opportunity presented itself and she were feeling out of sorts, as had been the case in England. According to them, Hodgson had set up a situation that encouraged and allowed Eusapia to cheat (Gauld 1968, p. 239). Eusapia's supporters pointed out that the kinds of tricks Hodgson detected were not sufficient to explain more than a small fraction of her phenomena (Gauld 1968, p. 240).

A full account of the Cambridge sittings was not published. Henry Sidgwick, in the *Journal of the Society for Psychical Research* (April 1896) explained: "It has not been the practice of the S.P.R. to direct attention to the performances of any so-called 'medium' who has been proved guilty of systematic fraud . . . In accordance, therefore, with our established custom, I propose to ignore her performances for the future, as I ignore those of other persons engaged in the same mischievous trade" (Gauld 1968, p. 240). Myers, on learning of more reports on Eusapia from the Continent, wanted to start a new series of tests, but Sidgwick refused to sanction them. Richet, however, continued his own experiments and became absolutely convinced of Eusapia's phenomena (Gauld 1968, p. 241).

Late in 1898, Richet convinced Myers to come to France for some experiments. Myers was present at two sessions, which took place on December 1 and December 3, at Richet's house in Paris. Also present were Theodore Flournoy (a Swiss psychologist), the Duc and Duchesse de Montebello (the French ambassador to Russia and his wife), and Emil Boirac (a paranormal researcher). The first sitting had good light—a lamp turned low, a fire, and moonlight. All details of Eusapia's dress and hands were visible. Her hands were placed far apart, both visible on the table, while an observer under the table held both of her feet. In other words, there was good control and visibility. A zither had been placed in a curtained-off window recess. The window itself was shuttered and bolted shut. The researchers noted movements of the zither and heard it play. The zither emerged from behind the curtain and moved to a position behind the researchers, so that the researchers were sitting between the floating zither and Eusapia. The zither played again and came over Myers's shoulder and descended onto the table (Gauld 1968, pp. 241–242). Similar phenomena occurred at the second sitting. Myers, now again convinced about Eusapia, wanted to publish. But at this time Hodgson was the editor of the SPR *Journal* and *Proceedings*. He would not publish any substantial report, just a brief letter from Myers, stating that recent investigations had led him to renew his faith in Eusapia (Gauld 1968, p. 242).

Investigations continued. At the Psychological Institute of Paris, a group of scientists, including Richet, carried out a long series of experiments with Eusapia (43 séances in all), during the years 1905–1907. According to Richet (1923, p. 420) the experiments yielded positive demonstrations of telekinesis. These are the experiments in which the Curies participated as members of an investigating committee. Other members of the committee included the philosopher Henri Bergon, Richet himself, and the physicist Jean Baptiste Perrin, who like the Curies won a Nobel Prize in physics. Bergson won a Nobel Prize in literature. So there were at least five Nobel laureates in the committee that investigated Eusapia Palladino. After the years of study, the committee issued a favorable report, which included observations such as this: "The two hands, feet and knees of Eusapia being controlled, the table is raised suddenly, all four feet leaving the ground; then two and again four feet; Eusapia closes her fists, and holds them towards the table, which is then completely raised from the floor five times in succession, five raps also being given. It is again completely raised, while each of Eusapia's hands is on the head of a sitter. It is raised to the height of one foot from the floor and suspended in the air for several seconds while Eusapia kept her hand on the table and a lighted candle was placed under the table; it was completely raised to a height of ten inches from the floor and suspended in the air for four seconds, M. Curie only having his hand on the table, Eusapia's hand being placed on top of his. It was completely raised when M. Curie had his hand on Eusapia's knees and Eusapia had one hand on the table and the other on M. Curie's head, her two feet tied to the chair on which she was sitting" (Carrington 1931, p. 135).

Richet was also favorably impressed with a series of experiments carried out with Eusapia in Naples. In 1908, Everard Feilding, present at the Cambridge séances, joined Hereward Carrington, and W. W. Baggally, a magician and skeptic, for some experiments with Eusapia in Naples. Carrington, a magician and author of a book exposing fraudulent mediums, gave his summary impressions of the Naples experiments: "In November and December, 1908, Mr. Everard Feilding and Mr. W. Baggally and myself held ten séances in our rooms at the hotel under perfect conditions of control, and we were convinced that authentic metapsychic phenomena were produced that no trickery could account for" (Richet 1923, p. 420).

The sittings were held in rooms rented by Carrington and his fellow investigators at the Hotel Victoria in Naples. The researchers carefully searched the rooms before the sittings. When Eusapia came, she herself was carefully searched, to insure there was nothing suspicious on her person or in her clothing. The rooms were on the fifth floor of the hotel, and the windows opened onto the street side of the building. After Eusapia entered the room chosen for the sitting, the door and windows were carefully locked and bolted. There was no possibility that any confederates could have entered. The researchers set up a "cabinet" by hanging two thin black curtains across a corner of the room. Upon a small table in the cabinet, the researchers placed objects such as a bell, guitar, and toy piano. The cabinet was inspected before each sitting, and several times during each sitting (Carrington 1931, pp 213–214). The researchers carefully controlled Eusapia's hands and feet, sometimes tying her to her chair at a table near the cabinet. Carrington (1931, p. 215) noted that "all three of the investigators were fully aware of all the methods of trickery employed by mediums in order to release their hands, feet, etc., and were fully prepared to detect it, should trickery of this kind exist." The researchers recorded levitations of a table and inexplicable movement of objects from the cabinet (Richet 1923, p. 420).

From 1909 to 1910 sittings were held in New York under the supervision of Carrington. The usual phenomena occurred under carefully controlled circumstances. Carrington (1931, p. 210) observed a table floating out of a curtained enclosure, noting that this happened "in a light sufficiently good to see that the medium was not touching it." The table rose four feet in the air, bounced five times against a wooden partition set up in the room, and then turned upside down and fell to the floor. While this was happening, Eusapia was being carefully controlled, with some experimenters holding her hands while Carrington was holding her feet with his hands.

During one of the New York sittings, the experimenters heard a mandolin playing inside the curtained enclosure. The striking of the strings was coordinated with the movements of Eusapia's fingers on the hands of one of the experimenters. Carrington (1931, p. 211) stated: "The mandolin then floated out of the cabinet, on to the séance table, where in full view of all, nothing touching it, it continued to play for nearly a minute—first one string and then another being played upon." During this demonstration, Eusapia was carefully controlled, her hands tightly gripped by the experimenters.

On another occasion the experimenters placed a flutelike musical instrument on a table in the curtained-off enclosure in the room. Suddenly the instrument appeared floating in front of the face of one of the experimenters. Carrington (1931, p. 211) stated: "No one saw how it got into its present position; but there it was, suspended in space, about five feet from Eusapia, and certainly too far for her to reach."

Carrington reported that he had often seen a wooden stool follow the movements of Eusapia's hand, moving forward, backwards, and from side to side. "During its various movements I repeatedly passed my hand and arm between her hand and the stool, showing that no threads, hairs, wires, etc., were utilized for purposes of its manipulation," said Carrington (1931, p. 121). He reported that sometimes Eusapia transferred the power to him by touching him, and that at such times the stool followed the movements of his hand, until Eusapia removed her hand from him.

Richet himself concluded (1923, p. 421): "I have insisted on the phenomena of telekinesis produced by Eusapia because there have perhaps never been so many different, skeptical, and scrupulous investigators into the work of any medium or more minute investigations. During twenty years, from 1888 to 1908, she submitted, at the hands of the most skilled European and American experimentalists, to tests of the most rigorous and decisive kind, and during all this time men of science, resolved not to be deceived, have verified that even very large and massive objects were displaced without contact."

Margaret Mead (Anthropologist)

Margaret Mead (1901–1978), a prominent American anthropologist, endorsed research into the paranormal. In 1942, she was elected as one of the trustees of the American Society for Psychical Research and was appointed to the Society's research committee in 1946. In 1969, she was influential in getting the American Association for the Advancement of Science to accept the Parapsychological Association as an affiliated organization. She herself was a former president of the AAAS.

Mead believed her own interest in psychical research might be connected with her family history. Mead's longtime friend Patricia Grinager wrote (1999, p. 195): "Two relatives in the family of her father's mother possessed psychic abilities: her great-grandmother Priscilla Rees Ramsay and her great-aunt Louisiana Priscilla Ramsay Sanders. Residents who lived around the Winchester, Ohio area a century ago spread word that this mother-daughter team diagnosed illnesses, read people's thoughts, and levitated tables. Margaret herself had been what her Ramsay kin called 'a psychic child.'" Mead thought she might be a reincarnated representative of her pair of psychic ancestors (Grinager 1999, p. 195).

Throughout her life, Mead consulted various mediums, psychics, and healers. For example, before she married Gregory Bateson in 1936, she consulted a Harlem medium about him. The medium approved (Howard 1984, p. 187). Toward the end of her life, Mead spent a lot of time with famous psychic Jean Houston and a Chilean healer named Carmen de Barraza. The first time Mead, accompanied by Houston, met de Barraza, she asked, "Do you see more people in the room than we do?" De Barraza said she could. Mead continued, "Do you see the tall one and the short one with me?" De Barraza said yes. Mead explained that these were her spirit guides, and that seers in all the tribes she had ever studied had noticed them (Howard 1984, p. 412).

At a conference on holistic medicine in Los Angeles, held shortly before her death, Margaret Mead said: "When I went away to college, I discovered that organized established science objected to the exploration of psychic abilities. Our culture suppresses them. It's just the opposite in Bali. The Balinese indulge every form of psychic activity: trance, prophecy, finding lost objects, identifying thieves, the whole range from trivial to important" (Grinager 1999, p. 252). Mead went on to say that we should study these capabilities and perhaps find ways to apply them in modern society.

John G. Taylor (Mathematical Physicist)

In 1974, Dr. John G. Taylor, a mathematical physicist at the University of London, appeared with Uri Geller on a BBC television show. Geller had become famous for his ability to bend and move metal in ways that seemed impossible in light of ordinary physics. Taylor's initial encounter with Geller was deeply upsetting. In his book *Superminds*, Taylor (1975, p. 49) said: "One clear observation of Geller in action had an overpowering effect on me. I felt as if the whole framework with which I viewed the world had suddenly been destroyed. I seemed very naked and vulnerable, surrounded by a hostile, incomprehensible universe. It was many days before I was able to come to terms with this sensation.

Some of my colleagues have even declined to face up to the problem by refusing to attend the demonstrations of such strange phenomena. That is a perfectly understandable position, but one which does not augur well for the future of science." Faced with the challenge of the Geller phenomena, Taylor decided to confront the challenge directly.

On February 2, 1974, Taylor performed carefully supervised tests with Geller in a laboratory. The results were mixed. Geller tried unsuccessfully to bend a metal rod that he was not allowed to touch. Some metal strips, to be used in the experiments, were lying nearby on a tray. "It was then observed," said Taylor (1975, p. 51), "that one of the aluminum strips lying on the tray was now bent, without, as far as could be seen, having been touched either by Geller or by anyone else in the room." Taylor then tested Geller's famous spoon-bending abilities, using one of his own spoons as the test object. Taylor (1975, p. 51) reported: "I held the bowl end while Geller stroked it gently with one hand. After about twenty seconds the thinnest part of the stem suddenly became soft for a length of approximately half a centimeter and then the spoon broke in two. The ends very rapidly hardened up again—in less than a second . . . Here, under laboratory conditions, we had been able to repeat this remarkable experiment. Geller could simply not have surreptitiously applied enough pressure to have brought this about, not to mention the pre-breakage softening of the metal. Nor could the teaspoon have been tampered with —it had been in my own possession for the past year."

Later in this series of experiments, Geller bent an aluminum strip without touching it. The strip was inside a wire mesh tube. In another experiment, Taylor found that Geller was able to bend a brass strip by ten degrees simply by touching it. He applied a pressure of half an ounce to the strip, but the strip bent in a direction opposite to that of the pressure. Taylor also noticed that the needle of the pressure scale was also bent in the course of the experiment. In another experiment, Geller attempted to bend a copper strip without touching it. He was also attempting to influence a thin wire. Nothing happened at first. "We broke off in order to start measuring his electrical output," said Taylor (1975, p. 160), "but turning round a few moments later I saw that the strip had been bent and the thin wire was broken. Almost simultaneously I noticed that a strip of brass on the other side of the laboratory had also become bent . . . I pointed out to Geller what had happened, only to hear a metallic crash from the far end of the laboratory, twenty feet away. There, on the floor by the far door, was the bent piece of brass. Again I turned back, whereupon there was another crash. A small piece of copper which had earlier been lying near the bent brass strip on the table had followed its companion to the far door. Before I knew what had happened I was struck on the back of the legs by a Perspex tube in which had been sealed an iron rod. The tube had also been lying on the table. It was now lying at my feet with the rod bent as much as the container would allow." In the course of his experiments, Taylor observed other strange happenings, such as pieces of metal scooting across the lab floor, from one wall to another, and a compass needle rotating. Taylor (1975, p. 163) said, "These events seemed impossible to comprehend; I should certainly have dismissed reports of them as nonsense if I had not seen them happen for myself. I could always take the safe line that Geller *must* have been cheating, possibly by putting me into a trance . . . Yet I was perfectly well able at the time to monitor various pieces of scientific equipment while these objects were 'in flight.' I certainly did not feel as if I was in an altered state of consciousness."

Taylor also went on to conduct experiments with a number of children who claimed to have metal-bending powers like those of Geller. He found that they were able to bend metal under laboratory conditions (Taylor 1975, p. 79). In one set of experiments, Taylor put straightened paper clips in a box. Two boys were able to make the straightened clips fold into s-shaped curves. Straightened clips were also folded without contact in other experiments. The children were also able to deflect compass needles and rotate metal rods. Taylor (1975, p. 89) thought that electromagnetism offered the best possible explanation, although he was not able to demonstrate it conclusively. He proposed that the mind was an electromagnetic entity that occupied not only the neural circuitry of the brain but an electromagnetic aura that extended outside the skull (Taylor 1975, p. 155).

In his next book, *Science and the Supernatural* (1980), Taylor underwent a strange transformation. Reviewing various paranormal phenomena, he summarily dismissed most of them, except for remote viewing and telepathy. Acknowledging that the evidence for them seemed strong, he said that this evidence nevertheless contradicted "modern scientific understanding." How could this contradiction be resolved? Taylor (1980, p. 69) proposed that most likely the evidence was defective. It was therefore necessary to carry out further investigations to find out exactly what the defects were. Regarding well documented cases of psychokinesis in connection with poltergeists, Taylor (1980, p. 108) said, "The only possible explanation left open to us in this whole poltergeist phenomenon is that of a mixture of expectation, hallucination and trickery . . . Such an explanation is the only one which seems to fit in with a scientific view of the world."

So what happened to Taylor between 1975 and 1980? In 1975, Taylor had accepted the paranormal events he witnessed during his own carefully controlled experiments with Uri Geller and a number of British children. He had hoped to explain these by one of the four fundamental forces accepted by modern physics, namely electromagnetism (the other three being the atomic strong force, the atomic weak force, and gravity). Philosopher David Ray Griffin (1997, p. 32) said, "Taylor soon learned, however, that this issue had been discussed for several decades by parapsychologists . . . In particular some Russian parapsychologists, given their Marxian materialistic orthodoxy, had devised experiments explicitly designed to show ESP and PK [psychokinesis] to be electromagnetic phenomena. Their experiments suggested otherwise." So when Taylor found he could not explain the paranormal phenomena he witnessed in terms of one of the forces accepted by modern physics, he developed an apparent case of amnesia about his own experiments and dismissed the experiments performed by others as the result of trickery, hallucination, and credulity. He did not offer any explanation as to exactly how Geller and the many children he tested had tricked him.

Edgar Mitchell (Astronaut)

Edgar Mitchell is an American astronaut who became interested in psychical research. During his trip to the moon he had a transcendental vision, giving him "new insight" (Mitchell 1996, p. 68). After returning to earth, he tried to gain understanding of his vision by studying mystical literature. He concluded (1996, p. 69): "What the ancients, who wrote in the Sanskrit of India, described as a classic *savikalpa samadhi* was essentially what I believe I experienced . . . this phenomenon is a moment in which an individual still recognizes the separateness of all things yet understands that the separateness is but an illusion. An essential unity is the benchmark reality, which is what the individual suddenly comes to comprehend." This also resembles the Vedic concept of *acintyabhedabheda-tattva,* inconceivable simultaneous oneness and difference. This generally refers to the relationship between God and God's energies. According to the teachings of Chaitanya Mahaprabhu all living beings have souls, and together these souls comprise an energy of God. The souls are simultaneously one with and different from God. They are one in spiritual substance and power but possess this spiritual substance and power in different quantities (Bhaktivinoda Thakura 1987, pp. 46–48).

In 1972, Mitchell left NASA and completely dedicated himself to the study of consciousness, which he believed bridged the gap between science and religion. "Mystical traditions assume, implicitly or explicitly, that consciousness is fundamental. Scientific tradition (epiphenomenalism) explicitly assumes it is secondary. It seemed to me that the study of consciousness provided the only unified approach to the questions of who we humans really are, how we got here, where we are going, and why" (Mitchell 1996, p. 72). To further his own studies and those of others, he organized the Institute for Noetic Sciences.

Edgar Mitchell participated in some spoon-bending experiments with psychic Uri Geller at the Stanford Research Institute. The normal procedure was for Geller to grasp the spoon in his hand, and lightly stroke the shaft of the spoon, at its narrowest point, with one finger. The shaft would then twist or bend. Skeptics claimed he could do the bending because he had unusually strong fingers. Others suggested he applied a solvent that caused the metal to soften. But Mitchell stated (1996, p. 86), "No one was aware of any such solvent that could be used in this way; the physicists in the group couldn't explain how he could be capable of twisting the metal so adroitly into such a neat little coil by merely touching it with a single finger." The experimenters found that he could not bend a spoon simply by mental effort. This was tested by placing a spoon under a glass cover.

When it became known that Mitchell was investigating Geller and his spoon bending, he received phone calls from parents of children who, after seeing Geller on television shows, were also bending spoons. Mitchell began investigating these children and, like Taylor in England, found them even more convincing than Geller. Mitchell (1996, p. 87) said: "I went to a number of homes around the country, sometimes with my own spoons in my pocket, or I would select one at random from the family kitchen. Typically it was a boy under ten years of age who would lightly stroke the metal object at the narrow point of the handle while I held it between thumb and forefinger at the end of the handle. The spoon would soon slowly bend, creating two 360-degree twists in the handle, perfectly emulating what Geller demonstrated on television. No tricks, no magic potions, just innocent children (with normal children's fingers) who had not yet learned that it could not be done."

Mitchell noted that during the six weeks of investigations of Geller at SRI, a number of unusual things occurred: "Video equipment that he had no access to would suddenly lose a pulley, which would later be found in an adjoining room. Jewelry would suddenly be missing, only to be found locked in a safe with a combination Uri could not have known" (Mitchell 1996, p. 87). In one psychokinetic experiment, Mitchell and the SRI researchers put a big ball bearing under a glass jar on a table. In Geller's presence, Mitchell says the ball bearing "began to jiggle, then roll this way and that" (Mitchell 1996, p. 88). The movement was recorded on videotape. But when the film was shown to SRI researchers out-side the group that was investigating Geller, the reaction was hostile. Mitchell stated, "They became red in the face, and some left, refusing ever to return to the lab. They accused Uri of being a fraud and the rest of us of being chumps in an elaborate charade. But their accusations flew in the face of the solid scientific work that had been done, and I believe they knew it" (Mitchell 1996, p. 88).

Modern Research into Paranormal Phenomena

In addition to isolated studies with single subjects like Geller, there is a great deal of experimental evidence for paranormal effects associat-ed with mental intention. The experiments mostly involve micro-psycho-kinetic effects and remote viewing. This type of research became promi-nent in the middle part of the twentieth century, and has continued up to the present day. A good review can be found in *The Conscious Universe: The Scientific Truth of Psychic Phenomena* (1997), by Dean Radin of the Consciousness Research Laboratory at the University of Nevada, Las Vegas. Let us first look at the remote viewing experiments.

Remote Viewing

The simplest kind of remote viewing experiment involves card guessing. The Nobel-prize-winning scientist Charles Richet carried out some card guessing experiments, and published a report in 1889. He hyp-notized his subjects and asked them to guess what cards were sealed in opaque envelopes (Radin 1997, p. 93). Later, in the mid-twentieth centu-ry, more systematic work was carried out by Dr. J. B. Rhine at Duke Uni-versity and Dr. S. G. Soal in England. These researchers conducted care-ful remote viewing experiments in which "receiver" subjects were able to correctly name images of cards viewed by isolated "transmitter" sub-jects. The number of correct identifications exceeded what could be ex-pected by chance. Results like this from Rhine and others prompted Professor H. J. Eysenck, chairman of the Psychology Department, Uni-versity of London, to say: "Unless there is a gigantic conspiracy involv-ing some thirty University departments all over the world, and several hundred highly respected scientists in various fields, many of these orig-inally hostile to the claims of the psychical researchers, the only conclu-sion the unbiased observer can come to must be that there does exist a small number of people who obtain knowledge existing either in other people's minds, or in the outer world, by means as yet unknown to science" (Radin 1997, pp. 96–97).

But not everyone was convinced. In 1955, Dr. George Price of the Department of Medicine at the University of Minnesota published in *Science* an article highly critical of the card guessing experiments. Price relied on David Hume's famous statement that it was more reasonable to believe that witnesses of miracles were deceived or lying than to accept violations of the well established laws of physics. On this basis, Price (1955) argued that Rhine and Soal's results, because they violated the laws of physics, must be the result of undetected fraudulent behavior. But some years later Price (1972) wrote a letter to *Science* about his 1955 article, saying, "During the past year I have had some correspondence with J. B. Rhine which has convinced me that I was highly unfair to him in what I said." He regretted his accusations of fraud. It is possible, of course, that cheating or inadvertent cueing of the subjects may have been involved. But Rhine and Soal had gone to great lengths to prevent such things.

Typical card tests made use of a deck of 25 cards. The cards were each marked with one of five symbols (star, wavy line, square, circle, or cross) so that each symbol was represented by five cards. In the earliest tests, experimenters gave a subject a shuffled deck of cards and asked the subject to guess the top card. After guessing, the subject turned over the top card, checking to see if the identification was correct, and then guessed the next card. Critics suggested that printing presses may have left impressions on the backs of the cards. The subjects could have detected these impressions by touch, and used this information to correctly guess the cards. To rule out this possibility, the cards were put into opaque envelopes. Critics suggested that the subjects could mark the cards with their fingernails, and feel the marks through the envelopes. Experimenters arranged things so that the subject no longer handled the envelopes. Critics suggested the experimenters might be giving subtle cues to the subjects. To prevent this, the subjects were separated from the experimenters and cards by opaque screens. Experimenters were later placed in remote rooms or buildings. Critics suggested that in recording the experimental results the experimenters often made errors, errors in favor of paranormal explanations. To solve this problem, experimental designs incorporated duplicate recording of results and double-blind checking. Monitors were employed to insure that experimenters followed procedures and did not engage in fraud. Critics suggested that experimenters sometimes stopped recording data when the results looked good. To solve this problem, experiments were run with a fixed number of trials (Radin 1997, pp. 94–95).

In 1997, Dean Radin published the results of his study of 34 card guessing experiments carried out with high levels of security. The experiments were conducted by two dozen researchers during the years 1934–1939, and involved 907,000 separate trials. The chance expectation would be correct guesses in one out of five trials, for a hit rate of twenty percent. Radin (1997, p. 96) arranged the studies in four groups, according to the kinds of security measures employed, and found that the hit rates were significantly above chance for all four groups. Critics propose that these hit rates might be the result of selective reporting. In other words, for every published report with favorable results, there might have been other studies with unfavorable results that the experimenters did not publish but kept in their file drawers. This is called "the file drawer problem." But in order to eliminate the positive results from the 34 published reports, there would have had to have been at least 29,000 unpublished studies, a ratio of 861 to 1 (Radin 1997, p. 97). Such a massive number of unpublished studies is exceedingly unlikely. Radin further noted: "If we consider *all* the ESP card tests conducted from 1882 to 1939, reported in 186 publications by dozens of investigators around the world, the combined results of this four-million trial database translate into tremendous odds against chance—more than a billion trillion to one." To eliminate this positive result, the number of unpublished studies in the "file drawer" would have to have been 626,000, for a ratio of more than 3,300 unpublished reports for every published report (Radin 1997, p. 97).

In 1974, *Nature,* the world's foremost scientific publication, printed a paper by physicists Harold Puthoff and Dr. Russell Targ, about paranormal experiments carried out at the Electronics and Bioengineering Laboratory of the Stanford Research Institute, associated with Stanford University. Targ and Puthoff sought to test the ability of a subject to give information about drawings of objects or scenes shielded from ordinary sense perception. The subjects included Uri Geller, whose psychic achievements were surrounded by accusations of fraud. Whatever one may think about those accusations, one should still be prepared to independently judge particular experiments as to whether or not adequate precautions were taken to prevent deception. Targ and Puthoff stated (1974, p. 602): "We conducted our experiments with sufficient control, utilising visual, acoustic and electrical shielding, to ensure that all conventional paths of sensory input were blocked. At all times we took measures to prevent sensory leakage and to prevent deception, whether intentional or unintentional."

Thirteen remote perception experiments were carried out with Uri Geller. In the first ten, either Geller or the researchers were placed in a shielded room. In the majority of cases, Geller was in the acoustically and visually isolated room, which had double steel walls with double locking doors. Only after this isolation procedure was carried out were target drawings made by the researchers and selected for Geller to identify. Geller did not know the identity of the researcher selecting the target or the method by which targets were selected. In most cases, the target drawings were made by SRI scientists who were not part of the experimental group. The target drawings were kept in a variety of locations, ranging from 4 meters to 7 miles away from the viewing site. Experimenters provided Geller with a pen and paper, and asked him to reproduce the target drawing, giving him the option to pass if he felt he could not detect the target. If he did produce a drawing, the researchers collected it before Geller was allowed to see the target drawing. In an additional three cases, drawings were made by computer. In one case the drawing was visually displayed on a computer screen. In another case it was kept in computer memory but not displayed on the screen. In the final case the target drawing was displayed on the screen but the contrast was adjusted so that the image was not actually visible to the human eye. During these three computer-screen tests, Geller was kept isolated in a Faraday cage, designed to weaken electrical signals. Geller gave responses to ten of the thirteen tests. To evaluate how well Geller's drawings matched the targets, they were submitted to two SRI scientists not part of the research team. The judges were asked to match subject drawings with target drawings. Targ and Puthoff (1974, p. 604) said, "The two judges each matched the target data to the response data with no error. For either judge such a correspondence has an *a priori* probability, under the null hypothesis of no information channel, of $P = (10!)^{-1} = 3 \times 10^{-7}$." In other words, in each case he submitted a drawing, or set of drawings, Geller was able to match the target.

In another set of remote viewing experiments, an SRI scientist made 100 target drawings, which were placed in double envelopes with black cardboard. Each day, twenty target drawings were selected for the experiment. Geller again had to try to make drawings that corresponded with the targets. The experiment was run once a day for three days. Targ and Puthoff (1974, p. 604) said, "The drawings resulting from this experiment do not depart significantly from what would be expected by chance." In a final set of ten experiments, Geller was presented with a closed metal box containing a die. Before presentation to Geller, the box was vigorously shaken. In each trial, Geller would write down which surface of the die was facing up. In two of the trials, Geller declined to write an answer. Targ and Puthoff reported (1974, p. 604): "In the eight times in which he gave a response, he was correct each time. The distribution of responses consisted of three 2's, one 4, two 5's, and two 6's. The probability of this occurring by chance is approximately one in 10^6 [1 in 1,000,000]."

In another set of experiments with a new subject, Targ and Puthoff attempted to determine whether the subject, Pat Price (a former city councilman and police commissioner in California), could identify geographical features several miles distant. Twelve locations within 30 minutes driving time of SRI were chosen by the director of the SRI Information Science and Engineering Division. The director also prepared travel directions for each of the selected locations. The set of locations and directions was not known to the experimenters and was kept under the director's control. For each trial, the director would give one of the sets of travel directions to a team of two to four experimenters, who would then proceed to the site. Price and another experimenter remained behind at SRI, and Price would provide a description of the target site to the experimenter. The descriptions were recorded on audio tape. Price took part in nine such trials. Targ and Puthoff (1974, p. 605) stated: "Several descriptions yielded significantly correct data pertaining to and descriptive of the target location . . . Price's ability to describe correctly buildings, docks, roads, gardens and so on, including structural materials, colour, ambience and activity, sometimes in great detail, indicated the functioning of a remote perceptual ability." Five independent judges from SRI visited the sites and examined transcripts of Price's descriptions. They then attempted to match the descriptions to the target sites they had visited. Targ and Puthoff (1974, p. 606) reported: "By plurality vote, six of the nine descriptions and locations were correctly matched." The probability of this occurring by chance was P = 5.6×10^{-4}.

In a final set of experiments, subjects (receivers) were tested to see if their brain wave activity could be correlated with that of persons (senders) being subjected to flashing lights at remote locations. In each trial, the sender would be subjected to ten seconds of flashing lights (at six or sixteen flashes per second) or ten seconds of no flashing lights. The receiver, in a visually and electrically isolated room, would hear a tone, indicating that a trial had begun. But the receiver would not know whether the trial involved flashing lights or not. The sequence of flashing or not flashing trials was random. The degree of correlation between the brain of the sender and the brain of the receiver was judged by measuring alpha waves in the brain of the receiver. Under normal circumstances, persons subjected to flashing lights show a decrease in the amplitude of alpha brain waves. So if the sender was exposed to flashing lights, the brain of the receiver should also show a decrease in the amplitude of alpha waves. One receiver's brain did show alpha waves that decreased in amplitude each time the sender was exposed to flashing lights. This subject was then selected for further testing, with the same result. The average power and peak power of alpha waves was consistently less in this receiver when the sender was being exposed to lights flashing sixteen times per second (Targ and Puthoff 1974, p. 607).

From all of these experiments, Targ and Puthoff (1974, p. 607) concluded: "A channel exists whereby information about a remote location can be obtained by means of an as yet unidentified perceptual modality." They also suggested that "remote perceptual ability is widely distributed in the general population, but because the perception is generally below an individual's level of awareness, it is repressed or not noticed." Finally, they stated, "Our observation of the phenomena leads us to conclude that experiments in the area of so-called paranormal phenomena can be scientifically conducted, and it is our hope that other laboratories will initiate additional research to attempt to replicate these findings."

Nature (1974, pp. 559–560) published an editorial along with the article by Targ and Puthoff. According to the referees who reviewed the article before publication, the descriptions about the precise manner in which experiments were carried out, including precautions taken to prevent unconscious or conscious leakage of information to the subjects, were "vague." I did not find this to be so, but readers can judge for themselves. The referees also thought that more care could have been taken in the target selection process. Again, I found the methods, as described, to be adequate. Favoring publication of the paper, said *Nature,* was the fact that the authors were "two qualified scientists, writing from a major research establishment." *Nature* found the phenomena worthy of investigation, even if many scientists were skeptical about their reality. As *Nature* put it, "If scientists dispute and debate the reality of extra-sensory perception, then the subject is clearly a matter for scientific study and reportage." *Nature* also recognized that failure to publish the article might add fuel to rumours circulating among scientists that "the Stanford Research Institute (SRI) was engaged in a major research programme into parapsychological matters and had even been the scene of a remarkable breakthrough in this field." It was felt that "publication of this paper, with its muted claims, suggestions of a limited research programme, and modest data, is . . . likely to put the whole matter in more reasonable perspective." The editorial concluded (1974, p. 560): "*Nature,* although seen by some as one of the world's most respected journals cannot afford to live on respectability. We believe that our readers expect us to be a home for the occasional 'high-risk' type of paper ... Publishing in a scientific journal is not a process of receiving a seal of approval from the establishment; rather it is the serving of notice on the community that there is something worthy of their attention and scrutiny."

But much more was happening at SRI than the experiments reported in *Nature*. The SRI experimenters were not only carrying out basic research establishing the reality of remote viewing but were actually carrying out remote viewing missions on behalf of the intelligence gathering agencies of the United States government and military. These programs involved substantial recruiting efforts. During screenings of large numbers of candidates, it turned out that about one percent possessed good remote viewing abilities (Radin 1997, p. 101).

On July 10, 1974, a physicist working for the CIA came to SRI with a test assignment. Analysts at the CIA were interested in a certain building complex in the Soviet Union. The physicist gave Targ the coordinates of a location in the Soviet Union, about ten thousand miles away from the SRI in Menlo Park, California. Targ and one of SRI's remote viewers, Pat Price, went into one of the electrically shielded rooms they used for their experiments. Price focused on the coordinates and began describing a site with buildings and a gantry moving back and forth on a track with one rail. He sketched the layout of the buildings and crane. He later drew a detailed picture of the crane. Over the next few days, additional details were added. "We were astonished," said Targ, "when we were told [later] that the site was the super-secret Soviet atomic bomb laboratory at Semiplatinsk, where they were also testing particle beam weapons ... The accuracy of Price's drawing is the sort of thing that I, as a physicist, would never have believed, if I had not seen it for myself" (Targ 1996, pp. 81–82; in Radin 1997, p. 26).

The remote viewing program at the Stanford Research Institute operated as part of Stanford University throughout the early 1970s, after which it became an independent organization, called Stanford Research International. The remote viewing program was founded by Harold Puthoff, who was joined early on by Targ and a few years later by physicist Edwin May. Puthoff left SRI in 1985, and May took over the leadership of the organization. In 1990, the remote viewing program moved to Science Applications International Corporation (SAIC), a big defense contractor. In 1994, the program ended (so we are told, anyway), after 24 years and $20 million from the CIA, Defense Intelligence Agency, Army intelligence, Navy intelligence, and NASA. Radin (1997,

p. 98) noted: "The agencies continued to show interest in remote viewing for more than twenty years because the SRI and SAIC programs occasionally provided useful mission-oriented information at high levels of detail."

In one test case in the intelligence-gathering program, supervisors gave a remote viewer only the barest amount of information about a target—that it was "a technical device somewhere in the United States." According to Radin the target was actually "a high-energy microwave generator in the Southwest." Unaware of this, the viewer made drawings and gave verbal descriptions of an object the same size and shape as the microwave generator. He correctly stated that its beam divergence angle was 30 degrees (May 1995, p. 204; in Radin 1997, p. 99).

In another case from the late 1970s, supervisors gave a remote viewer the map coordinates of a location in the United States. The remote viewer gave an accurate description of a super secret military installation. The very existence of this installation, located in Virginia, was at the time extremely confidential. Radin (Puthoff 1996; in Radin 1997, p. 99) said the viewer "was able to describe accurately the facility's interior and was even able to correctly sense the names of secret code words written on folders inside locked file cabinets." In 1977, a reporter, who had learned about the remote viewer's report, went to the spot to verify the existence of the military installation. The reporter saw just a hillside with sheep and concluded the report was not true. But the installation actually was at that spot—not on the surface, but underground (Radin 1997, p. 99).

In September of 1979, the National Security Council of the United States became interested in knowing what the Soviet Union was doing inside a large building in northern Russia. Spy satellite photos of activities around the building indicated some kind of heavy construction, but the NSC wanted to know exactly what was happening inside. A remote viewer working for the army, Chief Warrant Officer Joe McMoneagle, was assigned to the task (McMoneagle 1993, Schnabel 1997; in Radin 1997, pp. 194–195). The officers in charge of the project did not at first show McMoneagle the satellite photos or tell him anything about their content. They gave him only a set of map coordinates and asked what he could see at that location. He described large buildings and smokestacks in a cold location near a large body of water. After receiving this essentially accurate report, the officers showed McMoneagle the satellite photos of the building in which they were especially interested, and asked him to see what was going on inside. McMoneagle reported that a submarine was being constructed inside the building.

McMoneagle sketched a large vessel, much larger than any submarine in existence, with a long flat deck and tubes for eighteen or twenty missiles. The NSC officials were doubtful. The vessel was too big for a submarine, and the building was about a hundred yards from the water. Also, none of the intelligence services had picked up any reports of such a submarine under construction in the Soviet Union. Looking into the future, McMoneagle predicted that in four months time the Soviets would dig a canal from the building to the water to launch the submarine. In January of 1980, satellite photos revealed the submarine, the largest in the world, moving through a new artificial channel from the building to the harbor. The submarine had a flat deck and twenty missile tubes. It was the first *Typhoon* class submarine. Radin (1997, p. 195) said, "Scientists who had worked on these highly classified programs, including myself, were frustrated to know firsthand the reality of high-performance psi phenomena and yet we had no way of publicly responding to skeptics. Nothing could be said about the fact that the U.S. Army had supported a secret team of remote viewers, that those viewers had participated in hundreds of remote-viewing missions, and that the DIA, CIA, Customs Service, Drug Enforcement Agency, FBI, and Secret Service had all relied on the remote-viewing team for more than a decade, sometimes with startling results."

In 1988, Edwin May, director of Stanford Research International, reviewed the results of all psychical research tests carried out at SRI from 1973 to 1988, involving over 26,000 trials in the course of 154 experiments. The odds that the success rate in these trials could have been the result of chance guesses were 10^{20} to one, more than a billion to one (Radin 1997, p. 101). In 1995, the Congress of the United States asked the American Institutes for Research to review the CIA-sponsored remote viewing work carried out at Science Applications International Corporation (SAIC) during the years 1989–1993. The two chief reviewers were Dr. Jessica Utts, a statistics professor at the University of California at Davis, favorable to psychical research, and Dr. Ray Hyman, a long time critic of psychical research. Radin (1997, p. 101) noted, "The SAIC studies provided a rigorously controlled set of experiments that had been supervised by a distinguished oversight committee of experts from a variety of scientific disciplines. The committee included a Nobel laureate physicist, internationally known experts in statistics, psychology, neuroscience, and astronomy, and a retired U. S. Army major general who was also a physician."

In her evaluation, Jessica Utts concluded: "It is clear to this author that anomalous cognition is possible and has been demonstrated" (Utts

1996; in Radin 1997, p. 102). Utts also said: "The statistical results of the studies examined are far beyond what is expected by chance. Arguments that these results could be due to methodological flaws in the experiments are soundly refuted. Effects of similar magnitude to those found in government-sponsored research . . . have been replicated at a number of laboratories across the world. Such consistency cannot be readily explained by claims of flaws or fraud" (Utts 1996, p. 3; in Radin 1997, pp. 4–5).

Even Ray Hyman found little to criticize: "I agree with Jessica Utts that the effect sizes reported in the SAIC experiments . . . probably cannot be dismissed as due to chance. Nor do they appear to be accounted for by multiple testing, filedrawer distortions, inappropriate statistical testing or other misuse of statistical inference. . . . So, I accept Professor Utts' assertion that the statistical results of the SAIC, and other parapsychological experiments, 'are far beyond what is expected by chance.' The SAIC experiments are well-designed and the investigators have taken pains to eliminate the known weaknesses in previous parapsychological research. In addition, I cannot provide suitable candidates for what flaws, if any, might be present" (Hyman 1996, p. 55; in Radin 1997 p. 103). Nevertheless, he still was not prepared to admit that the tests confirmed psychical abilities. He proposed that although he was not able to identify any flaws, or even propose any possible flaws, that some flaws might be there. He therefore insisted on more "independent replication" of the results, although the results, in the course of twenty years, had already been independently repeated by different researchers at SRI and elsewhere.

Among the labs that had already independently replicated SRI's remote viewing work was the Princeton Engineering Anomalies Research (PEAR) Laboratory, at Princeton University. Remote viewing experiments started there in 1978. The published experiments involved 334 trials between 1978 and 1987. "The final odds against chance for the PEAR researchers' overall database were 100 billion to one," said Radin (1997 p. 105).

Ganzfeld Experiments

In recent years, psychical researchers have been conducting telepathic experiments with a technique called the ganzfeld (Radin 1997, pp. 69–72). The ganzfeld technique grew out of dream telepathy experiments carried out by psychiatrist Montague Ullman and psychologist Stanley Krippner at the Maimonides Medical Center in Brooklyn, New York, during the years 1966–1972. It appeared that if a waking person sent mental images to a dreaming person, the dreaming person would see those images in dreams. The dreamer would go to sleep in a closed room that was soundproofed and shielded from external electromagnetic waves. EEG monitoring of the sleeper's brain waves would signal the beginning of REM (rapid eye movement) sleep, during which dreaming occurs. During the REM period, a sender isolated at a different location would try to send to the dreamer an image, randomly selected from a group of images, in most cases eight. Experimental protocols kept contacts between the experimenters and the sender to an absolute minimum. The sender would simply hear a buzzer at the onset of the dreamer's REM sleep, and at this signal would begin sending the target image. At the end of the REM period, the sleeper would be awakened, and an experimenter would ask the sleeper to describe the dominant dream image. In some cases, the dreamer would go back to sleep and the process would be repeated. Afterwards, independent judges would compare the dream descriptions to the entire set of eight images from which the actual target image had been selected. The images would be ranked according to how well they matched the dreamer's description. The best match was assigned first place, the second best match second place, and so on. If it turned out that the actual target image sent by the sender was one of the four best matches, this was counted as a hit. If we assume there was nothing significant in the dream descriptions, and that the judges had no knowledge of the actual target image, then the matchings of the eight images to a particular dream description would be random. In that case we would expect that the actual target image would show up in the best four matches from the whole set of eight images only fifty percent of the time. Radin (1997, p. 70) noted: "In journal articles published between 1966 and 1973, a total of 450 dream telepathy sessions were reported . . . the overall hit rate is seen to be about 63 percent . . . the odds against chance of getting a 63 percent hit rate in 450 sessions, where chance is 50 percent and the confidence interval is . . . small [plus or minus 4 percent], is seventy-five million to one."

The dream experiments were based on the premise that psychical effects would operate more strongly on a receiver's mind when ordinary sensory inputs were lessened. Charles Honorton, a parapsychologist involved with the Maimonides dream experiments, sought to develop a method for putting subjects into an artificial state of dreamlike sensory deprivation. Researchers would thus have more control over the experimental process, as it no longer depended on waiting for the subject to fall asleep and enter the REM state. William Braud, a psychologist at the University of Houston, and Adrian Parker, a psychologist at the University of Edinburgh, Scotland, joined Honorton in producing what came to be called the ganzfeld method.

In their development of this method, the researchers were inspired by states of altered consciousness reported in ancient wisdom traditions. Radin (1997, p. 73) stated: "Honorton, Braud, and Parker had noticed that descriptions of mystical, meditative, and religious states often included anecdotes about psi experiences, and that the association between reduced mental noise and the spontaneous emergence of psi was noted long ago in the ancient religious texts of India, the *Vedas.* For example, in Patanjali's *Yoga Sutras,* one of the first textbooks on yoga dating back at least thirty-five hundred years, it is taken for granted that prolonged practice with deep meditation leads to a variety of *siddhis,* or psychic abilities." Statements to this effect are found throughout the Vedic literatures. In the *Shrimad Bhagavatam* (11.15.1), we read: "The Supreme Personality of Godhead said: My dear Uddhava, the mystic perfections of yoga are acquired by a yogi who has conquered his senses, steadied his mind, conquered the breathing process and fixed his mind on Me." In the Vedic conception, God is known as Yogesvara, the master of all mystic powers, and the yogi who stills the mind by focusing it on God within attains siddhis. One of these siddhis is named in the *Bhagavat Purana* (11.15.6) as *dura-shravana-darshanam,* the ability to see and hear things at a distance. The entire fifteenth chapter of the Eleventh Canto of the *Shrimad Bhagavatam* deals with the yogic siddhis and how they may be attained. Interestingly enough, the siddhis are actually considered obstacles for those on the path of complete spiritual perfection, because one who gets them tends to get absorbed in using them for selfish goals.

In the ganzfeld technique, the person who is to receive a psychic communication is placed in a soundproof room on a comfortable reclining chair. Halves of translucent white ping-pong balls are taped over the eyes, and a light is directed upon them, producing a uniform featureless visual field. Headphones, through which white noise is played, are placed over the ears. The receiver is also guided through some relaxation exercises to reduce inner tensions. The combined effect is a homogeneous state of reduced sensory input called in German the *Ganzfeld,* or "total field." When the receiver is in the ganzfeld state, a sender at another location looks at a randomly selected target image (a photograph or video tape clip) and mentally sends the image to the receiver. The session lasts for 30 minutes, during which the receiver continuously reports aloud all mental impressions, emotions, and thoughts. At the end of the session, four images are shown to the receiver, who is asked to select from among them the target. The receiver does this by judging which of the four images best matches the receiver's own stream of consciousness report. By chance, the hit rate should be 25 percent, but studies have shown that the receivers are able to correctly select the target image at a rate significantly greater than 25 percent. Psychologist D. J. Bem of Cornell University reported in 1996 (pp. 163–164): "More than 60 ganzfeld experiments have now been conducted, and a 1985 meta-analysis of 42 ganzfeld studies conducted in 10 independent laboratories up to that time found that receivers achieved an average hit rate of 35 percent—a result that could have occurred by chance with a probability of less than one in a billion. Supplementary analyses have demonstrated that this overall result could not have resulted from selective reporting of positive results or from flawed procedures that might have permitted the receiver to obtain the target information in normal sensory fashion."

The 1985 meta-analysis cited by Bem was conducted by Honorton (1985). A second study of the same cases was conducted by the skeptic Ray Hyman (1985a, 1985b). Even Hyman was forced to conclude that the results were not the result of improper use of statistics, sensory leakage, or cheating (Radin 1997, p. 82). He suggested that improper randomization techniques might have been responsible, although Honorton had given arguments against this. Radin (1997, p. 83) noted, "In this case, ten psychologists and statisticians supplied commentaries alongside the Honorton-Hyman published debate . . . everyone [including Honorton and Hyman] agreed that the ganzfeld results were not due to chance, nor to selective reporting, nor to sensory leakage. And everyone, except one confirmed skeptic [Hyman], also agreed that the results were not plausibly due to flaws in randomization procedures." Nevertheless, Honorton, in a joint communiqué with Hyman, did agree to modify the ganzfeld protocols to take into account Hyman's concerns (Hyman and Honorton 1986; in Radin 1997, p. 84). This had the good effect of getting Hyman to give his conditions in writing, so that he could not in the future simply raise vague possible objections to the ganzfeld results.

It turned out that Honorton had been conducting ganzfeld studies that complied with Hyman's stringent conditions since 1983, when the process of image selection had been taken out of the hands of human experimenters and given over to computers. The entire procedure of data recording was automated. Measures were taken to isolate the receiver more effectively, and the whole physical set-up and experimental protocol were reviewed by two professional magicians, who attested the experiments were not vulnerable to cheating (Radin 1997, pp. 85–86). Between 1983 and 1989, 240 persons participated in 354 automated ganzfeld experiments (Honorton and Schechter, 1987; Honorton et al. 1990). In these sessions, the hit rate was 37 percent. The odds against chance were 45,000 to one (Radin 1997, p. 86).

Hyman (1991), ever the skeptic, asked for independent replication. The Honorton experiments at the Psychological Research Laboratories were in fact later replicated by several researchers: Kathy Dalton and her coworkers at the Koestler Chair of Parapsychology, Department of Psychology, University of Edinburgh; Professor Dick Bierman, Department of Psychology, University of Amsterdam; Professor Daryl Bem, Cornell University Department of Psychology; Dr. Richard Broughton and coworkers at the Rhine Research Center, Durham, North Carolina; Professor Adrian Parker and coworkers at the University of Gothenburg, Sweden; and doctoral candidate Rens Wezelman, Institute of Parapsychology, Utrecht, Netherlands (Radin 1997, pp. 87–88). When combined with the experiments documented in the 1985 meta-analysis and the 1983–1989 series of Honorton, the total number of sessions was 2,549. "The overall hit rate of 33.2 percent is unlikely with odds against chance beyond a million billion to one," said Radin (1997, p. 88).

More recently, Bem was coauthor, with Honorton, of an important report on ganzfeld studies of telepathy. *Science News* said of the report, "New evidence supporting the existence of what most folks refer to as telepathy ... boasts a rare distinction: It passed muster among skeptical peer reviewers and gained publication in a major, mainstream psychology journal" (Bower 1994). In the *Science News* article, Bem said, "I used to be a skeptic, but we met strict research guidelines and the results are statistically significant. We hope the findings prompt others to try replicating this effect." The actual report was published in the January 1994 issue of *Psychological Bulletin.* Bem and Honorton, using statistical meta-analysis, combined the results of 11 studies involving 240 subjects. The hit rate was one in three, compared to the chance expectation of one in four. In one study, 29 dance, drama, and music students got a hit rate of one in two. One of the reviewers of the article for *Psychological Bulletin* was Robert Rosenthal, a psychologist at Harvard. He said, "Bem and Honorton's article is very sophisticated statistically and you can't dismiss their findings" (Bower 1994).

Not everyone was convinced. At a lecture on parapsychology at the Royal Institution, which I attended on February 5, 2000, psychologist Richard Wiseman of the University of Hertfordshire claimed that his own meta-analysis of the post 1987 ganzfeld studies gave a combined hit rate of 27 percent, which, according to him, does not exceed chance expectation. But he also admitted a subsequent study by one of his coworkers of the most recent studies, 1997–1999, yielded a hit rate of 37 percent. Altogether, it seems that there is a genuine paranormal effect in the ganzfeld experiments.

Modern Research into Psychokinetics

Having considered some of the recent scientific work in remote viewing and telepathy, let us now look at psychokinetics (pk), which according to my proposal involves the action of a subtle mind element on ordinary matter. In the nineteenth century and the early twentieth century, prominent scientists reported singular macro-psychokinetic effects such as floating tables. Later researchers have concentrated on reproducible micro-psychokinetic effects.

Dice tossing experiments, in which subjects attempt to mentally influence the results, are one example. In 1989, psychologist Diane Ferrari and Dean Radin, then at Princeton, did a meta-analysis of all such experiments in English-language journals up to that time (Radin and Ferrari 1991). They found 73 reports, from 52 different investigators, published between the years 1935 and 1987. These reports recorded the results of 2.6 million dice throws by 2,569 subjects in 148 experiments. The reports also recorded control studies, in which the subjects did not try to mentally influence the outcome of the dice throws. The hit rate for the control studies was 50.02 percent, about what would be expected by chance, while the hit rate for the experiments was 51.2 percent. Radin (1997, p. 134) noted: "This does not look like much, but statistically it results in odds against chance of more than a billion to one."

Radin and Ferrari tested their statistical results against various criticisms. Were most of the positive results concentrated in only a few of the many studies? After removing from the database the studies with the most positive results, the remaining studies still indicated a positive result with odds against chance of more than three million to one. Were positive results concentrated in a large number of studies done by a few researchers? Radin and Ferrari found that when they removed from their database the researchers who had done the most studies, the remaining results were still positive, with odds against chance of a billion to one. Were the positive results caused by selective reporting? It would have taken 17,974 unpublished studies with negative results to eliminate the positive results. This would amount to 121 unpublished studies for every published study (Radin 1997, 134–135).

One problem recognized by early researchers was the tendency of high numbers, like six, to turn up more often than lower numbers. The face of a die with six on it is made by scooping out six small depressions. This face is therefore lighter than the opposite faces with lower numbers and is more likely to turn up when the dice are thrown. So if the throwers were trying to get sixes, they would be likely to get a result higher than chance, not because of any paranormal mental influence but because of the natural tendency of sixes to come up more than lower numbers. Researchers established experimental protocols to control for this by varying the target numbers in a way that was carefully balanced. Of the 148 studies in the total sample analyzed by Radin and Ferrari, 69 were performed with this balanced protocol. They reported that for these studies "there was still highly significant evidence for mind-matter interactions, with odds against chance of greater than a trillion to one" (Radin 1997, p. 137).

In more recent times, random number generator (RNG) tests have replaced dice tossing tests. Random number generators incorporate an element that either emits particles from random radioactive decay or produces random electronic noise. Either of these will produce in the RNG circuitry random surges (spikes) in the signal. These spikes interrupt a special digital clock, which is emitting a stream of alternating ones and zeros (1010101010101 . . .), with the alternations occurring millions of times per second. The RNG circuitry is designed so that the apparatus records the state of the clock (one or zero) at the times the spikes interrupt the stream of alternating ones and zeros. If the spikes are coming randomly at a rate of ten thousand times per second, the RNG will therefore record a random sequence of ten thousand ones and zeros per second (for example, 10001101000111101010. . . .). The modern RNG machines are tamper-resistant and record data automatically. The percentage of ones from an RNG generating a random series of ones and zeros should, over a sufficiently large number of trials, be 50 percent. But when subjects are asked to will more ones than zeros, the percentage climbs to a level beyond what could be expected by chance.

Modern RNG studies began with the work of Helmut Schmidt, a physicist at Boeing Laboratories. Robert Jahn, dean of Princeton's School of Engineering and Applied Sciences, initiated his own program of RNG studies, and these studies have continued up to the present at PEAR, Princeton Engineering Anomalies Research. In 1987 Dean Radin and Roger Nelson, a Princeton psychologist, did a meta-analysis of all RNG experiments up to that time. Their report appeared in the prestigious mainstream science journal *Foundations of Physics.* Examining data from 597 experimental studies, carried out from 1959 to 1987, they found that the overall hit rate was about 51 percent. This might not sound like much, but the odds against this occurring by chance in the number of reported trials was over a trillion to one (Radin and Nelson, 1989, p. 140). Was selective reporting responsible for the results? To eliminate the evidence for a psychical effect would require 54,000 unpublished reports, or about ninety unpublished reports with negative results for each published report (Radin and Nelson 1989, p. 142). Another set of 1,262 experimental studies from PEAR, carried out from 1989 to 1996, was analyzed by York Dobyns, a mathematician at Princeton University. His analysis confirmed the previous studies (Dobyns 1996).

Analyzing the whole RNG research program, Nelson and Radin (1996) reported: "The primary overall findings, considering all available data, are that (a) nearly 40 years of experiments continue to show small but statistically unequivocal mental interaction effects, (b) the effect has been independently replicated by researchers at dozens of universities around the world, and (c) the effect has been replicated using a new experimental design involving skeptical third-party observers . . . A wide variety of theoretical models have been proposed for the interaction effect, ranging from observer effects in quantum mechanics to precognition."

Evaluations of Modern Laboratory Based Psychical Research

Several studies commissioned by various agencies of the United States government have given support to psychical research. A study by the Congressional Research Service, published in 1981, said, "Recent experi-ments in remote viewing and other studies in parapsychology suggest that there exists an 'interconnectedness' of the human mind with other minds and with matter" (U.S. Library of Congress 1983; in Radin 1997, p. 4). A few years later, the Army Research Institute commissioned a report on the status of parapsychology. Published in 1985, the report stated that the data reviewed in the report were "genuine scientific anomalies for which no one has an adequate explanation or set of explanations" (Palmer 1985; in Radin 1997, p. 4).

The U.S. Army in 1987 asked the National Research Council to review the state of parapsychological research. The NRC committee advised the Army to monitor parapsychological research in the United States and in the Soviet Union and to spend money in support of parapsychological research. The committee also admitted that for some categories of parapsychological experiments it could not provide alternatives to explanations involving paranormal influence. One of the committee members was the skeptical Dr. Ray Hyman, a psychology professor at the University of Oregon, who later said: "Parapsychologists should be rejoicing. This was the first government committee that said their work should be taken seriously" (*Chronicle of Higher Education*, September 14, 1988, p. A5; in Radin 1997, p. 4).

Macro Psychokinetic Effects

Although much of the recent work in parapsychology has focused on micro-psychokinetic effects and remote viewing, some experimental work in macro-psychokinetic phenomena, like that conducted in the late nineteenth and early twentieth centuries, has continued. Richard Broughton has discussed some of these cases in his book *Parapsychology: The Controversial Science* (1991), from which I will take two examples, one from Russia and the other from China. Both of these cases involve experiments conducted and reported by professional scientists. I shall also include here a particularly well documented poltergeist case, involving movements of objects by a variety of witnesses.

In Moscow, in June 1968, Soviet bloc scientists such as Dr. Zdenek Rejdak from Czechoslovakia, showed films of experiments with the Russian medium Nina Kulagina, giving Western scientists their first look at her abilities. Broughton (1991, p. 144) stated: "One film excerpt shows her moving a cigar tube standing upright on a playing card inside a closed, clear plastic case ... Other film excerpts show Kulagina selectively moving one or two matchsticks among several scattered on a table as well as moving several objects simultaneously in different directions. Soviet investigations of Kulagina were extensive. Besides studies by Soviet scientists openly interested in psychic phenomena, Kulagina was also investigated by committees and individuals from impartial scientific and medical institutes. The investigations appear to be quite competent regarding the elimination of fraud. Typically Kulagina was searched for magnets, strings, and other paraphernalia that might be used to simulate PK. For one series of filmed investigations she was examined by a physician and X-rayed for hidden magnets or traces of shrapnel from a war wound that could possibly act as a magnet. Often she was required to move nonmagnetic objects in sealed containers to eliminate magnetism or concealed threads as explanations."

In October of 1970, Kulagina was tested in St. Petersburg, Russia, by Gaither Pratt, who at the time was with the Division of Parapsychology at the University of Virginia at Charlottesville in the United States. He was accompanied by an associate, Champe Ransom. Also present were Kulagina's husband, a marine engineer, and two scientists, Genady Sergeyev, a physiologist who had been studying Kulagina, and Konstantin Ivanenko, a mathematician (Broughton 1991, p. 141). The meeting took place in a hotel room. Pratt and Ransom had with them some objects that could be used for tests, including a compass and a box of matches. Sergeyev placed them on a table in front of Kulagina, and then asked the group to step away from the table for a few minutes while Kulagina got herself into the proper mood. From a short distance, Pratt watched as Kulagina stretched her hands out over the objects. The matchbox moved towards her several inches. She put it back to its original position in the center of the table, and repeated the performance. The matchbox again moved toward her. She then declared herself ready to begin (Broughton 1991, p. 142).

One of the experiments involved a small nonmagnetic cylinder. Pratt filmed it with a home movie camera. Broughton (1991, pp. 142–143) wrote: "As Pratt set up the camera, Ransom spread a patch of aquarium gravel in the center of the table, placed the nonmagnetic cylinder upright in the midst of the gravel, and inverted a tall glass over it. Kulagina concentrated, Pratt filmed, and within moments the cylinder began tracing a path through the gravel. When the perimeter of the glass seemed to restrict the cylinder's movement, Ransom lifted it and Kulagina again concentrated. Again the upright cylinder plowed a path through the gravel as the camera rolled."

In April 1973, Benson Herbert, a British physicist, and his colleague Manfred Cassirer performed experiments with Kulagina in a temporary laboratory, set up in his room in a St. Petersburg hotel. Broughton (1991, p. 145) stated: "The centerpiece of this impromptu lab was a hydrometer, a glass-bulb-and-tube device used for measuring specific gravity, that floated upright in a saline solution. The entire system was surrounded by an electrically grounded screen. Herbert had hoped Kulagina might be able to depress the hydrometer, thus giving him a means of measuring the amount of psychic 'force' being used." Kulagina was somewhat ill at the time, and did not feel like making any attempts. Still, she was able to induce some small movements of the hydrometer. Exhausted from this effort, she sat down in a chair about three or four feet from the apparatus. From the chair, she focused her attention on the hydrometer. Broughton (1991, p. 145) stated: "Slowly she raised her arms in the direction of the apparatus. Within moments the previously motionless hydrometer floated in a straight line to the far side of the vessel. After resting there for about two minutes, it then retraced its path and continued to the near side. All of this took place under the close watch of the two British investigators, who were able to confirm there were no strings or hidden wires between Kulagina and the device several feet away." In the same session, Kulagina tried to rotate the needle of a compass, with some slight success. Herbert then saw the entire compass rotate counterclockwise about 45 degrees. "Over the next minute," said Broughton (1991, p. 145), "as Herbert ran his fingers over and under the table looking for threads and Kulagina sat motionless, the compass case did a zigzag dance about the table."

Between 1978 and 1984, Kulagina was investigated by physicists and other scientists in St. Petersburg at the Institute of Precise Mechanics and Optics and in Moscow at the Research Institute of Radio Engineering and Electronics as well as at the Baumann Higher School of Technology. The purpose of the research was not to verify her psychokinetic abilities (as these were taken as demonstrated), but to discover a biophysical force capable of explaining them. "In other experiments," said Broughton (1991, p. 145), "Kulagina reportedly decreased the intensity of a laser beam by affecting the physical properties of the gas through which it passed."

Zhang Baosheng was born in Bengxi City, in Liaoning province on China's northern coast. Local researchers learned of his paranormal abilities in 1976. Chinese scientists had for some time been studying paranormal phenomena under the name of "exceptional functions of the human body" (Broughton 1991, p. 166). Interest in this research became very strong in the late 1970s, causing a negative reaction from some scientists and Communist Party officials. In April 1982, the Party's National Committee of Science decided to resolve the dispute by inviting supporters of exceptional functions of the human body (EFHB) research and their critics to conduct joint experiments with leading psychics. Zhang was brought to Beijing and produced good results during these tests, which many other psychics failed (Broughton 1991, p. 166). For the next couple of years, Zhang was studied by researchers in several Beijing laboratories. During this period, much of the work with Zhang was done by Lin Shuhuang, a professor in the physics department of Beijing Teachers' College, who had also been involved in the April 1982 tests. Nineteen researchers conducted experiments under Lin in the period from December 1982 to May 1983.

Broughton (1991, p. 167) said, "In one experiment specially marked pieces of paper were chemically treated and placed in a glass test tube. The tube was melted to constrict it roughly at the midpoint. Into the top part were placed cotton wads that had been treated with a different chemical that would react if it came into contact with the chemical on the target papers. The top of the test tube was then irreversibly sealed with special paper. With four experimenters watching from different angles, the tube was placed in front of Zhang. Five minutes later the target papers were lying beside the empty tube. The seal on the tube was undamaged. . . . In another experiment of that series a live insect was marked and placed inside a tube. The tube was sealed so that any attempt to open it would break a fine hair glued inside. With two experimenters watching, the tube was placed on a table in front of Zhang. Several minutes later the insect, still alive, was outside the tube."

In 1984, research with Zhang came under the control of the Institute for Space-Medico Engineering (ISME), an agency connected with the Chinese military. This marked the end of regular publication of the results. But there were some occasional leaks. Broughton (1991, pp. 167 –168) stated: "In 1987 the Chinese scientific community received a shock when the Spaceflight Department awarded its Scientific Research Achievement Prize (second class) to the ISME team for a film of one of Zhang's experiments. Articles in the press and a Chinese science magazine reported that the ISME scientists filmed the movement of a medicine pill through an irreversibly sealed glass vial. The film was made in color using a high-speed (400 frames per second) Japanese camera. The reports say that three frames of the film clearly show the pill passing through the glass (entering the glass, halfway through, and exiting). Although no scientists outside of China seem to have seen the film, in late 1990 researchers both in and outside of China were surprised by the arrival of a new Chinese journal, the *Chinese Journal of Somatic Science*. In it was a report of new experiments with Zhang by the ISME team. Accompanying the report was a series of photos, reportedly from a 400-frame-per-second camera, showing a pill exiting from the bottom of a bottle held by Zhang. The report does not indicate whether the photos are from the prize-winning film."

Part One Conclusion: There Is a Mind Element

The experimental evidence accumulated by scientists of the past two centuries in the areas of telepathy, clairvoyance, and psychokinesis cannot be easily dismissed. Among the experimenters reporting positive results were several Nobel laureates, including the Curies, Richet, and Crookes. In later years, other scientists of lesser fame have conducted careful reproducible studies of a variety of paranormal phenomena. The phenomena were judged so reliable that governments and militaries invested considerable sums of money in practical applications of remote viewing. This body of paranormal evidence points to the existence of a mind element associated with the human organism. This mind element appears to be endowed with sensory abilities that enable it to perceive things at a distance and manipulate objects composed of ordinary matter in ways not explained by our current laws of physics.

PART TWO:
EVIDENCE FOR A CONSCIOUS SELF
THAT CAN EXIST APART
FROM THE BODY AND MIND

The mind is a subtle material element, which can, among other things, gather impressions of objects beyond the normal range of perception and manipulate ordinary matter in paranormal ways. But mind does not itself provide the human organism with conscious experience. Consciousness has another source, called, in Sanskrit, the *atma*, or self. The self, according to the Sanskrit Vedic literature, is a small particle of spirit that illuminates the body and mind with consciousness. Although we cannot see the *atma* directly, we can detect its presence through its symptom, consciousness. This conscious self can exist apart from the body and mind. We will now review scientific evidence for the existence of such a conscious self. As in the case of the mind element, I shall confine myself to evidence from the time period paralleling that of the modern evolution science, i.e., from the middle of the nineteenth century up to the present. I shall also confine myself to evidence suggesting that there is at this moment within the body a conscious self that is not a product of mind or matter. I shall consider evidence for the survival of this self after the death of the body in chapter 8.

William James on Consciousness

William James noted that "arrests of brain development occasion imbecility, that blows on the head abolish memory or consciousness, and that brain-stimulants and poisons change the quality of our ideas" (Murphy and Ballou 1960, p. 284). The totality of such observations led many scientists of his day to conclude that consciousness was produced by the brain and continually dependent upon the brain for its existence. When the brain ceased to function, the individual consciousness associated with it ceased to exist.

There was, however, no generally accepted explanation of exactly how consciousness is produced by the brain (and neither is there one today). Furthermore, any such theory of consciousness production would have to account for the production of millions of episodes of consciousness in an individual's daily life. This caused James to say, "The theory of production is therefore not a jot more simple or credible in itself than any other conceivable theory. It is only a little more popular" (Murphy and Ballou 1960, p. 294).

James (Murphy and Ballou 1960, p. 290) thought the brain might have a transmissive rather than productive relationship to consciousness. A prism has a transmissive function relative to light. It does not produce light. When light passes through a prism, the prism modifies it. According to this conception, the brain would transmit or obstruct consciousness to various degrees. James said: "According to the state in which the brain finds itself, the barrier of its obstructiveness may also be supposed to rise or fall. It sinks so low, when the brain is in full activity, that a comparative flood of spiritual energy pours over. At other times, only such occassional waves of thought as heavy sleep permits get by. And when finally a brain stops acting altogether, or decays, that special stream of consciousness which it subserved will vanish entirely from this natural world. But the sphere of being that supplied the consciousness would still be intact; and in that more real world with which, even whilst here, it was continuous, the consciousness might, in ways unknown to us, continue still" (Murphy and Ballou 1960, p. 292). James seems to prefer the image of a living stream of consciousness to that of a particulate conscious soul, but either way, consciousness exists apart from matter.

In connection with the idea that the brain simply transmits preexisting consciousness, James cited the following statement by British philosopher F. C. S. Schiller (1891): "Matter is an admirably calculated machinery for regulating, limiting, and restraining the consciousness which it encases. . . . If the material encasement be coarse and simple, as in the lower organisms, it permits only a little intelligence to permeate through; if it is delicate and complex, it leaves more pores and exists, as it were, for the manifestations of consciousness" (Murphy and Ballou 1960, p. 300).

Out-of-Body Experiences

Near death and out-of-body experiences (variously abbreviated as NDEs, OBEs, OOBEs) provide evidence demonstrating that consciousness may have an existence entirely apart from gross matter (the body) and subtle matter (the mind). Throughout history, people around the world have reported these experiences. In a cross-cultural study, Dean Sheils (1978, p. 697) stated: "Data from nearly 70 non-Western cultures were used to explore beliefs in out-of-the-body experiences (OOBEs). The data reveal that OOBE beliefs appear in about 95 per cent of the world's cultures and that they are striking in their uniformity even though the cultures are diverse in structure and location. Three conventional explanations of OOBE beliefs—social control, crisis, and the dream theories —were tested and found to be inadequate as explanations. Hence, it is possible that the specificity and generality of OOBE beliefs is simply a response to a genuine event; i.e., the actual occurrence of OOBE." By demonstrating that there is a conscious self that can experience sensations apart from the gross physical body, the OBE provides a foundation for the further conclusion that there is a conscious self that survives the death of the gross physical body. As Sheils himself says (1978, p. 700), "Before we can consider the issue of survival we are forced to establish that there is in fact 'something' that can survive." Apart from anecdotal cross-cultural evidence, there is medical and scientific research that supports the idea that there is a conscious self that can exist apart from the mind and body.

Some of the most systematic investigations into the near death experience (NDE) were carried out by Kenneth Ring. The popular books of Elisabeth Kübler-Ross and Raymond Moody on NDEs attracted the attention of Ring. Although he agreed with their conclusions, he felt the topic required a more scientific approach (Ring 1980, p. 19).

Ring assembled subjects, at least eighteen years old, who had been close to death either through illness, accident, or attempted suicide. Some subjects were enlisted through referrals from hospitals and psychiatrists, some responded to newspaper ads, and others, who had through various means learned of the survey, offered themselves as volunteers. In none of the attempts to enlist subjects was the topic of out-of-body experiences mentioned and none of the subjects were paid. A total of 102 subjects were enlisted. Subjects were first encouraged to give a "free narrative" of their near death episode. Then they were carefully questioned in order to determine "the presence or absence of the various components of the core experience as described by Moody" (Ring 1980, p. 28).

The subjects were told their identities would not be given in the final report. They were allowed to question the purpose of the study, but only after completing their interviews. The interviews were conducted between May 1977 and May 1978. Ring (1980, p. 29) stated: "A total of 102 persons recounting 104 near-death incidents were interviewed. Of these, 52 nearly died as a result of a serious illness; 26 from a serious accident; and 24 as a result of a suicide attempt." About half were male, half female, and all except 7 were white. Almost all were religious. The median age at the time of the reported near death incidents was about 38 years. One third of the subjects were interviewed within a year after their experience, sixty percent within two years.

Ring analyzed the interview reports in terms of a weighted list of features of the core near death experience derived from Moody's book *Life After Life*. The features and relative weights were (Ring 1980, pp. 32–33): a sense of being dead (1 point); feelings of pleasant peacefulness

(2 or 4 points, depending on the strength of the feeling); a sense of separating from one's body (2 or 4 points, depending on the distinctness of the description); entrance into a dark region (2 or 4 points, depending on the presence of movement); hearing a voice or feeling the presence of someone (3 points); reviewing one's life (3 points); seeing light (2 points); seeing beautiful colors (1 point); entering the light (4 points); encountering visible spirit beings (3 points). Scores could thus range from 0 to 29 points. Three judges had to agree on a subject's score for each item. Subjects with scores of less than six were deemed not to have had a Moody type NDE. Scores of from 6 to 9 points indicated a moderate NDE, and scores of 10 and over indicated a deep NDE. Ring found that 49 of his subjects (48 percent) reported experiences corresponding to Moody's description of the "core experience" (Ring 1980, p. 32). Of these, 27 persons (26 percent) had a deep NDE, and 22 (22 percent) had a moderate NDE.

Some of the narrative descriptions by Ring's subjects are of interest. One subject's sister worked as a nurse in the hospital in which the subject had an NDE during treatment for a heart attack. During the NDE, the subject saw a vision of her sister coming to the hospital. "She walked in shortly after the alert was sounded and got to the emergency room where she worked and someone told her what was going on and she came ripping upstairs. I could see her doing it, I could see her coming up the elevator." The subject's sister later confirmed to her that her vision represented exactly what had happened (Ring 1980, p. 51).

Ring also included in his book a case originally reported by British psychical researcher F. W. H. Myers in his classic book *Human Personality and Its Survival of Bodily Death*. The subject, Dr. A. S. Wiltse, was a medical doctor. In 1889, he came down with typhoid fever and almost died. As he entered a coma, he recalled feeling drowsy and then losing consciousness. Dr. S. H. Raynes, the doctor who was attending Wiltse, said that for four hours he showed no pulse or heart beat. It was during that time that Wiltse had the following experience: "I came again into a state of conscious existence and discovered that I was still in the body, but the body and I had no longer any interests in common." He felt that he, the living soul, was "interwoven" with the bodily tissues. But then the connections with the bodily tissues began to break, and he came out of the body through the head. "I seemed to be translucent, of a bluish cast and perfectly naked," said Wiltse. "As I turned, my left elbow came in contact with the arm of one of two gentlemen, who were standing at the door. To my surprise, his arm passed through mine without apparent resistance, the severed parts closing again without pain, as air reunites." Wiltse then gazed upon his own dead body. But then the body's eyes opened and

Wiltse found himself once more inside that body and said to himself, "What in the world has happened to me? Must I die again?" (Ring 1980, p. 230)

Ring (1980, p. 232) said that the near death experience is best explained as an out-of-body experience. Something separates from this body, but he prefers not to use the word soul, which for him does not function well as a scientific term because of all the different meanings attached to it by various religions. This could be avoided by giving a good definition for the term soul. But I have no objection to Ring's solution. He says (1980, p. 233): "I would content myself with saying that out-of-body experiences provide us with an empirical referent for the possible origin of the concept of soul. As such, I favor restricting its use to religious contexts. On the basis of the separation hypothesis, however, I do endorse the proposition that consciousness (with or without a second body) may function independently of the physical body."

In *Heading Toward Omega* (1984), Ring documented the results of further research. The results yielded more confirmation of his interpretation of the NDE as an out-of-body experience. Ring gave more accounts of NDEs, including ones in which the subjects entered into the light as "pure consciousness" and found themselves communicating telepathically with friendly spiritual beings who gave them messages of enlightenment. A subject identified as Mr. Dippong said that the last thing he remembered before entering into the NDE was praying to God. Then he found himself entering another state of consciousness. "I was in a heavenly pasture with flowers. It was another place, another time, and perhaps it was even another universe." His ears filled with otherworldly music. Everything that happened was beyond anything he had previously experienced, and yet was somehow familiar. Like many other subjects, he said the experience was really beyond words. In the midst of beautifully colored light he encountered a radiantly beautiful being that he felt could have been his creator. The golden-hued creature, who seemed strangely familiar to Dippong, was emanating light and love. He also became aware of other living beings. He felt that all living things were part of the light, and the light was part of them (Ring 1984, p. 61–66).

A subject named Ann described an NDE that occurred during the delivery of her second child in 1954. During a medical crisis, she felt herself being taken up swiftly toward a distant light. She left her pain behind and entered into feelings of peace and love. In this state, she felt that a being would soon approach her. When the being came, she felt she had met her dearmost friend. The being telepathically communicated that he had come for her child. Ann was happy, but soon became dejected when she realized she did not have a child. "He patted my hand in sympathy and reassured me that I was a mother, and I did have a child, but the child must have been delayed somehow," recalled Ann in a letter to Ring. "Then he waved his hand across the space in front of us and the haze cleared. I could see the nurses and doctor, and my baby, back in the delivery room." The being communicated to Ann that her child would live only four days. When Ann learned there was nothing she could do to prevent this, she said she did not want to go back. The being told her that she must go back. It was not time for her to go. He had come for her child, and would return for the baby in four days. Hearing this Ann was pleased, and willingly returned. She awoke to find a nurse slapping her face and calling her name. She learned she had given birth to a daughter, whom she called Tari. She felt there was something she wanted to tell the staff, but she could not quite remember what it was. On the second day, Ann's doctor learned that Tari was suffering from cerebral hemorrhaging and would most probably soon die. On the fourth day, the child did die. The physician told the nurses not to tell Ann, because he wished to break the news to her himself. But somehow this did not happen quickly enough. It came time for Ann to be discharged from the hospital, and at this time a nurse said, "Oh, God! Your doctor should have been here by now! I'm not supposed to tell you, but I can't let you go on believing Tari is alive. She died early this morning." At that time, Ann remembered her NDE (Ring 1984, pp. 77–84).

Ring used the Greek word *omega* for his study because it is the last letter of the Greek alphabet, and can be taken to mean the end of life, or, more positively, the goal of life. Ring (1984, p. 252) took this goal to be the evolution of consciousness. Ring (1984, p. 255) considered the NDE to be "only one of a family of related transcendental experiences" that were contributing to this evolution, characterized by "unlocking spiritual potentials previously dormant."

Another prominent researcher into NDEs and OBEs is Michael B. Sabom. When he was in his first year of cardiology practice at the University of Florida in Gainesville, he heard psychiatric social worker Sarah Kreutziger give a talk about Dr. Raymond Moody's book *Life After Life*. Sabom (1982, p. 3) recalled, "My indoctrinated scientific mind just couldn't relate seriously to these 'far-out' descriptions of afterlife spirits and such."

Nevertheless, Sabom, along with Kreutziger, decided to do a little research into the matter. Sabom chose patients that had been close to physical death, which he defined as "any bodily state resulting from an extreme physiological catastrophe, accidental or otherwise, that would reasonably be expected to result in irreversible biological death in the majority of instances and would demand urgent medical attention, if available" (Sabom 1982, p. 9). These states included severe injury, heart attacks, and deep comas. In interviewing subjects, Sabom and Kreutziger agreed they would at first avoid mentioning any interest in "near death experiences." They would simply ask subjects to tell their remembrances of what happened before they lost consciousness. Then they would ask if they could recall anything that happened during their unconscious state. Some subjects simply said they could remember nothing, except that they were unconscious. But other subjects would hesitate, and ask, "Why do you want to know?" At that point, Sabom or Kreutziger would explain that some patients had experienced things while they should have been unconscious and that as researchers they were sincerely interested in gathering more information about such experiences. The subjects would then usually share their experiences, first saying things like, "You won't believe this, but . . ." (Sabom 1982, pp. 9–10).

In his book, Sabom described many aspects of the NDE. I found most interesting the "autoscopic" experiences, in which the subjects found themselves observing their own bodies. For example, a fifty-seven-year-old construction worker found himself floating four feet above his body during an operation. He could see the doctors and nurses operating. At a certain point, he noticed one of the nurses looking in the direction of his floating face. It was obvious to him that she could not see anything (Sabom 1982, p. 10).

In another case, an American soldier in Vietnam was severely wounded in a mine explosion, losing two legs and one arm. While he was being transported away from the battlefield in a helicopter, in an unconscious state, he had an out-of-body experience. He remained close to his body and could see it. His body was taken to a field hospital. There he saw doctors operating on his body, but he wanted them to stop. In his interview he said, "I actually remember grabbing the doctor. . . . I grabbed and he wasn't there or either I just went through him or whatever" (Sabom 1982, p. 33). The same soldier reported traveling from the operating room back to the battlefield, where he witnessed other soldiers putting the dead into body bags and collecting the wounded. After trying to get one of the soldiers to stop, he found himself suddenly back in the hospital. He recalled, "It was almost like you materialize there and all of a sudden the next instant you were over here. It was just like you blinked your eyes" (Sabom 1982, p. 33). Other subjects also reported such "thought travel" experiences. A night watchman who had an autoscopic NDE during cardiac arrest reported traveling to locations near the operating room where he was being treated. These movements occurred according to his own desires. He recalled: "It was just like I said, 'Okay, what's going on in the parking lot?' and my brain would go over and take a look at what's going on over there and come back and report to me" (Sabom 1982, p. 34).

Sabom (1982, p. 34) stated, "All the people interviewed remarked that during the autoscopic NDE, they felt as if they had been truly 'separated' from their physical body." The autoscopic NDEs would usually end with the subject reporting reentering the body at the same time as some key event in their treatment. One of Sabom's subjects, a cardiac arrest patient, reported floating above his body. He could see the medical team putting pads (defibrillators) on his chest. He could not feel the first shock. Just before the second shock, he remembered his family, and thought he should reenter his body. He reported, "It was just as if I went back and got into my body" (Sabom 1982, p. 35).

Many of Sabom's subjects reported what Sabom (1982, p. 39) called "transcendental near-death experiences." The autoscopic experiences described above involve perception of the subject's own body and the surrounding environment, including other people, as they would be perceived by an observer in normal consciousness. The transcendental NDE's involve perceptions of being transported to realms beyond that of our normal experience, and perhaps also encountering deceased friends or relatives or personalities who seemed angelic or godlike. Forty-one of Sabom's subjects reported transcendental NDEs (Sabom 1982, p. 41). One of Sabom's heart attack patients recalled how he blacked out while being taken into a hospital for treatment. He saw his life flashing before him, including his acceptance of Jesus Christ. Then he entered a black tunnel, seeing at the other end an orange-colored light. Seeing this he entered into a peaceful state of consciousness. He could hear voices. He saw steps, which he took to be the steps leading up to the gates of heaven (Sabom 1982, p. 40). Some of Sabom's subjects reported experiences with both autoscopic and transcendental elements.

The most interesting of Sabom's subjects, from the scientific point of view, were those who gave detailed reports of their surgical procedures, observed during out-of-body experiences. In the beginning Sabom was skeptical of such reports. He thought it would be very easy for him to explain them. Sabom, a veteran of over a hundred resuscitations of cardiac arrest patients, said (1982, p. 7): "In essence, I would pit my experience as a trained cardiologist against the professed visual recollections of lay individuals. In so doing, I was convinced that obvious inconsistencies would appear which would reduce these purported visual observations to no more than an 'educated guess' on the part of the patient." But at the end of his study, Sabom came to a different conclusion.

Here is one of the cases that helped change Sabom's mind. The subject was a night watchman, 52 years old. He had undergone two heart attacks previous to the interview. He told Sabom about an OBE that occurred during his first heart attack, but hesitated to tell him about another experience he had undergone during his second heart attack, suggesting Sabom would probably not believe it. Upon further prompting from Sabom, the man went on to describe things he witnessed during his second heart attack (Sabom 1982, pp. 64–67). In his interview, he jumped back and forth in time, so in the following summary I have sorted out his observations in what appears to me to be the correct order. First he was administered an anesthetic intravenously, which caused him to become unconscious. But then he recalled, "All of a sudden I became aware of it . . . like I was in the room a couple of feet or so above my head, like I was another person in the room." He saw himself being draped with several layers of cloth. He saw his chest opened, and the chest cavity being held apart by a metal apparatus. He observed his heart, and saw that part of it was colored differently than the rest. He saw the doctors insert an apparatus into a vein. He heard them discussing a bypass procedure. He saw the doctors remove a piece of his heart. During the operation he saw the surgeons "injecting a syringe of something into my heart on two occasions." After the operation, he saw two doctors stitching him up. They worked first on the inside, and then the outside.

The subject's testimony matched very closely the surgeon's report, which the subject had never seen (Sabom 1982, p. 68; bracketed interpolations by Sabom): "A satisfactory general anesthesia [halothan] was introduced with the patient in the supine position. . . . He was prepped from the chin to below the ankles and draped in the customary sterile fashion . . . A long midline incision was made. . . . The sternum was sawed open in the midline, a self-retaining retractor was utilized . . . [After the heart had been exposed] Two 32 Argyle venous lines were placed through stab wounds in the right atrium [heart chamber]. . . . One of these tubes extended into the inferior vena cava and one into the superior vena cava [large veins which feed blood to venous side of heart]. . . . The patient was placed on cardiopulmonary bypass. . . . The ventricular aneurysm [large scarred area of heart which represented area of previous heart attack and would have appeared to be of a different color than the normal heart muscle that remained] was dissected free. . . . The left ventricle was then closed. . . . Air was evacuated from the left ventricle with a needle and syringe . . . The wound was closed in layers."

The subject's account contained many other details not mentioned in the surgeon's report, such as the insertion of sponges into the chest cavity to absorb blood. These details, too minor to be mentioned in the report itself, were, however, consistent with the report. Sabom gave other examples of very detailed accounts of perceptions of the details of surgical treatment, details not likely to be known by a patient. To Sabom, these detailed reports by subjects, matching the records kept by doctors about the exact surgical procedures, were good confirmation of the reality of the reported out-of-body experiences.

Thirty-two of Sabom's subjects reported details of their medical treatment (1982, p. 83). In order to judge the extent to which these reports could have been the result of educated guesses, Sabom interviewed a control group of twenty-five cardiac patients, with backgrounds similar to those reporting NDEs (1982, p. 84). They were familiar in a general way with hospital treatment of cardiac arrest and many admitted to having seen hospital dramas on television. Sabom asked the control subjects to imagine they were in an operating room watching doctors resuscitate a heart attack victim and to report to him in detail what they thought would be happening. Two of the control subjects could not come up with any description at all. Of the twenty-three who did supply descriptions, twenty made major errors. The most common error was including mouth-to-mouth breathing in the account. In hospitals, other methods are used to give oxygen to a patient. Three of those giving descriptions gave very limited ones without obvious error (Sabom 1982, p. 85). By way of contrast, of the 32 subjects reporting some recollection of their treatment during NDEs, 26 gave general descriptions that did not include any major errors. According to Sabom (1982, p.87), these descriptions "did correspond in a general way to the known facts of the near-death crisis event." According to these sub-jects, they were focusing more on the experience itself than on what the doctors were doing, and were thus not able to recall details (Sabom 1982, p. 86). Furthermore, six subjects gave remarkably detailed accounts that matched their medical treatment records. So, in the control group, 20 out of 23 subjects who gave reports made major errors, while in the NDE group of 32 subjects none made any mistakes and six gave very detailed reports that exactly matched their medical records, unseen by them. This led Sabom (1982, p. 87) to conclude that "these NDE accounts most likely are not subtle fabrications based on prior general knowledge." He said that further research was desirable, in order to strengthen the basis for this conclusion.

At the end of his study, Sabom (1982, p. 183) asked, "Could the mind which splits apart from the physical brain be, in essence, the 'soul,' which continues to exist after final bodily death, according to some religious doctrines?"

Sabom has his critics. One is Susan Blackmore. Once inclined to accept the reality of out-of-body experiences, Blackmore now believes that the out-of-body experience does not actually involve any conscious entity going out of the body. There are thus two interpretations of the OBE. The extrasomatic interpretation holds that there is a self which actually leaves the body. The intrasomatic interpretation holds that there is merely an internal impression of being out of the body. Most supporters of the intrasomatic interpretation would also deny that there is any kind of substantial conscious self at all, what to speak of one that could leave the body. Blackmore, who holds the intrasomatic view, stated (1982, p. 251): "Nothing leaves the body in an OBE and so there is nothing to survive." Under this intrasomatic view, the OBE is simply a dreamlike hallucination manufactured by the brain.

In his book *Parapsychology, Philosophy, and Spirituality: A Postmodern Exploration*, philosopher David Ray Griffin (1997, pp. 232–242) discussed objections to the intrasomatic hypothesis, the most significant of which I outline in the next few paragraphs. The most obvious objection is the intensity of the subject's feeling and perception of being out of the body. Most of those reporting OBEs are resolute in their conviction that they experienced something real, something distinct from a dream or hallucination.

Some subjects, not under anesthesia, reported a cessation of pain during their OBEs. This could possibly be explained by the action of the body's natural painkillers, such as endorphins. But the subjects reported that the pain returned as soon as they reentered their bodies. This should not happen if the pain relief was caused by endorphins. The most fitting explanation appears to be that the conscious self actually leaves the body and becomes temporarily detached from the sensations of the body.

The primarily visual nature of OBEs is also a problem for advocates of intrasomatic theories. When a person approaching death gradually becomes unconscious, normally the visual sensations cease before the auditory sensations. It would thus seem that subjects on the brink of death should be recalling sounds rather than sights. In this connection, it should also be noted that schizophrenic hallucinations are primarily auditory, not visual.

That the visual impressions of subjects, who should have been unconscious, correspond to their actual surroundings tends to rule out the theory that the subjects are making up their OBE reports as a defense against fear of death, to gain social approval, or to support a personal religious belief. It seems strange that such hallucinations should be limited to reconstructions of the actual surroundings.

The correspondence between the visual impressions and the actual surroundings also tends to rule out the hypothesis that the visions are hallucinations caused by anoxia (lack of oxygen in the brain) and hypercarbia (too much carbon dioxide). According to Sabom (1982, pp. 175–176), lack of oxygen produces a confused state of mind, contrasting with the mental clarity experienced by OBE subjects. Too much carbon dioxide can bring about flashes of light and other effects, but apparently not the perception of one's immediate surroundings. Furthermore, in one of Sabom's cases, the physicians actually took a blood sample for blood-gas analysis during cardiac treatment. The oxygen level was above average, and the carbon dioxide level was below average (Sabom 1982, p. 178).

Some have proposed that temporal lobe seizures account for the OBEs, but according to Sabom (1982, pp. 173–174) perception of the immediate environment is quite distorted during such seizures.

To account for the accuracy of the visual impressions reported in OBEs, Blackmore and others have proposed that the mind of a person losing consciousness uses touch and sound sensations to manufacture accurate visual imagery without actually leaving the body and seeing things from that perspective. But in many cases the visual perceptions extend to things the subject could not easily have learned about through touch or sound. One of Sabom's OBE subjects reported seeing gauge needles moving in an appropriately real fashion on a piece of medical equipment (a defibrillator). Blackmore (1993, pp. 118–119) suggested that the information could have been obtained after the operation (perhaps from a television program) and then incorporated into the subject's report. Of course, one can suggest anything, but according to the subject, he had not seen any television programs in which defibrillators were used (Griffin 1997, p. 246).

One of Sabom's patients reported seeing himself getting a shot in his right groin. Actually, it was not a shot. The doctors were withdrawing blood for a test. Sabom said this confusion would be natural for the subject, if he were actually viewing the action from outside his body, as a shot and blood withdrawal would look the same—the insertion of a needle. If the subject had manufactured an image of this from overheard words, it is unlikely that a withdrawal of blood would have been confused for a shot, because the doctors would clearly have been calling for a withdrawal of blood for testing. Blackmore replied that an image could have been reconstructed not from sound but from touch sensations. But here is an important detail: the medical reports said that the blood withdrawal was made from the left groin but the patient reported that incident, which he interpreted as a shot, had taken place in the right groin. If the subject had manufactured an image of what was happening from touch sensations, there should not have been any confusion. He should have felt the pricking on his left groin. But Sabom pointed out that if the subject had been looking down at his body from the foot of the bed, he would have seen, from his perspective, that the needle was going into the right groin. Blackmore chose to characterize the subject's entire report as uncorroborated, but neglects to mention that Sabom had interviewed the man's wife, who said that her husband had told her and her daughter the story soon after the event and had later repeated it several times, without any change. This tends to rule out the suggestion that the story was manufactured and gradually elaborated with newly acquired information about medical procedures (Sabom 1982, 109–111; Griffin, 1997, p. 248).

In view of Blackmore's objections, OBE accounts of events beyond the immediate area of subject would be important. In 1976, one of Sabom's subjects had a heart attack during a stay in a hospital. During his resuscitation he reported seeing his relatives. "I couldn't hear anything. Not one peep . . . And I remember seeing them down the hall just as plain as could be. The three of them were standing there—my wife, my oldest son and my oldest daughter and the doctor . . . I knew damn well they were there." From accounts of the man's resuscitation, it does not seem he would have been able to see his relatives or receive any information about them. The man was not expecting any visits from relatives that day, because he was due to be discharged. Even if he had been expecting a visit, it would have been hard for him to know who would be coming. He had six grown children and they had been taking turns coming to see him with their mother. On this particular day, the man's wife, eldest son, and eldest daughter had met and on the spur of the moment had decided to come visit him. They arrived at the hospital just as he was being taken out of his room back up to the operating rooms. The family members were stopped in the hallway, ten doors away from where their father, lying on a bed, was being worked on by doctors and nurses. The man's face was pointed away from his relatives. His wife recalled that she could only see the back of his head at a distance. He was immediately taken away to the emergency room without passing his relatives. The man's wife said, "He couldn't have seen us." Blackmore does not comment on this case (Sabom 1982, pp. 111–113; Griffin 1997, pp. 249–250).

Dr. Kimberley Clark, a professor of medicine at the University of Washington and a social worker at Harborview Medical Center, reported another case that is difficult to account for in terms of hallucinations formed from sound and touch impressions entering the mind of a person approaching complete unconsciousness. A migrant worker named Maria underwent treatment for cardiac arrest at Harborview. Afterwards, she told Clark she had experienced an OBE. She had been floating above her body and looking down at the doctors and nurses. Clark figured she could have imagined the scene, drawing upon things she saw and heard before she lost consciousness. Maria then told how she had found herself floating outside by the emergency room driveway. Clark concluded that she could have seen the driveway during her stay and incorporated it into her OBE. Maria further explained how she had noticed something sitting on the ledge of the third floor of the hospital building. She found herself floating right up next to the object, which turned out to be a tennis shoe. She described little details, such as a worn place in the spot where the little toe would have been, and a shoelace looped under the heel. Clark went to check, and at first saw nothing. She went up to the third floor, and after looking through many windows finally found one where she could see the shoe. The ledge was not easily visible from the window. One had to press one's face against the glass, and angle the eyes down. And from there she still could not see the details described by Maria. Clark stated: "The only way she would have had such a perspective was if she had been floating right outside and at very close range to the tennis shoe." When the shoe was retrieved it matched the description given by Maria (Clark 1982, p. 243; Griffin 1997, pp. 250–251). Blackmore (1993, p. 128) dismisses this case, calling it "fascinating but unsubstantiated." But Griffin (1997, p. 251) points out that "she does not make clear, however, what further substantiation, beyond the written testimony of a health-care professional, would be needed."

Kathy Kilne, a nurse at Hartford Hospital in Connecticut, told of a female cardiac arrest patient who had an OBE. The event took place in 1985. Recalling the patient's testimony, Kilne said: "She told me how she floated up over her body, viewed the resuscitation effort for a short time and then felt herself being pulled up through several floors of the hospital. She then found herself above the roof and realized she was looking at the skyline of Hartford . . . out of the corner of her eye she saw a red object. It turned out to be a shoe." Kilne told the story to a doctor who was doing his residency at the hospital. He mockingly dismissed the story. But later that day, he had a janitor take him up on the roof, where he saw a red shoe. He took the shoe and showed it to Kilne, who said by then he had become a believer (Griffin 1997, p. 251; Ring and Lawrence 1993, pp. 226–227).

These kinds of experiences are not uncommon. In 1954, Hornell

Hart published a summary study of out-of-body experiences during which the subject reported information that required some kind of paranormal knowledge. Hart (1954) found 288 cases mentioned in various publications and determined that in 99 of these cases the information reported by the subject was later confirmed. This indicated that the reports were genuine. Furthermore, in 55 cases, witnesses reported seeing an apparition of the subject at a location different from the subject's body (Griffin 1997, p. 254). In some cases the subjects voluntarily induced their OBEs, and in some cases the OBEs were spontaneous.

Ian Stevenson and coworker Pasricha Satwant have reported some interesting near death experiences from India (Satwant and Stevenson, 1986). Stevenson was a psychiatrist from the University of Virginia Medical School, and Satwant was clinical psychologist with the National Institute of Mental Health and Neurosciences at Bangalore, India. Satwant and Stevenson encountered the NDE stories as they were interviewing subjects in the course of their research into past life memories. All the sixteen subjects reporting NDEs were Hindus from northern India. The typical Indian NDE involved a subject being taken to the court of Yamaraja, the Hindu god of death, by messengers called Yamadutas, servants of Yamaraja. At the court of Yamaraja the subject encountered someone with a book or papers, corresponding to Chitragupta, who keeps a record of everyone's actions during life. This record is used to determine a person's next birth. In the NDE cases reported by Satwant and Stevenson, it would happen that the subject had been taken by mistake and had to be sent back to life on earth.

Here are some typical cases. Vasudeva Pandey, interviewed in 1975 and 1976, told of an experience that happened when he was about ten years old, around the year 1931. He had nearly died of a typhoid disease, the symptoms of death being so convincing that his body was taken for cremation. When signs of life were observed, he was taken to a hospital, where he remained unconscious for three days. In recollecting his NDE, he said he had been taken away by two persons, who eventually dragged him to Yamaraja, who said to his servants, "I had asked you to bring Vasudev the gardener ... You have brought Vasudev the student." The same two servants then brought Vasudev back to the world of the living. When Vasudev regained consciousness at the hospital he saw Vasudev the gardener among a group of friends and family who had come to see him. He looked healthy, but he died that night (Satwant and Stevenson 1986, p. 166).

Durga Jatav was fifty years old when he told his story in 1979. When he was about twenty years old, he was suffering from typhoid and at one point his family thought he was dead. He told his family that he had been taken away by ten persons. When he tried to escape, they cut his legs off at the knees. He arrived at a place where many people were sitting at tables. One of them said that Jatav's name was not on the list of people to be taken, and that he should be sent back. Jatav asked how he could go back with no legs. His lower legs were again attached to his knees, and he was told not to bend his knees for some time. Satwant and Stevenson (1986, p. 167) reported: "Durga's sister and a neighbor noticed, a few days after he revived, that marks had appeared on his knees; there had previously been no such marks there. These folds, or deep fissures, in the skin on the front of Durga's knees were still visible in 1979 . . . One informant for this case (the headman of the village where Durga lived) said that at the time of Durga's experience another person by the same name had died in Agra (about 30 km away)."

Chajju Bania reported that during his NDE four black messengers took him to the court of Yamaraja, where he saw an old woman with a pen and several clerks. Yamaraja was sitting on a high chair. He had a white beard and was wearing yellow cloth. "We don't need Chajju Bania," said one of the clerks. "We had asked for Chajju Kumbar. Push him back and bring the other man." Chajju Bania did not want to go back. He asked Yamaraja for permission to stay, but was pushed down, at which point he regained consciousness. Satwant and Stevenson (1986, p. 167) reported: "Chajju told us that he later learned that a person called Chajju Kumhar had died at about the same time that he (Chajju Bania) revived."

The cultural heritage of such accounts goes back a long time. The *Shrimad Bhagavatam*, one of India's ancient Sanskrit histories, tells the story of Ajamila (Canto 6, chpts. 1–3). As a boy, he was a saintly *brahmana,* but once he happened to see a debauched man embracing a prostitute in a public place. The vision stayed in his mind. He gave up his religious principles, and he in turn began consorting with a prostitute, by whom he had many children. He supported his family by gambling and robbery. He lived in this degraded way until the very end of his life. At the time of death, the servants of Yamaraja came to fetch him. Seeing them, Ajamila cried out the name of his youngest child, Narayana, who was standing nearby. The servants of Yamaraja nevertheless continued dragging Ajamila to the court of Yamaraja. Suddenly, some servants of Vishnu appeared and stopped the servants of Yamaraja from taking Ajamila to Yamaraja's court of judgement. The servants of Vishnu told the servants of Yamaraja that they had made a mistake. It seems that by chanting his son's name, Narayana, which happened to be one of the names of Vishnu, Ajamila had unwittingly become freed from the results of his sins. Ajamila, released by the servants of Yamaraja, returned to life, and gave up his sinful activities. Thus purified, he eventually died and was taken by the servants of Vishnu to the spiritual world to reside there eternally with God.

In another case reported by Satwant and Stevenson, an elderly man, Mangal Singh, was lying on a cot. Two people came and took him away. They came to a gate, where a man said, "Why have you brought the wrong person?" Mangal Singh saw two pots of water, which were boiling although there was no fire visible. The man, saying "Mangal must go back," pushed Mangal with his hand, which felt extremely hot. Mangal found himself awake, with a burning sensation in his left arm. Satwant and Stevenson (1986, p. 167) reported: "The area developed the appearance of a boil. Mangal showed it to a doctor, who applied some ointment. The area healed within 3 days but left a residual mark on the left arm, which we examined . . . Another person had died in the locality at or about the time he revived, but Mangal and his family made no inquiries about the suddenness of this person's death and did not even learn his name."

The Indian NDE reports differ from the Western ones. In most cases the Indian subjects did not report seeing their own physical body from a different perspective. In most cases, Western subjects did not report being taken away by messengers. Westerners who journey to other worlds might report seeing Christ or angels instead of Yamaraja or his messengers. On the basis of these and other differences, skeptics might conclude that all NDE reports are culturally influenced mental productions, and do not reflect real events. To this suggestion Satwant and Stevenson (1986, p. 169) replied: "If we survive death and live in an afterdeath realm, we should expect to find variations in that world, just as we find them in the different parts of the familiar world of the living. A traveler to Delhi encounters dark-skinned immigration officials, who in many respects behave differently from the lighter skinned immigration officials another traveler may meet when arriving in London or New York. Yet we do not say that the descriptions of the first traveler are 'real' and those of the second 'unreal.' In the same way, there may be different receptionists and different modes of reception in the 'next world' after death. They may differ for persons of different cultures."

As of this writing, medical professionals continue to document NDEs of the kind reported by Sabom and Ring. In February 2001, a team from the University of Southampton, in the United Kingdom, published a favorable study on NDEs in cardiac arrest patients in the journal *Resuscitation* (Parnia et al. 2001). The team was headed by Dr. Sam Parnia, a senior research fellow at the university. On February 16, 2001, the university published on its web site a report on the team's work (D'Arcy 2001): "University of Southampton researchers have just published a paper detailing their pioneering study into near death experiences (or NDEs) that suggests consciousness and the mind may continue to exist after the brain has ceased to function and the body is clinically dead. The team spent a year studying people resuscitated in the city's General Hospital after suffering a heart attack. The patients brought back to life were all, for varying lengths of time, clinically dead with no pulse, no respiration and fixed dilated pupils. Independent EEG studies have confirmed that the brain's electrical activity, and hence brain function, ceases at that time. But seven out of 63 (11 per cent) of the Southampton patients who survived their cardiac arrest recalled emotions and visions during unconsciousness. . . . This raises the question of how such lucid thought processes can occur when the brain is dead." Dr. Parnia stated: "During cardiac arrest brainstem activity is rapidly lost. It should not be able to sustain such lucid processes or allow the formation of lasting memories." The University of Southampton study took into account two common explanations for NDEs. The first is that the visions are produced by lack of oxygen or unusual drug treatments. But oxygen levels were carefully monitored in the study, and none of the survivors reporting NDEs had low oxygen levels. Neither did they have any unusual combinations of drugs. Another explanation is that the visions are an attempt by the mind to avoid confronting the uncomfortable fact of death. But Dr. Parnia observed, "The features of the NDEs in this study were dissimilar to those of confusional hallucinations as they were highly structured, narrative, easily recalled and clear." Dr. Parnia added: "The main significance of the NDE lies in the understanding of the relationship between mind and brain which has remained a topic of debate in contemporary philosophy, psychology and neuroscience. . . . Our findings need to be investigated with a much larger study. But if the results are replicated it would imply that the mind may continue to exist after the death of the body, or an afterlife."

Reincarnation Memories

The phenomenon of reincarnation memories lends strength to the idea that the OBE should be interpreted as a journey out of the body by a conscious self. Ian Stevenson and his associates have published numerous cases of young children spontaneously announcing a previous human existence. The published reports document evidence confirming the identity of the person the child claims to have been in a previous life.

This evidence is not likely to have been known to the child by normal means. The evidence has been verified by thorough cross examination of the child and persons professing to have knowledge of past life personalities and events named by the child. Stevenson has published 64 extensively documented case studies from all over the world, and has another 2,600 cases (investigated by himself and others) that appear genuine. Let us now consider two cases.

Sukla Gupta was born in 1954 in the village of Kampa, in West Bengal, India. From the time she was eighteen months old, her parents would see her playing with a block of wood. She wrapped it in a cloth, and treated it like an infant, calling it Minu. As she got older, she revealed that Minu was her daughter. She also spoke of having a husband. In a fashion typical of a married woman in India, she did not refer to her husband by name. She expressed a memory of having gone with her unnamed husband to a movie. She did mention by name two other men, Khetu and Karuna, indicating they were the younger brothers of her husband. She said they all lived in a neighborhood called Rathtala in Bhatpara, a village eleven miles south of Kampa, on the road to Calcutta. Stevenson (1974, p. 53) noted: "The Gupta family knew Bhatpara slightly; however, they had never heard of a district called Rathtala in Bhatpara nor of people with the names given by Sukla."

When she was about four years old, Sukla asked to be taken to Bhatpara, threatening that if her family did not take her, she would go herself. She said that if she were taken to Bhatpara, she could lead the way to the house of her husband's father. In the traditional Indian extended family, a young husband and wife would often stay in the household of the husband's father.

Sukla's father, K. N. Sen Gupta, a railway employee, mentioned his daughter's statements and recollections to another railway employee, S. C. Pal, who lived near Bhatpara. Through relatives, Pal learned that a man named Khetu did live in Bhatapara, in a neighborhood called Rathtala. Stevenson (1974, p. 53) stated, "Pal found further that the man called Khetu had a sister-in-law, one Mana, who had died some years back (in January, 1948) leaving an infant girl called Minu. When Sri Pal reported these facts to Sukla's father he became more interested in a visit by Sukla to Bhatpara; this was then arranged with the consent of the other family, of which Sri Amritalal Chakravarty was the head."

In the summer of 1959, Sukla and some of her family members went to Bhatapara. S. C. Pal either came with them or joined them in Bhatpara. At that time, Sukla led the group to the house of Amritlal Chakravarty, the father of Mana's husband. Stevenson (1974, p. 58) commented:

"Although the route available was straight, not curved, there were many houses and lanes into which Sukla could have turned if ignorant of the correct way. There is one main crossroad also. Sukla was ahead of the others. Only . . . Pal knew the way, and he was behind the girl."

Having arrived at the correct house, Sukla had some difficulty finding the main entrance door. Stevenson (1974, p. 58) commented: "Since the death of Mana, a former entrance to the house had been closed, and the main entrance moved to the side off the street and down an alley. Sukla's confusion was thus appropriate to the changes." While Sukla and the party were still in front of the house, Amritlal Chakravarty by chance came into the street. Immediately upon seeing him, Sukla gave a sign of recognition, dropping her eyes downward, as Indian women customarily do in the presence of an older male relative. Inside the house were between twenty and thirty people. Sukla was asked if she could pick out her husband. She correctly identified Haridhan Chakravarty as "Minu's father" (Stevenson 1974, p. 59). At the same time, she also pointed out Khetu, identifying him as "the uncle of Minu" (Stevenson 1974, p. 60). At another point during the visit, a man entered the room and a few minutes later asked Sukla, "Who am I?" (Stevenson 1974, p. 60) Sukla said, "Karuna," and also identified him as her younger brother-in-law. Most of those present did not know him by his given name Karuna, but by his nickname Kuti. When she saw Minu, Sukla began to shed tears and manifested other signs of intense affection for the girl, who was at the time twelve or thirteen years old (Stevenson 1974, p. 59). Sukla had just turned five years old. Sukla's grandmother, part of the party who had accompanied her, asked Sukla to point out her mother-in-law. Sukla correctly picked out the woman in the group of people present (Stevenson 1974, p. 60).

A week after Sukla visited Bhatpara, Haridhan Chakravarty (Mana's husband), Reba Nani Pathak (Mana's maternal aunt), and Minu visited Sukla at her home in Kampa. Reba Nani Pathak asked, "With whom did you leave Minu when you died?" Sukla replied, "With you." Stevenson (1974, p. 61) stated: "In fact, just before Mana died, her last words asked this aunt who would look after Minu, and the aunt had replied that she would do so." On this same occasion, Sukla had insisted that her family prepare a certain dish for Haridhan Chakrvarty, and it turned out to be his favorite dish. Reba Pathat recalled that during the visit, Sukla had been asked if she had any children besides Minu. Sukla correctly recalled having had a son who died as an infant, before Minu's birth. Sukla was asked, "Have you lived anywhere else besides Bhatpara?" She correctly replied that she had lived in Kharagpur. Haridhan Chakravarty and his wife Mana had in fact lived there for just over a year. Reba Pathak and

Haridhan Chakravarty questioned Sukla about her clothes. She stated correctly that Mana had three saris, two of them being fine silk saris from Benares. On a later visit to Bhatpara, two weeks after her first visit, Sukla picked out Mana's saris from among a large quantity of clothing that had not belonged to Mana (Stevenson 1974, p. 63). During this same visit, Sukla mentioned that the Chakravarty family had two cows and a parrot. The cows had died and the parrot had flown away after Mana's death. Sukla also mentioned that she had a brass pitcher in a certain room of the Chakravarty house. Stevenson (1974, p. 63) stated, "Sukla went to this room in the house and found the pitcher still there. She had not been to this room on her first visit. The room in question had been Mana's bedroom." Sukla correctly specified the former location of Minu's cot in her bedroom. On seeing a sewing machine, often used by Mana, Sukla began to shed tears.

Sukla developed a strong attraction for Haridhan Chakravarty, the husband of Mana. He confirmed Sukla's story about going to a movie. To some readers, accustomed to going to many movies a year, this might seem trivial. But Stevenson (1974, p. 58) states: "The occasion was memorable because it was the only time Mana ever went to a movie in her life, and she and her husband were afterwards reproached by her stepmother-in-law." Sukla looked forward to visits from Haridhan Chakravarty (he came several times). Whenever Sukla met Minu, she always showed extreme affection and always adopted the role of mother, even though Sukla was smaller and younger than Minu (Stevenson 1974, p. 57). Once, a member of the Pathak family who was visiting Sukla in Kampa told her, falsely, that Minu was very ill. Sukla wept until she was assured that Minu was not really sick. "On another occasion," stated Stevenson (1974, p. 57) "when Minu really was ill and news of this reached Sukla, she became extremely distressed, wept, and demanded to be taken to Bhatpara to see Minu. Her family could not quiet her until they actually took her the next day to see Minu, who was by then better."

Stevenson carefully considered the possibility that the two families could have been in communication with each other, thus providing a normal explanation for the knowledge displayed by Sukla. Stevenson stated (1984, p. 54): "The members of the two principal families concerned in the case denied that they ever had any knowledge of the other family prior to the attempts to verify Sukla's statements." The Guptas came to Kampa only in 1951, from East Bengal. Sukla's father had visited Bhatpara only once, to give a magic show at a school. The Chakravarty and Pathak families were long time residents of Bhatpara. Their denial of any contact with the Guptas is reinforced by the caste difference between the families.

The Chakravartys and Pathaks were of the *brahmana* caste while the Guptas were of one of the mercantile castes, the Banias. Sukla did not like to eat with the other children in her family. When she was three years old, she would say to them, "Why should I eat with you? I am a Brahmin" (Stevenson 1974, p. 57).

S. C. Pal, K. N. Sen Gupta's railway coworker, lived near Bhatpara, but he did not know anything about the Charkravarty and Pathak families until Gupta told him the story of his daughter's recollections of having lived in Bhatpara. At this time, Pal had known Gupta for only one month, and had never visited the Gupta house. So he could not possibly have been the source of the knowledge Sukla had been demonstrating for years prior to this (Stevenson 1974, p. 55). Another possible channel of information was Atul Dhar, another coworker of Sukla's father, who did have some slight contact with the Chakravarty family in Bhatpara. But Stevenson (1974, p. 55) noted that "Sri Atul Dhar never discussed the Chakravarty family with Sri Sen Gupta."

Here is another of Stevenson's cases. Imad Elawar was born in 1958, in the village of Kornayel, Lebanon. His family belonged to the Druse, an Islamic sect that accepts reincarnation. From the time he was two years old, Imad began telling of a previous life in the village of Khriby, in a family of the name Bouhamzy. He often spoke of someone with the first name Mahmoud. Other male persons he spoke of were Amin, Adil, Talil (or Talal), Said, Toufic, Salim, and Kemal. Imad also mentioned a female name, Mehibeh. Imad's father did not like these revelations and scolded his son for telling lies. But Imad's mother and grandparents were sympathetic. When Imad was still two years old, Salim el Aschkar happened to visit Kornayel. He was a resident of Khriby. Imad's grandmother testified that when Imad saw Salim, he rushed up to him and put his arms around him. "Do you know who I am?" asked Salim. Imad replied, "Yes, you were my neighbor" (Stevenson 1974, p. 276). Salim el Aschkar had in fact been a neighbor of a deceased member of the Bouhamzy family. Shortly thereafter, Imad's parents met a woman who lived in a village near Khriby. She confirmed that people with the same names as those mentioned by Imad did live there (Stevenson 1974, p. 276). In December of 1963, Imad's father attended a funeral in Khriby, and some of the people he met pointed out to him two men with names mentioned by Imad. This was his first visit to Khriby, and he did not at that time speak to any member of the Bouhamzy family.

Imad displayed unusual behaviors. As a child, the very first word that Imad uttered was Jamileh, the name of a woman, apparently known to him from his previous life. He described her beauty and her taste for

Western clothes. In many ways, he made known his attraction for this beautiful woman, showing an interest far beyond his young age of two or three years. Imad avoided children of his own age, and had a liking for strong tea and coffee, just like the village men. He would often ask his father to take him hunting. He indicated that in his previous life, he had a double barreled shotgun and a rifle. He said he had hidden his rifle in his house. In school, he was unusually quick in learning French. When a sister was born, he asked that she be named Huda. He also had a phobia of buses and trucks. He spoke repeatedly of two accidents. In one, a man driving a truck got into a wreck and lost his legs. There had been a quarrel between the man who lost his legs and the driver. In the second accident, Imad was the driver of a bus that got into an accident when for some reason he was not driving it. He also described the house in which he had lived. As a child, Imad often said he was very happy that he could walk.

From all of these things, Imad's parents concluded he had once lived in Khriby and that his name in his past life was Mahmoud Bouhamzy, who had a beautiful wife named Jamileh. The man had died after a truck hit him, causing him to lose both his legs. This had happened as a result of a quarrel with the truck driver. They also concluded that some of the names he mentioned were those of his sons, brothers, and other relatives. For example, they concluded he had a brother named Amin who lived in Tripoli and worked at the Tripoli courthouse. He had another brother Said. He had two sons, Adil and Talil (or Talal). He had another two sons, Kemal and Salim. He had a friend called Yousef el Halibi, and another called Ahmed el Halibi. He had a sister named Huda.

In 1962, Stevenson learned of the case from an informant, and in 1964 went to Lebanon to meet the Elawars. In March 1964, when Imad was five and a half years old, Stevenson took him and his father from their home in Kornayel to Khriby. Kornayel is in the mountains fifteen miles east of Beirut. Khriby lies 25 miles south from Kornayel. A distant relative of the Elawar family knew the Bouhamzy family. But Imad's father told Stevenson that this relative had never mentioned anything about the Bouhamzys.

When Stevenson, Imad, and his father got to Khriby on March 17, 1964, Stevenson interviewed a limited number of informants. Two residents said that in June 1943 a member of the Bouhamzy family died after having been run over by a truck. It was, however, not Mahmoud but Said Bouhamzy. As far as Jamileh was concerned, she was, they said, not the wife of Said Bouhamzy. On this visit, Stevenson managed to locate Yousef el Halibi, who was by this time quite old and ill. He said he had been a friend of Said Bouhamzy. Stevenson (1974, p. 279) stated: "On this occasion Imad pointed correctly in the direction of the house he claimed to have lived in, and made a couple of other statements suggesting paranormal knowledge of the village, but did not meet any members of the Bouhamzy family."

The next day Stevenson returned to Khriby, but without Imad and his father. He received additional confirmation that Said Bouhamzy had no connection with Jamileh. He also learned that the descriptions Imad had given of the house he had lived in did not match the house of Said Bouhamzy. Furthermore, there was already a man who claimed to have been Said Bouhamzy in a previous life.

Thus far the information obtained by Stevenson was confusing, and appeared to call into question Imad's story, as presented to him by his relatives. But then Stevenson learned about another member of the Bouhamzy family, a man named Ibrahim, a cousin of Said. Ibrahim did in fact have a relationship with a woman called Jamileh. She was his mistress. Ibrahim had died on September 18, 1949, suffering from tuberculosis. The disease had infected his spine, which caused him much pain in walking. Stevenson also learned that Ibrahim had an uncle named Mahmoud.

Upon further questioning of Imad and his relatives, Stevenson learned that Imad had never actually claimed to be Mahmoud. Nor had he ever actually claimed to have been the person who died in the incident with the truck. These were simply suppositions made by his parents, who had tried to put together all the names and places and events mentioned by Imad in a way that seemed most logical to them. Their interpretative errors tend to rule out the theory that they manufactured Imad's past life story, using information acquired by normal means from persons in Khriby.

Stevenson then began operating on the theory that Imad had been Ibrahim in his past life. Things began to fall together. Ibrahim's mistress Jamileh was locally famous for her beauty and did in fact dress in Western clothes—a red dress and high heels, for example—which would have been unusual for a village woman in Lebanon during the 1940s. Ibrahim was fluent in French, having learned it during his service in the army. Ibrahim did have a close relative named Amin who lived in Tripoli. Amin, a government employee, did have an office in the Tripoli courthouse building, as stated by Imad. Amin was not, however, Imad's brother, as originally supposed by Imad's parents when they heard Imad talk of him. It is common, however, for Lebanese males to call close friends and relatives "brother." Ibrahim had a female cousin, Mehibeh. Imad's parents had thought she was Imad's daughter in his previous existence. Ibrahim also had one male cousin called Adil and another called Khalil. Stevenson proposed that the name Imad gave, Talil, was a mispronunciation of Khalil. Both Talil and Adil were originally mistakenly identified by Imad's parents as sons of Imad in his previous life. Among the other names mentioned by Imad, Toufic, originally identified by Imad's parents as a brother, and Kemal, originally identified as a son, turned out to be additional cousins of Ibrahim. Salim, originally identified as a son, turned out to be an uncle of Ibrahim, with whom he lived. Ibrahim Bouhamzy did in fact have a sister Huda. Yousef el Halibi, named by Imad as a friend, was in fact a friend of the Bouhamzy family. Ahmed el Halibi, mentioned by Imad, was the brother of Yousef. Ibrahim Bouhamzy was in fact involved in an accident with a bus, of which he was the driver. The accident occurred, however, at a time when Ibrahim had pulled the bus to the side of the road and stopped. He had gotten out of the bus momentarily, when it began to roll and went off the road, injuring some of the passengers. Imad's statement that the bus accident occurred when he was not actually driving was thus confirmed. Ibrahim had indeed liked hunting and had owned a double-barreled shotgun, like the one mentioned by Imad. He also owned a rifle, which he kept hidden. It was illegal for a civilian to own such a gun (Stevenson 1974, pp. 286–290).

Imad had described his house as having been in the center of Khriby, near a slope. These details were correct for Ibrahim's house. The house, according to Imad, had two wells, one dry and one full. In this regard, Stevenson (1974, p. 293) reported: "During the life of Ibrahim there had been two 'wells' whose sites were pointed out to us. The 'wells' had been closed up since the death of Ibrahim. They were not spring wells, but rather concrete cavities or vats used for storing grape juice. The wells would be used alternately. During the rainy season one of these vats became filled with water, but the shallower one did not, because the water evaporated from it. Thus one would be empty while the other was full." Imad had talked about a new garden. Ibrahim's brother Fuad confirmed that at the time of Ibrahim's death, a new garden was in fact being built. Imad said, correctly, that it had cherry and apple trees. Stevenson saw the trees during his visit to the house. Imad had reported owning a small yellow car, a bus, and a truck. The members of the Bouhamzy family with whom Ibrahim lived did in fact own such vehicles.

On March 19, 1964, Stevenson made his third visit to Khriby, this time accompanied by Imad and his parents. They went to the house of Ibrahim Bouhamzy, where Imad made fourteen correct recognitions and statements (Stevenson 1974, p. 299). For example, he pointed out the place where Ibrahim had hidden his rifle. The place was confirmed by Ibrahim's mother, who said the place, in the back of a closet, was known only to her and Ibrahim. While at the house, Imad was shown a photograph of a man. Those showing the photograph to him suggested the man was Ibrahim's brother or uncle. But when asked to say who it was, Imad correctly said, "Me" (Ibrahim). One of the persons present in the house during the visit was Huda Bouhamzy, Ibrahim's sister. She asked Imad, "Do you know who I am?" Imad replied, "Huda" (Stevenson 1974, p. 301). Later Huda asked him: "You said something just before you died. What was it?" Imad replied, "Huda, call Fuad." Stevenson (1974, p. 301) stated: "This was correct because Fuad had left shortly before and Ibrahim wanted to see him again, but died immediately." Out of two beds in a bedroom of the house, Imad picked the one in which Ibrahim had died. He also correctly told where it had been in the room at the time of his death, a position different than at the time of Imad's visit. When asked how he had talked to his friends during his final illness, Imad pointed to a window in the room. Stevenson (1974, p. 300) noted, "During his infectious illness, his friends could not enter Ibrahim's room, so they talked with him through a window, the bed being arranged so that he could see and talk with his friends through the window."

Imad also told Stevenson and others of an intermediate life, between the death of Ibrahim in 1949 and his own birth in 1958. He said he had passed this brief life at a place called Dahr el Ahmar, but he could not remember enough details for Stevenson to conduct an investigation (Stevenson 1974, p. 318).

According to philosophy professor David W. Griffin (1997, pp. 193–194), several factors contribute to the authenticity of the past life memory cases reported by Stevenson: (1) The reports come spontaneously from young children, between two and four years old, and reports of such memories cease when they become older, usually disappearing when they are between five and eight years old. In fraudulent cases, the memories come much later in life. (2) There is usually a short time between the birth of the reporting child and the death of the reported past incarnation. Manufactured cases usually go back centuries. (3) The remembered person usually comes from the same culture and geographical area. In false cases this is not usually so. (4) Statements about the past life that are potentially verifiable turn out between 80 and 90 percent correct. (5) Persons other than the child's parents testify to the child's statements and behavioral patterns related to the previous existence. (6) Neither the reporting children nor the relatives have anything to gain in terms of money or status. (7) Memories of the past life are sometimes corroborated by behavioral patterns, talents and abilities, languages, and birthmarks or birth defects that can be associated with the previous existence.

Another interesting reincarnation case is that of William George, a Tlingit Indian from Alaska. He was known among his people for being a good fisherman. The Tlingits had a belief in reincarnation. George told his son Reginald and his son's wife, "If there is anything to this rebirth business, I will come back and be your son. And you will recognize me because I will have birthmarks like the ones I now have." He had one mole on his left shoulder and another mole on his left forearm. Later, he gave Reginald his gold watch, indicating that it should be kept for him in his next life. Reginald gave the watch to his wife and told her what his father had said. She put the watch in a jewelry box. A few weeks later, William George was lost at sea. Not long afterwards, Reginald's wife became pregnant. During her labor, she saw William George in a dream. He told her that he was waiting to see her son. The child, named William George, Jr., had two moles in the same places as his deceased grandfather's moles. William George had injured his right ankle while playing basketball as a youth and had throughout his life walked with a limp, with the right foot turned outwards. The child, when old enough to walk, walked with the same kind of limp. Once, when young William was almost five years old, his mother was looking through her jewelry box. The child saw the gold watch, grabbed it, and said, "That's my watch" (Griffin 1997, pp. 197–198; Stevenson 1974, pp. 232–34, 240). I will discuss more birthmark cases in chapter 8, which is concerned with evidence for paranormal modification of biological form.

Some have proposed alternative paranormal explanations for announcing dreams and birthmarks. Seeking to avoid the idea of a surviving conscious entity sending the announcing dream, Griffin (1997, p. 200) proposes that a person, Tom, while still living, could communicate to another person, Mary, his intention to return in another life. After Tom dies, the mother in whose womb he will take birth gets knowledge of his intention telepathically from Mary, who is still living. Alternatively, the mother could acquire such knowledge from Tom's own disembodied mind content, floating out in the ether. Again, this idea, of mind content existing after death, like some ethereal computer file, is meant to avoid the concept of a surviving conscious element, or soul. In any case, with the knowledge acquired from Mary or Tom's disembodied mind content, the mother subconsciously manufactures an announcing dream. In some cases, the knowledge is also communicated by the mother to the child in the womb, who after taking birth might announce he had intentionally taken birth after a previous existence, when in fact he had not existed before. His past life memories are not his at all. As for birthmarks, knowledge of them, obtained by telepathy, could be impressed on the fetal child by the mother through paranormal psychokinetic powers. Such explanations seem quite strained. Why, Griffin (1997, pp. 201–202) asks, would the mother herself not report a past life memory? Why would she communicate information to the child?

If past life memories are nothing more than living people accessing the mental impressions of dead persons, preserved somehow in some ethereal element, then there should be no memories extending beyond the death of the departed person. But Stevenson and others have recorded past life memory cases which contain events occurring after the death of the deceased. These "intermission memories" point towards reincarnation as the best explanation for the past life memories. Apparently, such memories are common. Out of Stevenson's 230 past life memory cases from Burma, 52 involved intermission memories. Out of 38 cases from Thailand, 21 involved intermission memories (Griffin 1997, pp. 202–203). An example of such a memory would be seeing one's own funeral, or observing one's new family before taking birth in it.

Many intermission memories are not verifiable, but some are. A four-year-old boy in India, Veer Singh, reported that he had in a previous life been a person named Som Dutt Sharma. Sharma had died eleven years before. Singh spoke about many events that had taken place in the Sharma family during those eleven years, including lawsuits and the birth of one male and two female children. Singh, upon first meeting these persons, immediately recognized and identified them (Griffin 1997, p. 203). A Burmese subject, Maung Yin Maung, said that after he died he was seen by someone at a particular place before he took his present birth (Griffin 1997, pp. 202–203).

Furthermore, if past life memories are created simply by reading the surviving mental content of a dead person, then it would seem that the subject should be reporting multiple existences, or existences containing mixed material, whereas subjects very consistently speak of only a single past life. After all, there should be a lot of mental content out there waiting to be accessed and incorporated into past life memories (Griffin 1997, pp. 206–207). All in all, the existence of a conscious self that survives one physical embodiment and moves into another physical embodiment seems the best explanation of reincarnation memories, and the associated phenomena of announcing dreams and birthmarks.

Fetal Memories

In her book *Changes of Mind,* published by the State University of New York Press, developmental psychologist Jenny Wade states that consciousness has been neglected in developmental psychology, and in science generally. But, according to Wade (1996, p. 2), recent developments in science are "introducing a new concept of reality more congruent with the Eastern and ancient mystical worldviews." She also believes that "a cosmology that accounts for the phenomena of consciousness may be the rightful paradigm of psychology" (1996, p. 4).

According to currently dominant ideas in psychology and the neurosciences, consciousness exists only in association with a pattern of neurons in the brain. But Wade says there is a body of evidence that challenges this assumption. "It comprises," says Wade, "empirically validated data of human consciousness functioning *independent of a physical substrate*" (1996, p. 18, her italics).

Included in this body of evidence are the NDE accounts and past life memories we've already discussed, but Wade, drawing on the research of D. B. Chamberlain, Helen Wambach, S. Grof, and others, brings to our attention a new category of evidence—fetal memories. About research in all of these areas, Wade (1996, p. 19) says, "These results are very new, and their implications are not fully understood; nevertheless they present a consistent pattern in the aggregate, suggesting that an individual's mature consciousness predates birth—in some cases, even conception—and survives death."

According to mainstream developmental studies, the pattern of neuronal development supporting conscious awareness appears rather late in the human fetus. Brain waves normally associated with the conscious state occur only in the seventh month of pregnancy, at 28–32 weeks (Spehlman 1981; in Wade 1996, p. 28). Even at that time, brain activity would be quite limited, because the neuronal connections between the brain cells develop mostly after birth. But there is, says Wade, compelling testimony for prenatal memories, memories indicating that conscious awareness is present in the fetus before the brain is properly organized.

Wade (1996, pp. 42–43) proposes that there are two kinds of fetal consciousness. The first is a limited consciousness, facilitated by the state of neuronal development in the fetal brain. The second is a more complete consciousness, experienced by a transcendent self associated with the fetus but not limited by its state of sensory and brain development. The two kinds of consciousness are related. As Wade (1996, p. 44) puts it, "These two sources of consciousness are clearly experienced as a continuity of the same self." One might therefore propose that consciousness is primarily a property of the transcendent self, and that it is sometimes channeled through the brain of the fetus, child, or adult, expressing itself according to the biological limitations of each stage of development. According to Wade (1996, pp. 13–14), the transcendent self associated with a fetus is an aspect of a larger conscious self. This would reflect the Vedic view that the individual *atma* is a permanently existing particle of the permanently existing *param atma,* or supreme self.

S. Grof (1985) and D. B. Chamberlain (1990) have reported prenatal memories, recovered by hypnotic regression, extending as far back as conception. These memories, according to Wade (1996, p. 44), have been verified by "information provided by the mother, relatives, obstetricians, and medical records." In addition to conception events, memories include attempted abortions. In most cases, it is unlikely that the subjects would have learned about the reported abortion attempts after birth, because, quite understandably, mothers and fathers would generally not wish to inform their children of such things. But in many cases parents would confirm the subjects' reports after they were recovered during hypnotic regressions. Here is one such report (Chamberlain 1990, p. 179): "I was hardly formed and my mom is using some kind of remedy to wash me away. It feels real hot . . . I know she is trying to get me out of there. I'm just a little blob. I don't know how I know, but I know. My aunt seems to be giving my mom directions. I can hear her voice and another woman in the background. She is not supposed to get pregnant. She doesn't know me...It didn't work either. It had a strong harsh smell, almost a disinfectant smell, like ammonia, strong, a vile strong smell. I can see where I was too; I was way up there, just teeny. I knew nobody really wanted me then . . . but I was determined. I was a fighter even then. Poor mom would die if she knew I knew all this stuff!"

Another category of memory is visual memory of the actual birth process. According to Wade (1996, p. 47), such accounts provide "one of the strongest arguments for a materially transcendent source of awareness." Physiologically, such accounts should not be possible because the infant should be unconscious. Furthermore, the fetal eyes are normally shut, and even when open an infant's eyes, right after birth, are not capable of normal sight.

Some birth memories come from hypnotic regressions, but others come spontaneously from very young children. Most of the spontaneous accounts come from children between two and three years old. Jason, at age three and a half, gave a birth account to his mother. He said he heard his mother crying and recalled trying hard to come out of the birth canal, in the midst of sensations of tightness and wetness. He felt something wrapped around his neck. Something hurt his head, and he said there were scratches on his face (Chamberlain 1988, p. 103; in Wade 1996, p. 48). Chamberlain (1988, p. 103) noted: "Jason's mother said she had 'never talked to him about the birth, *never*,' but the facts were correct. The umbilical cord was wrapped around his neck, he was monitored via an electrode on his scalp, and was pulled out by forceps. The photo taken by the hospital shows scratches on his face."

In evaluating reports of birth memories obtained by hypnosis, Chamberlain compared reports of children to those of their mothers, and found they matched. Before hypnosis, the children, averaging sixteen years old, could produce no birth memories. Regarding the reported memories obtained during hypnosis, Wade (1996, p. 49) said, "Narratives included accurate reportage of the time of day, locale, persons present, instruments used, position of delivery, and the medical personnel during the birth. Reports extended over the next several days, including correct feeding sequences (water, formula, and breast feedings), room layouts, details of discharge and arrival at home." Chamberlain found some disagreements between the reports of mothers and children, but they were of a minor nature, with no serious contradictions. Could the recollections of children have been derived from information passed on by mothers and later forgotten? Chamberlain thought not, because the children often gave details not known to the mothers.

Here is one set of memories (Wade 1996, p. 50). The mother recalled: "They sort of put her on my stomach but they're still holding onto her . . . lots of blood and white stuff. She's crying. I can see the umbilical cord. My hands are fastened down because I can't reach out and touch her. I would like them to move her, wrap her up. I'm talking to the doctors. . . . I think they had a white cap over my hair. They finally undo my hands and the nurse brings her over on my left side. But she doesn't hold her close enough so I can touch her. I really feel frustrated. I do say 'Hi!' to her. . . . I talk to the doctor about her weight."

The child recalled: "They put me on her stomach, sort of dumped me on her. He's talking to my mom. Everything seems to be okay and she's all right. . . . I feel bigger and heavier. I can see her but I'm not by her. Her hair is wrapped up, like in curlers or something. She looks tired, sweaty, Nobody's talking to me. They're talking about me, I think, but not *to* me. They act like they know I'm there but like *I* don't know I'm there. . . . The nurse kind of wiped me. Then they brought me over next to my mother. She wasn't crying but something like that. She's the first one that talked to me. She said 'Hi!' Nobody else seemed to think that I was really there. Then she talked to the doctor a little bit and they took me away again."

In another account, the subject, Deborah, tells how at birth she at first felt she was existing consciously apart from her infant body and then soon thereafter experienced her consciousness identifying with the body: "Then all of a sudden there was this yellow room and these people.

That's when I was beginning to figure out what was going on. Not very happy about it. . . . I didn't realize right off that I could make noises [cry] —that seemed to just kind of happen. . . . Starting to breathe was pretty strange, too. I had never done anything like that before. . . . I thought I was an intelligent mind. And so when the situation [of being born] was forced on me, I didn't like it too much. I saw all these people acting real crazy. That's when I thought I really had a *more* intelligent mind, because I knew what the situation was with me, and they didn't seem to. They seemed to ignore me. They were doing things *to* me—to the *outside* of me. But they acted like that's all there was" (Chamberlain 1988, pp. 155–157).

Helen Wambach (1981) hypnotically regressed over 750 subjects, and their reports of fetal life and birth are consistent with Wade's hypothesis of two sources of consciousness. Wade (1996, p. 52) says of Wambach's subjects: "They did not identify with the growing fetus or its stream of consciousness, although they accepted that the fetus was 'theirs.' Instead, they identified themselves with the physically transcendent source of consciousness, and tended not to become involved with 'their fetus' until six months after conception. In fact, many were extremely reluctant to join 'their consciousness' with the body-bound awareness of the fetus. Wambach's subjects characterized themselves as disembodied minds hovering around the fetus and mother, being 'in and out' of the fetus and having a telepathic knowledge of the mother's emotions throughout the pregnancy and birth. . . . Subjects ascribed their reluctance to join with the fetus to negative feelings about being born. Approximately 68 percent expressed antipathy and anxiety about being embodied. Their attitude was resigned toward physical life as an unpleasant duty they must perform in response to an unidentified imperative."

Taking into consideration reports of past life memories, the complete sequence of conscious development posited by Wade includes events consistent with the existence of a transcendent self before and after the present embodiment. According to some researchers, says Wade, the transcendent conscious self, during the process of conception and birth, comes to identify with subtle energy fields surrounding the gross physical body and finally with the body itself. "Broadly speaking," says Wade (1996, p. 243), "the theory emerging from this group seems to be that the individual's essence—his enduring consciousness as a form of life energy —including his karmic accumulation, 'steps down' from the outermost layer of the energy field surrounding the body to the one closest to the body and then into the body itself through cellular structures, when translated into incarnate life. . . . If karmic patterns are not resolved, more energy builds up during life to sustain the source of consciousness with highly charged material. Since it is not dissipated, this energy aggregate persists in time and incarnations." Wade's formulation mirrors the devolution concept, whereby a conscious self is gradually covered first with mind and then matter.

Summary of Chapter 6

Any scientific explanation must begin with certain axioms or assumptions that are not proven. If we demand proof of initial assumptions, then we fall into an endless regress of proofs of assumptions, and proofs of proofs of assumptions, and proofs of proofs of proofs of assumptions. So it is generally taken that initial assumptions should simply be reasonable on the basis of available evidence. Today, most scientific explanations of human origins begin with the assumption that human beings are composed solely of ordinary matter, the commonly known chemical elements. And this assumption, although not proved, is considered reasonable in terms of the available evidence. But in making this assumption scientists are not confronting all of the available evidence. I am, of course, speaking of the kinds of evidence described in this chapter. Even the highly skeptical Carl Sagan, who in his book *The Demon-Haunted World* attacked many claims for the paranormal, said therein, "At the time of this writing there are three claims in the ESP field which, in my opinion, deserve serious study: (1) that by thought alone humans can (barely) affect random number generators in computers, (2) that people under mild sensory deprivation can receive thoughts or images 'projected' at them; and (3) that young children sometimes report the details of a previous life, which upon checking turn out to be accurate and which they could not have known about in any other way than reincarnation" (Sagan 1995, p. 302). There are, I am convinced, other categories of such evidence worthy of study. And when all of this evidence is considered, the assumption that humans are composed of three substances—matter, mind, and consciousness, as I have defined them—becomes reasonable enough to serve as the foundation for an alternative research program for explaining human origins.

Such an alternative research program should be welcomed. Those who hold that mind and consciousness are produced, as emergent properties, from the matter in the neuronal circuitry of the brain are faced with major difficulties. They have not been able to explain in any detailed and convincing way how molecules interacting with each other according to known physical laws produce consciousness. This has led some researchers (Griffin 1997, p. 132) to propose that material atoms have, among other intrinsic properties, some slight degree of consciousness. When combined together these slight bits of consciousness can, some suggest, combine to form the intense and highly concentrated consciousness that we all experience. This idea is called panexperientialism. But if each atom possesses only a dim awareness, of what would it be aware? Most likely, an atom would only be aware of the atoms in its immediate neighborhood. Exactly how this local dim awareness of other atoms could transform into a concentrated, individualized, global awareness is not specified in any convincing way.

Griffin (1997, p. 133), following the philosophy of Alfred North Whitehead, and the earlier philosophy of Leibniz, suggests that "a multiplicity of individuals at one level can be subordinated to a 'dominant' individual with a higher level of experience and greater power." The idea seems to be that among all the individual atoms in the human body, each with its own little bit of awareness, there is one dominant atom with a much higher level of awareness, to which the others are subordinated. This takes one beyond the normal panexperientialism, and introduces something very akin to the *atma*, the unit of individual consciousness in the Vedic model. By introducing a quite radical distinction between the properties of different kinds of material particles, Griffin inadvertently reintroduces the matter/consciousness dualism he sought to avoid by his panexperientialist idea.

A "dualistic" atomic panexperientialism of this kind is potentially compatible with the Vedic model. According to Mantra 35 of the *Brahma Samhita*, a Sanskrit hymn to the universal creator, the Supersoul or *paramatma* enters into each atom. In a conversation with his disciples in London (August 17, 1971), my guru A. C. Bhaktivedanta Swami Prabhupada explained that an individual soul or *atma* is also present in the atom along with the *paramatma* (Conversations 1988, v. 2, p. 351). The bodies of living things would thus contain many atoms, each with soul and Supersoul. But the expression of the soul's consciousness is heavily covered in this condition. The bodies of living things would also contain a dominant soul-Supersoul pair that would be the soul and Supersoul not of a single atom but of the complete organism, giving the organism as a whole a developed individual consciousness connected to the global consciousness of God.

Some scientists suppose that consciousness may be a quantum mechanical effect. These scientists include physicist David Bohm, physiologist Karl Pribram, Nobel-prize-winning physicist Brian Josephson, mathematician Sir Roger Penrose, and neuroscientist Benjamin Libet. Stuart Hameroff, an anesthesiologist at the University of Arizona, has called attention to tiny structures called microtubules in brain cells as possible centers of quantum effects related to the generation of consciousness (Radin 1997, pp. 284–285). But there is no proof that consciousness is associated with microtubules in brain cells. Furthermore, left unexplained is why consciousness, of all things, should emerge as a result of a quantum mechanical effect in structures composed of ordinary molecules. At present, quantum mechanics says nothing about the origin of consciousness. Radin (1997, p. 287) points out: "An adequate theory of psi ... will almost certainly not be quantum theory as it is presently understood. Instead, existing quantum theory will ultimately be seen as a special case of how nonliving matter behaves under certain circumstances. Living systems may require an altogether new theory."

Physicist Helmut Schmidt did some of the original psi experiments with random number generators. As we have seen, RNGs use radioactive decay to interrupt streams of alternating ones and zeros. These radioactive decays are the result of quantum jumps in the states of atoms, causing the emission of electrons. Because these emissions are, according to quantum theory, random, the sequence of ones and zeros picked out by the emissions should also be random. This means that over time there should be fifty percent ones and fifty percent zeros. But in his experiments Schmidt found that by mental efforts subjects could cause an increase in either ones or zeros, beyond what could be expected by chance. Schmidt said (1993, p. 367): "The outcome of quantum jumps, which quantum theory attributes to nothing but chance, can be influenced by a person's mental effort. This implies that quantum theory is wrong when experimentally applied to systems that include human subjects." In other words, quantum theory is in this case wrong, because its predictions do not apply to the random number generator experiments. Schmidt added, "It remains to be seen whether the quantum formalism can be modified to include psi effects." It is doubtful that this can ever be achieved. This suggests the incompleteness of quantum mechanics as a description of reality. Accordingly, it may never be possible to give some simple set of equations that explains everything in the universe. Quantum mechanics may have its applications for a certain subset of reality, but it is not all encompassing. The goal of a mathematical theory of everything may therefore be forever beyond reach.

Any material explanation of consciousness, as an emergent property of neurons or as a quantum mechanical effect connected with microtubules in neurons, must confront the changeability of these brain components. The brain contains about 10 billion neurons. Each of these has about ten thousand connections with other neurons. Each day, a human loses an average of one thousand neurons in the brain (Radin 1997, p. 259). That consciousness and its mental contents can maintain their integrity in the face of such massive random disruptions in the brain circuitry that supposedly creates consciousness requires quite a leap of faith. It is more reasonable to suppose that the unitary consciousness of a living entity is an irreducible feature of reality and that it simply uses the brain as an instrument.

The interactions of matter, mind, and consciousness appear to sometimes violate the kind of bottom-up causation now generally favored by reductionist science. According to reductionist science, we start with molecules, and from molecules come mind and consciousness. Radin (1997, p. 260) and other researchers propose that living systems participate in a system with both upward and downward causation, in which states of matter can influence the states of mind and consciousness and vice versa. Radin (1997, p. 261) proposes that a comprehensive model of this causal system "might place quantum or subquantum physics at the bottom and a 'spirit' or 'superspirit' at the top." This echos the Vedic model, which does indeed place a "superspirit" at the top of the model (i.e. the paramatma, or Supersoul).

Radin gives this characterization of an adequate physical theory of living systems: "The theory will have to explain how information can be obtained at great distances unbound by the usual limitations of space or time . . . Such a theory must also explain not only how one can get information from a distance in space or time, but also how one can get *particular* information . . . The theory must account for why we are not overwhelmed with information all the time . . . The theory must also explain how random processes can be tweaked by mental intention . . . The theory of psi should explain phenomena associated with evidence suggesting that something may survive bodily death. These phenomena include apparitions, hauntings, out-of-body experiences (OBE), and near-death experiences (NDE) . . . The theory may need to account for poltergeist phenomena, which provide the primary evidence for large-scale mind-matter interaction effects" (Radin 1997, pp. 278–280).

A theory based on the Vedic model of the cosmos could account for all of the above. Matter, mind, and individual spirits emanate from God. God enters into each atom and accompanies each individual spirit as the Supersoul, or Paramatma. The Supersoul, by definition, is present in all phases of time and space, and is simultaneously beyond time and space. The Supersoul is also all knowing. Therefore, through the medium of the Supersoul, knowledge can be transmitted from one spirit to another beyond the usual limits of time and space. There are many examples of this in the Vedic literature. The *Bhagavad Gita* (15.15) says that it is from the Supersoul that each individual souls gets memory, knowledge, and forgetfulness. The Supersoul can therefore control the kind and amount of information that comes to each individual soul, whether through normal or paranormal means. Since the Supersoul is present in each atom of matter and is at the same time aware of conscious intentions, it is possible for the Supersoul to produce the effects associated with random number generators. Responding to the desires of experimenters and the intentions of subjects, the Supersoul could cause more ones or zeros to come up in the course of the experiments. The Vedic model, which posits the existence of an eternal conscious self (*atma*), would explain evidence for survival of bodily death. According to the Vedic model, the eternal conscious self, if it does not return to the spiritual level of reality, remains in the material world covered by a subtle mental body. This mental body is composed of a subtle material element (mind) that can, by the agency of Supersoul, affect ordinary matter. This would explain poltergeist effects and apparitions. The mental body also includes a subtle sensory apparatus, capable of operating without the assistance of the ordinary bodily sense organs. This would explain the visual perceptions that subjects report during out-of-body experiences. The Vedic model has considerable explanatory power.

This model overcomes the classic objection to the Cartesian duality of mind and matter. Descartes's terminology identifies mind with consciousness. A popular, but incorrect view, is that Descartes thought that the pineal gland in the brain mediated an interaction between mind (consciousness) and matter. This organ was, according to this account, sensitive to both mind and matter and could link them. Modern philosophers now believe that Descartes simply suggested that the pineal gland was the place where an interaction between mind and matter took place. As to how the interaction actually took place, Descartes could not say (Griffin 1997, p. 105). Nicolas Malebranche and Arnold Geulincx, two of the principal followers of Cartesian philosophy, accepted Descartes's formulation that mind and matter were distinct entities and concluded that they could not interact. They proposed to explain, however, their apparent interaction through the philosophical doctrine of occasionalism. Griffin (1997, p. 105) explains: "According to this doctrine, on the occasion of my hand's being on a hot stove, God causes my mind to feel pain, which leads me to decide to move my hand. My mind, unfortunately, cannot cause my body to move any more than my body could cause my mind to feel pain. On the occasion of my deciding to move my hand, accordingly, God obliges, moving it for me. All apparent interaction between mind and body is said to require this constant supernatural intervention."

The Vedic model of the relationships between matter, mind, and consciousness resembles occasionalism. In the Vedic model, mind (a subtle kind of matter) is placed along with ordinary matter on one side of the Cartesian divide. The soul, a unit of pure consciousness, is placed on the other side. The question still arises, how can any connection between the soul (consciousness) and matter in its two forms (ordinary matter and the subtle material mind) be established? The key is the Supersoul. The Supersoul is the ultimate source of the souls of living beings as well as the mind element and ordinary matter. The Supersoul monitors the desires and intentions of the souls of living beings and causes mind and matter to transform in response to those desires. The Vedic model also incorporates the property dualism of Spinoza, who proposed that there is actually only one substance, spirit, that is perceived differently according to its application, just as electricity can be used to heat or cool. The Supersoul possesses a spiritual potency which it can deploy in different ways. The spiritual potency when deployed to cover the original spiritual consciousness of the individual soul is known as matter. But the same potency can be changed back to its original spiritual form by the Supersoul.

Supersoul may explain a puzzling anomaly in consciousness studies. Benjamin Libet, a neuroscientist, has reported the results of experiments about intention and brain state. He asked his subjects to bend a finger at the exact time they made a decision to do so. Study of brain waves revealed that there was a gap of about one-fifth of a second between the time the subject decided to move their fingers and the time the muscles in the finger actually moved. But the same study also revealed that the brains of the subjects displayed activity a third of a second before the subjects consciously reported making a decision to move their finger. Libet took this to mean that our conscious free will is not really free, but is reflecting some unconscious brain action that precedes the decision's entry into our conscious awareness. Accordingly, free will is largely an illusion (Libet 1994; in Radin 1997, pp. 283–284). But this is not necessarily so. According to the Vedic model, the Supersoul, on a deep level, is monitoring the soul, the actual conscious self. Anticipating the desire of the soul to move the finger, the Supersoul could set the process in motion before the desire is manifested as a mental intention.

In their book *Margins of Reality* (1987), Robert G. Jahn and Brenda J. Dunne gave a theory that makes use of analogies from quantum mechanics and at the same time accounts for the action of consciousness in a way that is compatible with the Vedic model. Like the Vedic model, their model appears to accept unit consciousness as a feature of reality. Jahn and Dunne proposed that consciousness has a dual particle/wave nature, much like the atom or photon in quantum mechanics. They proposed that our normal individual embodied consciousness might be likened to "probability of experience waves" that are "confined to some sort of 'container,' or 'potential well,' representative of the environment in which that consciousness is immersed" (Jahn and Dunne 1987, p. 242). Ordinary conscious relations would be defined by the interactions of the confined waves, according to the conditions imposed by the physical body and environment. But just as in quantum mechanics there are tunneling effects, whereby the consciousness wave in a particular potential well can influence the consciousness wave in another potential well in ways not normally allowed. This might, according to Jahn and Dunne (1987, p. 243), "represent various types of anomalous information acquisition, including remote perception and remote PK effects." Jahn and Dunne added (1987, p. 243), "If any of the standing wave systems acquires sufficient energy to be elevated from cavity-bound to free-wave status, it may gain access to all consciousness space-time and interact with any other center in the configuration via that mode. Thus, this route could accommodate a variety of anomalies, including remote perception and remote man/machine interactions, as well as more extreme and controversial phenomena such as mystical union, out-of-body experiences, mediumship, and spiritual survival." The question is: how does a "standing wave system" (atma, or soul, in the Vedic model) acquire the "sufficient energy" to get out of an energy well? Here the Supersoul could play a role. Only the Supersoul would possess enough energy not to be bound in any way by any of the energies. But it could contribute enough energy to individual units of consciousness to break out of their limitations. But such units of consciousness could never achieve the same degree of freedom as the Supersoul and would require constant connection with the Supersoul to remain in the free state.

7

THE COSMIC HIERARCHY:
A CROSS-CULTURAL STUDY

Science provides substantial evidence supporting the assumption that a human being is composed of three things: matter, mind, and consciousness. This leads to the related assumption that our cosmos itself is divided into regions dominated by ordinary matter, mind, and spirit. Such cosmologies have existed in a vast number of cultures down through history.

These cosmologies include hierarchies of beings adapted to life at various levels. The structures of these hierarchies can often be complex, but one can see in them a basic pattern. At the top of the hierarchy is some kind of supreme guiding intelligence. Next comes a subordinate creator god, or demiurge. From the creator god come varieties of demigods, humans, plants, animals, ghosts, demons, and spirits. The highest level of the hierarchy, the level of the supreme guiding intelligence, God, is purely spiritual. The levels of the creator god and higher demigods are predominated by a mixture of spirit and the subtle material mind element. The lower levels, inhabited by minor demigods, humans, animals, and plants, are predominated by a mixture of spirit, mind, and a substantial amount of ordinary matter. These lower levels may include an underworld or hellish world, in addition to the ordinary terrestrial realm.

Humans, and all other living things we observe on earth, have a spiritual essence, or soul, which originates in the spiritual level of the cosmos. This spiritual essence is covered first by mind and then by matter, in a process that I call devolution. The process of devolution begins when the individual conscious self desires in a way that is incompatible with the spiritual harmony that exists between all beings in the spiritual world. According to their degree of departure from the original spiritual harmony, conscious selves receive subtler or grosser material bodies and fields of action. The higher demigods, who retain some considerable portion of their awareness of spiritual realities, receive bodies made primarily of the subtle material mind element, and act in an appropriate field. Those with grosser desires obtain not only a body of mind but also a body composed of a considerable amount of ordinary matter, capable of acting in the field predominated by ordinary matter. All of the bodies are programmed to last fixed durations of time. At the end of this duration, the soul obtains another body, according to the final state of its desires and consciousness. It is possible for a soul that has completely purified its desires to return to its original spiritual position. Otherwise, it receives another body, for another fixed term.

Cosmologies Material and Spiritual

There have always been various ways of looking at the world, some of them materialistic, focusing on matter and its purely mechanical transformations, and some of them mystical or spiritual, focusing on the influence of God, or of gods and goddesses, on transformations of gross and subtle matter. At a certain time and place, a particular cosmology may become dominant within the most powerful and influential social groups. But alternative cosmologies remain simultaneously in existence, perhaps among the general population or among subdominant elites. In ancient times, spiritual, or mystical, cosmologies were dominant, but materialistic cosmologies were also current. For example, during the time of the Greeks, some philosophers, such as Democritus, proposed that everything in the universe could be reduced to material atoms. But spiritual philosophers were more numerous and influential. Today the positions are reversed. Materialistic cosmologies are dominant in elite circles and a substantial percentage of the general population, but spiritual cosmologies have survived. Not only have they survived, but their influence is growing, and they may soon once more become dominant within leading circles of society.

Billions of people in the world are still under the influence of spiritual cosmologies. They include, in addition to the orthodox followers of the principal world religions, practitioners of voodoo, santeria, shamanism, wiccam, etc. Even in the most technologically advanced populations, a surprising number of people display commitment to spiritual cosmologies or phenomena identified with these cosmologies. In 1990, the Gallup organization presented Americans with a list of 18 kinds of paranormal experiences associated with spiritual cosmologies. Only 7 percent of the respondents denied belief in any of them. About 50 percent expressed belief in five or more (Gallup and Newport 1990, p. 1). For example, 70 percent of Americans said they believed in life after death, 49 percent said they believed in extrasensory perception, 36 percent said they believed in telepathy, 46 percent said they believed in psychic healing, and 29 percent said they believed in ghosts haunting houses (Gallup and

Newport 1990, p. 5). In addition to believing in such things, a good number claim to actually have experienced them. The Gallup report stated that "1 in 4 Americans believe they have had a telepathic experience in which they communicated with another person without using the traditional five senses, 1 in 6 Americans have felt they have been in touch with someone who had already died, [and] 1 in 10 claim to have seen or been in the presence of a ghost" (Gallup and Newport 1990, p. 1). Belief in paranormal phenomena connected with spiritual cosmologies is not limited to the general population. According to one survey (Wagner and Monet (1979), 57 percent of American college professors expressed belief in extrasensory perception. Another survey found that 30 percent of the heads of the divisions of the American Association for the Advancement of Science also believed in extrasensory perception (McClenon 1982).

But in the midst of this sea of persons committed to spiritual cosmologies there have arisen connected islands of scientific elites who are strongly committed to the materialistic cosmologies. And they have spread over the planet a web of economic, political, cultural, and intellectual institutions, founded on their materialistic cosmologies, and this web has somehow managed to attain a certain dynamic force and power, relative to the international institutional expressions of spiritual cosmologies. In this book, I am principally addressing myself to those people who have become entangled in this network of dominant materialistic institutions but who feel suffocated by it and wish to restore the planetary dominance of spiritual cosmologies. The first step must be a thorough critique of the assumptions underlying the materialistic cosmologies in their institutionalized manifestations, especially in educational institutions. To put it simply, students should begin to question the materialistic cosmologies imposed upon them by their teachers. And teachers can begin to question their administrative superiors, who in turn can question theirs. The representatives of institutionalized manifestations of materialistic cosmology should be confronted by advocates of spiritualist cosmologies in such a way that they begin to acknowledge them and negotiate with them. To some extent this is already happening.

In January 1999, I went to Capetown, South Africa, to present a paper on aspects of forbidden archeology at the World Archeological Congress, a major international conference. At one of the sessions I attended, a woman archeologist involved in major excavations at the Hittite site of Çatalhöyük in Turkey explained how the scientists in charge of the project, which is funded by such major multinational corporations as Shell, Glaxo-Wellcome, and Visa, were taking into account the alternative cosmologies of various parties interested in the site, including the New Age goddess worshipers. The cosmology of the modern goddess worshiper is a mystical one, quite different, in key respects, from that of a professional archeologist committed, as I assume most are, to the materialistic cosmology of modern science. But in this circumstance, the representatives of the materialistic cosmology found themselves compelled to negotiate with representatives of a spiritualistic cosmology.

The director of the Çatalhöyük site is archeologist Ian Hodder, of Cambridge University in England. While some members of the orthodox archeological establishment are striving to maintain their exclusive authority and control over the process of picturing the past for the rest of society, some few archeologists, such as Hodder, are starting to take notice of the evolving situation represented by personalities such as the goddess worshipers and this forbidden archeologist, with his roots in the ancient Vedic tradition of India. In a perceptive article in *Antiquity,* Hodder (1997, p. 699) wrote: "Day by day it becomes more difficult to argue for a past controlled by the academy. The proliferation of special interests on the 'fringe' increasingly challenges, or spreads to, the dominant discourse itself." The forbidden archeology phenomenon has done both. Over the past few years, I have certainly been working to challenge the "dominant discourse." Indeed, through my presentations at mainstream archeological conferences, sometimes resulting in my papers appearing in otherwise orthodox professional academic publications, the challenge has in fact spread into the realm of the dominant discourse itself. Of course, this is not just true of me and my work, but of that of many others working in the fields of alternative history and archeology. Hodder (1997, p. 699) took notice of the alternative knowledge communities springing up on the web, acknowledging that "many are extremely well informed." He then said that "it is no longer so easy to see who is 'in' the academy and who is 'outside'" (1997, p. 700). Hodder was instrumental in involving New Age goddess worshipers and ecofeminists in the ongoing exploration and development of the Çatalhöyük site. Hopefully, things will continue to progress in this direction, with academy-trained archeologists and well-informed representatives of alternative wisdom traditions cooperating to produce new ways of understanding the past. Hodder (1997, p. 694) cited efforts by North American archeologists to "work together with native Americans and integrate the use of oral traditions in archeological interpretation." The American archeologists involved in one such effort (Anyon et al. 1996, p. 15) said that it shows "scientific knowledge does not constitute a privileged view of the past . . . it is simply another way of knowing the past." My own effort has focused on bringing the spiritual cosmology of ancient India into mainstream archeo-logical discourse, thus contributing to our understanding of human origins.

Human Devolution and Cosmology

The human devolution concept can only be understood in the con-text of a spiritual cosmology, involving levels of matter, mind and spirit. In the first part of this chapter, I will review some of the expressions of spiritual cosmologies in the West, from the time of the Greeks and Rom-ans to the time of Newton. In this way, I hope to provide any new spiritual cosmology that may rise to prominence in the West with a cultural pedi-gree, and also the heritage of a longstanding and substantial evidential foundation.

In the second part of this chapter, I will demonstrate that spiritual cosmologies, greatly resembling those that were once dominant in the West can be found in many other times and places in the world's his-tory. The demonstration will be based upon reports of traditional beliefs of non-Western peoples gathered over the past two centuries by social scientists and scholars of comparative religion. Such scientists and scho-lars have advanced various theories about the origin and function of spiritual cosmologies, differing greatly in their conclusions. It is not, how-ever, my purpose to disentangle the history of their agreements and dis-agreements, but rather to point out that in the course of their presenta-tions they bring to our attention a wealth of detailed observations con-firming that the overwhelming majority of peoples and cultures on this planet have accepted, and still accept today, spiritual cosmologies.

My demonstration will take the form of soundings or test bores, spaced (or timed) widely and somewhat randomly. If we propose that there is an underground deposit of a certain kind of ore extended through a certain region, we may execute several widely spaced test drillings, and if all the test drillings over this particular region show the presence of that ore, then we may safely conclude our initial proposal is probably correct. Now to determine the exact boundaries of the ore deposit, horizontally and vertically, and the concentration and purity of the ore at different places, will take a much more intensive systematic mapping effort. But the initial test results will have justified that endeavor.

One problem with our cosmological test drillings is that the ter-minologies and conceptualizations of various historical cosmologies, al-though bearing a family resemblance, are somewhat different. This is to be expected, but for the purposes of analyzing the relationships among the members of this set of cosmologies, I wish to introduce a template cosmology against which the terminologies and conceptualizations of the others can be measured and compared, much as various world currencies are measured against the dollar. Actually, the currencies are separate, and have their roots in distinct economies; yet, there is a practical need for translation of one currency into another, and for this purpose, some standard of comparison has to be chosen. For this purpose, I am adopting a cosmological structure from the ancient Sanskrit writings of India. This, of course, reflects my own personal preferences as well as my belief that the cosmology expressed in the Sanskrit writings is objectively best suited for this purpose. I characterize the Indian Sanskrit writings as "Vedic," using the widest interpretation of the term to include not only the four original Vedas, but also the supplementary Vedic literatures such as the Puranas.

A Template Spiritual Cosmology

A clear expression of a template model of a mystical cosmology is found in chapters 25–29 of the Fourth Canto of the *Shrimad Bhagavatam,* also known as the *Bhagavata Purana.* These chapters present an elaborate cosmological allegory called "The City of Nine Gates." The sophistication of the allegory and the potential explanatory power of its elements invite modern researchers to consider alternatives to materialistic cosmologies.

The account of the City of Nine Gates is specifically identified as allegorical in the *Shrimad Bhagavatam* itself. The account was spoken by the sage Narada Muni, who was questioned by King Prachinabarhishat about the nature of the self, and Narada Muni himself explained all the elements of the allegory in the original text. In other words, it is not that I myself have identified some passages from the *Bhagavata Purana* as allegorical, and myself interpreted the passage in terms of a spiritual cosmology. The allegorical nature of the passages and their application to a spiritual cosmology are features of the text itself.

The central character in the allegory of the City of Nine Gates is a King named Puranjana. One meaning of the Sanskrit word *puran-jana* in the context of the allegory is "one who enjoys in a body." Soul/body dualism is thus hinted at in the King's name. King Puranjana originally existed as a spirit soul in a purely spiritual realm in relationship with a supreme conscious being, God. Materialists may oppose the introduction of this transcendental realm, which exists outside the material universe knowable by science. But even the materialist cosmology of modern science sometimes incorporates a "transcendental" realm, that is to say, a realm that exists beyond the universe knowable by the traditional methods of modern science, and from which that universe emerged at the time of the Big Bang. This transcendental reality, existing beyond time, space, and matter, is called the quantum mechanical vacuum, and is pictured as a pure energy field in which particles appear and instantly disappear. From this sea of virtual particles, some go through a process of expansion that keeps them in existence. According to many cosmologists, our universe is the outcome of one such expansion.

So both the *Shrimad Bhagavatam* and widely held versions of the Big Bang cosmology of modern science posit an eternal transcendental existence from which our universe of matter, with its features of time and space, arises. Once this is admitted, we can then decide which version of ultimate reality has the most explanatory power, when applied to the variegated reality of our experience. Modern cosmologists and other theorists have a great deal of difficulty in coaxing a sufficient amount of variety from the rather smooth and featureless universe that, according to theory, expands from the quantum mechanical vacuum. The origin of consciousness also poses a difficult problem. In light of this, an ultimate reality that is itself variegated and conscious might offer a solution.

In the spiritual world, King Puranjana originally existed in relationship with the Personality of Godhead, Krishna. Having departed from the spiritual world by misuse of independence, King Puranjana journeys through the material world. According to the Vedic cosmology, the material world is manifested by a special expansion of the Personality of Godhead. This expansion is called Maha Vishnu, who rests as if sleeping on the Causal Ocean. From the pores of the Maha Vishnu come millions of material universes. They emerge from the body of the Maha Vishnu in seedlike form, and then, energized by the glance of Maha Vishnu, expand in size. This provides an interesting parallel to some versions of the modern Big Bang cosmology, which also posit many expanding universes. Maha Vishnu then expands into each universe, and there emerges from Him in each universe a subordinate creator god called Brahma. Brahma is a soul who is given a very powerful material body with which to perform his creative functions. From Brahma come many other subordinate gods who control various aspects of the material universe. Surya is in charge of the sun, Chandra is in charge of the moon, Varuna is in charge of the waters, and so on. Brahma also creates the various material bodies that souls like Puranjana will enter. All together, there are 8.4 million kinds of bodies, ranging from microbes to demigods.

In his journey through the material world, Puranjana is accompanied by Avijnata Sakha ("the Unknown Friend"). The Unknown Friend corresponds to the Supersoul expansion of God into the hearts of all living beings. When Puranjana leaves God and the spiritual world, his memory of them becomes covered. But unknown to Puranjana, God accompanies him on his journey through the material world. According to the *Shrimad Bhagavatam*, God accompanies all spirit souls in the material world as their Unknown Friend, who observes and sanctions their activities.

In the West, mind/brain dualism is identified with the French philosopher René Descartes, who posited the existence of (1) matter extended in space and (2) mind existing outside space. Cartesian dualism is characterized by an interaction between mind and matter, but explaining how this interaction takes place proved problematic for advocates of the Cartesian model. How, for example, are impressions transmitted from the realm of matter to the completely different realm of mind?

According to the *Shrimad Bhagavatam*, both matter and the souls in the material world are energies of God, and as such both have a single spiritual source. The *Shrimad Bhagavatam* philosophy is thus both dualist and monist, simultaneously. The interactions of matter and the soul in the material world are mediated by Supersoul, who exists inside each material atom and also accompanies each spirit soul. By the arrangement of Supersoul, impressions of material experience can be channeled to the soul and the intentions of the soul can influence matter. How this takes place is the subject of the allegory of Puranjana.

Having left the spiritual world, Puranjana, accompanied by his Unknown Friend, the Supersoul, wanders through the material world. He desires to find a suitable place to enjoy himself. In other words, he searches for a suitable kind of body to inhabit. He tries many kinds of bodies on many planets. Here we note that each species of life consists of a soul inhabiting a particular kind of body. In this respect, the *Shrimad Bhagavatam* account differs from that of Descartes, who held that only humans have souls. For Descartes, animals were simply automatons.

Eventually, Puranjana comes to a place called Nava Dvara Pura, the City of Nine Gates. He finds it quite attractive. The City of Nine Gates represents the human male body, with its nine openings—two eyes, two nostrils, two ears, mouth, anus, and the genital opening. As Puranjana wanders through the gardens of the city, he encounters an extremely beautiful woman. Puranjana is attracted to her, and she is attracted to him. She becomes his Queen.

Puranjana, as we have seen, represents the conscious self. The beautiful woman represents Buddhi, intelligence. Up to this point, for the sake of simplicity, I have referred to the subtle material body of the living entity as mind. But according to the Vedic philosophy, the subtle material body is actually made up of the subtle senses, mind, intelligence and false ego. According to the *Shrimad Bhagavatam* philosophy, intelligence is a subtle material energy with discriminatory capabilities like those manifested by artificial intelligence machines. The attraction between King Puranjana and the Queen is the root of embodied consciousness. The King, it should be noted, has distinct conscious selfhood, with nonmaterial sensory capability, but this capability becomes dormant when he begins his relationship with the Queen.

The Queen (the subtle material element called intelligence) allows Puranjana (the conscious self) to enjoy the City of Nine Gates (the gross physical body). Employing a computer analogy, we might say Puranjana represents the user, the City of Nine Gates represents the computer hardware, and the Queen represents the software that allows the user to interface with the hardware and use it for practical purposes.

The Queen is not, however, alone but is accompanied by eleven bodyguards and a serpent with five heads. The bodyguards comprise the mind and the ten subtle senses. The ten subtle senses are made up of five knowledge-acquiring senses and five working senses. The five knowledge-acquiring senses are the senses of sight, smell, taste, hearing, and touch. The five working senses are those of walking, grasping, speaking, reproduction, and evacuation. All ten subtle senses are grouped around the mind. The ten subtle senses are considered servants of the mind. Each of these servants has hundreds of wives. The wives are desires for material experience, and the subtle senses act under their pressure. According to this system, the subtle senses are different from the physical sense organs. The subtle senses are part of the invisible subtle material covering of the soul, along with mind and intelligence. The physical organs of sensation (the eyes, nose, tongue, ears, skin, legs, arms, mouth, genitals, and anus) are part of the gross physical body that is visible to the eyes. The gross body and its physical organs are made up of five elements: earth, water, fire, air, and ether.

The distinction between subtle senses and physical sense organs is important, and offers consciousness researchers a valuable conceptual tool. Let us consider, for example, the problem of phantom limbs. Persons whose legs or arms have been amputated often report that they are able to distinctly feel the missing limb, and even experience quite distinct sensations, such as twinges of pain or itching. The City of Nine Gates allegory provides an explanation for this mysterious phenomenon. Let us take the case of someone whose arm has been amputated but who still feels the presence of the arm. The arm is one of the working senses. It is composed of two elements, the subtle grasping sense and the physical organ of the arm and hand. The process of amputation removes the physical organ through which the subtle sense operates. But the subtle sense itself remains, and therefore its presence may be mentally perceived.

Since the subtle sense is material, it may be able to act upon gross physical matter, without going through the related physical sense organ. This model may therefore explain some of the phenomena reported in connection with ghosts and apparitions, and in connection with mediums, particularly the mysterious movement of physical objects. This model may also explain how persons are able to experience sense data during near death experiences, during which the physical sense organs are incapacitated because of anesthesia or shock.

The subtle senses are compared to attendants of the Queen. They serve her by bringing information and by conducting activity. Together they comprise the array of material intelligence and sensory capabilities, all formed from subtle but nevertheless material energy. In combination, they manufacture a self picture, with which the King becomes entranced and falsely identifies. The body itself, the City of Nine Gates, is made of gross material energy, of the kind that can be manipulated by ordinary physics and chemistry. It is powered by five subtle airs, listed in the Ayur Veda, the Vedic medical science, as *prana, apana, vyana, samana,* and *udana.* In the Puranjana allegory the five airs, comprising the vital force, are represented by a five-headed serpent.

In the allegory, Puranjana asks about the identity and origin of the Queen and her attendants. The Queen replies, "O best of human beings, I do not know who has begotten me. I cannot speak to you perfectly about this. Nor do I know the names or the origins of the associates with me. O great hero, we only know that we are existing in this place. We do not know what will come after. Indeed, we are so foolish that we do not care to understand who has created this beautiful place for our residence. My dear gentleman, all these men and women with me are known as my friends, and the snake, who always remains awake, protects this city even during my sleeping hours. So much I know. I do not know anything beyond this. You have somehow or other come here. This is certainly a great fortune for me. I wish all auspicious things for you. You have a great desire to satisfy your senses, and all my friends and I shall try our best in all respects to fulfill your desires. I have just arranged this city of nine gates for you so that you can have all kinds of sense gratification. You may live here for one hundred years, and everything for your sense gratification will be supplied."

The King's questioning the Queen represents the self's interrogation of material intelligence for the answers to ultimate questions. The answers provided by the Queen, as well as her fundamental attitude, reflect those of modern science, which prides itself on avoidance of certain metaphysical questions and the tentativeness of whatever answers it may provide to other questions. "I cannot speak to you perfectly about this. . . . We only know that we are existing in this place." Essentially, the Queen provides a monist, materialist answer to the King's questions about his situation.

The *Shrimad Bhagavatam* then provides a more detailed description of the nine gates of the city inhabited by the King and Queen. Seven of the gates are on the surface (the two eyes, two ears, two nostrils, and mouth), and two of the gates are subterranean (the anus and genitals). Five of the gates face east.

The first two gates on the eastern side are called Khadyota (glowworm) and Avirmukhi (torchlight). In order to see, the King would exit these two gates, and go to the city called Vibhrajita (clear vision). On this journey he would be accompanied by his friend Dyuman (the sun, the ruler of the subtle visual sense).

In other words, the King encounters qualia by sensory contact through the physical gates of the body. Qualia are secondary properties of objects, such as color. In consciousness studies, the question of how we perceive qualia is a much debated topic. Do they exist in their own right, in the objects with which they are identified, or do they exist only in our own minds? According to the *Shrimad Bhagavatam* system, qualia, such as colors, exist as subtle sense objects. They thus have a reality of their own, and are not simply produced within the mind. The five subtle sense objects are sight, sound, taste, smell, and touch.

That the King goes out through the gates of the eyes to contact subtle sense objects in a city of visual impressions is interesting. This suggests that the seeing process is not simply one of passive reception, but may involve an active process of image acquisition (as in sonar, or radar). This may explain such phenomena as traveling clairvoyance, whereby a subject can mentally journey to a particular location, beyond the range of the physical sense organs, and then accurately report visual impressions. Visual sensations reported during out of body experiences could also be explained by this model. The exact relationships between the physical sense organs, the subtle senses, and subtle sense objects are not easily understood, but could perhaps be clarified by experimental work based on the overall model of the City of Nine Gates.

In the eastern part of King Puranjana's city there are, in addition to the eyes, two gates called Nalini and Naalini, representing the nostrils. The King would go through these two gates with a friend called Avadhuta (representing breathing airs) to the town of Saurbha (odor). The last gate on the eastern side is Mukhya (the mouth), through which the King would go with two friends to the towns of taste sensation and nourishment.

Through the two gates on the northern and southern sides (the ears), the King would go to places where different kinds of sound were heard. Through the gates on the western side of the city, the King would go to the towns where sensations of sexual pleasure and evacuation are experienced. During his journeys, the King would take help from two blind men, Nirvak and Peshakrit, who represent the arms and legs.

In all his activities, the King would follow the lead of the Queen. In other words, the conscious self in the material world becomes conditioned by material intelligence. The *Shrimad Bhagavatam* says: "When the Queen drank liquor, King Puranjana also engaged in drinking. When the Queen dined, he used to dine with her, and when she chewed, King Puranjana used to chew along with her. When the Queen sang, he also sang, and when the Queen laughed, he also laughed. When the Queen talked loosely, he also talked loosely, and when the Queen walked, the King walked behind her. When the Queen would stand still, the King would also stand still, and when the Queen would lie down in bed, he would also follow and lie down with her. When the Queen sat, he would also sit, and when the Queen heard something, he would follow her to hear the same thing. When the Queen saw something, the King would also look at it, and when the Queen smelled something, the King would follow her to smell the same thing. When the Queen touched something, the King would also touch it, and when the dear Queen was lamenting, the poor King also had to follow her in lamentation. In the same way, when the Queen felt enjoyment, he also enjoyed, and when the Queen was satisfied, the King also felt satisfaction."

As noted above, an important question that arises concerning dualist solutions to the mind/body question is how a nonmaterial conscious mind interacts with material sense objects. In this model, there is an answer to this question. The interaction is based on illusory identification.

To understand the nature of this illusory identification, we first need to readjust the familiar mind/body dualism to a triadic conception incorporating (1) a nonmaterial conscious self, (2) a subtle material body formed of mind, subtle senses, and intelligence, and (3) a physical body composed of gross matter. For the purposes of simplification, I sometimes reduce this triad to spirit, mind, and matter, with mind representing collectively all the elements of the subtle material body, namely, mind, the subtle senses, and intelligence.

In the more detailed model, however, the mind is a subtle material substance, associated with material intelligence. Mind is at the center of the subtle senses, which are in turn connected to the physical sense organs, which bring to the mind sense data in the form of subtle sense objects. Here yet another question arises.

In consciousness studies, one is faced with the problem of how the various kinds of sense data are presented in an integrated fashion. Even various elements of the visual sense, such as perception of color and movement and form are supposedly located in different parts of the brain. Sounds are processed in other parts of the brain. How are all these elements combined?

In the *Shrimad Bhagavatam* model, the integrating function is performed by the subtle mind element, which receives sensory inputs from the subtle senses grouped around it. The mind is not, however, conscious. The mind might, therefore, be compared to multimedia computer software capable of integrating audio and visual materials into a single, integrated display, making use of a variety of inputs and source materials. The material intelligence, represented by the Queen, directs the consciousness of the actual living entity to the integrated display of sense data. Intelligence, as a subtle material energy, is not itself conscious, but it mimics the behavior of consciousness. It thus attracts the attention of the conscious self, causing the self to identify with it, just as we identify with the image of an actor on a movie screen or the antics of a robot. By identification with material intelligence, which is in turn connected to the mind's integrated display of sense data, consciousness is connected with the sense data. This connection is not direct. The indirect connection of the conscious self with gross matter arises from the self's false identification with the action of a subtle material energy, intelligence. The extremely subtle material element that keeps the attention of the conscious self glued to the movements of the material intelligence is called *ahankara,* or false ego. The whole system is set up and directed by the Supersoul.

According to the *Shrimad Bhagavatam* picture, the conscious self originally experiences nonmaterial sense objects through nonmaterial senses. This takes place in the spiritual world, with God. But having turned from this original situation, the self is placed in a material body in the material world. Identifying with this artificial situation, the self forgets its own nature and that of God. But God remains with the self as Supersoul, the Unknown Friend. If the self tires of the artificial material reality and desires to return to its original position, the Unknown Friend will reawaken the original spiritual senses of the self and reconnect them with their spiritual sense objects.

The whole system of consciousness in the material universe therefore resembles a computer-generated virtual reality. In virtual reality systems, the user's normal sensory inputs are replaced by computer-generated displays. But just as a person can turn off the virtual reality display and return to normal sensory experience, so the conscious self in the artificial sensory environment of the material world can return to its original spiritual sensory experience.

In the *Shrimad Bhagavatam* allegory, King Puranjana and his Queen enjoy life for some time in the City of Nine Gates. Eventually, however, the City of Nine Gates comes under attack by a king named Chandavega. Chandavega represents time, and his name literally means "very swiftly passing away." Chandavega commands an army of 360 male Gandharva soldiers and their 360 female companions. Together, these represent the days and nights of the year. When Chandavega's army attacks, the five-headed serpent (the vital force) tries to defend the City of Nine Gates. The serpent fights the attackers for one hundred years but eventually becomes weak, causing anxiety for the King and his associates. Finally, the attacking soldiers overwhelm the defenders and set the City of Nine Gates ablaze. As it becomes obvious that the battle is being lost, King Puranjana is overcome with anxious thoughts of his wife and other relatives and associates. Then the commander of the invading forces arrests the King and takes him away along with his followers, including the five-headed serpent. As soon as they are gone, the attackers destroy the City of Nine Gates, smashing it to dust. Even as he is being led away, the King cannot remember his Unknown Friend, the Supersoul. Instead, he thinks only of his wife, the Queen. He then takes another birth, this time as a woman.

In this part of the allegory, we see how the conscious self leaves the gross physical body, accompanied by the intelligence, mind, and subtle senses. When they leave, the gross physical body disintegrates. The conscious self then receives another gross physical body. The kind of body received depends on the condition of the subtle material body, which is composed of intelligence, mind, and subtle senses. The subtle material body is the template upon which the gross physical body is constructed. This model allows one to account for reports of past life memories, such as those researched and verified by Dr. Ian Stevenson of the University of Virginia in his book *Twenty Cases Suggestive of Reincarnation*. In the *Shrimad Bhagavatam* model, the mind is the storehouse of memory, including memory of past lives.

In his next life, King Puranjana becomes Vaidarbhi, the daughter of King Vidarbha. When grown, Vaidarbhi becomes the Queen of King Malayadhvaja. At the end of his life, King Malayadhvaja retires to the forest and takes up the process of mystic yoga. The *Shrimad Bhagavatam* (4.28. 40) informs us: "King Malayadhvaja attained perfect knowledge by being able to distinguish the Supersoul from the individual soul. The individual soul is localized, whereas the Supersoul is all-pervasive. He became perfect in knowledge that the material body is not the soul but that the soul is the witness of the material body." In this state of higher awareness, Malayadhvaja, following the yoga process, deliberately leaves his material body and achieves liberation from material existence.

Queen Vaidarbhi (formerly King Puranjana) is overwhelmed with grief at her husband's departure. At this point, King Puranjana's Unknown Friend (the Supersoul), appears before Vaidarbhi as a *brahmana* (saintly teacher). The *brahmana* says to Vaidarbhi: "My dear friend, even though you cannot immediately recognize Me, can't you remember that in the past you had a very intimate friend? Unfortunately, you gave up My company and accepted a position as enjoyer of this material world. ... You were simply captivated in this body of nine gates." The *brahmana* then instructs Vaidarbhi further about her original position as a purely spiritual self in the spiritual world. The message is that we should return to our original spiritual position, in which we have a spiritual body with spiritual senses. But if we choose not to do this, then we can remain in the material world, in a body adjusted to our desires. The body could be that of a demigod in the heavenly material planets, or that of a human being on earth. It could also be that of a plant or animal. Human life therefore takes its place in a cosmic hierarchy of life forms.

In this summary, I have extracted only the principal elements of the City of Nine Gates allegory. The complete account is much more detailed, and allows one to make an even more subtle and refined model of self-mind-body interaction in the environment of a multilevel cosmos, divided principally into regions of gross matter, subtle matter, and spirit. This model does not fit easily into present categories of the mind-body debate. Although dualist, it partakes also of idealism and monism. It does, however, allow one to integrate many categories of evidence from normal and paranormal science, as well as evidence from humanity's wisdom traditions, into a rich synthesis, providing fruitful lines of research confirming and refining a complex model of self-mind-body interaction.

The potential explanatory power of this model, called by some the Gaudiya Vaishnava Vedanta (GVV) ontology, has been recognized by quantum physicist Henry P. Stapp, of the Lawrence Berkeley laboratory. Stapp observed (1994, p. 1), "The possibility that this ancient way of viewing Nature might be useful in science arises in the context of contemporary efforts to understand the empirically observed correlations between conscious processes and brain processes." Such efforts are, according to Stapp, hampered by the concepts of mind and matter inherited by modern science from previous centuries. He finds the self-mind-body triad helpful in explicating the ideas of knower and known: "GVV accomodates these ideas in a straight-forward way by making a clear distinction between the subjective conscious knower, the spiritual 'I', and a mental realm that contains certain things that he can know directly. This mental realm, in contrast to the Cartesian realm of mind, is material: it is constructed out of a subtle kind of matter. The introduction of this second material level, mind, provides . . . a basis for coherently extending the mathematical methods of the physical science from the gross physical world into the realm of mind, while leaving intact the knower, or self" (Stapp 1994, p. 9). All in all, Stapp considered GVV ontology to be "internally consistent and compatible with the available scientific data" (Stapp 1994, p. 3).

Elements of Spiritual Cosmology
In Western Thinkers of Classical Antiquity

We can now begin our review of elements of spiritual cosmology in Western thought. There are many ways in which such a survey could be arranged. I have chosen to proceed as much as possible in time order.

The Presocratic philosopher Empedocles (c.495–c.453) spoke of gods, demigods, humans, and other species, each with their natural realm of existence. Empedocles said that if a soul inhabiting the body of a demigod, blessed with long life, commits a sinful act, then for many thousands of years that soul must take birth "in the forms of all manner of mortal things and changing one baleful path of life for another" (Kirk and Raven 1957, fragment 115). Empedocles described himself as "a fugitive from the gods and a wanderer" (Kirk and Raven 1957, frag. 115). He said, "Already have I once been a boy and a girl, a fish and a bird and a dumb sea fish" (Kirk and Raven 1957, frag. 117). He held that by philosophical insight and a pious life a soul can return to its original position.

Ideas of reincarnation were also found in Orphism, the Greek mystery cult that influenced some Presocratic philosophers and Plato. George Mylonas (1950, p. 178), an archeologist and art historian, said the Orphics believed humans were made from the ashes of the Titans, representing matter and its powers. But because the Titans had previously devoured Zagreus, a son of Zeus, whose essence was deathless, humans contained both divine and material elements, the divine being immortal and the material temporary. Mylonas (1950, p. 181) said, "Through purification and ritual, through sacred literature and initiation into the mysteries, through the Orphic life and asceticism, man could hope that the divine essence in him, his soul, by the intervention of divine grace would free itself of the original impurity, would escape the Great Circle of Necessity and the ever recurring weary cycle of rebirth, would attain redemption. . . . That was the supreme aim of life."

According to his Greek and Roman biographers, Socrates communicated with a spirit being. "The familiar prophetic voice of my 'spiritual guide'," said Socrates, "has manifested itself very frequently all my life and has opposed me, even in trivial matters, whenever I was about to do something wrong" (Plato, *Apology of Socrates*, 39C1–40C3; in Luck 1985, p. 187). The Greek word for the "spiritual guide" was *daimonion*. Xenophon, a disciple of Socrates, said Socrates referred to his *daimonion* as "the voice of God" (Xen. *Apology* 12, in Luck 1985, p. 185). This is somewhat akin to the Vedic concept of *paramatma*, or Supersoul, which posits a localized personal expansion of God in the hearts of all living entities. Persons of a certain stage of spiritual advancement are able to directly communicate aurally with the Supersoul, and others may indirectly experience the promptings of the Supersoul in the form of intuitions and pangs of conscience. Of course, it may have been that Socrates was in communication not with Supersoul but with another kind of spirit being—for example, a minor demigod who had taken an interest in his activities.

In Plato's *Phaedo* (81C–D, in Luck 1985, p. 169), Socrates speaks of ghosts. He proposes that ghosts are souls who were not "pure" when they left the body. They retain some subtle yet visible substance, which enables them to be sometimes seen. Good souls do not become ghosts. As punishment for impious deeds during their earthly existence, ghosts are compelled to wander near inauspicious places such as tombs and burial grounds until they are once more allowed to enter a normal physical body. Many elements of Socrates's description of ghosts are familiar to me from Indian philosophy, which holds that the human organism is composed of three elements: a gross material body, a subtle material body composed of mind, and the soul itself, which is a particle of eternal consciousness. Under this view, ghosts are souls without gross material bodies. But they retain their subtle material forms (without, however, being allowed to enjoy subtle material pleasures) and in those forms haunt the living with a view to gaining control of a gross material body for gross material enjoyment. I propose that the action of the ghost's subtle material body upon the subtle senses of an embodied person's subtle body produces the perception of an apparition. After some time, the ghost is allowed to take on another physical form. If one properly uses this human form, one can become freed from both the subtle and gross material coverings, and attain to the realm of pure spiritual existence. A ghost is different from a demigod. The higher demigods and ghosts are both souls that have subtle material bodies. But demigods are pious souls who have been given positions in the universal system of management, and they are also given opportunities to experience subtle sensual pleasures surpassing those available to ordinary humans. Ghosts, on the other hand, are generally impious beings, whose subtle bodies are full of strong material desires that cannot be fulfilled. They are denied the subtle sensual pleasures available to the demigods. The only opportunities they have for satisfying their desires lie in commandeering the physical forms of humans, as in cases of possession.

In Book Ten of *The Republic,* Plato presents the story of the warrior Er, who died in battle (Eliade 1967, pp. 375–376). Twelve days after death, he revived, as he lay on his funeral pyre, and described what he had seen when his soul left his body. He and other souls came to a place where they saw two openings side by side in the heavens and two openings side by side in the earth. Through one of the openings in the earth souls were coming out and entering the opening leading into heaven. And through the second set of openings souls were coming down from heaven and entering the earth. The souls coming up through the opening in the earth described their sufferings in the hellish regions below, and those returning through the opening in the heavens described their enjoyment in the realm above. According to the Vedic cosmology, humans living on earth accumulate *karma.* Those with good *karma,* accumulated through pious acts, are elevated to the heavenly planets, but they return to earth when their good *karma* is exhausted. Those with bad *karma,* accumulated through impious acts, are sent to the hellish planets, but they return to earth when their bad *karma* is exhausted. If, however, one performs pure devotional service to God, one goes to the spiritual world, from which one does not have to return. Pure devotional service results in no karma, good or bad.

Aristotle, in the twelfth book of his *Metaphysics,* said that the stars and planets acted as an intermediary between his spiritual Prime Mover and the world of matter, composed of four elements (earth, water, fire, and air). The movements of the celestial bodies were therefore the intermediate cause of terrestrial life and movement (Thorndike 1923, v. 2, p. 253). Here we find a cosmology that depicts the universe as divided into three regions, resembling the Vedic cosmology.

Publius Cornellius Scipio Aemillanus (185–129 BC) was a member of a patrician Roman family. At a time when he was contemplating suicide, he saw his deceased father in a dream. In the course of warning him against suicide, his father instructed him on the nature of the soul. An account of this incident is given in Cicero's *On the Republic* (IV, 14–26). The father of Publius, from his place in the spiritual world, said: "Unless God whose temple is the whole visible universe releases you from the prison of the body, you cannot gain entrance here. For men were given life for the purpose of cultivating that globe, called Earth, which you see at the center of this temple. Each has been given a soul, from these eternal fires, which you call stars and planets, which are globular and rotund and are animated by divine intelligence.... Like all god-fearing men, therefore, Publius, you must leave the soul in the custody of the body, and must not quit the life on Earth unless you are summoned by the one who gave it to you; otherwise you will be seen to shirk the duty assigned by God to man.... be sure that it is not you who are mortal, but only your body; nor is it you whom your outward form represents. Your spirit is your true self, not that bodily form that can be pointed out with the finger. Know yourself, therefore, to be a god—if indeed a god is a being that lives, feels, remembers, and foresees, that rules, governs, and moves the body over which it is set, just as the supreme God above us rules this world. And just as that eternal God moves the universe, which is partly mortal, so an eternal spirit moves the fragile body" (Eliade 1967, pp. 373–374).

The views expressed by the father of Publius about the soul of the individual body and the soul of the universe are quite close to those found in our template Vedic cosmology. A. C. Bhaktivedanta Swami Prabhupada says in his commentary on *Bhagavad Gita* (7.6): "This material body is developed because spirit is present within matter; a child grows gradually to boyhood and then to manhood because that superior energy, spirit soul, is present. Similarly, the entire cosmic manifestation of the gigantic universe is developed because of the presence of the Supersoul. ... The cause of the big universe is the big soul, or the Supersoul. And Krishna, the Supreme, is the cause of both the big and small souls."

In his *Metamorphoses,* Ovid (43 BC–18 AD) declared that in the beginning "nature was all alike, a shapelessness, chaos ... in whose confusion discordant atoms warred." But he also spoke of an original, singular god "who out of chaos brought order to the universe, and gave it division, subdivision." Then came stars, the abodes of a plurality of gods, who seem to have been subordinate to the one who originally brought order out of chaos. Then "shining fish were given the waves for dwelling, and beasts the earth, and birds the moving air." Finally humans appeared. Ovid suggested "man was born, it may be, in God's image" (Sproul 1979, pp. 170–171). Here again we see an apparent tripartite division of the cosmos. The spiritual realm of the original singular god, the celestial realm of the subordinate gods (demigods), and the terrestrial realm of ordinary living beings, including humans.

The Greek philosopher Plutarch (c46–c120 AD) said in *On The Soul* that the journey of the soul at the time of death was like the experience of someone being initiated into mysteries, such as the Eleusinian mysteries. Plutarch wrote: "At first one wanders and wearily hurries to and fro, and journeys with suspicion through the dark as one uninitiated: then come all the terrors before the final initiation, shuddering, trembling, sweating, amazement: then one is struck with a marvelous light, one is received into pure regions and meadows, with voices and dances and the majesty of holy sounds and shapes: among these he who has fulfilled initiation wanders free, and released and bearing his crown joins in the divine communion, and consorts with pure and holy men, beholding those who live here uninitiated, an uncleansed horde. . . . huddled together in mud and fog, abiding in their miseries through fear of death and mistrust of the blessings there" (Eliade 1967, p. 302).

In the first century AD, Manilius composed an astrological treatise in which he compared the universe to a living creature permeated by a single spirit, which gives it form (Luck 1985, p. 332). Here we have further echoes of the Indian concept of God distributed in nature, and of the *vishvamurti,* or Universal Form, the universe conceived as the body of God. According to both Manilius and the sages of ancient India, God is the soul of the universe, giving it life. It is this unifiying presence of God's spirit in nature, said Manilius, that establishes a connection between human destiny and the stars (Luck 1985, p. 333). Furthermore, he says that this God "brings down from the heavenly stars the creatures of the earth" (Luck 1985, p. 333). I find this view quite compatible with my own, which also involves a descent of humans and other living things from higher planes of existence.

Around 217 AD, Philostratus composed *The Life of Apollonius,* recording the travels and teachings of the Pythagorean philosopher Apollonius of Tyana. Scholars agree that Apollonius was a genuine historical figure, but they disagree as to how well Philostratus's account reflects the actual life of Apollonius. In any case, the cosmological and metaphysical content of the *The Life* is of most interest to me, and whether it derives from Apollonius or Philostratus does not make much difference for my purposes. The citations I give from Philostratus are from the translation by Conybeare.

As a Westerner who has journeyed to India and taken up the practice of an Indian philosophical and religious system, I find it interesting that Apollonius, according to Philostratus, traveled to India, where he encountered *brahmanas* with mystic powers. These *brahmanas* could mys-teriously sense that Apollonius was coming, and sent a messenger to greet him by name while he was still far away from their dwelling place. The chief of the *brahmanas*, Iarchus, knew that Apollonius was carrying a letter for him, and correctly identified a particular misspelling in the unseen document (Philostratus III, 12, 16). Iarchus also displayed knowledge of many things that had happened to Apollonius during his life. According to the account, the *brahmanas* could make themselves invisible whenever they chose and could also levitate (III, 13, 17).

When the local king came to visit the *brahmanas*, Apollonius noted that vessels bearing food and wine appeared mysteriously from out of nowhere (III, 27). Iarchus and Apollonius also spoke of reincarnation (III, 19). In the course of this discussion, each gave details of his own previous existence. On being questioned by Apollonius, Iarchus claimed to be a reincarnation of an Indian warrior much like the Greek hero Achilles (III, 19), while Apollonius, on being questioned by Iarchus, revealed he had been in a previous life the pilot of an Egyptian seafaring boat (III, 23).

Apollonius asked Iarchus and his Indian companions about the composition of the universe. They said it was composed of elements. "Are there four?" asked Apollonius, referring to the earth, water, fire, and air of Greek cosmology. Iarchus replied that there were five: "There is the ether, which we must regard as the stuff of which gods are made; for just as all mortal creatures inhale the air, so do immortal and divine natures inhale the ether" (III, 34). Lists of the five elements mentioned by Iarchus, including ether, are found in *Bhagavad Gita* and other Vedic texts. Responding to questions by Apollonius, Iarchus said that the universe is to be seen as a living creature, with a soul. This soul adjusts the conditions of the universe to the actions of the creatures inhabiting it. "For example," said Iarchus, "the sufferings so often caused by drought are visited on us in accordance with the soul of the universe, whenever justice has fallen into disrepute and is disowned by men" (III, 34). Here we find an account of the laws of *karma*, which are administered by God in His form of Supersoul, the witness present in the hearts of all and even within the atom.

Iarchus compared the universe to a ship: "They set several pilots in this boat and subordinated them to the oldest and wisest of their number; and there were several officers on the prow and excellent and handy sailors to man the sails; and in the crew of this ship there was a detachment of armed men. . . . Let us apply this imagery to the universe and regard it in the light of a naval construction; for then you must apportion the first and supreme position to God the begetter of this animal, and subordinate posts to the gods who govern its parts; and we may well assent to the statements of the poets, when they say there are many gods in heaven and many in the sea, and many in the fountains and streams, and many round about the earth, and that there are some even under the earth. But we shall do well to separate from the universe the region under the earth, if there is one, because the poets represent it as an abode of terror and corruption" (Philostratus III, 25).

Once when the city of Ephesus was suffering from a plague, Apollonius determined that the cause was a demon disguised as an elderly beggar. Following the orders of Apollonius, citizens of Ephesus stoned the beggar. As soon as the order was given, fierce rays of light shot from the beggar's eyes. After the stoning, the people removed the stones and found instead of the beggar's body that of a demonic hound, smashed to a bloody pulp (Philostratus, IV, 10). Such incidents provide evidence that certain beings have the power to change the appearance and form of the gross physical body. If this can be done, perhaps beings with greater powers could be responsible not just for the changes of physical bodies, but their very production.

Some say Apollonius of Tyana died a natural death in Ephesus, attended by two maidservants. Others say he went to Lindus, where he entered the temple of Athena and mysteriously disappeared. Still others say he continued on to Crete, where he is also said to have disappeared in a temple, behind closed doors, outside which people heard a chorus of maidens singing, "Hasten thou from earth, hasten thou to Heaven, hasten" (Philostratus, VIII, 30).

After the death of Apollonius, a skeptical young man was studying philosophy in Tyana, the home town of Apollonius. He was doubtful about the existence of an immortal soul. He was particularly doubtful about the continued existence of the soul of Apollonius. "I myself," he said to his companions, "have done nothing now for over nine months but pray to Apollonius that he would reveal to me the truth about the soul; but he is so utterly dead that he will not appear to me in response to my entreaties, nor give me any reason to consider him immortal." Five days later, he awoke from a daytime sleep and asked those around him: "Do you not see Apollonius the sage, how that he is present with us and is listening to our discussions, and is reciting wondrous verses about the soul?" No one else could see or hear this. The young man repeated to them the following words from Apollonius (Philostratus, VIII, 31):

> The soul is immortal, and 'tis no possession
> of thine own, but of Providence,
>   And after the body is wasted away, like a
> swift horse freed from its traces,
>   It lightly leaps forward and mingles itself
> with the light air,
>   Loathing the spell of harsh and painful
> servitude which it has endured . . .

Alchemy, as practiced in the Hellenic world, had its basis in spiritual cosmology. In his book on magic in classical Greece and Rome, Luck (1985, p. 364) wrote: "The mystical side of alchemy is about as well documented as its practical side. It is marked by a quest for spiritual perfection, just as the search for precious metals involved the perfecting and refinement of raw materials. . . . Many alchemic operations can be understood as a sacrificial offering, as ceremonies to be accomplished after the alchemist himself has been initiated into some higher mysteries. A long period of spiritual preparation is indispensable. The ultimate goal of this process, as in the mystery religions, is salvation. Thus alchemy appears to be a Hellenic form of mysticism. Since the soul is divine in origin but tied to matter in this world and isolated from its spiritual home, it must, as far as possible, purify the divine spirit inherent in it from the contamination by matter. In his search for the *materia prima,* the alchemist discovers hidden powers within his own soul." The practice of alchemy continued for centuries in Europe. Sir Isaac Newton, renowned as the father of modern science, wrote extensively on alchemical subjects.

The similarity of alchemical transformations of metals and the purification of consciousness is noted in the following text from a sixteenth century Sanskrit work, the *Hari-bhakti-vilasa* (2.12), by Sanatana Goswami: "As bell metal is turned to gold when mixed with mercury in an alchemical process, so one who is properly trained and initiated by a bona fide spiritual master immediately becomes a *brahmana*" (*Chaitanya Charitamrita, Adi-lila,* 7.47). A *brahmana* is one whose consciousness has been purified of the grosser material influences. A *brahmana* is also defined as one who knows Brahman, or absolute spirit. The ultimate state of Brahman realization is knowledge of the soul's eternal loving relationship with God.

Elements of Mystical Cosmologies
In Europe Through the Middle Ages

Mystical cosmologies, with similarities to our Vedic template cosmology, continued to dominate European thought after the time of the Greeks and Romans. We shall now review a sampling of these cosmologies.

Kabbalah is a school of Jewish mysticism that became prominent during medieval times, but which was founded in earlier schools of Jewish esoteric wisdom. The principal text of the Kabbalah was the *Zohar*. In the *Zohar,* we find elements that are reminiscent of my template Vedic spiritual cosmology. For one thing, the Kabbalah's threefold concept of soul (*nefesh, ruah,* and *neshamah*) is related to the divisions of matter, mind, and spirit that form the basis of the human devolution idea. The *Zohar* says: "The 'soul' (*nefesh*) stands in intimate relation to the body, nourishing and upholding it; it is below, the first stirring. Having acquired due worth, it becomes the throne for the 'spirit' (*ruah*) to rest upon. . . . And when these two, soul and spirit, have duly readied themselves, they are worthy to receive the 'super-soul' (*neshamah*), resting in turn upon the throne of the spirit (*ruah*). The super-soul stands preeminent, and not to be perceived. There is throne upon throne, and for the highest a throne" (Scholem 1977, p. 44). The "super-soul" mentioned here is not the Vedic Supersoul, which is a localized manifestation of God Himself in the heart of each living entity. The *neshamah* of the Kabbalah would appear to correspond to the soul proper in the Vedic system, or, more to the point, the soul (*atma*) in touch with the Supersoul (*paramatma*). It might be correct to say that when the Vedic soul identifies principally with the gross physical body, it is like the *nefesh;* when it identifies with the subtle material body of mind and the vital force, it is like the *ruah;* and when it identifies with its own true nature as a particle of God's own spiritual energy, then it is like the *neshamah*.

That the Kabbalah may be speaking of one soul that reveals itself in three ways is hinted at in this passage from the *Zohar* (Scholem 1977, p. 44), in which the three souls are compared to parts of a single flame: "The study of these grades of the soul yields an understanding of the higher wisdom. . . . It is *nefesh,* the lowest stirring, to which the body adheres; just as in a candle flame, the obscure light at the bottom adheres close to the wick, without which it cannot be. When fully kindled, it becomes a throne for the white light above it, and when these two come into their full glow, the white light becomes a throne for a light not wholly discernible, an unknowable essence reposing on the white light, and so in all there comes to be a perfect light."

The Kabbalah also incorporates a multilevel cosmos. The *Zohar* says: "We have seen that when a man's soul leaves him, it is met by all his relatives and companions from the other world, who guide it to the realm of delight and the place of torture. If he is righteous, he beholds his place as he ascends and is there installed and regaled with the delights of the other world. But if no, then his soul stays in this world until his body is buried in the earth, after which the executioners seize on him and drag him down to Dumah, the prince of Gehinnom, and to his allotted level in Gehinnom" (Scholem 1977, pp. 57–58). The "realm of delight" also has several levels. The *Zohar* goes on to say about the pious soul: "It is first permitted into the cave of Machpelah up to a point, set in accordance with its merit. Then it comes to where the Garden of Eden stands, and there encounters the cherubim and the flashing sword which is found in the lower Garden of Eden, and if it is deemed worthy to do so, it enters. We know that there four pillars are waiting, and in their hands they hold the form of a body which the soul joyfully dons as its garment, and then it abides in its allotted circle of the Lower Garden for the stated time. After that a herald issues a proclamation and there is brought out a pillar of three hues, called 'the habitation of mount Zion' [*Isa.* 4:5]. By this pillar the soul ascends to the gate of righteousness, where are to be found Zion and Jerusalem. Happy is the lot of the soul deemed worthy to ascend higher, for then it is together with the body of the King. If it does not merit to ascend higher, then 'he that is left in Zion, and he that remaineth in Jerusalem, shall be called holy' [*Isa.* 4:3]. But when a soul is granted to ascend higher, then it sees before it the glory of the King and is vouschafed the supernal delight from the region which is called Heaven." The multilevel cosmology of the Kabbalah appears to correlate nicely with the template Vedic cosmology, in that both include hellish levels, earthly levels, paradisiacal levels of enhanced material enjoyment, and an ultimate spiritual level of transcendental delight in the association of the Personality of Godhead.

The ninth century Arab scholar Alkindi, known through summaries of his manuscripts by Latin authors in Europe, described a universe with similar features. Alkindi attributed occult influence to stars, and all things natural were a combination of stellar influences, carried by rays, acting on various aggregates of matter. According to Alkindi, each star has a different influence, and each kind of matter is especially receptive to a particular influence or combination of influences. In addition to occult stellar radiation, there are other kinds of radiation, such as sound and light. All of the various combinations of rays influencing natural objects are ultimately governed by a celestial harmony imposed by God.

Alkindi also spoke of the power of words uttered by humans to affect natural objects. These incantations, similar to the Vedic concept of *mantras*, were increased in potency by the faith and solemnity of the person uttering them as well as by favorable astrological influences (Thorndike 1923, v. 1, pp. 643–645).

About Alkindi's teachings on sound, Thorndike (1923 v. 1, p. 645) says: "The four elements are variously affected by different voices; some voices, for instance, affect fire most powerfully. Some especially stir trees or some one kind of tree. Thus by words motion is started, accelerated, or impeded; animal life is generated or destroyed; images are made to appear in mirrors; flames and lightnings are produced; and other feats and illusions are performed which seem marvelous to the mob. . . . He states that the rays emitted by the human mind and voice become the more efficacious in moving matter, if the speaker has fixed his mind upon and names God or some powerful angel."

During the early Christian era, apocryphal literatures such as the *Gospel of Enoch* were quite popular. The Enoch books spoke about angels controlling human destinies. The angels controlled the stars and planets, the years and seasons, the rivers and seas, as well as meteorological phenomena such as dew, hail, and snow (Thorndike 1923, v.1, pp. 342–343). The *Book of Enoch* also tells of fallen angels who mated with terrestrial human females. These angels instructed humans not only in magic, witchcraft, and astrology but also in practical sciences such as writing, mining metals, weapon making, botany, and pharmacy (Thorndike 1923, v.1, pp. 343–344). All this knowledge of "the secrets of the angels and violence of the Satans" was, according to Enoch, not good for humanity, "for man was created exactly like the angels to the intent that he should continue righteous and pure, . . . but through this their knowledge men are perishing" (Thorndike 1923, v.1, p. 344). The cosmology of the Enoch literature included a multilevel universe composed of seven heavens, or, in some manuscripts, ten heavens. Each level was inhabited by beings adapted to the conditions there (Thorndike 1923, v. 1, p. 346).

Hugh of St. Victor (1096–1141), one of the founders of Catholic scholastic theology, divided the cosmos into three levels: (1) the spiritual world, where God resides and everything is eternal; (2) the superlunar world, or the world beyond the moon, where things have a beginning but no end; and (3) the sublunar, or terrestrial world, where things have a beginning and an end (Thorndike 1923, v.2, p. 12). This is slightly different from the Vedic tripartite division of the cosmos, which includes the eternal spiritual world of God; the higher heavenly planets of the demigods (corresponding to Hugh's superlunar world), where a day is equivalent to millions of solar years; and the terrestrial realm of our human experience (corresponding to Hugh's sublunar world). The Vedic demigods are, like humans, subject to death, but their life span is far greater than that of human beings in the terrestrial realm. Hence the demigods are sometimes called *amara,* or deathless, but the word *amara* truly applies only to God and the liberated souls who exist with Him in the spiritual world. So in the planets of the Vedic demigods, things do have an end.

According to Hugh, the sublunar world is controlled by the planets and beings of the superlunar world. All terrestrial life and growth came "through invisible channels from the superior bodies" (Thorndike 1923, v. 2, pp. 12–13). The superlunar world is called Elysium, because it is char-acterized by peace and light. The sublunar world is called Infernum, because it is characterized by confusion and constant change. To the extent that humans identify with the sublunar nature, they are held in the grip of change by necessity. This is reminiscent of the Vedic concept of *karma*. All material change is carried out by karmic law, and living beings are forced to accept from material nature the results of their actions. But, according to Hugh, if they identify with their immortal nature they are connected to eternal Godhead (Thorndike 1923, v. 2, p. 3).

In the middle of the twelfth century, William of Conches wrote his *Dramaticon,* which takes the form of a philosophical dialogue between William and his patron Geoffrey Plantagenet, duke of Normandy and count of Anjou. In this work, William described three kinds of *daimons*, attributing his classification to Plato. The first class, which existed in the realm of ether between the starry heavens and the moon, were immortal beings blissfully engaged in contemplation of the sun. The second class inhabited a realm of rarified air near the moon. These immortal, rational beings transmitted the prayers of humans to God and made known to humans the will of God. The third class, inhabiting the realm of humid air near the earth, acted harmfully against humans, motivated by lust and envy. They would sometimes seduce terrestrial women (Thorndike 1923, v. 2, p. 55).

Bernard Silvester, in his *Di mundi universitate,* composed during the reign of Pope Eugenius III (1143–1153), gave a more complete list of supernatural creatures. He considered the stars to be living beings, "gods who serve God in person." In the realm of ether, they enjoy a life of eternal bliss, in constant contemplation of the divine. The human soul, upon leaving the material body, can return to this realm to become once more one of these gods. Next come the angels, who share with the stars the quality of deathlessness. But like humans they are influenced by passionate impulses. These angelic beings are of several kinds: (1) Benevolent angels serve as mediums between the Supreme Being and humans. They exist in the region between the sun and the moon. (2) In the aerial region just below the moon reside angelic beings who enjoy a tranquil and serene state of mind. (3) Next come genii, who are associated with particular humans, and guide them. It would seem that the *daimonion* of Socrates was of this category. (4) In the lower atmosphere, near the earth, resides a category of dark spirits, called by Bernard fallen angels. Sometimes they are assigned by superior powers the task of giving punishments to humans who deserve them. Sometimes, however, they act on their own, and possess humans, taking over their minds. They may also take on the forms of ghosts. (5) Finally, there are harmless nature spirits—gods and goddesses of mountains, rivers, lakes, and forests, with bodies composed of the pure forms of the physical elements. These bodies, though long lasting, are temporary (Thorndike 1923, v. 2, p. 104).

According to Bernard, the stars control nature and reveal the future. As the stars are living things, they accomplish their purposes not mechanically, but by receiving from the mind of God the knowledge of future events, which they then establish in the lower worlds, by arranging themselves in certain patterns (Thorndike 1923, v. 2, pp. 104–105). Those with proper intelligence would therefore be able to read the future from these stellar arrangements. Indeed, without the higher influences, there would be no movement of life in the lower world. But Bernard believed that humans, although in some ways subject to inevitable fate and variable fortune, could also exercise free will (Thorndike 1923, v. 2, p. 106). This seems to follow the concept of *karma*. The situations in which we find ourselves at present are determined by our past actions, but in each situation we have the freedom to choose different present actions, which in turn determine our future situations.

Henry Cornelius Agrippa (1486–1535) wrote *De Occulta Philosophia,* in which he divided the cosmos into three regions: elemental, celestial, and intellectual (Thorndike 1941, v. 5, pp. 134–135). In terms of our Vedic template cosmology, Agrippa's intellectual region appears to correspond to spiritual, celestial to mental, and elemental to material. Each kind of being in the elemental world is imbued with an occult virtue, implanted by the World Soul through the stars. The human soul originally belonged to the intellectual (Vedic spiritual) realm, but it has descended into the elemental realm, where it is bound and covered by the body. Agrippa believed that numbers, being of purer form than elemental objects, possessed more powerful occult virtues. The same was true of the letters of the alphabet, astrological signs, and geomantic figures. The book also deals with the lore of divine names, categories of demons, necromancy, and divination. According to legend, one of Agrippa's students once entered his private study while his teacher was gone and started reading one of his books of spells. Suddenly, a demon appeared, killing the youth or frightening him to death. When Agrippa came back some time later, he saw the dead body, and in order to avoid suspicion of murder, he summoned the same demon, causing him to enter the corpse. Thus animated, the body left the study and went walking around outside, in front of many witnesses. Thereafter, Agrippa caused the demon to depart from the body, which then fell down as if it had just been struck dead (Thorndike 1941, v. 5, p. 136).

Giordano Bruno (1548–1600) wrote several treatises on magic and occult properties of things. He believed in a World Soul, as well as a hierarchy of invisible spiritual beings, including those inhabiting the bodies of humans, plants, stones, and minerals. He believed that demons were the cause of various diseases. He believed it was possible to communicate with and influence these demons through signs, seals, and rituals. Bruno's concept of magic was based on a set of relationships between God and the lower worlds. God exercises influence over gods, corresponding to the Aristotelean Intelligences, and these in turn exercise influence upon the celestial bodies, including the earth. These celestial bodies are inhabited by *daimons,* who act upon the elements, which act upon compounds. The compounds act upon the senses, which act upon the soul, which acts upon the body of the animal or human. By magic, a human can attempt to influence higher beings in this ladder of relationships, with a view to obtaining specific results (Thorndike 1941, v. 6, pp. 425–426).

Johannes Kepler (1571–1630) is one of the most famous figures in the history of astronomy. Following on the work of Copernicus and Tycho Brahe, he calculated that the orbits of the planets were elliptical rather than circular. Nevertheless, he still accepted a spiritual cosmology. He wrote texts on astrology and also cast horoscopes himself. He said that the "geometry of the rays of the stars affects sublunar nature" (Thorndike 1958, v. 7, p. 21). In *Harmonice mundi* (1619), Kepler said there was "a soul of the whole universe, set over the movements of the stars, the generation of the elements, conservation of animals and plants, and finally the mutual sympathy of superiors and inferiors" (Thorndike 1958, v. 7, p. 26). He thought this soul most probably was located at the center of the cosmos, which for him was the sun. This soul of the universe controlled the movements of the stars and the generation of elements, as well as the manifestations of plant and animal life, and the occult properties of ob-

jects. Its influence was propagated by the sun's rays, just as the soul propagated its influence throughout the body of an animal. In his *Mysterium
cosmographicum*, Kepler said that each planet also had a soul. Kepler believed that the earth and living things on earth had a special faculty which
put them in sympathetic contact with stellar influences (Thorndike 1958,
v. 7, p. 26). The Earth, for Kepler, was like a living thing, like an animal,
not a quick one like a dog, but more like an elephant or cow (Thorndike
1958, v. 7, p. 31).

The German physician Sebastian Wirdig (1613–1687), in his book
Nova Medicina Spirituum, spoke of an immortal, nonmaterial, indivisible
soul in the human body. But between the soul and the body, there are,
said Wirdig, "spirits" (subtle yet material substances) that act as a medium. The condition of the spirits determines the health and sickness of the
body, the difference between life and death. These spirits are several, each
more subtle than the next: natural spirits associated with the simple bru-
tish and vegetative bodily activities; the vital spirits of the heart and arteries; the animal spirits of the brain and nerves; and the genial spirits of
the reproductive system. Altogether they form one complex vital spirit of
the body. This vital spirit acts in conjunction with astral and occult influences and powers. Wirdig held that the soul can through the vital spirits
influence matter. For example, strong feelings of lust can print moles on
embryos or produce monstrous children. Also, the vital spirits of one person can influence those of others, depending on relative strengths. This influence can be communicated by speech, song, gaze, touch, weapons, and
witchcraft. According to Wirdig, imagination is also controlled by the vital
spirits. If the vital spirits are too thin, or obstructed, then the impressions
of imagination on the soul are very weak. If the spirits are thicker, the
impressions on the soul are stronger (Thorndike 1958, v. 8, pp. 436–441).

Newton, widely regarded as the father of modern science, is most
known for his published works. But among his private papers are extensive manuscripts in which he reveals his commitment to the study of esoteric subjects connected with spiritual cosmologies. This caused Lord
Keynes, in a paper published on the three hundredth anniversary of Newton's birth, to call Newton "the last of the magicians" (Thorndike 1958,
v. 8, p. 588). Newton's unpublished writings contain hundreds of pages of
notes on alchemy, including extracts from books by various authors as
well as the results of Newton's own experimental work on transmutation
of metals, the philosopher's stone, and the elixir of life. Newton also analyzed sacred writings such as *Revelation* in his search for the key to the
mysteries of the universe. Lord Keynes noted, "The scope and character
of these papers have been hushed up, or at least minimized, by nearly all

those who have inspected them." It was clear Newton had dedicated years of his life to these experiments and writings, which Lord Keynes characterized as "wholly magical" and "devoid of scientific value" (Thorndike 1958, v. 8, p. 590). I disagree with Lord Keynes's latter remark. Newton's unpublished writings are of immense scientific value because they remind us that the best scientific minds are willing to consider all the evidence available to human experience in their attempts to comprehend life and the universe.

Newton believed that the human body was pervaded by subtle animal spirits. He said that the motions of the bodies of animals and humans were produced by the soul causing the subtle spirit element to move through the nerves, which then caused the muscles to act (Thorndike 1958, v. 8, p. 595). In an appendix to the 1713 edition of his *Principia,* Newton suggested there might be an all-pervading subtle spirit that was the ultimate cause of gravity, electricity, light, and sensation. But he did not believe he had yet enough experimental evidence to give "an accurate determination and demonstration of the laws by which this electric and elastic Spirit operates" (Thorndike 1958, v. 8, pp. 595–596). Newton, in a famous letter to Richard Bentley, said that "Tis unconceivable that inanimate brute matter should (without the mediation of something else which is not material) operate upon and affect other matter without mutual contact" (Griffin 1997, p. 19).

Non-Western Cosmologies

I deliberately began this review of mystical cosmologies with examples from the history of science and philosophy in the West, from the time of classical antiquity to the beginning of the scientific revolution. My purpose was to show that the evidence for psychic phenomena gathered by prominent scientists of the nineteenth and twentieth centuries should not necessarily be seen as strange anomalies, outside the realm of science. Of course, such things would be anomalous in the context of a science with metaphysical commitments to a strict materialism. But they would find a place in a science with a different set of metaphysical commitments, a science with the same kind of metaphysical commitments maintained by Kepler and Newton, for example. Another purpose was to provide a context for the introduction of spiritual cosmologies from outside the Western sphere. By showing that elements of these cosmologies have a strong presence in Western science and philosophy, I hope to show that the spiritual cosmologies of the world's great wisdom traditions are not alien to the intellectual tradition of the West.

Traditional Cosmology of China

The traditional wisdom of premodern China was a mixture of Buddhist, Confucianist, and Taoist elements, along with elements of a more primitive animism. The Taoist element was particularly influential. According to Taoism, the universe is pervaded by an order called Tao. The celestial aspect of this order (Tao T'ien) is revealed in the precise movements of the stars and planets. There is also a terrestrial aspect of the Tao revealed in the natural forces. But the original Tao existed before both of these manifestations of order. From this Tao come the principles of Yin, representing femininity, coldness, and darkness, and Yang, representing masculinity, warmth, and light (Day 1940, p. 56).

According to Day (1940, p. 165), the traditional Chinese cosmic hierarchy included many minor deities, such as the controller of small pox (Tou Shên), village patron protector (Chang Lao Hsiang Kung), spirit of wells (Tai Yi), and shop patron of prosperity (Kuan Kung). The Chinese also believed that they were surrounded by evil spirits (*kuei*) of many kinds. Latourette (1934, p. 163) reported: "On occasion they may take the forms of animals or even of men and women. A *kuei* may be in a man-eating tiger. Great numbers of stories are told of animals—*kuei*—who can take at will the body of a man or especially of a beautiful woman and in that guise work harm. *Kuei* may be in old trees, or in clothes, in objects of furniture, or in mountains or stones. Leaves driven before the wind may each be a *kuei*. . . . Insane persons are controlled by *kuei*" (Latourette 1934, p. 163). Among the *kuei* are the fox demons, who enter into humans, afflicting them with disease, mental illness, or death. Sometimes the fox takes on the shape of a beautiful young woman (Day 1940, p. 42).

The traditional Chinese believed they were being constantly protected from such evil spirits by their ancestors who had achieved spiritual liberation (De Groot 1912, p. 178). And they were also being protected by helping spirits. "There are, first of all," wrote Day (1940, p. 46), "the lesser officials Sui Hsing Shang Kuan and Hsi Fu Shang Kuan, who may be called in as demon-detectives; then the help of Hsing Tsai Szu, evil eradicator, or of the Hsing Tsai Wu Shêng, five sages who take away bad fortune, or of Hsiao Tsai Ta-Shêng, who assists in escaping calamities, may be secured. . . An extremely potent expeller of demons is Chung K'uei, usually represented as a fierce and powerful giant with sword in hand in the act of transfixing a demon underfoot. He is in the celestial Ministry of Exorcism (Chü Hsieh Uüan), associated with P'an Kuan as a god of demon-control."

A positive influence for good were the tutelary deities, who exercised guardianship over various aspects of Chinese life. There were, for example, the tutelary deities of the local land (T'u Ti), and the god of city walls (Ch'êng Huang). Higher than the tutelary deities were the gods of thunder (Lei Tsu), fire (Huo Te), and rain (Lung Wang). Lung Wang was the Dragon King, for whom many temples were built. Dragons are often featured in traditional Chinese art. Still higher were the planetary deities such as the god of Jupiter and Time (T'ai Sui), the moon goddess (T'ai Yin), and the sun god (T'ai Yang). In addition to the earthly and heavenly deities, there were also controllers of the underworld. These included the Taoist King of Hades, Tung Yüeh Ta Ti, and the Buddhist chief king of Hades, Yen-lo Wang (Day 1940, p. 165).

One interesting figure in the Chinese Buddhist pantheon is the savior of Hades, Ti-Ts'ang Wang, who mercifully delivers souls from the sufferings of the underworld to the heaven of Amitabha. About the savior of Hades, Doré (1922 v. 7, p. 252) stated: "With his magic wand, he opens the portals of this dismal land and rescues tortured souls from the grasp of Yama (Yen-lo Wang). According to the *Ti-Ts'ang Sutra* he uttered a vow before the throne of Buddha (deified), that he would devote himself to the salvation of suffering mankind, and would pursue that work until he had brought all living beings safely to the haven of Nirvana....On his birthday, which falls on the 30th of the 7th month, all the judges of the Ten Courts of Hades come and offer him their congratulations. On this occasion, he grants special favors to the damned. Those whose tortures are completed may leave the dismal realm of Hades and be reborn on earth as men, animals and plants. Others have their sufferings condoned [i.e., excused], and are transferred without further delay to the tenth court of Hades, where rebirth will soon take place."

The hierarchical nature of the traditional Chinese cosmos is further revealed in accounts of the Taoist saintly persons. One group called the Holy Men (Shêng Jên) live in the "highest heaven." Another, the Ideal Men (Chên Jên), live in the second heaven, and the Immortals (Hsien Jên) live in the third heaven and in remote parts of the earth such as the sacred central mountains called the K'un Lun. The latter group appears from time to time on earth to perform acts of mercy, including the curing of the sick (Latourette 1934, p. 162).

At the top of the Taoist cosmic hierarchy is the chief Taoist god, Yü Huang Shang Ti, who was called Father of the Gods (Day 1940, p. 125). He resides in the highest heaven, in the jade palace Ta Wei, situated in a constellation near the Pole Star. This celestial region was the source of all life and natural energy on the lower levels of the cosmic hierarchy (Day 1940, p. 132). In the Pole Star itself dwelled T'ai Yi, known as the Great Unity, or Supreme Spirit. The Pole Star, around which the universe revolved, became a symbol of the terrestrial emperors. There is also a Queen of Heaven (Burkhardt 1954, pp. 126–127).

According to Chinese traditional wisdom, humans are made of two elements or souls, *kwei* and *shen,* which are identified respectively with terrestrial matter (Yin) and the immaterial celestial substance (Yang). In a book called *Tsi,* Confucius said to Tsai Ngo, "The *khi* or breath is the full manifestation of the *shen,* and the *p'oh* is the full manifestation of the *kwei;* the union of the *kwei* with the *shen* is the highest of all doctrines. Living beings must all die, and the soul which must then return to earth is that which is called *kwei.* But while the bones and the flesh moulder in the ground and imperceptibly become the earth of the fields, the *khi* or breath departs to move on high as a shining light" (De Groot 1912, pp. 12–13).

It thus appears that according to Taoist and Confucian teachings, a human being, and all other living things, are composed of a material body (identified with *kwei* and *p'oh*) and a conscious self (identified with *shen* and *khi*). At birth they come together, and at death they separate. The material elements of the body merge back into Yin, earth, and the true soul, the *shen,* returns to Yang, or heaven. However, for the soul to remain in Yang, it has to be pure; otherwise, if infected with desires for lordship over matter, it comes again to earth in an earthly body.

The Taoist saint Chwang mentions another saint, Shen-pa, who lived in a cave, taking only water. He preserved his youthful complexion up to the age of seventy, at which time a tiger ate him. But Chwang noted that "this saint had nourished his inner man, and the tiger merely devoured the outward" (De Groot 1912, p. 88).

In the Taoist conception, souls who achieve liberation go to live in the abode of Shang-ti, the highest god, whose throne is the Pole Star. The other gods of nature, such as the gods of the sun, moon, stars, winds, clouds, thunder, and rain, surround Shang-ti in humanlike forms. The divine abode of Shang-ti is one of peace, stillness, and goodness, compared to the terrestrial realm, which is full of intense materially motivated action, which sometimes degenerates into dark savagery. This is somewhat like the Vedic conception of the three modes (*gunas*) of nature—*sattva-guna* (goodness), *raja-guna* (passion), and *tama-guna* (ignorance). In both the Chinese and Vedic systems, humans at death go to the place appropriate for the qualities they have acquired (De Groot 1912, pp. 170–180).

In the Chinese Taoist tradition, there are celestial warriors (*t'ien ping*), commanded by divine generals, who at the request of saintly persons sometimes come down to the terrestrial world to fight to establish principles of goodness (De Groot 1912, p. 180). The Buddhist strain of traditional Chinese cosmology also has personalities who descend to the terrestrial realm to mercifully assist humans. They are the *boddhisattvas,* who are worthy to enter *nirvana* but instead voluntarily take birth repeatedly in the material world to act for the benefit of others. We have already mentioned one such *boddhisattva,* Ti Ts'ang, the deliverer of souls from hell. Others are Kuan-yin, the goddess of mercy, and Wên-shu, lord of wisdom. Those who have attained complete supreme enlightenment are called Buddhas (MacNair 1946, p. 293).

In addition to the Taoist supreme god, Shang-ti, traditional Chinese cosmology also includes a creator god named P'an Ku. Emerging from an original cosmic egg, P'an Ku expanded in size, pushing the heavens (Yang) upward and spreading the earth (Yin) outwards. Then P'an Ku is said to have died. Harry Titterton Morgan (1942, p. 4) wrote: "In dying P'an Ku added to the completion of the Universe, for his head was transmuted into mountains, his breath into winds and clouds and his voice into thunder. His left eye became the light of the sun, his right eye the moon, his beard the stars; his four limbs and five extremities the four quarters of the globe and the five mountains. His veins and muscles became the strata of the earth, his flesh became the soil, his skin and the hairs therein changed into plants and trees, and his teeth and bones into minerals. The marrow in his bones became pearls and precious stones, his sweat descended as rain, while the parasites which infested his body, being pregnated by the wind, were the origin of the human race."

The Chinese understood that there were practical connections between different levels of the cosmic hierarchy. Such understanding is revealed in *feng shui*—the art of locating dwelling places, graves, and religious sites so as to receive the most favorable influences from the gods and goddesses of heaven and earth. If altars and temples are not properly situated, gods will refuse to dwell there. If graves and altars dedicated to ancestors are not properly situated, the ancestors cannot receive and distribute beneficial influences from higher powers (De Groot 1912, pp. 285–286). *Feng shui* means "wind and water." Valentine Rodolphe Burkhardt (1954, p. 130) said in *Chinese Creeds and Customs,* "The forms of hills, direction of watercourses, forms and heights of buildings, direction of roads and bridges, are all supposed to modify the *Ch'i,* or spiritual breath of the universe, and *Feng Shui* is the art of adapting the residences of the living and the dead to conform, as far as possible, with the local currents."

Altogether, the traditional Chinese cosmology appears to match our template Vedic cosmology quite well. Both have a high god, Vishnu or Krishna in the Vedic cosmology and Shang-ti in the Chinese cosmology. Both have a creator god, P'an Ku in the Chinese cosmology and Brahma in the Vedic cosmology. Both systems have a multilevel cosmos inhabited by various levels of demigods and demigoddesses. In both systems, humans have material bodies and nonmaterial souls.

Cosmology of the Ainu of Japan

The religion of the mysterious Ainu people of Japan is animistic. John Batchelor (1927, p. 345) noted in *Ainu Life and Lore*: "The Ainu certainly believe that whatever has life moves, and that whatever moves has life.... The welling up of the bubbling water spring, the rippling rivulet, the gliding stream, the rushing torrent, the tearing rapids, the whistling winds, the flying clouds, the pouring rain and falling snows, the mist and fog, fine weather and foul, the quiet lake and the restless oceans, thunder and lightning, the falling tree and the rolling of a stone down a mountain side; all such phenomena have, so they think, each a real life or soul, either good or bad, or both good and bad, abiding in it."

But such animism does not exhaust the cosmology of the Ainu. They have quite a developed picture of the universe, following the basic pattern of our template Vedic spiritual cosmology. For example, the Ainu have in their cosmology a creator god in addition to a supreme God. This subordinate progenitor god was called Aeoina. He descended from heaven and created the first human being on earth. He stayed on earth for some time, teaching humans how to live. During his time on earth, Aeoina dressed just as humans did. Upon finishing his task, he returned to heaven, still wearing terrestrial human clothes. The gods in heaven did not very much like the smell of these clothes, and they sent Aeoina back to earth to get rid of them. When he returned once more to heaven, he did so without any unpleasant human smell. Because of this incident Aeoina was sometimes called Ainu-rak-guur, which means "Person Smelling of Men" (Batchelor 1927, p. 115).

In each Ainu home is installed a fetish representing the household deity, generally pictured as an old man. The original fetish came not from the creator god Aeoina, but from the divine being said to be the True God. The Ainu Chief Penri told John Batchelor, "The deity who rules the household was first made by the True God, Who, after He had made him, sent him down from heaven to be the husband of the Goddess of Fire and to help her to attend to the wants of the Ainu. He is therefore called The Ancestral Governor of the House" (Batchelor 1927, p. 177). The Ainu distinction between the progenitor god and the true supreme being is parallel to the distinction between the creator god Brahma and the supreme being of the Vaishnava Vedic cosmology (variously named Vishnu, Narayan, Krishna, etc.).

The Ainu believe that the spirits of the dead live on in an afterlife. The household hearth is the gateway to the spirits of the dead. When the spirits of ancestors are invoked, they come through the hearth. The hearth is also the residence of the fire goddess, Kamui Fuchi. The household fire is carefully attended. Burning coals are covered with ashes during the night, during which time Kamui Fuchi is said to be sleeping. It is considered most inauspicious for a household woman to allow the fire to go completely out during the night. Neil Gordon Munro, in his book *Ainu Creed and Cult,* wrote (1963, p. 58): "There was no worse sin than neglect to provide fuel for Kamui Fuchi, who reared all Ainu at her hearth." Munro also noted (1963, p. 58), "All food . . . , at any ceremony, is supposed to be Kamui Fuchi's, and is placed on or near the hearth before distribution to guests."

In the cosmic hierarchy of the Ainu, the bottom region is called Chirama-moshiri, or "the Lowest World." This was not the place of judgement where souls went after death. They called that place Pokna-moshiri, "the Underworld." And the place of punishment for the wicked was called Nitne-kamui-moshiri, "the world of devils" or Teinci-pokma-moshiri, "the wet underground world." Chirama-moshiri, according to John Batchelor in his book *Ainu Life and Lore* (1927, p. 367), was not inhabited and represented "the bounds of material creation."

Elaborating on the Ainu view of Chirama-moshiri, Batchelor (1927, p. 368) explained: "As regards place, it is thought by them to be situated at the very confines of all created worlds. There are supposed by some to be six worlds beneath this upon which we dwell. The very lowest of these is called 'the lowest world' (*Chirama-moshiri*). . . . But as regards the nature of this land, it is not supposed by the Ainu to be a place of darkness, though it may have iron gates. It is said to be a very beautiful country, as full of light as this world; and it does not seem to be the prison house or abode of fallen angels or any other living beings, whether they be gods, men, or demons. The thunder demon, after having waged war upon this earth, is said to have proceeded to do so in heaven, because this world was unable to stand such a grievous conflict. The Creator, Who resides in heaven above, was much distressed at this, and sent the demon to fight in the 'lowest world.' Here the thunder demon was slain, but as no god or demon can actually die, his spirit again ascended to its original home, namely, the clouds of the lower skies."

The concept of there being six worlds below the terrestrial world is similar to the Vedic cosmology, which places the earth of our experience as the seventh of fourteen worlds, with six worlds beneath it and seven above it. The similarity of concepts might have resulted from diffusion of religious ideas throughout Asia, or from common perception of an existing spiritual reality, or from a common revelation by a supernatural being. That the accounts might differ in various respects and degrees does not rule out common perception or revelation. Once it is accepted that there is a supreme being, it becomes possible for the supreme being to reveal aspects of cosmology to greater or lesser degrees to various peoples, according to their particular structures of consciousness and sensory capabilities. Even if we wish to accept a purely local naturalistic explanation for the similarity of accounts, i.e., that the manufacture of such accounts is somehow favored by the process of evolution by natural selection, we must still take the accounts seriously and cannot dismiss the idea that they might reflect some underlying feature of reality. At the very least, we must wonder why the human physiology is so constructed as to produce mental cosmological pictures that so heavily govern human behavior. If we favor a simple diffusionist concept, we must still ask why the human mind, at all times and places, has the disposition to accept and incorporate into its deepest cultural concepts strikingly similar elements of our template cosmology. The most natural explanation for the similarity of accounts remains common perception or common revelation.

According to Ainu tradition, one of the worlds beneath the terrestrial world of our experience is a place where the wicked are sent after death. Another subterrestrial world is called Kamui-moshiri, the Land of the Gods. It is a place where good souls are sent. It is said that the inhabitants of this region walk with their feet pointed up toward the bottom of the terrestrial plane of existence and that the day of this heavenly region corresponds to the night of the terrestrial region (Batchelor 1927, p. 368). Batchelor concludes (1927, p. 368), "This myth shows very clearly that the Ainu believe the soul to exist apart from the present material body after death." Batchelor (1927, p. 346) also said about his conversations with the Ainu Chief Penri: "The old chief and I had much conversation on these matters soon after, and I learned many things from him. Particularly did I learn that in their idea, death in no way implied the extinction of the life or soul. He said they did not like the body to become a senseless corpse, but we must not imagine that because it became such, the soul also decomposed or got withered up."

From what we have seen above, the Ainu cosmology included heavens above and heavens below the earth. An Ainu chief told John Batchelor (1927, pp. 142–143) that the earth of our experience is, by arrangement of the supreme god, under the control of the fire goddess, who serves as his deputy. He sent her down from her home in heaven to rule the earth. A heavenly serpent, in love with her, desired to come with her. The goddess tried to dissuade him, telling him that if he came with her, he would have to endure fire. But the serpent still desired to make the journey, and the fire goddess gave him permission. He came down with her in a flash of lightning, which made a large hole in the ground. To this day, the descendants of the heavenly serpent sometimes come to earth to visit him, and they make their journeys, as he did, by lightning bolts, which also make holes in the ground. It is believed that these holes lead to underworlds in the subterrestrial regions of the cosmos, and it is there that the original serpent from heaven lives along with his serpent followers. The Ainu chief told Batchelor (1927, p. 143), "Snakes live in large communities in the underworld, and there they assume the bodily forms of men and women. They have houses and gardens just as we have, and their food consists largely of dew." They take the form of snakes when they come to our world. The Ainu chief said, "As his origin is divine, the snake is of a very haughty disposition. . . . From the very beginning the snake was desirous of doing evil; nevertheless, if fetishes are made of walnut wood and presented to him with the words 'Thou art a good God' he will be much pleased and render help. Again, if snakes are treated in a slighting manner they cause sickness. Yet, if they cause illness it may be cured by making fetishes of the walnut tree and offering these to them with worship."

Divine serpents living in subterranean realms, and taking the form of humans, are also a feature of the template Vedic cosmology. The Naga (serpent) race is said to live in a subterranean heavenly realm that is in some senses more opulent than the celestial heavens. In traditional Indian art, the Nagas are sometimes depicted in human or half-human forms.

Traditional Cosmology of Korea

Traditional Korean folk religion, like that of China, is a mixture of Confucianist, Buddhist, Taoist, and animist elements. It has a cosmic hierarchy that conforms to the pattern of our template cosmology.

According to Koreans, a person has three souls. One remains with the dead body in the grave. A second goes into the ancestor worship tablet kept in the home of the relatives. And a third goes into the afterworld (Clark 1932, p. 113).

The traditional Korean cosmic hierarchy includes gods of the heavens and earth, gods of mountains and hills, dragon gods, and gods who served as guardians of local districts. Some of these high ranking gods are the gods of the Buddhist pantheon. Below these are various household gods, including spirits of the kitchen and of possessions and furniture.

Some spirits take the form of animals, and others possess young girls and turn them into exorcists. Other spirits threaten humans in various ways. These threatening spirits include spirits that cause tigers to attack humans, spirits that cause people to die while traveling on roads, spirits that cause women to die in labor, and so on (Bishop 1898, p. 421). Almost any imaginable calamity is caused by some specific kind of evil spirit.

About this multitude of spirits, traveler Isabella Lucy Bishop wrote (1898, p. 404): "They fill the chimney, the shed, the living room, the kitchen —they are on every shelf and jar. In thousands they waylay the traveller as he leaves his home, beside him, behind him, dancing in front of him, whirring over his head, crying out upon him from earth, air, and water. They are numbered by thousands of billions."

Followers of traditional Korean religion are especially concerned with ghosts of departed humans, who are thought to be especially dangerous during the fall and winter. To appease the ghosts, the traditional Koreans offer them food in sacrifice. Younghill Kang (1931, p. 107), recalling his life in Korea, wrote: "All those who haunted around the tree-top from which they had fallen, those who had drowned and left their soul in the water, all who had died of hunger or of violence, was it not a pitying kindness toward them, to feed them now,—now especially, when hearts were anxious and the outlook dark?" Of all ghosts, the ghosts of persons who had drowned were considered most dangerous. Charles Allen Clark (1932, p. 203) wrote in *Religions of Old Korea,* "They are said to be in torment confined to the water until they can pull some other poor unfortunate in to take their places. Then they can come out on land. They wail around the side of the water and try to entice people near. The boatmen are terribly afraid of them."

Counteracting evil spirits is the business of the *mudangs* or exorcists. *Mudangs* are women and come from the lowest social class. J. Robert Moose (1911, pp. 191–192) says of the *mudang:* "She claims to be in direct league with the evil spirits which infest the world, and can appease them and persuade them to leave those in whom they have taken up their abode for the purpose of afflicting them in body or mind. The religious feeling of the people is so strong that even the highest and best educated classes do not hesitate to call for the *mudang* when they are in trouble."

Another kind of exorcist is the *pansu.* The *pansu* is male and, although he can come from any social level, his work is considered to be of a low kind, like that of the *mudang.* Moose (1911, p. 192) notes: "The *pansu* is always blind, and is supposed to be able to control the spirits not by persuasion but by power. They tell fortunes, and claim to be able to drive out evil spirits from sick people. The spirits are often soundly thrashed by these men, the evidence of which may be seen in the sticks with which they have been beaten. I have often seen bundles of these sticks, about as large as a broom handle and about two feet long, beaten into splinters at one end, caused by the severe thrashing which the poor, unfortunate spirit had received at the hands of the *pansu*. Sometimes an unruly spirit is driven into a bottle and corked up with a stopper made from the wood of a peach tree, and then delivered to a *mudang* to be carried away and buried."

In addition to a whole array of gods and spirits, the traditional Korean cosmology also appears to have a supreme being, Hananim. Homer B. Hulbert wrote (1906, p. 404): "This word *Hananim* is compounded of the words 'heaven' (sky) and 'master,' and is the pure Korean counterpart of the Chinese word 'Lord of Heaven.' The Koreans all consider this being to be the Supreme Ruler of the universe. He is entirely separated from and outside the circle of the various spirits and demons that infest all nature." Protestant missionaries used the word *Hananim* as a synonym for the Christian God. Catholics tended to use *Chun-ju* (or *Chunchon*), a Chinese word that means the same thing (Hulbert 1906, pp. 404–405).

Local legends say that Chunchon once looked into a small box, and found many letters inside, some of which spelled out the following message, "The '*ok*' (precious) Heaven controls all of the other thirty-six heavens, their inner apartments, and middle courts, the east and west lighted places, the depths and heights, the four departments and six places; also the '*yoosa*' officials and their departments. All of this is in order to control the five thunders and the three kingdoms. *Chunchon*, being infinitely great, personally surveys all of these matters. He does not even need to employ all of these agencies" (Clark 1932, p. 277).

J. Robert Moose, in his book *Village Life in Korea* (1911, p. 191), said about Hananim (Chunchon): "Strange to say, this the greatest of all the spirits, receives the least attention in the worship of the people. This is probably from the fact that he is considered good and the religion of Korea is one of fear and not of love. It is not worth while to bother the good spirits, since they will do no harm; but the bad ones must be placated. In times of severe drought, by special command of the king, sheep are sacrificed to *Hananim*. There are no temples or shrines dedicated to *Hananim* except the altars on which the above-stated sacrifices are offered. So it can hardly be said that the village religion has much to do with the great spirit *Hananim*."

William Elliot Griffis (1882, p. 301) distinguished several kinds of dragons in the Korean cosmology. The first kind, the celestial dragons, watched over the palaces of the gods in heaven. A second kind, from a position below heaven but above the terrestrial level, controlled natural forces, such as wind and water. And a third kind, the terrestrial dragons, determined the courses of rivers and streams. And a fourth kind ruled over mines and hidden treasures. These categories of dragons reflect a division of the cosmos into a spiritual realm, a realm of higher beings in charge of natural forces, an earthly realm, and a subterranean realm. About this last kind of dragon, Griffis (1882, p. 301) noted, "Intense belief in the dragon is one of the chief reasons why the mines in Cho-sen [Korea] are so little worked, and the metals disturbed. The dragon pursuing the invaders of their sanctuary or fighting each other to gain possession of the jewel balls or sacred crystals is a favorite subject in all art of Chinese parentage."

Tlingit Indian Cosmology

The Tlingit Indians, once spread widely on the northwestern coast of North America, now mainly live in southeastern Alaska. According to the Tlingit, all living things, including humans and animals, have souls. The souls are designated the "inhabitants" (*qwani*) of certain kinds of bodies. Bears are called *xuts,* and the souls of bears are called *xuts qwani.* Anthropologist Frederica de Laguna, in an article called "Tlingit ideas about the individual" (1954, p. 179), says, "The physical body of an animal at times seems to be a covering for the soul or spirit, with which, however, the latter remains closely associated after death, as long as the flesh is 'fresh," or even longer." Even the souls of animals are said to have human forms. The animals display these souls to each other in the wild, away from humans. Sometimes, however, animals also appear to humans in humanlike form, but de Laguna says it is not clear, from the myths, if the animal body transforms into a human body or the humanlike animal soul emerges from the animal body. The souls of the animals respond to human actions, punishing humans for wantonly harming animals and rewarding them for acts of kindness. De Laguna (1954, p. 179) says, "No sharp distinction separates animal from human souls, though the former would appear to be the more powerful."

Plants as well as animals have spirits. If the Tlingit cut a tree for building a house or boat, they have to offer respect to its spirit. Even things we normally regard as lifeless have spirits. Emmons (1991, p. 288) says, "Natural phenomena and inanimate objects all possessed something which made itself felt or became visible under certain conditions. The wind, whirlpool, thunder and lightning, or a glacier, were controlled by spirits."

Emmons (1991, p. 288) provides a more extensive account of how the Tlingit view the soul and its relationship to the human body: "As explained by an old native of the Hootz-ah-ta tribe, the Tlingit recognize three entities in man: (a) the material body; (b) the spirit, a vital central force through which the body functions during life and which, leaving the body, causes death; and (c) the soul, a spiritual element that has no mechanical connection with the body, and is eternal, dwelling in spirit land or returning from time to time to live in different bodies." The Tlingit also recognize a person's mind, thoughts, and feelings as a kind of inner self (Emmons 1991, p. 289). Altogether, this is strikingly similar to the distinctions made between body, mind, vital force, and soul in our template Vedic cosmology.

The Tlingit also recognize a "a personal guardian spirit, Ka kin-ah yage or Ka-hen-a yake, 'up above spirit'" (Emmons 1991, p. 368). This guardian spirit guides and protects a person. Sometimes the Tlingit will pray, "Watch over me carefully, my Spirit Above." The Spirit Above resembles the Supersoul of the Vedic cosmology. The Supersoul, or Paramatma, accompanies each soul in the material world, overseeing its activities and guiding it according to its own desires.

According to an individual's mode of death, there are different kinds of afterlives. There is a heaven for people who die of old age or disease. There is another such heaven for those who die from violence. Those who go to these heavens become the northern lights. They are then called "the people above." De Laguna (1954, p. 191) says of departed persons, "They may appear after their funeral to greet their friends, on other occasions they prophesy war or that a relative will die by violence." People who drown or become lost in the forest remain on this earth. They wander around as land-otter people. The Tlingit believe in reincarnation, although de Laguna noted (1954, p. 191) that in addition to the reincarnated self "there apparently remains a ghostly counterpart to be fed at potlatches, a dangerous presence still associated with the remains of the corpse, or something that may still be embodied in the form of the land-otter or in the northern lights."

The reincarnated self is the soul. Emmons (1991, p. 368) says: "After death, the 'soul' or 'shadow' (now a 'ghost') travels to a land of the dead, the place depending on the manner of death, and it may later be reincarnated in a living person." The Tlingit believe the soul in a human body can only return to another human body, usually in the same family or clan (Emmons 1991, p. 288). The return of a human soul to a human family group is recognized by announcing dreams and birthmarks. Citing a Tlingit informant, Emmons (1991, p. 288) says: "A . . . woman during pregnancy had dreams of her [maternal aunt], a woman of high caste who had many perforations in the rims of her ears—a sign of her social standing. The child, when born, had a number of scars and holes about the edges of the ears, which at once indicated that the spirit of the aunt had returned and entered the child." Another informant told of how a famous warrior returned in the body of his grandson. This warrior had suffered a fatal gunshot wound, the bullet entering the left breast and exiting through the back. The man's grandson had two large birthmarks in the same places as the entry and exit wounds (Emmons 1991, p. 288).

Kan (1989, p. 110), making use of a report initially recorded by de Laguna (1972, pp. 767–769), tells of a Tlingit man named Askadut who recalled a rebirth experience. In his past life, he had died. He recalled seeing his body during a wake held by his relatives in his house. He tried to reenter his body but could not do it. The body was then cremated, and he journeyed to the land of the dead. After some time, he left there. He followed a river until he found a suitable tree on its bank. He sat beneath this tree, leaning against its trunk for nine days, after which the bank caved in and he fell into the water. Kan (1989, p. 110) says, "The next thing he saw was his own sister holding him as her newborn infant."

The principal deity of the Tlingits is Yehl, the creator of the world. Frances Knapp and Rheta Louise Childe (1896, p. 153), commenting on the attitude of the Tlingit to their chief deity, stated: "He was their popular hero, and represented their ideal of wisdom and cunning. It mattered not that he was lazy and a glutton, or that he gained all his victories by fraud and knavery. Nor did it in the least conflict with their sense of the proprieties, that he should be a notorious thief and liar. They delighted in his cool impudence, his mad-cap pranks, the practical jokes he was continually playing on other spirits, and the miraculous means he employed to escape from the snares of his enemies."

Kanukh, the war god, was born before Yehl, and thus his descendants, the warriors of the Wolf family, consider him to be superior to Yehl. The god Chetl usually remains invisible, but reveals his birdlike form in storms. At such times, his eyes flash with lightning and his wings send forth sounds of thundering. His sister Ahgishanakhou rests beneath volcanos, supporting the earth on her shoulders, while waiting for her brother to finally come and relieve her of this duty. In addition to these main gods, the Tlingit also believed in three kinds of lesser gods called Yekh: gods of the air (Khikyekh), gods of land (Tahkiyekh), and gods of the sea (Tekhiyekh). Disguised as birds or beasts, they would come near human settlements (Knapp and Childe 1896, pp. 153–154).

The Tlingit religion is shamanistic. The shaman is called *ichta,* and his function is to communicate with spirits and influence them on behalf of the Tlingit people. Ethnologist Aurel Krause says (1956, p. 194), "For each spirit the shaman has a special mask, which he uses when he appeals to that spirit. The conjuring of a spirit consists of a wild dance around the fire during which violent contortions of the body take place. The shaman cures the sick by driving out evil spirits, brings on good weather, brings about large fish runs and performs other similar acts."

Ethnologist John Reed Swanton reported (1905, p. 465): "All kinds of tales are related of the power of these shamans. Thus it is said that some United States marines were going to cut the hair of a Sitka shaman, when his spirit came into him so powerfully that the arms of the big marine who was about to ply the shears were paralyzed and those of the other marines dropped to their sides." According to Swanton (1905, p. 466), the power of a shaman would usually pass to one of his nephews after his death. The shaman's chief spirit would tell the shaman shortly before his death where his body should be taken and what his clan should do. After this happened, the clan would gather in a house, and the successor shaman would invite a spirit to come in. When the spirit came in, there would be singing during which the new shaman would fall into a trance. And when he was awakened by the clan, the clan had a new shaman.

During sickness, a person's "spirit" (not the soul, but the vital force that causes the body to function) may leave the body, causing a dangerous situation. During such times, a shaman can summon a spirit helper to catch the spirit and bring it back to the body, thus restoring health, or ending the threat of death (Emmons 1991, p. 288).

Ojibwa Cosmology

The Ojibwa Indians, also known as the Chippewas, live on the northern shores of Lake Huron and Lake Superior in Canada. According to the Ojibwa, a human being is composed of a material body (*wijo*), a shadow (*udjibbom*), and a soul (*udjitchog*). After death the material body decays and disappears (Jenness 1935, p. 18).

The shadow is associated with the brain, but it also operates outside the body. It assists the soul in perception and knowledge. The shadow appears to correspond to the mind element or subtle material body of our model Vedic cosmology. The Ojibwa believe a man's shadow goes before him when he walks. Sometimes the shadow, moving ahead of a hunter, will cause his eyes to twitch, signalling that it has seen game (Jenness 1935, p. 19). Animals also have their shadows, which act in a similar fashion to protect them. But sometimes the animal shadow will fail to perceive an approaching human as a threat, and the human will kill the animal. On the other hand, the shadow of an animal, such as a deer, may become aware of a hunter and correctly perceive its intention. The deer's shadow then constantly watches the hunter, and therefore the hunter will never be able to approach the deer closely enough to kill it (Jenness 1935, p. 22).

If someone feels he is being watched, even though no one is visible, this is the shadow giving a warning to the soul. The shadow might also give a young Ojibwa a sensation that he will soon be visited by a *manitou,* or supernatural being, allowing him to make the proper preparations (Jenness 1935, p. 19). The shadow of a baby is especially sensitive and active. It moves beyond the body to observe and learn many things over wide distances, although the body remains stationary and quiet. Sometimes the baby smiles or laughs inexplicably. In such cases, the baby's shadow has apprehended something that gladdens its soul. Ojibwa parents are very protective of the baby's shadow. Rocking the baby's hammock carelessly may cause a disturbance to the shadow. The Ojibwa also believe that if the baby's father tortures an animal, the shadows of the baby and the father will suffer (Jenness 1935, p. 20)

At times, the shadow, which is normally not seen, becomes visible, taking the same form as the body (Jenness 1935, p. 20). This accounts for people seeing apparitions of someone who is in fact at a distance of many miles. The Ojibwa believe that a person's health requires a balance between body, shadow, and soul. Persons intent on harming others may employ witchcraft to disturb this balance. Sometimes the shadow may split in two, with one part pulling one way and the other part pulling in another. When this happens, the soul remains detached, waiting for a decision, while the body, under stress, falls victim to disease. If the conflict is not eventually resolved, the person dies and the shadow haunts the grave as a ghost (Jenness 1935, p. 20). Jenness says (1935, p. 19), "The shadow is slightly more indefinite than the soul, and the Indians themselves often confuse them, attributing certain activities of phenomena now to one, now to the other."

About the Ojibwa concept of the soul, Jenness (1935, p. 18) says: "The soul is located in the heart, and is capable of travelling outside the body for brief periods, although if it remains separate too long the body will die. . . . For the soul is the intelligent part of man's being, the agency that enables him to perceive things, to reason about them, and remember them. . . . Besides being the intelligent part of man the soul is the seat of the will."

A skilled medicine man can take a sleeping person's soul out of the body. Sometimes the intention may be innocent—to converse with the soul in the medicine man's tent before an audience of spirit beings and then let it go back to the sleeping body. But the intention may also be to kill the body by keeping the soul too long away from it. An Ojibwa said, "I had a lucky escape once. I was only sixteen years old. A conjurer drew my soul into his conjuring lodge and I knew at once that he wanted to kill me, because I had made fun of his son who was a 'humpy' [hunchback]. I said, 'I'm going out.' But the old man said, 'No! You can't go.' Then I saw my own head rolling about and the people in the lodge were trying to catch it [The "people" were the guardian spirits, *pawáganak,* of the conjurer—superhuman entities]. I thought to myself that if only I could catch my head everything would be all right. So I tried to grab it when it rolled near me and finally I caught it. As soon as I got hold of it I could see my way out and I left. Then I woke up but I could not move my legs or arms. Only my fingers I could move. But finally I managed to speak. I called out to my mother. I told her I was sick. I was sick for a couple of days. No one saw my soul go to and fro but I knew where I had been" (Hallowell 1955, p. 175, his insertions).

After death, the soul journeys to the west, to the land of souls. The land of souls is ruled by Nanibush, a great Ojibwa culture hero (Jenness 1935, p. 18). The soul is driven on its journey to the land of the dead by a supernatural being called the Shadow Manitou. The Shadow Manitou normally sleeps, but when an Ojibwa becomes very ill the person's wandering soul disturbs the Shadow Manitou. The Shadow Manitou walks around the wigwam of the Ojibwa but leaves no tracks. It tries to drive the soul to the land of the dead. If it does so, the body dies (Jenness 1935, p. 42). A good medicine man, if he acts quickly after death, can sometimes bring a soul back from the Land of the Dead. An Ojibwa Indian said, "Once I saw Owl do this. Tcètcebú was very ill. By the time Owl arrived where her father was encamped, she died. Owl tied a piece of red yarn around the girl's wrist at once [to enable him to identify her quickly in a crowd] and lay down beside her body. He lay in this position a long, long time. He was still; he did not move at all. Then I saw him move ever so little. The girl began to move a little also. Owl moved more. So did the girl. Owl raised himself up into a sitting posture. At the same moment the girl did the same. He had followed her to the Land of the Dead and caught her soul just in time" (Hallowell 1955, pp. 174–175).

Some authors, such as Vecsey (1983), have interpreted the distinction between shadow and soul given above as a dual soul concept. According to Vecsey (1983, p. 59), the first researcher to record this was Schoolcraft (1848, p. 127). An Ojibwa informant told Schoolcraft that one soul left the body during dreams, while another soul remained within the body to keep it alive. Following Hultkrantz (1953), Vecsey

(1983, pp. 59–63) says this about the two souls: "Located in the heart of each person, but with an ability to move about both within and without the body, the ego-soul provided intelligence, reasoning, memory, consciousness and the ability to act. It could leave the body for short periods of time, but lengthy separations resulted in sickness and permanent separation meant the body's death. This soul, the seat of the will, experienced emotions. Each person possessed one, receiving animation from it. The traveling soul, sometimes called a free-soul, resided in the brain and had a separate existence from the body, being able to journey during sleep at will. . . . It [also] perceived, sensed, acted as the 'eyes' of the ego-soul, seeing things at a distance." The free-soul corresponds to the shadow mentioned by other authors, and the ego-soul corresponds to the soul proper. In terms of Vedic concepts, the free-soul can be identified with the subtle material body (mind), and the ego-soul can be identified with the *atma* (conscious self).

According to the Ojibwa, not only humans but also animals, plants, and even water and stones possess bodies, shadows, and souls. They all have life, although varying in form and powers (Jenness 1935, p. 20). Nanibush, the great hero, would speak with the trees in their language, expressed in the sound of leaves moving in the wind. Jenness (1935, p. 20) said one of his Ojibwa informants told him, "Once when a man was walking along a flower cried to him 'Do not step on me,' for flowers are like little children."

The souls of witches can take on the forms of dogs or owls, and souls of animals can take on human forms (Jenness 1935, p. 27). Vecsey (1983, p. 60) says: "As souls traveled they could take other appearances, depending on their power. They could appear as plants, animals, and other forms; therefore, metamorphosis was an aspect of Ojibwa metaphysics." Sometimes humans were cursed to take on the forms of animals. In one case, the transformation of human forms into animal forms was arrested, resulting in an unusual type of creature. The Ojibwa Jonas King explained (Jenness 1935, p. 43): "Long ago the Indians discovered a sturgeon in a spring. Their elders warned them not to touch it, but some one imprudently cooked it and a number of people joined in the feast. When the hunters returned to the camp that evening they found all their relatives who had eaten of the sturgeon being rapidly transformed into fish. Some had changed completely, others remained half-human still; but all alike were struggling towards the water, or weeping near the shore with the water lapping their shoulders, while their unchanged kinsfolk strove in vain to draw them back. The medicine-men called on their *manidos* [manitous] for help, but the utmost they could accomplish was to check any further transformation." These half human, half fish creatures are called mermaids and mermen (*dibanabe*).

An Ojibwa named Jim Nanibush told Jenness (1935, p. 21): "The tree does not die; it grows up again where it falls. When an animal is killed its soul goes into the ground with its blood; but later it comes back and is reincarnated where its blood entered the ground. Everything, tree, birds, animals, fish (and in earlier times human beings also) return to life; while they are dead their souls are merely awaiting reincarnation. My uncle lived four or five lives, 500 years in all. But there are two very hard stones, one white and one black, that never die; they are called *meshkosh.*" Another Ojibwa, Pegahmagabow, said, "Sometimes a tree will fall when there is not a breath of wind. Its soul dies, just as the soul of a man dies and goes to the land of the west. But whither the tree's soul goes no one knows" (Jenness 1935, p. 21).

The animals have their own societies, organized much like human societies, complete with leaders, called bosses. The Ojibwa James Walker said, "Before the white man reached Georgian Bay a certain Indian gathered many beaver, otter, and other skins, which he kept in his wigwam in the woods. One still night he heard the crashing of a tree, and then a wailing of many voices 'Our King has gone!' When morning came he found that a giant white oak had fallen, being rotten at the base; the white oaks around it had bewailed its fall. He gathered up all his furs, laid them over the trunk as in burial, and returned to his wigwam. Night came, and as he slept he dreamed that a *manido* visited him and said, 'You have done well. Now take your furs again and travel east. There you will find a man who will give you clothing of a new kind in exchange for them.' The Indian travelled east and discovered French traders on the St. Lawrence River. He was the first Ojibwa to see or trade with white men" (Jenness 1935, p. 23).

As in our template Vedic cosmology, the Ojibwa cosmology has a multilevel universe. Jenness (1935, p. 28) says, "Even today some Indians believe there are six layers of worlds in the sky above and correspondingly six beneath; others assert that there are only two, one upper and one lower." Souls of animals go to Bitokomegog, a level below the earth of our experience. The number of animals on earth is tied to the number of animal souls that come up from the lower level. If there are many, the number of animals increases. If there are few, the number of animals decreases. The number of souls that come to earth is determined by the bosses of the animal species (Jenness 1935, p. 23).

Theresa S. Smith, in her study of Ojibwa cosmology (1995, p.44), echoes the theme of this chapter: "The notion of a multileveled world is not exclusive to the Ojibwe. Every shamanic society, from Siberia to Oceania, has shared this intuition of a many-storied universe. Like players in an intricate game of ladders and chutes, shamans travel routes mapped by myth and vision to power realms both above and below the sensible world. And returning from their travels they add their testimony to a continually growing corpus of descriptions regarding the structure and character of multileveled reality. Among the archaic traditions of the world—the Mesopotamian, Indian, Greek, and Japanese for instance—a hierarchy of worlds was the norm. Even contemporary non-shamanic world religions retain earlier cosmographies as symbolic expressions of sacrality both in and beyond this earth. . . . This means that contemporary people—including the Ojibwe—informed by a scientific understanding of cosmology, still find the hierarchical universe to be a resonant image."

The researchers and informants cited by Smith (1995, pp. 44–46) speak of a cosmos divided into three regions: upper, middle and lower. The upper region, inhabited by the Great Spirit Kitchie Manitou, the Thunderbirds, and various *manitous,* is divided into several levels. The lower region is also composed of several levels. Between the two is the earth of our experience, which is described as an island (Smith 1995, p. 47). Directly below the earth is the realm of underwater and underground creatures. Below this is the "mirror world," a place where night comes when it is day on earth. This place, described as "peaceful and abundant" (Smith 1995, p. 46), is the destination of souls of the dead. Below this is a place of constant darkness.

The gods and the spirits of the Ojibwa are of many kinds. One kind is similar to the fairies and brownies of Celtic mythology. They are called invisible people, and they are of two types—one with no name and the other called *bagudzinishinabe,* little wild people. Whoever sees either kind gets the blessing of a long life. The no-names hunt with foxes instead of dogs. "We see the tracks of the foxes, but not of their masters, except those they made on the rocks before the Indians came to this country," says Jenness (1935). "At that time the sun drew so close to the earth that it softened the rocks, and the feet of these invisible people left marks on them. When the sun withdrew the rocks hardened again and the footprints remained petrified on their surfaces." The little wild people are the size of children. Although mischievous they are not truly harmful. They are responsible for poltergeistlike effects, such as throwing pebbles onto the roofs of wigwams (Jenness 1935).

Above these are the *manitous.* They can be male or female, and display human attributes. Usually, they are invisible to humans of our kind, but they may become visible in any form they choose. The *manitous* possess different degrees of power (Jenness 1935, p. 29). "Highest in the scale of these supernatural beings," says Jenness (1935, p. 29), "is Kitchi-Manido, the Great Spirit, who is . . . the source of all the power inherent to a greater or less extent in everything that exists."

According to W. Vernon Kinietz (1947, pp. 152–153), the Great Spirit, Kitchi-Manitou (or Kijai Manitou), creates heaven, earth, and the lands from which the white people came. In these areas, he creates humans, animals and other things appropriate to each place. He rewards the virtuous and punishes the wicked. Kinietz (1947, p. 153) says, "Wiskendijac is next in power: he is said to be the Creator of all the Indian tribes, the country they inhabit and all it contains . . . The last of the deities is called Matchi Manitou, or the 'Bad Spirit.' He is the author of all evil, but subject to the control of Kijai Manitou."

Some modern researchers have tried to depersonalize the *manitou* concept, but even their accounts cannot avoid personality. Johnston (1995, p. 2), for example, says Kitchi-Manitou refers to "the Great Mystery of the supernatural order" and that it "cannot be known or described in human corporeal terms." Yet he goes on to say (1995, pp. 2–3), "According to the creation story, Kitchi-Manitou had a vision, seeing, hearing, touching, tasting, smelling, sensing, and knowing the universe, the world, the *manitous*, plants, animals, and human beings, and brought them into existence. The story represents a belief in God and in creation, an explanation of the origin of things; it also serves as an example for men and women to emulate. Following the example set by Kitchi-Manitou, every person is to seek a dream or vision within the expanse of his or her soul-spirit being and, having attained it, bring it into fulfillment and reality." Each person must therefore go on a quest to discover his or her own dream or vision, along with the talent or ability to fulfill it. Stressing the personalistic nature of Ojibwa cosmology, Smith (1995, p.48) says: "The . . . [Ojibwa] . . . experience of the world, whether awake or in a dream, is an experience of a world controlled by the actions of persons, human and otherwise. The levels and directions are not 'animated' or 'anthropomorphized' by humans who, in a purely cognitive exercise, posit souls and spirits and ascribe them to things in the world. Rather, the cosmos is experienced as a place literally crowded with 'people.'"

Besides the *manitous* mentioned above, there are other *manitous* who control various natural powers. For example, there is a chief *manitou*, who, assisted by various subordinate manitous, controls the winds and breezes (Jenness 1935, p. 34). Another group of *manitous* controls the thunder. After the Great Spirit, the thunder *manitou* are considered the strongest. The subordinate *manitous* have souls, like human beings and other living things (Vecesey 1983, p. 61).

Some Indians have supernatural powers obtained from the *manitous*. An Ojibwa named Pegahmagabow said: "Long ago the *manidos* or supernatural powers gathered somewhere and summoned a few Indians through dreams, giving them power to fly through the air to the meeting-place. The Indians (i.e., their souls) travelled thither, and the *manidos* taught them about the supernatural world and the powers they had received from the Great Spirit. Then they sent the Indians to their homes again" (Jenness 1935, p. 29). One type of especially empowered human is the *wabeno*, a kind of medicine man who specializes in curing diseases with plant medicines. According to the Ojibwa, the first *wabeno*, Bidabbans (Day-dawn), got his curing powers from the moon god (Jenness 1935, p. 62).

Human beings and *manitous* are sometimes threatened by supernatural water serpents, whose boss is called Nzagima. The Ojibwa Pegahmagabow said that Nzagima has seven heads (Jenness 1935, p. 39). Vedic histories describe how a many headed water serpent called Kaliya entered a sacred river, the Yamuna, and was driven away by the Personality of Godhead, Krishna, who danced on the serpent's heads (*Shrimad Bhagavatam* 10.16). The water serpents led by Nzagima can travel beneath the surface of the earth and sometimes take away the souls of humans. "So if lightning strikes a tree near an Indian's wigwam it is the thunder-*manido* driving away some water serpent that is stealing through the ground to attack the man or his family," says Jenness (1935, p. 35). According to the Ojibwa elder John Manatuwaba, the serpent *manitous* live under the earth and jointly control the lives of plants and trees (Jenness 1935, p. 40). This resembles the Vedic accounts of a race of serpents (*Nagas*) who live in subterranean heavenly planets (*Shrimad Bhagavatam* 1.11.11).

Another malevolent being is the *windigo*. A human who in the hard times of winter resorts to cannibalism to avoid starvation becomes a *windigo*. *Windigos* are gigantic in size and possess supernatural powers. In winter, the *windigos* roam about seeking victims to eat. They are indestructible by ordinary means. Sometimes an Ojibwa will cut off a *windigo's* head but it will grow back. A good medicine man using the right methods can, however, actually destroy a *windigo* (Jenness 1935, pp. 40–41). The wolf is considered to be the dog of the *windigo* (Jenness 1935, p. 25).

Other American Indian Cosmologies

The world of the Hopi is full of spirits, including a sun god, moon god, and star gods. Atmospheric gods control the rain, wind, lightning, thunder, and rainbows. In certain springs live serpent gods, who control the supply of water (Talayesva 1942, p. 17). But in the beginning, there was only Taoiwa, the creator, who existed in Tokpela, a realm of endless, timeless space. In order to bring about the finite creation, Taiowa manifested Sotuknang, unto whom he said, "I have created you, the first power and instrument as a person, to carry out my plan for life in endless space. I am your Uncle. You are my Nephew. Go now and lay out these universes in proper order so they may work harmoniously with one another according to my plan" (Sproul 1979, p. 271). Sotuknang manifested seven universes for habitation by the living entities he would generate. In addition to these seven worlds, he manifested his own realm, and, of course, Taiowa had his realm. Then from Sotuknang came Kokyangwuti, the Spider Woman, who from the earth created humans of different colors. Sotuknang then gave them the powers of speech and wisdom, along with the power to generate offspring. He said to the humans, "With all these I have given you this world to live on and to be happy. There is only one thing I ask of you. To respect the Creator at all times. Wisdom, harmony, and respect for the love of the Creator who made you. May it grow and never be forgotten among you as long as you live" (Sproul 1979, p. 272).

A highly visible and famous part of Hopi religion is the Kachina cult. *Kachi* means "life or spirit" and *na* means "father," so Kachina literally means "life father" or "spirit father" (Dockstader 1985, p. 9). The word *kachi* can also be taken to mean "sitter," and thus a Kachina can be taken to be a supernatural being who sits among the Hopi, listening to their petitions for material and spiritual blessings. Dockstader (1985, p. 9) says that the Kachinas "have the power to bring rain, exercise control over the weather, help in many of the everyday activities of the villages, punish offenders of ceremonial or social laws, and in general act as a link between gods and mortals." Their main function is to take messages from the Hopi to their gods. Today masked people take on the role of the Kachinas in ceremonies, and the Hopi accept that they to some extent have the same supernatural qualities as the original Kachinas. According to Dockstader (1985, p. 10), the Hopis held that "the Kachinas were beneficent spirit-beings who came with the Hopis from the Underworld, whence came all people." According to one view, they remained with the Hopis for some time, giving them many benedictions. Then, after the Hopis began to take them for granted, the Kachinas returned to the Underworld. Before leaving, they instructed some good young men how to dress themselves as Kachinas and perform the rites. "When the other Hopis realized their loss," says Dockstader (1985, p. 11), "they remorsefully turned to the human substitute-Kachinas, and the ceremonies have continued since that time."

In the cosmology of the Hopis, we find key elements of the template Vedic cosmology. In both there is a distinction between an ultimate high god and a creator god, or gods, responsible for manifesting the forms of humans and other creatures. In both, there is a multilevel universe.

The Lenape or Delaware Indians are Algonguins. They believed in many gods, *mani 'towuk*, but among the *mani 'towuk,* one was supreme. He was called Gicelemu 'kaong, which means "creator" or "great spirit." All of the other *mani 'towuk* were his servants. Through them Gicelemu 'kaong manifested the earth and all of its creatures. The Lenape directed most of their worship to the agents of the great spirit, considering them more closely involved in their daily life. The great spirit lived in a distant place, the twelfth and highest heaven above the earth (Eliade 1967, pp. 12–13).

Lenape chiefs would recite this prayer during ceremonies held in the tribal Big House: "Man has a spirit, and the body seems to be a coat for that spirit. That is why people should take care of their spirits, so as to reach Heaven and be admitted to the Creator's dwelling. We are given some length of time to live on earth, and then our spirits must go. When anyone's time comes to leave this earth, he should go to Gicelemu`kaong, feeling good on the way. We all ought to pray to Him to prepare ourselves for days to come so that we can be with Him after leaving the earth . . . When we reach that place, we shall not have to do anything or worry about anything, only live a happy life. We know there are many of our fathers who have left this earth and are now in this happy place in the Land of Spirits . . . Everything looks more beautiful there than here, everything looks new, and the waters and fruits and everything are lovely. No sun shines there, but a light much brighter than the sun, the Creator makes it brighter by his power. All people who die here, young or old, will be of the same age there; and those who are injured, crippled, or made blind will look as good as the rest of them. It is nothing but the flesh that is injured: the spirit is as good as ever" (Eliade 1967, p 160). The parallels with the Vedic cosmology are striking. In *Bhagavad Gita* (2.22), the body is described as a garment for the soul. The purpose of life is characterized as journeying to the realm of God. The *Bhagavad Gita* (15.6) specifically says that the realm of God is luminous, but without the light of the sun or moon.

The Lenape Big House is a model of the universe. "The centre post is the staff of the Great Spirit, with its foot upon the earth, its pinnacle reaching to the hand of the Supreme Deity. The floor of the Big House is the flatness of the earth. . . . The ground beneath the Big House is the realm of the underworld while above the roof lie the extended planes or levels, twelve in number, stretched upward to the abode of the Great Spirit, even the Creator" (Speck 1931, pp. 22–23). The Big House also included a White Path, corresponding to the Milky Way, the path by which the soul goes to the spiritual realm of the Great Spirit.

The supreme being of the Omaha Indians is called Wakonda. The process of humans coming into being expressed by the Omaha Indians is similar to the concept of human devolution expressed in this book. An Omaha Indian informant said, "At the beginning, all things were in the mind of Wakonda. All creatures, including man, were spirits. They moved about in space between the earth and the stars (the heavens). They were seeking a place where they could come into bodily existence." First they went to the sun and moon, but these were not fit places for them. Then they came to the earth, which at first was covered by water. When the water receded dry land was revealed. The Omaha informant said, "The host of spirits descended and became flesh and blood. They fed on the seeds of the grasses and the fruits of the trees, and the land vibrated with their expressions of joy and gratitude to Wakonda, the maker of all things" (Eliade 1967, pp. 84–85).

Cosmology of the Aranda People of Australia

The Aranda are one of the aboriginal peoples of Australia. They believe that in the beginning there were great personalities called Numbakulla. The meaning of this word is "always existing" and "out of nothing." The greatest of them, according to the members of the southern, central, and northern groups of aboriginals, is the Numbakulla who came out of nothing at Lamburkna, in the south. He created the land and water, and established the main features of the landscape, such as mountains, rivers, hills, and deserts. He also brought into being plants and animals. He also established totem places (*knanikilla*), which he would use in the future in populating the earth (Spencer and Gillen 1927, p. 356).

Below Numbakulla in the Aranda cosmology come gods and goddesses of nature. The sun goddess is called Alinga or Orthika. She is said to have come out of the ground at a place near Alice Springs, along with two woman associates. The eldest of the women carries a young child. The sun goddess leaves them each day and rises into the sky. At night the sun returns to the spot where it rose (Spencer and Gillen 1927, p. 496). The Water Men (Atoakwatje) supply water to earth from the clouds, wherein they dwell. The moon god, Atninja, is regarded as male and is therefore sometimes called Atua Oknurcha, big man. There is also an underworld.

Returning to his *tmara marakirna* (great camp) at Lamburkna,

Numbakulla carved a cavelike storehouse in the rock and surrounded it with gum tree boughs. He did this in preparation for the creation of the first ancestors of humans. The process begins with the making of *churingas,* objects imprinted with signs associated with totem groups. When Numbakulla later made the *churingas* he would put them in the rock cave (Spencer and Gillen 1927, p. 356). The time and place associated with Numbakulla, the original ancestor, and his various first creations is called *alchera.* The cave where the *churingas* were to be stored was called the *pertalchera,* the rock of the *alchera* (Spencer and Gillen 1927, p. 357).

Before the *churingas* could be made, Numbakulla had first to make the *ilpintiras,* the signs that would be imprinted on the *churingas.* On the floor of the *pertalchera,* Numbakulla painted a *churinga-ilpintira,* a sign for the *churinga* of a totem group, or *knanj.* This first *churinga-ilpintira* was for the *achilpa knanj,* or wild cat totem. He painted another *achilpa churinga-ilpintira* on the ground outside the *pertalchera.* In the center of it, he raised a pole called *kauwa-auwa.* Numbakulla then made the first *churinga* for the *achilpa* totem. He did this by marking a rock or other object with the *achilpa churinga-ilpintira,* the sign of the wildcat totem. He placed in this first *achilpa churinga* the *kuruna* (soul or spirit) of the first Achilpa man, and placed this *churinga* on the *churinga-ilpintira* in the Pertalchera cave. Out of the *churinga* came Inkata Achilpa Mara-knirra, the first Achilpa man, who was called *inkata* (leader) and *mara-knirra* (very great).

Numbakulla then manifested many more *kurunas,* souls, from within himself. Each *kuruna* was connected with an original *churinga,* one for each *knanj* (totem group): *achilpa* (wildcat), *erlia* (emu), *arura* (kangaroo), etc. Numbakulla gave these original *churingas* to Inkata Achilpa Maraknirra, and also taught him the ceremonies for each totem group. Inkata Achilpa Maraknira carried the original *churingas* to the totem places (*knani-killa*) previously designated by Numbakulla. In each original *churinga* there was the *kuruna* of an *inkatat oknirra,* a headman, as well as many additional *churingas* and *kurunas.* These original *churingas* are called *churinga indulla-irrakura.* After the headman for a totem group appeared from a *churinga* in a specific place, he would make use of the *churingas* and *kurunas* in the *churinga indulla-irrakura* to make more people. He would also use *churingas* and *kurunas* stored in his own body (Spencer and Gillen 1927, p. 361).

The origin of males and females is explained as follows. The original stone *churingas* of the totem groups were split in two, making pairs. These pairs were tied together. Spencer and Gillen (1927, p. 359) say, "One *Churinga* of each pair had an *atua* or man's spirit, the other an *arragutja* or woman's. Each *Churinga* had also an *Aritna churinga*, or sacred name, associated with it and its *Kuruna* and all these names were given, originally, by Numbakulla. Later on, the *Kurunas* emanated from the *Churinga* and gave rise to men and women, each of whom bore as his or her sacred name, the one given to the *Churinga* by Numbakulla." Neither Numbakulla nor the original Achilpa Inkata Maraknirra, or the first forefathers of the totem groups had mates, but all subsequent *kurunas* were manifested in male and female pairs (Spencer and Gillen 1927, pp. 361–362).

A child is born after a *kuruna* enters a woman. The *kuruna* will have existed previously in another body, and the old men of the totem group have ways of telling which *kuruna* has reincarnated into the group (Spencer and Gillen 1927, p. 103). About the birth process, W. E. H. Stanner says in his paper "The Dreaming" (1956), "The means by which, in aboriginal understanding, a man fathers a child, is not by sexual intercourse, but by the act of dreaming about a spirit-child. His own spirit, during a dream, 'finds' a child and directs it to his wife, who then conceives. Physical congress between a man and a woman is contingent, not a necessary prerequisite" (Lessa and Vogt 1958, p. 515).

The *churinga* from which the *kuruna* (soul) of the child came remains in the *pertalchera* of the child's original totem group. A double of the *kuruna*, called the *arumburinga*, remains with the *churinga* in the *pertalachera*. The *arumburinga* can travel outside the *pertalchera* and sometimes goes to visit its embodied *kuruna* double. The embodied *kuruna* is called *ulthana*. At death, the *ulthana kuruna* goes to the *churinga* in the *pertalchera* in which it was originally placed in the original time, *alchera* (Spencer and Gillen 1927, p. 103).

The relationships between soul, body, and *churinga* are complex, as is the language related to these relationships. The word *aradugga* (or *aradukka*) refers to the physical birth of a child from the womb. The word *knailjalugga* refers to the *kuruna* or soul coming out of the *churinga*. In the birth process, a *kuruna* leaves the *churinga* and enters the body of the woman who is to be its mother. In the body of the mother, the *kuruna* receives its own body, which is called *mberka* (Spencer and Gillen 1927, p. 358). The *kuruna* is said to be small, like a tiny pebble, and colored red. The body of the child within the womb is called *ratappa* (Spencer and Gillen 1927, p. 363).

At the end of a person's life, two spirit brothers called Inchinkina, who normally exist as stars in the heavens, come down to earth to hasten the person's death (Spencer and Gillen 1927, p. 429). Another evil spirit called Eruncha sometimes helps them. If the dead person tries to rise from the grave, Eruncha forces him back (Spencer and Gillen 1927, p. 430).

The embodied *kuruna* soul (called *ulthana*) remains with the body of the dead person for some time, watching over it in its burial mound until the final burial ceremony is performed. Sometimes the *ulthana* is with the body in the grave, sometimes it is observing the relatives of the deceased, and sometimes it is visiting with its spirit double, the *arumburinga*, which stays with the person's *churinga* in the *pertalchera* (Spencer and Gillen 1927, p. 432).

For the Australian aboriginal, existence between birth and death is just a transient phase. A. P. Elkin, in his book *The Australian Aborigines* (1964), says, "Found by his parent in a spiritual experience, he is incarnated through his mother and so enters profane life. But a few years later, through the gate of initiation, he partially re-enters the sacred dream-time or sky-world which he has left for a season. After passing farther and farther into it, so far as the necessities of profane life allow, he dies, and through another gate, the transition rite of burial, he returns completely to his sacred spirit state in the sky, the spirit-home . . . perhaps to repeat the cycle later" (Eliade 1967, p. 162).

Similar beliefs are found among the Ngaju Dayaks in nearby Borneo. Hans Schärer, in his book *Ngaju Religion: The Conception of God Among a South Borneo People* (1963), says, "Man originated from the godhead. The godhead has guided him through the various stages of life until his death, until he returns to the godhead and is given new life and a new existence in the Upperworld from which he once departed and from which there will be no more separation" (Eliade 1967, p. 170). Schärer adds: "This idea has nothing to do with any Christian influence; it is an ancient Dayak concept which is understandable in relation to the primeval sacred events and the mode of thought connected with them" (Eliade 1967, pp. 155–156).

Cosmology of the Easter Islanders

The Polynesians of Easter Island regarded the Great God, Etua, as superior to other gods and goddesses. The particular personal name of Etua was Makemake. He rewarded good and punished evil, and spoke to people through male and female priests. Thunder was the expression of his anger. The Easter Islanders did not have in their system an equivalent to the Christian devil. Makemake was seen as the creator of the heavens and earth. The Easter Islanders offered Makemake the first products of the land. He was honored in the form of wooden images, but was not directly worshiped (Métraux 1940, p. 312).

Métraux (1940, pp. 312–313) records an account of the appearance of Makemake from a skull: "There was a priestess watching over a skull on a rock in the bay of Tonga-riki ... One day a wave came and took the skull that was watched on the rock in front of the bay of Tonga-riki. The wave swept away the skull from above; it floated. The eyes of the priestess saw the skull. She leaped to take it, she swam behind the skull which floated ahead. She arrived in the middle of the sea, she was tired, she landed on the island of Matiro-hiva. Haua saw this woman who was a priestess. He asked: 'where do you come from?' 'I am pursuing my skull.' Haua said: 'It is not a skull, but the god Makemake.' The priestess stayed." Later, at the suggestion of Makemake, all three (Haua, Makemake, and the priestess) went back to the people of the priestess and taught them to utter the names of Haua before taking food.

Makemake did not have a female consort, but other gods did have consorts and children. By the will of Makemake, the first man and first woman sprang up from the earth like plants. They were known as Tive and Hiva. They and their offspring had souls that lived forever. These souls could travel outside the body during dreams, and could be victimized by evil spirits (Métraux 1940, p. 312, 315; Routledge 1919, p. 238).

The lesser gods of the Easter Islanders were known collectively as *akuaku*. They had residences at various places on the island, and existed in relationship to the local residents. The gods were of different kinds. Métraux (1940, pp. 316–317) says: "They were supernatural beings who belonged to a certain district or family. A few of them were real gods, others were demons or nature spirits, and others were spirits of deified dead. All lesser gods are now grouped under the general term *akuaku*, which is applied also to the spirits of the dead when they appear as ghosts. ... it is difficult to distinguish between minor gods who were worshipped and legendary characters who were endowed with superhuman power but who never functioned as actual gods. ... *Akuaku* were both male and female. They were often represented as human beings, who might have been mistaken for ordinary creatures had the story teller not classified them as *akuaku* or *tatane*. They married ordinary men or women, had children by them and died. They could even be killed if their adversary was strong enough or sly enough. At times their supernatural power manifested itself in the ability to fly through the air and change rapidly from one place to another. Some *akuaku* were embodied in animals, in natural or artificial things, or in phenomena. ... Spirits embodied in things or phenomena bear the names of their material representation. ... Thus, Te Emu is a 'Landslide'; Mata-vara-vara 'the Rain-with-heavy-drops'. Men are indebted to the minor gods or demons for many important discoveries and improvements in their culture. The art of tattooing was introduced by the sons of two *akuaku*—Vie Moko (The Lizard Woman) and Vie Kena (The Gannet Woman). The female *akuaku*, in the form of birds, taught men to extract dye from turmeric (*Curcuma longa*). The first bone fishhooks were made by Ure, a capricious and strange character of Easter Island folklore. An *akuaku* bird (the frigate) brought a new kind of yam as a gift to a man called Rapu."

Some of the *akuaku* were inimical to humans, functioning as demons. A legendary man named Raraku killed thirty of these demons long ago, but some survived and continued to trouble the people (Métraux 1940, p. 317). Occasionally, a demon would help a human. Métraux (1940, p. 317) says: "Paepae-a-Tari-vera (Stone-house-of-Tari-vera) saved a famous warrior (*matatoa*), whose soul (*kuhane*) was kidnapped by another spirit."

Easter Islanders worshiped the *akuaku* by offering them portions of food cooked in their houses. Sometimes the *akuaku* appeared to favored persons and spoke with them. In these communications, some times they revealed the future and other secret things. Métraux (1940, p. 317) says, "I was told by Viriamo's son that in her youth Viriamo had been seen at night speaking familiarly with the two spirits, Tare and Rapa-hango. The voices of these spirits were always high-pitched and recognizable."

The rain god was Hiro. In times of drought, the people would ask the king for help. The king would then send a priest (*ariki-paka*) to conduct a ceremony and make prayers to Hiro. The king of Easter Island was called *ariki man*. This divine chief traced his lineage to the gods Tangaroa and Rongo (Métraux 1940, p. 330). The king possessed supernatural power (*mana*). The concept of *mana* is found throughout Polynesia. In his publication *Polynesian Religion* (1927), E. S. Craighill Handy says: "*Mana* was thought to come into individuals or objects only through the medium of gods or spirits. . . . The primal *mana* was not merely power or energy, but procreative power, derived from an ultimate source and diffused, transmitted, and manifested throughout the universe. This was the original *mana* which was believed to be continuously passed down through the gods, the *mana atua*" (Lessa and Vogt 1965, p. 258). A Maori teacher explained to Handy that the *mana atua* were "godlike powers" that originally came "from Io, the Supreme God" (Lessa and Vogt 1965, p. 258).

Cosmology of the Black Carib People of Central America

The cosmology of the Black Carib people of Central American countries such as Belize (formerly British Honduras) is a mixture of

Christian, African, and Caribbean elements. Most Black Caribs believe that God's throne in heaven occupies the central position in the universe. Over the throne of God the Father is the Holy Ghost. Jesus Christ, the Virgin Mary, and the saints stand at God's right hand, and to his left stand the angels and a group of beings called blessed souls, or *gubida* (Coelho 1955, p. 235).

Outside the gates of the heavenly realm of God lies Sairi, the paradisiacal realm of pagan spirits, apparently of African origin. Below Sairi are roads leading to earth. Below the earth is Hell, the residence of Satan, who like God, has assistants sitting to his right and left. Coelho (1955, p. 235) says: "On earth, places such as cemeteries, crossroads, clearings within forests, the bottom of the seas, and the tops of mountains and hills, are considered to be the abode of 'pagan' spirits, while churches and sanctuaries constitute the strongholds of heavenly forces, especially the centers of pilgrimage, Suyapa in Honduras, and Kaquipulas in Guatemala." The "masters of the land," called *labureme ubau*, were the gods worshipped by the vanished Indian civilizations of old and they are now thought to be "wild," completely outside the control of the current spiritual hierarchy (Coelho 1955, p. 237).

The universe itself is a cosmic battleground, in which several (i.e., more than two) parties of combatants are constantly fighting. But the makeup of each group changes, because of shifting alliances (Coelho 1955, pp. 235, 237). In other words, there is not a fixed duality of good and evil forces. Saints, angels, and spirits have a considerable degree of independence, and don't always use it in harmony with God's own will. In the Carib cosmology, saints are given control of the universe on their name day. But people are often afraid of this. For example St. Francis of Gordon is feared because he loves storms and might take advantage of his day of control to cause floods (Coelho 1955, p. 237).

The independence manifested by the Carib saints, angels, and spirits has a parallel in Vedic cosmology. Vedic demigods sometimes oppose the Supreme Lord, Krishna, when he enters this world as an avatar. Once Krishna arranged for the residents of the village of Vrindavan to stop their sacrifices to Indra, the god of heaven who controls the rain. In retaliation, Indra poured incessant rain on Vrindavan. Krishna protected the inhabitants by raising with his hand a hill called Govardhan, employing it like a huge umbrella. Seeing his attempt to drown the residents thwarted, Indra came to his senses and returned to his normal position of worshipful subordination to Krishna (*Shrimad Bhagavatam* 10.24–25).

The *gubida*, who live in Sairi, are souls of persons who formerly lived on earth. Valentine (1993, p. 12) says, "The word *Gubida* means dead." Sometimes called "the Carib angels," they are officially under the command of the traditional Christian angels, like St. Gabriel and St. Michael, but they sometimes act indepedently for the welfare of Carib people with whom they had family connections during their lives on earth (Coelho 1955, p. 237). Such interactions between the *gubida* and their living descendants are not always favorable. According to Staiano (1986, p. 125), the *gubida* return to earth fifteen or twenty years after their deaths, demanding favors from their descendants. If their demands are not met, or they feel offended, they may cause illness or allow an illness to take place (Staiano 1986, p. 125).

Following Catholic teaching, Caribs believe that departed souls must spend some time in purgatory before going to the final spiritual destination, God's paradise in heaven. Purgatory is sometimes identified with Sairi. A soul who is remembered by relatives with masses and ceremonies spends only a short time in purgatory. A soul who dies without relatives to offer such help must spend a long time in purgatory. Such souls are called lonely souls (*animas solas*). Sometimes, someone who is not a relative of a lonely soul will conduct a ceremony that helps the soul get deliverance from purgatory. In such cases, that soul will then act for the benefit of the person who gave it assistance (Coelho 1955, p. 237).

Pagan spirits, called *hiuruha*, live permanently in Sairi, as opposed to other souls who pass through on their way to heaven. The *hiuruha* are technically subordinate to the higher angels but, like the *gubida*, display some independence. Sometimes they help fortunetellers and soothsayers to understand the future and hidden things. They also help healers cure diseases brought on by spirits. Traditional healers are mostly female, and are called *buyai* (Foster 1986, p. 17). A woman becomes a *buyai* by virtue of being possessed by *hiuruha*, or spirit helpers. According to Foster (1986, p. 17), *hiuruha* are "the spirits of mediums of the past." Generally, a medium will have a principal *hiuruha*. Foster (1986, pp. 17–18) states: "The medium's possession by spirit helpers enables her to differentiate between illnesses of natural origin (*lisandi ubau*, 'sickness of the world') and those caused by the malevolence of ancestral spirits. In fact it is believed to be the spirit helpers themselves who, in their petulant voices, communicate diagnoses to the afflicted in a séance (*arairaguni*, 'descension of the spirits') held either in the cult houses (*dabuyaba*) or in a domestic house." As mentioned previously, illnesses are sometimes caused by *gubida*, departed ancestors. Healers will therefore conduct curing rituals to placate the *gubida*. During these rituals the *gubida* responsible for the illness are summoned by the *buyai* to a cult house, where they make their presence known by possessing one or more of the participants (Foster 1986, pp. 41–44).

Nature spirits (*kolubi*) have an even greater degree of independence than *hiuruha* (Coelho 1955, p. 237). The nature spirits included evil bush spirits (*mafia*, or *maboya*). Coelho (1955, p. 153) says, "The spirits called *mafia*, who wander through the streets at night, sometimes entering the house, are responsible for domestic accidents, and may strangle people in their sleep. They also attract women coming from gardens in the hills ... The chief is named Uinani, often identified with Satan." One Carib informant said that Uinani is "a monster seen by the soul or spirit alone." Sometimes it appears like an alligator, a demon, or a dragon. It generally appears at night, from eleven o'clock to three or four o'clock. Seeing the Uinani in dreams makes one ill. A medical doctor may not be able to help, but a spirit medium may deliver a cure (Staiano 1986, p. 125).

The *agauima* is a female evil spirit found in pools or cascades of rivers. The *agauima* can capture a man's soul, bringing sickness or death. She assumes the form of a beautiful woman with long hair (Staiano 1986, pp. 122–124). She usually appears during the middle of the day, from 11:30 to 12:30, when things are calm and peaceful, according to a Carib informant (Staiano 1986, p. 124). This informant, who was sixty years old at the time, said: "When I saw her, I was quite young. She dashed herself into the bush backwards when she became aware of our presence. There were a group of us going to the river bank to do some fishing. When I saw her, I turned back at speed. The others, having become alarmed, followed me. Four days later, one of my youngest brothers died. He was only five at the time. On the second day after we returned he had fits. He had been well until then. *Agaiuma* may be harmful to the human body and may cause death. I believe it was the effects of the haunting which caused him to die" (Staiano 1986, p. 124). An *agaiuma* can also appear in male form. A Carib woman said, "She can make you sick. Your illness may start with a fever or chills. She appears to a sick person in their dreams. If it is a woman who is ill, she will come to her like her husband" (Staiano 1986, p. 124). The disease brought on by an *agaiuma* can be cured only by a spirit medium, not an ordinary medical doctor.

Among the evil spirits is the *ogoreu* (Coelho 1955, p. 256). It usually appears as a blue lizard, but sometimes appears in other forms, such as an armadillo, snake, or crab. It lives in a burrow in the corner of the house. The Carib believe it must be offered milk, cheese, cassava, and manioc beer. If this is not done, the *orogeu* will cause accidents in the home. The *orogeu* attaches itself to women and will cause stillbirths and deaths of babies. Intervention by a spirit medium can prevent this. It is said by some that the *orogeu* will follow the woman to whom it is attached wherever she goes. If a man believes an *orogeu* is attached to a woman and causing problems, he may give up his relationship with her (Coelho 1955, p. 152).

The *duendu* and *pengaliba* are also evil spirits, resembling the devils of Christianity. They live inside large trees and come out for a few hours at noon and again at midnight. Ambitious people will sometimes make pacts with the *duendu* in order to acquire property or money. For example, a *duendu* may reside near a cattle ranch. The *duendu* is fond of items such as silk, cheese, and butter. The rancher desires to prosper by expanding his herd. In exchange for the items he desires, the *duendu* causes this to happen (Coelho 1955, p. 154). The *duendu* appears like a short man with a big chest. He wears a red cap that gives him an air of authority, like an official of the Church. Sometimes a pact with the *duendu* requires that the soul of a family member be signed over in return for quick wealth. Similar pacts are made with the *pengaliba*. If it is seen that a family becomes suddenly rich after the death of a younger member of the family, people may attribute this to a deal that an elder member of the family has made with a *pengaliba*. The soul, or *afurugu,* of the victim must serve the *penga-liba* until the Judgement Day. In some cases, the death of the younger member may be postponed. For example, it was seen that the son of a wealthy cattle rancher mysteriously disappeared a few years after the rancher acquired his riches. In this regard, it is said that a poor old woman went to the town of Trujillo to purchase some entrails to cook for food. But she arrived many hours before the market was scheduled to open at 4 o'clock in the morning. So she was waiting for the opening of the market, which happened to be near a cemetery. At midnight she saw in the road a tall man dressed in a black uniform with golden metal insignia. He asked the old lady what she was doing. She said she was waiting for the market to open. The man said he had some private business with someone, and to get rid of the woman, he gave her some money and told her to go buy some fish in her home village. Normally, she would not have been able to afford fish, so she took the money and left. Before she left, she asked who was coming. She learned it was the cattle raiser. This incident happened a short time before the cattle raiser's son disappeared (Coelho 1955, p. 155).

According to the Black Carib, the human soul has three parts. The first is the vital force or animal spirit (*anigi*). It is located in the heart. Generally, it ceases to exist at death, although it may sometimes persist for a few months after the death of the body. The *anigi* can be perceived in the beating of the heart, the pulsing of blood in the arteries, the drawing of the breath, and other bodily functions (Coelho 1955, p. 136). In infants, the pulsing of the blood can be seen in the veins of the head. The Carib thought the vital force of the infant was in need of special protection, and relied upon magical means to accomplish this (Ceolho 1955, p. 137).

The second part of the Carib soul is the *iuani,* located in the head. Whereas the *anigi* is material, the *iuani* is immaterial and normally invisible, although it can appear in dreams (Staiano 1986, p. 96). It corresponds to the soul in Christian thought. It leaves the body immediately after death. Staiano (1986, p. 96) says that "death is defined as the absence of the *iuani.*" The physical body itself is called *ubugu* (Staiano 1986, p. 98). There are different ideas about what happens to the *iuani* at death. According to one view, at death the *iuani* leaves the body and goes by a long road to Sairi, crossing a river along the way. Valentine (1993, p. 11) says: "This journey is a long one. It is beset with many obstacles. The spirit has to travel through deserts, wilderness, mud and rough seas. Sometimes the spirit is in the company of other spirits, but most of the time it finds itself alone. Most of the time it is wet with sweat, rain and dew; full of dust and grime. There are times when the distant lights of Seiri [Sairi] are visible. Other times, the way is total darkness, beset with many dangers and seemingly, without direction." The length of the journey depends on the character of the soul. For souls who have manifested goodness during their life, the journey is short—about three months. Therefore, about three months after death, most families will hold a bathing ceremony for the departed soul, who thus cleansed from the journey can enter Sairi. For those who have behaved badly, the journey is longer, and through a medium such a soul will request another bathing, sometimes long after the one that was given three months after death (Valentine 1993, pp. 11–12). Sairi is the world of the pagan spirits (*hiuruha*). Upon entering the gate to Sairi, the soul sees a land of thatched houses and rich agricultural fields. The inhabitants greet the newcomer with food and drink. But if the time is not right for the soul to enter Sairi, a barking white dog chases the soul back across the river and the soul reenters its body (Taylor 1951, p. 107).

If the disembodied soul (*iuani*) remains near its home after death, it is called *pantu,* or ghost. In such instances, the *iuani* may stay for days or weeks as *pantu.* One of Staiano's informants said (1986, p. 96): "When my mother died, she came back plain and walked around the house for about half an hour." Another said that one can sometimes see the *pantu* moving rapidly in the light of the moon, looking like a bundle of fire. Staiano (1986, p. 125) says that the spirit becomes a *pantu* "only if at death it was discontented or had committed some crime or misdeed. The *pantus* do not cause much trouble, but the person who sees a *pantu* becomes disturbed. In such cases, the person will announce the problem, and others will join in prayer, causing the *pantu* to go away.

Another kind of ghost is called *ufie*. According to some, they are, like *pantus*, the spectres of persons recently dead, and according to others, they are not connected with the recently dead. Murderers can become *ufie* ghosts. Persons whose bodies thrown into the bush instead of being properly buried can become *ufie*. Persons who are too attached to some possession or place can remain as *ufie*. Such ghosts can be driven out of haunted places by an exorcist (Coelho 1955, p. 256). The *ufie* are normally difficult to see, but people with sufficient mental powers may be able to detect them. The *ufie* is seen surrounded by a thin vapor, and the *ufie's* feet do not touch the ground, although they remain close to it. After some time, the feet rise higher off the ground and the *ufie* grows dimmer and disappears. Coelho (1955, p. 143) observes that "the proper attitude in the presence of ghosts is one of impassiveness, since any display of emotion would give the *ufie* an opportunity to seize upon the spiritual double of the living person."

The spiritual double (*afurugu*) is the third part of the Carib soul concept. Situated between the vital air and the soul, it is "an astral body reproducing the shape of a person in all its details, but composed of a substance akin to that of supernatural entities" (Coelho 1955, p. 138). Coelho further says (1955, p. 138): "The astral body is the intermediary between the supernatural and everyday realms of reality. It possesses faculties of discernment, even clairvoyance, which enable it to know of dangers threatening the individual to whom it is attached before he is aware of them. It gives its owner warning of these dangers by well-known signs, such as itching of arms and shoulders. . . . At times the signs are not so clear, and must be interpreted with the aid of an aged person, or any one conversant with supernatural lore."

According to the Carib, the *afurugu* can wander away from the body for short periods of time, while remaining connected to it (Coelho 1955, p. 138). The same is true of the subtle, or astral body, in the Vedic conception. For example, while the gross physical body is sleeping, the subtle body may remain active and leave the gross physical body in a kind of astral travel in dreams. But unless the person dies, the subtle body remains connected with the gross physical body and returns to it.

When the *afurugu* suddenly departs from the body, as when a person is unexpectedly frightened, the person may fall into a stupor. If the *afurugu* stays away from the body for long enough, the person dies, or becomes a living corpse, without normal use of the mental faculties. Separation between the *afurugu* and the body may be brought about by "workers of evil magic." Sometimes the worker of evil magic will be paid by a person's enemy to capture the *afurugu* and deliver it to an evil spirit, in exchange for wealth and power. Or the motive may simply be to cause the person's downfall. According to the Carib, a person's *afurugu* is particularly vulnerable to capture by an evil spirit or sorcerer when it is wandering away from the body during dreams. *Afurugus* may be heavy or light, according to the nature of the individual. A heavy *afurugu* is less vulnerable to evil spirits and sorcerers than a light *afurugu*. Those with heavy *afurugus* "may abandon themselves to dream experiences, which are valued by the Black Carib as a source of prophetic knowledge and a means of communicating with the dead, through which the ancestors make their will known to their descendants, indicating processes of obtaining large catches of fish, or revealing the secret designs of enemies, or the perils that must be faced by those who embark upon long journeys" (Coelho 1955, p. 139).

A famous spirit medium named Ding, who lived in the early twentieth century, reputedly restored people to life after their *afurugus* had been stolen by evil spirits. An old woman said that when she was twelve she had died. Her parents summoned Ding, and he told them that their daughter's *afurugu,* or spirit double, had been stolen by one of the leading evil spirits, Uinani. Ding sent six of his spirit helpers to retrieve the *afurugu.* They found that Uinani had closed himself up within a mountain with the girl's *afurugu* and would not let them enter. Ding sent six more spirit helpers, along with some rum. With the rum, they enticed Uinani to open the way into the mountain. When he took the rum and became intoxicated, the spirit helpers took the girl's *afurugu* and brought it back to her body, thus reviving her. Ding lived in the village of Kauéch, near Livingston, in Belize, the former British Honduras (Taylor 1951, p. 111).

The Black Carib conception of self, composed of *anigi, inuani*, and *afurugu,* resembles the Vedic conception. According to the Vedic literature, a person has a material body that is powered by the vital airs. A person also has a soul, a unit of consciousness or spirit that survives the death of the body. A person also has a subtle material body made of the subtle material elements (mind, intelligence, ego). The subtle body carries the soul from one gross physical body to another, until such time as the soul is liberated from all contact with matter, either gross or subtle, and returns to the purely spiritual plane of existence to be with God. The higher demigods of the Vedic cosmology have bodies made principally of the subtle material elements. So it could be said that the subtle material body of a human being partakes of the nature of the bodies of the demigods.

According to Coelho, the multipart Carib soul is derived from the similar multipart soul concepts of West Africa. The Africans of Dahomey believe in a four part soul. *Se Djoto* is the first part. It comes from the ancestors and serves as a guardian spirit. *Se Medo* is the personal soul, which survives death. Coelho (1955, p. 255) describes the next part of the soul as "*Se Lido,* a particle of Mawu, the creator god, which resides in every individual." This resembles the Vedic concept of Supersoul: every individual has a spirit soul and along with it exists a manifestation of the Supersoul, or Paramatma, who serves as a witness and permitter. A fourth part of the Dahomey soul is related to Fa, destiny personified (Coelho 1955, p. 255). This fourth part may correspond to the subtle material body in the Vedic conception. The subtle material body carries the *karma* of the individual. The *karma* stored in the subtle body determines the destiny of the soul, including the kind of physical body it will receive and the kind of experiences it will undergo.

Cosmology of the Gilyak of Siberia

The Gilyak are among the tribal peoples that inhabit the eastern most part of Siberia, including the island of Sakhalin and the coastal region around the Amur River. The world of the Gilyak is not one of dead matter. It is alive with deities. According to the Gilyak, deities are connected with each element and feature of nature. For example, in connection with mountains, there is a master of the mountains, a Mountain Man (Coxwell 1925, p. 119). Mountains are called *pal.* The master of the mountains is called *pal-yz.* Many clans of animals are subordinate to him, and he sends them to the Gilyak hunters. Without his sanction, they would not get a single animal. He lives on the highest mountain (Shternberg 1933, p. 55). In connection with the sea there is a master of the sea, a Sea Man, known by the name *tol-yz,* or *tayrnadz.* Shternberg (1933, p. 55) says, "The god of the sea, Tayrnadz, lives on the bottom of the Sea of Okhotsk. He is a very old man with a white beard, who lives with his old wife in an underwater yurt. In the yurt there is a huge number of boxes with all kinds of spawn, which he throws by the handful into the sea from time to time. It is he who, at the appointed time, sends the countless detachments of salmon, without which the life of the Gilyak would be impossible; it is he who sends out the *kosatki* [killer whales] to establish order in the sea and drive all kinds of sea animals toward the Gilyak." In connection with the earth, there is an Under Earth Man. These deities resemble the Gilyak in their outer appearance, but they are endowed with mystical powers, including the ability to take the forms of the animals, trees, or stones under their control. Sometimes the Gilyak may be seen worshiping these forms, but the real deities are the masters (Shternberg 1933, p. 54).

The Gilyak regard the bear as a particularly sacred animal who carries out the divine will. For example, the bear punishes evildoers during their lifetimes. The soul of a Gilyak who is killed by a bear is said to enter the body of a bear. Schrenck (1881–1895, p. 749) says, "The belief in the transmigration of souls with reference to the bear may be the basis of a number of pictorial representations among the Gilyaks—amulets or small idol-images that are worn around the neck in case of sickness. Among them one finds double figures of a human being and bear. This is ordinarily a small piece of wood which at one end branches out into two parts, one representing a human head, the other a bear's head."

In addition to the deities of the more important forces and creatures of nature, there are also many less important ones who watch over every aspect of Gilyak life. There are also categories of deities who are quite distant from the Gilyak, such as the sun, the moon, and "the heavenly people," called *tly-nivukh*. Shternberg (1933, p. 55) says, "Out of mischievousness a heavenly man will lower a fishing rod with hooks to the earth in order to catch some Gilyak. This does not always work, however. For example, the young Gilyak, Il'k, from the village of Arkovo told me that *tly-nivukh* once caught his father with a golden hook, and he just saved himself by grabbing a tree, thus getting away with only a scare and a torn coat." Another of Shternberg's informants told him (1933, p. 363), "A certain man once met the master of the sky. He was riding on a sled pulled by wolves, but, upon encountering the Gilyak, the wolves turned upward and disappeared into the sky with their rider."

The Gilyak also worship clan gods. The clan gods are Gilyaks who after death have entered into the association of one of the nature gods. Shternberg (1933, p. 58) says, "If, while hunting, a Gilyak was killed by a bear, if he fell prey to the waves on the water, if he was murdered or burned to death through his own carelessness, if, according to the shaman's explanation, a woman died from a bear's love for her, etc.—all such persons do not travel to the ordinary kingdom of the shades, but go over into the clan of the gods—masters who took a liking to them, of the mountain, water, fire, etc., and then become the smallest 'masters' and protect their clansmen. In this way the clan *pal'-nivukh'i*—forest people, *tol'-nivukh'i*—sea people, etc. took form. It is to these gods-clansmen that the entire clan offers sacrifices." These departed Gilyak, having become clan gods, appear before the living in the form of certain animals. The forest clan gods appear as bears, the sea clan gods as beluga whales or killer whales (Shternberg 1933, p. 58). The clan gods act for the benefit of their living descendants. The clan gods remain in their positions for up to two generations (Shternberg 1933, p. 89). Gilyak who become clan gods are remembered through special shrines. For example, if a Gilyak drowns and becomes a clan god associated with the master of the sea, the Gilyak put at his place of cremation a boat, with all equipment for sea or river travel.

The Gilyak gods are sometimes worshiped in the form of idols. Sometimes the Gilyak wear small idols on strings around their necks. These are called *sawa* (Schrenck 1881–1895, p. 745). The person wearing the idol gives it a little of the food he eats by touching it to the idol's mouth. The idols are not simply representations. The Gilyak believe that spirits reside in them. The resident spirit is known by the name *kobold.* Schrenck (1881–1895, p. 240) says, "If an idol is 'heavy' it means that its inhabitant, the *kobold*, is at home, but when it gets 'lighter' than usual, the spirit is roaming about somewhere." The Gilyak consider fire, and the fire deity, to be the medium by which humans can communicate with the other more powerful deities. For example, the hunter offers sacrifices into fire for the Lord of the Forest, so that he will be successful in killing animals (Coxwell 1925, p. 118).

Some spirits are actively hostile to the Gilyak. These are called *melk,* which means, roughly, devil. Like the other deities, they are connected with elements and features of nature (Coxwell 1925, p. 120). So there are sea devils, mountain devils, forest devils, etc. The sea devils ride in boats, and if they see the Gilyak coming in boats to hunt seals, they shout, "What are you doing here?" One of the evil spirits is called Ge-nivukh. He lives in an earthen mound near Tekhrvo. He comes to the home of a Gilyak, and through the window he asks for something, gesturing with two fingers extended. If he gets something, he departs. Sometimes the Gilyak give him a coal. Not quite understanding, Ge-nivukh begins tossing the hot coal from hand to hand, saying, "It is hot, if you do not have (anything), do not give!" But Ge-nivukh is not always so easily put off. He is known to kidnap people, especially children. For a person faced with kidnaping by Ge-nivukh there is something that can be done to prevent it: "the only way is to inflict a wound upon oneself, for Ge-nivukh is afraid of blood" (Shternberg 1933, p. 321). The Gilyak believe that except for the attacks of the evil spirits, they would live forever in their earthly bodies. Sickness is interpreted as the attack of evil spirits who have invaded the body. Shternberg (1933, p. 73) says, "Just as he, the Gilyak, lies in wait for a beast and tries in every way to kill him, so an evil spirit lies in wait for the Gilyak himself at every step in order to devour him."

The supreme being, creator, and moral authority is called Kiskh. According to the Gilyak, a sick person has offended Kiskh. This offense leaves the person subject to the influence of evil spirits. An offering is made to the evil spirit, to induce it to leave the person. The Gilyak don't make offerings to Kiskh for the relief of disease or any other purpose. The Gilyak worshiper's relationship with Kiskh appeared mysterious to observers such as Charles H. Hawes, who wrote (1903, p. 162): "So vague is his notion of him that he can only be said to exist in his mind as a nebulous conception." Schrenck (1881–1895, p. 740) says: "Among the Gilyak there is an obscure and hazy conception of 'God,' of a supreme being, who has the attribute of the 'Good One' in full measure and without any admixture of evil and who is revered by human beings. But this conception is a wholly abstract, completely empty one and does not at all fit into the life, into the customs and practices of the Gilyaks; there is nothing concrete about it for them, and therefore they only know the word 'pray,' but not the act itself. Also, they know nothing about 'God,' in view of the complete emptiness of the concept, except that he is *kíngulatsch,* the 'Good One.'"

Still, it appears that the Gilyak did recognize some intervention by their God in their affairs, and did sometimes give him some attention. Schrenck (1881–1895, p. 239) noted, "In one village, however, I heard that God is very angry if a shaman is put to death" and "when a Gilyak crosses a dangerous passage on his journey, he pours a bowl of spirits on the earth or in the waters: this is the sacrifice to God."

According to some, the name of the supreme God is Kurn. The same word is also given to the universe. Shternberg (1933, p. 49) says the Gilyak regard their supreme God (Kurn) as "personal, man-like." In the beginning there was only water, and then Kurn made the earth. Kurn then lost his reindeer, which made tracks across the land. These tracks became the great rivers. As Kurn pursued his reindeer, he waved his lash at it, and the marks of the lash on the ground became the streams (Shternberg 1933, p. 320).

The Gilyak of Sakhalin call their island *mif,* meaning "the earth." They consider it to be "a living, divine creature" says Shternberg (1933, p. 49). Its head lies in the Sea of Okhotsk to the north, and its two legs, represented by two peninsulas, stretch to the south, in the La Perouse Strait. Shternberg (1933, p. 50) says: "Here is Kryuspal, a marvelous cone, one of the highest peaks of Sakhalin, which impresses everyone approaching the island from the sea with its grandeur, a lonely, stern demon of the sea . . . And even the lonely cliffs sticking out of the water all along the shore of the island—all of this is alive, gods who ran away from their clans under the influence of internecine wars. All the rest of nature is equally alive: the menacing *tol* (the sea), the somber forests of the mountainous island, the fast mountain rivers, etc. When cutting down a tree, the Gilyak is afraid to destroy its soul and places upon its stump a special being, the *inau* [in the form of a sharpened stick] . . . which returns soul and life to it. The mountains, the ocean, cliffs, trees, animals—this is only a mask under which the gods conceal themselves from the curiosity of man."

Sometimes, a smaller killer whale (*kosatka*) accompanies a larger one in the sea. A Gilyak explained to Shternberg that the smaller *kosatka* is the sword of the larger one. It only seemed to be a *kosatka*. Actually, it was a sword. And as for the big *kosatka*, its actual form was like that of a Gilyak hunter. Shternberg (1933, p. 50) said his Gilyak informant told him that what to us seems like a sea animal is actually the boat of the Gilyak spirit of the *kosatka*. The *kosatka* is considered a sacred animal, and it is not hunted. When the dead body of a *kosatka* happens to wash up on the shore, the Gilyak give it a ceremonial burial (Shternberg 1933, p. 54).

According to the Gilyak, humans have several souls, of various sizes. The large souls are the same size as the human body, and a person may have different numbers of these, with those of higher rank, such as shamans, having more than those of lower rank. A person also has a number of small egg-shaped souls. These are located in the head of the large soul. When the large soul ceases to exist, a small soul expands to large size, duplicating it. (Shternberg 1933, p. 78) It is the small soul that experiences itself in dreams (Shternberg 1933, p. 79). Sometimes it is said that a person has three souls. The principal soul is called *cheg:n,* and the other two are called shadows, or assistants. Shternberg (1933, p. 306) says that "when the *cheg:n* of a shaman is wounded, the shaman dies." If a dream is very clear and comes true, it is produced by the main soul. If it does not come true, then it is produced by one of the shadow souls.

Gilyak shamans provide a connection between the visible world and the invisible world. Shternberg (1933, p. 74) says that there are shamans "who in night visions or in a trance receive a revelation from the god-protector about their high calling." Their primary activity is to cure diseases by driving out evil spirits. They also predict the future and perform sacrifices. They can control natural forces. For example, they can prevent rain or cause rain. They can also use their powers to cause harm to others. They can cause a person to die, or can punish a village by sending a flood (Seeland 1882, pp. 242–243). The shamans have two kinds of divine beings who serve as their assistants. They are called *kekhn* and *kenchkh*. The *kekhn* are the most important assistants. They help the shaman cure diseases by making a disease-causing devil leave a person's body. They can also help the shaman retrieve a person's soul, if it has been taken by a devil. The *kekhn* can take the forms of wolves, seals, eagles, reindeer, and owls, among others (Shternberg 1933, p. 74).

The shaman may cure a person in three ways. By the first method, the shaman takes help of dreams to find a cure. By the second method, the shaman drives out the evil disease-causing spirit by loud chanting and dancing. By the third method, the shaman, in addition to chanting and dancing, summons *kekhn* to help him (Shternberg 1933, p. 74). The chanting and dancing puts the shaman into a state of consciousness in which he can directly perceive the *kekhn*, his spirit helpers and protectors. "We can fully believe that he actually hears and sees them," says Shternberg (1933, p. 75). "I hope that no one will suspect me of a partiality for the shamans, but I can calmly testify that in my presence the ecstasy of the shaman ... brought the Gilyak to such a state that they ... saw everything that the shaman himself saw in his trance. The shaman skillfully has recourse to first one, then another of his *kekhn,* depending on the circumstances. Thus, if the devil has stubbornly settled inside the organism and does not want to leave, the shaman calls on the *ar-rymnd-kekhn,* which turns into a fiery ball and makes its way into the belly of the shaman and from there to the most distant parts of his body, so that during the seance the shaman emits fire out of his mouth or nose or from any part of his body. After being thus filled with fire, he touches the sore spot with his lips and lets in fire, which conclusively drives out the devil."

In the case of a drowning, the shaman will send a *kekhn* after the soul of the drowned person. The *kekhn* will go to the place of the master spirit of the sea, taking along a white reindeer. There the soul of the drowned man is kept in the yurt of the master spirit of the sea. When the sea spirits see the white reindeer, an animal strange to them, they come out of the yurt to look at it in wonder. At that time, the *kekhn* goes into the yurt and takes the soul of the drowned man, to bring it back to the world of the living (Shternberg 1933, p. 75).

The shaman, despite his many *kekhn,* is at times not able to help a person, especially if the person is being attacked by the very powerful devils of the mountains or seas. These devils destroy the body of the person, and carry away the soul. However, the soul, freed of the burden of the gross physical body, may be able to exercise its own powers to escape to the protection of the friendly mountain and sea deities. Afterwards, the soul may take human form and journey to Miyvo, the "settlement of the dead." Under some circumstances, the evil spirits leave the soul of a dead person alone, allowing it to peacefully journey to Miyvo (Shternberg 1933, p. 79).

Miyvo is said to be located in the center of the earth. The residents engage in hunting an unending supply of animals and catching an unlimited supply of fish (Hawes 1903, p. 163). Shternberg (1933, p. 79) says: "There everything is as it is here: the same earth, the same sky, sea, rivers, and forest; only there the sun shines when we have night, and the moon when we have day. The dead come to life and continue to live there in the same settlements as on earth, fish, kill beasts, celebrate clan festivals, marry and procreate. Only the material status changes: the poor man becomes rich and the rich man poor. . . . Even in the new world, however, sickness and death await man. From there the soul must migrate into a third world, and so on until such time as the soul degenerates and turns into ever smaller and smaller beings, a small bird, a gnat, and, finally, ashes. Sometimes souls are born again on our planet, completing again the infinite series of transformations." Concerning rebirth in this world, there is a legend telling of a Gilyak who died in a fight with a bear. The Gilyak body had a certain pattern of wounds on the face. Later, a boy was born to a Gilyak family, with the exact same pattern of scars on his face (Shternberg 1933, p. 368).

The souls of persons who committed suicide and persons who have been murdered go directly to Miyvo. Others must make a journey that can last several days (Hawes 1903, p. 163). After a person dies, there is a ceremonial preparation for the journey. Hawes witnessed such a ceremony for a recently deceased woman. The body was kept in a hut for four days. During this time, the woman's soul was visiting the four principle gods of the Gilyak with the purpose of giving an account of her life and receiving instructions for the afterlife. Her relatives kept her company, remembering and reciting her good deeds and qualities. Because the god of fire serves as a channel of communication to the other gods, a fire is kept burning constantly in the hut. The body of a dead person is dressed in new garments and provided with the best nets, spears, rifles, and bows for the journey to Miyvo (Shternberg 1933, p. 80). The dead person receives a new name, and according to Shternberg (1933, p. 368), the Gilyak consider it a sin to call the dead person by the person's old name.

Cosmology of the Incas

The main god of the Incas of South America was called Viracocha. Rowe (1946, p. 293) said that Viracocha was "the theoretical source of all divine power, but the Indians believed that He had turned over the administration of his creation to a multitude of assistant supernatural beings, whose influence on human affairs was consequently more immediate." Viracocha dwells in the celestial region, but descends to the terrestrial region, appearing to humans in times of crisis. This is similar to the

Vedic concept of the avatar, "one who descends." In the *Bhagavad Gita* (4.7), the Supreme Lord Krishna says, "Whenever and wherever there is a decline in religious practice and a predominant rise in irrelgion, at that time I descend myself." After he created the earth, Viracocha wandered through it, exhibiting miracles and giving instruction to the people. After reaching the place called Manta, in Ecuador, he set off to the West, walking on the waters of the Pacific Ocean (Rowe 1946, p. 293).

There was a golden idol of Viracocha, the supreme creator, in the main temple in Cuzco, capital of the Inca empire. It was of manlike form, but about the size of a boy of ten years (Rowe 1946, p. 293). Temples for worship of Viracocha were established throughout the Inca empire, along with farming fields to provide income for servants and sacrificial performances (de Molina 1873, p. 11).

One prominent early historian, Garcilaso de la Vega (1539–1616), identified Viracocha with another supreme creator called Pachacamac. Garcilaso de la Vega was the son of an Inca princess and a Spanish conquistador, and therefore his knowledge of Inca religion was acquired from an Inca perspective. *Pacha* means universal and *camac,* according to Garcilaso de la Vega (1869–1871, p. 106), is "the present participle of the verb *cama,* to animate, whence is derived the word *cama,* the soul." Thus Pachacamac means "He who gives animation to the universe", or, more accurately, "He who does to the universe what the soul does to the body" (Garcilaso de la Vega 1869–1871, p. 106). This corresponds to the Vedic concept of Supersoul, which exists in several forms. One form of the Supersoul resides within the body of each living entity, along with the individual soul. Another manifestation of the Supersoul animates the entire universe.

The name of God, Pachacamac, was held in great reverence, and the Incas never uttered it without special gestures such as bowing, or raising the eyes to heaven, or raising the hands. Garcilaso de la Vega (1869–1871, p. 107) says, "When the Indians were asked who Pachacamac was, they replied that he it was who gave life to the universe, and supported it; but that they knew him not, for they had never seen him, and that for this reason they did not build temples to him, nor offer him sacrifices. But that they worshipped him in their hearts (that is mentally), and considered him to be an unknown God." But there was one temple to Pachacamac in a coastal valley of the same name. Garcilaso de la Vega (1869–1871, p. 552) says, "This temple of Pachacamac was very grand, both as regards the edifice itself and the services that were performed in it. It was the only temple to the Supreme Being throughout the whole of Peru."

According to some historians, the Incas originally worshiped the sun as supreme. But one of the early Inca rulers noted that the sun was always moving, without any rest. It could also be seen that even a small cloud could cover the sun. For these reasons he concluded that the sun could not be the supreme god. Therefore, there must be a higher being who controlled and ordered the sun. This ultimate supreme being he called Pachacamac (de Molina 1873, p. 11).

After Virococha (or Pachacamac), the god next in importance in the Inca system of worship was the sun god, the chief of the sky gods. Inca royalty were accepted as the children of the sun, and were taken to be divine beings themselves (Garcilaso de la Vega 1869–1871, p. 102). The first Inca queen was called Mama Uaco. She was a beautiful woman and also a sorceress. She could speak with demons, and she also empowered sacred stones and idols (*huacas*) to speak. She was the daughter of the sun and moon. Somehow, with no earthly husband, she had a son, the Mango Capac Inca, whom she married, taking a dowry from her father, the sun god. The later Inca kings were descended from her. The sun god presided over the growing of crops, and thus his worship was very important among the primarily agricultural Inca people. There was an idol of the sun in the main Inca temple in Cuzco (Rowe 1946, p. 293).

Next in importance was the moon goddess. She was called Mama-Kilya, "Mother Moon." She was the wife and sister of the sun. Her movements guided calculations of time and determined the calendar of Inca festivals (Rowe 1946, p. 295). The Thunder God was the god of weather. The Incas prayed to him for rain. His form was that of a man in the sky, holding in one hand a war club and in the other a sling. Thunder was produced by the loud crack of his sling, and lightning was the flash of his shining garments. In producing rain, he took water from the Milky Way, a heavenly river, and poured it down on the earth. He was called by the names Ilyap'a, Intil-ilyap'a, or Coqu-ilya, and was identified with a constellation similarly named (Rowe 1946, pp. 294–295).

The stars were regarded as the handmaidens of the moon (Garcilaso de la Vega 1869–1871, p. 115). Among the stars, the Incas worshiped the Pleiades, which they called Collca. Certain stars presided over different earthly affairs, and were specifically worshiped for this reason. For example, shepherds worshiped the star Lyra, which they called Vrcuchillay. They considered this star to be a many-colored llama, with powers to protect livestock (Polo de Ondegardo 1916, pp. 3–4). Incas in the mountains worshiped the star Chuquichinchay, which means moutain lion. It was in charge of lions, jaguars, and bears, from which the Incas desired protection. This star is part of the constellation Leo. The Incas worshiped the star Machacuay, which ruled over snakes. According to Polo de Ondegardo (1916, p. 5), Machacuay represented the crab, corresponding to a star in the constellation Cancer. Other stars represented the divine mother (Virgo), the deer (Capricorn), and rain (Aquarius).

The earth was called Pacha Mama (Earth Mother), and the sea was called Mama Qoca (Mother Sea). They were worshiped as supernatural goddesses (Rowe 1946, p. 295). The Inca people also paid homage to many local gods, down to the level of household deities. They worshiped plants, trees, hills, and stones, such as the emerald. They also worshiped animals such as jaguars, mountain lions, foxes, monkeys, great snakes, and condors (de la Vega 1869–1871, p. 47).

Idols of the principal gods would regularly receive offerings of food and a beverage called *chicha*. The food was burned and the *chicha* poured on the ground. Wherever the god or departed soul actually was, it would receive the offering. In the case of the sun god, the Inca, the ruler, would burn the offering of food, but the *chicha* was poured into a large gold jar behind a statue of the sun god, and from there the *chicha* was poured into the hollow of a stone lined with gold. This stone stood in the plaza before the altar (Cobo 1893, p. 83).

The idols were worshiped in temples. The main temple of the Incas was in Cuzco. People came there from all over the Incan empire to worship. Rowe (1946, p. 293) says, "The 'Temple of the Sun' in Cuzco housed images of all the sky gods of the Inca and a host of lesser supernaturals besides; its most important image was not of the Sun but of Viracocha. The fields attributed to the Sun supported the whole Inca priesthood, not just the ministers of the Sun, and the Chosen Women served all the deities in the temples, not the Sun alone. Although a very important power in Inca religion, the Sun was merely one of many great powers recognized in official worship, and his importance was more theoretical than real."

The Chosen Women, mentioned above, were dedicated to the service of the temple deities from childhood. They lived in cloisters near the temples of the Sun found in important towns throughout the empire. The virgins who lived in the cloister were called Mamaconas, "lady mothers." The Mamaconas were considered to be the wives of the gods (Cobo 1893, pp. 146–147). The Mamaconas tended the sacrificial fire in the main temple at Cuzco, feeding it carved and painted pieces of a special kind of wood. Rising at dawn each day, they prepared the food for the Sun god, who was represented by a golden figure called Punchao (Cobo 1893, pp. 147–148). The figure was "a golden disk with rays and a human face" (Rowe 1946, p. 293). The figure stood facing the East, so that it was bathed with the first light from the rising sun. At this time, the priestesses offered the food into the sacrificial fire, saying, "Sun eat this food prepared for you by your wives." The remnants of the offerings not placed in the fire were then taken by the temple priests, officials, and guards, as well as the priestesses. In the temples of the gods of the Vedic cosmology, there are daily offerings of food and drink. As in the case of the Incas, the remnants of such offerings are consumed by the servants of the deities.

The *amautas* were the philosopher priests of the Incas. They taught that human beings were composed of body and soul. The soul was an immortal spiritual substance, while the body was a temporary, material substance. The *amautas* equated the body with earth, because they saw that at death the body turned into earth. The *amautas* therefore called the body *allpacamasea,* which means "animated earth." The human body was, however, distinguished from the bodies of animals, by adding the word *runa,* which refers to reason and intelligence (Garcilaso de la Vega 1869–1871, p. 126). The Incas accepted a future life. The pious souls went to reside with the sun god, whereas the impious went to a cold underworld, where there are only stones to eat.

The Incas practiced divination, consulting the supernatural to "diagnose disease, determine the truth of a confession, locate lost property, identify hostile sorcerers, choose between possible heirs, determine the most acceptable sacrifice to a deity being worshiped, and, in general, to settle any doubtful question" (Rowe 1946, p. 302). They also relied upon omens to determine their future conduct.

Divination could also be carried out by sorcerers (*omo*), who were in direct communication with spirits. People consulted them to find lost or stolen objects. The sorcerers could also provide information about things happening in distant places. The sorcerers called spirits by chanting spells or drawing figures on the ground. Some established communication with spirits while unconscious after drinking intoxicating beverages. Generally, they talked to spirits in the dark, and people could hear the voices of the sorcerer and the spirits (Rowe 1946, p. 302).

Zulu Cosmology

The Zulus are a Bantu speaking tribe living in the northeastern part of the Natal province of the Republic of South Africa. According to some Zulu informants, their cosmology includes not only a creator god but a more distant ultimate high god. The creator god, responsible for manifesting the visible world and the bodies of living entities, is called Umvelinqangi. The forefather of human beings is called Unkulunkulu. A Zulu informant of Callaway (1870, p.97) said that Unkulunkulu is the same as Umvelinqangi, the creator god given above. The informant said the ultimate god who existed before the creator god is simply called the King. The distinction is like that found in the Vedic system, between the ultimate god (known by names such as Krishna, Narayan, Vishnu) and the creator god (Brahma), who manifests the material planets and the forms of living things, including humans.

Sometimes it is said that the Zulu idea of an ultimate, or high, god came from contact with Christianity. But one of Callaway's Zulu informants said (1870, p. 19), "And the King which is above we did not hear of him [first] from white men. In summer time, when it thunders, we say, 'The king is playing.' And if there is one who is afraid, the elder people say to him, 'It is nothing but fear. What thing belonging to the king have you eaten?' This is why I say, that the Lord of whom we hear through you, we had already heard of before you came. But he is not like that Unkulunkulu who, we say, made all things. But the former we call a king, for we say, he is above. Unkulunkulu is beneath; the things which are beneath were made by him."

Callaway's informant explained that it is the heavenly king, the high god above, who responds to sinful activities by striking one with misfortune. That is how his action is recognized. The informant said, "We know nothing of his mode of life, nor of the principles of his government. His smiting is the only thing we knew." The heavenly king god does not come from Unkulunkulu, as everything else does. The informant said, "There is no connection between our knowledge of Unkulunkulu and of him. For we can give some account of what belongs to Unkulunkulu; we can scarcely give any account of what belongs to the heavenly king. We know much of what belongs to Unkulunkulu, for he was on this earth, and we can give an account of matters concerning him. The sun and moon we referred to Unkulunkulu together with the things of this world" (Callaway 1870, pp. 20–21).

Callaway's informant objected to Christians who told the Zulus that the king of heaven made all things visible in this world. "We said that Unkulunkulu alone made them" (Callaway 1870, p. 21). The informant added, "And we black men, although some missionaries tell us that this king and that Unkulunkulu is the same, did not say that Unkulunkulu was in heaven; we said, he came to be, and died; that is all we said." This parallels the Vedic conception, in which Brahma, the creator god, is mortal, and the ultimate high god, Krishna, is immortal. Apparently, Unkulunkulu has a heavenly abode. When asked about the whereabouts of the creator, some Zulu elders replied, "The Creator of all things is in heaven. And there is a nation of people there too" (Callaway 1870, p. 53).

A twentieth century Zulu philosopher, Laduma Madela, gives the following account of the creation. The creator god's name is Umvelinqangi, which means "who created everything except the world which created him." His wife's name was Ma Jukujukwini. She is named after the place where creation took place, Ema Jukujukwini. At this place, the creator and his wife appeared "like mushrooms" (Bodenstein and Raum 1960, p. 169). After their appearance, they produced three children—Sitha, Nowa, and Nomkhubulwana, "the Princess who does not marry" (Bodenstein and Raum 1960, p.169). The earth is called Umhlaba. On the earth, the creator god erected four pillars. The creator god also created earths below the earth we see and heavens above the heaven we see. One of the Zulu informants said (Bodenstein and Raum 1960, p. 172), "Just as if you reach the horizon you always find another one beyond, so it is with the vault of heaven!"

A Zulu woman described Nomkhubulwana, the daughter of Umvelinqangi, as a heavenly princess (Berglund 1976, p. 70): "She loves human beings. So she opens the heaven, allowing them to see things in there. That is when the rainbow is seen. It is when she ... lets them see it. The arches are the colours. They are beautiful having all the colours." When the people see the rainbow, they say, "The Princess surely loves us. Now the rain will stop and give us sunshine. Then after a time she will bring rain again."

In the early days, the first humans saw her directly. Now she is rarely seen. If she meets a man, she hides and asks him to turn his back and not look at her because she is naked. If one looks at her, one will become sick and die very soon. But she will sometimes speak, and her messages have great importance. She may tell a man in his garden, "This year you shall have food; although for a long time there has been famine, it shall be so no longer" (Callaway 1870, p. 254). She also gives various instructions, which the Zulu do not hesitate to follow. She is apparently sometimes seen by women. Krige (1968, p. 180) says, "A woman who claims to have met her this spring (1966) described her as a tall human figure in the mist near a thicket almost completely covered by a cape, greyish black in colour like the rain clouds." She is also seen partially dressed with vegetable plants, reflecting her powers over agriculture.

The various forces of nature are also seen as manifestations of living entities. A Zulu man's home was struck by lightning, and afterwards he claimed to have seen a lightning creature. He said (Berglund 1976, p. 39), "We were all in the house when suddenly the door was flung open and lightning came in, taking this one and that one.... Looking, I saw the thing. It was fearful to see and moved very quickly. But I saw it clearly. It was a bird. The feathers were white, burning. The beak and legs were red with fire, and the tail was something else, like burning green or like the colour of the sky. It ran quickly, saying nothing, simply snatching those whom it took. Then it touched the grass with its fire. It vanished through the door again."

Concerning the origin of humans, Raum (1973, p. 76) says: "The Zulu do not consider that mankind originated by sexual reproduction but by a process resembling vegetative reproduction. There occurred a hiving-off, a division from a pre-existing entity. This entity is either called *uhlanga* (reed-bed) or *umhlaba* (earth). The agent responsible for the splitting off is Unkulunkulu." Because humans are said to have come from a reed, reeds are held sacred and can only be cut by permission of a Zulu chief (Raum 1973, p. 76). Unkulunkulu is not directly part of any particular Zulu tribal lineage, but is the origin of all of them (Raum 1973, p. 76). It appears that there were sub-Unkulunkulus who were the creators of the members of specific tribes and races in addition to the "Unkulunkulu of all men" (Callaway 1870, p. 96).

Among the Zulu are female "diviners," who give medicines and perform cures. They are called *isangoma*. In her book *Body and Mind in Zulu Medicine,* Harriet Ngubane (1977, p. 102) says: "A person does not choose to become a diviner (*isangoma*), but is said to be chosen by her ancestors, who bestow upon her clairvoyant powers. A neophyte learns about medicine from a qualified diviner to whom she is apprenticed for some time, but in addition some medicines are said to be revealed to her by her ancestors. I have already mentioned that the ancestral spirits do not take possession of the body, but they are close to the diviner—they 'sit' on her shoulders and whisper into her ears."

The Zulus also have various categories of "doctors." Some cure diseases with the aid of spirits. Another kind of doctor, the heaven doctor, operates on the weather and other natural forces, relying on his own knowledge of magic. Such doctors are often called heaven herds, because they herd storm clouds, with their dangerous lightning and hail, just like boys herd cattle. Eileen Jensen Krige (1968, p. 310) says, "They run out with their weapons and rain-shields and shout to the lightning, telling it to depart and go elsewhere, and whistling as cattle-herds do. No matter how old a heaven-doctor may be, he is always called 'a young man who herds.'"

Part of the lore of sorcery and magic are "familiars," spirits, often embodied in animals, who serve witches or wizards. The most important familiar among the Zulus is the wild cat called *impaka*. It can take control of dogs, cattle, snakes and other animals, inducing them to cause trouble to targeted people. Krige says (1968, p. 325), "To expel the animal and discover the wizard, a diviner will immediately be employed."

The Zulu concept of the life-soul is connected with a person's reflection. The Zulus hesitate to look at their reflection in a dark pool of water, fearing that a beast hidden in the pool will take it, thus depriving them of life (Raum 1973, p. 123). A pregnant woman believes she gives life to her child through her reflection. By custom, she therefore keeps a water pot in which only she can look. If someone else looks, the stranger may take away the child's life. The reflecting surfaces of lakes and rivers are considered gateways to other worlds. One who loses one's life in the water may find a new life on the other side of the surface (Raum 1973, p. 123). The Zulu also believe that the life-soul (called *iklozi* or *ithongo*) is connected with a person's shadow (*ithunzi*). After death the shadow passes some time in the bush or veld. The name for the dead is *abaphansi,* the people below. The departed ancestors depend on the prayers and sacrifices offered by their descendants, who in turn depend on the intercession of their ancestors. Raum (1973, p. 76) says that the ancestors "have control over the good and bad fortune of their descendants."

Cosmology of the Igbo of West Africa

The Igbo people of West Africa live mostly in the present day country of Nigeria. According to the Igbo, each human being has a spirit double called the *chi*. Anthropologist Charles Kingsley Meek (1970, p. 55) states that the *chi* is a "transcendent self" and "closely resembles the Egyptian conception of the *ka,* which was the double or genius of a man, an ancestral emanation, apparently, which guided and protected him during his lifetime and to which he returned after death." Conceptions of the *chi* vary somewhat, but Okpewho (1998, pp. 90–91) says: "It is at least generally recognized that *chi* is the spirit which helps the protoself negotiate a prenatal destiny before the supreme divinity; it either remains in the spiritual world to ensure the individual's welfare as (s)he acts out his/her choice or accompanies him/her to the world as some kind of protective spirit-double."

The connection between person and *chi* is established at the time of conception. The Igbo, who believe in reincarnation, say that the *chi* in one life is different from that in the next. This might result in a person being rich in one lifetime and poor in another. Further describing the *chi,* Meek (1970, p. 55) says, "A man's abilities, faults, and good or bad fortune are ascribed to his *chi,* and this explains, to some extent, the fatalistic attitude of the Ibo. If a man's conduct gets him into trouble he excuses himself by saying (and believing) that his *chi* and not himself is responsible." Animals also have their *chi*. When an Igbo hunter finds his arrow misses its animal target, he attributes this to the protective action of the animal's *chi*. Meek (1970, p. 55) adds: "An animal may become the *chi* of a man, and people who behave in a brutal manner are believed to have the *chi* of an animal. It is said that the children of hunters are liable to have the *chi* of animals slain by their fathers. In this way animals revenge themselves on men."

The *chi* is, however, different from the real self. According to Ogbuene (1999, p. 112), the unchanging spirit self is called *mmuo*—the spirit that activates all living things. For the Igbo, says Ogbuene (1999, p. 112), "Reality is the hierarchy of Mmuos—spirits, which all originate from Chukwu, the ultimate Mmuo-Spirit." Departed ancestors are called *alammuo*—spirits alive in the spirit world, but dead in this world (Ogbuene 1999, p. 112). But such spirits can return to this world. Ogbuene (1999, p. 116) says: "Parents and relatives who knew a spirit in a former existence will recognize that spirit in a new incarnation and can recall the events of that spirit's life. We believe that many children are born resembling their past spirits closely."

The body that the soul inhabits is called *aru* (Ogbuene 1999, p. 164). There is also another element connected with a living thing—*obi*, which Ogbuene (1999, p. 164) characterizes as breath, and which Meek (1930, p. 56) characterizes as a person's "vital essence." Ogbuene (1999, p. 164) also recognized an element called *eke*, which he calls "the ancestral guardian." *Mmuo, chi, aru, obi,* and *eke* might be compared respectively to the Vedic concepts of *atma* (individual spirit soul), *mana* (subtle material body), *deha* (gross physical body), *prana* (vital air), and *paramatma* (the accompanying Supersoul).

The Igbo feel a close connection with their departed ancestors. The living behave as if the dead were still with them. Victor Chikenzie Uchendu (1965, p. 102) writes about the spirits of the dead: "They are reprimanded for failing in their duty to their children, by closing their eyes to the depredations of evil spirits which cause death in the family, cause crop failure, and make trade unprofitable." In simple household rituals, they are offered ordinary foods. According to Igbo beliefs, their ancestors sometimes reincarnate again in their same families. Uchendu (1965, p. 102) notes, "Belief in reincarnation [rebirth in human form] gives the Igbo hope of realizing their frustrated status goals in the next cycle of life. Transmigration [reincarnation into nonhuman species], on the other hand, is regarded as the greatest possible punishment for the incestuous, the murderer, the witch, and the sorcerer. *'lsdigh uwa na mmadu'* 'May you not reincarnate in the human form'—is a great curse for the Igbo." This corresponds with Vedic concepts of reincarnation, in which those souls who have accumulated bad karma reincarnate in lower forms, such as those of animals.

Among the Igbo, certain animals are sacred or taboo for certain kin groups. For example, at Lokpanta the leopard is sacred to the Um-Ago kinship group. Um-Ago means "the children of leopards." The Um-Ago do not kill leopards or eat their flesh, believing that if anyone did so, that person would die untimely. Members of the Um-Ago are said to possess the ability to become leopards and act against enemies by killing their livestock (Meek 1970, p. 252).

The Igbo also have a belief in shape-changing children. If a child cannot walk or crawl by the age of three, the Igbo conclude that it is a creature that has come from a river or stream. Among one group of Igbo, the child is taken to a nearby river, along with an offering of a plate of mashed yams, whereupon, it is said, the child turns into a python and glides into the water. In another Igbo group, a ceremony for such a child takes place in the house. Sometimes the child turns into a snake, and in that case it is killed. Sometimes the child turns into a monkey. Northcote W. Thomas wrote in his anthropological report on the Igbo (1914, p. 29): "A changeling is known as *nwa di mwo,* and I have been seriously assured by more than one person that they have actually seen the transformation."

The gods of the Igbo are described as follows by Charles Kingsley Meek (1970, p. 20): "Firstly, there is a pantheon of high gods, headed by Chuku or Chineke the Supreme Spirit, Anyanu (the Sun), Igwe (the Sky), Amadi-Oha (Lightning), and Ala (the Earth deity). Then there are innumerable minor deities: water and agricultural godlings; spirits which are the personification of fortune, destiny, wealth, strength, divination, and evil; spirits which are the counterparts of living human beings; and finally the ancestors, who control the fortunes of their living descendants. The Supreme Being, or it might be more correct to say the Supreme Spirit or World-Oversoul, is known as Chuku, a word which is a contraction of Chi=Spirit and uku=great. . . . In his creative aspect he is known as Chineke, or Chukwoke, or Chi-Okike."

Ogbuene (1999, pp. 113–114), like Meek, makes a distinction between Chukwu or Chuku ("God, the big Spirit . . . the first ancestor . . . the self existent Being and wellspring of all that exists") and Chineke ("God the creator"). In the Vedic cosmology there is a similar distinction between Krishna, the Supreme Personality of Godhead, known as the source of everything, and the creator god Brahma, who, using the ingredients supplied by Krishna, manifests the earth and other celestial bodies in the universe. Okpewho (1998, p. 90) believes that the traditional God concept of today's Igbo has been to some extent influenced by Christian missionaries, but even Okpewho accepts there is some kind of "supreme divinity" and gives traditional accounts of humans meeting with a personal God (1998, pp. 73–74). As Okpewho puts it (1998, p. 74): "It is significant ... that the Ijo [Igbo] imagination can conceive of an encounter with the supreme divinity." Ogbuene (1999, p. 108) states that "Chukwu ... is a God who acts and speaks, from whom help and assistance is sought in sacrifices." At the same time he is indescribable, and is therefore sometimes called Ama-ama-Amasi Amasi, "One who is known but can never be fully known." Ogbuene (1999, p. 108) says, "This is different from saying that Chukwu could be anything at all, or nothing. It is rather saying there is a reality which cannot be described; but towards which His actions point."

Of Chukwu, Meek (1970, p. 20) says: "He is the author of heaven and earth, he sends the rain, makes the crops grow, and is the source from which men derive their *chi* or accompanying soul. He is the father of the gods, for some at least of the gods are said to be his 'sons'. But he is a distant deity of vague personality, and sacrifice is seldom offered to him directly. Yet he is regarded as the ultimate recipient of all sacrifices. Thus, if sacrifice is offered to Anyanu, the officiant asks Anyanu to accept the sacrifice and bear it to Chuku."

This relationship of the minor Igbo gods to the high god Chuku is similar to the relationship among gods found in our template Vedic cosmology. In the *Bhagavad Gita* (9. 23), Krishna, the Supreme God, says, "Those who are devotees of other gods and who worship them with faith actually worship only Me, O son of Kunti, but they do so in a wrong way."

According to Ogbuene (1999, p. 109), the various gods and creatures, including Chineke, are seen as simultaneously one with and different from Chukwu: "The Igbo recognizes that Chukwu is one, vast, and that He informs and unifies every other being. The so-called gods or spirits are not themselves Chukwu, but simply reflect certain aspects of His principles, ways and consciousness." This is remarkably similar to the doctrine of inconceivable simultaneous oneness and difference (*acintya-bhedaabeda-tattva*), characteristic of the school of Vedic philosophical thought to which I adhere (Gaudiya Vaishnavism). The teachers of this school explain that just as the rays of the sun are simultaneously one with and different from the sun, all souls are simultaneously one with and different from the Supreme Soul.

According to the Vedic cosmology, God, Krishna, has three features: *sat*, the feature of eternal existence; *cit*, the feature of unlimited knowledge; and *ananda,* the feature of ever increasing transcendental pleasure. This last feature is manifested in loving exchanges of spiritual pleasure between Krishna and His eternal associates. These exchanges are characterized as *nitya-lila,* eternal pastimes. Material loving affairs are considered imperfect reflections of the original spiritual pastimes. Chukwu, the supreme god of the Igbo, also displays the three features of existence, knowledge and pleasure pastimes. The existence feature of Chukwu is displayed as Okike, in which "He is manifested in the creation of everything visible and invisible" (Ogbuene 1999, p. 109). The sum total of everything that exists, material and spiritual, as well as existence itself, is called *ife* (Obguene 1999, p. 112). Chukwu also displays a knowledge feature. According to Ogbuene (1999, p. 110), "Chukwu is a living God who knows the secrets of all hearts." Ogbuene (1999, p. 163) goes on to say, "The Supreme Being Chukwu is not only an ocean of consciousness [knowledge] and being [existence], but also an ocean of love and bliss. His purpose in creation is to play the game of love with Himself, through his creatures but in different capacities."

Humans are called *oke-chukwu,* which means "the portion from Chukwu." When Chukwu manifested the first humans, he uttered *mmadu,* "may beauty be" (Ogbuene 1999, p. 160). According to Ogbuene (1999, p. 162), the Igbo believe that "*mmadu* manifests the divine thought, translates the infinite into the finite, the divine spirit into sensory phenomena." Humans are the creatures closest to God, and their relationship to God, Chukwu, is established by *aja,* sacrifice and prayer. "Every day, first thing in the morning, a typical traditional Igbo family gives gratitude to Chukwu in the form of prayers. This is introduced by the washing of the hands, making lines on the floor with *Nzu*—a kind of white chalk, and sometimes painting the toes with the substance. The colour white symbolizes the pure, the unspotted, the spiritual" (Ogbuene 1999, p. 235).

The universe of the Igbo, with its multiplicity of gods and spirits, is highly personalized. Richard Neal Henderson (1972, p. 117) wrote: "Men know that there are gods, spirits and ghosts . . . and know that the agencies may act upon them directly. However, while the courses of human lives and communities are presumed to be set by these wills, they are largely unknown to men. Men therefore continually seek to bring them into personal or public awareness through acts of communication." This communication is facilitated by "messenger spirits" such as the vulture.

The Igbo cosmology has several levels or worlds. Different accounts mention various numbers of worlds—eight, seven, or four. Henderson (1972, p. 109) states that "from the viewpoint of men occupying this one, the other worlds are all 'lands of the dead' into which all persons who die should subsequently be incarnated." These other worlds are also the sources of souls incarnating into this world of our experience. The Igbo consider themselves to be in rather constant communication with these other worlds and their inhabitants, who retain an interest in the affairs of this world. Some of the dead, who have retained too much attachment to this world, remain here as ghosts. Henderson (1972, p. 109) states that "these are the 'bad dead' who have violated the world order."

Final Remarks on Multilevel Cosmology

Our "test drillings" in the field of cosmologies of various peoples throughout the world reveal some significant degree of family resemblance to our template Vedic cosmology. We find that humans and other living entities are possessed of souls that survive the death of the gross physical body. We find that in addition to a gross physical body, living entities have a subtle material body, through which the soul can act in ways that surpass actions performed through the medium of the gross physical body alone. We find that humans exist as part of a cosmic hierarchy of beings, in a multilevel cosmos. At the topmost level, we find a supreme conscious being, living in a purely spiritual domain. We find a creator god, who manifests the bodies and dwelling places for souls who enter the world of matter. We find that this creator god is assisted by many other demigods and demigoddesses. We find that souls can travel from body to body, and from level to level of the cosmos, by transmigration or other forms of travel.

8

APPARITIONS, ANGELS, AND ALIENS

Sometimes when hiking, one looks back on the route traversed before moving onward. In this book, we began our journey with a review of evidence for extreme human antiquity. This archeological evidence, which contradicts current Darwinian theories of human evolution, suggested that we need to look for a new explanation for the origin of human beings. But before starting to look, we decided we should first answer the question "what is a human being?" In that way, we could be sure that any explanation we proposed actually did the job of explaining what needed to be explained. Today, many scientists assume that a human being is simply a combination of matter, by which we mean the elements listed in the periodic table. But we saw that it is more reasonable to start with the assumption that a human being is composed of three distinct things: matter, mind, and consciousness (or spirit). We saw that modern science itself provides sufficient evidence for this assumption. Therefore, if we are going to explain the origin of human beings, we have to explain from where matter, mind, and consciousness each came and how they came together in the form of human beings. The existence of matter, mind, and consciousness in the human form suggests that the cosmos is arranged in regions where matter predominates, where mind predominates, and where consciousness predominates. In other words, there is a multilevel inhabited cosmos, in which we humans find our particular place. We reviewed testimonial evidence for this multilevel cosmos in classical Western culture, and then showed how this same understanding has been present historically in varieties of cultures throughout the world. This multilevel cosmos is inhabited by varieties of extraterrestrial and extradimensional humanlike beings.

Up to this point, the evidence I have cited for the existence of these extraterrestrial and extradimensional beings has consisted of reports from peoples of the distant past, or from peoples of today who are not totally integrated into modern developed society. In this chapter, our sources will be mostly observations from persons representative of modern developed society, from the dawn of modern science to the present. This evidence adds credibility to traditional accounts of extraterrestrial and extradimensional beings, who, I propose, are responsible for producing the bodily forms of the living things within our normal experience. In chapter 9, we will see that it is in fact possible to produce changes in biological organisms by the action of mind and consciousness on matter. In chapter 10, we will consider the cosmological anthropic principle, some versions of which entail the idea that the entire universe has been designed with human existence in mind. And in chapter 11, I will bring together all the elements of the human devolution concept—the concept that we have not evolved up from matter, but have devolved from pure consciousness, or spirit, in a process guided by intelligent agents. I will relate various parts of this argument to their sources in the ancient Vedic writings of India, which inspired and guided my research.

In this chapter's review of various categories of observational and experimental evidence demonstrating the existence of extradimensional, conscious, humanlike personalities, we will begin with examples of communications from departed humans now apparently existing in some other part of the multilevel cosmos. We shall then consider apparitions of departed human personalities and possessions of terrestrial humans by departed human personalities. Reports like these reinforce the evidence presented in chapter 6 for the existence of an embodied conscious self that is distinct from mind and ordinary matter. But the cases in this chapter particularly focus on the continued existence of this conscious self long after the death of its body composed of gross matter. We shall go on to consider another category of apparition and possession cases, involving beings of apparently superhuman type. We shall then consider the modern scientific search for extraterrestrial intelligence, which will lead us into the realm of extraterrestrial and extradimensional beings revealed in the modern UFO and alien abduction reports, particularly those with a paranormal element. In this manner, I plan to show that the idea of extraterrestrial and extradimensional conscious beings is not something entirely alien to modern scientific thought.

Communications from Departed Humans

Several prominent scientists have investigated communications from departed humans. If their reports are accepted, we find ourselves in possession of evidence for some part of the multilevel cosmos and cosmic hierarchy of beings described in the last chapter.

Evidence of departed human intelligences continuing to have contact with terrestrial humans comes from a variety of sources, including mediums. William James, a prominent American scientist of the early twentieth century, and one of the founders of modern psychology, was especially impressed by the mediumship of Mrs. Piper.

During her trances, Mrs. Piper's normal personality was apparently replaced by that of her "control," a long departed spirit called Phinuit, who spoke through her, revealing paranormal knowledge of living persons. However, not everyone was convinced that Phinuit either existed or was the source of Mrs. Piper's revelations about the living. For example, Richard Hodgson, of the American Society for Psychical Research, at first favored the hypothesis that Mrs. Piper was obtaining her knowledge telepathically from living persons. But in March 1892, Mrs. Piper's communicator Phinuit was replaced by George Pellew, a young man who had died in a riding accident a short time before. One hundred fifty living subjects were introduced to Mrs. Piper when, in trance, she was under the control of Pellew. Out of these subjects, Pellew, speaking through Mrs. Piper, recognized thirty, and these thirty happened to be only those who had known Pellew when he was alive. Pellew conversed with them in a familiar fashion, demonstrating extraordinary knowledge about them. This convinced Hodgson that Mrs.Piper was indeed in communication with a departed spirit, George Pellew (Gauld 1968, pp. 254–261).

Hodgson himself died on December 20, 1905. By December 28, messages from him were supposedly coming to Mrs. Piper. William James believed that the evidence suggested Hodgson, or perhaps some remnant of him (in what we might call a cosmic memory bank), was communicating with Piper. The messages communicated by Piper from Hodgson, and others, were sometimes garbled, observed James. He nevertheless said that "there would still appear a balance of probability . . . that certain parts of the Piper communications really emanate from personal centers of memory and will, connected with lives that have passed away" (Murphy and Ballou 1960, p. 140). More specifically, he said, "Most of us felt during the sittings that we were in some way, more or less remote, conversing with . . . a real Hodgson" (Murphy and Ballou 1960, p. 143).

James said about the Piper communications: "When I connect the Piper case with all the other cases I know of automatic writing and mediumship, and with the whole record of spirit-possession in human history, the notion that such an immense current of experience, complex in so many ways, should spell out nothing but the word 'humbug' acquires a character of unlikeliness. The notion that so many men and women, in all other respects honest enough, should have this preposterous monkeying self annexed to their personality seems to me so weird that the spirit theory immediately takes on a more probable appearance" (Murphy and Ballou 1960, p. 147).

Frederick Myers, a leading member of the Society for Psychical Research (SPR), died in 1901. In that same year, Mrs. Margaret Verrall, the wife of the English classical scholar A. W. Verrall, took up automatic writing to let Myers communicate through her. In automatic writing, a medium allows her hand to form letters and words spontaneously. After some months Mrs. Verrall began getting cryptic messages signed by Myers, some with quotations from obscure Latin and Greek works. In 1902, Mrs. Piper, in Boston, also began producing similar writings signed "Myers." These contained allusions to Mrs. Verrall's writings. Mrs. Verrall's daughter, Helen Verrall, also began receiving writings, without seeing her mother's. Helen's writings contained allusions to the same topics. Piper and the Verralls began sending their writings to Alice Johnson, secretary of the SPR. In 1903, Mrs. Alice Kipling Fleming, a sister of Rudyard Kipling, also began receiving messages from Myers through automatic writing. She began sending them to Johnson, under the name "Mrs. Holland." Johnson filed them away, but in 1905 she began comparing the messages from all the writers and noticed some interesting correlations among them. Johnson and other investigators concluded that these "cross correspondences" were deliberate attempts by Myers to demonstrate his survival (Griffin 1997, pp. 162–163).

Purported communications from dead persons through mediums are sometimes explained away by appealing to telepathy. A medium engaging in automatic writing may consciously or unconsciously tap into memories of various living persons who knew the dead person and thus obtain the confidential information that appears in the messages. In other words, although the information in the message may have been acquired by paranormal means, the information might not be coming from a surviving spirit. One might therefore ask, "How could a dead person attempting to communicate with the living overcome this objection?"

H. F. Saltmarsh, in his book on the Myers communications, explained (1938, pp. 33–34): "Suppose a message in cryptic terms be transmitted through one automatist [receiver of automatic writing], and another message, equally incomprehensible, through a second at about the same time, and suppose that each automatist was ignorant of what the other was writing, we have then two meaningless messages entirely disconnected with each other. Now, if a third automatist were to produce a script which, while meaningless taken by itself, acts as a clue to the other two, so that the whole set could be brought together into one whole, and then show a single purpose and meaning, we should have good evidence that they all originated from a single source. . . . Telepathy between the automatists . . . would not explain these facts, for none of them is able to understand the meaning of their own particular fragment, and so could not possibly convey to the other automatists the knowledge required to supply the missing portions. In most cases [involving the Myers communications] the puzzle . . . has been solved by an independent investigator, in fact, frequently the automatists themselves have remained in ignorance of any scripts but their own." In other words, the cross correspondences among the independent communications, each apparently meaningless on its own, reveals the action of a departed intelligence.

Here is an example of such a cross correspondence. Early in 1907, Mrs. Margaret Verrall got a communication from the departed Myers that mentioned "celestial halcyon days." This inspired her to telepathically send back to Myers a Greek quotation from Plotinus: *autos ouranos akumon*, which means "the very heavens waveless" (Saltmarsh 1938, p. 73). In the passage in which this phrase occurs, Plotinus had said that the soul, in order to attain enlightenment, must be peaceful, that the earth, sea, and air should be calm, and "the very heavens waveless." Verrall knew that Myers had used this Greek phrase as a motto for a poem he had written about Tennyson. She also knew that he had included an English translation of the phrase in his book *Human Personality and Its Survival of Bodily Death.* Mrs. Verrall telepathically sent the phrase to Myers on January 29, 1907, in the presence of the medium Mrs. Piper.

On January 30, Mrs. Verrall noticed the names of the trees "larch" and "laburnum" appearing close to each other in a communication to Mrs. Piper from Myers (Saltmarsh 1938, p. 74). She recalled that these trees are mentioned in a poem by Tennyson, "In Memoriam." The verse that mentioned larches ended with the line "the sea-blue bird of March." This is the kingfisher, and another name for the kingfisher is halcyon. According to ancient legend, when the kingfisher nests by the sea around the time of the winter solstice, this causes the seas to become calm and waveless, recalling the phrase from Plotinus, *autos ouranos akumon* ("the very heavens waveless"). Mrs. Verrall believed that Myers was deliberately responding to her by introducing these subtle allusions into his communications with Mrs. Piper.

On February 25, Mrs. Verrall received another phrase from Tennyson: "the lucid interspace of world and world." On February 26, the communication from Myers contained the above mentioned quotation from Plotinus (*autos ouranos akumon*) written in Greek characters. The script also contained these words: "And may there be no moaning of the bar—my pilot face to face." This was a reference to Tennyson's poem "Crossing the Bar." The names of Tennyson and Browning were also in the script. On March 6, Mrs. Verrall's script from Myers contained many references to calm, including a passage from "In Memoriam" by Tennyson: "And in my heart if calm at all. If any calm, a calm despair." In her final script in this series, produced on March 11, one can, according to Saltmarsh (1938, p. 75), find allusions to Plato and Tennyson, with "phrases about unseen and half-seen companionship—voiceless communings—unseen presence felt." Tennyson's poem "In Memoriam" is about the poet communing with a departed friend. That these particular references should appear in the Myers scripts is, of course, meaningful, especially in the context of the complicated connections between Plotinus, Tennyson, the Greek phrase about the stillness of the heavens, and the many references to stillness and calm that appeared in the scripts. Some of these connections were discovered long after the scripts were produced.

Cross correspondences to these references in the communications to Mrs. Verrall occurred in separate communications received by Mrs. Piper. On March 6, 1907, these words from Myers appeared in the Piper communications: "Cloudless sky horizon, followed by a cloudless sky beyond the horizon; in the waking stage following came the words: moaning at the bar when I put out to sea . . . Goodbye. Margaret." Mrs. Verrall's name was Margaret. The references to calm heavens and the bar are strikingly similar to images in the scripts of Mrs. Verrall, which are references to Tennyson's poems "In Memoriam" and "Crossing the Bar." According to Saltmarsh (1938, p. 77), neither Mrs. Piper nor the person sitting with her during this session, Mr. Piddington, had enough knowledge to bring these obscure literary allusions together on their own. Saltmarsh (1938, p. 77) also said, "As regards Mrs. Verrall, it must be noted that she had not grasped the significance of the combination of quotations from 'In Memoriam' and 'Crossing the Bar' until after this sitting with Mrs. Piper." So that means it would not have been possible for Mrs. Piper to access this information from Mrs. Verrall's mind by some kind of telepathic process, indicating that the best explanation for the information was the surviving persona of Myers himself.

On April 29, Mrs. Verrall sat with Mrs. Piper, whose scripts revealed not only words connected with "halcyon days" but also some mysterious and apparently disconnected references to Swedenborg, St. Paul, and Dante. On the next day, Myers, in a script produced by Mrs. Piper, said the Greek quotation from Plotinus reminded him of Socrates and Homer's *Iliad*. The connection between Plotinus, who lived in the third century AD, and Socrates, who lived in the fourth century BC, and Homer, who lived in the eighth century BC, was not immediately apparent. On May 1, Mrs. Verrall's automatic writing session produced the words "eagle soaring over the tomb of Plato." Mrs. Verrall recalled that Myers, in his book *Human Personality*, had used this phrase to describe Plotinus. Investigating further, she found that in the epilogue to *Human Personality*, Myers had mentioned a vision of Plotinus. Just before this comes the story of how Socrates had a vision of a fair woman dressed in white robes. (This story is from Plato's *Krito*.) The woman in the vision of Socrates recites a line from the *Iliad* of Homer. Saltmarsh (1938, p. 78) notes: "A further, and even more significant discovery was made. On the same page that contains the phrase 'eagle soaring over the tomb of Plato,' there is a list of 'the strong souls who have claimed to feel it' (ecstasy) and among these, after Plotinus and before Tennyson occur Swedenborg, St. Paul and Dante." So here we can see that elements in the scripts of one medium gave clues to the meaning of elements in the scripts of another medium, which at first appeared meaningless, showing all the elements were known to Myers and associated by him in particular ways in obscure passages of his written works. Finally, on May 6, 1907, SPR member Mrs. Henry Sidgwick was about to ask Myers the name of the author of the Greek phrase originally sent to him by Mrs. Verrall. But Myers interrupted her inquiry, saying, through a script recorded by Mrs. Piper, "Will you say to Mrs. V. [Verrall] Plotinus?" Myers then said this was "my answer to *autos ouranos akumon*" (Saltmarsh 1938, p. 78).

Explaining the significance of this case, Saltmarsh (1938, pp. 78–79) says: "It seems to me to be one of the best examples which we have of the complex type of cross correspondence. The knowledge shown in the Piper sittings was completely outside Mrs. Piper's own range, also was unknown to the sitter, Mr. Piddington and to Mrs. Verrall, but it had been in the possession of Fred Myers and was characteristic of him. The answers given were allusive and indirect, and thus avoided the possibility of explanation by direct telepathy; moreover, on more than one occasion the scripts themselves gave guidance to the investigators by supplying the necessary clues which led them to discover the associations, as, for example, when the phrase 'eagle soaring over the tomb of Plato' directed Mrs. Verrall's attention to that part of *Human Personality* where she found the unlikely association between Plotinus, Socrates, Homer, Swedenborg, etc."

Saltmarsh studied a huge amount of the Myers cross correspondence scripts, which accumulated over thirty years from many different mediums. He pointed out, "Were we to find in the scripts of several automatists one or two scattered cases of cross correspondence, we might reasonably attribute them to chance coincidence, but should they occur in large numbers, the tenability of that hypothesis is much lessened. Further, when this large number of cross correspondences is accompanied by definite indications of intention, and indeed, by explicit statements in the scripts that they are parts of a planned experiment, then explanation by chance alone can be confidently rejected" (Saltmarsh 1938, p. 126). And this is indeed the case with the Myers material, from which I have selected only one of hundreds of examples. That leaves survival of the Myers personality after death as the best explanation for the cross correspondences. The list of intricate cross correspondences in the communications received by various mediums in this particular case goes on and on. Interested readers should consult Saltmarsh's book to get an idea of their full impact.

Sir William F. Barrett (1918, pp. 184–185), a physicist and Fellow of the Royal Society, was a founder of the Society for Psychical Research. He investigated an interesting case of communication with the dead. During the First World War, Mrs. Travers Smith, wife of a prominent Dublin medical doctor, and Miss C., daughter of another medical man, were attempting, with others, to establish communication with the dead through an ouija board. In using an ouija board, one places one's fingers lightly on a movable pointer, and the spontaneous movements of the pointer toward letters printed on the board spell out words. Miss C.'s cousin, an officer in the British Army, had been killed in France a month before the sittings. During one sitting, the name of the dead officer was unexpectedly spelled out by the ouija board. Miss C. then asked, "Do you know who I am?" In reply came her name and the following message: "Tell mother to give my *pearl tie-pin* to the girl I was going to marry, I think she ought to have it." None of the sitters knew of this engagement. They asked for the name and address of the girl. The full name of the girl was given, along with an address in London. But when the sitters sent a letter to that address, it was returned as undeliverable. The sitters concluded the message had not been genuine. Six months later, the sitters learned from personal papers of the deceased officer sent by the War Office that he had in fact been engaged to the very lady whose name was given by the ouija board communication. She was mentioned in the officer's will. The officer had, however, never mentioned her to any of his relatives. Among his personal effects there was a pearl tie pin. Barrett (1918, p. 185) noted "Both the ladies have signed a document they sent me, affirming the accuracy of the above statement. The message was recorded at the time, and *not* written from memory after verification had been obtained. Here there could be no explanation of the facts by subliminal memory, or telepathy or collusion, and the evidence points unmistakably to a telepathic message from the deceased officer."

Sir Oliver Joseph Lodge (1851–1940) made important contributions to research in electromagnetic radiation and radio communications. He also documented a famous case of communication with a departed human, his son Raymond. In his biographical encyclopedia of famous scientists, Isaac Asimov (1982, p. 530) wrote about Lodge: "He became a leader of psychical research, and is one of the prime examples of a serious scientist entering a field that is usually the domain of quacks." I don't agree with Asimov that psychical research is the domain of quacks. The number of serious scientists conducting psychical research, and getting positive results, is quite impressive. It is Asimov's statement that seems rather quacklike.

Lodge (1916, p. 83) wrote: "I have made no secret of my conviction, not merely that personality persists, but that its continued existence is more entwined with the life of every day than has been generally imagined; that there is no real breach of continuity between the dead and the living; and that methods of intercommunication across what has seemed to be a gulf can be set going in response to the urgent demand of affection."

On September 17, 1915, Lodge received news of his son Raymond's death in military action in Europe during World War I. On September 25, Mrs. Lodge was having a sitting with a medium, Mrs. Leonard. At that time, Mrs. Lodge's identity was unknown to the medium. The medium and her guests were sitting at a round table. The medium would begin to recite the letters of the alphabet until the table tilted. The letter sounded at the moment of the tilt would be recorded, and then the process would be repeated until a message was spelled out. (This may seem less quaint in light of today's handheld internet communication devices, which compel one to spell out messages in ways hardly less cumbersome and time consuming.) From the standpoint of spiritualists, the tilting of the table was accomplished by the departed spirits. Skeptics would claim the medium controlled the table and composed messages using surreptitiously obtained information about the living and the dead. To counter such doubts, one has to demonstrate that the medium had no knowledge of the persons involved, as appears to be the case here. During her anonymous séance with Mrs. Leonard, Mrs. Lodge received the following message from a spirit called Raymond: "Tell father I have met some friends of his." Mrs. Lodge asked for the name of one of these friends. Raymond gave the name Myers, the departed psychical researcher, who was in fact known to Lodge.

On September 27, Lodge himself showed up for a sitting, which had been arranged anonymously through a Mrs. Kennedy. According to Lodge, Mrs. Leonard did not know his identity. At this sitting, the communication with departed spirits was not through table tilting, but through the medium's contact with her control, a young girl named Feda. When the medium went into trance, and came under the control of Feda, Lodge was told that there was present a young man, whose description matched Raymond. Feda said through Mrs. Leonard: "He finds it difficult, he says, but he has got so many kind friends helping him. He didn't think when he waked up first that he was going to be happy, but now he is, and as he is a little more ready he has got a great deal of work to do" (Lodge 1916, p. 98).

On September 28, Lodge and his wife together attended a sitting with Mrs. Leonard. The communication was through table tilting (Lodge 1916, pp. 140–142). The first spirit contacted was named Paul, who said, in answer to a question posed by Lodge, that, yes, he had brought Raymond. The next message from Paul said, "Raymond wants to come himself." Lodge asked Raymond to give the name of an officer. Lodge was anticipating that he would give the name of Lieutenant Case, who was one of the last persons to see Raymond alive, after he was wounded. Instead, Raymond spelled out the name Mitchell. Mrs. Lodge later said, "Raymond, I don't know Mitchell." Raymond answered, "No." Lodge then asked, "Well, that will be better evidence?" Raymond said, "Yes." Lodge asked, "Is that why you chose it?" Raymond again replied, "Yes." Raymond then gave three letters: "a," "e," and "r." The medium said, "No, that can't be right?" But the letters continued coming, spelling out the word "aeroplane." Lodge asked, "You mean that Mitchell is an aeroplane officer?" The answer was a firm "yes." Also, Lodge asked Raymond to give the name of a brother. The tilting table gave the letters "n," "o," "r," "m," and "a." Lodge interrupted the communication, thinking that the intended name, Norman, was a mistake. During this session, Lodge asked Raymond how he was working the table. The message, received letter by letter, was, "You all supply magnetism gathered in medium, and that goes into table, and we manipulate" (Lodge, 1916, p. 146).

The name "Mitchell" given by Raymond in connection with the word "aeroplane" was quite significant. No one present at the sitting knew an officer of that name. Lodge conducted extensive research, and for weeks obtained no results. Relevant personnel lists had not yet been published (Lodge 1916, p. 146). Lodge eventually did obtain some information about Mitchell: "After several failures at identification I learnt, on 10 October, through the kind offices of the Librarian of the London Library, that he had ascertained from the War Office that there was a 2nd Lieut. E. H. Mitchell now attached to the Royal Flying Corps. Accordingly, I wrote to the Record Office, Farnborough; and ultimately, on 6 November, received a post card from Captain Mitchell." In his letter to Lodge, Mitchell said "I believe I have met your son, though where I forget" (Lodge 1916, p. 149).

The name "Norman," of no apparent significance to Lodge and his wife when they heard it, turned out to be a name that Raymond used in a general way to refer to his brothers, especially when they were playing field hockey. This information was supplied to Lodge later by his surviving sons, who had not been present at the sitting (Lodge 1916, p. 147). The practice is believable to me, because I, and children in my neighborhood, jokingly used to do the same thing when I was young, using names such as "Holmes" to refer to almost anyone.

Some of the communications from Raymond gave interesting information about the spirit world. The following descriptions were obtained during a sitting Mrs. Lodge had with Mrs. Leonard on February 4, 1916. Raymond, speaking through the control Feda, indicated that the spirit world was divided into different spheres. For example, he said his sister (Lily) had "gone right on to a very high sphere, as near celestial as could possibly be" (Lodge 1916, p. 229). In the spirit world, like spirits gravitated towards each other. Raymond said, "I've seen some boys pass on who had nasty ideas and vices. They go to a place I'm very glad I didn't have to go to, but it's not hell exactly. More like a reformatory—it's a place where you're given a chance, and when you want to look for something better, you're given a chance to have it" (Lodge 1916, p. 230). Raymond himself was on a middle level, the third, called Summerland, or Homeland. Beings from higher realms could visit there, and the persons on Summerland could come to the earth. He called it a "happy medium" (Lodge 1916, p. 230).

Raymond told his mother he was once taken up to another level: "I was permitted, so that I might see what was going on in the Highest Sphere. . . . He [Christ] didn't come near me, and I didn't feel I wanted to go near him. Didn't feel I ought. The Voice was like a bell. I can't tell you what he was dressed or robed in. All seemed a mixture of shining colours" (Lodge 1916, pp. 230–231). Raymond explained that he was somehow transported back to Summerland, with a sense that he was to be engaged in a spiritual mission, "helping near the earth plane" (Lodge

1916, p. 232). He said, "I was told Christ was always in spirit on earth—a sort of projection, something like those rays, something of him in every one" (Lodge 1916, p. 232). Raymond said, "Some people ask me, are you pleased with where your body lies? I tell them I don't care a bit, I've no curiosity about my body now. It's like an old coat that I've done with, and hope some one will dispose of it. I don't want flowers on my body" (Lodge 1916, p. 235).

Lodge was concerned that many scientists would never take seriously any evidence for survival and other psychical phenomena. To such scientists, Lodge (1916, p. 379) addressed the following remarks: "They pride themselves on their hard-headed scepticism and robust common sense; while the truth is that they have bound themselves into a narrow cell by walls of sentiment, and have thus excluded whole regions of human experience from their purview."

In the case of Lodge and Raymond, the communicator, Raymond, was of course known to Lodge and others in the presence of the medium. There are, however, some cases in which communicators not known to the sitters or the medium "drop in" to séances. These are of interest because one cannot easily propose that the medium has obtained the knowledge revealed by the drop-in communicator from the other persons at the séance. Nor would the medium have much reason to manufacture such a personage, given that the sitters have come to her specifically to communicate with some departed friend or relative, well known to them, not some unknown person.

Ian Stevenson and Erlendur Haraldsson (1975a) report an interesting case from Iceland. The medium was Hafsteinn Bjornsson. In 1937, a group of people began having séances with Bjornsson at a private home in Reykjavik. In the course of the sittings, a drop-in began to communicate through Bjornsson. He refused to identify himself, giving obviously false names such as Jon Jonsson, the Icelandic equivalent of John Doe. When asked what he wanted, the communicator said, "I am looking for my leg," adding that it was "in the sea" (Haraldsson and Stevenson 1975a, p. 37). In the fall of 1938, the same communicator appeared in another series of sittings. He still asked for his leg and still refused to properly identify himself. In January 1939, Ludvik Gudmundsson started coming to the sittings. He owned a house in the village of Sandgerdi, near Reykjavik. The communicator seemed pleased that Gudmundsson was present, but Gudmundsson could not understand why this should be so. When asked about this, the communicator said that Gudmundsson had his leg in his house at Sandgerdi.

After Gudmundsson became impatient with the communicator's

refusal to identify himself, the communicator finally said in one sitting: "Well, it is best for me to tell you who I am. My name is Runolfur Runolfsson, and I was 52 years old when I died. I lived with my wife at Kolga or Klappakot, near Sandgerdi. I was on a journey from Keflavik in the latter part of the day and I was drunk. I stopped at the house of Sveinbjorn Thordarsson in Sandgerdi and accepted some refreshments there. When I wanted to go, the weather was so bad that they did not wish me to leave unless accompanied by someone else. I became angry and said I would not go at all if I could not go alone. My house was only about 15 minutes' walk away. So I left by myself, but I was wet and tired. I walked over the *kambinn* [beach pebbles] and reached the rock known as Flankastadaklettur which has almost disappeared now. There I sat down, took my bottle [of alcoholic spirits], and drank some more. Then I fell asleep. The tide came in and carried me away. This happened in October, 1879. I was not found until January 1880. I was carried in by the tide, but then dogs and ravens came and tore me to pieces. The remnants [of my body] were found and buried in Utskalar graveyard. But then the thigh bone was missing. It was carried out again to sea, but was later washed up again at Sandgerdi. There it was passed around and now it is in Ludvik's house" (Larusdottir, 1946, pp. 203–204; in Haraldsson and Stevenson 1975a, p. 39).

Runolfsson said that his account could be verified by looking at the records of the church in Utskalar. These records confirmed that a person bearing his name had in fact died on the date he had given, and also that the person was of the age given by him (Haraldsson and Stevenson 1975a, p. 40). Other records confirmed that he had lived at Klopp and later at another place near the Flankastadaklettur rock. And a report by a church clergyman said that the dismembered bones were found much later, apart from his clothes, which also washed up on the beach. But there was no mention of the missing leg bone. Gudmundsson asked old men in the village of Sandgerdi if they knew anything about any leg bones. Some of them recalled hearing something about a thigh bone being passed around. One of them said that he recalled something about a carpenter who put a leg bone in one of the walls of Gudmundsson's house. Gudmundsson and others looked around the house, trying to guess what wall might be concealing the bone. Someone made a suggestion, but the bone was not found. Later, the carpenter himself was located and he pointed out the place where he had put the bone, and the bone was found there (Haraldsson and Stevenson 1975a, p. 41). The femur was long, consistent with Runolfsson's statements in his communications that he was tall. The bone was found in 1940, three year's after Runolfsson first mentioned it. If this bone can be relocated, it may be possible to compare it genetically to the other buried bones of Runolfsson.

In 1969, a story about the case appeared in a Reykjavik newspaper, and a reader wrote in giving another source of information about Runolfsson's death. This was a manuscript written in the nineteenth century by Reverend Jon Thoraeson, who had been a clergyman in Utskalar at the time. The manuscript was, however, published in 1953, many years after the sittings in which Runolfsson revealed himself.

As far as the medium was concerned: (1) He said he had never been to Sangerdi or met anyone from there prior to the sittings connected with Runolfsson. (2) He had visited the National Archives, where some records related to the case are kept, in November 1939, but this was six months after Runolfsson had identified himself and told his story. (3) He had never read the Utskalar church records. In any case, in none of these accounts is the missing leg bone mentioned. Residents of Sandgerdi who did know about a leg bone had not connected it with Runolfsson, who was also known by the knickname Runki (Haraldsson and Stevenson 1975a, p. 43). Haraldsson and Stevenson (1975a, p. 57) concluded that the simplest explanation of all the facts was "Runki's survival after his physical death with retention of many memories and their subsequent communication through the mediumship of Hafsteinn."

Here is another case. On January 25, 1941, the medium Hafsteinn Bjornsson was holding a séance for Hjalmar Gudjonsson, who was expecting to hear from dead persons known to him. The medium's control was a spirit called Finna. But Finna, instead of passing on messages from persons known to Gudjonsson, passed on messages from a person unknown to him. This drop-in communicator, who called himself Gudni Magnusson, mentioned a place called Eskifjordur. He said he had died there from an accident involving a motor vehicle. Asmundur Gestsson, who heard about the drop-in communicator after the sitting, had a cousin, Gudrun Gudmundsdottir, who lived in Eskifjordur. Gudmundsdottir was married to a physician, Einar Astrads. On February 26, 1941, Gestsson wrote to his cousin, asking if her husband had ever treated a man named Gudni Magnusson. And if so, had the man died in an automobile accident? (Haraldsson and Stevenson 1975b, pp. 246–247)

On March 14, Gudrun Gudmundsdottir wrote back to Asmundur Gestsson, confirming that her husband had treated a man named Gudni Magnusson who had died, adding more details: "There is a married couple here [in Eskifjordur] by the name of Anna Jorgensen and Magnus Arngrimsson.... One of their sons ... who was about 20–21 years of age, was a truck driver and had been for the past two or three years. He had often worked with his father in road building. Last fall this young man, whose name was Gudni Magnusson, was very busy with his truck driving and he left in the morning to go to Vidifjordur, a rather long and strenuous journey. Then later in the day he went to Reydarfjordur. After reaching there he left for home. His truck was not running well and the trip took longer than usual. He was alone. When he was crossing the mountain pass between Reydarfjordur and Eskifjordur, the truck ran out of gasoline. So he left the truck and went down to Eskifjordur to obtain some gasoline in a can. That meant a walk of four miles each way and when he returned home he was exhausted. During the night he experienced extremely severe pain in the stomach. Einar was sent for and went to him, but could not diagnose his condition at first. The next day Einar had to go to Reydarfjordur and stayed there the whole day. In the evening he received a telephone call at Reydarfjordur asking him to come quickly [back to Eskifjordur] because Gudni's condition had become very critical. Einar was also asked to bring with him the army doctor stationed at Reydarfjordur if that would make it easier to help Gudni. The [two] physicians arrived at nine o'clock in the evening and they saw immediately that the young man was in a very critical condition and probably suffering from some internal rupture or intestinal obstruction. They could do nothing with the patient where he was. They therefore decided to send the young man at once to the hospital at Seydisfjordur. They could not use an airplane because, being October, it was already dark. They therefore took Gudni in a motorboat, but he died on the way between Nordfjordur and Seydisfjordur" (Haraldsson and Stevenson 1975b, p. 249).

Gestsson then obtained a more detailed account of the séance, written by Gudjonsson on March 31, 1941: "The first thing that Finna said to me was that a young man was with me and that he was of average height, blond, and with thin hair at the top of his head. He was between 20 and 30 years of age and was called Gudni Magnusson. She could easily see him. She said that he had known some of my relatives, and also that he and his death were connected with Eskifjordur and Reydarfjordur. He had been a car or truck driver. She saw clearly how he had died. He had been repairing his car, had crawled under it, stretched himself, and then had ruptured something inside his body. Then he had been brought by boat between fjords to medical care, but died on the way. That is all I remember" (Haraldsson and Stevenson 1975b, p. 247). Gudjonsson later said that he wrote this before he had any knowledge of the letter to Gestsson from Gudrun Gudmundsdottir in Eskifjordur (Haraldsson and Stevenson 1975b, p. 260).

Gudrun Jonsdottir, who had also attended the séance, also provided a statement, dated June 6, 1941. Hansina Hansdottir, the only other person at the séance, also signed Jonsdottir's statement, saying it was correct. Here is Jonsdottir's statement: "Hjalmar [Gudjonsson] . . . did not recognize in any way at all the man Finna described to him. I had the impression that he did not want to hear anything further from this unknown man, so I asked Finna about him myself. Finna said: 'This man has living parents. . . .' I asked: 'Did he die immediately?' Finna said: 'No, he managed to get to his home, and then I see he was carried by boat. He was brought to a doctor. I see the boat between fjords and that he died on the way in the boat.' I asked: 'Can you tell me between what fjords he was to be brought?' Finna said: 'I cannot get that, but Eskifjordur is what he has most on his mind.' I asked: 'How long do you think it is since he died?' Finna said: 'I cannot see that clearly. I believe it to be some months, about four or five, but it could be more or less. This man seems to have become well oriented [in the after-life], but he does not feel secure.' I asked: 'What do you think he wants from Hjalmar? Something specific?' Finna said: 'He just came to him since they are both from the same part of the country and he is also trying to get strength from him. You should think well of him. That gives him strength'" (Haraldsson and Stevenson 1975b, pp. 247–248).

In June 1941, Asmundur Gestsson went to Eskifjordur and confirmed details about Gudni Magnusson, such as the fact he had blond hair, thinning on the top of his head. Later, Erlendur Haraldsson interviewed Gudni's brother Otto and sister Rosa, who also confirmed the details of the reports from the séance. Haraldsson also, with some difficulty, obtained a copy of Gudni's death certificate, which listed the cause of death as "intestinal perforation" (Haraldsson and Stevenson 1975b, p. 249).

On November 7, 1940, an Icelandic newspaper published a brief obituary of Gudni, but it did not give many details, and would not in itself have been of much help to the medium Hafsteinn in manufacturing the communications from Gudni. Neither the medium nor any of the sitters had any connection with Gudni or his family. Haraldsson and Stevenson (1975b, pp. 260–261) concluded: "Despite extensive inquiries we have not been able to find any channel for normal communication to the medium of the correct information he had about Gudni Magnusson and expressed at the séance under consideration."

Possession by Departed Humans

The mediumistic communications we have just examined help establish that personalities of humans who existed on earth are still existing in some other, apparently nearby, dimension of the universe and are capable of interacting with us here through special channels. Frederick Myers, one of the principal researchers in this field, wrote that "the evidence for communication with the spirits of identified deceased persons through the trance-utterances and writings of sensitives apparently controlled by those spirits is established beyond serious attack" (Myers 1903, v. 1, p. 29). Some of the communications gave information of even higher levels or dimensions of the universe, inhabited by higher beings.

We shall now consider another category of evidence that conscious entities exist at some other level of the cosmos—reports of terrestrial humans possessed by departed human personalities. Mediumistic communications also represent a kind of possession, because the medium appears to be temporarily possessed by the communicating spirit. The possession cases that follow are, however, different in that they involve longer and more intense periods of possession. It also seems that the motivation of the possessing spirit to enter a terrestrial human body plays a larger role than in the mediumistic communication cases.

Psychologist William James was willing to consider the reality of spirit possession. The theory that a demonic spirit might take control of a living human body could explain some mental illnesses. In fact, up to the nineteenth century, many physicians in Europe and America did accept this theory. "That the demon theory will have its innings again is to my mind absolutely certain," said James (Murphy and Ballou 1960, p. 207).

I found the case of the "Watseka Wonder" (Stevens 1887; Myers 1903, v. 1, pp. 361–367) especially interesting because of its detailed documentation of a possession. Watseka, a town of five or six thousand people, is the capital of Iroquois County in the state of Illinois. The Watseka Wonder was a girl named Lurancy Vennum. The daughter of Thomas J. and Lurinda J. Vennum, she was born on April 16, 1864 near Watseka. One night in early July of 1877, Lurancy felt the presence of persons in her room at night. They called her by her nickname, Rancy, and she felt them breathing on her face. The next day, she told her parents about this. On the evening of July 11, 1877, Lurancy was sewing. At six o'clock, her mother asked her to help make dinner. Lurancy said, "Ma, I feel bad: I feel so queer" (Stevens 1887, p. 3). She then fell upon the floor, and lay there, her body quite rigid. After five hours, she regained consciousness but reported she still felt "very strange and queer" (Stevens 1887, p. 3). She then rested for the night.

The next day, her body again became rigid, and during this state she was apparently aware of both her present physical surroundings and another dimension—a world of spirits. Among the spirits she saw a sister and brother who had died and called out, "Oh, mother! can't you see little Laura and Bertie? They are so beautiful!" (Stevens 1887, p. 3) Lurancy's visions of spirits and angels continued for several weeks, ending in September. On November 27, 1877, Lurancy suffered severe pains in her stomach, and these attacks continued for two weeks. On December 11, in the middle of these attacks, she entered into a trancelike state and again began speaking of spirits and angels she could see in a place she called heaven (Stevens 1887, p. 4).

On the advice of relatives and friends, Lurancy's parents considered sending her to an asylum. Asa B. Roff and his wife Ann, on hearing of this, tried to persuade the Vennums not to do it and asked for permission to see Lurancy. Mr. Vennum finally agreed, and on January 31, 1878, Mr. Roff came, along with Dr. E. W. Stevens of Janesville, Wisconsin. Stevens was a medical doctor with spiritualist leanings. When he saw Lurancy, she was sitting on a chair near the stove, having adopted the bodily expressions and voice of an "old hag." She refused to speak to anyone except Dr. Stevens. She said that only he could understand her, because he was a spiritualist. Stevens asked her name, and she answered without hesitation, "Katrina Hogan." Further questions revealed the personality of an old woman from Germany, sixty-three years old, controlling Lurancy's body from the spirit world. After some time, Lurancy's personality changed. She was now Willie Canning, the delinquent son of a man named Peter Canning. He had run away from home and lost his life (Stevens 1887, pp. 5–6).

When Dr. Stevens and Mr. Roff were getting ready to leave, Lurancy rose up and then fell flat on the floor, her body rigid. Stevens ministered to her, using mesmeric and spiritualist techniques, and soon Lurancy was manifesting her own personality, although she was still in a trance state. She said she was in heaven. Stevens convinced her that she should not allow herself to be controlled by bad spirits such as Katrina and Willie. She should find a nicer spirit. Lurancy agreed and after searching announced she had found one who desired to make use of her. Lurancy said, "Her name is Mary Roff." Mr. Roff recognized Mary as his daughter, who had died twelve years previously, when Lurancy was one year old. During her life, Mary Roff had displayed clairvoyant and other psychic powers, and these were tested and verified by leading citizens of Watseka. Mr. Roff advised Lurancy that Mary was a good spirit and that she should let Mary communicate through her. Lurancy accepted this suggestion (Stevens 1887, pp. 6–8).

After a few hours, Lurancy came out of her trance. But the next day, February 1, 1878, she claimed to be Mary Roff. Her father then went to Mr. Roff's office and told him, "She seems like a child real homesick, wanting to see her pa and ma and her brothers" (Stevens 1887, p. 9). But Lurancy did not go immediately to be with the Roffs. She remained at home, continuing to manifest Mary Roff's personality there. After a few more days, Mrs. Ann B. Roff and her daughter Mrs. Minerva Alter came to see Lurancy. The girl recognized them through a window as they were coming up the street, saying, "There comes my ma and sister Nervie!" (Stevens 1887, p. 13) When the two women entered the house, Lurancy cried for joy, and threw her arms around their necks in greeting, as if she knew them intimately. After this visit, she seemed quite homesick and desirous of going to the Roffs. The Vennums, on the advice of friends, finally allowed their daughter to go, on February 11, 1878.

When Lurancy was being taken by the Roffs to their house, she tried to get them to go to another house on the way. She insisted it was her house. The Roffs had to take her past this house, almost by force. It was the house in which Mary Roff had died. The Roffs had then moved to another house, the one to which they were taking Lurancy (Myers 1903, v. 1, p. 367).

Richard Hodgson, of the American Society for Psychical Research, published a report on Lurancy's stay with the Roffs, during which "almost every hour of the day some trifling incident of Mary Roff's life was recalled by Lurancy" (Myers 1903, v. 1, p. 366). Indeed, Lurancy appeared to forget her identity as the daughter of the Vennums. Once, Lurancy told Dr. Stevens about a cut on her arm. As she rolled up her sleeve to show him the scar, she said, "Oh, this is not the arm; that one is in the ground," meaning that the cut was on the arm of Mary Roff, whose body was now buried. Lurancy (as Mary) recalled seeing her own burial, indicating the soul of Mary Roff had hovered near her body after death or observed the scene from heaven (Griffin 1997, p. 172).

On February 19, 1878, Mr. Roff stated to Dr. Stevens: "Mary is perfectly happy; she recognizes everybody and everything that she knew when in her body twelve or more years ago. She knows nobody nor anything whatever that is known by Lurancy. Mr. Vennum has been to see her, and also her brother Henry, at different times, but she don't know anything about them. Mrs. Vennum is still unable to come and see her daughter. She has been nothing but Mary since she has been here, and knows nothing but what Mary knew. She has entered the trance once every other day for some days. She is perfectly happy. You don't know how much comfort we take with the dear angel" (Stevens 1887, p. 17).

Lurancy had predicted the angels would let her stay as Mary with the Roffs until May. (Stevens 1887, pp. 13–14). Minerva Alter, Mary's sister, wrote on April 16, 1878: "My angel sister says she is going away from us again soon, but says she will be often with us. She says Lurancy is a beautiful girl; says she sees her nearly every day, and we do know she is getting better every day. Oh, the lessons that are being taught us are worth treasures of rare diamonds; they are stamped upon the mind so firmly that heaven and earth shall pass away before one jot or one title shall be forgotten. I have learned so much that is grand and beautiful, I cannot express it; I am dumb. A few days ago Mary was caressing her father and mother, and they became a little tired of it, and asked why she hugged and kissed them. She sorrowfully looked at them, and said, 'Oh, pa and ma! I want to kiss you while I have lips to kiss you with, and hug you while I have arms to hug you with, for I am going back to heaven before long, and then I can only be with you in spirit, and you will not always know when I come, and I cannot have you as I can now. Oh, how much I love you all!'" (Stevens 1887, p. 18)

On May 7, 1878, Mary told Mrs. Roff that Lurancy was coming back. As she was sitting with her eyes closed, Lurancy regained control of her body. When she opened her eyes, she was surprised by her surroundings, and displaying anxiety, said: "Where am I? I was never here before" (Stevens 1887, p. 19). She cried and said she wanted to go home. In five minutes, Mary returned, and began singing her favorite childhood song, "We are Coming, Sister Mary" (Stevens 1887, p. 20). Mary continued to inhabit Lurancy's body for some more time. During this period, she continued communicating her visions of heaven to the Roffs, including an encounter with the baby that Minerva Alter had recently lost to death.

From time to time, during these last days, the personality of Mary would recede enough for the personality of Lurancy to partially appear. When the girl was asked, "Where is Lurancy?" she would reply, "Gone out somewhere," or "She is in heaven taking lessons, and I am here taking lessons too" (Stevens 1887, p. 26). On May 19, 1878, Mr. Roff was sitting with Mary in the parlor of his house. Mary then departed, and Lurancy took full control of her body. Henry Vennum, Lurancy's brother, happened to be visiting the Roffs and was called in from another room. Lurancy, weeping, threw her arms around his neck and kissed him. Everyone present began to cry. Henry left to get Lurancy's mother, and while he was gone, Mary returned briefly. But when Mrs. Vennum came, Lurancy returned again. Stevens (1887, p. 35) said, "Mother and daughter embraced and kissed each other, and wept until all present shed tears of sympathy; it seemed the very gate of heaven." Lurancy returned home, married, and lived a fairly normal life except that when she would see the Roffs sometimes "Mary" would briefly return (Stevens 1887, p. 35).

Is it possible that the Watseka Wonder can be explained as a hoax manufactured by Dr. Stevens, the author of a book about the case? This seems unlikely. Both the Vennum and Roff families testified to the accuracy of the account given by Stevens. Many details can also be corroborated from newspaper reports, and the case was thoroughly investigated by outside researchers such as Richard Hodgson, of the American Society for Psychical Research. Furthermore, William James, a world renowned psychologist, accepted the case and published it in his *Principles of Psychology*. In a footnote, James (1890 v. 1, p. 398, footnote 64) wrote, "My friend Mr. R. Hodgson informs me that he visited Watseka in April 1890, and cross-examined the principal witnesses of this case. His confidence in the original narrative was strengthened by what he learned; and various unpublished facts were ascertained, which increased the plausibility of the spiritualistic interpretation of the phenomenon." What about Lurancy? Could she have been responsible? It does not seem likely that she could have acquired by natural means the extensive knowledge she displayed about numerous details of the lives of Mary Roff and members of the Roff family. Mary died when Lurancy was one year old, and the Roff and Vennum families had little contact with each other (Griffin 1997, p. 173).

The obvious paranormal explanation is that the soul of Mary Roff temporarily possessed the body of Lurancy Vennum. This would, of course, support the idea that there is a conscious self that can survive the death of the body. Supporters of the "superpsi" hypothesis might suggest that Lurancy picked up information about Mary from the minds of her living relations. But this would not easily account for her forgetting her identity as Lurancy Vennum and functioning for fourteen weeks, without a break, as Mary Roff. One researcher (Griffin 1997, pp. 173–174) has proposed that although Mary's personality did not survive, perhaps some of her memories survived in a recoverable form and were used by Lurancy to construct the personality of Mary. But these memories should have stopped with Mary's death. This would leave unexplained Lurancy's account of Mary witnessing her own funeral. All things considered, the idea that the surviving personality of Mary Roff temporarily possessed the body of Lurancy Vennum seems the most economical and reasonable explanation of the facts.

The Watseka Wonder was cited by Frederick Myers of the Society for Psychical Research as one of the main evidences for survival of the human personality after death. From the total body of evidence available to him, Myers drew the following conclusions about spirits and the spirit world: "Spirits may be able to recognize spatial relations (so that they can manifest at an agreed place) but they are themselves probably independent of space; their interactions with each other are all telepathic, and the laws of telepathy are non-spatial laws . . . The spirits of the recently dead may retain telepathic links with spirits still in the flesh and may endeavor to contact them, or to 'guide' their activities. Beyond and behind such spirits, but still with affinities to them, are the spirits whose advancement in knowledge and understanding has linked them in fellowship to higher souls" (Gauld 1968, pp. 309–310). These are, according to Myers, linked to still higher ones, and all are linked to a Universal Spirit, the source of love and wisdom.

Ian Stevenson, known for his work on past life memories, also did work on xenoglossy cases, in which subjects manifest inexplicable abilities to speak foreign languages. Xenoglossy cases can sometimes involve past life memories, but possession is another possible explanation. One of Stevenson's principal xenoglossy studies involved an Indian woman, Uttara Huddar, and her case does seem to involve possession.

Uttara Huddar was born on March 14, 1941, in the town of Nagpur, in the Indian province of Maharashtra. Like most of the inhabitants of this province, Uttara was of the Maratha group and spoke the Marathi language. Both of Uttara's parents were Marathas. In her twenties she was hospitalized for some physical disorders. During her stay in the hospital, she took lessons in meditation from a yogi, and afterwards, during altered states of consciousness, began speaking a new language and manifesting a new personality. Dr. Joshi (pseudonym), one of the physicians at the hospital, recognized the language as Bengali. Because the Bengali she spoke contained no English loan words, it appeared to date to the nineteenth century. After Uttara returned from the hospital, her parents began to try to find an explanation for their daughter's strange behavior. They consulted M. C. Bhattacarya, a Bengali who served as a priest at a temple of goddess Kali, in Nagpur. To Bhattacarya, Uttara identified herself as a Bengali woman named Sharada, and gave many details about her life. All of this was communicated in Bengali. From the information given by Sharada, it appeared to Bhattacarya that she considered herself to be living some time in the past. She said her father, whose name was Brajesh Chattopadaya, lived near a Shiva temple in the town of Burdwan. Her mother's name was Renukha Devi, and her stepmother's name was Anandamoyi. She gave her husband's name as Swami Vishwanath Mukhopadaya, and said her father-in-law's name was Nand Kishore Mukhopadaya. When asked where she had been living before she came to Nagpur, Sharada replied that she had been living with her maternal aunt in the town of Saptagram. This information was recorded in Bhattacarya's diary for the year 1974 (Stevenson 1984, pp. 73–75).

In May of 1975, Dr. R. K. Sinha, making use of this information, visited the Saptagram region of Bengal, and attempted to verify some of the details of Sharada's life. Satinath Chatterji, a living member of the Chattopadaya family, gave a genealogy of his male ancestors in which the name of Brajesh Chattopadaya appeared. Dr. Sinha got from Chatterji further names of Brajesh Chattopadaya's relatives and contemporaries. Returning to Nagpur, Dr. Sinha questioned Uttara, without revealing any of the new genealogical information he had obtained. Stevenson (1984, pp. 88–89) reported: "The names Sharada gave for her father, grandfather, one brother (Kailasnath), and two uncles (Devnath and Shivnath) all appear in the genealogy with the relationship she attributed to them. In addition, she told him the name of another male relative, Mathuranath, without specifying how he was related to her. The genealogy does not include the name of Srinath, one of the brothers mentioned by Sharada. His existence, however, is established in a deed of agreement for the settlement of property between Devnath, on the one hand, and Kailasnath and Srinath, on the other. The deed is dated March, 1827. This property settlement between the uncle and two nephews indicates tacitly that the nephews' father, Brajesh, had died by March 1827, and presumably not long before the property settlement. Satinath Chatterji had another deed (also dated in 1827), which identified Mathuranath as the grandson of Shivnath, who was one of Sharada's (presumed) uncles."

How are Uttara's impressions to be explained? One explanation is that she was getting this information from living sources, by a process of "super-extrasensory perception." In other words, perhaps she had drawn on knowledge existing in the mind of Satinath Chatterji and other persons living in Bengal in the 1970s. But Stevenson pointed out that Sharada's language abilities could not have been acquired by simple extrasensory perception. Such a skill requires actual practice for its acquisition. Stevenson (1984, pp. 160–161) therefore concluded: "Any person (or personality) demonstrating the ability to speak a language must have learned the language himself some time before the occasion of demonstrating this ability. And if we can further exclude the possibility that the person concerned did not learn the language earlier in his life, it follows that it was learned by some other personality manifesting through him. That other personality could be a previous incarnation of the person concerned or it could be a discarnate personality temporarily mani-

festing through the living subject—possessing the subject, we might say."
In the case of Uttara, Stevenson showed that she had not learned Bengali
before the time of the manifestation of the personality of Sharada. She
had learned a few words of Bengali, but did not possess the fluent command of the language demonstrated by Sharada (Stevenson 1984, pp.
134–135, 137–138, 140, 146).

Philosopher David Ray Griffin proposes that Uttara was very unhappy with her childless, husbandless life, and wanted to adopt another
personality (Sharada had a husband and children). Making use of his
theory of surviving mental impressions (as opposed to surviving
souls with memories), he concluded that Uttara, using a superpsi faculty,
selected Sharada's memories from some cosmic reservoir of memories
and constructed from them an alternate personality for herself (Griffin
1997, pp. 180–182). This does not, however, account for Uttara's mastery
of Bengali. Recollection would allow only simple repetition of things
said in the past, not the ability to compose new speech. Possession of
Uttara's body by the surviving Sharada personality seems to be the most
reasonable explanation.

Here is a final detail. Uttara, speaking as Sharada, recalled that she
had been bitten on her right toe by a snake and had died. Uttara's mother
said that when she was pregnant with Uttara, she repeatedly dreamed that
a cobra was about to bite her on the right toe. The dreams stopped upon
Uttara's birth. Uttara herself had a great fear of snakes as a child. When
the personality of Sharada overtook Uttara, she would sometimes experience physical transformations suggestive of a snake bite. Her tongue and
mouth became dark, and there was a black area on her toe. During one
such episode she pointed to the toe and said that a king cobra had just
bitten her there. Stevenson (1984, p. 112) noted: "A present-day member
of the Chattopadaya family, furthermore, reports hearing that during the
time of his great grandmother a female member of the family had died
of a snakebite."

Apparitions of Departed Humans

Having considered cases of communication through mediums and
cases of possession as evidence for spirits of departed humans continuing
to exist in some other level of a cosmic hierarchy, let us now look at cases
of apparitions of departed humans. Prominent scientists have taken such
cases seriously. For example, William James said: "Science may keep saying: 'Such things are simply impossible'; yet so long as the stories multi-
ply in different lands, and so few are positively explained away, it is bad
method to ignore them. They should at least accrete for further use. As I

glance back at my reading of the past few years ... ten cases immediately rise to my mind" (Murphy and Ballou 1960, pp. 62–63). Let's now look at a few cases. I agree with James that it is "bad method to ignore them."

The astronomer Camille Flammarion (1909, p. 303) accepted "the possibility of communication between incarnate and discarnate spirits." He added (1909, p. 303) that his own research had led him to conclusions favoring "the plurality of inhabited worlds ... and the indestructibility of souls, as well as of atoms." Flammarion's masterpiece was *Death and Its Mystery,* a three volume compilation of evidence for the existence of the soul apart from the body and its survival after the death of the body. The book contains several apparition cases.

The following is an account of an apparition that appeared about two hours after death (Flammarion 1923, v. 3, pp. 133–136). It was recorded by Charles Tweedale of the Royal Astronomical Society of London in *The English Mechanic and World of Science* (July 20, 1906). Tweedale recalled an incident from his boyhood. He went to bed early on the evening of January 10, 1879. He awoke and saw a form taking shape before him in the moonlight. He noticed that the moonlight was coming in from the window on the south side of his room. The form gradually became clearer until he recognized his grandmother's face. She was wearing "an old-fashioned cap which was fluted in a shell-like design." After a few seconds, the form gradually disappeared. At breakfast, Tweedale told his parents about his vision. His father left the table without speaking. His mother explained, "This morning your father told me that he had waked up in the night, and that he had seen his mother standing near his bed, but just at the moment when he wished to speak to her she had disappeared." A few hours later the family received a telegram bearing the news of the death of Tweedale's grandmother. Tweedale later learned that his father's sister (Tweedale's aunt) had also seen the apparition on the night of the old woman's death. The death occurred at fifteen minutes past midnight. Tweedale's father had noted the time of his vision as two o'clock in the morning. Tweedale himself did not have a timepiece, but from the position of the moon, he estimated that his vision had also taken place at two in the morning. The vision of Tweedale's aunt also took place well after the reported time of death. Tweedale stated: "This proves that we are not concerned with a telepathic or subjective manifestation, occurring before death or at the very moment of death, but with a really objective apparition occurring *after* life had left the body. We may conclude, therefore, that the dead woman, though apparently lifeless, was sufficiently *alive* some hours later to manifest herself to different persons separated by considerable distances" (Flammarion 1923, v. 3,

p. 135). Details of the report given by Tweedale were confirmed by his mother and his aunt's surviving husband.

From all the evidence recorded in his books, Flammarion (1923 v.3, p. 348) arrived at five conclusions: "(1) The soul exists as a real entity, independent of the body. (2) It is endowed with faculties still unknown to science. (3) It may act at a distance, telepathically, without the intermediary of the senses. (4) There exists in nature a psychic element, the character of which is still hidden from us. . . . (5) The soul survives the physical organism and may manifest itself after death."

Concerning the relationship of the soul to the body, Flammarion (1923 v. 3, p. 346) said: "The body is but an organic garment of the spirit; it dies, it changes, it disintegrates: the spirit remains. . . . The soul cannot be destroyed." This is remarkably similar to the following statement from *Bhagavad Gita* (2.22): "As a person puts on new garments, giving up old ones, the soul similarly accepts new material bodies, giving up the old and useless ones."

On a Friday night in April of 1880, Mrs. N. J. Crans went to sleep in New York. She reported in a letter to Richard Hodgson, of the American Society for Psychical Research: "After lying down to rest, I remember feeling a drifting sensation, of seeming almost as if I was going out of the body. My eyes were closed; soon I realized that I was, or seemed to be, going fast somewhere. All seemed dark to me; suddenly I realized that I was in a room; then I saw Charley lying in a bed asleep; then I took a look at the furniture of the room, and distinctly saw every article—even to a chair at the head of the bed, which had one of the pieces broken in the back." Charley was her son-in-law, Charles A. Kernochan, who was living in Central City, South Dakota. Mrs. Crans continued: "In a moment the door opened and my spirit-daughter Allie came into the room and stepped up to the bed and stooped down and kissed Charley. He seemed to at once realize her presence, and tried to hold her, but she passed right out of the room about like a feather blown by the wind." Allie was the daughter of Mrs. Crans and the wife of Charles Kernochan. She had died in December 1879, about five months before this incident. Mrs. Crans told several people about her dream, and then on Sunday wrote a letter to Charles. Meanwhile, Charles himself had written a letter which crossed hers in the mail, delivery of which took about six days between New York and South Dakota. In this letter, Charles wrote, "Oh, my darling mamma Crans! My God! I dreamed I saw Allie last Friday night!" Mrs. Crans said that Charles described Allie "just as I saw her; how she came into the room and he cried and tried to hold her, but she vanished." After Charles sent this letter, he received the letter sent by Mrs.

Crans, and wrote another letter in reply. Mrs. Crans said that Charles "wrote me all that I had seen was correct, even to every article of furniture in the room, also as his dream had appeared to him" (Myers 1903, v. 1, p. 244). In this case, it appears that both percipients were in the dream state when Allie appeared to them. One might propose that there was an unconscious telepathic link between Mrs. Crans and Charles, and that together they manufactured the joint appearance in an intersubjective dream state. But there is hardly any less reason to suppose that there could have been a third party to this intersubjective encounter, namely Allie herself, in some subtle material form.

General Sir Arthur Becher was serving with the British Army in India when he saw an apparition (Myers 1903, v. 1, pp. 250–251). In March, 1867, he went to the hill station of Kussowlie (Kussoorie) to inspect a house where he and his family were planning to reside during the hot season. He was accompanied by his son. During the night, the General woke up to find an Indian woman standing near his bed. As he got up, the figure went through a door leading from the bedroom into a bathroom. The General followed, but the woman was not there. He noticed that aside from the door by which he had entered, the only other exit, a door leading from the bathroom to the outside of the house, was securely locked. The General went to sleep again, and in the morning wrote in pencil on a doorpost a brief note that he had seen a ghost. But he mentioned the matter to no one.

After a few days, the General and his family, including his wife Lady Becher, arrived to set up residence in the house. Lady Becher decided to use the room in which the General had slept as her dressing room. On her first evening in the house, Lady Becher was dressing for dinner in this room when she saw an Indian woman standing in the bathroom. Thinking the woman to be her own *ayah,* or maidservant, Lady Becher asked her what she wanted. There was no reply, and when Lady Becher went into the bathroom she found the woman gone and the door to the outside locked.

At dinner, Lady Becher mentioned the strange occurrence to the General, who replied with his own account. Later they went to sleep in their bedroom. Their youngest son, who was eight years old, was sleeping in a bed in the same room. He had no knowledge of the apparition. His bed was near the door to the dressing room and bathroom. During the night, the boy woke up, and his parents heard him cry out in Hindi, "What do you want, *ayah*? What do you want?" He had obviously seen the form of an Indian woman. On this occasion neither the General nor his wife saw the form. In fact, none of them ever saw it again. The

General wrote about this last appearance: "It confirmed our feeling that the same woman *had appeared to us all three,* and on inquiry from other occupants we learned that it was a frequent apparition on the first night or so of the house being occupied. A native Hill, or Cashmere woman, very fair and handsome, had been murdered some years before in a hut a few yards below the house, and immediately under the door leading into the bath and dressing room, through which, on all three occasions, the figure had entered and disappeared. . . . I could give the names of some other subsequent occupants who have told us much the same story" (Myers 1903, v. 1, p. 251).

Charles Lett, a military man, recalled the following apparition incident, noteworthy because of the multiple simultaneous percipients (Griffin 1997, pp. 218–219). On April 5, 1873, his wife's father, Captain Towns, had died in his house. Six weeks later, Lett's wife was in one of the bedrooms of the house and saw reflected on the polished surface of a wardrobe a very detailed and lifelike image of the head and torso of Captain Towns. Accompanying her was a young lady, Miss Berthon, who also saw the image. At first they thought someone had hung a portrait of the Captain. At that moment Mrs. Lett's sister, Miss Towns, entered the room, and before either Mrs. Lett or Miss Berthon had a chance to say anything, Miss Towns said, "Good gracious! Do you see papa?" Several household servants were summoned individually, and one after another they expressed astonishment at the apparition. Charles Lett recalled, "Finally, Mrs. Towns was sent for, and seeing the apparition, she advanced towards it with her arm extended as if to touch it, and as she passed her hand over the panel of the wardrobe the figure gradually faded away, and never again appeared."

Was the apparition really caused by the surviving soul of Captain Towns, who manifested his form in space? Superpsi theorists would say no. But such multiple perception cases are difficult to account for by the superpsi explanation. One would have to propose that the main percipient generated in her mind an image of Captain Towns, acquiring it from her own mind or by extrasensory perception from the mind of a living person. The main percipient would then have to experience this image in the context of the room. By a process called telepathic contagion, the same image would then be transmitted to the minds of others. But extensive experiments in telepathic image transmission, reviewed in chapter 6, show that it is not easy to transmit a complete image from one mind to another. Another possible explanation is a kind of super psychokinetic (super-pk) ability, whereby the main percipient generates an actual form in three dimensional space. But whether we are talking about superpsi or super-pk, there are difficulties. In this particular case, seven individuals saw the image and it looked the same to all of them. Also, the individual percipients were standing in different places in the room, and the image was placed in proper perspective for each of them. It is also significant that the percipients saw the image only as they entered the room, and later it faded at the same time for all of them. This discussion is based on an analysis given by Griffin (1997, pp. 219–221), who, after noting that multiple perceptions of apparitions are not uncommon, said (1997, p. 221), "The view that at least some of the apparitions are due to postmortem agency of the apparent could certainly provide the simplest explanation."

Superpsi and super-pk explanations of apparitions with multiple percipients usually place the motivation for the apparition in the mind of the main percipient. This requires that the main percipient know the deceased person, and have some reason for wanting to perceive the person. Otherwise, the motivation would then lie with the deceased, which would give evidence for survival, the very thing the superpsi and super-pk explanations are meant to exclude. But there are cases of collective apparitions where the primary percipient did not know the deceased. Here is one such case from Myers's *Human Personality*. On Christmas Eve of 1869, just as a woman and her husband, Willie, were about to go to sleep, the woman saw a man dressed in a naval uniform standing at the foot of the bed. She touched her husband, who was facing away from the image, and drawing his attention to it, said, "Willie, who is this?" Her husband said loudly, "What on earth are you doing here, sir?" The figure said reproachfully, "Willie, Willie!" The figure then moved toward the wall of the bedroom. The woman recalled, "As it passed the lamp, a deep shadow fell upon the room as of a material person shutting out the light from us by his intervening body, and he disappeared, as it were, into the wall." After the disappearance, Willie told his wife that the image had been that of his father, a naval officer, who had died fourteen years earlier. She had never seen him. Her husband had been in anxiety about a large financial transaction, and he took the apparition of his father as a warning for him not to proceed (Griffin 1997, p. 222,). Taking the wife as the principal percipient and the apparition as a hallucination, it is unusual that she should hallucinate an image of her husband's dead father, whom she had never met or seen. A paranormal researcher might propose that by super-esp the wife picked up on her husband's anxiety and his unconscious thoughts of his father, and from that material manifested a real apparition by super-pk, causing it to be visible not only to her but her husband. But this is straining perhaps too much to avoid the survival hypothesis. In this case, it is simpler to propose that the surviving spirit of Willie's father, desiring to save his son from financial ruin, was responsible for his own apparition. Griffin (1997, p. 223) points out that in such cases "Frederick Myers suggested that the postmortem soul, or some element thereof, produces quasi-physical effects in the region of space at which the apparition is seen."

Evidence for Superhuman Personalities
In the Cosmic Hierarchy

In the apparition, possession, and communication cases we have considered above, the appearing, possessing, or communicating entity appears to be a departed human. But in some cases the entity appears to be superhuman, giving evidence for contact with beings at a different level of the cosmic hierarchy than that occupied by departed humans.

Demonic Possession

On January 15, 1949 members of the Doe family in the Georgetown district of Washington, D. C., heard strange knocking and scratching noises in their house (Doe is a pseudonym used in the reports of the case). At first they thought it was the ghost of a departed relative. Eventually, the sounds stopped, and small objects began to disappear and reappear in the house. Pieces of furniture moved inexplicably, and paintings shook on the walls. After a few weeks, the Does' son Roland, thirteen years old, began to manifest strange symptoms. He talked in his sleep and shouted obscenities. One night the family members heard him screaming and went into his room to see him. They found him and his mattress floating in mid air. The Does, who were Lutherans, sought help from a clergyman. A few nights later, this clergyman witnessed a similar levitation by Roland. These levitations were repeated, not only in the Doe home, but in other houses and hospitals. After the levitations started, Roland started manifesting symptoms of possession. He suffered violent seizures, and a demonic personality took control of his body and speech (Rogo 1982, pp. 41–42).

At this point, the parents concluded that the only cure was a Roman Catholic exorcism. Church officials accepted their petition, and Roland was taken to a Catholic hospital in St. Louis for the exorcism. The priests conducting the exorcism were Father Raymond Bishop, Father F. Bowdern, and Father Lawrence Kenny. They kept a diary, which recorded the many supernatural events that took place during the exorcism. Roland levitated, read the minds of the exorcists, manifested understanding of Latin, and exercised unusual strength, breaking away from attendants who were trying to hold him down on his bed. Father Charles O'Hara, of Marquette University in Milwaukee, was present for some of the sessions. He later said to Father Eugene Gallagher of Georgetown University: "One night the boy brushed off his handlers and soared through the air at Father Bowdern standing at some distance from his bed [with] the ritual [book] in his hands. Presumably, Father was about to be attacked but the boy got no further than the book. And when his hand hit that—I assure you I saw this with my own eyes—he didn't tear the book, he dissolved it. The book vaporized into confetti and fell in small fine pieces to the floor" (Rogo 1982, p. 43).

After several weeks, Roland was finally freed from the demon's control. Rogo (1982, p. 43) says: "Unfortunately, a large portion of the diary kept by Roland's exorcists is now lost. The case report written by the priests was in the possession of Father Gallagher until 1950, at which time he lent it to a colleague. Somehow a number of its sixteen pages were misplaced at that time. However, many of the original witnesses who took part in the case, in both St. Louis and Georgetown, are still alive." It was on this case that William Peter Blatty based his novel *The Exorcist,* which was turned into a film that became a classic of its kind.

On December 22, 1693, Carlo Maria Vulcano, a boy sixteen years old, entered the monastery of the Hieronymite order in Naples for training as a novice (Gauld and Cornell 1979, pp. 158–166). During the night of May 4, 1696, stones mysteriously fell into the hallway outside the room where Carlo and some other novices were sleeping. The same thing happened the next night. The novices rushed into the hallway, but saw only the stones lying on the floor of the hallway. Later that night, Carlo, alone in his room, noticed some movements in the dark. Then a voice cried out in his room, pleading for a prayer to be said for him. Carlo ran out the room screaming, "Jesus, Jesus, help me, help me" (Gauld and Cornell 1979, p. 162). One of the masters, Master Squillante, pacified Carlo, blessed the room, and told Carlo to go to sleep. When Carlo was lying in his bed, he saw a figure dressed as a Benedictine monk in the doorway. It came into the room, again crying out for prayers to be said on its behalf. Carlo and the novices ran to the prayer room, where they said prayers and chanted the rosary. As they did so, they heard a great commotion in the hallway, and then everything was quiet.

During the first part of the next day, stones fell in different rooms throughout the monastery, and then things became quiet. That night, as Carlo was trying to go to sleep, he again heard a voice calling him. He ignored it, thinking it a product of his imagination. But then the voice challenged, "You do not want to reply?" At that moment, his bed collapsed and the sheets and blankets flew into the air. Carlo ran out of the room, as behind him all the furniture crashed down and the window burst open. On the days that followed, stones continued to fall in various places. The demon pounded on doors, all the while crying out loudly. During the attacks, mattresses, sheets, and pillows were flung wildly around. The demon put pots of excrement in front of sacred images, threw excrement at Carlo, and threw paving stones at other persons.

On the night of May 11, the demon addressed the master of the novices in loud impolite language. The demon, upon being interrogated, identified himself as "the devil of the inferno" and declared that he had been ordained by God "to ceasely torment that novice" (Gauld and Cornell 1979, p. 163). On May 13, two brothers of the order, bearing sacred relics, posted themselves at the door to Carlo's room, to prevent the demon from entering. Nevertheless, that night Carlo woke to find sitting near his bed a fiery-faced figure dressed in black. The demon shouted, "Now I will make you know who I am" (Gauld and Cornell 1979, p. 163). Carlo took a sacred image and pushed it into the demon's face. In response, the demon burst into activity, scaring away the two brothers. The master and some novices came to the door of the room. Carlos tried to come out, but the demon grabbed him by his cassock and pulled him back. Recitation of the names of Jesus and Mary caused the demon to loosen his grip, and Carlos released himself. But upon his cassock was the print of a hand. The mark could not be removed. Demonic figures impressed in the wall of the room also could not be erased, and therefore the plaster was removed.

The boy was taken to the home of an uncle, Domenico Galisio. On May 22, Carlo was taken to Sorrento to see the remains of Saint Anthony, and there again the demon started to cause trouble. Carlo was then taken back to the monastery in Naples, where demonic phenomena resumed with increased ferocity. At times, the buildings shook as if being hit by earthquakes. Once Carlo and some monks were in a room, and part of the ceiling crashed down on them. No one was injured. The master of the novices commanded the demon to restore the ceiling, and to their amazement those present saw all the pieces of wood and plaster rise up and reassemble themselves. Still the disturbances continued. Cardinal Ursini performed an exorcism, but it failed to stop the activities of the demon. Carlo was sent from place to place, but the phenomena followed wherever he went. At another monastery in Capri, a Father Pietro wanted to perform an exorcism, but could not do it because he had left in Naples a book containing the proper procedures. When he began to pray, the demon appeared and threw the book at his feet. The demon said, "To my great confusion, I am obliged by that accursed name of that lad to bring you this book" (Gauld and Cornell 1979, p. 165).

On January 12, 1697, Carlo returned to his home. Sometimes when Carlo was away from the house, attending church services, the demon appeared in the shape of Carlo and beat Carlo's brother and tormented his mother. Shortly thereafter things quieted down for a couple of months. On March 30, Carlo therefore returned to the monastery, but immediately the phenomena began again. At that point the leaders of the monastery decided that Carlo should give up all plans for becoming a monk. After that, the demon never returned.

Gauld and Cornell (1979, p. 158) explain: "The case was recorded by one of the brothers . . . who seems to have kept notes of the occurrences, and his account survives (or survived) in two identical contemporary manuscripts, entitled *Caso successo in Napoli nell'anno 1696 a 4 maggio nella casa dei P.P. Gerolomini* (Case which happened in Naples, in the year 1696 on the 4th of May in the house of the Hieronymite Fathers). One of these manuscripts was obtained by a well-known Italian writer on psychic subjects, Francesco Zingaropoli, and was published by him with introduction and notes in a small and extremely rare book *Gesta di uno 'spirito' nel monastero dei P.P. Gerolomini in Napoli* (Naples, 1904)."

Laurence G. Thompson of the University of Southern California, in his book *Chinese Religion: An Introduction,* includes an account of an exorcism by a Taoist priest. The exorcism was witnessed by Peter Goullart, who recorded it in a book published in 1961.

Goullart and his traveling companions arrived at a Taoist temple in China. In a courtyard in front of the temple, they saw a young man, twenty-five years old, who had been possessed by a demon of a kind the Taoists call *kuei.* The emaciated young man, who had a wild look in his eyes, was lying on a straw mat placed on an iron bedstead. A Taoist priest and two assistants were standing nearby, with ritual paraphernalia on a small portable altar. Four strong men stood guard around the possessed young man. After repeating mantras from a book of incantations, the priest approached the possessed man. Goullart said, "His eyes were filled with malice as he watched the priest's measured advance with a sly cunning and hatred. Suddenly he gave a bestial whoop and jumped up in his bed, the four attendants rushing to hold him." The priest said to the *kuei* who had possessed the man, "Come out! Come out! I command you to come out." From the mouth of the young man came the words "No! No! You cannot drive us out . . . Our power is greater than yours!" These words and more were spoken rapidly "in a strange, shrill voice, which sounded mechanical, inhuman—as if pronounced by a parrot" (Nicola 1974, p. 102).

The priest repeated his commands, while the four strong men held the violently struggling young man down on the iron bed. He howled like an animal, showing his teeth like fangs. Suddenly, he broke out of the arms of the men holding him and threw himself at the priest's throat. The four men dragged him back down on the bed and tied him to it with ropes. Then the young man's body began to swell. Goullart stated, "On and on the dreadful process continued until he became a grotesque balloon of a man.... Convulsions shook the monstrous, swollen body.... It seemed that all the apertures of the body were opened by the unseen powers hiding in it and streams of malodorous excreta and effluvia flowed on to the ground in incredible profusion.... For an hour this continued" (Nicola 1974, p. 103). After this ordeal, the man resumed his normal size.

The priest then took a ritual sword, and standing over the possessed man, commanded the demons: "Leave him! Leave him, in the name of the Supreme Power who never meant you to steal this man's body!" (Nicola 1974, p. 103) Now the possessed man's body became rigid and heavy, causing the bed to bend beneath his weight. The four guards could not lift him. Only when three other men joined them from the onlookers gathered around could they move him. Then the possessed man suddenly became light. The guards placed him on a wooden bed. The Taoist priest again began to recite mantras from his book of incantations. Then he sprinkled the possessed man with holy water and came up to him with the sword. This time his efforts were successful. He cried out to the demons, "I have won! Get out! Get out!" (Nicola 1974, p. 103) The possessed man went into convulsions, foaming at the mouth and clawing his body with his fingernails until it became covered with blood. From his foaming lips came the words, "Damn you! Damn you! We are going but you shall pay for it with your life!" Goullart stated, "There was a terrible struggle on the bed, the poor man twisting and rolling like a mortally-wounded snake and his colour changing all the time. Suddenly he fell flat on his back and was still. His eyes opened. His gaze was normal, and he saw his parents who now came forward to reclaim their son" (Nicola 1974, p. 104).

Marian Apparitions

Earlier in this chapter, we considered postmortem apparitions of ordinary people as evidence for the existence of disembodied human beings. We then considered demonic possession as evidence for the existence of superhuman beings, albeit of the malevolent type. We shall now consider evidence for the existence of benevolent superhuman beings, beginning with Marian apparitions, apparitions of the Virgin Mary.

Juan Diego was an Aztec Indian who converted to Christianity shortly after the Spanish conquest of Mexico. He lived in a town called Quahutitlan, near Mexico City. Each day, he would walk to a church in a place called Tlatiloco. On the way, he would pass a hill called Tepeyacac. On the morning of December 8, 1531, as Juan Diego was passing by Tepeyacac, he heard music coming from the top of the hill. The music stopped, and then he heard a female voice calling his name. He climbed the hill and saw the glowing form of a beautiful young woman with a dark complexion, like an Indian. She spoke to him in Nahuatl, the language of the Aztecs. She identified herself as the Blessed Virgin Mary and asked him to tell the local bishop to build a church for her on the Tepeyacac hill. Interestingly enough, the Tepeyacac hill was the site of a temple to the Aztec earth goddess Coatlique (Mini 2000, p. 92).

Juan Diego went to the residence of Bishop Zumárraga and waited until he was allowed to see him. The bishop listened for a short time, and then suggested that they could talk more later. It was apparent to Juan Diego that the bishop did not believe his story. He went again to Tepeyacac and saw the apparition, who told him to go once more to the bishop. The next day, he again went to Mexico City, and with great difficulty, again managed to see the bishop. This time Zumárraga was more receptive. He told Juan Diego to ask the apparition for a sign that would authenticate her divine nature. Juan Diego said he would do this and left. When he saw the apparition for a third time, she told him she would give him the sign he requested on the next day.

On the next day, Juan Diego found that his uncle had become sick. His uncle wanted a priest. So instead of going to the hill to see the Virgin, Juan Diego went searching for a priest. On his way to get a priest, he passed the hill and heard the voice of the apparition calling him to see her, as he had promised. He replied that he would come, but he must first get a priest for his uncle. The voice replied, accusing Juan Diego of not having faith. The voice said his uncle would recover from his illness. Hearing this, Juan Diego agreed to come up to the top of the hill, but only if the apparition would give him the miraculous sign she had promised. She agreed. When Juan Diego reached the top of the hill, he saw it had been transformed. Where previously there had been only weeds and cactus plants, there was now, on December 12, 1531, in the iciest part of winter, a beautiful garden of blossoming, fragrant flowers, including Castilian roses and other Spanish flowers, all out of season. The apparition gathered some of these flowers, and placed them in the cloak that Juan Diego was wearing. She told him to present the flowers to the Bishop as the sign he had asked for. She also told Juan Diego not to open the cloak and show the flowers until he saw the Bishop.

Juan Diego came to the Bishop's residence, and after making his way through hostile servants and guards who tried to see what he was carrying, came before the Bishop himself. When he opened his cloak, not only did the flowers fall out, but there was visible on the cloak itself a colorful image of the Virgin Mary. The radiant image was that of a beautiful young dark-skinned woman in prayer. She was standing on a crescent moon, and the crescent moon was being held by an angel. It could be seen that it was not a painted image, but was part of the fabric of the cloak. Bishop Zumárraga was overwhelmed by this miraculous sign, and agreed to build a church on the hill. The cloak, with its image unfaded, is on display even today in the Church of the Virgin of Guadalupe in Villa Madero (Rogo 1982, pp. 117–120).

Rogo (1982, p. 120) says, "Between 1531 and 1648, no fewer than thirty-three documents describing the events of December 1531 were placed on record. As Father José Bravo Ugarte, an expert on Mexican history, states in his *Cuestiones historicas guadalupanas* (1946), 'There can be little doubt that the story of the Guadalupe miracle rests on firm historical fact.' Even Zumárraga apparently wrote out an account of the miracle, though his description was destroyed in 1778 by a fire that struck the archive room of the monastery where it had been deposited. In 1666 the Church officially investigated the miracle, retraced its history, and documented the evidence supporting its authenticity." As part of the 1666 investigations, a group of painters examined the image and concluded it could not have been made by even the finest human artists. They stated: "It is impossible for any human craftsman to paint or create a work so fine, clean and well formed on a fabric so coarse" (Mini 2000, p. 167).

Over the years, there have been many investigations of the cloak and its image. The miraculous preservation of the maguey fabric was noted long ago. In 1660, Father Florencia wrote in his historical book *La estrella del norte de Mexico,* "The permanence of the coarse maguey canvas ... has lasted more than a hundred years. This is miraculous, since it is as entire and strong as it was the first day; especially when we consider the place in which it is subject to wind and saline dust and the heat of the candles and the incense which the devout continuously offer—without fading, or darkening or cracking" (Rogo 1982, p. 120).

In the twentieth century, enlarged photographs of the eyes of the Virgin showed a human face, apparently that of Juan Diego, reflected in each eye. In 1956, a group of eye and vision specialists looked at these images. Mini (2000, p. 169) stated: "They found that the images were reflected not only from the corneas of both of her eyes, but also from the lenses. . . . The image of Juan Diego's face appears three times in each of the Virgin's eyes. It appears once at the surface of the cornea, again at the anterior surface of the lens, and a third time at the posterior surface of the lens. . . . The images of Juan Diego in the Virgin's eyes maintain perfect optical proportions under the closest scientific scrutiny. The scientists discerned that the images in each eye are in the exact locations required by optical physics."

In 1979, Philip Callahan, a biophysicist from the University of Florida, tested the image on the cloak and found no brushstrokes or any "underdrawn blueprint" (Rogo 1982, p. 121). He also confirmed that the image has suffered no fading or cracking, which is unusual for an image produced by painting four hundred years ago. Callahan did find that there had been some additions to the original image. A sunburst had been painted around the Virgin's figure and some stars and a golden border had been added to the Virgin's cape. But Callahan pointed out that these additions had faded, while the original image retained its full colors. The cloak bearing the image is made of maguey cactus fiber, which should have rotted away hundreds of years ago. Callahan inspected the fibers to see if the cloak had been treated to prevent rotting, and found that this was not the case (Rogo 1982, p. 120).

The village of Pontmain is near the city of Le Mans in northwestern France. On the evening of January 17, 1871, Eugene Barbadette, who was twelve years old, and his brother Joseph, who was ten years old, were working in the barn on their father's farm. Eugene decided to take a break from their work and went outside into the winter night. The sky was clear and filled with stars. Then Eugene noticed the figure of a beautiful woman floating in the sky. She was dressed in a blue robe, studded with golden stars, and wore a blue veil. At first, Eugene took the vision as a sign that his brother, who was in the French army, had died in battle with the Prussians, who had invaded France in the Franco-Prussian War of 1871. But he then noticed that the woman was smiling, and decided the vision must mean something favorable. Jeanette Detais, a neighborhood woman who had come for a visit, was standing nearby. But she could not see the apparition. Eugene's father Mr. Barbadette and Eugene's younger brother Joseph also came out. The father could not see anything, but Joseph could. Joseph and Eugene then began speaking to each other about what they were seeing. During the course of the evening, the boys continued to see the apparition, while others arriving on the scene, including Mrs. Barbadette, her maid, and a local nun, Sister Vitaline, could not.

Sister Vitaline concluded that perhaps the apparition was visible only to children. She went back to her convent to get two girls who were staying there. The girls were Francoise Richer, who was eleven years old, and Jeanne-Marie Lebosse, who was nine years old. Sister Vitaline deliberately did not tell them anything about the vision, but as soon as the girls came out into the street, they started telling Sister Vitaline about the apparition. They could see a beautiful woman in the sky, wearing a blue robe with stars on it. Soon thereafter, Joseph Barbadette came over from his house, and, as previously, he also saw the vision. Other children were also brought to the scene, and they could all see the apparition, although the adults could still see nothing. The children then began to describe changes in the apparition. An oval frame with four candles appeared around the figure of the woman. Then, letter by letter, a message began to form under the woman in the sky. The final message was *Mais priez, Dieu vous exaucera en peu de temps Mon Fils se laisse toucher*, which means: "But pray, God will hear your prayers in a short time. My Son allows himself to be moved." By the time the message was being spelled out, the children had dispersed to separate locations, and were thus out of communication with each other, but the same letters appeared to all of them.

At the same time, a messenger arrived in Pontmain, saying that the Prussians were marching in the direction of the village. After the message in the sky was spelled out, the woman in the sky, identified by the faithful Catholics of Pontmain as the Blessed Virgin Mary, raised her arms in benediction. Then the message faded, and the Virgin began to frown as a crucifix formed on her chest. Finally, after the apparition had been visible for two hours, it faded away. The Prussian armies mysteriously stopped their advance at the town of Laval, and did not proceed any further. In 1875, the Bishop of Laval attested to the reality of the Marian apparition at Pontmain and a church was erected at the place where the apparition was seen (Rogo 1982, pp. 214–217).

Fatima, in Portugal, was in 1917 the site of the most famous of Marian apparitions. The apparition was seen several times by three children: Lucia dos Santos (nine years old), Francisco Marto (eight years old), and Jacinta Marto (six years old). All three were shepherds, and would take out their flocks together. They were related as cousins.

The Marian apparitions were preceded by apparitions of angels. The first angel apparition occurred to Lucia in 1915, when she was out herding sheep with three other girls. Lucia recalled: "We saw a figure poised in the air above the trees; it looked like a statue made of snow, rendered almost transparent by the rays of the sun. . . . We went on praying, with our eyes fixed on the figure before us, and as we finished our prayer, the figure disappeared" (Maria Lucia 1998, p. 61). Lucia and her friends saw the figure twice more.

By 1916, Lucia was herding sheep with Francisco and Jacinta. One day they were watching their sheep in an olive grove at the foot of a hill. After taking their lunch, they chanted their rosary prayers and then began to play a game they called "pebbles." Then a strong wind moved the branches of the trees. The children thought this unusual, because it had been a calm day. Then the same figure Lucia saw in 1915 appeared again, but this time she could see it more clearly. It was moving toward them over the olive trees. "It was a young man," said Lucia, "about fourteen or fifteen years old, whiter than snow, transparent as crystal when the sun shines through it, and of great beauty. On reaching us, he said, 'Don't be afraid, I am the Angel of Peace. Pray with me'" (Maria Lucia 1998, p. 63). Some time later, during the summer, the angel appeared again, near a well on property owned by Lucia's family.

About these experiences, Lucia wrote (1998, pp. 161–162): "The force of the presence of God was so intense that it absorbed us and almost completely annihilated us. It seemed to deprive us even of the use of our bodily senses for a considerable length of time. During those days, we performed all our exterior actions as though guided by that same supernatural being who was impelling us thereto. The peace and happiness which we felt were great but wholly interior, for our souls were completely immersed in God. The physical exhaustion that came over us was also great."

On May 13, 1916, the children, out with their sheep, were playing on a slope at a place called the Cova da Iria. Suddenly they saw a flash of light. "We'd better go home," said Lucia. "That's lightning; we may have a thunderstorm." The children took their sheep down the slope. As they were going, they saw another flash of light near a large holmoak tree. "We had only gone a few steps further," said Lucia, "when, there before us on a small holmoak, we beheld a Lady all dressed in white. She was more brilliant than the sun, and radiated a light more clear and intense than a crystal glass filled with sparkling water, when the rays of the burning sun shine through. We stopped, astounded before the Apparition. We were so close, just a few feet from her, that we were bathed in the light which surrounded her, or rather, which radiated from her" (Maria Lucia 1998, p. 164).

The lady said to the children, "Do not be afraid. I will do you no harm." Lucia asked, "Where are you from?" The lady replied, "I am from heaven" (Maria Lucia 1998, pp. 165–166). She told the children she wanted them to come on the same day and hour for the next six months. She said, "Later on, I will tell you who I am and what I want." Lucia asked if she (Lucia) would go to heaven. The lady said yes. In response to further questions from Lucia, she said Jacinta would also go, and so would Francisco. The lady asked if they were willing to offer themselves to God and, for the sake of the sinners of the world, bear all the troubles He would send to them. The children replied that they were willing. The lady said the grace of God would be their comfort. Then, said Lucia, the lady "opened her hands for the first time, communicating to us a light so intense that, as it streamed from her hands, its rays penetrated our hearts and the innermost depths of our souls, making us see ourselves in God, Who was that light, more clearly than we see ourselves in the best of mirrors" (Maria Lucia 1998, p. 166). The lady asked the children to pray the rosary every day, to end World War I and bring peace. "Then she began to rise serenely," said Lucia, "going up towards the east, until she disappeared in the immensity of space. The light that surrounded her seemed to open up a path before her in the firmament."

On the spot, at Lucia's urging, the children agreed to keep silent about the apparition. But that very night Jacinta spoke about it to her family. Once the word was out, they all found themselves speaking. Lucia experienced a lot of opposition from her family, particularly her mother. Lucia said, "My mother was getting worried, and wanted at all costs to make me deny what I had said. One day, before I set out with the flock, she was determined to make me confess that I was telling lies, and to this end she spared neither caresses, nor threats, nor even the broomstick. To all this she received nothing but a mute silence, or the confirmation of all that I had already said. . . . She warned me that she would force me, that very evening, to go to those people whom I had deceived, confess that I had lied and ask their pardon" (Maria Lucia 1998, pp. 32–33).

On June 13, the children waited at the appointed time and place for the lady to appear. Once more they saw a flash of light, and then the lady appeared again in the same holmoak tree as before. This time about fifty villagers were present, but they saw nothing. Lucia said to the lady, "I would like to ask you to take us to heaven." The lady replied, "Yes, I will take Jacinta and Francisco soon. But you are to stay here some time longer. Jesus wishes to make use of you to make me known and loved." The lady assured Lucia that she would not be alone. Then the lady opened her hands, and light streamed forth. Lucia said, "We saw ourselves immersed in this light, as it were, immersed in God. Jacinta and Francisco seemed to be in that part of the light which rose towards heaven, and I in that which was poured out on the earth" (Maria Lucia 1998, p. 169). The revelation that Jacinta and Francisco would soon be taken to heaven was the first of three famous secrets of Fatima, later revealed by Lucia. In 1918, both Jacinta and Francisco were struck by influenza. Francisco died in 1919, and Jacinta died in 1920. Before her death, Jacinta had some personal visions of the lady.

Although no one else saw the figure of the lady on June 13, some of the people present did notice some paranormal phenomena. Reverend V. Dacruz, a Spanish priest who studied the history of the Fatima events very deeply, noted: "The day was bright and hot as it usually is in Portugal in the month of June. Now, during the entire period of the apparition the light of the sun was dimmed in an exceptional manner, without any apparent cause. At the same time, the topmost branches of the tree were bent in the form of a parasol, and remained thus as if an invisible weight had come to rest upon them. Those nearest the tree heard quite distinctly Lucy's [Lucia's] words, and also perceived in the form of an indistinct whispering, or the loud humming of a bee, the sound of the Lady's answer, alternating regularly with the girl's voice. At the end of the apparition, there was heard near the tree a loud report which the witnesses compared to the explosion of a rocket, and Lucy cried: 'There! She is going away.' At the same time the onlookers saw rise from the tree a beautiful white cloud which they could follow with their eyes for quite a while as it moved in the direction of the East. Further, at the Lady's departure, the upper branches of the tree, without losing the curved shape of a parasol, leaned towards the East, as if in going away the Lady's dress had trailed over them. And this double pressure which had bent the branches, first into a curve and then towards the East, was so great that the branches remained like this for long hours, and only slowly resumed their normal position" (Rogo 1982, pp. 224–225). After this second apparition, news of the strange happenings began to circulate all over Portugal.

On July 13, a much larger number of people, four or five thousand, gathered with the children to await the scheduled apparition. The lady appeared in the same way as before. Once again, onlookers, although they could not see the lady herself, saw the sun become dimmer, saw an orb of light over the tree where the lady was apparently standing, and heard a whispering voice reply indistinguishably to Lucia (Rogo 1982, p. 225). Lucia put a request to the lady: "I would like to ask you to tell us who you are, and to work a miracle so that everybody will believe that you are appearing to us." The lady replied, "Continue to come here every month. In October, I will tell you who I am and what I want, and I will perform a miracle for all to see and believe." The lady also asked the children to sacrifice themselves for the sake of the world's sinners. Then the lady, light streaming from her hands, gave the children a terrible vision. Lucia said, "The rays of light seemed to penetrate the earth, and we saw as it were a sea of fire. Plunged in this fire were demons and souls in human form, like transparent burning embers." Lucia added, "It must have been this sight which caused me to cry out, as people say they heard me" (Maria Lucia 1998, p. 170). The lady explained to the children that what they saw was the hell where sinners go and that if they followed her instructions they could prevent many souls from going there. This would also insure peace in the world. The lady told them, "The war [World War I] is going to end; but if people do not cease offending God, a worse one will break out during the pontificate of Pius XI. When you see a night illumined by an unknown light, know that this is the great sign given you by God that he is about to punish the world for its crimes by means of war, famine, and persecutions of the Church and of the Holy Father." The lady said she would later come to ask for the conversion of Russia, saying that otherwise Russia "will spread her errors throughout the world, causing wars and persecutions" (Maria Lucia 1998, pp. 170, 174). The lady specifically said: "In the end, my Immaculate Heart will triumph. The Holy Father will consecrate Russia to me, and she will be converted, and a period of peace will be granted to the world" (Maria Lucia 1998, p. 110). The lady asked that this revelation be kept secret. This is the famous second secret of Fatima.

According to the revelation, a second great war was to start during the reign of Pope Pius XI. But he died on February 10, 1939, several months before World War II began with the German invasion of Poland in September of that year. Father Louis Kondor, editor of Lucia's writings on Fatima, stated: "To the objection that the Second World War . . . actually started during the Pontificate of Pius XII, she [Lucia] replied that in fact the war began with the occupation of Austria in 1938." Kondor also stated, "Lucia presumed that the 'extraordinary' aurora borealis during the night of 25th to 26th January, 1938, was the sign given by God to announce the imminence of war." The lady's promise to come back was fulfilled by an appearance to Lucia in 1925. Lucia took the fall of the communist regimes in East Europe and Russia to be a fulfillment of the lady's revelations concerning Russia" (Maria Lucia 1998, p. 110).

After revealing the two secrets mentioned above, the lady revealed the famous third secret of Fatima. It was later written down by Lucia on January 3, 1944, and it was then kept secret until June 26, 2000, when it was released in English by the Vatican. Here is the text: "At the left of Our Lady and a little above, we saw an Angel with a flaming sword in his left hand; flashing, it gave out flames that looked as though they would set the world on fire; but they died out in contact with the splendor that Our Lady radiated towards him from her right hand; pointing to the earth with his right hand, the Angel cried out in a loud voice: 'Penance, Penance, Penance'. And we saw in an immense light that is God (something similar to how people appear in a mirror when they pass in front of it) a Bishop dressed in White (we had the impression that it was the Holy Father). Other Bishops, Priests, men and women Religious going up a steep mountain, at the top of which there was a big Cross of rough-hewn trunks as of a cork-tree with the bark; before reaching there the Holy Father passed through a big city half in ruins and half trembling with halting step, afflicted with pain and sorrow, he prayed for the souls of the corpses he met on his way; having reached the top of the mountain, on his knees at the foot of the big Cross he was killed by a group of soldiers who fired bullets and arrows at him, and in the same way there died one after another the other Bishops, Priests, men and women Religious, and various lay people of different ranks and positions. Beneath the two arms of the Cross there were two Angels each with a crystal aspersorium in his hand, in which they gathered up the blood of the Martyrs and with it sprinkled the souls that were making their way to God." One might take it that the fall of Communism in Russia indicated that the Virgin was pleased, and that therefore her third prediction did not come to pass. Some have suggested that the attempted assassination of Pope John Paul II was partial fulfillment of the prediction.

As the apparitions continued, the anticlerical government of Portugal saw the Fatima events as the focal point for a dangerous resurgence of Catholic religious sentiment, with political implications. The government, having concluded that priests had encouraged the children to manufacture the apparitions, assigned a district official, Arthur d'Oliveira Santos, to expose the children as liars. Santos arrived in Fatima on August 11 and questioned them there. Despite his threats, the children refused to confess they were telling lies in collusion with local priests (Rogo 1982, p. 226).

On August 13, as huge crowds gathered for the apparition, Lucia and her cousins were taken away by government officials. Although the children were not present at the appointed time, some unusual things did happen. Rogo (1982, p. 226) said, "The crowd heard a loud detonation and a flash of lightning illuminated the sky at the very time the woman should have appeared. The sun dimmed, and a kaleidoscope of colors bathed the Cova. A white cloud appeared by the oak tree, remained for an instant, and then rose and moved quickly away."

Meanwhile the children were forcefully interrogated by Santos at Ourem, and then kept in a prison (Maria Lucia 1998, p. 77). The children were threatened with death. In fact, when Santos spoke with each one separately, he told them the others had already been killed and that the one being questioned would also be killed if he or she did not confess to having manufactured the Fatima apparitions. Lucia said (1998, p. 36) that even after this they were all together threatened with being "fried alive." When the children were in their cell, other prisoners tried to convince them to admit to being liars and thus get out of prison. But desiring to preserve the secrecy the lady asked for, they said they would rather die. Unable to extract confessions from them, Santos soon released them.

Although the children were not able to keep their appointment with the apparition on August 13, the lady again appeared to the children on August 19 as they were herding sheep at a place called Valinhos. There was another appearance at the usual place on September 13. This time, thirty thousand people came. Around noon they saw the sun become dim and they could see stars in the sky. They also saw a globe of white light settle on the tree where the lady normally appeared. Monsignor John Quareman, the vice-general of the town of Leiria, said, "To my surprise, I saw clearly and distinctly a globe of light advancing from east to west, gliding slowly and majestically through the air. . . . My friend looked also, and he had the good fortune to see the same unexpected vision. Suddenly the globe with the wonderful light dropped from sight" (Rogo 1982, p. 227). On this occasion there was also a rain of white flower petals, which mysteriously disappeared before they reached the ground.

Finally, the time came for the October 13 apparition, the last and most important of the series. Government officials were certain that the promised miracle would not occur, and were preparing to take advantage of this to launch a large propaganda campaign to discredit the whole Fatima phenomenon (Rogo 1982, p. 228). Lucia said (1998, p. 177): "We left home quite early, expecting that we would be delayed along the way. Masses of people, about seventy thousand, thronged the roads. The rain fell in torrents." Among the crowds were church officials, government and military officials, and reporters from Portugal's leading papers. The government also had troops standing by.

Then Lucia and her cousins reached the tree where the lady usually appeared. Lucia told the crowds of people gathered there to close their umbrellas and start saying the rosary prayers. The rainfall turned to a drizzle. Then came a flash of light, and the lady appeared to the children.

She identified herself as the Lady of the Rosary and exchanged words with Lucia, on the same themes as previously. "Then," said Lucia, "opening her hands, she made them reflect on the sun, and as she ascended, the reflection of her own light continued to be projected on the sun itself." At this moment Lucia asked the people to look at the sun, which up to that moment had been hidden by thick clouds (Maria Lucia 1998, p. 177). People who looked in that direction saw a glowing silvery disk. Some researchers believe this was a UFO. Others believe the movements were those of the sun itself. The glowing disk revolved on its axis, sending rainbow-colored beams of light in all directions. This continued for twelve minutes. Then the disk, moving in zigzag fashion, plunged earthward. The fall was accompanied by a rapid increase in atmospheric temperature, causing panic among the crowds of witnesses. Suddenly the disk rose back into the sky. The astonished people present found that the blazing heat had dried the rain-soaked ground along with their own clothing. Reports of these events were carried in most major newspapers, including the anticlerical *O Seculo*. In the 1940s and 1950s researchers came to Portugal and interviewed many of the surviving witnesses and recorded their testimonies (Walsh 1947, Haffent 1961).

Dr. Almeida Garrete, a professor at the University of Coimbra, described his experience at Fatima: "The radiant sun had pierced the thick curtain of clouds which held it veiled. All eyes were raised towards it as if drawn by a magnet. I myself tried to look straight at it, and saw it looking like a well-defined disc, bright but not blinding. . . . This chequered shining disc seemed to possess a giddy motion. It was not the twinkling of a star. It turned on itself with an astonishing rapidity. Suddenly a great cry, like a cry of anguish, arose from all this vast throng. The sun while keeping its swiftness of rotation, detached itself from the firmament and, blood-red in colour, rushed towards the earth, threatening to crush us under the immense weight of its mass of fire. There were moments of dreadful tension. All these phenomena, which I have described, I have witnessed personally, coldly and calmly, without the slightest agitation of mind" (Rogo 1982, p. 230).

The disk and its movements were seen by others, distant from the Fatima site. In 1931, Father Ignatius Lawrence Pereira told how he witnessed the event when he was nine years old, attending a school nine miles from Fatima. He said: "Our teacher rushed out, and the children all ran after her. In the public square people wept and shouted, pointing to the sun. . . . I looked fixedly at the sun, which appeared pale and did not dazzle. It looked like a ball of snow turning on itself. . . .Then suddenly it seemed to become detached from the sky, and rolled right and left, as if it were falling upon the earth. Terrified, absolutely terrified, I ran towards the crowd of people. All were weeping, expecting at any moment the end of the world. . . . During the long minutes of the solar phenomena, the objects around us reflected all the colours of the rainbow. Looking at each other, one appeared blue, another yellow, a third red, etc., and all these strange phenomena only increased the terror of the people. After about ten minutes the sun climbed back into its place, as it had descended, still quite pale and without brilliance" (Rogo 1982, p. 231). Just after the lady disappeared, Lucia saw apparitions of Mary, St. Joseph, and Jesus (Maria Lucia, pp. 177–178).

On June 24, 1981, two girls, Ivanka Ivankovic and Mirjana Dragicevic, were walking through a sheep pasture near the village of Medjugorje in Croatia, which was then part of Yugoslavia. Ivanka saw on the slopes of Mt. Podbrdo, at a distance of a few hundred yards, a glowing figure of a young woman floating in the air on a grey cloud. Ivanka called to her friend Mirjana, telling her that "Our Lady" was there. At first, Mirjana, not believing her, did not look, and they went off to meet some friends. Later the same day, Ivanka and Mirjana returned to the site of the apparition with a friend, Milka Pavlovic, and they all saw the apparition. Then three other young people (Vicka Ivankovic, Ivan Ivankovic, and Ivan Dragicevik) arrived and also saw it. This time all six identified the apparition as the Virgin Mary, holding the child Christ. The young people silently gazed at the apparition for forty-five minutes, until she disappeared (Hancock 1998, pp. 25–26).

When they returned to their village, they spoke about what they had seen, but no one believed them. Milka's sister, Marija, told her she had been hallucinating, and Vicka's sister sarcastically suggested she had seen a UFO. The next day, Ivanka, Mirjana, Vicka, and Ivan Dragicevic returned to the place where they had seen the apparition, accompanied by two other children (the skeptical Marija Pavlovic and a boy, Jakov Colo) as well as two adults (Hancock 1998, pp. 27–28).

Ivanka saw on Mt. Podbrdo the apparition, summoning them to come up to her. Vicka later recalled: "We ran quickly up the hill. It was not like walking on the ground. Nor did we look for the path. We simply ran toward Her. In five minutes we were up the hill, as if something had pulled us through the air. I was afraid. I was also barefoot, yet no thorns had scratched me" (Hancock 1998, p. 27). Normally, it should have taken twenty minutes, walking very quickly, to ascend the hill. When the children came near the apparition, they felt themselves forced to their knees. One of the children, Vicka, asked Mirjana what time it was. Mirjana said that when she looked at her watch, she saw that the number twelve had changed to the number nine. The children took this as a minor miracle, a sign from the apparition that her appearance was real. The next day, June 26, thousands of people came with the children to the base of the mountain. Anne Marie Hancock (1998, p. 28) wrote, "For the first time, the Madonna's apparition was preceded by a brilliant light that was witnessed not only by the children, but the spectators as well. The light illuminated not only the area, but the entire village!" Three of the children, Ivanka, Mirjana, and Vicka, fainted. When they returned to consciousness they observed the apparition for thirty minutes.

On Saturday, June 27, 1981, the police examined the children, testing their mental and physical health. They found the children normal. Then, on the theory that perhaps one of the children was influencing the others to tell stories about an imaginary vision, they split the children into two groups. One group went to the top of the mountain, and the other group stayed at the bottom. The apparition appeared to both groups, and the group at the bottom of the hill outran their adult supervisors to the top of the hill. Then the apparition disappeared. All the children then fell to their knees, and the apparition appeared to them again, preceded by a brilliant light, which was seen by the crowds of people gathered for the event. As usually happened, the apparition itself was visible only to the children. For the first time, the apparition explicitly identified herself to the children as the Virgin Mary. On this same occasion, the apparition also appeared to another one of the children, Ivan, who had been kept home by his parents (Hancock 1998, p. 29).

On Sunday, June 28, 1981, fifteen thousand people gathered at Mt. Podbrdo. Concerned government officials brought the children to the town of Citluk for more examinations. The officials, hoping to find evidence of psychological unfitness, had the children examined by another doctor, who also found them physically and psychologically fit. That evening the children returned once more to Mt. Podbrdo, and when they saw the apparition, they begged her to give some sign that the onlookers could also see (Hancock 1998, p. 31).

The children specifically asked the apparition to cure a mute boy named Daniel. Daniel, who was two and a half years old, was also unable to walk. The apparition told the children to ask Daniel's parents, who were present in the crowd along with Daniel, to have firm faith that he would be cured. When the family left Mt. Podbrdo to go home, they stopped at a restaurant along the way. At this restaurant, Daniel struck the table with his hands and said, "Give me something to drink." Later, he began to walk and run (Hancock 1998, p. 59).

Hancock (1998, p. 58) says: "There have been numerous reported healings at Medjugorje. Fifty-six have been documented by Father Rupcic in his book. Physical healings relate to eye and ear diseases, arthritis, vascular problems, neurological disease, wounds, tumors, and a plethora of others. The strength to overcome addictions and smoking, after repeated attempts, has been documented. Psychological healings have also been reported. Various modes of healing have been identified." The lady said to the children, "I cannot heal; only God can."

On June 30, 1981, government officials tried to put an end to the crowds of people gathering to see the apparitions by removing the children. Two female social workers came from the town of Bijakovici to get the children. Their orders were to make sure that the children would not be at Mt. Podbrdo at the usual time of the apparition. As the children were being driven away in a car, they demanded that the driver stop the car. The children got out of the car and prayed. They saw a brilliant light moving towards them from the mountain. The two social workers could also see it. Then the Virgin appeared to the children at the usual time (Hancock 1998, pp. 31–32). Afterwards, the two social workers resigned their government positions. To put an end to the matter, the police decided themselves to keep the children away from the place of the apparitions.

On July 1, 1981, Father Jozo, the local Catholic priest, was praying in his church, when something unusual happened. Father Jozo later recalled, "Something happened that for me was important and decisive. . . . a turning point and a moment of revelation. While I was praying, I heard a voice say, 'Come out and protect the children'" (Hancock 1998, p. 33). At this moment, the children were running toward the church, with the police chasing after them. Father Jozo hid the children in the church. When the police arrived and asked him about the children, he pointed in the direction of the town of Bijakovici. Father Jozo kept the children for some time in the church. Later, he informed the parents about a law forbidding police to question minor children without the consent of their parents. When the police approached the parents to question the children, the parents withheld consent. Up to this time, Father Jozo, although he wanted to shelter the children, did not himself believe in the apparitions. But later that summer, Father Jozo himself saw the apparition (Hancock 1998, p. 33).

On August 12, 1981, the police banned the public from gathering at the apparition site at Mt. Podbrdo. Thereafter, the apparitions continued in the presence of the children in homes and other places. The gatherings were kept as secret as possible. The police kept up their pressure by arresting Father Jozo. They also seized his church records, which contained the best documentation of the apparitions (Hancock 1998, pp. 34–35).

During the days of Father Jozo's trial (October 21–22, 1981), villagers saw a cross on Mt. Krizevak become a column of light. They also saw an apparition of the Virgin. Father Jozo was given a prison sentence of three and a half years, but when villagers protested, he was released after eighteen months (Hancock 1998, p. 35).

The apparitions continued in the presence of the children in the Church of St. James and in other places. The Madonna is then said to have revealed ten secrets to each of the children. The revelations took place over the course of many months. Mirjana was the first to receive all ten, the last secret coming on December 25, 1982. Thereafter, other children claimed they started to receive messages from the apparition through the heart.

Appearing to Ivan Dragicevic, the apparition asked that the villagers fast and pray for three days prior to the Madonna's 2,000th birthday, which the apparition gave as August 5, 1984 (the official Church date for the Madonna's appearance is September 8). On August 5, 35,000 people gathered at Medjugorje. Hancock (1998, p. 39) states: "It was on this day, early in the morning, for the first recorded time, that many would personally witness a vision of the Madonna on Mt. Krizevak. There were thousands who had camped outside the church, itself. They saw what has been described as the silhouette of a woman clothed in brilliant white, her hands raised towards the sky. Some reported seeing the figure in colored garments.... Many others reported other signs and wonders that day, including the sun spinning furiously in its orbit." According to Hancock (1998, p. 62) the witnesses to the solar miracle saw the sun "spinning on its own axis" as it moved toward them and then receded.

Describing her own experience on another occasion, Hancock (1998, p. 62) wrote, "The finest artist could never adequately reproduce the sight that was so graphically sculpted and colored across the sky before my eyes. I was truly in awe. For myself, I experienced a spinning that was almost hypnotic, and I found myself staring at this vortex of gold, seemingly covered by a disc that protected my eyes. It was a pulsating brilliance that defies description. As it spun, it seemed to move towards us, yet still remain in its orbit. It seemed as if it could move in any direction at any given moment. The colors were vibrant fuschia, violet, lavender, silver, and emerald. As soon as one color could be identified, it immediately melted into another, gently blending into its next spectrum. It is known that staring into the sun for an extended period of time can, and has, damaged the retina in the eyes. Yet, after thirty minutes of staring directly at the sun, my eyes had absolutely no damage to them. Many observers have subsequently had their eyes tested by optometrists. The results have always been the same: no damage, no explanation!" Hancock noted (1998, p. 63), "Others say they have seen the Holy Mother, with the Sacred Heart, and a herald of angels, during their experiences."

Several of the original visionaries continue to see the apparition and give reports about messages received, including secrets to be revealed at appropriate times by specially chosen priests.

Chaitanya Mahaprabhu: A Modern Incarnation of Godhead

The Bible gives records of appearances of God on earth in periods from perhaps 6,000 to 2,000 years ago. But the Gaudiya Vaishnava tradition of India records such appearances as recently as the fifteenth century. According to Gaudiya Vaishnava historical records, Chaitanya Mahaprabhu, who appeared at Mayapur, West Bengal, in 1486, was an avatar, a descent of the Godhead to the earthly plane of existence. He disappeared from this world in 1534. Among the contemporaries of Chaitanya Mahaprabhu in Europe were Magellan (1480–1521), Copernicus (1473–1543), da Vinci (1452–1519), Columbus (1451–1506), and other figures of the early modern period. India itself was at this time recognized as a prosperous land, with a reputation for learning in philosophy and the sciences. Biographical accounts recognizing the divinity of Chaitanya Mahaprabhu became classics of Bengali literature. For the sketch of his life that follows, my main source is the *Chaitanya Charitamrita,* by Krishnadasa Kaviraja Goswami, who lived in the sixteenth century. He composed this work shortly after the departure of Chaitanya Mahaprabhu from this world. One thing that is quickly apparent from this biography is that Gaudiya Vaishnavas were cautious in accepting the divinity of Chaitanya Mahaprabhu, basing their judgement upon a combination of scriptural evidence predicting his appearance, displays of superhuman powers, and experimental tests of his symptoms.

One of the predictions of Chaitanya Mahaprabhu's appearance can be found in the *Shrimad Bhagavatam,* sometimes called the *Bhagavata Purana.* In the fifth chapter of the eleventh canto of *Shrimad Bhagavatam,* the great sage Narada Muni tells Vasudeva the identity of the principal avatar worshiped in each of the four ages (*yugas*) in the Vedic *yuga* cycle (Satya Yuga, Treta Yuga, Dvapara Yuga, Kali Yuga). Having described the avatars for the first three *yugas,* Narada Muni then described the avatar for the fourth. Because Narada Muni was speaking at the end of the third *yuga,* his statements about the fourth avatar, the one for the Kali Yuga, were therefore predictive. According to the *Shrimad Bhagavatam* itself, the text itself was composed five thousand years ago. And even modern scholars, who attribute a younger age to the work, say it is at least one thousand years old. Either way, the descriptions of the fourth avatar predate the appearance of Chaitanya Mahaprabhu. Narada Muni said: "In Kali-yuga also people worship the Supreme Personality of Godhead by following various regulations of the revealed scriptures. Now kindly hear of this from me. In the age of Kali, intelligent persons perform congregational chanting to worship the incarnation of Godhead who constantly sings the names of Krishna" (*Shrimad Bhagavatam* 11.5.31–32). When Chaitanya Mahaprabhu was present, he traveled widely all over India, chanting the names of Krishna in the form of the Hare Krishna mantra: Hare Krishna, Hare Krishna, Krishna Krishna, Hare Hare, Hare Rama, Hare Rama, Rama Rama, Hare Hare. Millions of people joined him in this congregational chanting.

Chaitanya Mahaprabhu predicted that this chanting would spread to every town and village in the world, and within recent times, this prediction has come true. In 1965, my spiritual master, His Divine Grace A. C. Bhaktivedanta Swami Prabhupada, a guru in the line of succession coming from Chaitanya Mahaprabhu, came by sea from India to New York, and began to introduce the chanting of the Hare Krishna mantra worldwide, in fulfillment of Chaitanya Mahaprabhu's prediction. And now the chanting can be seen and heard in the streets of cities and villages everywhere.

The birth of Chaitanya Mahaprabhu was preceded by announcing dreams. His father Jagannatha Mishra told his wife Sachi Devi, "In a dream I saw the effulgent abode of the Lord enter my heart. From my heart it entered your heart. I therefore understand that a great personality will soon take birth" (*Chaitanya Charitamrita, Adi-lila* 13.84–85). The birth of Chaitanya Mahaprabhu coincided with a lunar eclipse. According to custom, during a lunar eclipse Vaishnava Hindus take baths in sacred rivers like the Ganges while loudly chanting the Hare Krishna mantra. Thus at the moment of Lord Chaitanya's birth, in Navadvipa, West Bengal, on the banks of the Ganges, the atmosphere was filled with the chanting of the Hare Krishna mantra, giving a prophetic glimpse of his future mission. The horoscope of Chaitanya Mahaprabhu confirmed that he was a great godlike personality who would deliver humankind from the miseries of existence in the material world. His feet, hands, and body also displayed an auspicious combination of features and marks indicating he was an incarnation of the Personality of Godhead.

Chaitanya Mahaprabhu spent his first twenty-four years in Navadvipa, performing many miracles. Then he became a *sannyasi,* a member of the renounced spiritual order of life. *Sannyasis* take a lifelong vow of celibacy, and travel widely to give their spiritual teachings. Chaitanya

Mahaprabhu first went to the home of one of his chief associates, Advaita Prabhu. There he showed Advaita Prabhu his universal form, thus confirming his status as an incarnation of the Personality of Godhead (*Chaitanya Charitamrita, Madhya-lila* 17.10). The universal form is an awe inspiring display whereby all of the planets and celestial bodies become present in the form of the incarnation, which becomes simultaneously present in all of them.

Afterwards, Chaitanya Mahaprabhu journeyed to the sacred city of Jagannatha Puri, in the state of Orissa. Upon arriving, he entered the famous temple of Jagannatha, a form of Vishnu, and, displaying signs of spiritual ecstasies, fainted when he saw the altar deity. The temple guards were used to seeing pilgrims imitate ecstatic symptoms, in hopes of passing themselves off as incarnations of God. Thinking that Chaitanya Mahaprabhu was another such imposter, they came forward to expel him from the temple. But they were stopped by Sarvabhauma Bhattacharya, one of the leading teachers of Jagannatha Puri. He sensed that *sannyasi* lying on the floor might not be the usual kind of fake.

A. C. Bhaktivedanta Swami Prabhupada comments in his introduction to his *Shrimad Bhagavatam* translation and commentary: "Sarvabhauma Bhattacarya, who was the chief appointed pandit in the court of the King of Orissa, Maharaja Prataparudra ... could understand that such a transcendental trance was only rarely exhibited. . . . The Lord was at once carried to the home of Sarvabhauma Bhattacarya, who at that time had sufficient power of authority due to his being the *sabha-pandita*, or the state dean of faculty in Sanskrit literatures. The learned *pandita* wanted to scrutinizingly test the transcendental feats of Lord Caitanya because often unscrupulous devotees imitate physical feats in order to flaunt transcendental achievements just to attract innocent people and take advantage of them. A learned scholar like the Bhattacarya can detect such imposters, and when he finds them out he at once rejects them. In the case of Lord Caitanya Mahaprabhu, the Bhattacarya tested all the symptoms in the light of the *shastras* [Sanskrit literatures]. He tested as a scientist, not as a foolish sentimentalist. He observed the movement of the stomach, the beating of the heart and the breathing of the nostrils. He also felt the pulse of the Lord and saw that all His bodily activities were in complete suspension. . . . Thus he came to know that the Lord's unconscious trance was genuine, and he began to treat Him in the prescribed fashion."

After staying briefly in Jagannatha Puri, Chaitanya Mahaprabhu embarked on a six-year journey throughout southern India. In one village he met a *brahmana* named Vasudeva, who suffered from a severe case of leprosy. He embraced Vasudeva, and immediately the leprosy disappeared (*Chaitanya Charitamrita, Madhya-lila* 7.141).

Upon returning to Jagannatha Puri, Chaitanya Mahaprabhu took part in the famous annual Rathayatra festival. In this festival, the temple deities are mounted on huge wooden chariots with towering colorful canopies, and are taken on a procession through the city. Millions of pilgrims attend the festival and thousands assist in pulling the giant chariots with long ropes. The imposing nature of the scene has come down to us in the term "juggernaut," which has come to mean an unstoppable force. Juggernaut is a corruption of *jagannatha* ("lord of the universe"). During one festival, Chaitanya Mahaprabhu divided his followers into seven groups. Each group, equipped with hand cymbals and drums, loudly danced and chanted. Looking at the scene, Sarvabhauma Bhattacharya and the King of Orissa could see that Chaitanya Mahaprabhu had expanded himself into seven forms, and was chanting and dancing in each of the seven groups simultaneously (*Chaitanya Charitamrita, Madhya-lila* 13.52).

Chaitanya Mahaprabhu then visited the sacred town of Vrindavan, the site of Krishna's appearance in this world five thousand years ago. Chaitanya Mahaprabhu is an incarnation of Krishna, who is recognized in the *Shrimad Bhagavatam* and *Bhagavad Gita* as the Supreme Personality of Godhead, the source of all incarnations. In Vrindavan, Chaitanya Mahaprabhu learned of some reports of a new appearance of Krishna, who was repeating some of his original pastimes. Crowds of people came to Chaitanya Mahaprabhu saying, "Krishna has again manifested Himself on the waters of Kaliya Lake. He dances on the hoods of the serpent Kaliya, and the jewels on those hoods are blazing. Everyone has seen Lord Krishna Himself. There is no doubt about it" (*Chaitanya Charitamrita, Madhya-lila* 18.94–95). For three days, people repeated this to Chaitanya Mahaprabhu. On the third day, Chaitanya Mahaprabhu's personal assistant said that he wanted to go and see Krishna. Chaitanya Mahaprabhu sharply replied: "You are a learned scholar, but you have become a fool, being influenced by the statements of other fools. . . . Foolish people who are mistaken are simply causing agitation and making a tumult. Do not become mad. Simply sit down here, and tomorrow night you will go see Krishna." The next morning, some respectable, intelligent, experienced gentlemen came to see Chaitanya Mahaprabhu, and he asked them about the events at the Kaliya Lake. They replied, "At night in Kaliya Lake a fisherman lights a torch in his boat and catches many fish. From a distance, people mistakenly think that they are seeing Krishna dancing on the body of the Kaliya serpent. These fools think that the boat is the Kaliya serpent and the torchlight the jewels on his hoods. People also mistake the fisherman for Krishna." The gentlemen then said, "Actually Lord Krishna has returned to Vrindavana. That is the truth, and it is also true that people have seen Him. But where they are seeing Krishna is their mistake." The gentlemen were indirectly indicating that they knew Chaitanya Mahaprabhu was actually an avatar. The special feature of Chaitanya Mahaprabhu was that he for the most part concealed his identity as an incarnation of Godhead, so that he could instead teach about how to understand and worship God. For this reason he is sometimes called the *channa*, or hidden, avatar.

Chaitanya Mahaprabhu spent the last eighteen years of his life in the sacred city of Jagannatha Puri. For the final twelve of these years, he was absorbed in spiritual trance and lived in seclusion in a room in one of the houses near the famous temple complex. Krishnadasa Kaviraja Goswami stated in *Chaitanya Charitamrita* (*Madhya-lila* 2.8) that although the doors to the house were locked, Chaitanya Mahaprabhu would sometimes be found at night lying unconscious at the main gate to the Jagannatha Puri temple. Chaitanya Mahaprabhu disappeared in 1534, merging into the deity of Krishna on the altar of the Tota Gopinatha temple.

The Search for Extraterrestrial Intelligence (SETI)

Although supported by credible observational reports, avatars and Marian apparitions are a religious manifestation of the idea of extraterrestrial intelligence, an idea central to my human devolution concept. The idea of extraterrestrial intelligence involved in the origin of the human species can also be approached from another angle—from the angle of modern science. The search for extraterrestrial intelligence is a genuine part of modern materialistic science, which assumes that any extraterrestrial intelligence would be connected with a biological form made of ordinary chemical elements. But, as we shall see, if followed carefully to its natural conclusion, there is an eventual convergence between the kind of extraterrestrial intelligence posited by some modern scientists and the kind posited by various religious traditions, which are more extradimensional than simply extraterrestrial.

In the nineteenth century several scientists proposed making huge mirrors or landscaped signs on the earth that would be visible from great distances in outer space, as a means of signaling our presence to extraterrestrial intelligences. These intelligences would then initiate communication with us. Swift (1990, p. 6) noted: "Mathematician Karl Friedrich Gauss suggested planting broad bands of forests in Siberia in the shape of a right-angled triangle. Inside the triangle wheat would be planted to provide a uniform color. An elaboration of this basic scheme would have included squares on each side of the triangle, to form the classic illustration of the Pythagorean theorem. . . . Joseph von Littrow, a Viennese astronomer, is said to have suggested that canals be dug in the Sahara Desert to form geometric figures twenty miles on a side." This is quite interesting, in connection with modern reports of crop circles. Perhaps alien intelligences have decided that placing landscaped signs on the earth is a good way to communicate with us.

The foundations for modern SETI programs began in 1959, when Cornell University physicists Giuseppe Cocconi and Phillip Morrison advocated a systematic search for signals from outer space. They proposed that the signals would most likely be radio signals. Starting in 1960, Frank Drake, who had independently arrived at the same conclusion, began using radio telescopes at the U.S. National Radio Astronomy Observatory at Green Bank, West Virginia, to actually search for such signals. His Project Ozma targeted two close stars resembling our sun. Then in 1961, Drake, Cocconi, Morrison, and other scientists, including Carl Sagan, attended a conference on SETI organized by the U.S. National Academy of Sciences at Green Bank (Swift 1990, p. 8). Sponsorship by America's top national science organization removed extraterrestrial intelligence from the fringes of science and placed it within the mainstream. But for the first years of SETI, there was not much funding, and most radio telescope searches focused on only a few stars and a few radio frequencies. In the 1980s searches increased in scope, expanding to full sky surveys on millions of frequencies. These searches were endorsed by scientific committees and supported by modest U.S. government funding of 1.5 million dollars a year. The government of the Soviet Union was also funding SETI research, to an even greater extent than the American government. The Soviet effort was organized by the Section on the Search for Cosmic Signals of Artificial Origin within the Soviet Council on Radio Astronomy (Swift 1990, pp. 16–17).

In 1992, NASA began a SETI program, funded for 10 years with a budget of 100 million dollars. The program was conducted with two teams. One team, at the Ames Research Center, conducted a "targeted search" focused on 800 stars within 80 light years of the earth. This search was based on the assumption that it was quite likely that human civilizations like ours had arisen many times in our galaxy. A second team, based at the Jet Propulsion Laboratory in Pasadena, California, did a wider search called the All Sky Survey. It was based on the assumption that advanced intelligent life forms were not so common and that we should have to search widely for them in the universe. In 1993, the NASA SETI program lost its government funding. The All Sky Survey stopped, but the target search program survived by transforming itself into Project Phoenix, run by the SETI Institute, a nongovernmental organization, which raises private funds (Lamb 1997, p. 224). A recent article in *Nature* (2001, p. 260) reveals that much of the funding for the SETI Institute and other such organizations comes "primarily from wealthy technology pioneers such as William Hewlett, David Packard, Gordon Moore, Paul Allen and Barney Oliver."

All of these programs assumed the standard materialistic cosmologies of modern science, which involve a universe and life forms composed only of the standard material elements and energies acting according to the known laws of physics. Following these assumptions, scientists calculated in various ways the likelihood of intelligent life forms coming into existence, their likely levels of technological advancement, and the likely times necessary for them to conduct interstellar or intergalactic communication or colonization efforts. Some scientists find a high probability for many extraterrestrial civilizations, some find a low probability that there is even one. I am not going to explore the details of the various calculations different researchers have made, because the fundamental assumptions upon which these calculations are made are flawed. There is more to the universe than ordinary matter and energy (in all their exotic varieties, including dark matter and dark energy). There is more to life than chemicals. And there are more ways to communicate than radio signals.

Alien Visitors

A good many SETI researchers assert that as of now we have no evidence whatsoever that extraterrestrial beings have visited the earth or tried to communicate with us. Some take this as evidence no such beings exist. They say that if humanlike civilizations did exist elsewhere in the universe, they would have already explored or colonized every habitable planet in the universe. Other researchers counter that perhaps they are here, or have been here, but we have not noticed them yet. But perhaps some researchers have noticed them. This brings us to the topic of UFOs and alien abductions, as evidence for the existence of extraterrestrial intelligences.

Since time immemorial religious traditions, including the Judeo-Christian tradition, have reported not only visitations by angels and superhuman beings, coming and going without the use of machines, but also visitations that involve some kind of machines. The Vedic literatures of India are full of descriptions of various kinds of *vimanas,* or spacecraft, a topic explored in depth by Richard L. Thompson in his book *Alien Identities.* Modern UFO reports are therefore not new, but represent a continuing set of observations of extraterrestrial or extradimensional craft.

The modern UFO phenomenon began in 1947 and has continued to the present. The UFO phenomenon has several components. The first is observations of machinelike flying objects that cannot be explained in terms of existing human technologies. The second is humanoid beings associated with such machines. And the third is paranormal phenomena connected with such machines and humanoids and their interactions with humans.

Observations of UFOs have been reported by professional scientists. In a letter to *Science,* J. Allen Hynek, chairman of the astronomy department at Northwestern University, said, "some of the very best, most coherent reports have come from scientifically trained people" (Markowitz 1980, p. 255). Hynek served as a scientific consultant to the U.S. Air Force on UFOs from 1948 to 1968, and he was later director of the civilian Center for UFO Studies.

In 1952, a survey of 40 professional astronomers revealed that five of these astronomers had seen UFOs. The survey was included in a section of a government-sponsored report on the UFO phenomenon. The author of this section said about the sightings: "Perhaps this is to be expected, since astronomers do, after all, watch the skies." He further noted that astronomers "will not likely be fooled by balloons, aircraft, and similar objects, as may be the general populace" (Condon 1969, p. 516).

UFO researcher Jacques Vallee was previously employed as a professional astronomer. He recalled: "l became seriously interested in 1961, when I saw French astronomers erase a magnetic tape on which our satellite tracking team had recorded eleven data points on an unknown flying object which was not an airplane, a balloon, or a known orbiting craft. 'People would laugh at us if we reported this!' was the answer I was given at the time. Better forget the whole thing. Let's not bring ridicule to the observatory" (Vallee 1979, p. 7).

In 1967, James McDonald, a physicist and meteorologist at the University of Arizona, stated: "An intensive analysis of hundreds of outstanding UFO reports and personal interviews with dozens of key witnesses in important cases, have led me to the conclusion that the UFO problem is one of exceedingly great scientific importance." McDonald favored "the hypothesis that the UFOs might be extraterrestrial probes" as being "the least unsatisfactory hypothesis for explaining the now-available UFO evidence" (McDonald 1967, p. 1).

In the 1970s, astrophysicist Peter Sturrock sent a questionnaire on UFOs to 2,611 members of the American Astronomical Association. The results, published in 1977, revealed that 1,300 members replied, and their reports contained 60 UFO sightings (Sturrock 1977). In July 1979, the journal *Industrial Research/Development* polled 1,200 scientists and engineers about UFOs. They were asked, "Do you believe that UFOs exist?" Among these scientists and engineers, 61 percent said yes, they did believe in UFOs. In fact, 8 percent said they had seen UFOs, and an additional 10 percent thought they might have seen them. Fully 40 per cent said they believed UFOs originated in outer space (Fowler 1981, pp. 221–222).

Probably the most famous scientist to comment favorably on the existence of UFOs was psychiatrist Carl Jung, who said: "So far as I know it remains an established fact, supported by numerous observations, that Ufos have not only been seen visually but have also been picked up on the radar screen and have left traces on the photographic plate ... It boils down to nothing less than this: that either psychic projections throw back a radar echo, or else the appearance of real objects affords an opportunity for mythological projections" (Jung 1959, pp. 146–147).

After initial reports of UFO sightings in 1947, some high officers in the American Air Force became concerned with the phenomenon. Edward Condon said in his official report on the American military's research on UFOs: "Within the Air Force there were those who emphatically believed that the subject was absurd. . . . Other Air Force officials regarded UFOs with utmost seriousness and believed that it was quite likely that American airspace was being invaded by secret weapons of foreign powers or possibly by visitors from outer space" (Condon 1969, p. 503).

General Nathan Twining, chief of staff of the U. S. Army and commanding general of the Army Air Force, wrote on September 23, 1947 about the flying disks reported in various parts of the country: "1. The phenomenon reported is something real and not visionary or fictitious. 2. There are objects probably approximating the shape of a disc, of such appreciable size as to appear to be as large as man-made aircraft. 3. There is a possibility that some of the incidents may be caused by natural phenomena such as meteors. 4. The reported operating characteristics such as extreme rates of climb, maneuverability (particularly in roll), and action which must be considered evasive when sighted or contacted by friendly aircraft and radar, lend belief to the possibility that some of the objects are controlled either manually, automatically, or remotely" (Condon 1969, p. 894).

To carry out Twining's directives for a study group, the Air Force organized Project Sign, which continued until February 1949. The research work, which took the extraterrestrial nature of UFOs as a serious possibility, was carried out by the Air Technical Intelligence Center (ATIC) at Wright-Patterson Air Force Base near Dayton, Ohio. Thereafter, work by the ATIC continued under the name Project Grudge. But there was a change in attitude toward the phenomenon. J. Allen Hynek, who worked on the project said, "The change to Project Grudge signaled the adoption of the strict brush-off attitude to the UFO problem. Now the public relations statements on specific UFO cases bore little resemblance to the facts of the case. If a case contained some of the elements possibly attributable to aircraft, a balloon, etc., it automatically became that object in the press release" (Hynek 1972a, p. 174). Captain Edward J. Ruppelt, a project officer, said, "This drastic change in official attitude is as difficult to explain as it was difficult for many people who knew what was going on inside Project Sign to believe" (Hynek 1972a, p. 175). The final report of Project Grudge, released in August 1949, said there was no evidence of any high tech devices, and explained away UFO reports as mistakes, illusions, or fabrications. Project Grudge was formally dissolved in December 1949.

General C. B. Cabell, director of Air Force intelligence, reactivated Project Grudge in 1951, putting Captain Ruppelt in charge. Ruppelt was fairly open minded, but even he had his limits. Although he was ready to take unidentified *flying* objects a little seriously, he had problems with reports of UFOs that *landed.* And there were quite a number of such accounts. Ruppelt later wrote that he and his team systematically eliminated such accounts from their reporting system (Vallee 1969b, p. 28).

The CIA was also interested in UFOs. On September 24, 1952, H. Marshall Chadwell, the CIA's assistant director for scientific intelligence, wrote a memo to CIA director Walter Smith about UFO publicity and the high rate of reports of UFO activity coming into the Air Technical Intelligence Center at Wright-Patterson Air Force Base. His main concern was public opinion: "The public concern with the phenomenon, which is reflected both in the United States press and in the pressure of inquiry upon the Air Force, indicates that a fair proportion of our population is mentally conditioned to the acceptance of the incredible. In this fact lies the potential for the touching-off of mass hysteria and panic" (Thompson 1993, p. 81). Chadwell feared that false reports of UFOs could distract the military from real observations of attacking Soviet bombers. He also feared that the mentality of the American public could be used by the enemies attempting to engage in psychological warfare against the United States.

In 1953, the CIA formed a panel to study the UFO phenomenon.

It came to be known as the Robertson panel, after Dr. H. P. Robertson, director of the weapons systems evaluation group for the Secretary of Defense. The Robertson panel included several prominent physicists. They decided that UFOs were not any real threat to national security, i.e. they were not machines from foreign powers or outer space. But they did say "that the continuous emphasis on the reporting of these phenomena does . . . result in a threat to the orderly functioning of the protective organs of the body politic" (Condon 1969, p. 519). The panel recommended that "the national security agencies take immediate steps to strip the Unidentified Flying Objects of the special status they have been given and the aura of mystery they have unfortunately acquired" (Condon 1969, pp. 519–520). The panel recommended a systematic program of debunking. "The 'debunking' aim would result in reduction in public interest in 'flying saucers' which today evokes a strong psychological reaction" (Condon 1969, pp. 915–916).

In 1953, in a development perhaps related to the Robertson panel's conclusions, the U.S. Air Force enacted Air Force Regulation 200-2, restricting public reporting of military UFO sightings. "In response to local inquiries resulting from any UFO reported in the vicinity of an Air Force base, information may be released to the press or the general public by the commander of the Air Force base concerned only if it has been positively identified as a familiar or known object" (Thompson 1993, pp. 83–84). In other words, anything that could not be identified as a weather balloon, ordinary airplane, planet, or meteor would not be announced. The effect of this policy is that if there are observations of extraterrestrial UFOs, there will be no public reports about them coming from official military and governmental sources.

Air Force UFO reports did, however, continue to be collected by Project Grudge. In 1959, the name of the Air Force UFO research program was changed to Project Blue Book. In 1964, the nongovernmental National Investigating Committee on Aerial Phenomena published a report called *The UFO Evidence,* which contained 92 UFO sightings by aircraft crews of the United States military. The sightings took place in the period 1944–1961. Of these cases, 44 involved U.S. planes being chased or buzzed by UFOs, U.S. aircraft chasing UFOs, or UFOs flying low over U.S. military bases (Hall 1964, pp. 19–22). In 1969, the Air Force stopped its official Project Blue Book UFO investigations. A summary and evaluation of the entire effort appeared in the Condon Report, which was released in that same year.

Although the Condon Report contained many detailed accounts of unexplained sightings, the report's conclusion said "nothing has come from the study of UFOs in the past 21 years that has added to scientific knowledge" and "further extensive study of UFOs probably cannot be justified in the expectation that science will be advanced thereby" (Condon 1969, p. 1). In answer to the question what should be done with UFO reports that come to the government and military from the public, the report advised "nothing should be done with them in the expectation that they are going to contribute to the advance of science" (Condon 1969, p. 4). And finally, the authors said: "We strongly recommend that teachers refrain from giving students credit for school work based on their reading of the presently available UFO books and magazine articles. Teachers who find their students strongly motivated in this direction should attempt to channel their interests in the direction of serious study of astronomy and meteorology, and in the direction of critical analysis of fantastic propositions that are being supported by appeals to fallacious reasoning or false data" (Condon 1969, pp. 5–6).

Since this time, the official policy of the U.S. government and military has been to keep silent about the UFO phenomenon. Nevertheless, high government officials have reported UFO experiences and have sought to get government agencies to release information on UFOs. President Ronald Reagan, while governor of California, reported sighting a UFO while flying in a plane over southern California. In 1972, shortly after the incident, Reagan told Norman Miller, Washington bureau chief for the *Wall Street Journal*: "We followed it for several minutes. It was a bright white light. We followed it to Bakersfield, and all of a sudden to our utter amazement, it went straight up into the heavens" (Burt 2000, p. 308). The pilot also recalled the incident, saying, "The UFO went from a normal cruise speed to a fantastic speed instantly. . . . the object definitely wasn't another airplane. But we didn't file a report on the object for a long time because they considered you a nut if you saw a UFO." U.S. President Jimmy Carter's science advisor wanted NASA to form a committee to conduct an inquiry on UFOs. NASA rejected the request because it feared ridicule (Henry 1988, p. 122).

Major foundations have shown interest in UFO research. Marie Galbraith, wife of Evan Griffin Galbraith, U.S. ambassador to France from 1981 to 1985, traveled around the world to get information about UFOs from scientists involved in UFO research. She and others then put together a report called *Unidentified Flying Objects Briefing Document, The Best Available Evidence,* which was distributed to high government officials in the United States. Galbraith's work was supported by Laurence Rockefeller. She also helped organize a colloquium on the scientific evidence for UFOs, which took place in September 1997 at the Rockefeller Brothers Fund property at Pocantico, New York, again with the assistance of Laurence Rockefeller. The moderator of the meeting was Peter Sturrock, an astrophysicist (COMETA 1999, p. 51).

Governments and military organizations around the world have shown strong interest in UFOs. On November 2, 1954, Brigadier General João Adil Oliveira, chief of Brazil's air force general staff information service, said to members of the Army war college, "The problem of flying discs has polarized the attention of the whole world. But it's serious and it deserves to be treated seriously. Almost all the governments of the great powers are interested in it, dealing with it in a serious and confidential manner, due to its military interest" (Burt 2000, p. 311). In a letter dated May 5, 1967, Air Marshall Rosenun Nurjadin, commander-in-chief of the Indonesian air force, wrote, "UFOs sighted in Indonesia are identical with those sighted in other countries. Sometimes they pose a problem for our air defence and once we were obliged to open fire on them" (Burt 2000, pp. 313–314). In 1974, in an interview with *UFO News*, General Kanshi Ishikawa, chief of staff of Japan's air self-defense force, said, "Much evidence tells us that UFOs have been tracked by radar, so, UFOs are real and they may come from outer space. . . . UFO photographs and various materials show scientifically that there are more advanced people piloting the saucers" (Burt 2000, p. 314). China's Academy of Social Sciences has had a branch called the China UFO Research Organization. In the August 27, 1985 edition of the newspaper *China Daily,* Professor Liang Renglin of Guangzhou Jinan University said, "More than six hundred UFO reports have been made in China during the past five years" (Burt 2000, p. 322).

In 1984, the Soviet Union's Academy of Sciences established a commission on anomalous atmospheric phenomena. The chairman was Vsesvolod Troitsky, of the Academy, and the vice chairman was General Pavel Popovich, a famous cosmonaut. In 1988, the Academy of Sciences held a conference on UFOs, attended by 300 scientists (Clark 1998, p. 978). In June 1989, General Igor Maltsev, Soviet chief of air defense forces, discussed military encounters with UFOs in an article in *Soviet Military Review*: "For skeptics and non-skeptics, this information can serve as officially documented proof of UFO validity. We hope that this open acknowledgment of the phenomenon will put an end to ambiguous speculations and will make the fact of its existence beyond doubt. Now we have grounds to tell that UFOs are not optical or hallucinated objects, which were allegedly caused by global psychosis. The objects have been spotted by technological means. Pictures are available for specialists" (Burt 2000, p. 315).

The French government has an active UFO research program. The first organized studies began in 1976, when the Institute des Hautes Etudes de Défense Nationale (IHEDN), formed a committee to study UFOs. It was chaired by General Blanchard of the Gendarmerie National. This led to the formation of the Groupe d'Etude des Phénomènes Aérospatiaux Non Indentifiés (GEPAN). In 1977, GEPAN published a five volume report. The report focused on eleven cases, studied in great detail. Sociologist Ronald Westrum said in 1978, "In nine of the eleven cases, the conclusion was that the witnesses had witnessed a material phenomenon that could not be explained as a natural phenomenon or a human device. One of the conclusions of the total report is that behind the overall phenomenon there is a 'flying machine whose modes of sustenance and propulsion are beyond our knowledge'" (Fowler 1981, pp. 224–225). GEPAN later became the Service d'Expertise des Phénomènes de Rentrée Atmosphérique (SEPRA), which is part of the Centre National d'Etudes Spatiales (CNES), the French equivalent of NASA (COMETA 1999, p. 7).

In 1999, a group of high ranking scientists, military officers, and government officials presented a report on UFOs to the French government. The report, titled *UFOs and Defense: What Should We Prepare For?*, was produced by the Committee for In-Depth Studies (COMETA). The guiding force behind COMETA was French air force general Denis Letty. COMETA included in addition to General Letty: air force general Bruno Le Moine; Admiral Marc Merlo; Denis Blancher, chief of the ministry of the interior's national police force; Françoise Lépine of the Foundation for Defense Studies; Christian Marchal, research director of ONERA, the National Aerospace Study and Research Office; Michael Algrin, state doctor of political science; Alain Orszag, a doctor of physical sciences and weapons engineer; Pierre Boscond, also a weapons engineer; and Jean Dunglas, an engineer. Several other high ranking military and government officers also contributed to the report (COMETA 1999, p. 6).

General Norlain, director of the IHEDN, said about COMETA: "Almost all of its members have, or had during the course of their careers, important responsibilities in defense, industry, teaching, research, or various central administrations." General Norlain also said, "I express the wish that the recommendations of COMETA, which are inspired by good sense, will be examined and implemented by the authorities of our country" (COMETA 1999, p. 5). Professor André Lebeau, former chairman of the Centre National d'Etudes Spatiales (CNES), wrote a foreword to the COMETA report. He said, "The report is useful in that it contributes toward stripping the phenomenon of UFOs of its irrational layer" (COMETA 1999, p. 2).

Governing and military officials in the United Kingdom have long been interested in UFOs. In the July 11, 1954 edition of London's *Sunday Dispatch,* Air Chief Marshal Lord Dowding, Commander-in-Chief of RAF Fighter Command, said about UFOs: "More than 10,000 sightings have been reported, the majority of which cannot be accounted for by any scientific explanation. . . . I am convinced that these objects do exist and that they are not manufactured by any nation on earth. I can therefore see no alternative to accepting the theory that they come from some extraterrestrial source" (Burt 2001, p. 312).

Since 1964, the British Ministry of Defence (MOD) has studied UFOs through Department 2a of the Secretariate (Air Staff) division, abbreviated Sec(AS)2a. Nick Pope, who headed the division from 1991 to 1994, has described its activities in his book *Open Skies, Closed Minds.* Pope afterwards remained an official of the Ministry of Defence. About Pope, the COMETA report says, "He has given interviews to the press and participated in television programs. He has cooperated with ufological organizations, giving their address and phone number to witnesses who have written to him. In his letters of response he admitted that a small proportion of UFO sightings defied explanation and that the MOD was keeping its mind open regarding these. . . . In his book, Nick Pope evokes various hypotheses to explain certain unidentified cases that were the subject of credible and detailed reports. He strongly favors the extraterrestrial hypothesis" (COMETA 1999, pp. 52–53).

In 1987, in his foreword to Timothy Goode's book *Above Top Secret,* Lord Hill-Norton, Chief of Defence Staff, Ministry of Defence, wrote about UFOs: "A very large number of sightings have been vouched for by persons whose credentials seem to me unimpeachable. It is striking that so many have been trained observers, such as police officers and airline or military pilots. Their observations have in many instances been supported either by technical means such as radar or even more convincingly by . . . interference with electrical apparatus of one sort or another" (Burt 2001, pp. 312–313).

Let us now consider some representative UFO cases. We will consider cases in four categories: 1. sightings of flying objects that display intelligently guided flight characteristics beyond those of known aircraft; 2. sightings such of UFOs involving landings that leave physical traces; 3. sightings of UFOs that involve not only landings but also humanoid occupants; 4. abductions.

Sightings of Unidentified Flying Objects

On March 8, 1950, pilots on a Trans World Airways flight saw a UFO near Dayton, Ohio. About twenty other reports from the same area came in to the nearby Wright-Patterson Air Force Base. Military personnel at the Air Technical Intelligence Center there also saw the UFO. Four military aircraft were sent up to intercept the UFO. Two military pilots established visual contact with the UFO, describing it as large, round, and metallic. The object also showed up on radar. After the sightings by the military aircraft, the object flew straight up into the sky at great speed and disappeared (Hall 1964, p. 84).

There are many military reports that involve UFO contacts on radar. Sometimes these radar contacts are explained as "anomalous propagation effects." In the Condon Report, an atmospheric scientist writing on UFO radar contacts said: "There are apparently some very unusual propagation effects, rarely encountered or reported, that occur under atmospheric conditions so rare that they may constitute unknown phenomena. . . . This seems to be the only conclusion one can reasonably reachfrom examination of some of the strangest cases." In other words, the only way to explain some UFO radar sightings is to postulate *unknown* radar signal propagation effects (Condon 1969, p. 175). Of course, the other way to explain them is by postulating extraterrestrial flying machines with unknown capabilities.

During the nights of August 13–14, 1956, military air traffic controllers, military radar operators, and military pilots reported sightings of UFOs moving at high rates of speed and engaging in inexplicable stop and start flying patterns above and around the joint American and British air force bases at Lakenheath and Bentwaters. At 22:00 on August 13, radar operators at Bentwaters detected an object moving from east to west at 2,000-4,000 miles an hour. At the same time, personnel in the Bentwaters air traffic control tower saw a bright light moving over the ground in the same direction at "an incredible speed," at a height of 1,200 meters. A pilot of a military transport plane flying at about the same altitude reported seeing a bright light pass from east to west just under his plane, moving "at an incredible speed."

The radar operator at Bentwaters reported the radar sighting to the radar control center at Lakenheath. One of the operators detected an object motionless in the air about 40 kilometers southwest of Lakenheath. The object was on the line of flight of the object observed visually and by radar from Bentwaters. Then the Lakenheath radar operators saw the object instantly start moving at 600–950 kilometers per hour.

The object started and then stopped several times. Each time it started moving, it would travel between 13 and 30 kilometers in a different direction. The stops and starts (all involving instant acceleration to 950 kilometers per hour) were observed not only on radar but by visual sightings from the ground.

The RAF sent a fighter to pursue the object. Guided by radar operators from the ground, the fighter pilot saw the object and also had it on his radar. Then he lost it. Radar operators then guided him to a second encounter with the object. The pilot then again lost sight of the object, which had moved rapidly behind him and was now trailing him. The pilot then began a series of climbs, dives, and turns to get the object off of his tail, but the object, as confirmed by radar observation, followed him, maintaining a constant distance. The pilot, low on fuel, started to return to his base. The object followed him for a short distance, and then came to a stop in midair. It then began moving again to the north, at 950 kilometers per hour and disappeared from radar. A second fighter sent in pursuit did not find the object.

The Lakenheath report to Project Blue Book said, "The fact that rapid accelerations and abrupt stops of the object were detected by radar and by sight from the ground give the report definite credibility." The Condon Commission, which gave a report on the U. S. Air Force's Project Blue Book records of UFO sightings, classified the Lakenheath sightings as "unidentified." The COMETA report dismissed attempts by Phillip Klass to explain the case as a combination of meteor sightings and radar anomalies (COMETA, 1999, pp. 12–13; Condon 1969, pp. 250–256; Thompson 1993, p. 89).

On March 21, 1990, UFOs were sighted by the Russian air force in the Pereslavl-Zalesski region, to the east of Moscow. General Igor Maltsev, Soviet Air Defense Forces commander, reported on the incident in the newspaper *Rabochaya Tribuna* (*Worker's Tribune*). He said combat aircraft were sent to intercept the first UFO, which was tracked by radar and sighted visually by one hundred observers. General Maltsev stated: "I am not a specialist in UFOs, and therefore I can only link the data together and express my own hypothesis. Based on the data collected by these witnesses, the UFO was a disk 100 to 200 meters in diameter. Two lights were flashing on its sides. In addition, the object turned around its axis and performed an S-shaped maneuver in both the vertical and horizontal planes. Next the UFO continued to hover above the ground, then flew at a speed two to three times greater than that of modern combat aircraft." Other UFOs were also sighted. General Maltsev stated, "The objects flew at altitudes ranging from 100 to 7000 meters. The movement of the UFOs was not accompanied by any type of noise and was characterized by an astounding maneuverability. The UFOs appeared to completely lack inertia. In other words, in one fashion or another they had overcome gravity. At present, terrestrial machines can scarcely exhibit such characteristics" (COMETA 1999, p. 16; *Rabochaya Tribuna* 1990).

On the night of March 30, 1990, a captain of the Belgian national police reported a UFO sighting to the Belgian Air Force Headquarters. The headquarters officers immediately acted to confirm the sighting. The officers received additional reports of visual sightings of the object, and radar contact was established by the NATO radar center at Glons and the Belgian national radar control center at Semmerzake. Analysts at Belgian Air Force Headquarters ruled out the usual explanations for false radar contacts, especially temperature inversions. F-16s were sent to intercept the object. They established radar contact. An article in *Paris Match* stated: "The object had speeded up from an initial velocity of 280 kph to 1,800 kph, while descending from 3,000 to 1,700 meters ... in one second! This fantastic acceleration corresponds to 40Gs. It would cause immediate death to a human on board. The limit of what a pilot can take is about 8Gs. ... It arrived at 1,700 meters altitude, then it dove rapidly toward the ground at an altitude under 200 meters, and in so doing escaped from the radars of the fighters and the ground units at Glons and Semmerzake. This maneuver took place over the suburbs of Brussels, which are so full of man-made lights that the pilots lost sight of the object beneath them. During the next hours the scenario repeated twice. This fantastic game of hide and seek was observed from the ground by a great number of witnesses, among them 20 national policemen who saw both the object and the F-16s. The encounter lasted 75 minutes." One strange feature: there was no sonic boom even though the object exceeded the speed of sound. This was just one of several hundred sightings around this time in Belgium. The Belgian Air Force cooperated with civilian UFO organizations in reporting and investigating the sightings (Thompson 1993, pp. 100–101).

On January 28, 1994, Air France flight 3532 was on its way from Nice to London. The captain was Jean-Charles Duboc, and the copilot was Valérie Chauffour. At 1:14 in the afternoon, the plane was at an altitude of 11,900 meters about 50 kilometers west of Paris. The chief steward, pilot, and copilot observed a roundish object at a distance of about 50 kilometers and judged it to be flying at an altitude of 10,500 meters. They deduced the object was quite large. It appeared to change shape, from a bell-like shape to a disklike shape. Then the object suddenly disappeared from their view. The captain reported the incident to the Reims air navigation control center. The center had no record of any other flights in the region. But the Taverny air defense operations center found that the Cinq-Mars-la-Pile control center reported a radar track near flight 3532. The track persisted for 50 seconds and then disappeared at the same moment that the air crew members reported that the object disappeared. Investigations by the air defense operations center showed no flight plans for any other aircraft in the vicinity, and ruled out the hypothesis of a weather balloon. The case was also investigated by the French northern regional air navigation center (COMETA 1999, p. 11).

Landings and Physical Traces

Dr. William T. Powers, an engineer, wrote in a letter published in the April 7, 1967 issue of *Science*: "In 1954, over 200 reports over the whole world concerned landings of objects. . . . Of these, about 51 percent were observed by more than one person. . . . In 18 multiple-witness cases, some witnesses were not aware that anyone else had seen the same thing at the same time and place. In 13 cases, there were more than 10 witnesses. How do we deal with reports like these? One fact is clear: we cannot shrug them off" (Powers 1967). Many of these landings left physical traces.

In 1981, Ted R. Phillips, a UFO investigator, issued a report on 2,108 UFO landing cases from 64 countries. In 705 of these cases, the UFOs were seen by more than one witness. Phillips stated, "The UFOs observed by multiple witnesses appear to have been solid constructed bodies under intelligent control. . . . They produced physical traces that, in many cases, have no natural or conventional explanation." Physical traces included vegetation altered by heat, pressure, and dehydration, as well as marks made by landing gear (Thompson 1993, pp. 67–68).

Let us now consider a few cases of this type. In May 1957, American astronaut L. Gordon Cooper was at Edwards Air Force Base commanding a camera crew that was filming the installation of a precision landing guidance system. Cooper recalled: "I had a camera crew filming the installation when they spotted a saucer. They filmed it as it flew overhead, then hovered, extended three legs as landing gear, and slowly came down to land on a dry lake bed! These guys were all pro cameramen, so the picture quality was very good. The camera crew managed to get within 20 to 30 yards of it, filming all the time. It was a classic saucer, shiny silver and smooth, about 30 feet across. It was pretty clear it was an alien craft. As they approached closer, it took off. After a while, a high-ranking officer said that when the film was developed I was to put it in a pouch and send it to Washington. That's what I did when it came back from the lab and it was all there just like the camera crew reported" (Burt 2000, p. 317; Clark 1998, p. 666).

Jean-Jacques Velasco, head of GEPAN, the French governmental agency that investigated UFOs in the 1970s, reported on the Collini case. On February 8, 1981, at five in the afternoon, Mr. Collini saw an oval-shaped UFO sitting near a garden where he was working. The object remained on the ground for less then a minute. It rose into the air and moved away. Collini went to the spot and observed round marks on the ground, along with a crown-shaped imprint. On the orders of GEPAN, local police came and collected samples of the soil and nearby vegetation. Later, a GEPAN team came to investigate the site. They found the witness had no psychological problems. They found signs that the ground at the spot of the landing had been heated to between 300 and 500 degrees Centigrade and also detected traces of zinc and phosphate. Study of plants at the site showed a 30–50 percent reduction in chlorophyll pigments in alfalfa (Velasco 1987, pp. 56–57).

Humanoids

At a symposium on UFOs sponsored by the American Association for the Advancement of Science in 1969, J. Allen Hynek said: "There are now on record some 1,500 reports of close encounters, about half of which involve reported craft occupants. Reports of occupants have been with us for years, but there are only a few in the Air Force files; generally Project Bluebook personnel summarily, and without investigation, consigned such reports to the 'psychological' or crackpot category" (Hynek 1972b, pp. 47–48). Of the 2,108 cases reported by Ted R. Phillips in his 1981 study on UFO landing cases, 460 involved observations of humanoids. Of these humanoids, 310 were smaller than average humans, 87 were of normal human size, and 63 were larger than average humans (Thompson 1993, pp. 67–68).

The case of the UFO crash at Roswell involved humanoids. In July of 1947, people in Corona, New Mexico, about 75 miles northwest of Roswell, reported seeing a flying silvery disk pass by overhead. The next day, William "Mac" Brazel found debris on a ranch near Corona. Military officers from Roswell Air Force Base, including Major Jesse Marcel, an intelligence officer, came to investigate. Marcel said he found extremely light metal beams with strange inscriptions carved on them, as well as paper-thin sheets of metal that could not be dented even by heavy hammering. The Roswell air base commander, Colonel William Blanchard, issued a press release stating that a crashed flying disc had been recovered and was being shipped on board a B-29 to Wright Field in Ohio.

Afterwards, General Roger Ramey, commander of the Eighth Air Force, authorized a press release saying that the wreckage was actually that of a weather balloon. But Major Jesse Marcel testified on videotape: "One thing I was certain of, being familiar with all our activities, is that it was not a weather balloon, nor an aircraft, nor a missile." Marcel also said that his commanding officer told him to conceal the actual wreckage from the site. Robert Shirkley, the assistant base operations officer at Roswell, was present when a B-29 arrived at Roswell to take the wreckage. He saw parts of what he understood to be a flying saucer, including a metal beam with strange letters on it, being loaded onto the plane. General Arthur E. Exon was a lieutenant colonel at Wright Field in Ohio when the wreckage arrived from Roswell. About the wreckage, he said, "The metal and material was unknown to anyone I talked to. Whatever they found, I never heard what the results were. A couple of guys thought it might be Russian, but the overall consensus was that the pieces were from outer space" (Randle and Schmitt 1991, p. 110). Exon also said: "There was another location where . . . apparently the main body of the spacecraft was . . . where they did say there were bodies. . . . They were all found, apparently outside the craft itself but were in fairly good condition" (Randle and Schmitt 1991, p. 110). The wife of an Air Force pilot testified that her husband told her he had ferried wreckage and bodies from the Roswell site to Dayton, Ohio, near Wright-Patterson Air Force Base (Thompson 1993, pp. 103–107).

In 1997, Colonel Philip Corso published a remarkable book, *The Day After Roswell.* From 1953 to 1957, Colonel Corso was on the National Security Council Staff. In his book, he stated that the Roswell crash was that of an extraterrestrial spacecraft, and he also testified that he saw the body of one of the aliens. From 1961 to 1962, Corso served in the U.S. Army's department for research and development as chief of foreign technology. He said that during this time he helped introduce technological breakthroughs derived from extraterrestrial equipment from the Roswell debris into the U.S. military and private industry. Senator Strom Thurmond, chairman of the U.S. Senate's armed services committee, contributed a foreword to the first printing of the book, but this foreword was withdrawn from later printings (COMETA 1999, p. 52; Corso 1997).

On July 1, 1965, at Valensole, in the department of Alpes-de-Haute Provence in France, Maurice Masse, a farmer, was going to look at his lavender field when he saw in the field a round metallic object, the size of a small car, standing on six legs. There was a metal shaft protruding from the center of the object to the ground. As Masse approached the object, two small humanoids turned a tubelike instrument towards him, and he felt himself paralyzed. The two humanoids entered the craft, which then lifted off, retracting its six legs and central shaft. The object flew upwards with extreme rapidity and disappeared. The case was investigated in-depth by the Gendarmerie Nationale. They found a depression at the spot where the vehicle had been sighted, and in the middle of the depression was a round hole 19 centimeters in diameter and 40 centimeters deep. The investigators found that the lavender plants for a hundred yards along the direction of the object's departure were dried up. For years after the incident, no plants would grow there. The investigators turned up no evidence of psychopathology or hoaxing (COMETA 1999, p. 20).

On August 29, 1967, near Cussac in the department of Cantal, France, two children herding cows saw four small humanoids standing near a bright spherical object on the other side of a country road. One of the humanoids blinded the children with an object that looked like a mirror. The humanoids then entered their craft in a strange way, floating into the air and then diving headfirst through the top of the sphere. The sphere, making a hissing sound, then flew off rapidly in an upward spiraling flight path. The children noticed a strong smell of sulfur. In 1978, GEPAN, the French governmental agency responsible for UFO studies, opened an investigation. The investigators interviewed a gendarme who had arrived on the scene shortly after the incident. The gendarme had noted tracks on the ground and a strong smell of sulfur. A second witness, who had been working nearby, testified that he heard a hissing sound. The investigators learned from a physician and the children's father (the mayor of the village) that the children themselves had smelled of sulfur after the incident, and that their eyes were tearful for days afterwards. The GEPAN judge for the case stated, "There is no flaw or inconsistency in these various elements that permit us to doubt the sincerity of the witnesses or to reasonably suspect an invention, hoax, or hallucination. Under these circumstances, despite the young age of the principal witnesses, and as extraordinary as the facts that they have related seem to be, I think that they actually observed them" (COMETA 1999, p. 21).

In January of 1975, businessman George O'Barski, 72 years old, was driving from his shop in New York City's Manhattan Island to his home in New Jersey. As he was driving through North Hudson Park, he heard static on his car radio while a brightly shining flying object, emitting a humming sound, passed by his car. Ahead of him, he saw the object land in a park. The object, about 30 feet long, with a row of narrow glowing windows, was floating at a height of ten feet. Then it descended to four feet. From a door between two windows, several small humanoid figures with helmets came out. After digging up some earth, they went back into the craft, which rose into the air and moved north. The time was one or two in the morning. The next day, O'Barski returned to the site and saw on the ground the holes left by the creatures. UFO investigator Budd Hopkins interviewed people who lived in the area to see if they had noticed anything. Bill Pawlowski, doorman at the Stonehenge apartment complex near the site, said that at two or three o'clock in the morning one day in January, he saw a dark object with 10 or 15 lighted windows in the nearby park floating about 10 feet off the ground. He later mentioned this to Al Del Gaudio, a police lieutenant who lived in the building. Another doorman, Al Gonzalez, saw the same kind of object at the same place six days before the sighting by O'Barski and Pawlowski. The Wamsley family lived about 14 blocks from the Stonehenge apartments. Their residence was on the path O'Barski said the object had taken after leaving the park. Late one Saturday night in January, Robert Wamsley, age 12, had seen, through a window in the Wamsley home, a round brightly lit flying craft with rectangular windows. Robert and other family members went outside and observed the craft for two minutes as it moved slowly away (Hopkins 1981, pp. 23–28; Thompson 1993, pp. 51–53).

The existence of extraterrestrial humanlike entities is damaging to the Darwinian theory of evolution. Today, evolutionists claim that the existence of humans on this planet is the result of a strictly terrestrial process of physiological evolution. Therefore, if there are humans from elsewhere, they must have arisen by an entirely separate evolutionary process somewhere else in the cosmos. That creatures with humanlike intelligence and bodies could have arisen in this way is very unlikely. For reasons explained in chapter 4, the origin of life of any kind from chemicals is very unlikely. Even granting the formation of simple unicellular organisms, there is no necessity for them to form multicellular creatures. Then granting the existence of multicellular creatures, there is no reason that they should be animal-like rather than plantlike, or terrestrial rather than aquatic. Even if we suppose that somehow or other, some small quadruped vertebrate mammals evolved in some other part of the universe, it is not at all probable that they would develop into something like a human being. Let's go back 50 million years, to the Eocene period on earth. During that time, the first primates came into existence. Theodosius Dobzhansky (1972, p. 173), a prominent founder of modern evolutionary theory, said, "Man has at least 100,000 genes, and perhaps half of them (or more) have changed at least once since the Eocene. The probability is, to all intents and purposes, zero that the same 50,000 genes will change in the same way and will be selected again in the same sequence as they were in man's evolutionary history." The most recent estimate of the number of human genes is about 30,000, but Dobzhansky's basic point still holds. This suggests that if we ran the tape of evolution again (to borrow a phrase from Stephen J. Gould), it is practically impossible that human beings would be the result. Of course, one could propose that humans evolved elsewhere, and that our planet was seeded with human genes at some point in history. But that takes us quite far from today's evolutionary theories and leaves unresolved the very difficult question of how human beings evolved elsewhere. The simplest explanation for similar human types from different parts of the cosmos is a common intelligent source.

Abductions

Cases involving landings and humanoids can also include abduction experiences. In 1985, David Webb published a study of abduction reports. Out of 300 abduction cases, he found that 140 were well investigated, with no signs that there was any hoaxing and no signs that the witnesses were mentally deranged (Webb 1985).

The first abduction case to attract wide attention involved Betty and Barney Hill (Clark 1998, pp. 489–499). On September 26, 1961, Betty wrote a letter about a UFO encounter to Donald E. Keyhoe, a former Marine Corps major who was then serving as the director of NICAP, the National Investigating Committee on Aerial Phenomena. NICAP referred the case to Walter N. Webb, an astronomer in Boston who was also a UFO investigator. Webb conducted a series of interviews.

Betty Hill was 41 years old at the time of the encounter. She was a social worker employed by the state of New Hampshire, and did volunteer work for the National Association for the Advancement of Colored People. Barney Hill, 39 years old, worked as a dispatcher at the U.S. post office in Boston. He was also on the board of directors of a local poverty relief program and served as an advisor to the U.S. Civil Rights Commission.

On the evening of September 19, 1961, the Hills were driving from Quebec, Canada, to their home in Portsmouth, New Hampshire. As they were driving through New Hampshire, they saw a bright light in the sky. It crossed the moon, and then it began moving toward them. As a precaution, Barney stopped the car, got a pistol from the trunk, and started driving again. Betty looked at the object with binoculars. Now its flight path was lower and closer to the car. She saw a spinning disk shape, with a row of lighted windows along the edge. Barney suggested to his wife that the object might be an airplane, but when he himself looked through binoculars he didn't see any wings, and they didn't hear any sound of airplane engines. They stopped again. The object had moved farther away, and they saw it pass behind a mountain peak a mile away. They started driving, and the object moved closer again. It descended in a clearing on their right, hovering about 100 feet in the air. It was no longer spinning. It appeared the size of a four-engine airplane.

Barney stopped the car on the road and got out to look at the craft through binoculars. The object moved silently from one side of the road to the other, still hovering at 100 feet from the ground. Then it began to descend. Through his binoculars, Barney could see in the craft's windows several humanoids moving about inside, and looking out at him. Then, all except one of the humanoids left the windows and busied themselves with what appeared to be control instruments. The craft then moved towards Barney, approaching to within 75 feet. Barney could see the one humanoid who remained at the windows staring intensely at him. He felt that the humanoids wanted to capture him. So he ran back to the car, shouting, "They're going to capture us." When he got into the car, he immediately drove away. Near a place called Indian Head, the couple heard a loud beeping sound, apparently coming from the rear of the car, and at the same time the car shook. Barney and Betty experienced a tingling feeling and, overcome by drowsiness, entered a semi-sleep state. After some time, they again heard the beeping sounds. They were still driving in their car, but had lost track of time. They noticed they were in Ashland, about 35 miles from where they heard the first set of beeps. Gradually, they returned to normal waking consciousness.

At home, the Hills felt uncomfortable. Barney thought there might be something wrong with his lower abdomen. Betty noticed a pink powder on her dress. They could not clearly recall what had happened after they left Indian Head, where they had seen the saucer hovering close to the ground near their car. Barney reported the sighting to an Air Force officer at Pease Air Force Base. Project Blue Book listed the case as one with insufficient evidence to form any judgment, but noted the planet Jupiter as a possible explanation. Betty noticed a dozen round marks on the trunk of the car, and when she put a compass over the marks, the needle started spinning, although the needle remained steady when the compass was held over other parts of the car.

In the weeks after the incident, Betty Hill had a series of vivid troubling dreams. In November, she recorded her memories of the dreams in great detail. Here is a summary of her accounts. Betty and Barney were taken by the aliens through the forest to the craft. One of the aliens told her they were to be examined and then released. Inside the craft, Barney was led away to one room, and Betty remained in another. There she was examined and tested in various ways by the aliens, who also took some tissue samples. After the examination, Betty conversed with one of the humanoids. During the talk, she saw a book in a strange script and a three-dimensional star map, showing the home of the humanoids. Afterwards, Barney was brought back into Betty's presence. As they were being escorted out of the craft, Betty was carrying a book in the humanoids' script. She wanted it as proof of their existence. But the humanoids intervened and took the book away. The humanoids also told her she would not remember what took place inside the craft. The humanoids took Betty and Barney to their car. They stood by their car and watched the craft lift off and depart. They then got into the car and continued their drive home.

During an interview with NICAP researchers that took place on November 25, the Hills realized that their whole journey should normally have taken about four hours. Instead, it had taken seven hours. Even allowing for the stops that the Hills remembered, there were about two hours of "missing time." The Hills tried to reconstruct their memories of the entire journey, but they found they had only vague memories of what happened between Indian Head and Ashland. Betty began to wonder if her strange dreams were the explanation for the missing time. Meanwhile, a circle of warts formed on Barney's lower abdomen, and he had them removed surgically. He also began to experience anxiety attacks and an old drinking problem came back. To deal with these problems, he began seeing a psychiatrist.

Later the Hills tried hypnosis to recover their memories of the missing time and thus explain their dreams and uneasy feelings. From January to June 1964, the Hills visited Benjamin Simon, a Boston psychiatrist who practiced hypnosis. Barney was the first to undergo hypnosis. He was hypnotized alone, away from Betty, and Simon instructed him to forget anything that he recalled under hypnosis. Barney's recollections under hypnosis were as follows. After observing the UFO at close range, he and Betty got back into their car and drove away. At the point where they heard the beeping sounds for the first time, near a place called Indian Head, he drove off the highway (Route 3) into the forest, against his will, as if controlled by some higher power. He saw six humanoids on the small road, who motioned him to stop. The humanoids told him to not be afraid and to close his eyes. With his eyes closed, he could feel himself being led out of the car and then up a ramp. When he opened his eyes, he was inside the craft, in a place he described as an "operating room." He again closed his eyes. He underwent a medical examination, during which he felt a cup being placed over his groin, to extract a semen sample.

After the examination, with his eyes still closed, he was led out of the craft and down the ramp. When he opened his eyes, he saw his car and then Betty. He didn't know why they were there. They drove twenty miles back to Route 3, and after driving down Route 3 for some time heard the beeping sounds a second time, near a place called Ashland. Betty also underwent hypnosis, and her recollections basically matched what she reported from her dreams, and were also consistent with what Barney reported under hypnosis. They later estimated their onboard experiences had taken about two hours, which accounted for the missing time. Barney and Betty believed that the humanoids communicated with them telepathically.

Simon tried to convince Barney that his experiences recovered under hypnosis were derived from his recollections of Betty's dreams. But Barney Hill rejected this explanation, pointing out that his experiences contained elements not found in Betty's dreams (such as his being stopped on the forest road by six humanoids). In any case, the treatment by Simon was successful, in that the Hills felt relieved of their anxieties.

Afterwards, newspapers began to report on the Hill case, and in 1965 their experience was the subject of a book titled *The Interrupted Journey,* by John G. Fuller. The book was excerpted in *Look* magazine, and was turned into a television movie called *The UFO Incident.* The Hills became celebrities. Barney died in 1969, but I met Betty Hill a couple of years ago when I spoke at a Mutual UFO Network (MUFON) conference in Portsmouth, New Hampshire.

There is some corroboration for the Hill incident. There was a radar sighting of a UFO near the landing approach to Pease Air Force Base in New Hampshire on the night of the Hill sighting, although not exactly in the same area where the Hills had their encounter. An amateur astronomer, Marjorie Fish, produced a three dimensional map of stars near our sun that matched the star map drawn from memory by Betty Hill. From the information supplied by Hill, Fish determined that the points of origin for the humanoids were the stars Zeta 1 Reticuli and Zeta 2 Reticuli. In December 1974, Terence Dickinson, editor of the journal *Astronomy*, wrote for that publication an article about the star map. Dickinson asked scientists to give their opinions, and many were intrigued by the apparent match between the map and the actual stars. Throughout the next year, the magazine carried letters from scientists debating the merits of the star map.

Another abduction experience was reported in what came to be called the Buff Ledge Case. The principal investigator was Walter N. Webb, director of the planetarium at the Boston Museum of Science. On August 7, 1968, a boy sixteen years old and girl nineteen years old were working at a private summer camp for girls near Buff Ledge on the shores of Lake Champlain in the state of Vermont. According to the boy, he and the girl were sunbathing on the dock when a large UFO appeared, and three smaller UFOs emerged from it. One of the three UFOs approached, emitting sounds that appeared synchronized with its pulsating aura. The object was as big as a small house. The boy could see inside the craft some humanoid entities with large heads, big eyes, and small mouths. They were wearing silvery uniforms. The boy received from them a telepathic communication that they were from another planet and that he would not be harmed. When he tried to reach up and touch the bottom of the UFO, which was then floating over his head, he saw a beam of light, and felt a sensation of losing consciousness and moving up while holding on to the girl. The next thing he remembered was being again with the girl on the dock, at night, as the UFO floated overhead and then disappeared. The boy and girl went to their residences separately. The boy felt very tired, but before going to sleep he called nearby Plattsburgh Air Force base to report his experience. The person he spoke to said that other calls had been received, but military planes were not responsible. The boy never spoke about the incident to the girl, and after they left the camp, they did not see each other. After some initial attempts to speak about his experience to disbelieving friends and relatives, the boy stopped saying anything about it. But after ten years, he was still privately wondering about what had happened to him, so he contacted Walter Webb, who decided to thoroughly investigate the case. Webb located the woman who had been with the subject at the time of the incident. Webb had the two subjects separately hypnotized by two professional clinical psychologists in an attempt to recover their memories. They both reported similar experiences, which involved their being taken by the UFO to a "mother ship" in space above the earth. During the journey both the subjects were subjected to medical tests and probes by the aliens. The male subject reported that the aliens communicated with him telepathically. During his return to earth, the male subject reported that he passed through a television screen on the UFO that showed him and the girl lying on the dock. The woman's recollections of the events before entering the UFO were very close to those of her male companion. Both subjects took psychological tests that showed they were normal (Webb 1988; Thompson 1993, pp. 116–122). That the accounts given by the two subjects, who had not communicated with each other, were similar to a remarkable degree, including minor details, convinced Webb that the incident they reported actually took place.

There have been hundreds of such alien abduction reports, most of them with very similar features. In abduction accounts there is often a strong sexual element. In some cases the aliens are said to collect sperm or eggs, or engage in other kinds of medical activities connected with the human reproductive system and process. In other cases, aliens themselves engage in sexual activities with their human subjects. A Brazilian farmer named Antonio Villas Boas in 1957 was abducted and taken aboard a craft manned by beings of the "gray" type (i.e., small, with large heads and thin limbs). While he was on board, he was approached by a naked woman who appeared like a normal human, and she seduced him. After this, he was left on the ground (Creighton 1969; Thompson 1993, pp. 135–136). Women report being impregnated, either mechanically or by sexual contact with aliens, and bearing alien/human hybrids (Hopkins 1987; Jacobs 1992; Fowler 1990; Thompson 1993, pp. 137–138).

Psychological evaluations of abductees have been carried out, and researchers have found them to be sane. In 1981, psychologist Dr. Elizabeth Slater tested and interviewed nine abductees without knowing anything about their UFO experiences. She found they were normal, although somewhat anxious (Slater 1983a, p. 18). After learning about their experiences, she reported: "The first and most critical question is whether our subjects' reported experiences could be accounted for strictly on the basis of psychopathology, i.e., mental disorder. *The answer is a firm no.*" Slater also concluded that the anxiety they displayed was what one might expect from an abduction experience, which she said could be characterized as "a trauma of major proportions." She said that in this respect the abduction experience's "psychological impact might be analogous to what one sees in crime victims or victims of natural disaster" (Slater 1983b, p. 33; Thompson 1993, p. 153).

Conclusions similar to those of Dr. Slater were reached by other psychiatrists and psychologists. In her studies, psychiatrist Rima Laibow found no evidence of psychosis in abductees. She did find symptoms of post traumatic sress disorder, and pointed out that PTSD normally occurs only in cases where people have undergone very stressful physical experiences. It normally does not occur in response to purely psychological events such as nightmares or hallucinations. Laibow also pointed out that psychotic fantasies tend to be bizarrely unique, whereas the abduction accounts were quite similar to each other (Conroy 1989, pp. 237–240). Dr. Jean Mundy worked at St. Vincent's Hospital in New York City as a senior clinical psychologist. In her studies of abductees, she, like Slater, found they were not psychotic and displayed classic symptoms of post traumatic stress disorder: "This is how people who have experienced terrible trauma react—people who were holocaust victims, or Vietnam veterans, or rape victims. We don't know the nature of the trauma they experienced, but we know it's not their imagination. It's something that hit them from the outside, and in that sense it's something 'real'" (Stark 1990, p. 30; Thompson 1993, pp. 154–155).

Dr. John E. Mack, a psychiatrist at Harvard University, got his introduction to abductee reports through UFO researcher Budd Hopkins. After studying some of the reports collected by Hopkins, Mack (1994, p. 2) concluded they were genuine: "Most of the specific information that the abductees provided . . . had never been written about or shown in the media. Furthermore, these individuals were from many parts of the country and had not communicated with each other." This seemed to rule out collusion and repetition of media stereotypes as an explanation for the similarity of the reports coming from these individuals. Mack (1994, p. 2) added: "They seemed in other respects quite sane, had come forth reluctantly, fearing the discrediting of their stories or outright ridicule they had encountered in the past. They had come to see Hopkins at considerable expense, and, with rare exceptions, had nothing to gain materially from telling their stories. . . . What Hopkins had encountered in the more than two hundred abduction cases he had seen over a fourteen-year period were reports of experiences that had the characteristics of real events: highly detailed narratives that seemed to have no obvious symbolic pattern; intense emotional and physical traumatic impact, sometimes leaving small lesions on the experiencers' bodies; and consistency of stories down to the most minute details."

Mack then conducted his own interviews with several of Hopkins's subjects. Mack (1994, p. 3) concluded: "None of them seemed psychiatrically disturbed except in a secondary sense, that is they were troubled as a consequence of something that had apparently happened to them. There was nothing to suggest that their stories were delusional, a misinterpretation of dreams, or the product of fantasy. None of them seemed like people who would concoct a strange story for some personal purpose." He then began research with his own subjects. By 1994, he had accumulated studies on 76 subjects that satisfied his "quite strict criteria," which included "no apparent mental condition that could account for the story" (Mack 1994, pp. 3–4).

Mack got into trouble with his Harvard colleagues for his research on alien abductees. A report in the *Boston Globe* says, "After a yearlong investigation the Harvard Medical School has decided not to censure psychiatrist John Mack. . . . Mack had become a *cause célebrè* at Harvard after the 1994 publication of his best-selling book *Abduction*. In countless television and newspaper interviews, he was inevitably dubbed 'the

Harvard professor who believes in UFOs,' causing considerable anguish to many of his colleagues" (Beam 1995, p. 1). A special faculty committee at the medical school carried out the investigation. The *Boston Globe* reported, "The Medical School committee's preliminary report . . . chastised Mack for 'affirming the delusions' of his many patients who claim to have been abducted by aliens. The committee also found Mack to be 'in violation of the standards of conduct expected by a member of the faculty of Harvard University'" (Beam 1995, p. 1). There were suggestions that Mack's tenure should be revoked. After mounting a vigorous defense, Mack escaped any punitive action by the University.

Paranormal Aspects of Alien Encounters

Many abductees report paranormal phenomena. Betty Andreasson provides one example. In 1975, Andreasson wrote a letter to J. Allen Hynek, head of the Center for UFO Studies, and former director of the U. S. Air Force's Project Blue Book. In the letter, she told of an encounter with aliens that took place in 1967. Hynek referred the letter to the Humanoid Study Group of the Mutual UFO Network. Investigators connected with the group looked into the case.

Andreasson's experiences began on January 25, 1967 in South Ashburton, Massachusetts (Clark 1998, pp. 86–89). She was at home with her seven children, ranging from three to eleven years old. Her mother and father were also there. At 6:35 in the evening, the lights in the house went out. Andreasson, in the kitchen, saw a pinkish light coming in through the window, from the dark, foggy back yard. When her children entered the kitchen, she turned away from the window and took them back into the living room. Meanwhile, Andreasson's father, looking through a pantry window into the back yard, saw several humanoids. One of them looked at him, and he felt strange.

The next thing Andreasson remembered was waking up the next morning, feeling uneasy, as if something strange had happened. Her oldest child Becky, eleven years old, felt as if she had had a nightmare. Over the next few years, Betty Andreasson herself would from time to time experience brief images of beings and places not of this earth. After contacting UFO researchers, she underwent hypnosis, and recalled what happened after she saw the light coming through her kitchen window.

Everyone in the house except her was overcome by a kind of paralysis, in which time seemed to stop. Five humanoids passed through the closed front door of the house, and came into the kitchen. They were typical "grays," small in stature, with large heads, and large eyes. Betty, who was a fundamentalist Christian, believed they might be angels. They communicated with her telepathically. The leader of the entities was called Quazgaa. She handed him a Bible. In return, Quazgaa gave her a blue book. (Under hypnosis, Betty's daughter Becky said she could see her mother standing with little men, one of whom was holding a blue book.) Then Quazgaa waved his hand over the copy of the Bible he was holding, and several Bibles appeared. Each of the other humanoids took one and started looking through it. Betty noticed that each of the pages was a luminous white. When Betty looked at the blue book that Quazgaa had given her, she saw the first three pages were luminously white, and that there were strange images on the other pages.

The humanoids said they had come to help save the world from self-destruction and asked Betty to follow them. Quazgaa told her to stand behind him. Then Betty and all the humanoids passed through a closed door and then floated through the hazy air to a craft shaped like a disk. The craft became transparent, and Betty could see inside some rotating globes made of a crystalline substance. Betty and the humanoids then floated into the craft. Betty was then taken to a room, for an examination.

After the examination, which involved some intrusive investigation with strange instruments, Betty was taken on a tour by two humanoids. They floated through a black tunnel, and passed through a glowing glass wall at the end of the tunnel into a realm in which everything was of a glowing reddish color. There she saw creatures that were not humanoid. They had eyes on the ends of long stalks coming from roundish bodies with thin arms and legs. Betty, still accompanied by the two humanoids, then entered a green world full of plantlike entities. Then she entered a crystalline world, where her strange experiences continued. Betty was thinking she had been led into this realm by Jesus or God Himself, although there was no specifically Christian imagery. She then journeyed back through the other two worlds to her starting place.

There Quazgaa told her that the humanoids were friends and well wishers of the human race. They hoped humans would try to get knowledge through spiritual means. He then said he would send her back to her home. She would forget her experiences for some time, but secrets would remain locked in her mind for later retrieval. Two humanoids led her out of the craft, through her backyard, and into her house. There she saw her children and parents standing motionless. The humanoids directed them into their respective bedrooms. One of the humanoids, named Joohoop, told Betty she could keep the blue book, still in her hands, for ten days. Then Betty was led to her bedroom, where she was put to sleep.

Hynek wrote in a foreword to one of Raymond Fowler's books on

Betty Andreasson: "Here we have 'creatures of light' who find walls no obstacle to free passage into rooms and who find no difficulty in exerting uncanny control over the witnesses' minds. If this represents advanced technology, then it must incorporate the paranormal. . . . Somehow, 'they' have mastered the puzzle of mind over matter" (Fowler 1979, p. 9).

There are many cases similar to Andreasson's. These have led to a major split in the UFO research community. One group wishes to focus on the purely "scientific" evidence for extraterrestrials visiting the earth in craft superior to our own but still operating according to known physical laws. Another group, like Hynek, says the totality of evidence suggests that we might be encountering in the UFO phenomenon not just extraterrestrial beings, but extradimensional beings, with connections to the kinds of beings normally called supernatural. I favor this latter interpretation of the reports of the UFO phenomenon.

One of the earliest paranormal interpretations of the modern UFO phenomenon was offered by N. Meade Layne, founder of Borderland Sciences Research Associates. He called the UFOs "ether ships." In 1950, Layne wrote about UFOs: "The aeroforms are thought-constructs, mind constructs. As such, they are in effect, the vehicle of the actual entity who creates them. Just as our own terrestrial minds rule and become identified with our bodies, so does the entity of the Etheric world make for himself a body or vehicle out of etheric substance. This body may be of any shape or size, any one of a hundred *mutants*—such as the indefinite and changing shapes reported by observers of flying saucers throughout the world. . . . The impenetrable steel of landed discs is, as it were, a sort of etheric isotope of our terrestrial steel, or we may call it 'etheric steel.' The shapes and vehicles and entity operating them form one being, just as a human being is a psychophysical mind-body unity. The body of this Etherian entity is a thoughtform which can go anywhere, and penetrate our earth and sea as easily as our air" (Layne 1950; in Clark 1998, p. 697).

Although most "conservative" UFO researchers rejected Layne's view, Jerome Clark notes "some more conservative ufologists nonetheless considered it possible that if UFOs did not come from outer space, perhaps they were visiting from a 'fourth dimension'—the etheric realm by another name" (Clark 1998, p. 697).

The paranormal trend picked up strength in the 1960s and has continued to the present. Gordon Creighton, a frequent contributor to *Flying Saucer Review,* wrote in 1967: "Some of the UFO beings allegedly encountered could . . . be said to correspond to our Western, Christian, idea of 'Angels' . . . or to what Hindus and other peoples of Asia might term 'Devas.' And ... there is abundant evidence that there are other and altogether different creatures which correspond very closely indeed to the traditional concepts held in all parts of our world, of 'demons,' 'goblins,' 'trolls,' and so on" (Creighton 1967; Clark 1998, p. 699). In 1969, *Flying Saucer Review* assistant editor Dan Lloyd, wrote: "There could be no greater distortion of what is actually happening at the present time in man's relation to the spiritual world than to spread the delusion that physical machines are coming to earth with physical beings from outer space" (Lloyd 1969; Clark 1998, p. 699).

Another controversial UFO theorist was John Alva Keel, an early proponent of the paranormal theory. He said about UFOs: "The objects may be composed of energy from the upper frequencies of the electromagnetic spectrum. Somehow they can descend to the narrow (very narrow) range of visible light and can be manipulated into any desirable form ... including dirigibles, airplanes, and 'flying saucers.' ... They ... simply adopt a form which would make sense to us. Once they have completed their mission and, say, led another police officer on a wild goose chase, they ... revert to an energy state and disappear from our field of vision" (Keel 1969; Clark 1998, pp. 550–551).

Jacques Vallee became one of the most prominent advocates of the supernatural explanation of UFOs. In 1959, he received a bachelor's degree in mathematics from the University of Paris. In 1961, still in France, he received a master's degree in astrophysics, from Lille University. In 1962, Vallee moved to the United States, where he studied at the University of Texas and worked at an observatory. In 1963, he went to Northwestern University in Chicago, and got a Ph.D. in computer science, working under J. Allen Hynek, who was head of the astronomy department and head of the U. S. Air Force UFO research program, Project Blue Book. In his early writings, Vallee stuck to the "nuts and bolts" view of UFOs, but in his book *Passport to Magonia*, he came out firmly in support of the paranormal explanation. *Magonia* is a Latin word meaning "magicland." In medieval France, some used it to mean a place in the sky from where ships come sailing in the clouds (Clark 1998, p. 702). UFO researcher Jerome Clark (1998, p. 969) said about *Passport to Magonia*: "In it Vallee argued that UFO phenomena are better understood when related to folk traditions about supernatural creatures (elementals, fairies, angels, demons, ghosts) than to astronomers' speculations about life on other planets." Vallee (1988, p. 253) himself said, "I believe that the UFO phenomenon represents evidence for other dimensions beyond spacetime; the UFOs may not come from ordinary space, but from a multiverse which is all around us, and of which we have stubbornly refused to consider the disturbing reality in spite of the evidence available to us for centuries."

Hynek's ideas eventually began to come close to those of Vallee, his former student. Hynek rejected the idea that UFOs were mechanical spacecraft, mainly because the distances between the earth and star systems outside our solar system seemed too great. In 1978, Hynek said at a conference sponsored by MUFON (Mutual UFO Network) that a super-civilization somewhere out there in the universe might use "ESP, psychokinesis, teleportation, mental telepathy as part of their everyday technology as we incorporate transistors and computers in ours. . . . UFOs could well be the product of such a technology. To such a technology, the idea of building nuts and bolts spacecraft and blasting them off from some space Cape Canaveral would seem archaic and childlike. Perhaps all they have to do to get someplace is to think themselves there, projecting a thought form, or a force field, to any part of space they want and causing it to manifest there, on that plane" (Hynek 1978; Clark 1998, p. 704).

The paranormal explanation of the UFO phenomenon continued to gain strength. In a doctoral dissertation for the University of Pennsylvania, Peter M. Rojcewicz said that the UFO phenomenon "constitutes a multi-faceted continuum of experience with and belief in fairies, demons, angels, ghosts, apparitions . . . spectre ships, *kachinas* . . . *vimanas* [Vedic spaceships], mysterious unmarked helicopters and planes, mysterious airships, and various 'monsters' reported in association with unknown aerial phenomena" (Rojcewicz 1984; Clark 1998, p. 706).

Many of the cases studied by Harvard University psychiatrist John E. Mack contain strong paranormal elements. In May 1997, Mack (1999, pp. 166–177) met Sequoyah Trueblood, 56 years old and an American Indian of the Choctaw nation. In July 1970, Sequoyah had just returned to the United States from Vietnam, where he had served as a United States Army officer. On July 4, he and his wife were sitting and watching their children swimming in the pool of their townhouse in Laurel, Maryland. Without knowing why, he left them and drove to the Washington/Baltimore airport, where he boarded a flight for Oklahoma City. When he arrived there, he called a friend, who took him to the house of another friend in nearby Norman. There he went into a bedroom to rest. As he was resting on a bed, breathing deeply, he felt himself sucked into a whirlpool of colored lights and found himself in a garden, in which he saw a silver disk. Standing on steps coming from the bottom of the craft was a small, androgynous, grayish humanoid with large eyes. It communicated telepathically with Sequoyah, telling him that it was from another place and that it was going to take him there.

Mack (1999, p. 175) stated, "Sequoyah does not distinguish the beings who he says took him into a spacecraft from the guardian spirits that have guided and protected him all his life. The use of the word extraterrestrial by whites, Sequoyah believes, is just another expression of our separation from spirit. There are many other planets, stars, and universes, populated, he believes, by a virtually infinite number of beings. Such beings are always among us and become visible in humanoid form so they can interact with us and bring us back to Source. . . .The form in which spirit chooses to manifest on any given occasion—as human, humanoid, or animal creature, for example—is itself a sacred mystery. According to Sequoyah, we are all in a sense extraterrestrial, for star beings took part in the creation of the human species and have always been our teachers."

Sequoyah willingly entered the craft with the androgynous humanoid. Then the craft started its voyage. Through a small window, Sequoyah saw the moon and the sun and then countless stars pass by as if in an instant. The voyage ended in what seemed to be another universe or another dimension of reality. The craft was hovering over a city with beautiful white buildings. Sequoyah and the androgynous being descended to the city by what Sequoyah characterized as a process of "dematerialization and rematerialization" (Mack 1999, p. 177). The people in the city were of male and female gender, and they wore white garments. Sequoyah and his androgynous humanoid guide walked down a street lined with white buildings three hundred stories high, and came to a clearing in some parklike woods. Sequoyah learned that the people there lived in peace in this timeless realm and received nourishment through breathing. One of the leaders of the people indicated to Sequoyah that he had been brought there to see the potential of the human race on earth. He would be sent back to earth to teach his own native people, and then other people on earth, about the peace and love he had seen. He was told that he could, if he desired, stay for some time before returning to earth. But Sequoyah suddenly felt very strong memories of his wife and children, his car, his home: "I almost went into a psychosis, for this was my first lesson in realizing how attached I was to the material world" (Mack 1999, p. 177). The beings told Sequoyah, "This is one of the big problems on Mother Earth. You're only here temporarily. These bodies of yours are just tools that you've been given to learn with" (Mack 1999, p. 177). Attachment to these material bodies is the source of suffering for the conscious self within the body. Sequoyah said he wanted to return. During the return voyage, he again saw the stars passing. Then came the sun and the moon. He found himself in the garden where he had first seen the craft, and then he went through the vortex of swirling colored light and found himself once more on the bed in the house of his friend in Norman, Oklahoma.

For Mack, the paranormal aspect of the UFO phenomenon assumes great importance. Mack (1999, pp. 268–269) said, "Efforts to pin down physical evidence for the existence of UFOs and the material aspects of abductions will and probably should continue, if for no other reason than the fact that they corroborate the actuality of the phenomena. But I am increasingly convinced that the subtle and elusive nature of the abduction phenomenon is such that its secrets will be denied to those using a purely empirical approach, who try to keep observer and observed, subject and object, totally separate." Mack (1999, p. 269) added, "It appears ever more likely that we exist in a multidimensional cosmos or multiverse. . . . The cosmos . . . far from being an empty place of dead matter and energy, appears to be filled with beings, creatures, spirits, intelligences, gods . . . that have through the millennia been intimately involved with human existence."

Conclusion

In 1999, I gave a lecture on forbidden archeology to the faculty and students of the University of Olsztyn in Poland. As usual, I presented evidence for extreme human antiquity that problematizes the current Darwinian theories of human origins. During the question session, I was asked if I had an alternative to the Darwinian theory. I presented a brief summary of the human devolution concept. I mentioned also that Poland was the homeland of Copernicus, who made a revolution in astronomy, ending its geocentric focus. I suggested to the audience that it was now time for a Copernican revolution in biology, ending its geocentric focus. I was surprised when the audience burst into loud applause. Yes, it is time for not only an extraterrestrial biology, but an extradimensional biology, with a cosmic hierarchy of beings ranging from a supreme intelligent being, to demigods, to human beings of our type. Within this system, the origin of human beings would have to be explained in relation to the other beings present in the hierarchy.

9
PARANORMAL MODIFICATION AND PRODUCTION OF BIOLOGICAL FORM

For thousands of years, humans have been involved in the intelligent modification of biological form and development, through selective breeding. In this way, one can produce plants and animals with desirable features, including desirable size, color, and rate of growth. Darwin himself used the results of such intentional modification of biological form as one of the pillars of his theory of evolution by natural selection. He reasoned that if in a short period of time we humans can induce such changes on a small scale, then just imagine what mutation and natural selection can accomplish over millions of years. In other words, Darwin appealed to something visible to us (selective breeding within an existing species) to demonstrate something invisible to us (the origin of new species). But there is another visible kind of intelligent modification of biological form and development. It goes beyond the conventional processes of selective breeding that Darwin used as evidence for the possibility of evolution of complex new forms. I am talking about paranormal modification of biological form and development. This paranormal modification can take place in many ways, including the mentally transferred intentions of human agents, the transference of impressions from mothers to embryos within their wombs, the transference of physical modifications from one life to another by agency of a surviving soul, and the influence of superhuman beings from the lower levels of the cosmic hierarchy on the human organism. If we can detect within our experience such visible modification of biological form and development by paranormal means, we are justified in assuming that more powerful agents might be able to accomplish more. Instead of simply making changes within an existing species, they might be able to manifest new biological forms by their greater paranormal powers. The reasoning is essentially the same as Darwin's. In this chapter, we shall review cases involving both human and apparently superhuman modification and production of biological form.

Modern Scientific Reports on
Cellular Modification in Laboratories

We begin our review with cases of human agents acting on single-celled organisms under laboratory conditions. Some of these cases are summarized by Dossey (1993, p. 190). In one set of experiments Barry (1968) had ten persons try to slow the growth of fungus cultures. From a distance of 1.5 yards, the experimenters concentrated on 194 culture dishes for fifteen minutes, willing them not to grow. The cultures were then placed in incubation for several hours. Out of the 194 culture dishes, 151 showed slower than normal growth. Tedder and Monty (1981) replicated Barry's experiment, this time using a group of subjects who were stationed at distances from one to fifteen miles from the fungus cultures. This group was able to retard the growth of the fungus in sixteen out of sixteen attempts. Nash (1982) had sixty subjects attempt to influence the growth of bacteria cultures. He reported that the subjects were able to retard and increase the growth rate to a significant degree.

Describing another set of experiments by Nash (1984), Dossey (1993, p. 190) stated, "Sixty university volunteers . . . were asked to alter the genetic ability of a strain of the bacteria *Escherichia coli,* which normally mutates from the inability to metabolize the sugar lactose ("lactose negative") to the ability to use it ("lactose positive") at a known rate. The subjects tried to influence nine test tubes of bacterial cultures—three for increased mutation from lactose negative to lactose positive, three for decreased mutation of lactose negative to lactose positive, and three tubes uninfluenced as controls. Results indicated that the bacteria indeed mutated in the directions desired by the subjects." This is significant, because the subjects were able to affect not only growth but the genetic structure of the organism.

Dossey (1993, pp. 191–192) noted: "Although skeptics often criticize spiritual healing as being simply the result of suggestion or a placebo response, the above experiments show that this cannot be true, unless skeptics wish to attribute a high degree of consciousness to bacteria and yeast. These results suggest that the effects of spiritual healing can be completely independent of the 'psychology' of the subject."

Beverly Rubik conducted laboratory research on "volitional effects of healers on a bacterial system" while director of the Institute for Frontier Sciences at Temple University in Philadelphia, Pennsylvania. The experiments were performed using the bacterium *Salmonella typhimurium,* a very well studied organism. The chief subject in the study was faith healer Olga Worrall, who had demonstrated positive abilities in other experiments.

One set of experiments involved volitional effects on bacterial cultures infused with low and high concentrations of the antibiotics tetracycline and chloramphenicol, which inhibit growth to various degrees. To influence the cultures, Worrall would hold her hands close to, but not touching, the culture dishes. After about 20 generations of bacterial reproduction (bacteria reproduce by dividing in two), the cultures that Worrall acted upon were compared with the control cultures. In all cases there was a significant increase in growth of the bacteria in the cultures treated by Worrall.

In the experiments in which the bacterial samples were infused with low concentrations (1 microgram per milliliter) of tetracycline, samples treated by Worrall showed 121 percent more growth than the control samples. In experiments with concentrations of 10 micrograms/ml of tetracycline, samples treated by Worrall showed 28 percent more growth than the control samples. In experiments with concentrations of 10 micrograms/ml of chloramphenicol, samples treated by Worrall showed 70 percent more growth than the control samples. In experiments with concentrations of 100 micrograms/ml of chloramphenicol, samples treated by Worrall showed 22 percent and 24 percent more growth than the control samples (Rubik 1996, p. 105).

Another set of experiments involved studies of motility of bacteria. The bacteria were placed on slides in a solution of phenol sufficient to immobilize but not kill them. The slides of bacteria were then observed under a microscope. Rubik (1996, p. 108) stated, "Application of . . . phenol completely paralyzes the bacteria within 1 to 2 minutes. Worrall's treatment inhibited this effect . . . such that on the average up to 7% of the bacteria continued to swim after 12 minutes exposure to phenol compared to the control groups which were completely paralyzed in all cases."

Distance Healing on Humans

Today, many people around the world are using alternative medical treatments in addition to, or instead of, modern Western medical treatment. Many alternative medical treatments involve spiritual and paranormal influences, such as prayer. A study published in the *Journal of the American Medical Association* (Eisenberg et al. 1998) found that 35 percent of all Americans had used prayer to help solve health problems. Another national study, published in *Time* magazine (Wallis 1996), found that 82 percent of all Americans believe that prayer has healing power. A study published in the *Annals of Internal Medicine* (Astin et al. 2000) found that "a growing body of evidence suggests an association between religious involvement and spirituality and positive health outcomes."

In support of this assertion the authors of the study cited reports from a variety of scientific and medical journals.

In their study, Astin and his coworkers did a thorough review of published medical reports on "distant healing." Their definition of distant healing includes "strategies that purport to heal through some exchange or channeling of supraphysical energy" as well as prayer (Astin et al. 2000, p. 903). Searching through the professional literature, Astin's group found 100 clinical trials of distant healing. They then analyzed these according to a stringent set of criteria. This resulted in many being excluded from consideration. They stated (2000, p. 904), "The principle reasons for excluding trials from our review were lack of randomization, no adequate placebo condition, use of nonhuman experimental subjects or nonclinical populations, and not being published in peer-reviewed journals." After this strict selection procedure, 23 clinical trials remained. Astin's group noted that even these had some minor methodological shortcomings that could be improved with better experimental design and controls. Nevertheless, they found that 13 of the 23 studies (57 percent) showed a positive treatment outcome. They concluded (2000, p. 910): "Despite the methodologic limitations that we have noted, given that approximately 57% (13 of 23) of the randomized, placebo controlled trials of distant healing that we reviewed showed a positive treatment effect, we concur ... that the evidence thus far warrants further study." Regarding studies on nonhuman subjects, such as bacteria, Astin's group, citing a review by Benor (1990), said (2000, p. 904): "The findings of controlled trials of distant healing in nonhuman biological systems are provocative enough to merit further research."

Local Healing by Faith Healers

Let us now consider some specific cases of healing by spiritualists. Kathryn Kuhlman, a Christian faith healer who worked from the 1940s to the 1970s, was responsible for some interesting cures that appear to be well documented, such as the case of George Orr. In 1925, Orr was working at the Laurence Foundry Company in Grove City, Pennsylvania. A drop of molten iron splashed into his eye, injuring it severely. Dr. C. E. Imbrie determined that the cornea of the eye was covered by scar tissue, causing almost complete loss of vision. In 1927, the Pennsylvania State Department of Labor and Industry said the injury was equivalent to the loss of an eye, and granted Orr complete compensation. On May 4, 1947, Orr and some family friends attended one of Kuhlman's meetings, in Franklin, Pennsylvania. Orr prayed for a healing. He felt a tingling in his eye, which began to shed tears. Later, on the drive back home, he realized he could see. The scar on his eye had disappeared. Dr. Imbrie later examined Orr and was astonished by the cure (Rogo 1982, pp. 275–277). The Orr case is significant because the healing was not just the result of an activation of the body's own powers of regeneration. Rogo (1982, p. 277) stated: "Because scar tissue on the eye does not simply vanish or dissolve, George Orr's cure must be considered a legitimate miracle . . . It was not of a sort that might occur naturally, Orr was under no medical treatment at the time, and the healing was instantaneous, complete, and permanent."

In 1948, Karen George was born in Conway, Pennsylvania, with a clubfoot. Rogo (1982, p. 277) said, "The bottom of her left foot faced upward and a walnut-sized ball of flesh was embedded in its surface. The toes were pushed together as well, and the kneecap was twisted over to the side of the leg." A doctor put a brace on Karen's leg when she was three months old, the first of many braces. None of them worked.

Karen's mother recalled, "When we saw no improvement from the first brace, we changed doctors. Karen was four months old then. We took her to another orthopedist who was recommended to us. He immediately put her in a cast that encased the whole leg and left it on for a month. She cried almost constantly. When they took the cast off, the leg flopped back exactly as it had been before. The doctor let her go about a month and then tried another cast. More crying almost day and night. And when he took off that cast, the leg promptly went back into its twisted position" (Spraggett 1970, pp. 77–78).

The orthopedist told the Georges that when their daughter was two and a half years old, she could have surgery. But the Georges did not want to wait that long. And they did not have faith in the operations. Mrs. George said, "We met other parents with children who had the same problem in the doctor's waiting room and they told us of repeated operations, and sometimes after years of treatment the child was still deformed. We knew, too, from talking to other parents and seeing their children that Karen's was a very serious case" (Spraggett 1970, p. 79).

Having heard of Kathryn Kuhlman, the Georges brought their daughter to one of her meetings. Kuhlman and her congregation prayed for Karen's healing. Within two days, the lump on Karen's foot was gone. Spraggett (1970, p. 80) said, "Karen George received no further medical treatment for her foot. Her mother took her to Kathryn Kuhlman's miracle services regularly. Over a period of a month the child's foot imperceptibly improved until one day Mrs. George examined it and it was perfectly normal." When Karen was twenty years old, Spraggett (1970, p. 80) visited her and personally observed her perfectly normal foot.

Healing by Distance in Time

Sometimes miraculous healings occur in connection not only with living humans, but with humans long departed, as in the case of healings by departed saints. John Fagan, a dock worker in Glasgow, Scotland, underwent such a cure (Rogo 1982, pp. 266–271). On April 26, 1967, the middle-aged Fagan found himself vomiting blood. He entered the Glasgow Royal Infirmary, and underwent medical testing, which showed he had stomach cancer. The doctors, without telling him he had cancer, recommended surgery. Rogo (1982, p. 267) stated, "The resulting surgery revealed that the cancer had eaten through the stomach and into the transverse colon. The stomach was greatly ulcerated, and the cancer had apparently spread far by the time of the operation. The cancerous tissue could not be completely removed, and the doctors duly advised Mrs. Fagan that her husband had only from six months to a year to live. Again, Fagan was not told of this prognosis." Fagan was released from the hospital, and as predicted, his condition grew worse. He went back into the hospital on December 21, 1967. Doctors informed Mrs. Fagan that inoperable secondary tumors had developed. There was nothing they could do for Mr. Fagan other than give him medications to reduce the pain he was suffering. Mrs. Fagan cared for her husband at home. He remained in bed, getting weaker as he approached death. A Catholic priest, Father John Fitzgibbon, of the Church of Blessed John Ogilvie, started visiting the Fagans, who were Catholic. Expecting the worst, Father Fitzgibbon gave Fagan the last rites. As a last hope, he gave Mrs. Fagan a medal of Blessed John Ogilvie, a Scottish Catholic martyr killed by Glasgow Protestants in 1614, and suggested she pray to him. Mrs. Fagan followed the priest's advice. Friends of the Fagan's would also come and pray to Blessed John Ogilvie. Rogo (1982, p. 268) states, "By March, Fagan was so weak that he could neither get up from bed, eat, or even talk. He could only vomit repeatedly, since by now his stomach was literally dissolving itself. . . . The Fagans' doctor, Archibald MacDonald, arrived . . . [March 6] . . . and was so shaken by his patient's condition that he could do nothing but advise Mrs. Fagan that he would return after the weekend to sign the death certificate. He gave her husband a pain killer and left. Fagan then fell into a deep sleep." The next day, Fagan's condition changed completely. His pain and vomiting stopped, and he felt hungry. Dr. MacDonald was astounded by the recovery, which was soon complete.

When Fagan's miraculous cure became known, Catholic Church officials in Scotland hoped to use it to convince the Vatican to take the final step in canonizing John Ogilvie as a saint. In order to accomplish this, the Church officials had to extensively document Fagan's cure. They convened a panel headed by Father Thomas Reilly. This panel obtained an account of the case from Dr. MacDonald, and then chose a committee composed of three Glasgow doctors to investigate further. After two years' study, the committee could find no medical explanation for the cure. In 1971, the Vatican sent Dr. Livio Capacaccia, an expert on diseases of the stomach and intestines at the University of Rome, to Scotland. Although Dr. Capacaccia was inclined to believe Fagan's cure was miraculous, Father Reilly encouraged him to carefully consider possible natural explanations for the cure. Dr. Capacaccia made some proposals, which were studied by the committee. For example, he proposed that perhaps the secondary cancerous growths had undergone spontaneous remission. The committee concluded that the medical evidence ruled this out. Another theory was that something other than secondary cancerous growths caused Fagan's relapse. Along these lines, Dr. Gerard Crean, an expert on diseases of the stomach and intestines from Edinburgh, suggested that the original operation had removed all the cancerous growths, and that Fagan's relapse had been caused by discharge from an abscess that later healed itself. Rogo (1982, p. 270) states, "Crean's theory was finally rejected on the basis that (1) Fagan was too near death to have been suffering from a simple abscess; (2) the original surgeon was ready to confirm that not all of Fagan's cancer had been removed during the surgery; and (3) Fagan's decline was consistent with his doctor's original diagnosis and prognosis. The panel could find no alternative explanation and concluded that Fagan was suffering from a secondary malignant cancer that had—for no apparent medical reason —suddenly healed of its own accord."

In May 1971, Fagan underwent thorough medical testing at Western General Hospital in Edinburgh. The examiners concluded that Fagan's relapse was "entirely consistent with the natural history of a patient with recurrent gastric carcinoma" and that there was "no satisfactory explanation" for his cure (Rogo 1982, p. 270). Dr. Capacaccia returned to Glasgow in October 1971 and reviewed all of the medical evidence in consultation with the doctors involved in the investigation. He found that the cure was miraculous and reported his conclusion to the Vatican. Pope Paul VI declared the cure a miracle caused by John Ogilvie, who was soon thereafter declared a saint.

Postmortem healings also took place in connection with St. Martin de Porres of Peru, who was born in 1579 and died in 1639. The Catholic process of declaring sainthood goes in two main stages. The first is beatification and the second is canonization. The beatification of St. Martin de Porres came in 1837. His canonization came in 1857. In connection with the beatification process, Pope Gregory XV on March 19, 1836 approved the following cure as miraculous. A woman in Lima broke a piece of pottery, and a sliver entered her eyeball, causing all the fluid to leak out. This injury left the eye incurably blind. Rogo (1982, p. 265) stated, "The master of a nearby monastery, however, sent the woman a small bone fragment, a relic of Martin de Porres, and instructed her to hold it to the damaged eye. She did as she was directed and woke the next morning to find her eye and sight totally restored. Though this was medically impossible, the cure was authenticated by the woman's own doctor, who had examined the original wound." The second cure connected with the beatification of St. Martin of Porres also took place in Lima. A Peruvian child fell eighteen feet from a balcony and split his skull. The child went into convulsions. A doctor looked at him and found his case hopeless. The child's mother, and the Spanish noblewoman who employed her, prayed to Martin de Porres, and after the hours, the child got up from bed, having recovered completely. Two more recent cures were recognized by the Vatican in 1962. In 1948, Dorothy Caballero Escalante, an elderly woman in Paraguay, was suffering from an inoperable intestinal blockage. Her daughter, having been informed that her mother was near death, prayed to Martin de Porres, and she recovered fully. In 1956, Anthony Cabrera Perez, a boy four years old, was playing in a construction site in Tenerife, in the Canary Islands. A large block of cement fell on his leg, crushing it. Gangrene later infected the leg. Doctors at St. Eulalia's Hospital treated it with medicine, which failed to act. The doctors then decided to amputate the leg to save the boy's life. But the parents prayed to Martin of Porres, and the next morning the gangrene was gone and the boy's leg soon healed.

Stigmatics

Over the centuries, certain persons of Christian faith, including, but not limited to, saints, have developed marks (stigmata) on their bodies corresponding to the wounds Christ suffered during the crucifixion. These persons, called stigmatics, usually develop wounds in the palms of the hands and in the feet, corresponding to nail wounds, and sometimes also develop a wound on the side of the chest, corresponding to the place where a Roman soldier stabbed Christ with a spear. Several authors have explained these stigmata as psychosomatic effects, produced on the body by the mind of the stigmatic, who imagines the crucifixion scene. One argument in favor of this is that the wounds sometimes appear in slightly different places (Stevenson 1997, pp. 34–42), just as they do in different artistic representations of the crucifixion. In other words, just as artists may imagine the marks on the body of Christ in a slightly different way, so might the stigmatics. Alternatively, the stigmata could be manifested on the body of the stigmatic directly by some supernatural being, or by some combination of the psychosomatic and supernatural influences. I favor the latter suggestion, but in either case, the stigmata do represent a paranormal modification of biological form. Stevenson (1997, p. 34) noted that usually a variety of paranormal phenomena, in addition to stigmata, manifest in the lives of stigmatics, including "visions, bilocations, healing powers, extrasensory perception, the ability to live normally without food and water, and postmortem incorruptibility of the physical body."

The German psychiatrist A. Lechler studied the stigmata case of Elisabeth K. Although he does not give her last name, he does provide extensive documentation of his thorough study of her hypnotically induced stigmata, including photographs. Elisabeth K. was born in 1902, and suffered from many psychiatric disorders. Lechler began treating her in the late 1920s. Stevenson (1997, pp. 43–52) gives a summary of a report on Elisabeth K. by Lechler (1933).

Elisabeth identified with the sufferings of others. For example, if she saw someone with a limp, she developed a limp herself. Once she heard of someone with an inflamed tendon in the arm, and thereafter her own arm developed the symptoms of tendonitis, including redness, pain, and swelling. Lechler (1933, p. 11) wrote: "Whenever she read in the Bible stories about the healing of the lame, she had the feeling that she herself was lame and numb in her legs. She attended a lecture (illustrated with lantern slides) about the suffering and death of Jesus; as she looked at the picture of the Savior on the cross, she felt severe pain in her hands and feet at the places where nails had been driven into Jesus."

This incident occurred in 1932. Lechler wanted to see if the actual stigmata might appear. He hypnotized Elisabeth and told her to continue thinking, while she was asleep that night, about nails being driven through her hands and feet. The next morning, Elisabeth, very much alarmed, showed her hands and feet to Lechler, who noted (1933, p. 11): "The sites I had indicated during the hypnosis all had areas (about the size of a small coin) that were red and swollen with the skin somewhat opened up and showing moisture. Elisabeth calmed down when I explained to her the cause [his hypnotic suggestions] of the wounds. Then with her consent I gave her, in a waking condition, the further suggestion that the wounds would become deeper and also that she would weep bloody tears." The wounds did in fact become deeper, exposing the underlying tissues, which appeared bloody. There were, however, no bloody tears. Lechler gave further hypnotic suggestions, and before two hours had passed, Elisabeth came to him with bloody tears running down her cheeks from her eyes. Lechler took photographs, which he later published, of the wounds and the face with tears. He then gave Elisabeth a suggestion that the tears would stop. They did. He also gave a suggestion that the wounds would close up, and within 48 hours they did. Lechler soon thereafter induced the stigmata on Elisabeth's hands and feet a second time, during which he observed actual bleeding more distinctly than the first time. Another time, Lechler suggested to Elisabeth that he was putting a crown of thorns on her head. The next morning, her forehead was red and swollen and covered with wounds, triangular in shape, like those made by a thorn. When Lechler suggested the wounds would bleed, within an hour they did.

Lechler did not keep Elisabeth under continuous observation during these experiments. Realizing that he could not be one hundred percent sure she had not inflicted the wounds upon herself, he performed another series of experiments, during which she was kept under continuous observation by either him or nurses from a hospital. The same stigmata were produced in this second set of experiments—the wounds on the hands and feet, the bloody tears, and the wounds on the forehead. In some of these cases, Lechler personally observed the wounds begin to bleed.

Therese Neumann (1898–1962) was another stigmatic who achieved wide recognition (Rogo 1982, pp. 65–69). As a devoutly Catholic girl living in the Bavarian village of Konnersreuth, she dreamed of becoming a missionary to Africa. But on March 10, 1918, she was injured while fighting a fire at a nearby farm. A few weeks later, she fell down some stairs, and went to a hospital suffering from internal injuries and convulsions. After she was released, she remained at home, a bedridden invalid, her body covered with bedsores. Her left foot began to decay from lack of use. She also lost her sight. By this time, Therese had become devoted to Thérèse of Lisieux. Rogo (1982, p. 66) stated, "On April 29, 1925—the very day Thérèse of Lisieux was beatified—Neumann was spontaneously healed of her blindness. A few days later her left foot . . . regenerated new skin after rose leaves from St. Thérèse's grave were placed under its bandages. On May 17, 1925—the date of Thérèse of Lisieux's formal canonization— Neumann's paralysis immediately disappeared. And on September 10, the anniversary of St. Thérèse's death, Neumann found her strength so revitalized that she could leave her bed without aid." Rogo (1982, p. 66) pointed out that Neumann's paralysis and blindness could have been purely psychological in origin. Nevertheless, the healing of the foot did seem mysterious.

During Lent of 1926, Neumann had dreams of Christ, and developed stigmata, with bleeding wounds on her hands and feet, and a deep bleeding wound on her chest. She said: "The five wounds hurt me constantly, although I have already become accustomed to pain. It is as though something is penetrating into my hands and feet. The wound in the side seems to be really one in the heart. I feel it at every word I utter. If I draw a deep breath when speaking forcibly or hurrying, I feel a stabbing pain in my heart. If I keep quiet, I don't notice this. But I suffer this pain willingly. Actually, the wounds close up during the week. The real pain lies much deeper inside" (Rogo 1982, p. 67). Later, in November, Neumann developed on her forehead eight wounds, the stigmata associated with the crown of thorns. In 1927, the wounds on her feet deepened, going from her instep all the way through to the soles. Similarly, the wounds on the backs of her hands went all the way through to the palms. Rogo (1982, p. 67) said, "Protuberances resembling nail heads slowly appeared within the wounds on her hands. These nail-like structures, apparently formed from hardened skin, were examined by several doctors and priests. They passed completely through her feet and hands, taking up most of the area of the wounds. The 'nails' could be seen on the backs of her hands, bent to the sides of her palms, and also on her feet. A soft, membranelike tissue surrounded them. During her ecstasies this membrane would break to allow blood to flow."

Each Friday, Neumann would have a vision of the crucifixion, and during these visions her wounds would exude large amounts of blood, which would be soaked up by continuous application of bandages. In addition to her stigmata, Neumann also exhibited other paranormal abilities, such as miraculous healing of others, clairvoyance, and appearing in two places simultaneously.

Stevenson (1997, p. 49) notes this interesting incident in connection with the Neumann stigmata: "A physician of Silesia, Dr. A. Mutke . . . had steeped himself in information about the case of Therese Neumann, which received immense publicity during the 1920s and 1930s. During this period, the physician became severely ill. As he was recovering, a colleague visited him one day and said to him: 'What has happened to your hands? You are stigmatized.' On the back of each of the physician's hands there was a dark red, almost bloody area that was fairly well defined and about the size of a 2 mark piece (of that period in Germany) . . . The stigmata appeared and disappeared—on both hands—five times in all. In November 1934 Dr. Mutke wrote a report of his experience to the Bishop of Regensburg, but the case never became publicly known, and we lack further details."

Gemma Galgani (1878–1903) provides another well documented case of stigmata (Thurston 1952, pp. 52–54). Her stigmata appeared each Thursday evening and continued until Friday afternoon. Her biographer, Father Germano di St. Stanislao, described the appearance of the stigmata: "Red marks showed themselves on the backs and palms of both hands; and under the epidermis a rent in the flesh was seen to open by degrees; this was oblong on the backs of the hands and irregularly round in the palms. After a little the membrane burst and on those innocent hands were seen marks of flesh wounds. The diameter of these in the palms was about half an inch, and on the backs of the hands the wound was about five-eighths of an inch long by one-eighth wide." Father Germano said the wounds "seemed to pass through the hand—the openings on both sides reaching each other." Within the wound in each hand, he said, one could on some rare occasions see tissue that was "hard and like the head of a nail raised and detached and about an inch in diameter" (Thurston 1952, p. 53).

Not long after each appearance, the stigmata disappeared, leaving hardly a trace. Father Germano said, "As soon as the ecstasy of the Friday was over, the flow of blood from all the five wounds ceased immediately; the raw flesh healed; the lacerated tissues healed too, and the following day, or at latest on the Sunday, not a vestige remained of those deep cavities, neither at their centres, nor around their edges; the skin having grown quite uniformly with that of the uninjured part. In colour, however, there remained whitish marks" (Thurston 1952, p. 54).

Maternal Effects

Some medical professionals and other scientists have long believed that a strong mental impression in a pregnant woman can influence the developing body of the child within her womb. For example, if a woman sees someone with an injured foot and then constantly remembers this, her child might be born with a malformed foot. Such incidents are called "maternal impressions." The view was common among the Greeks and Romans, and among European physicians until the nineteenth century (Stevenson 1992, p. 353–356). In 1890, W. C. Dabney reviewed in a medical encyclopedia 69 reports published between 1853 and 1886 documenting a close correspondence between the mother's mental impression and the physical deformation in her child. Stevenson (1992, p. 356), describing Dabney's conclusions, stated, "He found that defects related to errors of embryological development [such as a deformed or missing limb] tended to be associated with maternal impressions received early in pregnancy; in contrast, birthmarks and other abnormalities of the skin and hair tended to be associated with maternal impressions occurring later in pregnancy" (my interpolation). By the end of the nineteenth century, however, many physicians had given up belief in the phenomenon of maternal impressions. Dabney (1890, p. 191) offered the explanation that "thinking men came to doubt the truth of those things which they could not understand." Such doubts became all-pervasive in the twentieth century. By this time medical science had become exclusively materialistic in its assumptions about the nature of the human organism. Stevenson (1992, p. 356) suggested that the failure of Western medical professionals to find any materialistic explanation for maternal impressions "eventually led to denial that there were any phenomena to be explained." Nevertheless, in many parts of the world, the phenomenon of maternal impressions on children is still accepted even today.

Stevenson (1997) reviewed 50 cases of maternal impressions. For example, Sylvia Hirst Ewing believed she was a reincarnation of a deceased woman named Julia Ford. Ford had a small hole in her skin near the middle of her right eye. Sylvia Ewing had a similar cavity. It would sometimes exude pus, or mucus, or a tearlike liquid. When she became pregnant, Sylvia Ewing constantly worried that her child would be born with a similar disfiguring hole. The child, Calvin Ewing, was born on January 28, 1969, with a hole at exactly the same place as his mother (Stevenson 1992, p. 364).

In some cases, the maternal impressions occur in dreams (Stevenson 1992, p. 364). Brydon (1886) reported a case in which a woman four months pregnant dreamed that a rat had chewed off the big toe of her right foot. When her child was born, it was missing the big toe of its right foot. Hammond (1868) reported a case in which a pregnant woman dreamed about a man who had lost part of his ear. Her child was born with a defective ear, matching the one the woman saw in her dream. Hammond (1868, p. 19) stated: "I have examined this child, and the ear looks exactly as if the portion had been cut off with a sharp knife."

Karl Ernst von Baer (1792–1876) was the founder of modern embryology. He told how his sister, while away from her home, saw a fire in the distance and strongly feared it was her own house burning. At the time, she was six or seven months pregnant. When her daughter was born, she had a red mark on her forehead. The red mark was pointed at the tip, like a flame (Stevenson 1997, pp. 105–106).

The Druse are an Islamic sect, living mostly in Israel, Syria, and Lebanon. Tamimi Mishlib was an Israeli Druse woman. The Druse have a belief that a pregnant woman can produce a birthmark on a child within the womb under the following conditions: (1) she develops a desire to eat a certain food, (2) she does not eat that food, (3) while resisting the desire to eat the food she presses her finger on a part of her body. The result should be that the child is born with a birthmark at the same place on its body. For this psychosomatic operation to work, it should be carried out during the period when the child within the womb is particularly sensitive to this effect, i.e., the first three months of pregnancy. Tamimi Mishlib decided to test this folk belief. One day she felt a strong desire to eat some honey. She did not eat the honey, but simply looked at it. While looking at the honey, she pressed her right forearm with the thumb of her left hand. Her son, Hamad Mishlib, was born with a birthmark on his right forearm, corresponding to the place she pressed her own forearm (Stevenson 1997, pp. 150–151).

Reincarnation Effects on Biological Form

As we saw in chapter 6, psychiatrist Ian Stevenson has documented cases of past life memories spontaneously reported by young children. Out of 895 cases of children who claimed to remember a previous life, unusual birthmarks and/or birth defects were reported in 309 of the subjects (Stevenson 1993, p. 405). These birthmarks or defects corresponded in appearance and location to wounds or other marks on the deceased person whose life the child remembered. The marks on the deceased person were verified by statements from living witnesses who knew the deceased person. In 49 cases, Stevenson was able to also use postmortem medical reports and death certificates to verify the wounds or marks on the prior personality. A correspondence between a birthmark on the living child and a wound on the deceased person was judged satisfactory if both the birthmark and wound occurred within an area of 10 square centimeters at the same anatomical location. Stevenson noted that out of the 49 cases where medical documentation was available, the marks corresponded in 43 (88 percent) of the cases (Stevenson 1993, p. 405). This strong correlation increased the confidence in the accuracy of informants' memories concerning wounds and other marks on deceased persons for the other cases. For 18 cases in which two birthmarks on a subject corresponded to gunshot wounds of entry and exit, in 14 cases the evidence clearly showed that the smaller birthmark corresponded to the wound of entry and the larger birthmark corresponded to the wound of exit. Exit wounds are nearly always larger than entry wounds. According to Stevenson (1997, pp. 1131–1137), the probability that the location of a single birthmark would correspond to a wound from a previous life is about 1 in 160. The probability that the locations of two birthmarks would correspond to the locations of two wounds is 1 in 25,600. Stevenson

(1997, p. 1135) cites cases in which the birthmarks and wounds occur within 5 centimeters of each other. In the case of single birthmark/wound correlations, the probability for such occurrences is 1 in 645, and the probability of double birthmark/wound correlations is 1 in 416,025.

Let us now consider some examples of unusual birthmarks related to wounds suffered in a past life. Henry Demmert III was born with a mark corresponding to a knife wound suffered by Henry Demmert, Jr. (Stevenson 1997, pp. 417–421). Henry Demmert, Jr., was born in Juneau, Alaska, on December 6, 1929. He was the son of Henry Demmert, Sr., and his wife Muriel. Because they were Tlingit Indians, Henry and Muriel also gave their son the Tlingit name Shtani. Muriel Demmert died soon thereafter, and in 1932 Henry Demmert, Sr., married his second wife, Gertrude. When Henry Demmert, Jr., grew up, he worked as a fisherman in Juneau. On March 6, 1957, he went to a party where he and others drank a lot of alcohol. A fight broke out around 5:30 the next morning, and Henry Demmert, Jr., was stabbed in the heart. He died at the Juneau hospital at 6:45 A.M. The death certificate said the attacker's knife cut and wounded the left lung and heart.

Henry Demmert, Sr., and his second wife, Gertrude, had a daughter Carole. She married Cyrus Robinson, and they had a child, Henry Robinson. Shortly before Henry was born Gertrude Demmert had a dream about him. The child was searching for Henry Demmert, Sr., and Gertrude. Henry Robinson was born on October 5, 1968. When Henry Demmert, Sr., and Gertrude saw their newly born grandson, they both noticed a birthmark at the same place as the stab wound that had killed Henry Demmert, Jr. Shortly after Henry was born, his parents separated. Henry Demmert, Sr., and Gertrude adopted him. They gave him the name Henry Demmert III, believing him to be a reincarnation of their son Henry Demmert, Jr. They also gave him the same Tlingit name (Shtani) they had given Henry Demmert, Jr. When Henry Demmert III was about two years old, he made some statements to his grandfather about his wound. Stevenson (1997, p. 420) reported, "Pointing to his birthmark he said that he had 'got hurt there.' He added that this had happened when he 'was big.'"

In 1978, Ian Stevenson examined Henry Demmert III and photographed the birthmark. Stevenson (1997, p. 420) said: "The birthmark was inferior and slightly lateral to the left nipple. It was located at approximately the level of sixth rib. It was ... approximately 3 centimeters long and 8 millimeters wide. The medial end of the birthmark was slightly more pointed than the lateral end. The birthmark was not elevated. It may have been fractionally depressed below the surrounding skin." Stevenson (1997, p. 420) added: "A knife-entering the chest at the site of the birthmark, or near it, would penetrate the heart if directed medially and upward. No other member of the family had a birthmark in this location." The birthmark had an approximately triangular shape. Stevenson (1997, p. 421) commented: "The suggestion of triangularity in the birthmark may provide an indication that the weapon stabbing Henry Demmert, Jr., had a single cutting edge, like a clasp knife or a kitchen knife, instead of having two cutting edges like a dagger."

Ekouroume Uchendu was a member of the Igbo tribe in Nigeria. He was, as Stevenson (1997, p. 1652) puts it, "a practitioner of indigenous medicine." He had a sister named Wankwo. When Wankwo was grown up and married, she and a man named Kafor quarreled. Kafor threatened to kill Wankwo. Upon being threatened in this way, Wankwo went to her brother Ekouroume Uchendu for help. He killed Kafor by sorcery. Wankwo later died.

Ekouroume Uchendu had several wives. In 1946, a daughter, Nwanyi, was born to Onyenyerego, one of his senior wives. From an oracle, Ekouroume Uchendu learned that Nwanyi was a reincarnation of his sister Wankwo. Nwanyi died when she was just one year old. Believing that Nwanyi's departure from this world was deliberate, Stevenson (1997, p. 1633) stated: "He thought that the least she—the reincarnation of his sister Wankwo—could have done, given the trouble he had taken to kill Kafor, was to stay in the family for longer than a year. In what can only be regarded as a fit of rage, he cut off some of the dead Nwanyi's fingers and toes. In addition, he tied her legs together with some cord, symbolically preventing her from ever walking again. To block the Wankwo/Nwanyi personality from ever returning, he put some of the amputated fingers and toes, along with some 'medicines,' in a little bag and hung this up in his house. This ritual was intended to banish Wankwo/Nwanyi permanently and prevent her from ever being reborn in Ekouroume Uchendu's family."

After this, Ekouroume Uchendu took yet another wife, named Irodirionyerku, who knew nothing about Nwanyi and the ritual mutilation carried out after her death (to stop her from coming back into Ekouroume Uchendu's family). Over the course of eleven years, Irodirionyerku had three children. Then one day, while doing some remodeling of the house, she took down the bag that contained the toes and fingers of Nwanyi, without knowing what it was. Stevenson (1997, pp. 1635–1636) said she was pregnant at the time this happened. When Irodirionyerku's child Cordelia was born in 1958, in the village of Umuokue, Imo State, Nigeria, she had birth defects. Stevenson (1997, p. 1636) described them:

"Several fingers on each hand were markedly shortened, and some had no nails. . . . There was a deep constriction of the left lower leg above the ankle. (This was said to correspond to the groove made by the cord with which Ekouroume Uchendu had tied Nwanyi's legs.) The right leg had a similar, but much less prominent mark at about the same level . . . All the toes (except the right great toe) were shortened, none had nails . . . Ekouroume Uchendu said that he had amputated some but not all of Nwanyi's fingers and that the birth defects of Cordelia's fingers 'corresponded exactly' to the mutilations he had made on Nwanyi's body."

Irodirionyerku's pregnancy was normal, except that Cordelia remained within the womb slightly longer than normal and the labor was also longer than normal. Irodirionyerku was in good health, and did not take alcohol or drugs. Her previous three children were normal, and a subsequent child was also normal. But she and her husband said that no members of their families had birth defects (Stevenson 1997, p. 1638). Several tribes in West Africa mark the bodies of dead infants by mutilation so that they might recognize the person if the person reincarnates into the same family as a "repeater child" (Stevenson 1997, p. 1626).

Sunita Khandelwal was born on September 19, 1969, in the small town of Laxmangarh, near the city of Alwar, in the eastern part of the province of Rajasthan in India. She was the sixth child of Radhey Shyam Khandelwal, a grain dealer, and his wife, Santara Bai. At birth, Sunita had on the right side of her head a large birthmark.

When she was two years old, Sunita began to speak of a previous life. The first thing she said was, "Take me to Kota." Kota is a city in the southeast part of Rajasthan, about 360 kilometers from Laxmangarh. When Sunita's family inquired about what was in Kota, she said, "I had two brothers. I was the only daughter. I have a mummy and pappa. We have a silver shop and a safe. We have a car and a scooter. My mother has many saris." In some of her statements she was less clear about the nature of the shop, simply stating there were silver coins in the shop. She also revealed that she had a paternal uncle older than her father. Pointing to the birthmark on her head, she said, "Look here, I have fallen" (Stevenson 1997, p. 468).

When she was three years old, Sunita asked to be taken to Kota, refusing to eat until her wish was carried out. Her parents thought to take her to the nearby city of Jaipur, telling her it was Kota. But Sunita said, "This is not Kota. This is Jaipur. You are telling lies and will be punished" (Stevenson 1997, p. 468).

Thereafter, Sunita gave further revelations about her life in Kota. She said her father was of the Bania, or merchant, caste, and that his shop was in the Chauth Mata Bazaar. The family house was in the Brijraj-pura quarter. Revealing more of the circumstances of her death, she said, "I was a girl and died at the age of eight," and, "My cousin pushed me down the stairs because I had asked for water" (Stevenson 1997, p. 469).

In 1974, H. N. Banerjee, a reincarnation researcher in Jaipur, learned of Sunita's case through a friend of the Khandelwal family. Although initially reluctant, the Khandelwals agreed to let Banerjee take them and their daughter to Kota. Their first stop in Kota was the shop of a photographer, Pratap Singh Chordia, who knew many of the residents. From the information supplied to him, Chordia suggested Sunita's father in her previous life may have been Prabhu Dayal Maheshwari. Sunita had once mentioned the name "Prabhu" in connection with her father. Also, Prabhu Dayal's shop was a jewelry shop (with silver jewelry), and the shop was in the Chauth Mata Bazaar. Chordia did not know, however, that Prabhu Dayal had a daughter who died from a fall.

Taking Chordia's advice, the party went to the Chauth Mata Bazaar to search for Prabhu Dayal's shop. Stevenson (1997, p. 470) says, "Sunita, according to her mother, recognized a shop with a man in it who was writing. Sunita said that he was her father. This man was Prabhu Dayal Maheswari, and he was sitting in his own jewelry shop. The matter was explained to him. . . . Prabhu Dayal then invited Sunita to come to his home. Sunita led the way and found Prabhu Dayal's house. She then made a number of other recognitions and some further statements about the life she was remembering. Prabhu Dayal and his wife had lost their only daughter in April 1968. This child, Shakuntala, had fallen over the low railing of a balcony and landed head first on a cement floor below. She died a few hours later. With a few exceptions everything Sunita had said in Laxmangarh was correct for the life and death of Shakuntala in Kota." Stevenson (1997, p. 487) listed some of the correct items: "She was the only daughter; she died at the age of 8; her parents were both living; a paternal grandmother had died, but a paternal grandfather was living; she had no uncle younger than her father, but one older than he; she had two brothers and a girl cousin." Stevenson also detailed other statements and behaviors of Sunita, of a more personal nature, such as food preferences and nicknames for relatives, that matched those of Shakuntala.

The members of the families of Sunita and Shakuntala had never met, with one exception. Sunita's maternal uncle, a jeweler who lived in Delhi, had occasionally met Prabhu Dayal in Kota, but their meetings were strictly commercial, not social. He had never visited Prabhu Dayal's home, and knew nothing about the death of Prabhu Dayal's daughter

(Stevenson 1997, pp. 473–474). So it was unlikely that Sunita could have learned of details of Shakuntala's life and death from her own family members.

Stevenson visited Kota and verified the following details about the death of Shakuntala. On April 27, 1968, during the late afternoon, Shakuntala was on the balcony of the inner courtyard of her house, playing with her younger cousin. The balcony had a low railing. Her mother, Krishna Devi, heard her fall down from the balcony to the concrete floor, a distance of about five meters. Krishna Devi found her daughter unconscious and bleeding from one ear. She called her husband, who quickly returned home from his shop. Stevenson (1997, p. 474) stated, "Prabhu Dayal said that when he had come home he had noticed that Shakuntala had injured the top of her head and that there was some slight bleeding from a wound there." He then took his daughter to the M. B .S. Hospital in Kota. The medical records show that Shakuntala was admitted and that she died nine hours later from "head injury" (Stevenson 1997, p. 475).

When Sunita was born she had a large birthmark on the top of her head. It bled for three days. Stevenson (1997, p. 487) described the birthmark as it appeared when photographed in 1979: "The mark was approximately round in shape with irregular edges and about 2.5 centimeters in diameter. It was . . . hairless . . . slightly raised and slightly puckered." A relative said no other member of the family had a birthmark like this.

Recollecting what happened during the time between her fatal accident and her rebirth, Sunita said, "I went up. There was a baba (holy man) with a long beard. They checked my record and said: 'Send her back.' There are some rooms there. I have seen God's house. It is very nice. You do not know everything that is there" (Stevenson 1997, p. 484).

Here are some brief accounts of other cases documented by Stevenson. A woman in Thailand was born with three linear scars in the middle of her back. When she was a child, this woman remembered a previous life as a woman who was killed by three strokes of an axe on her back (Stevenson 1993, p. 410). A Burmese woman was born with two round birthmarks on her chest. The marks overlapped, and one was larger than the other. When she was a child, she recalled dying in a previous life after being shot accidentally with a shotgun. According to a witness who knew the dead woman, the shotgun that killed her had been loaded with two kinds of shot (Stevenson, 1993, pp. 410–411). A female Burmese child was born with a long, vertical birthmark near the middle of her lower chest and upper abdomen. She recalled having previously existed as one of her aunts. This aunt had died during heart surgery. Stevenson (1993,

p. 411) obtained the aunt's medical records and found that the incision for theheart surgery matched the birthmark. "Two Burmese subjects," said Stevenson (1993, p. 411), "remembered as children the lives of persons who had died after being bitten by venomous snakes, and the birthmark of each corresponded to therapeutic incisions made at the sites of the snakebites on the persons whose lives they remembered." A Turkish boy was born with a malformed right ear, and the right side of his face was underdeveloped. The boy remembered a previous life as a man who died after someone shot him in the head with a shotgun. Stevenson (1993, p. 411), having verified the existence of this man, examined his medical records and found that he died in the hospital six days after a shotgun wound to the right side of the skull.

An Indian child was born with small stubs instead of fingers on one hand. The child remembered existing in a previous life as a child who put his hand in a farm machine and lost his fingers. Stevenson noted that in most medical cases of brachydactyly (shortened fingers) the bones are still present in the fingers. Usually, only the middle finger bone is shortened. But in this case, there were no finger bones present at all. Also, cases where the fingers of only one hand are affected are rare. Stevenson (1993, p. 411) said he could not find a single published case in the medical literature. A Burmese girl was born with the lower part of her right leg missing. Stevenson (1993, pp. 411–412) reported, "She said that she remembered the life of a girl who was run over by a train. Eyewitnesses said that the train severed the girl's right leg first, before running over the trunk."

Some might suppose that children, aware of their birthmarks, may have invented imaginary past lives with histories that corresponded with the birthmarks. But we should remember that in many cases Stevenson has verified not only the existence of the past life person but has, through examination of the deceased person's medical records, also verified the wound or incision matching the living subject's birthmark.

Stevenson (1997, pp. 2099–2100) offered this explanation of this kind of evidence: "I believe that the cases I have described in this work strongly suggest . . . an influence by a deceased person on the embryo of a person who will be born later and (in most cases) come to have memories of the events in the life of that deceased person. . . . they further suggest an interaction between mind and body during life and the survival of mind after death. They also suggest that the form of a deceased person concerned in such a case can influence the form of the succeeding person who will remember the first person's life. And finally, they suggest that memories of the first person's life exist on some intermediate vehicle between death and presumed rebirth." Putting it a little more directly, Stevenson (1997, p. 2102) concluded that "sometimes mental images in the mind of a deceased person who has survived death can influence the form of an embryo or fetus so as to cause birthmarks and birth defects."

Paranormal Healings by Humans Acting as Mediums for Spirits

João Texeira da Faria, later known as João de Deus (John of God), is a Brazilian psychic healer of international fame. Hereafter, I will call him John of God. I have relied on Pelligrino-Estrich (1997) for the accounts of his activities found in this section. John of God was born in 1942 in a small town in the state of Goias, Brazil. His family was very poor, and he had little formal education. When he was sixteen years old and wandering jobless, he stopped to bathe in a creek near Campo Grande. He then heard a woman's voice calling him. He saw in the shade of some trees a beautiful woman with fair hair. He spoke with her for some time. That night, he concluded it must have been Saint Rita of Cascia (1386–1456), the "saint of the impossible," a patron of the dispossessed and desperate. He returned to the creek the next day, but instead of the woman, he saw a beam of light. When he turned away, he heard the woman's voice say, "João. You must go to the Redemptor Spiritual Center in Campo Grande. They are waiting for you there." Simultaneously, the beam of light disappeared. John went to the center, where a man greeted him, saying he was expected. John lost consciousness, and woke three hours later to find people congratulating him. He was informed that he had been possessed by "the entity of King Solomon" and had healed many persons. John remained at the center for three months as a healer and decided this was his life's mission. He traveled from place to place, moving when physicians, dentists, or priests would have the local police charge him with criminal offences, such as medical malpractice. Finally, he set up his permanent clinic in its present location at Abadiania, Brazil, in 1978. In 1981, he was brought into court for practicing medicine illegally, but a jury acquitted him (Pelligrino-Estrich 1997, pp. 32–39). In 1987, John of God himself suffered a stroke, which partially paralyzed half his body. Eventually, he successfully cured himself (Pelligrino-Estrich 1997, pp. 26–27).

John of God's clinic is in the village of Abadiania in the Goias Plateau. Thousands of people from around the world have come there for healings. The clinic is a small white building. Inside, early in the morning of a typical day, John rests in a small room, decorated with pictures of Christ, the Madonna, and Dom Inacio, the principal entity who works through John to give cures. In fact, the clinic is called Casa de Dom Inacio, the House of Dom Inacio. The cures start each day at eight o'clock in the morning and continue into the night. John of God has received honorary degrees and awards from many famous persons, governments, and institutions. For example, the President of Peru gave him that country's Medal of Honor for curing his son (Pelligrino-Estrich 1997, pp.15–16).

There are several rooms in the clinic. There is a small room where John of God begins his day by calling upon one of thirty-three spirit entities to enter him. Pelligrino-Estrich (1997, p. 42) says, "The entities are spirits of deceased doctors, surgeons, healers, psychologists and theologians who are of such high soul elevation they need no longer reincarnate to our physical plane. They do, however, continue to elevate in the spirit plane by the extent of their benevolence and charitable works." Over all the entities are Jesus Christ, the Virgin Mary, and Dom Inacio (St. Ignatius of Loyola, the founder of the Jesuit order). After the entity enters him and takes over his body, John of God begins his work. Although he can incorporate only one entity, he can change entities at will. Also, entities can work on patients without entering into John of God's body (Pelligrino-Estrich 1997, p. 44).

People coming before him first pass through two rooms, called "current rooms," where mediums sit on both sides, for the purpose of generating spiritual energy, or current. In the first current room are twenty or thirty mediums in meditation; in the second, or main, current room are fifty mediums. As the patients walk through the two rows of mediums in the second current room, they come before John of God, who is sitting on a seat covered with white cloth. As the patient comes before John of God, the entity within him assesses the patient's past lives, medical condition, spiritual consciousness, and present circumstances. Depending on the nature of the case, the entity prescribes various treatments, including herbal remedies, invisible operations, or visible operations. Herbal remedies are provided by the clinic's pharmacy. Those requiring invisible operations go to a treatment room. The most severe cases lie down in beds and enter into a coma while entities operate invisibly upon them. Others sit upon their beds, guided in prayer and meditation by twelve special healing mediums, while they also undergo invisible operations by the entities. Twice a day, John of God enters this room and says, "In the name of Jesus Christ you are all cured. Let what needs to be done be done in the name of God" (Pelligrino-Estrich 1997, p. 19). At this time, the invisible operations are completed internally. Pelligrino-Estrich (1997, p.19) says, "Scientific teams have found by X-rays, following these invisible operations, that there are incisions and stitches internally."

In a large hall, John of God carries out the visible operations. Patients first go to the main current room, where they remain for a half hour in meditation. John of God then leads some of them into the main hall, where they undergo visible surgery. John of God, possessed by the spirits of entities with different medical specialties, then carries out the operations with surgical instruments like scalpels (Pelligrino-Estrich 1997, pp. 20–22). Pelligrino-Estrich (1997, pp. 42–43) says about John of God, "His fingers work with skilled precision, even when his head is turned or his attention is diverted elsewhere. Many of the surgical routines cannot be done by highly skilled surgeons." John of God says, "It is not me who cures. God is the healer—I am simply the vessel" (Pelligrino-Estrich 1997, p. 44). Patients undergoing these operations, under the influence of a kind of spiritual anesthesia, feel no pain (Pelligrino-Estrich 1997, p. 45). John of God also possesses a mystical antiseptic power. Pelligrino-Estrich (1997, p. 45) says, "There has never been a known case of infection in the house even after hundreds of thousands of physical operations over the past thirty years." Another strange feature of the operations, which sometimes involve large incisions, is the small amount of blood that flows out (Pelligrino-Estrich 1997, p. 46).

The cures are not simply the result of surgical procedures, visible or invisible. Their success may also depend on removing the negative influence of harmful entities that may have attached themselves to the patients (Pelligrino-Estrich 1997, p. 90). Another factor to be considered is the patient's record of karmic debt. Pelligrino-Estrich (1997, p. 96) says, "The record is imprinted in the superconscious mind and carried in the soul which brings with it the debt and the disease or malady it chooses to endure when it is reincarnated. The affliction may be immediately apparent, as in the case of birth defects or deformity, or they may develop at any time in the life cycle. Karmic illness brought from a previous life cannot be cured except by way of repayment of the debt. . . . It can be paid by unselfish service to mankind or by personal suffering in the manner in which the debt was incurred. The ultimate aim is awareness, learning and cleansing of the soul." All of the operations are videotaped, and the tapes can be seen and studied at the clinic or purchased and taken away. At the end of the day, John of God has a special session with all of his assisting mediums, and then he allows the possessing entity to leave his body.

The healings of John of God have been subjected to many scientific studies. For example, a group of physicians and scientists from the faculty of clinical biophysics at the Dr. Bezerro de Menezes University in Brazil, led by Dr. A. Arlete Savaris, observed and tested John of God for two years. The results, favorable to the authenticity of the cures, were published in the book *Curas Paranormais Realizadas por João da Faria*, available from the university, but only in Portuguese (Pelligrino-Estrich 1997, p. 100). In 1984, Dr. Klaus Schubert of Germany carried out a series of investigations with a group of scientists. The conclusions of the group were positive. One outcome of this research effort was a documentary film titled *Medium João de Deus* (Pelligrino-Estrich 1997, p. 111).

Another set of tests was carried out by Alexander Moreira de Almeida, Tatiana Moreira de Almeida, and Angela Maria Gollner, all of the faculty of medicine of the Federal University de Juis de Fora, in the state of Minais Gerais, Brazil. The authors, who chose to focus on the visible surgeries, stated: "We filmed and photographed a series of operations, the patients were interviewed and examined and all of the organic substances were collected and removed for pathological testing at the university. None of the patients received any form of anaesthetic and only one of them said he felt a mild form of pain during the operation. . . . No form of antiseptic was observed. . . . Our conclusions firmly uphold that the surgery is genuine. The pathological tests reveal that the removed substances are compatible with their origins and that they are human tissues" (Pelligrino-Estrich 1997, pp. 103–105).

The relationship between the visible surgical intervention and the actual healing event is sometimes quite mysterious. One of John of God's techniques is to insert scissorlike surgical clamps into the nose of a patient. He then twists the clamps. Strangely enough, this technique is used to accomplish cures in all parts of the body. Pelligrino-Estrich (1997, p. 110) says, "In one observed case this technique was used to rejoin six compound fractures in a man's feet. The man came into the center on knee pads and walked out on his reassembled feet! He went back to work within a week."

Of course, the invisible operations are of more interest to us, as they are a better demonstration of modification of biological form by paranormal methods. Dr. Klaun of the Minas Gerais state, a recent graduate of medical school, became ill with a brain tumor. He went to America for treatment. He was told that an operation was possible, but he would have only a fifty percent chance of living. And if he lived, it would be most likely for a short time, and he would be a paralyzed below the waist. Dr. Klaun's father was a physician and an official for the Brazilian government's ministry of health. As such he was familiar with John of God, having received complaints from doctors accusing him of medical malpractice as well as testimonials from satisfied patients. Dr. Klaun's family thus decided to try a spiritual operation at John of God's clinic at

Abadiania. In November 1994, Klaun came to Abadiania with his father and two doctors. These two doctors had participated in the original diagnosis of his brain tumor (Pelligrino-Estrich 1997, p. 107).

Pelligrino-Estrich (1997, pp. 108–109) stated: "He [Klaun] was placed in the intensive operations room and went into a coma for three days, during which he was operated on by spirit. For three days and nights his body all but shut down physical functions—no food, no elimination and no movement. When he finally awoke on the third day he was advised to have another X-ray. The enormous tumour had completely disappeared. The before and after X-rays and the critical observations of such qualified medical practitioners constituted a medically observed phenomenon. All were prepared to participate in a statement which verified the pre-operation and post-operation conditions. On 15 November, 1994, a testimonial video was produced before hundreds of people in which each doctor and the patient testified to their observations and the successful result. Firstly the radiologist showed the pre-operative X-rays and made his statement. In his opinion there was no chance of survival by normal surgery. . . . Dr. Maureso de Veta of the Brazilian Ministry of Health . . . gave his professional opinion of the inoperability of the tumour and declared that the tumour was indeed gone, without any sign of surgical entry to the skull." Klaun himself said his doctors "were stunned that the X-rays showed no sign of any surgical cut to across the tumour and that I was in such remarkably good health" (Pelligrino-Estrich 1997, p. 109).

Dr. Ronei Pappen is a Brazilian medical doctor. His offices are at Rua Santo Antonio 653 in Porto Alegre. On August 22, 1995, Dr. Pappen was in an automobile accident. His skull was crushed, injuring his eyes and optic nerves. As a result, he became totally blind. He also suffered extensive internal injuries. His colleagues told him he would never see again. Aware of John of God's work, Dr. Pappen went to Abadiania, on October 12, 1995. He there underwent invisible operations, and after some time fully regained his sight. Since then, he has worked as an assistant to John of God, in addition to continuing his own medical practice (Pelligrino-Estrich 1997, p. 55).

On October 26, 1996, Deanna Rovacchi of Florence, Italy, gave this signed testimonial of her treatment: "I had been fighting cancer for eight years. I had one mastectomy (removal of the right breast) and for the past eight years I have been under the care of one of the most reputed cancer clinics in Europe, the Steiner Clinic in Bern, Switzerland. With careful diet, drugs and injections I was able to slow down the spread of the disease but ultimately, by early 1995, the best I could expect was another twelve months of life . . . I had two tumours on my neck, a larger one in my abdomen and small nodules on my left breast. . . . In the first week in July 1996 I flew to Brazil with . . . my best friend Mara who had a similar condition to mine. We were operated invisibly by João Teixeira da Faria, given herbs and returned to Italy. . . . On 11 October 1996 Mara and I went for our regular check-up at the Steiner Clinic. The doctors were amazed. Mara was declared totally clear of tumours and all of my tumours had disappeared except for one on my neck which was shrinking rapidly. The doctors said they had never seen anything like it in all their years at the clinic. Not only were the tumours gone but the disease was in full remission" (Pellegrino-Estrich 1997, pp. 136–137).

Surprisingly, some of John of God's enemies have become his satisfied patients. For example, on July 3, 1996, John of God spotted among the patients waiting in line to see him police commissioner Firto Franki, one of the prosecutors who filed cases against him. John of God, under the control of one of his entities, said, "You have pursued me for more than ten years. You have made my life hell and now you come to me for help?! Let me show you, once and for all, the extent of my work" (Pelligrino-Estrich 1997, p. 40). John of God had six of his patients testify to their cures. Then John of God said, "You came to me ten years ago under the pretences of being ill and then testified against me as a fraud based on your own lies. You knew my work was authentic because you sent your friends to me for treatment, but still you continued to persecute me. Do you publicly acknowledge here before these witnesses that my work is genuine?" (Pelligrino-Estrich 1997, p. 41) Franki agreed to give a statement that John of God's cures were genuine.

Healings by Supernatural Beings at Lourdes

Lourdes is a town in southern France, at the base of the Pyrenees Mountains. It is the site of one of the most famous Marian apparitions and has become synonymous with miraculous healings. The Lourdes healings are not mediated by a human intercessor, such as John of God. At Lourdes, the influence of the entity apparently acts directly on the subjects. The entity, whether or not correctly identified as the Virgin Mary, appears to occupy a higher place in the cosmic hierarchy than an ordinary departed human.

On February 11, 1858, three girls from Lourdes (Bernadette Sourbirous, her sister, and a friend) went out to search for firewood. While the other two girls crossed a stream called the Gave, Bernadette, afraid of catching a cold, remained behind, watching. While her friends were gone, she saw a golden cloud emerge from a rocky hillside grotto on the other side of the stream. In the middle of the golden cloud she saw a beautiful young lady dressed in white. Bernadette knelt in prayer. When the other two girls returned, they saw Bernadette kneeling, but could not see the entity. Bernadette told the girls what she had seen and asked them not to tell anyone, but they did. At first, no one in Lourdes took the story seriously. Bernadette felt compelled to return to the grotto and did so on February 14, accompanied by some townspeople. Bernadette saw the entity, but the townspeople did not. The same thing happened on February 18. During these visitations, the people who came along could see Bernadette enter into a trancelike state, as she replied to the words of the invisible entity only she could see and hear. With each visitation the crowds grew larger (Rogo 1982, pp. 284–285).

On February 25, Bernadette, as usual, knelt on the ground and went into her trance. At one point, she stood up. She walked a short distance and then fell to the ground. She began digging, and some water began to fill the hole. Later she explained, "Whilst I was in prayer, the Lady said to me in a friendly but serious voice, 'Go, drink and wash in the fountain.' As I did not know where this fountain was, and as I did not think the matter important, I went towards aside the Gave. The Lady called me back and signed to me with her finger to go under the grotto to the left; I obeyed but I did not see any water. Not knowing where to get it from, I scratched the earth and the water came. I let it get a little clear of the mud, then I drank and washed" (Estrade 1958, p. 94). Over the next few days, the water continued to flow out, forming a pool. The miraculous appearance of the spring increased the faith of the people who gathered there.

Another paranormal occurrence was recorded by Dr. Pierre Romain Dozous, who was present at the grotto during one of Bernadette's trances. He stated: "Her rosary was in her left hand, and in her right she held a blessed candle which was alight. . . . She suddenly stopped, and placed the lighted candle under . . . her left hand. The fingers were sufficiently apart to allow the flame to pass through . . . but I could not see any sign of burning on the skin. . . . taking my watch, I observed her in this position for a quarter of an hour. . . . Bernadette rose, and was about to leave the Grotto. I retained her a moment, and asked her to show me her left hand, which I examined most carefully. There was not the slightest trace of a burn" (Bertrin 1908, pp. 49–50).

Others witnessed similar episodes involving Bernadette and candle flames. The significant fact is that Bernadette's flesh was not burned. Bertrin (1908, pp. 50–51) stated, "A nervous state may cause insensibility, but it could not prevent fire from consuming the flesh with which it comes into contact.... where is the delusionary who can put his hand over a strong flame and keep it there for fifteen minutes without being burnt?"

Residents of Lourdes began taking water home from the spring in the grotto, and they claimed that it cured a variety of illnesses. Today there is a church at the site, and the spring water has been channeled into bathing pools. Pilgrims seeking cures are monitored and regulated, and since 1884 cures have been carefully documented by physicians of the Bureau des Constatations Médicales, the BCM. The membership of the BCM is not restricted to Catholics. The BCM has an office directly at Lourdes and also has an advisory committee in Paris that reviews cases of special interest (Rogo 1982, pp. 285–286).

Rogo (1982, pp. 286–287) describes the procedures the BCM employs for documenting cases: "When a Lourdes pilgrim believes that he has been cured, he is taken immediately to the BCM's offices where he is examined by a physician, who also takes possession of all pertinent medical data and documents the patient may have brought with him. This initial evaluation at the BCM is intended to determine whether the patient was actually sick or injured at the time of his journey, was actually cured at the shrine, and was cured in a medically inexplicable way. If the healing seems to meet these three tests, a doctor registered with the bureau in the patient's hometown or district is contacted. The patient is sent home, and the doctor there is given the responsibility of observing him for one year. This procedure serves as a precaution against the occurrence of a relapse that might not otherwise come to the attention of Lourdes officials. The doctor is also expected to interview the patient's own physician and collect any medical records from him that may bear on the case. The patient is then asked to return to Lourdes after the year has expired, at which time he is once again examined by the BCM. Only when all the doctors involved in this evaluation agree that the cure seems inexplicable is the case given candidate status as a miracle. In making its final evaluation, the BCM looks for several characteristics that they consider differentiate a miraculous healing from a biological one. They verify that the cure was instantaneous, that it led to the termination of the patient's convalescence, that it wasn't consistent with the normal process the condition in question undergoes while healing biologically, and that it occurred at a time when the patient was no longer receiving any conventional treatment. Also subject to this careful analysis are cases in which a damaged limb or organ—such as a permanently damaged eye—is miraculously restored to use."

In 1868, Pierre de Rudder, of Jabbeke, Belgium, broke his leg when he fell from a tree. Large pieces of broken bone had to be taken from the wound. The missing bone made it impossible to set the two pieces of the broken leg back together. The leg was held together only by muscle and skin. Doctors recommended amputation, but de Rudder would not consent. After eight years of tolerating this painful condition, he went to Oostacker, Belgium, home to a statue of Our Lady of Lourdes. Before he went, he saw Dr. van Hoestenberghe in Jabbeke. The doctor found an open wound at the place of the break, and he could see that the two pieces of broken bone were separated by a space of three centimeters. De Rudder made the trip to Oostacker in great pain, his wound oozing pus and blood. Three men had to carry him off the train. When he arrived at the shrine of Our Lady of Lourdes, by aid of crutches, he began to pray. In the midst of the prayer, he was overcome by a strange feeling. He stood up without his crutches and began to walk. The broken leg bone had healed (Rogo 1982, pp. 293–294).

When de Rudder returned to Jabbeke, Dr. van Hoestenberghe examined him and was astonished to see the transformation. The doctor then wrote to the medical bureau in Lourdes: "Pierre is undoubtedly cured. I have seen him many times during the last eight years, and my medical knowledge tells me that such a cure is absolutely inexplicable. Again, he has been cured completely, suddenly, and instantaneously, without any period of convalescence. Not only have the bones been suddenly united, but a portion of bone would seem to have been actually created to take the place of those fragments I myself have seen come out of the wound" (Rogo 1982, p. 294).

In 1898, de Rudder died, and in 1900 Dr. van Hoestenberghe got permission to exhume the corpse and conduct an autopsy. His studies were documented with photographs. Rogo (1982, p. 294) states: "These photos clearly show that the two parts of de Rudder's leg bone had been fused together by a new piece of healthy bone over an inch long that had formed, apparently instantaneously, over its broken ends. Such growth or regeneration of bone is medically unprecedented.... Today de Rudder's leg bones are preserved at the University of Louvain in Belgium."

Dr. Prosper Gustave Boissarie, a doctor with the Bureau of Medical Authentication (Bureau de Constatations Médicales, or BCM), tells of the case of Joachime Dehant. She had on her leg "a sore a foot long by six inches wide, reaching to the bone and attended by gangrene, and which had lasted twelve years" (Boissarie 1933, p. 3). The sore was the result of cholera and typhus. Dehant, who was 29 years of age, weighed only 60 pounds.

Dehant, who lived in Belgium, was sent to Lourdes at the request of the Countess of Limminghe. Dehant was so sure she would be cured, she wanted to buy a shoe and stocking for her injured leg. But Dehant stated, "There was no means of taking the measurement of my sore leg and foot. A large sore about a foot long from the ankle to the knee covered the leg, and the foot, which was all turned around, was thinner and smaller than the other. I had to be content with the measurement of the other foot" (Boissarie 1933, p. 3).

Joachime Dehant set out from Belgium on September 10. The journey by train was painful, not only for Dehant but for her traveling companions. Her sore was constantly oozing blood and pus, accompanied by a horrible smell. From time to time she changed her bandages, each time removing pieces of dead flesh. She reached Lourdes on September 13, and was taken to the bathing place. Before she went, she once more changed her bandages: "This task required more than an hour. I removed pieces of decayed bone and gangrenous flesh, which I left on the floor" (Boissarie 1933, p. 4). Her first bath did not result in a cure. The next morning, she again went to the bathing place and remained in the water for 27 minutes. When she came out, her companion, Léonie Dorval, removed the bandages and said: "Joachime, there is no longer any sore; you are cured!" Joachime replied, "Blessed be Our Lady of Lourdes! See how well she knows how to do things! She has not only put new skin on my leg, but she has made new flesh and a calf!" (Boissarie 1933, p. 5) Everyone who had seen Joachime Dehant before her cure was amazed. Dr. Boissarie stated (1933, p. 3) that she came out of the water "radically cured, with skin covering the wound."

The next day, Joachime bathed again, and another extraordinary transformation took place. Joachime had suffered not only from a large sore but from deformation of her hip, knee, and foot. Describing what happened the day after the cure of Dehant's sore, Bertrin (1908, pp. 105–106) stated: "Both she and her companion saw her deformed foot straighten itself until it was as straight as the hands on a clock. The leg stretched to its full length, the muscles uncontracted, and the knee resumed its normal shape. In the hip a movement was felt which caused unutterable pain. Joachime swooned, and Léonie thought she was dying. But after a time she regained consciousness and opened her eyes. All was over. The pain had completely gone, and her body which had been deformed so long had become straight and agile."

Upon returning to Belgium, Joachime Dehant was examined by Dr. Gustave Froidbise, who verified the cure. He also gave testimony that he saw the wound just before Dehant's departure from Belgium, thus defusing any thought that Dehant had been cured before going to Lourdes

(Boissarie 1933, p. 8). Here is the text of the statement he gave after examining Dehant just before her departure from Lourdes: "I, the undersigned, Gustave Froidbise, doctor of medicine, etc., at Ohey, in the province of Namur, Belgium, declare that I have examined Mlle. Joachime Dehant, aged twenty-nine, born at Wanfercée-Baulet, resident at Gesves, and I certify as follows: Dislocation of the hip-joint on the right side. Retraction of the lateral tibial muscles of the right leg which causes club-foot (talipes varus). An ulcer which covers two-thirds of the outer surface of the right leg. Hence my present declaration, Ohey, September 6, 1878. Dr. G. Froidbise" (Bertrin 1908, p. 106). To this document he added the results of his examination of Dehant on the day she returned from Lourdes: "I, the undersigned, doctor of medicine, etc. at Ohey, province of Namur in Belgium, declare that I have examined Mlle. Joachime Dehant, aged twenty-nine, born at Wanfercée-Baulet, and resident at Gesves, and I affirm that the lesions mentioned in the accompanying certificate have completely disappeared. A simple redness shows the place where the ulcer existed.—Dr. G. Froidbise. Gesves, Sep. 19th, 1878" (Bertrin 1908, p. 107). Dr. Henri Vergez, of the faculty of medicine at the University of Montpellier, stated: "The sudden cure of a sore, or rather of a spreading chronic ulcer, in a very decayed constitution, and the spontaneous reduction of dislocation of the hip, are facts quite outside natural explanation" (Bertrin 1908, p. 107).

Some extreme skeptics went so far as to suggest that Dehant had no wound at all. But the testimony of many credible witnesses eliminated this suggestion. Simon Deploige, professor of law at the Catholic University of Louvain, and a physician, Dr. Royer, conducted a careful investigation of the evidence for the wound. Dr. Boissarie (1933, pp. 8–9) reviewed their procedures: "Taking Dr. Froidebise's certificate of September 6th as a starting point, they followed the history of this ulcer, so to speak, from hour to hour, up to the time of its disappearance. They questioned…:1st. Joachime Dehant's neighbors who saw the ulcer immediately before the departure for Lourdes; 2nd. The fellow travelers on the journey; 3rd. The managers of the hotel where Joachime stopped at Lourdes. Not one of these witnesses questioned was related to the cured girl. . . . All the witnesses questioned were interviewed in their homes without preliminary notice and without having had any opportunity of collusion among them. All read over their depositions and certified their being a faithful and exact account."

Deploige and Royer stated in their conclusion: "Two facts seem duly established by this inquiry. 1st fact: The existence on Mlle. Joachime, at least up to September 12, 1878, at ten o'clock in the evening, if not up to the morning of the 13th, of an ulcer covering nearly the whole right leg from the knee to the ankle, exposing the raw flesh, which was broken out in pimples, inflamed and blackish in places; disgusting to the sight, suppurating profusely, giving out a foul odor and, according to medical testimony, incapable of being cured, naturally, in thirteen days, and making no progress towards improvement. 2nd fact: The entire disappearance of the same ulcer and its replacement by new, dry, healthy skin from September 13, 1878, in the forenoon or, at the very latest, towards nine or ten o'clock in the evening" (Boissarie 1933, p. 9). Church officials, after reviewing all the medical evidence, declared the cure miraculous.

Early in the history of Lourdes, there were suggestions that the cures may have been the result of medicinal properties of the water. A chemical analysis showed the water to have a mineral content similar to other waters in the region (Bertrin 1908, p. 116). Others proposed that the power of suggestion may have caused the cures. But even very young children, unable to comprehend such suggestion, have been cured of physical defects. Bertrin (1908, pp. 142–143) states, "George Lemesle, aged two years and seven months, was cured of infantile paralysis (1895); Fernand Balin, aged two years and six months, was cured of a crooked knee (1895); little Duconte, two years old, whom his doting mother carried to the Grotto in an almost dying condition (1858), was restored to health; Yvonne Aumaître, whom the doctor, her father, plunged into the miraculous water in spite of her cries, was taken out cured of a double club-foot (1896); at the age of nineteen months, A. Mertens was cured of paralysis in the right arm (1895); Pierre Estournet, an unweaned baby, had his eyes cured (1864); and lastly, Paul Mercère was cured of two congenital ruptures when a year old (1866). Of course there is no question of psychotherapeutics in such cures." Dr. Alexis Carrel, who won the Nobel Prize for medicine and physiology in 1912, was a vocal supporter of the Lourdes healings (Rogo 1982, p. 261).

In November 1882, Francois Vion-Dury, a soldier, suffered burns on his face as he rescued people trapped in a fire at a hotel café in Dijon, France. As a result of the burns, the retinas of his two eyes became detached, causing almost complete blindness. He was released from the army with a pension on July 11, 1884. In the course of a proceeding to get the amount of his pension increased, he was examined by Dr. Dor, of Lyon, France, who on September 16, 1884, stated: "Although the retina in the left eye has returned to place, this eye is still unable to distinguish night from day. With the right eye, M. Vion-Dury has difficulty in counting fingers held a foot away. He is thus incapable of doing any work and must be considered completely and incurably blind in both eyes" (Agnellet 1958,

p. 52). In 1890, Vion-Dury entered a hospital at Confort, France. Nuns at the hospital convinced him to pray for the intercession of Our Lady of Lourdes and gave him a bottle of Lourdes water. The next day, after his prayers, he put some of the water on his eyelids. "My sight came back in a flash," he later recalled. "I didn't believe it myself" (Agnellet 1958, p. 53). Dr. Dor, a Protestant, reported to a conference of eye specialists in Paris: "Vion-Dury was nearly blind. His visual acuity was one-fiftieth, about the same in each eye. . . . The detachment of the retinae was diagnosed by a large number of specialists and had resisted all treatment. Vion-Dury's condition was static for seven and a half years. Then, without any special treatment . . . his sight became about normal" (Agnellet 1958, p. 53). The Church recognized Vion-Dury's cure as miraculous.

In 1887, Catherine Lapeyre had a cancerous tumor on her tongue. A doctor recommended an operation. Instead, Lapeyre went to Lourdes, but after washing her mouth and bathing in the waters was not cured. In January 1889, Lapeyre was admitted to the main hospital in Toulouse, France. After unsuccessful attempts at treatment, a surgeon decided to remove the tumor. Before the operation, a photograph of the tongue was taken. Boissarie (1933, p. 40) said the photograph showed "a malignant tumor, jagged and vegetating, which had developed on her tongue." Three months after the operation, the tumor returned. The surgeon proposed another operation, but Lapeyre did not want it, and left the hospital for a room in Toulouse. In July 1889, she was refused a place on a pilgrimage to Lourdes, as she had already gone in 1887. Her friends advised her to simply pray with them to the Virgin for nine days. Lapeyre did this and also washed herself with Lourdes water. On the ninth day she was cured. Boissarie (1933, p. 41) stated: "Her tumor diminished and disappeared. The glands of her neck were no longer swollen; she was able to eat and to talk. The dreadful pains in her head which had followed the path of the nerves of the tongue and caused corresponding pains in the ear had completely disappeared. In a few hours this trouble, which had seemed incurable and which had reappeared after the operations, had ceased without leaving any trace other than a very ordinary scar." Boissarie (1933, p. 42) added, "Thus, according to the statements of the doctors, and from the progress of the disease as shown by the photograph, which gives a very exact idea of the lesion, there is no doubt that Catherine Lapeyre had a cancer of the tongue and consequently an incurable affection, which would have proved fatal in a very short time. Her cure, happening within a few hours, with no treatment, upsets every calculation. We never experience such results in the practice of medicine." When Lapeyre was examined at the medical bureau in Lourdes in 1897, doctors saw the tongue was healed and that there was no chance of reappearance of the cancer.

Amelie Chagnon was born in France in 1874. As a child she was very much devoted to the Virgin Mary. At age thirteen her foot became red and swollen. In 1889, she went to Lourdes, but was not cured. By age seventeen, a bone in her foot had become thoroughly decayed from tuberculosis. This bone had become soft, and its articulations with other foot bones had been detached. Around the bone was a deep oozing sore. She also had a swollen knee. Treatments at a hospital in Poitiers were not effective, and her maladies were deemed incurable. For three months, she remained in bed, unable to move. During this time she expressed a desire to go once more to Lourdes, and refused further medical treatment (Boissarie 1933, pp. 10–14).

Amelie arrived at Lourdes on August 21, 1891. So convinced was she of a cure that she brought with her a new pair of shoes, although she had not been able to wear shoes for four years. She was dipped once into the waters, but nothing happened. But upon being placed in the water a second time, she felt a sudden snapping of her knee and an intense outflow of pain from her foot. She was cured. Boissarie (1933, pp. 10–11) said: "Caries, sores, tuberculosis of the bone, destroyed articulation—all were cured in a few moments. The sore was replaced by a firm scar. The decayed, movable bone, which marked a bluish trail under the skin, had resumed its normal aspect and firmness. It was joined to the neighboring parts. In the knee there was no more swelling or pain but an entirely healthy articulation."

One of Amelie's attendants, Madame de la Salinière, recalled: "There were six of us to support the young girl upon the sheet in the water ... Between the two immersions, at the moment when we lifted the child upon her sheet to take her out of the water, I perceived the sore upon her foot very distinctly. Upon Amélie's urgent request: 'If you will put me back into the water, I am sure I will be cured,' we went back down the three steps which we had just ascended. . . . At the end of a minute or two, what was our astonishment to see the girl jump out of the sheet and walk, saying: 'I feel nothing more; the Blessed Virgin has cured me.' I immediately knelt to examine her foot and saw very distinctly a pink surface which seemed freshly healed."

Amelie Chagnon then went to the medical bureau, where she was examined by doctors, including Dr. Boissarie, who said (1933, pp. 15–16): "She showed us her certificates declaring that she was afflicted with white swelling of the knee and a sore with decay of the bone. We looked in vain for any trace of these lesions. There was none in the foot or in the knee. . . . The cure . . . had been instantaneous in its essential parts."

Testimony was gathered from physicians who had treated Amelie Chagnon in Poitiers. Dr. Dupont stated: "For several months I attended Mademoiselle Amélie Chagnon for caries of the bone of the foot and white swelling of the knee. I had decided to extract the whole diseased bone and to inject chloride of zinc into the tissues of the knee. The young girl begged me to defer this treatment until after her return from Lourdes. On the eve of her departure I saw her suffering so much that I wondered how she could stand the fatigue of the journey. She had not left her bed for several months. Upon her return . . . her foot had healed. . . . There was no sensitiveness along the line of the bone. In the knee every movement was possible without pain. The girl knelt, got up and walked without experiencing the slightest suffering" (Boissarie 1933, p. 16). Dupont added, "I have received more than a hundred letters in which I am asked for information about the case. The majority of these letters were signed by colleagues. To all I replied: 'The disease and the cure are indisputable'" (Boissarie 1933, p. 16). The medical bureau also gathered supporting testimony from the nurses who had attended Chagnon in Poitiers and pilgrims who had accompanied her on her journey to Lourdes.

Marie Briffaut became ill in August 1888. For four years, she had her leg in a cast and could not rise from her bed. She suffered from coxalgia, a disease of the hip joint. The bones of the joint were decaying, and an oozing open sore had formed, from which came pieces of decayed bone. Briffaut's entire leg was swollen, and she felt intense pain. The infection also poisoned her blood (Boissarie 1933, pp. 22–23). Describing her condition, Briffaut said, "For two years, my tongue was black, my mouth was dry, and I vomited everything I drank, for I took no solid nourishment. One day, when they wished to change the linens, my back and my leg stuck to the cast, and it was necessary to tear the skin before they could raise me; I was all blood. . . . The doctors gradually discontinued their visits. They declared I would not get well and that death would soon come" (Boisarrie 1933, p. 23).

Unable to walk, she made the journey to Lourdes in a coffinlike box. Her neighbors thought she would die on the way. Somehow she survived the rail journey of over seven hundred miles, and arrived at Lourdes in September 1893. Her first bath in the pool at Lourdes gave no result. When she was lowered into the water the next day, she felt something happening. "The pains ceased. My leg was no longer heavy; it seemed as if some one had lifted an enormous weight which was bearing me down" (Boissarie 1933, p. 23). After she was raised out of the water, she said, "I am cured" (Boissarie 1933, p. 23). Her attendants then examined her.

Marie Briffaut said, "There was no longer a sore; the leg was neither black nor swollen; they touched it without giving pain—I was cured!" (Boissarie 1933, p. 23)

In the 1950s, Ruth Cranston, a Protestant researcher, was given access to the BCM records at Lourdes, and produced one of the most authoritative books on the cures there, titled *The Miracle of Lourdes* (1955). Here is one of the cases she documented. In 1924, Charles McDonald, of Dublin, Ireland, came down with tuberculosis. The next year, his health improved somewhat, and he moved to South Africa, where he again became ill in 1931. He returned to Dublin, where his condition worsened and was deemed untreatable. In November 1935, he moved into a hospice to prepare for death. As a last chance, he decided to go to Lourdes. At this time he was suffering from Pott's disease, involving destruction of bone in the twelfth thoracic vertebra, resulting in curvature of the spine. The bone of his right shoulder showed the effects of tubercular arthritis, and he also had nephritis, an acute destructive inflammation of the kidney. McDonald arrived in Lourdes on September 5, 1936. At that time he was unable to walk. The day after bathing in the Lourdes water, he was walking, and when he returned to Ireland a medical examination showed that his tuberculosis, arthritis, and nephritis were cured. Following the BCM procedures, McDonald returned to Lourdes a year later, in September 1937. Thirty-two physicians of the BCM examined him and studied his medical records, which included a statement by McDonald's doctor that he went to Lourdes with an advanced case of tuberculosis with various complications. The BCM found that McDonald's case satisfied its criteria for a miraculous healing (Rogo 1982, pp. 287–288).

The BCM report stated: "Charles McDonald has been afflicted with (1) tuberculosis of the left shoulder . . . ; (2) tuberculosis of the dorsal spine . . . ; (3) chronic nephritis characterized by the presence of pus, blood, albumin. These three conditions were in full evolution at the moment of the pilgrimage to Lourdes . . . They were abruptly halted in their evolution on September 7 [1936]. An immediate functional healing after a bath in the piscine was followed in less than four days by . . . return of normal urinary secretion rid of its infectious germs; cessation of pain, return of partial movements of the left arm and lumbar region. . . . No medical explanation, in the present state of science, can be given; considering the extraordinary rapidity of the healing of these tuberculous affections, judged incurable by the specialists called in to treat him, and whose beginning was noted by general infection, later by bony localizations" (Rogo 1982, pp. 288–289).

On July 4, 1921, Dr. Pierre Cot provided this statement about the medical condition of Mademoiselle Irène Salin, then twenty-one years old, in order to help her qualify for a place on a pilgrimage to Lourdes: "I, the undersigned, Pierre Cot, doctor of the Faculty of Montpellier, living at Maussanne, declare and certify that I have had under my care for two years Mademoiselle Irène Salin, suffering from Pott's disease in the lumbar region. Actually the patient presents evidence of disease in the last three lumbar vertebrae, with persistent pain in the whole of that region. She has to wear a plaster corset" (Marchand 1924, p. 51). Pott's disease is tuberculosis of the spine with destruction of bone resulting in curvature of the spine. Dr. Cot's diagnosis of Pott's disease was supported by four other physicians and evidence provided by X-rays (Marchand 1924, p. 55).

Salin's condition was such that she could not walk without assistance. Dr. Cot was not very much in favor of allowing Salin to go on the pilgrimage. He allowed it only on the condition that she remain in her plaster corset and wear a brace called "Bonnet's splint." She was also to be supported by a cradlelike apparatus called a gouttière. Salin arrived in Lourdes on August 18, 1921, after a painful journey. During her stay in Lourdes, she was bathed in the pool twice, with no immediate result. On August 23, Salin boarded a train for her home in Provence, expressing her hope that she would in fact someday be cured at Lourdes. During the train ride, she found she could walk. While Salin was riding in a carriage from the train station to her home, Dr. Cot happened to pass by in his car and was astonished to see her cured. On August 26, Dr. Cot visited Salin, removed her splint, and found that all of her symptoms of disease had disappeared.

On September 14, Dr. Cot wrote: "Mademoiselle Irène Salin, aged twenty-one, suffering from Pott's disease in the lumbar-sacral region, was put in a Bonnet's splint from March, 1919, to June, 1920; then, as painful symptoms still persisted and walking was impossible, a plaster corset was applied, which she wore from April 5, 1921, to August 26 of the same year. At that date I removed the plaster corset, and state, that then Mademoiselle Salin presented none of the classical signs of Pott's disease. The movements of antero- and postero-flexion of the spine, as well as the lateral movements, were perfectly free and painless. The patient walked without pain, and felt no fatigue therefrom. I am obliged to avow, with all the impartiality which certificates of this kind ought to have, that it is impossible to explain otherwise than supernatural such a complete and rapid cure" (Marchand 1924, p. 54).

In 1927, at age 13, Louise Jamain was diagnosed with tuberculosis at the Saint-Louis Hospital in Paris. In 1930 she underwent operations at another hospital, which did not arrest the spread of the disease. By 1937, Jamain entered the Laënnec Hospital near death, suffering from pulmonary, intestinal, and peritoneal tuberculosis. Although she could not feed herself and was coughing blood, she decided she wanted to go to Lourdes. On March 28, she boarded a train for Lourdes. On the train and after her arrival in Lourdes, she had severe attacks of coughing, bringing up blood. On April 1, she was taken to see the evening procession at Lourdes, but after fainting she was taken to the hospital, where she lay in her bed motionless, as if dead. Jamain later recalled, "It was 3 o'clock in the morning and I was lying on my bed in the Saint-Michel Hospital at Lourdes. Three friends around my bed were talking about the difficulties of arranging for my funeral and having my body taken back to Paris. They recalled that I had no family, that my father was dead, having been gassed in the war, and that my mother and four brothers had died from tuberculosis. But the first thing I did was to ask for something to eat. My friends brought me some white coffee. You can guess their astonishment because for six months I had been fed only be injections and by serum" (Agnellet 1958, p. 110). After drinking her coffee, Jamain went to sleep. The next morning she got up from her bed feeling hungry and ready to eat something.

Jamain then went to the medical bureau. The doctors were amazed at her recovery. By the time she left on the train to Paris a few hours later, all signs of her illness had disappeared. On arriving in Paris, she was taken to the Laënnec Hospital. Agnellet (1958, p. 111) stated, "The staff were astonished to see walking along the corridor of the chest section a patient who should by rights have been in the cemetery. In the ward where she had been dying a few days before there were incredulous exclamations to check the cure—and perhaps to disprove it. But their efforts resulted in confirmation. There were no signs of the pulmonary lesion on the X-rays and no trace of Koch's bacilli in the sputum. The cure was clinically established. It was certified by the signatures of Dr. Bezancon and Dr. Cachin, who could hardly be supposed to have received a bribe from the Basilica at Lourdes." In 1951, Jamain's cure was certified as miraculous by Church officials.

Gérard Baillie was born in 1940 in France. As a young child he became blind from chorio-retinitis. Agnellet (1958, p. 118) stated: "This disease consists in the infective degeneration of the internal layers of the eye, the choroid and the retina, and is progressive. As the cones and rods which form the sensory nerve endings in the eye and make up the retina are gradually destroyed, the field of vision contracts as though the circular shutter of a camera were being closed in front of the eye. When the destruction reaches the intra-ocular end of the optic nerve, the nerve itself atrophies in its turn. Blindness is then complete and absolutely incurable, since nerve cells never regenerate once their nucleus is destroyed. Only the axon can be restored and in the case of chorio-retinitis the degeneration affects the whole of the cell."

At two years old, Baillie was placed in the Institute for Blind Children at Arras, France, and specialists there confirmed he was suffering from chorio-retinitis. Two years later, Baillie was taken by his parents to Lourdes. Agnellet (1958, p. 119) stated: "Gérard's complete blindness on arrival at Lourdes is confirmed by fifteen certificates and the testimony of a hundred people." After a few days at Lourdes, Baillie started recovering his sight in stages. Doctors at the medical bureau, as well as other eye specialists, confirmed that he could see again. In 1950, the cure was complete and a medical examination "showed that the retinal layers of the eye and the optic nerves were entirely restored" (Agnellet 1958, p. 120).

Gertrude Fulda and her sister were famous music hall dancers in Austria. In 1937, she felt intense pains in her abdomen, and an operation revealed an intestinal perforation and inflammation of the peritoneum, the membrane that lines the abdominal cavity. A few days later, she came down with nephritis, a severe infection of the kidneys. The infection spread to the adrenal glands, which stopped functioning, thus bringing on Addison's disease. She developed the usual symptoms of the disease. Her skin turned brownish, and she lost her appetite. Soon her body lost almost all of its flesh. Only by injections of hormones did she avoid death for seven years. But finally, a physician announced to Gertrude Fulda's grandmother that she would soon die. Fulda's grandmother sent to France for a bottle of Lourdes water. Gertrude washed herself with the water, without result. She then decided that she wanted to go to Lourdes, but was not able to make the journey until 1950. On July 10, she was examined by doctors at the medical bureau, who recommended hormone treatments and would not allow her to bathe at Lourdes. Fulda refused the treatments, and said she would die if not allowed to bathe in the Lourdes waters. On August 8, the Lourdes doctors gave their consent for her to bathe, and she was cured right away. Agnellet (1958, pp. 141–142) stated, "This was not a question of progressive improvement or of convalescence. Gertrude Fulda was cured instantly. The Medical Bureau noted this cure on the 16th August 1950, stating that all symptoms of the illness had disappeared in spite of the suspension of treatment. Her skin lost its discoloration, her pains went and all organic functions immediately became normal. The blood count confirmed the cure and her blood pressure also returned to normal. The suprarenal glands, destroyed by the abscesses around the kidneys, had suddenly been regenerated and were once again secreting into the bloodstream normal amounts of hormones which it had been necessary up to then to introduce artificially into the circulation." Her cure was verified by her doctor in Vienna and by the doctors of the Lourdes medical bureau when Fulda returned there in 1952.

Paranormal Production of Partial and Complete Biological Forms

In the case of Lourdes, we see modification or restoration of existing or previously existing biological form by the action of a being higher in the cosmic hierarchy. Now we want to consider the new production of partial or complete biological forms. We have already encountered some instances of this in the accounts of mediums found in previous chapters.

For example, as we learned in chapter 5, Sir Alfred Russel Wallace, cofounder with Darwin of the theory of evolution, saw a form manifested in the presence of the medium Haxby in London. Haxby, seated behind a curtain in a small room separated by a curtain from the drawing room in which Wallace and other witnesses were sitting, entered into a trance, and from behind the curtain appeared a white-robed human form, which then began to move about the room. Wallace stated that he was able to feel the hands and touch the garments of the form. This human personage was of a different size than the medium, Haxby, ruling out impersonation by the medium (Wallace 1905, v. 2, pp. 328–329). After the human form disappeared behind the curtain, Wallace and others looked in. Wallace stated: "Haxby was found in a trance in his chair, while no trace of the white-robed stranger was to be seen. The door and window of the back room were securely fastened, and often secured with gummed paper, which was found intact" (Wallace 1905, v. 2, pp. 328–329). If Wallace's observations are to be trusted, this rules out the idea that a man other than Haxby secretly entered and carried out a deception.

Wallace witnessed another materialization of a complete human form in the presence of the medium Eglington. While Eglington was sitting behind a curtain hung across a corner of a room, a robed male figure emerged. Just before the materialization, Wallace and others had carefully searched the walls and floor behind the curtain and found no secret entrances. Immediately afterwards, every item of Eglington's clothing was carefully searched, and the investigators found no robes. Meanwhile, Wallace and another person checked the walls and floor behind the curtain and found nothing out of the ordinary. Nor had Eglington left anything behind the curtain. So here again impersonation by either Eglington or a confederate was ruled out (Wallace 1905, vol. 2, p. 329).

In the presence of the medium Monk, Wallace witnessed the actual production of a humanlike form. The place was an apartment in London. It was broad daylight. A cloudy figure emerged from the side of Monk's body. It was connected to him by a cloudy band. Wallace (1905 v. 2, p. 330) stated: "Monk . . . passed his hand through the connecting band, severing it. He and the figure then moved away from each other till they were about five or six feet apart. The figure had now assumed the appearance of a thickly draped female form, with arms and hands just visible. Monk . . . clapped his hands. On which the figure put out her hands, clapped them as he had done, and we all distinctly heard her clap following his, but fainter. The figure then moved slowly back to him, grew fainter and shorter, and was apparently absorbed into his body as it had grown out of it." Hensleigh Wedgwood told Wallace how he had more than once seen a tall, robed, male figure appear alongside Monk. Wedgwood touched the figure, feeling its clothes and body. Once the figure lifted the chair upon which one of Wedgwood's fellow investigators was seated (Wallace 1905, vol. 2, p. 331).

In 1874, Wallace saw in London some materializations of human forms in the presence of the medium Kate Cook, who was sitting in a chair behind a curtain hung across a corner of a room. The materialized form was that of a white-robed woman taller than Cook, and with different features. Wallace (1905 vol. 2, p. 328) said: "I could look closely into her face, examine the features and hair, touch her hands." After a half hour, the materialized form would disappear behind the medium's curtain. Within just a few seconds, Wallace and others looked in and saw only Kate Cook, dressed in black, sitting in trance.

Sir William Crookes, who won a Nobel Prize in physics and served as president of the Royal Society, saw many materializations by Kate Cook. The usual skeptical explanation is that she quickly changed clothes behind the curtain and came out before the audience as the materialized figure. But Crookes testified that he once accompanied the materialized person behind the curtain and observed Kate Cook lying on the floor in trance (Wallace 1896, p. 189). Furthermore, once the electrician C. F. Varley, a Fellow of the Royal Society, attached electrical monitoring equipment to Cook, in order to detect any movement by her as she rested in trance behind the curtain. Wallace (1896, pp. 188–189) noted: "The apparatus was so delicate that any movement whatever was instantly indicated . . . under these conditions, the spirit-form did appear, exhibited its arms, spoke, wrote, and touched several persons . . . at the conclusion of the experiment Miss Cook was found in a deep trance."

In his book *Lights and Shadows of Spiritualism,* the medium D. D. Home devotes two chapters to "trickery and exposure." He showed how false mediums created various illusions, such as materializations of human forms and limbs, materializations of objects, and so forth. He also showed that these fake effects depended upon conditions of darkness and lack of proper experimental control. His own effects were demonstrated in the light and under the control of prominent scientists and other leading members of society. Home, although very skeptical of materializations, did believe that some materializations were genuine: "I need hardly remind my readers that the carefully conducted experiments of Mr. Crookes with Miss Cook were repaid by evidence giving undeniable certainty of the phenomenon" (Home 1879, p. 415).

Materializations of limbs also took place in the presence of Home himself. Recalling a sitting with Home, Sir William Crookes described, "A beautifully formed small hand rose up from the opening in the dining table and gave me a flower; it appeared and then disappeared three times at intervals, affording me ample opportunity of satisfying myself that it was as real in appearance as my own. This occurred in the light, in my own room, whilst I was holding the medium's hands and feet." Crookes noted several other appearances of hands in the presence of Home, at times when the medium was carefully observed and controlled (Carrington 1931, pp. 175–176).

Productions of various parts of the human form were observed in the presence of the medium Eusapia Palladino. On July 27, 1897, the astronomer Camille Flammarion participated in a séance with her in the home of the Blech family in Paris. As usual, a cabinet was prepared by stretching a curtain across the corner of a room. The medium sat outside this cabinet. Among items placed inside the cabinet were two trays of putty, one large and one small. They were placed on the floor. The purpose of the trays of putty was to catch the imprints of materialized hands or feet (Flammarion 1909, p. 68). As usual, Flammarion and another participant physically controlled the medium by grasping her hands and feet. During parts of the séance, Flammarion and the others then felt the touches and slaps of invisible hands. De Fontenay saw a detached hand remove a pad of paper from the table (Flammarion 1909, p. 72).

During a break in the sitting, Mrs. Blech checked the trays of putty on the floor of the cabinet. They were untouched. She put the small tray on the round table outside the cabinet, and the large tray on the chair in the cabinet. The séance resumed in the dim red light. De Fontenay and

Flammarion resumed controlling the medium, holding her hands. Flammarion felt her fingers digging deeply into his hand. After some time, she said, "It is done." When the small tray of putty was examined, it had the impressions of four fingers, in the same positions as the fingers that had gripped Flammarion's hand (Flammarion 1909, p. 74).

Later, the chair within the cabinet moved out and took up a position near Mrs. Blech. It then rose up and rested on top of Mrs. Blech's head. The large tray of putty resting on the chair, weighing nine pounds, floated across the table into the hands of Mr. Blech. Eusapia exclaimed, "It is done." Blech felt no pressure on the tray of putty in his hands. When they looked at the tray, the sitters saw the imprint of the profile of a human face in the putty. Mrs. Blech moved forward and kissed Eusapia on her cheeks, and detected no odor from the putty, which had a strong scent of linseed oil. The imprint of the face resembled Eusapia's (Flammarion 1909, pp. 74–75).

Flammarion took the tray of clay, walked into the nearby dining room, and placed the tray on a table there, so they could examine the facial imprint more carefully. Eusapia came with the party. Flammarion observed her carefully. During the entire time, she stood motionless with both hands on the table. Eusapia then moved back into the other room. Flammarion (1909, p. 77) said, "We followed her, observing her all the while, and leaving the clay behind upon the table. We had already got into the chamber when, leaning against one of the halves of the double door, she fixed her eyes upon the tray of clay which had been left upon the table. The medium was in a very good light: we were separated from her by a distance of from six to ten feet, and we perceived distinctly all the details. All of a sudden Eusapia stretched her hand out abruptly toward the clay, then sank down uttering a groan. We rushed precipitately towards the table and saw, side by side with the imprint of the head, a new imprint, very marked, of a hand which had been thus produced under the very light of the lamp, and which resembled the hand of Eusapia."

On November 16, 1897, Flammarion conducted a sitting with Eusapia at his home in Paris. Arthur Levy came with an attitude of distrust and skepticism. Eusapia and the researchers sat at a table close to a curtain hung across a corner of the room. Levy and another sitter, George Mathieu, controlled the hands and feet of Eusapia. During the sitting, a hand appeared and disappeared above Eusapia's head (Flammarion 1909, p. 89). At another séance with Eusapia in Flammarion's home, a Mr. and Mrs. Pallotti were present. The room was lit dimly by a night lamp set some distance from the table. Two of the sitters, Mr. Brisson and Mr. Pallotti, were controlling the medium. Mrs. Flammarion and Mrs.

Brisson were sitting away from the table, some yards away, facing Eusapia. Mr. and Mrs. Pallotti expressed a desire to see their daughter. Flammarion (1909, p. 128) said, "There was a great movement of the curtain. Several times I see the head of a young girl bowing to me, with high-arched forehead and with long hair. She bows three times, and shows her dark profile against the window." The Pallottis talked to the figure, and felt the face and hair of the apparition. "My impression was that there was really there a fluidic being," said Flammarion (1909, p. 128). But he believed the Palottis were simply imagining the materialized figure to be their departed daughter.

Other careful researchers also observed fluidic limbs materialize from Eusapia Palladino. During a sitting with Eusapia, Mrs. Frederick Myers, reported armlike protrusions extending from Eusapia's body (Gauld 1968, p. 236–237). On another occasion, a Mrs. Stanley saw a similar armlike protrusion. Just after this incident, Mrs. Meyers, who was also present, assisted other witnesses in undressing and searching Eusapia. They found nothing suspicious (Gauld 1968, p. 237). Fluidic limbs, of the kind noticed by Mrs. Myers and Mrs. Stanley, were seen at other séances with Eusapia. Nobel laureate Charles Richet reported (1923, p. 419): "Venzano saw a fluidic hand take shape and emerge from the right shoulder of the medium to get a glass full of water and carry it to the medium's mouth. Professors Morselli and Porro were present at these experiments." Giuseppe Venzano was a physician, Enrico Morselli a psychiatrist, and Francesco Porro an astronomer. When a special commission of researchers investigated Eusapia in Naples, they reported fluidic limbs. The commission reported: "Mr. Feilding, while holding and seeing Eusapia's two hands, was touched behind the curtain by a living hand, three fingers below and the thumb above, and grasped so that he felt the fingernails in his flesh. These hands occasionally became visible. Mr. Baggally, while seeing and holding the hands of the medium, was touched on the back of his own hand by a hand stroking it and proceeding up his arm" (Richet 1923, p. 420). Carrington (1931, p. 175) cited a report by Professor Felippe Botazzi, from a sitting with Eusapia at the University of Naples: "Botazzi felt a hand grasp the back of his neck. He moved his own left hand to the place of contact and reported: "I found the hand which was touching me: a left hand, neither cold nor hot, with rough, bony fingers which dissolved under pressure; they did not retire by producing a sensation of withdrawal, but they *dissolved, dematerialized, melted.*" He then felt a hand placing itself on his head and quickly moved his own hand to touch it, reporting, "I felt it, I grasped it; it was obliterated and again *disappeared in my grasp.*" Later, the hand rested on his forearm.

Botazzi grasped it with his left hand, reporting, "I could *see* and feel at the same time; I saw a human hand, of natural colour, and I felt with mine the fingers and the back of a lukewarm nervous, rough hand. The hand dissolved, and (I saw it with my eyes) *retreated as if into Mme Palladino's body, describing a curve"* (Carrington 1931, pp. 174–175).

Hans Driesch (1867–1941) was a German philosopher and scientist. He was one of the last important biologists to support the doctrine of vitalism (Berger 1991, pp. 113–114), which holds that the laws of material science alone are not sufficient to explain life. He was also actively involved in psychical research, and served as president of the Society for Psychical Research. He found a close connection between psychical phenomena and his vitalistic approach to biology. According to Driesch, some guiding nonmaterial agent was involved in the development of biological form. He used the Aristotelian word entelechy to name this vital principle.

Driesch's interest in vitalism began with some experiments with sea urchins. He found that when he separated individual cells from the early embryonic stage of a sea urchin, they would each grow into an adult sea urchin. He attributed this to a vital principle that guided and ordered the development of ordinary matter. The materializations of ectoplasmic limbs and bodies produced by Eusapia Palladino and other mediums, were, according to Driesch, another variety of this same principle. He considered his vitalistic biology to be "a bridge leading into physical parapsychological phenomena" (Berger 1991, p. 114).

He explained the connection between vitalist biology and psychical materializations as follows: "Think of the little material body, called an egg, and think of the enormous and very complex material body, say, an elephant, that may come out of it: here you have a permanent stream of materializations before your eyes . . . a spreading of entelechial control" (Berger 1991, p. 114).

Bilocation Events

Another form of paranormal production of biological form occurs in the phenomenon of bilocation, in which a duplicate form of a person appears in another place. Much of the documentation for this can be found in accounts of the lives of Christian saints. Rogo (1982, p. 81) states: "It shouldn't be presumed, though, that bilocating saints are sending only some apparitional or ethereal representations of themselves to far-off places during the production of this miracle. For according to traditional mystical lore, this 'second self' is able to eat, drink, and carry out any physical act the body is capable of performing. In fact, according to

Church doctrine, during the process of bilocation the human body is actually duplicated through the grace of God."

One day in the year 1226, St. Anthony of Padua (1195–1231) was giving a sermon in a church in Limoges, France. While speaking, he remembered he had promised to conduct a service at a monastery on the other side of Limoges. Stopping his sermon, he knelt in prayer. At this moment, monks in the monastery saw St. Anthony walk in and conduct the service, after which he stepped away into the shadows. Meanwhile, in Limoges, he ended his prayers and rising to his feet again began speaking (Rogo 1982, pp. 81–82).

Many bilocations were documented in the life of St. Martin de Porres, born in Peru in 1579. As a young man, he entered the monastery of the Holy Rosary in Lima. He did not become a priest, but served as a lay helper. He lived at the monastery, humbly serving the priests, until he died in 1639. After his death, various Church commissions interviewed witnesses to his miracles, including bilocations. Rogo (1982, pp. 82–83) stated: "The original documents containing these eyewitness testimonies of the saint's miracles include the *Processus ordinaria auctoritate fabricatus super sanctitae vitae, virtutibus heroicis et miraculis* (1664) and the *Beatificationis et canonizationis Servei Dei Fratis Martine Porres* (1712), both of which are housed in the archives of the Order of Friars Preachers, Santa Sabina, in Rome. Another source of information on the saint's bilocations is the *Responsio ad novas animadversions R.P.D. fidei promotes super dubio an constet de virtutibus ecc* issued in Rome in 1742. Also useful are the official volumes on St. Martin's beatification and canonization processes published in Italy in 1960 and 1962 respectively."

Once at the monastery in Lima, Brother Francis, a friend of Martin de Porres, became severely ill. As he lay on his bed in his room, the door of which was locked, he saw St. Martin, who brought hot coals for a fire. He also sponged the body of Brother Francis and remade his bed, before disappearing (Rogo 1982, pp. 83–84). Other residents in the monastery reported similar experiences. In addition, there are reports of appearances of St. Martin de Porres in Japan and China. He had often expressed a desire to be a missionary in the East.

Once when St. Martin was in Lima, his sister Joan and her husband were hosting a family reunion at their home outside Lima. Shortly after an argument broke out among the relatives, St. Martin appeared at the door, carrying food and drink. He seemed to know all about the cause of the argument, and negotiated a peaceful resolution. Martin remained in the home of his sister for the rest of the evening, and departed for Lima the next morning. Joan visited the monastery a few days later. She told the monks how he had appeared at her home just in time to solve the quarrel that had broken out there. The monks were astonished, because he had been busy tending patients in the monastery's infirmary at that time (Rogo 1982, p. 84).

In 1970, a yogi named Dadaji visited a family of his followers in Allahabad, India. He went alone into a room of their house for solitary meditation. When he came out, he told his hosts that he had bilocated to the house of his sister-in-law in Calcutta, 400 miles away. This was verified by the Allahabad followers, and later confirmed by parapsychology researchers Karlis Osis and Erlendur Haraldsson (1976). Interviewing the Mukherjee family in Calcutta, Osis and Haraldsson found that they had seen an apparition of Dadaji in their house at the time of the yogi's meditation in Allahabad. Roma, the Mukherjee's daughter, said she was reading a book in the study when she saw the figure of Dadaji, who first appeared partly transparent and then became solid. Dadaji indicated that he wanted some tea. Roma got a cup of tea and a biscuit, and passed them into the study through the partly opened door. Roma's mother and father saw the figure through a crack in the door. The family members did not enter the study, but remained in the living room. Later, after hearing a noise in the study, they entered and found the figure gone. But the tea cup was half empty and the cookie was gone. Although Roma was a follower of Dadaji, the other family members were not (Rogo 1982, pp. 90–91).

Conclusion

I have presented in this chapter only a sampling of the vast accumulation of observations related to paranormal modification and production of biological form. Just as Darwin used observations of intentional modification of biological form through selective breeding as evidence for evolution on a larger scale, we can take the observations in this chapter as evidence for the paranormal modification and production of biological form on a larger scale—the initial production of a large variety of biological forms, including the human form, by intelligent causation.

10
A UNIVERSE
DESIGNED FOR LIFE

The universe itself appears designed for life. Certain fundamental constants of nature, certain ratios between the forces of nature, appear to be very finely tuned. If their numerical values were even slightly different, the universe as we know it would not exist. Stable atoms, stars, and galaxies could not form (Barrow and Tipler 1996, p. 20). And thus, life itself, as we know it, could not exist. The values of the constants and ratios appear to be entirely arbitrary. In other words, as far as scientists today can tell, the values are not determined by any law of nature or property of matter. It is as if the values had been set by chance. But the odds against this are so staggering, in some cases trillions to one, that we are confronted with a genuine problem in cosmology, called the fine tuning problem. One possible explanation is that the finely tuned values were set by a providential intelligence. In these times, this is the last thing most scientists would concede. One way to avoid the God conclusion is to suppose that there are innumerable universes. Therefore cosmologists have begun to favor theories that result in the production of such universes. They imagine that in each universe, the fundamental constants and ratios have, by chance, different values. And we just happen to live in the universe where all the values are properly adjusted for life to exist. We should not be surprised at this. After all, if the values of the constants and ratios were not just the way they are, then we would not be here to observe them. Another way to avoid the God conclusion is to find some as yet undiscovered physical explanation, a new theory of everything, such as superstring theory, that would yield the fine tuning we observe in this universe.

All of the current discussions about the fine tuning problem take place within the general framework of the Big Bang cosmology. Under the general heading of the Big Bang cosmology, there are dozens of Big Bang theories, almost as many as there are Big Bang cosmologists. It is not my purpose here to explore all the technicalities of these theories. I just want to give a general composite picture of what they involve. First, the universe emerges as a fluctuation of the quantum mechanical vacuum, which is compared to a sea of energy. In the case of multiverse theories, many universes emerge as fluctuations of the quantum mechanical vacuum. These universes in their beginning stages are immeasurably small, dense, and hot. Then they began to expand rapidly for a short period of time. As they continue to expand, they are filled with a super hot plasma. Later, after more expansion, and cooling, the super hot plasma condenses into subatomic particles, which later begin to condense into the gases hydrogen, helium, and deuterium. More exotic types of matter and energy, called dark matter and dark energy, are also produced. In regions of more dense concentrations of dark matter and energy, the atomic gases condense into stars and galaxies. Within the superheated cores of these stars, heavier elements form. And when the stars finally explode into supernovas, still heavier elements form in the heat and shock. And after billions of years, we have the universe we observe. Its fate is not precisely known, but according to some cosmologists the universe will eventually contract into a black hole, and perhaps rebound again, emerging through a white hole.

The Big Bang theory grew out of observations that the universe appears to be expanding. In the 1920s, astronomer Edwin Hubble discovered that light coming to us from distant galaxies was shifted toward the red end of the spectrum. The more distant the galaxies, the larger the red shift. Toward the red end of the spectrum, light waves become longer. So the wavelengths of light coming from these galaxies had been stretched. If the galaxies were moving away from us, that would explain the stretching of the light waves. Imagine a paddle boat in an otherwise still lake, with the paddle turning at a certain fixed rate. You are observing the boat from the shore. If the boat was anchored and held its position, the waves would come toward you at regular intervals. But if the boat started moving away from you, then the waves reaching you would be coming in further apart, even though the paddle on the boat was still turning at the same fixed rate. The wavelength of light coming from receding galaxies would get longer in the same way. And that is what scientists actually observe. The wavelengths of light are stretched. Scientists also say that the Big Bang theory predicted the temperature of the cosmic microwave background radiation. The cosmic microwave background is the heat left over from the initial superheated expansion of the universe billions of years ago. Furthermore, scientists say that the Big Bang theory predicts the abundances of hydrogen, deuterium and helium that we observe today in the universe.

There are many critics of the Big Bang theory. Among them is astronomer Tom Van Flandern, who has compiled a list of twenty principal problems with the Big Bang theory. These do have to be taken into account. To some, these problems suggest that the universe did not expand from an initial small state, as most cosmologists now believe. They suggest a steady state universe. To me, the current problems with the Big Bang theory suggest only that the expansion of the universe from a tiny seedlike form cannot be completely described without taking into account God and His powers. Aside from that, many elements of the Big Bang theory correspond to accounts of the origin of the universe found in the ancient Sanskrit writings of India.

Here is a brief summary of the Vedic account of the origin of the universe, taken from the *Shrimad Bhagavatam* and the *Brahma Samhita*. Beyond time and space as we know them, Maha Vishnu floats in cosmic slumber upon the waves of the Causal Ocean. From the pores of the Maha Vishnu emerge numberless universes in seedlike form. When Maha Vishnu glances upon these seedlike universes, energizing them with His potencies, they begin to expand in a flash of golden light. Within each universe, ele-ments are gradually formed beginning with the lighter ones and proceeding toward the heavier. While this is happening the celestial bodies are formed. And the universe continues to expand. The universes exist for the length of one breath of the Maha Vishnu. The universes come out from His body when He exhales and reenter his body when He inhales. The length of one breath is estimated to be 311 trillion years. Within this vast period of time, each universe continuously undergoes subcycles of manifestation and nonmanifestation lasting about 8.6 billion years each.

Both the Big Bang cosmology and the Vedic cosmology posit a sea of transcendental energy existing before the material manifestation of universes. Some cosmologists propose that universes expand from white holes and contract into black holes. White holes spit out universes, black holes eat them up. The Vedic version also proposes that universes expand from and contract into holes, the skin holes of Maha Vishnu. Both accounts propose that there is an initial period of rapid inflation. Both accounts propose an initial burst of light, or radiation. Both accounts propose that the universe goes on to expand. Both accounts involve many universes.

When the Big Bang theory was originally presented to my guru, Bhaktivedanta Swami Prabhupada, he was opposed to it. His disciples presented it to him as an explosion of an original lump of matter, with no involvement by God. Of course, a simple explosion like that could not produce the universe we observe. But that was not an accurate picture of what the Big Bang picture actually says. When more realistic accounts of the theory were reported to him, he was more favorably inclined toward them. He accepted the principle of an expanding universe, as can be seen in a conversation with disciples that took place in Los Angeles, on December 6, 1973 (Conversations 1989, v. 6, pp. 228–229).

> *Bali Mardana:* Prabhupada, when the universes are emanated
>   from the body of Maha-Vishnu, they begin to expand.
> *Prabhupada:* Yes, yes.
> *Bali Mardana:* Is the universe still expanding?
> *Prabhupada:* Yes. . . .
> *Karandhara:* While the exhaling is going on, the universe is
>   expanding . . .
> *Prabhupada:* Yes.
> *Karandhara:* In the inhaling, the universe is contracting.
> *Prabhupada:* Yes.

And in his commentary on one of the verses of *Shrimad Bhagavatam* (3.29.43), he stated that "the total universal body is increasing." The entering and reentering of the universes into the body of the Maha Vishnu is described in *Brahma Samhita* (5.48), which characterizes the Maha Vishnu as an expansion of God "into whom all the innumerable universes enter and from whom they come forth again simply by His breathing process."

Nevertheless, the Vedic expanding universe cosmology is distinct from the modern materialistic Big Bang cosmology in that the substance of the Vedic universe emerges from God, as one of His energies, and the further deployment of this energy is accomplished and controlled by God. In the following discussion, I will show how careful examination of the modern Big Bang cosmology leads one *toward* the same conclusion. The argument takes this basic form: even if one assumes, as modern cosmologists do, that the origin and development of the universe are to be explained solely in terms of the interaction of various kinds of matter and physical forces, then one is led to the conclusion that the finely tuned nature of these interactions implies a cosmic intelligence behind them. Once that conclusion is reached, we may then have to go back and reevaluate the initial assumptions of the modern Big Bang cosmology, and we may be warranted in making substantial changes in those assumptions, so as to bring the Big Bang cosmology and the Vedic cosmology into sharper agreement. In my discussion of the Big Bang cosmology, it may appear that I am accepting its assumptions as fundamentally correct. But I am simply saying that if, for the sake of argument, we accept the assumptions underlying the current state of Big Bang cosmology as correct, then certain conclusions follow. It would not be practical for me, however, to qualify each and every reference I make to Big Bang cosmology in this way.

The Anthropic Principle

Hundreds of years ago, most astronomers believed the earth was the center of the universe. Then the astronomer Copernicus introduced the idea that the earth rotated around the sun. Astronomers adopted what they called the Copernican Principle, the idea that the earth and its human inhabitants do not occupy any special place in the universe. But in the twentieth century astronomer Brandon Carter proposed that our position is to some extent special, returning to some degree to the previous view, which is also found in the Vedic cosmology. In order for humans to exist as observers, said Carter, we have to find ourselves in a certain position in a universe with certain characteristics. Carter (1974, p. 291) called this the anthropic principle. For one thing, according to current ideas about cosmology, the universe would have to be of a certain age in order for there to be human observers—about ten billion years old. According to current theories, it would take that long for successive generations of stars to convert helium and hydrogen into the heavier elements, such as carbon, one of the main ingredients of organic life. In an expanding universe, the size of the universe is related to its age. This means, say modern cosmologists, that we should expect a universe capable of supporting carbon-based human life to be at least ten billion light years in diameter, and our universe is of that size, according to currently accepted observations and calculations (Barrow and Tipler 1996, p. 3). I do not necessarily agree with the exact size and age estimates given for the universe by modern cosmologists and note that these are constantly changing.

Some versions of the anthropic principle hold that human observers should not only expect to find themselves in a universe of a certain age and size, but also in a universe where the values of physical constants and ratios of natural forces are finely tuned to allow the very formation of that universe and the human life in it. It is this initial fine tuning which is of most interest to me. My discussion of the fine tuning problem will be based primarily on two main sources: the book *Just Six Numbers* by Sir Martin Rees, the astronomer royal of Great Britain, and the book *The Cosmological Anthropic Principle* by astronomer John D. Barrow and physicist Frank J. Tipler.

Fine Tuning

Physicist John Wheeler, known for his many worlds interpretation of quantum mechanics, wrote (Barrow and Tipler 1986, p. vii), "It is not only that man is adapted to the universe. The universe is adapted to man. Imagine a universe in which one or another of the fundamental . . . constants of physics is altered by a few percent one way or the other. Man could never come into being in such a universe. That is the central point of the anthropic principle. According to this principle, a life-giving factor lies at the center of the whole machinery and design of the world." Let us now look at the numerical values associated with some of these fundamental constants and ratios of natural forces, and see exactly what would happen if each of them were changed only slightly.

The Large Number N and Gravity

According to modern cosmology, the size of the universe and the sizes of the objects and living things in it are related to the ratio between the force of electromagnetism and the force of gravity (Rees 2000, pp. 27–31). Atoms are composed of subatomic particles with different electric charges. Among these subatomic particles are electrons and protons. Electrons have negative charge and protons have positive charge. The electromagnetic attraction between the positive and negative charges of electrons and protons is one of the factors holding the atom together. The force of gravity also acts among the subatomic particles making up the atom. But the force of gravity is much weaker than the electromagnetic force. The ratio of gravity to electromagnetism is obtained by dividing the strength of the electromagnetic force by the strength of the gravitational force. The resulting number (N) is 10^{36}, which means that the gravitational force is 1,000,000,000,000,000,000,000,000,000,000,000,000 times weaker than the electromagnetic force.

On the atomic scale, gravity does not have much of an effect. But on the larger scale, gravity does have a very noticeable effect, even though it is much weaker than electromagnetism. The positive and negative charges in atoms cancel each other out. This means that on the large scale we do not feel very much of an effect from electromagnetism (unless the electromagnetic charges in an object are aligned, as in a magnet or an electric current). But gravity is always positive. The more mass present in an object, the greater its gravity. So when there are large aggregates of atoms their masses add up, and the force of gravity increases proportionately. The combined force of the gravity in the mass of all the atoms in the earth holds us down on the surface of the earth. In fact, the force of gravity determines how big living things can be on a particular planet. If the force of gravity were slightly stronger, the maximum size of living things would decrease. Let us imagine that N was 10^{30} instead of 10^{36}. Then gravity would be "only" 1,000,000,000,000,000,000,000,000,000,000 times weaker than electromagnetism. As a result of this small change (just a few zeroes), the force of gravity on earth would be so heavy, that no creatures larger than insects would be able to survive the pressure. And even these little insect sized creatures would have to have massive legs. And that's not all.

Everything in the universe would be much smaller. For example, it would take a billion times fewer atoms to make a star. According to current thinking, stars form when the gravitational force of the atoms in hydrogen and helium gas clouds causes the gas to condense. As the gas condenses it becomes heated, and when the gas becomes dense enough and hot enough, it triggers fusion reactions. The heat of the fusion reactions pushes the star's material outwards, but the force of gravity holds it in. The balance between the outward expansion and inward contraction causes stars to assume a particular size. The star has to be big enough to have enough gas molecules to collapse into a core with enough pressure to start the atomic fusion process. And the star has to retain enough mass to keep the heat generated by that fusion process from forcing all the materials of the star out into empty space. In general, stars normally have to be quite big. If, however, the force of gravity were greater, it would take fewer atoms to start the fusion process and fewer atoms to overcome the outward expansion. If N were 10^{30} instead of 10^{36}, it would take a billion times fewer atoms to overcome the force of outward expansion. This means that stars would be much smaller. They would also burn their nuclear fuel much more quickly. A fire with a little bit of fuel is normally going to go out more quickly than a fire with large amount of fuel. According to Rees (2000, p. 31), the average lifetime of a star would be ten thousand years rather than ten billion years. That would have quite a negative impact on the possibility of biological evolution of the kind scientists now imagine. Galaxies would also be much smaller, and would be more densely packed with stars. The dense packing of stars would interfere with the orbits of planets circling those stars. And we have to remember that the presence of life depends on stable orbits for planets. If our own planet's orbit were not stable the extremes of temperature on earth would be too great for life as we know it to survive. Why does N have the precise value it does? Rees (2000, p. 31) says, "We have no theory that tells us the value of N. All we know is that nothing as complex as humankind could have emerged if N were much less than 1,000,000,000,000,000,000,000,000,000,000,000,000."

The Binding Energy ε

The binding energy ε is another cosmic number that greatly influences the characteristics of our universe (Rees 2000, pp. 43–49). It determines how atoms are formed, and how nuclear reactions take place. Of course, this is also very important for the existence of life forms.

Atoms of different elements have different binding energies. For us, the most important is the binding energy of helium. According to today's astrophysicists, the first generation of stars converts hydrogen into helium by fusion. The nucleus of a hydrogen atom contains one proton. The nucleus of deuterium, an isotope of hydrogen, contains one proton and one neutron. When two deuterium atoms fuse, they form an atom of helium, with two protons and two neutrons. The nucleus of the helium atom has a mass equivalent to .993 (99.3 percent) of the mass of the two protons and two neutrons it contains. In the process of fusion, .007 (0.7 percent) of the mass is converted into energy, mostly heat. This number .007 is ε, the binding energy of atomic nuclei. It is related to the strong nuclear force, which keeps the protons in the atom together. Rees (2000, p. 48) says, "The amount of energy released when simple atoms undergo nuclear fusion depends on the strength of the force that 'glues' together the ingredients in an atomic nucleus." The greater the binding energy, the greater the strength of the strong nuclear force. The protons in the nucleus have positive charge, and normally positive charges will repel each other, thus blowing the atom apart. But the strong nuclear force is just strong enough to overcome this repulsion, and holds the protons together in the nucleus. We do not feel this force, because it operates only within the nucleus of the atom.

If the value of ε were even slightly different, there would be major effects on atomic structure. If, for example, the value of ε were .006 instead of .007, this would mean that the strong nuclear force was slightly weaker than it is now. But this would be enough to interrupt the formation of elements heavier than hydrogen. Heavier elements are formed by adding protons to the nuclei of atoms. Hydrogen, with one proton, is the lightest element. Iron has 26 protons. But to get to iron and the heavier elements, we first have to go from hydrogen to helium. The helium nucleus usually contains two protons and two neutrons, while the simple hydrogen nucleus consists of just one proton. So to go from hydrogen to helium requires a middle step, the conversion of hydrogen to its isotope deuterium, which consists of one proton and one neutron. Then two deuterium nuclei can fuse to form a helium nucleus, with two protons and two neutrons. The strength of the nuclear binding force between the protons and neutrons in the helium nucleus causes the release of part of their mass as energy, the binding energy. Now if this binding energy were .006 of the total mass of the protons and neutrons, instead of .007, the strong nuclear force would be weaker. It would be just weak enough so that a neutron could not bind to a proton. Deuterium nuclei could not form, and therefore helium nuclei could not form. The hydrogen atoms would still condense into heavy masses, and these masses would heat up. But there would be no fusion reactions to keep the star going. No other elements would be formed. There would be no planets and no life as we know it.

What if ε was .008 instead of .007, indicating that the strong nuclear force was slightly stronger than it is today? That would lead to a problem of another kind in the process of element formation. As we have seen, the strong nuclear force is needed to bind protons together. Today, the strong force is not strong enough to bind just two protons together. A combination of two protons is called a diproton. There are no stable diprotons in the universe today. This is because the repulsion between the two positively charged protons is stronger than the binding energy of the strong nuclear force. But the binding energy, at its current value of .007, is strong enough to cause a proton to bind to a neutron, thus forming deuterium. And then two deuterium atoms can combine to form helium. This happens because the neutrons supply the extra binding energy needed to bring the two protons together. Because the neutrons are neutral in electric charge, they do not add any additional force of repulsion. Now if ε were .008, then two protons could join together, forming a diproton, an isotope of helium with two protons and no neutrons. This means that *all* of the hydrogen atoms (each with one proton) in the early universe would quickly combine into diprotons. Today, only some of the hydrogen atoms form deuterium and normal helium, over long periods of time. This leaves hydrogen in the universe for the formation of hydrogen compounds necessary for life. Barrow and Tipler (1996, p. 322) put it like this: "If the strong interaction were a little stronger, the diproton would be a stable bound state with catastrophic consequences—all the hydrogen in the Universe would have been burnt to He^2 during the early stages of the Big Bang and no hydrogen compounds or long-lived stable stars would exist today. If the diproton existed *we* would not!" The most important hydrogen compound is water, and in a universe in which ε was .008, there would be no water. The stable stars would not exist because they require hydrogen for fuel and there would be no hydrogen.

Going from helium to carbon also requires some fine tuning (Barrow and Tipler 1996, pp. 250–253). According to cosmologists, the first generations of stars burn hydrogen nuclei by a fusion process that yields helium nuclei. Eventually, the star runs out of hydrogen, and the helium core of the star begins to become denser. The condensation raises the temperature of the star to the point where helium begins to fuse into carbon. A helium nucleus has two protons. A carbon nucleus has six protons. Theoretically, three helium nuclei could fuse to form a carbon nucleus. But in practice this does not happen, because it is not very likely that three helium nuclei could collide at the same instant in just the way necessary to produce a carbon nucleus. Instead, there is a two step process. First two helium nuclei combine to form a beryllium nucleus, with four protons. Then a beryllium nucleus combines with another helium nucleus to form carbon. The problem is that the beryllium nuclei are unstable and rather quickly break back down into helium nuclei. Therefore, physicists would expect that very little carbon would be produced, certainly not the amounts of carbon present in the universe. But then the English astronomer Fred Hoyle showed that the carbon nucleus just happens to have a particular resonant energy level that lies just above the combined energy levels of beryllium and helium. The additional energy supplied to beryllium and helium by the heat of the solar core brings the beryllium and helium nuclei up to this level, enabling them to combine into carbon nuclei much more rapidly than might otherwise be expected. It is possible that all of the carbon produced in this way could have been immediately converted into oxygen, if the carbon nuclei combined with helium nuclei. But the oxygen nucleus has a resonant energy level that is below the combined energies of carbon and helium. This lucky circumstance means that the fusion reaction between carbon and helium becomes less likely. And therefore we have enough carbon for carbon-based life forms. Rees (2000, p. 50) noted: "This seeming 'accident' of nuclear physics allows carbon to be built up, but no similar effect enhances the next stage in the process, whereby carbon captures another helium nucleus and turns into oxygen. The crucial 'resonance' is very sensitive to the nuclear force. Even a shift by four per cent would severely deplete the amount of carbon that could be made. Hoyle therefore argued that our existence would have been jeopardized by even a few percentage points' change in ε." Commenting on the finely tuned resonances that enabled the production of heavy elements in the stellar interior, Hoyle said, "I do not believe that any scientist who examines the evidence would fail to draw the inference that the laws of physics have been deliberately designed with regard to the consequences they produce inside the stars" (Barrow and Tipler 1996, p. 22).

Ω (Omega) and the Cosmic Balance of Forces

According to modern cosmologists, the expanding universe in its very beginnings had three possible fates. (1) The force of gravity could have overwhelmed the force of expansion, and the universe could have rapidly collapsed back on itself, before any stars and galaxies could have formed. (2) The force of expansion could have overwhelmed the force of gravity, so that the universe would have expanded too rapidly for stars and galaxies to form. (3) The forces of gravity and expansion could have been adjusted very carefully so that the universe expanded at just the right speed for stars and galaxies to form and persist over billions of years.

The fate of the universe therefore depends upon a critical average density of matter. According to cosmologists, the critical density is 5 atoms per cubic meter. If the density is more than 5 atoms per cubic meter, gravity will be strong enough to cause the universe to collapse. If the density is much less than 5 atoms per cubic meter, the universe will expand too rapidly for stars and galaxies to form.

The cosmic number omega is the ratio between the critical density and the actual density (Rees 2000, pp. 72–90). If the critical density and the actual density are equal, then the ratio is 1, and hence Ω (omega) = 1. This allows a slowly expanding universe in which stars and galaxies can form, as is the case with our universe. But in our universe, the actual density of visible matter is far less than the critical density. If all visible matter, in the form of stars, galaxies and gas clouds, is taken into account, the actual density is only .04 of the critical density. But observations of the movement of the visible matter have convinced scientists that there must exist another form of matter in the universe, called dark matter. For example, spiral galaxies are shaped like rotating pinwheels, with two or more curving "arms" of stars streaming from a bright central core. When astronomers look at spiral galaxies, they see that they do not contain enough ordinary visible matter to keep the arms curving as closely as they do toward the centers of such galaxies. According to the current laws of gravity, the arms should be less curved. For the galaxies to maintain their observed shapes, they should have ten times more matter than they visibly have. This means there is some "missing matter." What form does it take? Some astrophysicists suggest the dark matter may be made of neutrinos, strange particles generated during the Big Bang with very small mass, or myriads of black holes of extremely great mass. "It's embarrassing," said Rees (2000, p. 82), "that more than ninety per cent of the universe remains unaccounted for—even worse when we realize that the dark matter could be made up of entities with masses ranged from 10^{-33} grams (neutrinos) up to 10^{39} grams (heavy black holes), an uncertainty of more than seventy powers of ten."

When the dark matter is added to the visible matter, the actual density of matter in the universe becomes about .30 of the critical density.

For this to be the situation now, after billions of years of expansion, the ratio of the actual density of matter in the universe to the critical density had to be extremely close to unity (i.e., one to one). Rees (2000, p. 88) stated, "Our universe was initiated with a very finely-tuned impetus, almost exactly enough to balance the decelerating tendency of gravity. It's like sitting at the bottom of a well and throwing a stone up so that it just comes to a halt exactly at the top—the required precision is astonishing: at one second after the Big Bang, Ω cannot have differed from unity by more than one part in a million billion (one in 10^{15}) in order that the universe should now, after ten billion years, be still expanding and with a value of Ω that has certainly not departed wildly from unity."

λ *(Lambda): Levity in Addition to Gravity?*

If gravity were the only force operating in connection with the expansion of the universe, then astronomers should detect that the rate of expansion is decreasing. Gravity should be slowing down the rate at which all the material objects in the universe are moving away from each other. In short, we should observe deceleration of the expansion. The force of gravity depends on the total density of matter. The more density, the more gravity. The more gravity, the more deceleration. Depending on the exact density of matter in the universe, the rate of deceleration could be faster or slower. But there should be some deceleration, as the force of gravity counteracts the expansion. Instead, scientists have noted an apparent acceleration in the rate of expansion. This was somewhat unexpected, as it indicates that in addition to gravity there may be another fundamental natural force that is repulsive, rather than attractive. In other words, there may be antigravity in addition to gravity.

The antigravity force was discovered by scientists who were hoping to find the total amount of dark matter in the universe (Rees 2000, pp. 91–95). The visible matter in the universe contributes only .04 of the critical density. The critical density is the exact amount of matter necessary for a Big Bang expanding universe to exist for long periods of time with relatively stable stars and galaxies. There must be enough matter to slow the rate of expansion so that all the matter in the universe does not quickly disperse into a featureless gas. But there must not be so much matter as to thoroughly overcome the expansion, causing the universe to quickly recollapse into a black hole. Because the visible matter in the universe is distributed in ways not possible according to the laws of gravity, scientists have inferred the existence of clumps of dark matter, which although invisible possess gravitational force. Taking into account the gravitational force of these clumps of invisible dark matter allows cosmologists to explain the distribution of visible matter. But when the clumped dark matter is added to the visible matter, the total amount of matter is still only .30 of the critical density. Some scientists have proposed that the present state of our universe would most easily be explained if the actual density of matter in the universe very closely approached the critical density, so that their ratio (Ω) was one to one ($\Omega = 1$). But that would require that there should be some more dark matter in the universe. Therefore, some scientists have proposed that there might be large amounts of extra dark matter evenly distributed throughout the universe. Unlike the clumped dark matter, this evenly distributed dark matter would not exert noticeable gravitational force on individual galaxies. And it would therefore not show its influence in the form of anomalies in the distribution of matter in and among galaxies. However, the evenly distributed dark matter might be slowing down the overall expansion of the universe.

To test their ideas, scientists measured the red shifts of a particular type of supernova: "A distinctive type of supernovae, technically known as a 'Type 1a', signals a sudden nuclear explosion in the center of a dying star, when its burnt-out core gets above a particular threshold of mass and becomes unstable," stated Rees (2000, p. 93). "It is, in effect, a nuclear bomb with a standard yield. . . . What is important is that Type 1a supernovae can be regarded as 'standard candles', bright enough to be detected at great distances. From how bright they appear, it should be possible to infer reliable distances, and thereby (by measuring the red shift as well) to relate the expansion speed and distance at a past epoch. Cosmologists hoped that such measurements would distinguish between a small slowdown-rate (expected if the dark matter has all been accounted for) or the larger rate expected if—as many theorists suspected—there was enough extra dark matter to make up the full 'critical density.'" Two groups of researchers were surprised to find that their measurements of these supernova red shifts showed no deceleration effect at all. Instead, their measurements showed the rate of the expansion of the universe was actually *increasing*. This meant two things. First, there was not any significant amount of extra dark matter. Second, in order to explain the increase in the rate of the universe's expansion, scientists had to propose a kind of antigravitational force.

The idea of an antigravitational force goes back to Einstein. In the 1920s, Einstein was working on the assumption that the universe was static. But his equations would not allow a universe to exist in a static state. The attractive force of gravity would cause all the matter in the universe to contract. To balance this attractive force, Einstein added to his equations a "cosmological constant," called λ (lambda), to balance the force of gravity. When cosmologists accepted an expanding universe, they lost interest in the idea of a cosmological constant tied to equations describing a static universe. But now it turns out that the expanding universe model itself appears to require λ. What exactly does λ measure? It does not measure the force of any kind of light or dark matter. Cosmologists have been reduced to proposing that λ "measures the energy content of empty space" (Rees 2000, p. 154).

The current measured value of λ appears to be quite special. "A higher-valued λ would have overwhelmed gravity earlier on, during the higher-density stages," stated Rees (2000, p. 99). "If λ started to dominate before galaxies had condensed out from the expanding universe, or if it provided a repulsion strong enough to disrupt them, then there would be no galaxies. Our existence requires that λ should not have been too large."

Q

According to the Big Bang cosmology, our universe started out as a small dense globular mass of extremely hot gas. As it expanded, it became cooler. If the globe of gas had been perfectly smooth, then as the expansion continued the atoms of gas would have distributed themselves evenly in space. In order for matter to have organized into structures like stars, galaxies, and clusters of galaxies, there had to have been some variations in the smoothness of the original globular cloud of gas. Some regions had to have been slightly denser than others. In these slightly more dense regions, the atoms became attracted to each other by the force of gravity, eventually becoming stars and galaxies. Rees (2000, p. 106) explains the measure of this force: "The most conspicuous structures in the cosmos—stars, galaxies, and clusters of galaxies—are all held together by gravity. We can express how tightly they are bound together—or, equivalently, how much energy would be needed to break up and disperse them—as a proportion of their total 'rest-mass energy' (mc^2). For the biggest structures in our universe—clusters and superclusters—the answer is about one part in a hundred thousand. This is a pure number—a ratio of two energies—and we call it Q." In other words, it would not take very much energy to overcome the force of gravity holding galaxies and clusters of galaxies together.

Q is necessarily related to the original density variations in the fireball of the early stages of the Big Bang. If there were no density variations at all, then the matter in the universe would have expanded completely evenly, so that there would have been no clumping of matter in the more dense regions. So according to the present value of Q (one in a hundred thousand, i.e. 10^{-5}), the initial variations in the energy of the Big Bang universe were no greater than one hundred thousandth of its radius. Scientists plan to confirm this with space satellites that can very accurately measure minute variations in the cosmic microwave background radiation, which scientists take to be the remnants of the original Big Bang fireball.

It turns out that **Q**'s present value (10^{-5}) is just about the only one that allows for the kind of universe in which there can be stable stars and planets on which life as we know it could exist. What if **Q** were *smaller* than 10^{-5}? Rees (2000, p. 115) said "the resulting galaxies would be anaemic structures, in which star formation would be slow, and inefficient, and 'processed' material would be blown out of the galaxy rather than being recycled into new stars that could form planetary systems." If **Q** were still smaller (smaller than 10^{-6}), then "gas would never condense into gravitationally bound structures at all, and such a universe would remain forever dark and featureless" (Rees 2000, p. 115). But what would happen if **Q** were much greater than 10^{-5}? Rees (2000, p. 115) said in such a universe most matter would quickly collapse into huge black holes and any remaining stars "would be packed too close together and buffeted too frequently to retain stable planetary systems." So although the current value of **Q** is critical for our existence, there is no particular reason why **Q** has that value. As Rees (2000, pp. 113–114) put it, "The way **Q** is determined . . . is still perplexing."

I do not want to leave the impression that there are no problems with the general scenario of galaxy formation implicit in this discussion. Although scientists do believe that stars and galaxies form more or less automatically according to physical laws during the condensation of gas clouds in space, they have not been able to accurately model the process on computers. Rees (2000, p. 110) noted that "nobody has yet performed a simulation that starts with a single cloud and ends up with a population of stars." In other words, the evidence for the fine tuning of constants combined with the inability of scientists to accurately model the process of star and galaxy formation may lead us to the conclusion that more is required than matter acting according to certain laws. The overall active intervention of a supreme being may also be required. In other words, God is not necessary just to fill in the gaps, but as an overall enabling and coordinating factor.

D: The Number of Dimensions

The number of spatial dimensions, **D**, determines important features of our universe. For our universe **D** is three. If **D** were two or four or some other number, life as we know it could not exist.

In our universe gravity and electricity obey the inverse square law. If you move an object twice as far away from you as it is now, the force of its gravity upon you will be only one quarter of what it was. Four is the square of two ($1/2 \times 1/2$), and one quarter is the inverse square of two (2×2). If the object is moved four times as far away, its gravitational force becomes one sixteenth of what it was, one sixteenth being the inverse square of four.

In a four dimensional world, gravity would follow an inverse cube law instead of an inverse square law. This would have a devastating effect, according to Rees (2000, p. 135): "An orbiting planet that was slowed down—even slightly—would then plunge ever-faster into the Sun, rather than merely shift into a slightly smaller orbit, because an inverse-cube force strengthens so steeply towards the center; conversely, an orbiting planet that was slightly speeded up would quickly spiral outwards into darkness." Only an inverse square law of gravity allows for stable orbits of planets. The same is true for orbits of electrons. If gravity and electromagnetism operated according to anything other than an inverse square law, there would be no stable atoms (Rees 2000, p. 136; Barrow and Tipler 1996, pp. 265–266).

If there were only two dimensions, it would be difficult for a functioning brain to exist. Barrow and Tipler (1996, p. 266), citing the work of Whitrow (1959), said, "He argues that if the spatial structure were of dimension two or less then nerve cells (or their analogues) would have to intersect when superimposed and a severe limitation on information-processing of any complexity would result."

It also appears that reliable electromagnetic signaling (of the kind we use in radios, televisions, computers, and telephone systems, as well as in biological neural systems) is possible only in a three dimensional universe. Barrow and Tipler (1996, p. 268) explained, "In two-dimensional spaces wave signals emitted at different times can be received simultaneously: signal reverberation occurs. It is impossible to transmit sharply defined signals in two dimensions." Reliable transmission requires not only that waves are without reverberation but also without distortion. Barrow and Tipler went on to say, "Three-dimensional worlds allow spherical waves . . . to propagate in distortionless fashion. . . . Only three-dimensional worlds appear to possess the 'nice' properties necessary for the transmission of high-fidelity signals because of the simultaneous realization of sharp and distortionless propagation. . . . If living systems require high-fidelity wave propagation for their existence to be possible, then we could not expect to observe the world to possess other than three spatial dimensions." Also, the gravity waves of Einstein's general theory of relativity could only propagate in a universe with three spatial dimensions and one time dimension (Barrow and Tipler 1996, p. 273). A modern cosmological theory, string theory, relies on a universe with ten spatial dimensions and one time dimension; however, all but three of the spatial dimensions are compacted on the microscopic level and have no visible effect on wave propagation (Barrow and Tipler 1996, pp. 274–275).

How to Explain the Fine Tuning

The existence of a universe in which human life as we know it is possible depends on the fine tuning of several constants and ratios of physical forces. How did this fine tuning come about? Today, theorists recognize three main possibilities. First, the fine tuning in the universe of our experience might be determined by an as yet undiscovered physical law. Second, it could be that our universe is only one of an infinite number of universes, each with different values for the constants and ratios, and we just happen to be living in the one with the values that will allow life to arise. Third, the fine tuning could be the result of providential design. Let us now consider each of these possibilities, beginning with physical determination of the fundamental constants and ratios.

In modern cosmology, some theorists propose that the fine tuning of universal constants and ratios of fundamental forces of nature will eventually be predicted by a grand unified theory of everything. At the present moment the biggest obstacle to a theory of everything is the unification of quantum mechanics and Einstein's general relativity theory. Quantum mechanics does very well in explaining the world of atoms and subatomic particles, where the main forces are electromagnetism, the atomic weak force, and the atomic strong force. Relativity theory does very well in explaining the action of gravity on the larger scale of the universe. At present no theory has successfully integrated both quantum mechanics and relativity theory, and this unification is especially necessary to explain the very early history of the Big Bang universe, when all the forces of nature were unified. One theory that promises to unify gravity with the other three fundamental forces is superstring theory. According to superstring theory, the basic units of matter are very tiny circular "strings" of energy. The various subatomic particles are strings vibrating at different frequencies in ten dimensional space. Superstring theorists claim that many of the fine tunings of fundamental constants and ratios of natural forces could be directly derived from the theory. But at the present moment there is no physical verification of superstring theory. "Strings" are many orders of magnitude smaller than the smallest subatomic particles visible in the biggest particle colliders. Rees (2000, p. 145) calls attention to the "unbridged gap between the intricate complexity of ten-dimensional string theory and any phenomena that we can observe or measure." Until some kind of verification can be obtained, superstring theory remains in the realm of speculation and cannot be called upon to resolve the fine tuning problem.

In the absence of a physical theory that determines the finely tuned fundamental constants observed in our universe, one can consider the possibility that some intelligent designer adjusted the constants. A good many cosmologists would rather not have it come down to this, so they appeal to the existence of innumerable other universes, in which the constants vary randomly. Among these universes is ours.

There are varieties of ways to get many universes. One proposal is that the Big Bang is cyclical. A Big Bang universe ends in a "Big Crunch," compacting itself into a singularity, a point of unlimited density, and then bounces back into existence in another Big Bang. And the process repeats itself endlessly, with each universe having a different set of fundamental constants. But Barrow and Tipler (1996, pp. 248–249) stated: "Only in those cycles in which the 'deal' is right will observers evolve. ... The problem with this idea is that it is far from being testable. .... Also, if the permutation at each singularity extends to the constants of Nature, why not to the space-time topology and curvature as well? And if this were the case, sooner or later the geometry would be exchanged for a noncompact structure bound to expand for all future time. No future singularity would ensue and the constants of Nature would remain forever invariant. .... However, why should this final permutation of the constants and topology just happen to be the one which allows the evolution of observers!" For our purposes, the main point is that the cyclic universe idea is an untestable speculation motivated by the desire to avoid the idea that God finely tuned the fundamental constants and ratios we observe in our universe.

One of the main interpretations of quantum mechanics also assumes many universes. Quantum mechanics involves transforming the deterministic equations of ordinary physics to yield a wave function specifying a range of statistical probabilities. The situation we observe in the universe of our experience represents only one of these statistical probabilities. According to the "many worlds" interpretation of quantum mechanics, the other possibilities are simultaneously realized in separate universes.

Yet another way to introduce many universes is to propose that just after the initial Big Bang many regions of the universe had their own

Mini Bangs and moved away from each other so quickly that light signals were no longer able to pass between them. Thus isolated from each other, these noncommunicating regions are in effect separate simultaneously existing universes.

No matter how they get many universes, cosmologists concerned with the fine tuning question go on to propose that in each of these universes the fundamental constants are adjusted differently, by chance. And we just happen to find ourselves in the universe where all these constants are adjusted so as to allow the presence of stable stars, planets, atoms, and the development of life forms.

Among modern cosmologists, Rees (2000, p. 4), for example, favors this many universe explanation. But he himself has admitted it is "speculative" (Rees 2000, p. 11). There is no way of demonstrating by the methods of modern materialistic science that these many alternative universes actually exist. And even if it could be shown they existed, one would have to further show that in each of them the fundamental constants varied randomly. According to the Vedic cosmology, alternative material universes do exist. An unlimited number of them emanate from Maha Vishnu. But in each one of them there is life, according to the Vedic accounts, indicating that in each universe the fundamental constants of nature would show the appropriate fine tuning. In short, the hypothesis of many universes does not in itself provide an escape from the fine tuning problem or rule out providential design. In the absence of a physical theory that yields the observed values of the fundamental constants, and in the absence of experimental evidence for a multiplicity of universes with randomly varying fundamental constants, the fine tuning of physical constants that we observe in our own universe, the only one that we can observe, points directly to providential design. In essence, all the attempts by modern cosmologists to come up with alternative explanations are motivated by the desire to avoid the default conclusion that God is responsible for the fine tuning.

11

HUMAN DEVOLUTION:
A VEDIC ACCOUNT

Let us now review the path we have taken. The evidence documented in *Forbidden Archeology* shows that humans of our type have existed on this planet for the duration of the current day of Brahma, about two billion years. This archeological evidence, along with genetic evidence, contradicts current evolutionary accounts of human origins and opens the way to new kinds of explanations. We then decided that before we ask how humans came into existence, we should first of all ask the question, "What is a human being?" Today most scientists assume that humans are simply a combination of the ordinary chemical elements. We concluded, however, that it is more reasonable, on the basis of all available scientific evidence, to start with the assumption that humans are composed not just of one thing, ordinary matter, but of three things—ordinary matter, subtle matter in the form of mind, and consciousness. With this established, we found it natural for us to assume that the cosmos is divided into regions with different balances of these three substances. We also found it natural to suppose that in each region conscious beings exist, of different grades and powers, with bodies adapted to the conditions there. With these basic elements in place, it is now time to integrate them all into a comprehensive account of what I call human devolution, in a specifically Vedic form. To put the Vedic account in its most simple terms, we did not evolve up from matter; rather, we have devolved, or come down, from the level of pure spiritual consciousness.

Today, most people favor relatively simple accounts of human origins. They favor either a simple creation account, or a simple Darwinian evolutionary account, or a simple extraterrestrial intervention account. The Vedic account of human devolution involves elements of all three. In common with the usual creation account, the Vedic account posits the existence of an overall conscious designer and controller, God. But the Vedic account also incorporates something from the evolutionary ac-

487

count. By evolution, Darwinists mean reproduction with modification. As we shall see, the Vedic account also involves reproduction with modification, a kind of intelligently guided genetic engineering, which starts with the more complex and subtle life forms and then moves on to simpler and grosser life forms. The Vedic account also includes an extraterrestrial element. The Vedic tradition may support variants of the account I am about to give, but these variants all share a family resemblance with each other, and, more generally, with creation accounts from others of the world's wisdom traditions.

The conscious self originally exists on the level of pure consciousness, in relationship with the supreme self, God, known in Sanskrit by many names, including the name Krishna, which means all attractive. The constitutional relationship of the particulate conscious self with the supreme conscious self is one of eternal reciprocal enjoyment. If a conscious self departs from its constitutional relationship with the supreme self, it descends to the level of the material energies. The basic motivation for this descent is the desire to assume the position of independent enjoyer, apart from the supreme conscious self. Because one cannot assume this position in the domain of pure consciousness, one must try to assume it in another domain, that of the material energies. The particulate conscious self then takes on a material body for action within the material energies.

The material energies are of two basic kinds: the subtle material energies and the gross material energies. Conscious selves existing in levels or regions of the cosmos dominated by the subtle material energies have bodies composed principally of the subtle material energies—mind (*manas*), intelligence (*buddhi*), and false ego (*ahankara*). Conscious selves existing in the realm dominated by the gross material energies have, in addition to a bodily covering made of the subtle material energies, a bodily covering made of the gross material energies—earth (*bhumi*), water (*apa*), fire (*anala*), air (*vayu*), and ether (*kham*).

God himself (Krishna) is not directly involved in the affairs of manifesting the material universes to accommodate the conscious selves who have departed from the spiritual level of reality. For this purpose Krishna expands himself as the Maha Vishnu, who lies in the Causal Ocean. From the pores of Maha Vishnu come numberless universes. By His glance, the Maha Vishnu injects conscious selves into each universe. The Maha Vishnu also expands into each universe as the Garbhodakashayi Vishnu. From the Garbhodakashayi Vishnu in each universe comes a subordinate creator god, Brahma. Brahma is one of the conscious selves injected into a universe. He is charged with populating the universe. He does this by manifesting bodies to serve as vehicles for conscious selves.

Brahma exists on the highest, most subtle level of the material universe. His place is called Brahmaloka. The body of Brahma is composed primarily of the subtle material elements. In his commentary on *Chaitanya Charitamrita* (*Adi Lila* 5.22), Bhaktivedanta Swami Prabhupada said, "The residents of Brahmaloka do not have gross material bodies to change at death, but they transform their subtle bodies into spiritual bodies and thus enter the spiritual sky." From his mind, Brahma directly produces mental sons (*manasa putras*), such as the sage Kardama Muni. Then from his body, Brahma produces other sages and the first sexually reproducing pair—Svayambhuva Manu and his consort Shatarupa. The Sanskrit word *svayambhuva* means self born. Svayambhuva Manu and Shatarupa have sons and daughters. The daughters are given in marriage to some of the mental sons of Brahma, and they begin to produce children. This reproduction of great sages, demigods, and demigoddesses takes place on the higher more subtle levels of the material universe.

When it is time for the production of the forms for souls who require bodies made of the grosser material elements, the demigods and demigoddesses engage in reproductive activities to produce them. In the course of these reproductive activities they make use of *bijas*, or seeds. These *bijas* contain the plans for the forms of the bodies. Modern biologists have difficulty explaining exactly how the process of development takes place. Each plant or animal generally begins as a single cell, which begins to divide. Each cell contains the same DNA, the same set of genes. So it is not easy to explain how and why, in the course of the progressive division of a few cells into millions of cells (trillions in the case of humans), that the cells sequentially differentiate and arrange themselves into complex forms of bodily tissues. I propose that associated with each form is not only the DNA but also a *bija*, or subtle seed, containing the developmental plan for the particular kind of body.

In *Bhagavad Gita* (14.4) Krishna says, "I am the seed-giving father of all living entities." And in *Bhagavad Gita* (7.10) Krishna says, "I am the original seed of all existences." The word used for "seed" in this case is *bija*. It could be taken to mean the *atma* (conscious self), which comes from Krishna. Bodies are vehicles for conscious selves, and without the presence of a conscious self, a body would not exhibit symptoms of life. But the presence of the conscious self is not itself sufficient to explain the form of a particular body. All bodies, according to Vedic thought, have conscious selves, including plants and animals. But each unit of conscious selfhood resembles the others. If the conscious self is the same in all bodies, then how do we explain the generation of different kinds of bodies?

We can do so by considering an additional meaning of the word *bija*, or seed. In his commentary to *Chaitanya Charitamrita* (*Madhya Lila* 19.152), Bhaktivedanta Swami Prabhupada said, "Everything has an original cause, or seed. For any idea, program, plan or device, there is first of all the contemplation of the plan, and that is called the *bija*, or seed." I propose that the development of bodily forms involves a seed of this type, in addition to the seed of the soul. This subtle developmental seed contains the plan for the body. In his commentary on *Shrimad Bhagavatam* (3.10. 7), Bhaktivedanta Swami Prabhupada explained that in the beginning "the living entities were all already generated in seedling forms by the Supreme Personality of Godhead, and Brahma was to disseminate the same seedlings all over the universe." From this it can be taken that the seeds (or seedlings) were given to the demigods, demigoddesses, and sages, who then used them in their reproductive processes to produce the forms of bodies to serve as vehicles for conscious selves.

Bodies of living things are manifested in the course of cyclical creations and destructions of universes and the planets within them. The basic unit of Vedic cyclical time is called the day of Brahma. The day of Brahma lasts for 4,320,000,000 years and is followed by a night of Brahma, which also lasts for 4,320,000,000 years. During the nights of Brahma, the conscious selves enter the body of the Garbhodakashayi Visnu in each universe and remain there until the next day of Brahma begins. Each day of Brahma is divided into 14 *manvantara* periods, each lasting about 300,000,000 years. There is normally a partial devastation between each *manvantara* period. During this period, the planets of the higher demigods are not touched, but the earthly planetary system is devastated. After each *manvantara* period, the demigods must again manifest the bodily vehicles for conscious selves. We are now in the seventh *manvantara* period. This means there have been six devastations, after which the earth has again been repopulated. This is interesting, because according to modern paleontology, the history of life on earth has been interrupted by six major extinction events, spaced at intervals of about the same order of magnitude as the devastations between the *manvantara* periods.

The fourth chapter of the sixth canto of *Shrimad Bhagavatam* contains a description of how repopulation occurred at the beginning of the sixth *manvantara* period. The repopulation was carried out by Daksha, a *prajapati* (generator of population). *Shrimad Bhagavatam* (6.4.19–20) says, "With his mind, Prajapati Daksha first created all kinds of demigods, demons, human beings, birds, beasts, aquatics and so on. But when Prajapati Daksha saw that he was not properly generating all kinds of living entities, he approached a mountain near the Vindhya mountain range, and there he executed very difficult austerities." After this, Daksha and his wife Asikni had sixty daughters. The daughters were given to various demigods and sages. The sage Kashyapa received seventeen daughters as wives. In *Shrimad Bhagavatam* (6.6.24–26), Shukadeva Goswami said to King Parikshit, "O King Parikshit, now please hear from me the names of Kashyapa's wives, from whose wombs the population of the entire universe has come. They are the mothers of almost all the population of the entire universe, and their names are very auspicious to hear. They are Aditi, Diti, Danu, Kashtha, Arishta, Surasa, Ila, Muni, Krodhavasa, Tamra, Surabhi, Sarama and Timi." Some of the wives of Kashyapa gave birth to various kinds of demigods. According to *Shrimad Bhagavatam* (6.6.26–31), others produced various species of animals: "From the womb of Timi all the aquatics took birth, and from the womb of Sarama the ferocious animals like the tigers and lions took birth. My dear King Parikshit, from the womb of Surabhi the buffalo, cow and other animals with cloven hooves took birth, from the womb of Tamra the eagles, vultures and other large birds of prey took birth.... The sons born of Krodhavasa were the serpents known as dandasuka, as well as other serpents and the mosquitoes. All the various creepers and trees were born from the womb of Ila.... animals whose hooves are not split, such as the horse, were born from the womb of Kashtha." One of the wives of Kashyapa was Aditi, and one of her sons was Aryama. *Shrimad Bhagavatam* (6.6. 42) states: "From the womb of Matrka, the wife of Aryama, were born many learned scholars. Among them Lord Brahma created the human species, which are endowed with an aptitude for self-examination."

Exactly how the demigods use their reproductive processes to generate the bodily forms for conscious selves is not specified in the *Shrimad Bhagavatam*. But from other parts of the Vedic literature, we get some clues. The *Mahabharata* (*Adi Parva* 118) tells us that once the sage Kindama and his wife transformed themselves into deer to engage in sexual intercourse. Not understanding their identities, King Pandu killed them, and was cursed. Similarly, we learn in the seventeenth chapter of the *Ramayana* of Valmiki that various demigods took on the forms of monkeys and engaged in reproductive activities to generate a population of monkeys with humanlike intelligence. Therefore, it is possible that the demigods take on the forms of a particular species and then, using *bijas* supplied by God, engage in a special kind of sexual reproduction in order to produce bodies of that same kind, as vehicles for conscious selves. Once this happens, reproduction of that species can continue in the ordinary way. There are, however, instances where demigods and humans on this planet produce offspring. For example, Arjuna, the hero of the

Bhagavad Gita was born of a terrestrial mother, Kunti, and a celestial father, the demigod Indra.

The process by which conscious selves descend to the realm of the material energy, and are placed in material bodily vehicles, is the primary meaning of devolution, as I have defined it. But there is another sense in which conscious selves devolve. According to its quality of consciousness, a conscious self can receive any kind of body. The human body is especially valuable, because in the human form the conscious self can understand the difference between spirit and matter, and make progress on the way back to its original spiritual home. However, if a conscious self misuses the human form, it will after death take birth in a body not as well equipped for self realization. The conscious self can descend into the animal and plant species. If this happens, the conscious self must then usually pass through births in several species before again attaining the human form. This process may be characterized as a kind of spiritual evolution.

There is yet another sense of devolution. That is the decline of human qualities and characteristics in the course of *yuga* cycles. Each day of Brahma is made up of one thousand *yuga* cycles. Each cycle lasts 4,320,000 years and consists of four *yugas,* or ages: a Satya Yuga, a Dvapara Yuga, a Treta Yuga, and a Kali Yuga. With the passing of each *yuga* in the cycle, humans decrease in their physical, mental, and spiritual qualities. We are now in the Kali Yuga of one of the *yuga* cycles. This Kali Yuga began about five thousand years ago. The *Shrimad Bhagavatam,* which according to the text itself was compiled at just about that time, contains predictions for the Kali Yuga. For example, the *Shrimad Bhagavatam* (1.1.10) says, "O learned one, in this iron age of Kali men have but short lives. They are quarrelsome, lazy, misguided, unlucky and, above all, always disturbed." More details can be found in the twelfth canto of *Shrimad Bhagavatam* (12.2.1–22): "Sukadeva Gosvami said: Then, O King, religion, truthfulness, cleanliness, tolerance, mercy, duration of life, physical strength and memory will all diminish day by day because of the powerful influence of the age of Kali. In Kali-yuga, wealth alone will be considered the sign of a man's good birth, proper behavior and fine qualities. And law and justice will be applied only on the basis of one's power. Men and women will live together merely because of superficial attraction, and success in business will depend on deceit. Womanliness and manliness will be judged according to one's expertise in sex. . . . A person's spiritual position will be ascertained merely according to external symbols. . . . A person's propriety will be seriously questioned if he does not earn a good living. And one who is very clever at juggling words will be considered a learned scholar. A person will be judged unholy if he does not have money, and hypocrisy will be accepted as virtue.... and beauty will be thought to depend on one's hairstyle. Filling the belly will become the goal of life, and one who is audacious will be accepted as truthful.... As the earth thus becomes crowded with a corrupt population, whoever among any of the social classes shows himself to be the strongest will gain political power ... Harassed by famine and excessive taxes, people will resort to eating leaves, roots, flesh, wild honey, fruits, flowers and seeds. Struck by drought, they will become completely ruined. The citizens will suffer greatly from cold, wind, heat, rain and snow. They will be further tormented by quarrels, hunger, thirst, disease and severe anxiety. The maximum duration of life for human beings in Kali-yuga will become fifty years.... The path of the Vedas will be completely forgotten in human society, and so-called religion will be mostly atheistic. The kings will mostly be thieves, the occupations of men will be stealing, lying and needless violence, and all the social classes will be reduced to the lowest level ... family ties will extend no further than the immediate bonds of marriage. Most plants and herbs will be tiny, and all trees will appear like dwarf ... trees. Clouds will be full of lightning, homes will be devoid of piety, and all human beings will have become like asses. At that time, the Supreme Personality of Godhead will appear on the earth. Acting with the power of pure spiritual goodness, He will rescue eternal religion.... After all the impostor kings have been killed, the residents of the cities and towns will feel the breezes carrying the most sacred fragrance of the sandalwood paste and other decorations of Lord Vasudeva, and their minds will thereby become transcendentally pure. When Lord Vasudeva, the Supreme Personality of Godhead, appears in their hearts in His transcendental form of goodness, the remaining citizens will abundantly repopulate the earth." This will take place about 427,000 years from now. At that time, another Satya Yuga will begin.

Among all the understandings of the devolution concept, the one related to the question of human origins is the most important for this book. Although I have used modern scientific evidence to draw attention to the Vedic account of human origins, I have not used such evidence to try to prove the Vedic account. The Vedic account, as divine revelation, has its own epistemological certainty, and is, in that respect, in no need of proof. In fact, the Vedic account, accepted on its own terms, can provide a means for evaluating the sometimes contradictory body of evidence provided by material science, and for evaluating the historical processes by which certain categories of this body of evidence have been privileged over others. It turns out that the entire body of scientific evidence related to the question of human origins can be evaluated in such a way that it does not contradict the Vedic account, and, indeed, is quite consistent with it. My thought in writing this book was that if the Vedic account of human origins were to be accepted as true, then there should be some correspondence between that account and the evidence available to us through our senses. I have shown that such a correspondence does exist, and my hope is that this should generate interest in the Vedic literatures among scientists and the general public.

If, following the Vedic account, we accept that humans, and other living things, have by a process of devolution come down from an original state of pure consciousness, in connection with the supreme conscious self, God, then we should become interested in what can be called re-evolution, the process of returning to that original state. The Vedic literature provides a range of techniques for transforming consciousness for this purpose. In the present age, the most highly recommended technique is the process of mantra meditation, specifically meditation on mantras composed of names of God. Almost every religious tradition in the world's history recommends such meditation. Such meditation is best practiced under the guidance of a perfected teacher (spiritual master). I myself began to practice meditating upon the Hare Krishna mantra, composed of Sanskrit names for God, under the guidance of my spiritual master Bhaktivedanta Swami Prabhupada. My studies of human origins and antiquity have encouraged me to take up the actual purpose of human existence, the transformation of materially covered consciousness to pure consciousness harmonized with the supreme conscious self, Krishna, the reservoir of pleasure.

Om Tat Sat

BIBLIOGRAPHY

- Unless otherwise noted in the text, quotations from entries followed by (*) have been translated into English by Michael Cremo.
- HRAF stands for Human Relations Area File.

Adler, T. (1995) Lineage of Y Chromosome boosts Eve theory. *Science News, 147*: 326.

Agnellet, Michel (1958) *I Accept These Facts: The Lourdes Cures Examined.* London, Max Parrish.

Alberts, B., Bray, D., Lewis, J., Raff, M., Roberts, R. and Watson, J. D. (1994) *Molecular Biology of the Cell.* 3rd edition. New York, Garland.

Ameghino, Florentino (1909) Le Diprothomo platensis, un précurseur de l'homme du pliocène inférieur de Buenos Aires. *Anales del Museo Nacional de Historia Natural de Buenos Aires, 19:* 107–209. (*)

Anderson, R. V. V. (1927) Tertiary stratigraphy and orogeny of the northern Punjab. *Bulletin of the Geological Society of America, 38:* 665–720.

Anderson, S., Bankier, A. T., Barrell, B. G., de Bruijn, M. H. L., Coulson, A. R., Drouin, J., Eperson, I. C., Nierlich, D. P., Roe, B. A., Sanger, F., Schreier, P. H., Smith, A. J. H., Staden, R. and Young, I. G. (1981) Sequence and organization of the human mitochondrial genome. *Nature, 290*: 457–465.

Anyon, R., Ferguson, T. J., Jackson, L., and Lane, L. (1996) Native American oral traditions and archaeology. *American Archaeological Bulletin, 14(2):* 14–16.

Arthur, W. (1987) *Theories of Life.* London, Pelican.

Asimov, Isaac (1982) *Asimov's Biographical Encyclopedia of Science and Technology.* 2nd revised edition. Garden City, New Jersey, Doubleday.

Astin, John A., Harkness, Elaine and Ernst, Edzard (2000) The efficacy of "Distant Healing": A systematic review of randomized trials. *Annals of Internal Medicine, 132(11)* (June 6): 903–911.

Ayres, W. O. (1882) The ancient man of Calaveras. *American Naturalist, 25(2):* 845–854.

Baker, D. M., Lillie, R. J., Yeats, R. S., Johnson, G. D., Yousuf, M., Zamin, A. S. H. (1988) Development of the Himalayan frontal thrust zone: Salt Range, Pakistan. *Geology, 16:* 3–7.

Ballou, W. H. (1922) Mystery of the petrified 'shoe sole' 5,000,000 years old. *American Weekly* section of the *New York Sunday American,* October 8, p. 2.

Barrett, Sir William F. (1918) *On the Threshold of the Unseen.* New York, E. P. Dutton.

Barrow, John D. and Tipler, Frank J. (1996) *The Cosmological Anthropic Principle.* Oxford, Oxford University Press.

Barry, J. (1968) General and comparative study of the psychokinetic effect on a fungus culture. *Journal of Parapsychology, 32:* 237–43.

Barth, G. (1853) Adolphe Didier's clairvoyance. *The Zoist, X* (January): 405–410.

Batchelor, John (1927) *Ainu Life and Lore; Echoes of a Departing Race.* Tokyo, Kyobunkwan. HRAF AB6 Ainu No. 7, p. 115.

Beam, Alex (1995) Harvard takes 'no adverse action' on UFO researcher. *The Boston Globe,* August 3, pp. 1, 22.

Becker, George F. (1891) Antiquities from under Tuolumne Table Mountain in California. *Bulletin of the Geological Society of America, 2:* 189–200.

Behe, Michael (1994) Experimental support for regarding functional classes of proteins to be highly isolated from each other. In Buell, J. and Hearn, G., eds. *Darwinism: Science or Philosophy.* Dallas, Foundation for Thought and Ethics, pp. 60–71.

Behe, Michael (1996) *Darwin's Black Box: The Biochemical Challenge to Evolution.* New York, Free Press.

Behe, Michael J. (1998) Intelligent design theory as a tool for analyzing biochemical systems. In Dembski, William A., ed. *Mere Creation: Science, Faith, and Intelligent Design.* Downers Grove, Illinois, Intervarsity Press, pp. 177–194.

Beloff, J. (1993) *Parapsychology: A Concise History.* London, Athlone Press.

Bem, D. J. (1996) The ganzfeld: A procedure for obtaining replicable evidence for an anomalous process of information transfer. In *Consciousness Research Abstracts. Toward A Science of Consciousness 1996 "Tucson II"*. pp. 163–164.

Benor D. (1990) Survey of spiritual healing research. *Complementary Medical Research, 4*: 9–33.

Berger, Arthur S. (1991) *The Encyclopedia of Parapsychology and Psychical Research*. New York, Paragon House.

Berglund, Axel-Ivar (1976) *Zulu Thought: Patterns and Symbolism*. Uppsala, Sweden, Swedish Institute of Missionary Research in Cooperation with David Philip, Publisher. HRAF FX20 Zulu, Doc # 8.

Bertrand, P. M. E. (1868) Crane et ossements trouvés dans une carrière de l'avenue de Clichy. *Bulletins de la Société d'Anthropologie de Paris (Series 2), 3:* 329–335. (*)

Bertrin, Georges (1908) *Lourdes: A History of Its Apparitions and Cures*. Translated by Mrs. Philip Gibbs. Vol. 13. International Catholic Library, xv. London, K. Paul, Trench, Trübner & Co.

Bhagavad-gita As It Is (1986) Sanskrit text, Roman transliteration, English equivalents; translated with elaborate purports by Bhaktivedanta Swami Prabhupada. Los Angeles, Bhaktivedanta Book Trust.

Bhaktivinoda Thakura (1987) *Sri Chaitanya Mahaprabhu: His Life and Precepts*. New York, Gaudiya Press.

Bishop, Isabella Lucy (Bird) (1898) *Korea and Her Neighbors: A Narrative of Travel, with an Account of the Recent Vicissitudes and Present Position of the Country*. New York, F. H. Revell. HRAF AA1 Korea, No. 46, p. 421.

Blackmore, Susan J. (1982*) Beyond the Body: An Investigation of Out-of-Body Experiences*. Chicago, Academy Chicago Publishers.

Blackmore, Susan (1993) *Dying to Live: Near-Death Experiences*. Buffalo, Prometheus Books.

Bodenstein, W. A. and Raum, Otto F. (1960) A present day Zulu philosopher. *Africa, 30:* 166–180. HRAF FX20 Zulu, Doc # 27.

Boissarie, Prosper Gustave (1933) *Healing at Lourdes; From the French of Dr. Boissarie*. Baltimore, The John Murphy Company.

Boman, Eric (1921) Los vestigios de industria humana encontrados en Miramar (Republica Argentina) y attribuidos a la época terciaria. *Revista Chilena de Historia y Geografía, 49(43):* 330–352. (*)

Bonnette, Dennis (2001) *Origin of the Human Species.* Studies in the History of Western Philosophy. Value Inquiry Book Series, no. 106. Edited by Peter A. Redpath. Amsterdam-Atlanta, Georgia, Editions Rodopi.

Bourguignon, Erika, ed. (1973) *Religion, Altered States of Consciousness, and Social Change.* Columbus, Ohio State University Press.

Bower, Bruce (1994) Scientists peer into mind's psi. *Science News, 145(5):* 68.

Bower, Bruce (2000a) 'Y guy' steps into human-evolution debate. *Science News, 158*: 295.

Bower, Bruce (2000b) Salvaged DNA adds to Neandertals' mystique. *Science News, 157*: 213.

Bower, Bruce (2000c) Gene test probes Neandertal origins. *Science News, 158*: 21.

Bower, Bruce (2001) Gene, fossil data back diverse human roots. *Science News, 159*: 21.

Bradley, Walter L. (1998) Nature: Designed or designoid. In Dembski, William A., ed. *Mere Creation: Science, Faith, and Intelligent Design.* Downers Grove, Illinois, Intervarsity Press, pp. 33–50.

Breguet, G., Butler, R., Butler-Briunner, E. and Sanchez-Mazas, A. (1990) A worldwide population study of the Ag-system haplotypes, a genetic polymorphism of a human low-density lipoprotein. *American Journal of Human Genetics, 46*: 502–517.

Brooks, Rodney (2001) The relationship between matter and life. *Nature, 409* (January 18): 409–411.

Broughton, Richard (1991) *Parapsychology: The Controversial Science.* New York, Ballantine Books.

Brown, F., Harris, J., Leakey, R., and Walker, A. (1985) Early *Homo erectus* skeleton from west Lake Turkana, Kenya. *Nature, 316*: 788–793.

Brydon, J. (1886) Maternal impressions. *British Medical Journal, i:* 670.

Burkhardt, Valentine Rodolphe (1954) *Chinese Creeds and Customs.* Hong Kong, South China Morning Post. HRAF AF1 China, Doc # 55.

Burt, Harold (2000) *Flying Saucers 101.* Los Angeles, UFO Magazine.

Butler, R. W. H., Coward, M. P., Harwood, G. M., and Knipe, R. J. (1987)

Salt control on thrust geometry, structural style and gravitational collapse along the Himalayan Mountain Front in the Salt Range of Northern Pakistan. In Lerche, I., and O'Brian, J. J., eds. *Dynamical Geology of Salt and Related Structures.* Orlando, Academic Press, pp. 339–418.

Callaway, Henry (1870) *The Religious System of the Amazulu. Izinyanga Zokubula; or Divination as Existing Among the Amazulu, in Their Own Words.* London, Trübner & Co. HRAF FX20 Zulu, Doc #12.

Cann, R. L., Stoneking, M., and Wilson, A. C. (1987) Mitochondrial DNA and human evolution. *Nature, 325:* 31–36.

Carrington, Hereward (1931) *The Story of Psychic Science.* New York, Ives Washburn.

Carter, Brandon (1974) Large number coincidences and the anthropic principle in cosmology. In M. S. Longair, ed. *Confrontation of Cosmological Theories with Observational Data.* Dordrecht, Reidel, pp. 291–298.

Chaitanya Charitamrita—see *Sri Caitanya-caritamrta.*

Chamberlain, D. B. (1988) *Babies Remember Birth: And Other Extraordinary Scientific Discoveries About the Mind and Personality of Your Newborn.* Los Angeles, Tarcher.

Chamberlain, D. B. (1990) The expanding boundaries of memory. *Pre- and Peri-Natal Psychology Journal, 4(3):* 171–189.

Chen, Jian (1990) Australopithecus in China. *China Today, 39(8):* 17–18.

Choffat, Paul (1884) Excursion à Otta. *Congrès International d'Anthropologie et d'Archaéologie Préhistoriques, Lisbon 1880, Compte Rendu,* pp. 61–67. (*)

Christie, W. A. K. (1914) Notes on the salt deposits of the Cis-Indus Salt Range. *Records of the Geological Survey of India, 44:* 241–264.

Clark, Charles Allen (1932) *Religions of Old Korea.* New York, Fleming H. Revell. HRAF A11 Korea.

Clark, Jerome (1998) *The UFO Encyclopedia.* 2nd edition. 2 vols. Detroit, Omnigraphics.

Clark, Kimberly (1982) Clinical interventions with near-death experiences. In Gregson, B. and Flynn, C. P., eds. *The Near Death Experience.* Springfield, Illinois, Charles C. Thomas, pp. 242–255.

Coates, J., Crookshank, H., Gee, E. R., Ghost, P. K., Lehner, E., and

Pinfold, E. S. (1945) Age of the Saline Series in the Punjab Salt Range. *Nature, 155:* 266–277.

Cobo, Bernabé (1893) *Historia del Nuevo Mundo* [History of the New World]. Vol. 4. Edited by Don Marcos Jiménez de la Espada. Sevilla, Sociedad de Bibliofilos Andaluces. HRAF SE13 Inca, Doc # 4.

Coelho, Ray Galvao de Andrade (1955) *The Black Carib of Honduras: A Study in Acculturation.* Ann Arbor, University Microfilms [0013076, 1989 copy]. HRAF SA12 Garifuna, Doc # 8.

COMETA (1999) *UFOs and Defense: What Should We Prepare For?* Levallois-Perret, G. S. Presse Communication.

Condon, Edward U. (1969) *Scientific Study of Unidentified Flying Objects.* Edited by D. S. Gillmor. New York, E. P. Dutton.

Conroy, Ed (1989) *Report on Communion.* New York, William Morrow.

Conversations with Srila Prabhupada (1988–1991) Los Angeles, Bhakti-vedanta Book Trust.

Cornet, B. (1989) The reproductive morphology and biology of *Sanmiguela lewisii,* and its bearing on angiosperm evolution in the Late Triassic. *Evolutionary Trends in Plants, 3(1):* 25–51.

Cornet, B. (1993) Dicot-like leaf and flowers from the Late Triassic Tropical Newark Supergroup Rift Zone, U.S.A. *Modern Geology, 19:* 81–99.

Corso, Philip J. (1997) *The Day After Roswell.* New York, Simon and Schuster.

Cotter, G. de P. (1931) Some recent advances in the geology of North-West India. Presidential address, section of geology. *Proceedings of the Eighteenth Indian Science Congress, Nagpur, 1931 (Third Circuit).* Calcutta, Asiatic Society of Bengal, pp. 293–306.

Cotter, G. de P. (1933) The geology of the part of the Attock District west of longitude 72° 45' east. *Memoirs of the Geological Survey of India, 55(2).* Calcutta, Geological Survey of India.

Coxwell, C. Fillingham (1925) *Siberian and Other Folk-tales.* London, C. W. Daniel. HRAF RX2 Gilyak, Doc # 10.

Cranston, Ruth (1955) *The Miracle of Lourdes.* New York, McGraw-Hill.

Creighton, Gordon (1967) Three more Brazilian cases. *Flying Saucer Review, 13(3)* (May/June): 5–8.

Creighton, Gordon (1969) The amazing case of Antonio Villas Boas. In Michel, Aimé. *The Humanoids.* Edited by Charles Bowen. Chicago, Henry Company, pp. 200–238.

Cremo, Michael A. and Thompson, Richard L. (1993) *Forbidden Archeology: The Hidden History of the Human Race.* San Diego, Govardhan Hill Publishing.

Crookes, Sir William (1871a) Experimental investigation of a new force. *Quarterly Journal of Science,* July 1.

Crookes, Sir William (1871b) Some further investigations on psychic force. *Quarterly Journal of Science,* Oct. 1.

Crookes, Sir William (1874). *Researches in the Phenomena of Spiritualism.* London, J. Burns.

Crookes, Sir William (1889) Notes of séances with D. D. Home. *Proceedings of the Society for Psychical Research, VI*: 98–127.

Culotta, E. (1999) A new human ancestor? *Science, 284*: 572–573.

Dabney, W. C. (1890) Maternal impressions. In Keating, J. M., ed. *Cyclopaedia of the Diseases of Children.* Vol. 1. Philadelphia, J. B. Lippincott, pp. 191–216.

D'Arcy, Kim (2001) Research body will shed more light on near death experiences. In sotONLINE [daily electronic news and events service] Southampton, University of Southampton, 2001[cited 16 February 2001]. Available from http://www.soton ac.uk/~pubaffrs/0128.htm.

Darrah, W. C. (1937) Spores of Cambrian plants. *Science, 86:* 154–155.

Darwin, Charles R. (1936) *On the Origin of Species.* Reprint. New York, Modern Library; (1859) London, John Murray.

Darwin, Charles R. (1988) *The Origin of Species.* 6th edition. New York, New York University Press, p. 151; (1872) London, John Murray.

Darwin, Francis, ed. (1887) *Life and Letters of Charles Darwin.* Vol. II. London, John Murray.

Davidson, Eric (1991) Spatial mechanisms of gene regulation in metazoan embryos. *Development, 113*: 1–26.

Dawkins, Richard (1986) *The Blind Watchmaker.* New York, Norton.

Day, Clarence Burton (1940) *Chinese Peasant Cults.* Shanghai, Kelly and Walsh. HRAF AF1 China, Doc. # 27.

Day, M. H., and Molleson, T. (1973) The Trinil femora. *Symposia of the*

Society for the Study of Human Biology, 2: 127–154.

De Groot, Jan Jakob Maria (1912) *Religion in China; Universism: A Key to the Study of Taoism and Confucianism.* New York, Putnam. HRAF AF1 China, Doc. # 11.

De Laguna, Frederica (1954) Tlingit ideas about the individual. *Southwestern Journal of Anthropology, 10*: 172–191. HRAF NA12 Tlingit, Doc #5.

De Laguna, Frederica (1972) *Under Mount Saint Elias: The History and Culture of the Yakutat Tlingit.* Washington, Smithsonian Institution Press.

De Molina, Christoval (1873) The fables and rites of the Yncas. In Markham, Clements R., trans. and ed. *Narratives of the Rites and Laws of the Yncas.* London, Hakluyt Society, pp. 1–64. HRAF SE13 Inca, Doc #8.

De Mortillet, G. (1883) *Le Préhistorique.* Paris, C. Reinwald. (*)

De Quatrefages, Armand (1884) *Hommes Fossiles et Hommes Sauvages.* Paris, B. Baillière. (*)

Deo Gratias, Rev. [D. Perrando] (1873) Sur l'homme tertiaire de Savone. *Congrès International d'Anthropologie et d'Archéologie Préhistoriques, Bologna 1871, Compte Rendu*, pp. 417–420. (*)

Devlin, T. M. (1992) *Textbook of Biochemistry.* New York, Wiley-Liss, pp. 938–954.

Didier, Alexis (1856) *Le Sommeil Magnétique Expliqué par le Somnambule Alexis en l'État de Lucidité.* Paris.

Dimroth, E. and Kimberley, M. M. (1976) Pre-Cambrian atmospheric oxygen: Evidence in sedimentary distribution of carbon, sulfur, uranium, and iron. *Canadian Journal of Earth Sciences, 13*: 1161–1185.

Dingwall, Eric J., ed. (1967) *Abnormal Hypnotic Phenomena: A Survey of Nineteenth Century Cases.* Vol I. France, J. & A. Churchill.

Disraeli, Benjamin (1852) *Lord George Bentinck: A Political Biography.* 2nd edition. London, Colburn.

Disraeli, Benjamin (1927) *Tancred.* Vol. 10 of *Novels and Tales of Benjamin Disraeli, 1st Earl of Beaconsfield.* Bradenham edition. London, Peter Davies; (1847) Philadelphia, Carey & Hart.

Dobyns, York H. (1996) Selection versus influence revisited. New methods and conclusions. *Journal of Scientific Exploration, 10(2):* 253–268.

Dobzhansky, Theodosius (1972) Darwinian evolution and the problem of extraterrestrial life. *Perspectives in Biology and Medicine, 15(2):* 157–175.

Dockstader, Frederick J. (1985) *The Kachina and the White Man: The Influences of White Culture on the Hopi Kachina Cult.* Albuquerque, University of New Mexico Press.

Doré, Henry (1922) *Researches into Chinese Superstitions.* 10 Vols. Translated by M. Kennelly. Shanghai', Usewei Printing Press.

Dossey, Larry (1993) *Healing Words: The Power of Prayer and the Practice of Medicine.* San Francisco, Harper-San Francisco.

Dyson, Freeman (1985) *Origins of Life.* Cambridge, Cambridge University Press.

Eigen, Manfred and Schuster, P. (1977) The hypercycle: A principle of natural self-organization. Part A: Emergence of the hypercycle. *Naturwissenschaften, 64:* 541–565.

Eigen, Manfred and Schuster, P. (1978a) The hypercycle: A principle of natural self-organization. Part B: The abstract hypercycle. *Naturwissenschaften, 65:* 7–41.

Eigen, Manfred and Schuster, P. (1978b) The hypercycle: A principle of natural self-organization. Part C: The realistic hypercycle. *Naturwissenschaften, 65:* 341–369.

Eisenberg, D. M., Davis, R. B., Ettner, S. L., Appel, S., Wilkey, S., Van Rompay, M., et al. (1998) Trends in alternative medicine use in the United States, 1990–1997: Results of a follow-up national survey. *Journal of the American Medical Association, 280:* 1569–75.

Eliade, Mircea (1967) *From Primitives to Zen: A Thematic Sourcebook of the History of Religion.* New York, Harper and Row.

Elinson, Richard (1987) Changes in developmental patterns: Embryos of amphibians with large eggs. In Raff, R. A. and Raff, E. C., eds. *Development as an Evolutionary Process.* New York, Alan Liss, pp. 1–21.

Elkin, A. P. (1964) *The Australian Aborigines.* Garden City, New York, Anchor Books.

Emmons, George Thornton (1991) *The Tlingit Indians.* Seattle, University of Washington Press.

Eschenmoser, Albert (1999) Chemical etiology of nucleic acid structure. *Science,* 284: 2118–2124.

Esdaile, James (1846) *Mesmerism in India, and Its Practical Application in Surgery and Medicine.* London, Longman, Brown, Green, and Longmans.

Esdaile, James (1852) *Natural and Mesmeric Clairvoyance, With the Practical Application of Mesmerism in Surgery and Medicine.* London, H. Baillière.

Estrade, Jean Baptiste (1958) *The Appearances of the Blessed Virgin Mary at the Grotto of Lourdes.* Translated by J. H. Le Breton Girolestone. Lourdes, Imprimerie de la Grotte.

Ewing, Katherine P. (1994) Dreams from a saint: Anthropological atheism and the temptation to believe. *American Anthropologist, 94(3):* 571–583.

Feder, K. (1994) *Forbidden Archeology.* Book review. *Geoarchaeology, 9(4):* 337–340.

Fermor, L. L. (1935) General report of the Geological Survey of India for the year 1934. *Records of the Geological Survey of India, 69(1):* 1–108.

Flammarion, Camille (1909) *Mysterious Psychic Forces: An Account of the Author's Investigations in Psychical Research, Together with Those of Other European Savants.* Boston, Small, Maynard and Company.

Flammarion, Camille (1922) *Death and Its Mystery: At the Moment of Death —Manifestations and Apparitions of the Dying.* Vol. II, *"Doubles;" Phenomena of Occultism.* Translated by Latrobe Carroll. New York, The Century Co.

Flammarion, Camille (1923) *Death and Its Mystery: After Death—Manifestations and Apparitions of the Dead.* Vol. III, *The Soul after Death.* Translated by Latrobe Carroll. New York, The Century Co.

Foote, Michael and Gould, Stephen J. (1992) Cambrian and recent morphological disparity. *Science, 258:* 1816.

Fos, M., Dominguez, M. A., Latorre, A. and Moya, M. (1990) Mitochondrial DNA evolution in experimental populations of *Drosophila subobscura. Proceedings of the National Academy of Sciences, USA, 87*: 4198–4201.

Foster, Byron (1986) *Heart Drum: Spirit Possession in the Communities of Belize.* Belize, Cubola Productions. HRAF SA12 Garifuna, Doc # 6.

Fowler, Raymond (1979) *The Andreasson Affair.* Englewood Cliffs, New Jersey, Prentice Hall.

Fowler, Raymond (1981) *Casebook of a UFO Investigator.* Englewood Cliffs, New Jersey, Prentice Hall.

Fowler, Raymond (1990) *The Watchers.* New York, Bantam Books.

Fox, Cyril S. (1928) A contribution to the geology of the Punjab Salt Range. *Records of the Geological Survey of India, (2):* 147–179.

Franzen, J. L. (1985) Asian australopithecines? In Delson, E., ed. *Hominid Evolution: Past, Present and Future.* New York, Alan R. Liss, pp. 253–263.

Frayer, David W., Wolpoff, Milford H., Thorne, Alan G., Smith, Fred H. and Pope, Geoffrey G. (1993) Theories of modern human origins: The paleontological test. *American Anthropologist, 95(1)*: 14–50.

Gallup, George H., Jr., and Newport, Frank (1990) The paranormal: Belief in psychic and paranormal phenomena widespread among Americans. *The Gallup Poll News Service, 55(13)* (Monday, August 6): 1–7.

Garcilaso de la Vega, el Inca (1869–1871) *First Part of the Royal Commentaries of the Yncas.* Translated and edited by Clements R. Markham. 2 vols. London, Hakluyt Society. HRAF SE13 Inca, Doc # 3.

Gauld, Alan (1968) *The Founders of Psychical Research.* London, Routledge & Kegan Paul.

Gauld, Alan and Cornell, A. D. (1979) *Poltergeists.* London, Routledge & Kegan Paul.

Gee, E. R. (1934) The Saline Series of North-western India. *Current Science, 2:* 460–463.

Gee, E. R. (1945) The age of the Saline Series of the Punjab and of Kohat. *Proceedings of the National Academy of Sciences, India. Section B, 14:* 269–310.

Ghosh, A. K., and Bose, A. (1947) Occurrence of microflora in the Salt Pseudomorph Beds, Salt Range, Punjab. *Nature, 160:* 796–797.

Ghosh, A. K., and Bose, A. (1950a) Microfossils from the Cambrian strata of the Salt Range, Punjab. *Transactions of the Bose Research Institute Calcutta, 18:* 71–78.

Ghosh, A. K., and Bose, A. (1950b) Microfossils from the Vindhyans. *Science and Culture, 15:* 330–331.

Ghosh, A. K., and Bose, A. (1951a) Recovery of vascular flora from the Cambrian of Kashmir. *Proceedings of the Indian Science Congress, Part III,* pp. 127–128.

Ghosh, A. K., and Bose, A. (1951b) Evidence bearing on the age of the Saline Series in the Salt Range of the Punjab. *Geological Magazine, 88:* 129–132.

Ghosh, A. K., and Bose, A. (1952) Spores and tracheids from the Cambrian of Kashmir. *Nature, 169:* 1056–1057.

Ghosh, A. K., Sen, J., and Bose, A. (1948) Age of the Saline Series in the Salt Range of the Punjab. *Proceedings of the Indian Science Congress, Part III,* p. 145.

Gibbons, Ann (2001) Modern men trace ancestry to African migrants. *Science, 292:* 1051–1052.

Gilbert, S. (1991) *Developmental Biology.* 3rd edition. Sunderland, Mass., Sinauer.

Gingerich, P. (1985) Nonlinear molecular clocks and ape-human divergence times. In Tobias, P. V., ed. *Hominid Evolution: Past, Present, and Future.* New York, Alan R. Liss, pp. 411–416.

Griffin, David Ray (1997) *Parapsychology, Philosophy and Spirituality: A Postmodern Exploration.* Albany, State University of New York Press.

Griffis, William Elliot (1882) *Corea: The Hermit Nation.* New York, Charles Scribner's Sons. HRAF AA1 Korea.

Grinager, Patricia (1999) *Uncommon Lives: My Lifelong Friendship with Margaret Mead.* New York, Rowman & Littlefield Publishers, Inc.

Grof, S. (1985) *Beyond the Brain: Birth, Death and Transcendence in Psychotherapy.* Albany, State University of New York Press.

Gurney, Edmund, Myers, Frederic W. H. and Podmore, Frank. (1886) *Phantasms of the Living.* 1st edition. Vol. 1. London, Rooms of the Society for Psychical Research, Trübner and Co.

Haeckel, Ernst (1866) *Generelle Morphologie der Organismen.* Vol. 1. Berlin, G. Reimer.

Haeckel, Ernst (1892) *The History of Creation.* Translated by E. R. Lankester. London, Trübner and Co.

Haeckel, Ernst (1905) *The Wonder of Life.* Translated by J. McCabe. London, Watts.

Haffent, John (1961) *Meet the Witnesses.* Washington, New Jersey, Ave Maria Institute.

Halder, G., Callaerts, P. and Gehring, W. J. (1995) Induction of ectopic eyes by targeted expression of *eyeless* gene in Drosophilia. *Science, 267*: 1788–1792.

Hall, Richard H., ed. (1964) *The UFO Evidence.* Washington, D.C., National Investigating Committee on Aerial Phenomena.

Hallowell, A. Irving (1955) *Culture and Experience.* Philadelphia, University of Pennsylvania Press. HRAF NG6 Ojibwa, Doc # 21.

Hammer, M. F., Spurdle, A. B., Karafet, T., Bonner, M. R., Wood, E. T., Novelletto, A., Malaspina, P., Mitchell, R. J., Horal, S., Jenkins, T. et al. (1997) The geographic distribution of human Y chromosome variation. *Genetics, 145(3):* 787–805.

Hammer, M. F., Karafet, T., Rasayanagam, A., Wood, E. T., Jenkins, T., Griffiths, R. C., Templeton, A. R. and Zegura, S. L. (1998) Out of Africa and back again: Nested cladistic analysis of human Y chromosome variation. *Molecular Biology and Evolution, 15(4):* 427–441.

Hammond, W. A. (1868) On the influence of the maternal mind over the offspring during pregnancy and lactation. *Quarterly Journal of Psychological Medicine and Medical Jurisprudence, 2*: 1–28.

Hancock, Ann Marie (1998) *Be A Light: Miracles at Medjugorje.* Westchester, Pennsylvania, Whitford Press.

Handy, E. S. Craighill (1927) *Polynesian Religion.* Honolulu, Bernice P. Bishop Museum, Bulletin 34.

Haraldsson, Erlendur and Stevenson, Ian (1975a) A communicator of the 'drop-in' type in Iceland. The case of Runolfur Runolfsson. *Journal of the American Society for Psychical Research, 69:* 33–59.

Haraldsson, Erlendur and Stevenson, Ian (1975b) A communicator of the 'drop-in' type in Iceland. The case of Gudni Magnusson. *Journal of the American Society for Psychical Research, 69*: 245–261.

Harrison, Edward R. (1928) *Harrison of Ightham*. London, Oxford University Press.

Hart, Hornell (1954) ESP projection: Spontaneous cases and the experimental method. *Journal of the American Society for Psychical Research, 48(4)* (October): 121–146.

Hawes, Charles H. (1903) *In the Uttermost East*. London, Harper and Brothers. HRAF RX2 Gilyak, Doc # 9.

Henderson, Richard Neal (1972) *The King in Every Man; Evolutionary Trends in Onitsha Ibo Society and Culture*. New Haven, Yale University Press. HRAF FF26 Igbo, Doc # 22.

Henry, Richard C. (1988) UFOs and NASA. *Journal of Scientific Explanation, 2(2):* 93–142.

Hodder, Ian (1997) Always momentary, fluid, and flexible: Toward a reflexive excavation methodology. *Antiquity, 71*: 691–700.

Holland, T. H. (1903) *General Report on the Work Carried Out by the Geological Survey of India for the Year 1902/03*. Calcutta, Geological Survey of India.

Holmes, William H. (1899) Review of the evidence relating to auriferous gravel man in California. *Smithsonian Institution Annual Report 1898–1899*, pp. 419–472.

Home, D. D. (1879) *Lights and Shadows of Spiritualism*. New York, G. W. Carleton.

Honorton, C. (1985) Meta-analysis of psi ganzfeld research: A response to Hyman. *Journal of Parapsychology, 49:* 51–91.

Honorton, C. and Schechter, E. I. (1987) Ganzfeld target retrieval with an automated testing system: Model for initial ganzfeld success. In Weiner, D. B. and Nelson, R. D. *Research in Parapsychology 1986*. Metuchen, New Jersey, Scarecrow Press, pp. 36–39.

Honorton, C., Berger, R. E., Vargolis, M. P., Quant, M., Derr, P., Schechter, E. I. and Ferrari, D. C. (1990) Psi communication in the ganzfeld. Experiments with an automated testing system and a comparison with a meta-analysis of earlier studies. *Journal of Parapsychology, 54:* 99–139.

Hopkins, Budd (1981) *Missing Time*. New York, Ballantine Books.

Hopkins, Budd (1987) *Intruders*. New York, Ballantine Books.

Howard, Jane (1984) *Margaret Mead: A Life.* New York, Simon and Schuster.

Hrdlička, Ales (1912) *Early Man in South America.* Washington, D.C., Smithsonian Institution.

Hulbert, Homer B. (1906) *The Passing of Korea.* New York, Doubleday. HRAF AA1 Korea.

Hultkrantz, Ake (1953) *Conceptions of the Soul among North American Indians.* Monograph Series, 1. Stockholm, The Ethnographical Museum of Sweden.

Hurwic, Anna (1995) *Pierre Curie.* Translated by Lilananda Dasa and Joseph Cudnik. Paris, Flammarion.

Huxley, Thomas H. (1869) On the physical basis of life. *The Fortnightly Review, 5*: 129–145.

Hyman, Ray (1985a) Parapsychological research: A tutorial review and critical appraisal. *Proceedings of the IEEE, 74:* 823–849.

Hyman, Ray (1985b) The ganzfeld psi experiment: A critical appraisal. *Journal of Parapsychology, 49:* 3–49.

Hyman, Ray and Honorton, C. (1986). A joint communiqué: The psi ganzfeld controversy. *Journal of Parapsychology, 50*: 351–364.

Hyman, Ray (1991) Comment. *Statistical Science, 6:* 389–392.

Hyman, Ray (1996) Evaluation of a program on anomalous mental phenomena. *Journal of Scientific Exploration, 10*: 31–58.

Hynek, J. Allen (1972a) *The UFO Experience.* Chicago, Henry Regnery Company.

Hynek, J. Allen (1972b) Twenty-one years of UFO reports. In Sagan, Carl, and Page, Thornton, eds. *UFOs—A Scientific Debate.* Ithaca, Cornell University Press, pp. 37–51.

Hynek, J. Allen (1978) UFOs as a space-time singularity. In Andrus, Walter H., Jr., ed. *MUFON 1978 UFO Symposium Proceedings.* Sequin, Texas, Mutual UFO Network, pp. 113–120.

Issel, Arthur (1868) Résumé des recherches concernant l'ancienneté de l'homme en Ligurie. *Congrès International d'Anthropologie et d'Archéologie Préhistoriques, Paris 1867, Compte Rendu,* pp. 75–89. (*)

Jacob, K, Jacob, C., and Shrivastava, R. N. (1953) Evidence for the existence of vascular land plants in the Cambrian. *Current Science, 22:* 34–36.

Jacobs, David M. (1992) *Secret Life.* New York, Simon and Schuster.

Jahn, Robert G. and Dunne, Brenda J. (1987) *Margins of Reality: The Role of Consciousness in the Physical World.* Orlando, Harcourt, Brace, Jovanovich.

James, William (1886–1889) Report of the committee on mediumistic phenomena. *Proceedings of the American Society for Psychical Research, 1:* 102ff.

James, William (1890) *The Principles of Psychology.* 2 vols. New York, H. Holt and Company.

James, William (1896) Address by the President. *Proceedings of the Society for Psychical Research* (London), *Part XX. XII* (June).

James, William (1897) *The Will to Believe and Other Essays in Popular Philosophy.* New York, Longmans, Green and Company.

James, William (1909) Report on Mrs. Piper's Hodgson-Control. *Proceedings of the American Society for Psychical Research, III.* In Murphy, Gardner and Ballou, Robert, O., eds. (1960) *William James on Psychical Research.* New York, Viking Press, pp. 115–210.

James, William (1911) *Memories and Studies.* New York, Longmans Green.

Jaumé, S. C. and Lillie, R. J. (1988) Mechanics of the Salt Range-Potwar Plateau, Pakistan: A fold-and-thrust belt underlain by evaporites. *Tectonics, 7:* 57–71.

Jenness, Diamond (1935) *The Ojibwa Indians of Parry Island: Their Social and Religious Life.* Ottawa, National Museum of Canada. HRAF NG6 Ojibwa, Doc # 1.

Jessup, M. K. (1973) *The Case for the UFO.* Garland, Texas, Uaro Manufacturing Company.

Jian, Gao, Xu, C., Wang, L. and Han, K. (1975) Australopithecine teeth associated with *Gigantopithecus. Vertebrata PalAsiatica, 13*: 81–87.

Johanson, Donald C. and Edey, M. A. (1981) *Lucy: The Beginnings of Humankind.* New York, Simon and Schuster.

Johanson, Donald C., Masao, F. T., Eck, G. G., White, T. D., Walter, R. C., Kimbel, W. H., Asfaw, B., Manega, P., Ndessokia, P., and Suwa, G. (1987) New partial skeleton of *Homo habilis* from Olduvai Gorge, Tanzania. *Nature, 327:* 205–207.

Johnston, Basil (1995) *The Manitous: The Spiritual World of the Ojibway.* New York, HarperCollins.

Joyce, Gerald F. and Orgel, Leslie E. (1993) Prospects for understanding the origin of the RNA world. In Gesteland, R. F. and Atkins, J. F., eds. *The RNA World.* Cold Spring Harbor, New York, Cold Spring Harbor Laboratory Press, p. 18.

Jung, Carl (1959) *Flying Saucers, A Modern Myth of Things Seen in the Skies.* New York, Harcourt Brace and Co.

Kan, Sergei (1989) *Symbolic Immortality: The Tlingit Potlatch of the Nineteenth Century.* Washington, Smithsonian Institution Press.

Kang, Younghill (1931) *The Grass Roof.* New York, Scribner. HRAF AA1 Korea.

Ke, Yuehai; Su, Bing; Song, Xiufeng; Lu, Daru; Chen, Lifeng; Li, Hongyu; Qi, Chunjian; Marzuki, Sangkot; Deka, Ranjan; Underhill, Peter; Xiao, Chunjie; Shriver, Mark; Lell, Jeff; Wallace, Douglas; Wells, R. Spencer; Seieistad, Mark; Oefner, Peter; Zhu, Dingliang; Jin, Jiazhong; Huang, Wei; Chakraborty, Ranajit; Chen, Zhu and Jin, Li (2001) African origin of modern humans in East Asia: A tale of 12,000 Y chromosomes. *Science, 292*: 1151–1153.

Keel, John A. (1969) The principle of transmorgification. *Flying Saucer Review, 15(4): 27–28, 31.*

Keith, A. (1928) *The Antiquity of Man.* Vol. 1. Philadelphia, J. B. Lippincott.

Kerr, R. (1980) Origin of life: New ingredients suggested. *Science, 210*: 42–43.

Kinietz, W. Vernon (1947) *Chippewa Village: The Story of Katikitegon.* Bloomfield Hills, Michigan, Cranbrook Press. HRAF NH6 Ojibwa, Doc #14.

Kirk, Geoffrey S. and Raven, J. E., trans. (1957) *The Presocratic Philosophers.* Cambridge, Cambridge University Press.

Knapp, Frances and Childe, Rheta Louise (1896) *The Thlinkets of Southeastern Alaska.* Chicago, Store & Kimball. HRAF NA12 Tlingit, Doc #9.

Kok, R. A., Taylor, J. A. and Bradley, W. L. (1988) A statistical examination of self-ordering of amino acids in proteins. *Origins of Life and Evolution of the Biosphere, 18:* 135–142.

Koken, E., and Noetling, F. (1903) Geologische Mittheilungen aus der Salt

Range. No. 1. Das permische Glacial. *Centralblatt für Mineralogie, Geologie, und Päleontologie,* 45–54.

Krause, Aurel (1956) *The Tlinget Indians: Results of a trip to the Northwest Coast of America and Bering Straits.* Translated by Erna Gunther. Seattle, University of Washington Press for the American Ethnological Society.

Krige, Eileen Jensen (1968) Girls' Puberty Songs and Their Relation to Fertility, Health, Morality and Religion Among the Zulus. *Africa, 38*: 173–198.

Krings, Matthias, Stone, Anne, Schmitz, Rolf W., Krainitzki, Heiki, Stoneking, Mark and Pääbo, Svante (1997) Neandertal DNA sequences and the origin of modern humans. *Cell, 90*: 19–30.

Laing, S. (1893) *Problems of the Future.* London, Chapman and Hall.

Lamb, David (1997) Communication with extraterrestrial intelligence: SETI and scientific methodology. In Ginev, D. and Cohen, R. S., eds. *Issues and Images in the Philosophy of Science.* Netherlands, Kluwer Academic Publishers, pp. 223–251.

Larusdottir, E. (1946) *Midillinn Hafsteinn Bjornsson* (The Medium Hafsteinn Bjornsson). Iceland, Nordri.

Latourette, Kenneth Scott (1934) *The Chinese: Their History and Culture.* Vol. 2. New York, Macmillan. HRAF AF1 China, Doc #34.

Layne, N. Meade (1950) *The Ether Ship and Its Solution.* Vista, California, Borderland Sciences Research Associates.

Leakey, Louis L. S. B. (1931) *The Stone Age Cultures of Kenya Colony.* Cambridge, Cambridge University.

Leakey, Louis L. S. B. (1960) *Adam's Ancestors.* 4th edition. New York, Harper & Row.

Leakey, Louis L. S. B. (1971) *Homo sapiens* in the Middle Pleistocene and the evidence of *Homo sapiens'* evolution. In Bordes, F., ed. *The Origin of Homo sapiens.* Paris, United Nations Educational, Scientific, and Cultural Organization, pp. 25–28.

Leakey, Mary (1979) Footprints in the ashes of time. *National Geographic, 155:* 446–457.

Leakey, Meave G., Spoor, F., Brown, F. H., Gathogo, P. N., Kiarie, C., Leakey, L. N. and McDougall, I. (2001) New hominin genus from eastern Africa shows diverse middle Pliocene lineages. *Nature, 410:* 433–440.

Lechler, A. (1933) *Das Rätsel von Konnersreuth im Lichte eines neues Falles von Stigmatisation.* Elbersfeld, Licht und Leben Verlag.

Leclerq, S. (1956) Evidence for vascular plants in the Cambrian. *Evolution, 10:* 109–114.

Lee, Thomas E. (1966) Untitled editorial note on the Sheguiandah site. *Anthropological Journal of Canada, 4(4):* 18–19.

Lemonick, Michael D. and Dorfman, Andrea (2001) One giant step for mankind. *Time,* July 23, pp. 54–61.

Lessa, William A. and Vogt, Evon Z. (1958) *Reader in Comparative Religion.* Evanston, Row, Peterson and Company.

Lessa, William A. and Vogt, Evon Z. (1965) *Reader in Comparative Religion,* 2nd edition. New York, Harper and Row.

Libet, B. (1994) A testable field theory of mind-brain interaction. *Journal of Consciousness Studies, 1(1):* 119–126.

Lindsay, Robert Bruce (1970) *Men of Physics: Lord Rayleigh—The Man and His Work.* New York, Pergamon Press.

Lloyd, Dan (1969) Let's take off our blinkers. *Flying Saucer Review, 15(1):* 9–11.

Lodge, Oliver J. (1916) *Raymond or Life and Death: With Examples of the Evidence for Survival of Memory and Affection after Death.* New York, George H. Doran Company.

Lovejoy, C. O., et al. (1993) The mtDNA common ancestor of modern humans was a member of *Homo erectus.* Manuscript in David W. Frayer's personal archives.

Luck, George (1985) *Arcana Mundi: Magic and the Occult in the Greek and Roman Worlds.* Translated by George Luck. Baltimore, Johns Hopkins University Press.

Macalister, R. A. S. (1921) *Textbook of European Archaeology.* Vol. 1, *Paleolithic Period.* Cambridge, Cambridge University.

Mack, John E. (1994) *Abduction: Human Encounters with Aliens.* New York, Charles Scribner's Sons.

Mack, John E. (1999) *Passport to the Cosmos: Human Transformation and Alien Encounters.* New York, Random House, Inc.

MacNair, Harley Farnsworth, ed. (1946) *China.* Berkeley, University of California Press. HRAF China AF1, Doc # 20.

MacNaughton, Robert D. (1989) *The Seventh Goswami: A Biography* of His Divine Grace Srila Saccidananda Bhaktivinoda Thakura. Mumbai, Sri Sri Sitaram Seva Trust.

MacRae, A. F., and Anderson, W. W. (1988) Evidence for non-neutrality and mitochondrial DNA haplotypes in *Drosophila subobscura. Genetics, 120*: 485–494.

Maddison, D. R. (1991) African origins of human mitochondrial DNA reexamined. *Systematic Zoology, 40*: 355–363.

Marchand, Alfred (1924) *The Facts of Lourdes and The Medical Bureau.* Translated by Dom Francis Izard. New York, Benziger Brothers.

Maria Lucia, Sister (1998) *Fatima in Lucia's Own Words.* Fatima, Secretariado dos Pastorhinos.

Markowitz, William (1980) Physics and metaphysics of unidentified flying objects. In Goldsmith, D., ed. *The Quest for Extraterrestrial Life.* Mill Valley, California, University Science Books, pp. 255–261.

Marks, Jonathan (1994) Blood will tell (won't it?): A century of molecular discourse in anthropological systematics. *American Journal of Physical Anthropology, 94*: 59–79.

Markzke, M. W. (1983) Joint function and grips of the *Australopithecus afarensis* hand, with special reference to the region of the capitate. *Journal of Human Evolution, 12:* 197–211.

May, E. C. (1995) AC technical trials: Inspiration for the target entropy concept. In Zingrone, N. L., ed. *Proceedings of Presented Papers, 38th Annual Parapsychological Association Convention.* Fairhaven, Massachusetts, The Parapsychological Association, pp. 193–211.

May, E. C. and Spottiswoode, S. J. P. (1996) Toward a physical interpretation of extrasensory perception. In *Consciousness Research Abstracts. Toward A Science of Consciousness 1996 "Tucson II,"* p. 164.

Maynard-Smith, John (1979) Hypercycles and the origin of life. *Nature, 280*: 445–446.

McClenon, J. (1982) Survey of elite scientists: Their attitudes toward ESP and parapsychology. *Journal of Parapsychology, 46*: 127–152.

McDonald, James E. (1967) UFOs: Greatest Scientific Problem of our Times. Paper presented at the annual meeting of the American Society of Newspaper Editors, 22 April, Washington, D.C.

McDougal, I. (2001) New hominin genus from eastern Africa shows diverse middle Pliocene lineages. *Nature, 410*: 433–440.

McDougall, J. W. and Khan, S. H. (1990) Strike-slip faulting in a foreland fold-thrust belt: The Kalabagh Fault and Western Salt Range, Pakistan. *Tectonics, 9:* 1061–1075.

McMoneagle, J. (1993) *Mind Trek.* Charlottesville, Hampton Roads.

Meacham, Standish (1970) *Lord Bishop; The Life of Samuel Wilberforce, 1805–1873.* Cambridge, Massachusetts, Harvard University Press.

Medhurst, R. G. & Goldney, K. M. (1972). *Crookes and the Spirit World. A Collection of Writings by or Concerning the Work of Sir William Crookes, O.M., F.R.S., in the Field of Psychical Research.* Souvenir Press, London.

Medlicott, H. B. and Blandford, W. T. (1879) *Manual of the Geology of India, Part 2.* Calcutta, Geological Survey of India.

Meek, Charles Kingsley (1970) *Law and Authority in a Nigerian Tribe; A Study in Indirect Rule.* New York, Barnes & Noble, Inc. HRAF FF26 Igbo, Doc # 8.

Meister, William J. (1968) Discovery of trilobite fossils in shod footprint of human in "Trilobite Bed"—a Cambrian formation, Antelope Springs, Utah. *Creation Research Quarterly, 5(3):* 97–102.

Melleville, Maximilien (1862) Foreign Intelligence. *The Geologist, 5:* 145–148.

Métraux, Alfred (1940) *Ethology of Easter Island.* Honolulu, Bernice P. Bishop Museum. HRAF OY2 Easter Islanders, Doc # 1.

Meyer, Stephen C. (1998) The explanatory power of design: DNA and the origin of information. In Dembski, William A., ed. *Mere Creation: Science, Faith, and Intelligent Design.* Downers Grove, Illinois, Intervarsity Press, pp. 113–147.

Middlemiss, C. S. (1891) Notes on the geology of the Salt Range, with a reconsidered theory of the origin and age of the Salt Marl. *Records of the Geological Survey of India, 24:* 19–42.

Miller, Stanley L. (1953) A production of amino acids under possible primitive earth conditions. *Science, 117*: 528–529.

Mini, John (2000) *The Aztec Virgin: The Secret Mystical Tradition of Our Lady of Guadalupe.* Sausalito, California, Trans-Hyperborean Institute of Science.

Mitchell, Edgar (1996) *The Way of the Explorer: An Apollo Astronaut's Journey Through the Material and Mystical Worlds.* New York, G. P. Putnam's Sons.

Moir, J. Reid (1916) Pre-Boulder Clay man. *Nature, 98:* 109.

Moir, J. Reid (1924) Tertiary man in England. *Natural History, 24:* 637–654.

Monypenny, William F. and Buckle, George E. (1929) *The Life of Benjamin Disraeli, Earl of Beaconsfield.* Rev. edition. Vol. 2. New York, Macmillan.

Moose, J. Robert (1911) *Village Life in Korea.* Nashville, Publishing House of the Methodist Episcopal Church, South. HRAF A11 Korea.

Morgan, Harry Titterton (1942) *Chinese Cymbols and Superstitions.* South Pasadena, P. D. and Jane Perkins. HRAF China AF1, Doc # 18.

Munro, Neil Gordon (1963). *Ainu Creed and Cult.* Seligman, B. Z., ed. New York, Columbia University Press. HRAF AB6 Ainu, No. 7, p. 58.

Murphy, Gardner and Ballou, Robert, O., eds. (1960) *William James on Psychical Research.* New York, Viking Press.

Murray, T. (1995) *Forbidden Archeology.* Book review. *British Journal for the History of Science, 28:* 377–379.

Myers, Frederick W. H. (1903) *Human Personality and Its Survival of Bodily Death.* 2 vols. New York, Longmans, Green and Co.

Mylonas, George Emmanuel (1950) Mystery Religions of Greece. In Ferm, Virgilius. *Ancient Religions.* New York, Philosophical Library, pp. 171–191.

Nash, C. B. (1982) Psychokinetic control of bacterial growth. *Journal of the American Society for Psychical Research, 51:* 217–21.

Nature (1974) Investigating the paranormal. *251(5476)* (October 18): 559–560.

Nature (2001) News: Search for alien life reasserts its credibility. *412 (6844)* (July 19): 260.

Nelson, Paul A. (1998) Applying design within biology. In Dembski, William A., ed. *Mere Creation: Science, Faith, and Intelligent Design.* Downers Grove, Illinois, Intervarsity Press, pp.148–174.

Nelson, R. D., and Radin, Dean L. (1996) Evidence for direct interaction between consciousness and physical systems: Princeton Engineering Anomalies Research Laboratory, Princeton University, Princeton, N.J., USA. In *Consciousness Research Abstracts. Toward A Science of Consciousness 1996 "Tucson II."* Journal of Consciousness Studies, p. 161.

Ngubane, Harriet (1977) *Body and Mind in Zulu Medicine: An Ethnography of Health and Disease in Nyuswa-Zulu Thought and Practice.* London, Academic Press. HRAF FX20 Zulu, Doc # 2.

Nicola, John J. (1974) *Diabolical Possession and Exorcism.* Rockford, Illinois, Tan Books and Publishers, Inc.

Oakley, K. P. (1980) Relative dating of the fossil hominids of Europe. *Bulletin of the British Museum (Natural History), Geology Series, 34(1):* 1–63.

Oakley, K. P., and Montagu, M. F. A. (1949) A re-consideration of the Galley Hill skeleton. *Bulletin of the British Museum (Natural History), Geology Series, 1(2):* 25–46.

Ogbuene, Chigekwu G. (1999) *The Concept of Man in Igbo Myths. European University Studies, Series XX: Philosophy.* Vol. 597. Frankfurt, Peter Lang.

Okpewho, Isidore (1998) *Once Upon a Kingdom: Myth, Hegemony, and Identity.* Bloomington, Indiana University Press.

Oldham, R. D. (1893) *A Manual of the Geology of India.* 2nd edition. Calcutta, Geological Survey of India.

Oparin, Alexander I. (1938) *The Origin of Life.* Translated by S. Margulis. New York, Macmillan.

Oparin, Alexander I. (1968) *Genesis and Evolutionary Development of Life.* Translated by E. Maass. New York, Academic Press.

Osborn, Henry Fairfield (1921) The Pliocene man of Foxhall in East Anglia. *Natural History, 21:* 565–576.

Osis, Karlis and Haraldsson, Erlendur (1976) OBEs in Indian swamis: Satya Sai Baba and Dadaji. In Morris, Joanna, Morris, Robert and Roll, W. G., eds. *Research in Parapsychology 1975.* Metuchen, New Jersey, Scarecrow Press.

Oxnard, Charles E. (1975) *Uniqueness and Diversity in Human Evolution.* Chicago, University of Chicago.

Oxnard, Charles E. (1984) *The Order of Man.* New Haven, Yale University.

Page, Roderic D. M. and Holmes, Edward C. (1998) *Molecular Evolution: A Phylogenetic Approach.* Oxford, Blackwell Science, Ltd.

Palca, J. (1990) The other human genome. *Science, 249:* 1104–1105.

Palmer, J. (1985) An Evaluative Report on the Current Status of Parapsychology. U. S. Army Research Institute, European Science Coordination Office, Contract No. DAJA 45-84-M-0405.

Parnia, S. MBBS, MRCP, Waller D., G MD FRCP, Yeates R., BA RN, Fenwick, P., MBBChir, FRCPsych. (2001) A qualitative and quantitative study of the incidence, features and aetiology of near death experiences in cardiac arrest survivors. *Resuscitation, 48* (Feb): 149–156.

Pascoe, E. H. (1920) Petroleum in the Punjab and North West Frontier Province. *Memoirs of the Geological Survey of India, 40(3).* Calcutta, Geological Survey of India.

Pascoe, E. H. (1930) General report for 1929. *Records of the Geological Survey of India, (63):* 1–154. Calcutta, Government of India Central Publications Branch.

Pascoe, E. H. (1959) *A Manual of the Geology of India and Burma.* Vol. II. Calcutta, Geological Survey of India.

Pearson, K. (1914) *Francis Galton: Life and Letters.* Vol. 2. London, n. p.

Pellegrino-Estrich, Robert (1997) *The Miracle Man: The Life Story of João de Deus.* Australia, Triad Publishers.

Pennock, E. S., Lillie, R. J., Zaman, A. S. H., and Yousaf, M. (1989) Structural interpretation of seismic reflection data from Eastern Salt Range and Potwar Plateau, Pakistan. *The American Association of Petroleum Geologists Bulletin, 73:* 841–857.

Phillips, Ted R. (1981) Close encounters of the second kind: Physical traces? *1981 MUFON UFO Symposium Proceedings.* Seguin, Texas, MUFON, Inc., pp. 93–129.

Philostratus (1912) *The Life of Apollonius of Tyana.* Translated by F. C. Conybeare. 2 vols. London, William Heinemann.

Polo de Ondegardo, Juan (1916) *Informaciones Acerca de la Religión y Gobierno de los Incas* [Information concerning the religion and government of the Incas]. Lima. HRAF SE13 Inca, Doc # 5.

Pomerol, C. (1980) *Geology of France.* Paris, Masson.

Powers, William T. (1967) Analysis of UFO reports (letter). *Science, 156:* 11.

Prestwich, J. (1892) On the primitive character of the flint implements of the Chalk Plateau of Kent, with reference to the question of their glacial or pre-glacial age. *Journal of the Royal Anthropological Institute of Great Britain and Ireland, 21(3):* 246–262.

Price, George R. (1955) Science and the supernatural. *Science, 122*: 359–67.

Price, George R. (1972) Apology to Rhine and Soal. *Science, 175:* 359.

Price-Williams, Douglass and Hughes, Doreen J. (1994) Shamanism and altered states of consciousness. *Anthropology of Consciousness, 5(2):* 1–15.

Puthoff, H. E. (1996) CIA-initiated remote viewing program at Stanford Research Institute. *Journal of Scientific Exploration, 10:* 63–76.

Quiring, R., Walldorf, U., Kloter, U. and Gehring, W. J. (1994) Homology of the *eyeless* gene of Drosophilia in the *small eye* gene in mice and *Aniridia* in humans. *Science, 265*: 785–789.

Rabochaya Tribuna (1995) UFOs on air defence radar. April 19, 1990. Translated by U.S. Foreign Broadcast Information Service. Cited by Don Berliner, Marie Galbraith, and Antonio Honneur in Unidentified Flying Objects Briefing Document, private publication, December 1995.

Radin, Dean L. (1997) *The Conscious Universe: The Scientific Truth of Psychic Phenomena.* San Francisco, Harper Edge.

Radin, Dean L. and Ferrari, D. C. (1991) Effects of consciousness on the fall of dice: A meta-analysis. *Journal of Scientific Exploration, 5:* 61–84.

Radin, Dean L. and Nelson, R. D. (1989) Evidence for consciousness-related anomalies in random physical systems. *Foundations of Physics, 19:* 1499–1514.

Raff, R. and Kaufman, T. (1991) *Embryos, Genes, and Evolution.* 2nd edition. Bloomington, Indiana University Press.

Ragazzoni, Giuseppe (1880) La collina di Castenedolo, solto il rapporto antropologico, geologico ed agronomico. *Commentari dell'Ateneo di Brescia,* April 4, pp. 120–128. (*)

Randle, Kevin D. and Schmitt, Donald R. (1991) *UFO Crash at Roswell.* New York, Avon Books.

Raum, Ott Friedrich (1973*) The Social Functions of Avoidances and*

Taboos Among the Zulu. Berlin, Walter de Gruyter. HRAF FX20 Zulu, Doc #15.

Rayleigh, Lord (1919) Presidential Address to the Society for Psychical Research. *Proceedings of the Society for Psychical Research, XXX:* 275–290.

Reck, Hans (1914) Zweite vorläufige Mitteilungen über den Fund eines fossilen Menschenskeletts aus Zentral-afrika. *Sitzungsbericht der Gesellschaft der naturforschender Freunde Berlins, 3:* 81–95. (*)

Rees, Martin (2000) *Just Six Numbers: The Deep Forces That Shape the Universe.* New York, Basic Books.

Richet, Charles Robert (1884) La Suggestion Mentale et le Calcul des Probabilités. *Revue Philosophique, 18:* 609.

Richet, Charles Robert (1923) *Thirty Years of Psychical Research; Being a Treatise on Metapsychics.* New York, The Macmillan Company.

Ring, Kenneth (1980) *Life at Death: A Scientific Investigation of the Near-Death Experience.* New York, Coward, McCann & Geoghegan.

Ring, Kenneth (1984) *Heading Toward Omega: In Search of the Meaning of the Near-Death Experience.* New York, William Morrow.

Ring, Kenneth, and Lawrence, Madelaine (1993) Further evidence for veridical perception during near-death experiences. *Journal of Near-Death Studies, 11(4)* (Summer): 223–229.

Ritter, Malcolm (1995) Study: Y chromosome traced to one male. *Santa Barbara News Press.* 23 November, p. A6.

Robinson, J. T. (1953) *Meganthropus,* australopithecines and hominids. *American Journal of Physical Anthropology, 11:* 1–38.

Rogers, A. R. and Jorde, L. B. (1995) Genetic evidence on modern human origins. *Human Biology, 67(1):* 1–36.

Rogo, D. Scott (1982) *Miracles: A Parascientific Inquiry into Wondrous Phenomena.* New York, The Dial Press.

Rojcewicz, Peter M. (1984) *The Boundaries of Orthodoxy: A Folkloric Look at the UFO Phenomenon.* 2 vols. Ph.D. Dissertation, University of Pennsylvania, Philadelphia.

Routledge, Katherine (1919) *The Mystery of Easter Island.* London, Sifton, Praed. HRAF OY2 Easter Islanders, Doc. #15.

Rowe, John Howland (1946) Inca Culture at the time of the Spanish Conquest. In Steward, Julian H., ed. *Handbook of South Ameri-*

can Indians. Vol. 2. Washington, D.C., Government Printing Office, pp. 183–330. HRAF SE13 Inca, Doc #1.

Rubik, Beverly (1996) Volitional effects of healers on a bacterial system. In Rubik, B., ed. *Life at the Edge of Science*. Philadelphia, Institute for Frontier Science, pp. 99–117.

Rusch, W. H., Sr. (1971) Human footprints in rocks. *Creation Research Society Quarterly, 7:* 201–202.

Ruse, Michael (1982) *Darwinism Defended: A Guide to the Evolution Controversies*. Reading, Addison-Wesley, Advanced Book Program/World Science Division.

Sabom, Michael B. (1982) *Recollections of Death: A Medical Investigation*. New York, Harper & Row.

Sagan, Carl (1995) *The Demon Haunted World*. New York, Random House.

Sahni, Birbal (1944) Age of the Saline Series in the Salt Range of the Punjab. *Nature, 153:* 462–463.

Sahni, Birbal (1945) Microfossils and problems of Salt Range Geology. *Proceedings of the National Academy of Sciences, India, 1944*. Section B, Vol. 14, pp. i–xxxii.

Sahni, Birbal (1947a) The age of the Saline Series in the Salt Range (Second Symposium). Concluding remarks. *Proceedings of the National Academy of Sciences, India, 1945*. Section B, Vol. 16, pp. 243–247.

Sahni, Birbal (1947b) Microfossils and the Salt Range Thrust. *Proceedings of the National Academy of Sciences, India, 1945*. Section B, Vol. 16, pp. i–xlx.

Saltmarsh, H. F. (1938) *Evidence of Personal Survival from Cross Correspondences*. London, G. Bell & Sons, Ltd.

Salvini-Plawen, L. and Mayer, Ernst (1977) On the evolution of photoreceptors and eye. *Evolutionary Biology, 10:* 207–263.

Sanford, J. T. (1971) Sheguiandah reviewed. *Anthropological Journal of Canada, 9(1):* 2–15.

Satwant, Pasricha and Stevenson, Ian (1986) Near-Death experiences in India: A preliminary report. *The Journal of Nervous and Mental Disease, 143(3):* 165–170.

Schärer, Hans (1963) *Ngaju Religion: The Conception of God among a South Borneo People*. Translated by Rodney Needham. The Hague, M. Nijhoff.

Schiller, F. C. S. (1891) *Riddles of the Sphinx*. London, Swan Sonnenschein.

Schindewolf, O. H. and Seilacher, A. (1955) Beiträge zur Kenntnis des Kambriums in der Salt Range (Pakistan). *Akademie der Wissenschaften und der Literatur. Abhandlungen der Mathematisch Naturwissenschaftlichen Klasse, (10)*. Wiesbaden, Verlag der Akademie der Wissenschaften und der Literatur in Mainz, in Kommision bei Franz Steiner Verlag.

Schmidt, Helmut (1993) Observation of a psychokinetic effect under highly controlled conditions. *Journal of Parapsychology, 57*: 351–372.

Schnabel, J. (1997) *Remote Viewers: The Secret History of America's Psychic Spies*. New York, Dell.

Scholem, Gershom, ed. (1977) *Zohar: The Book of Splendor. Basic Readings from the Kabbalah*. New York, Schocken Books.

Schoolcraft, Henry Rowe. (1848) *The Indian in His Wigwam, or Characteristics of the Red Race of America*. New York.

Schrenck, Leopold von. (1881–1895) *Die Völkner des Amur-Landes. Reissen und Forschungen im Amur-Lande in den Jahren 1854–1856*. [The Peoples of the Amur Region. Travels and research in the Amur region in the years 1854–1856]. Vol. 3. St. Petersburg, Kaiserliche Akademie der Wissenchaften. HRAF RX2 Gilyak, Doc # 2.

Seeland, Nicolas (1882) Die Ghiliaken: eine ethnographische Skizze [The Gilyaks: An Ethnographic Sketch]. *Russische Revue, 21*: 97–130. HRAF RX2 Gilyak, Doc. # 13.

Sergi, Giuseppe (1884) L'uomo terziario in Lombardia. *Archivio per L'Antropologia (Rome), 17*: 199–216. (*)

Sheils, Dean (1978) A cross-cultural study of beliefs in Out-of-The-Body Experiences, waking and sleeping. *Journal of the Society for Psychical Research, 49(775)* (March 1978): 697–741.

Shipman, Pat (1986) Baffling limb on the family tree. *Discover, 7(9)*: 87–93.

Shrimad Bhagavatam—see *Srimad Bhagavatam*.

Shternberg, Lev Íakovlevich (1933) *Giliaki, orochi, gol'dy, negidal'tsy, ainy; stat'i I materialy* [The Gilyaki, Orochi, Goldi, Negiadal, Ainu; articles and materials]. Edited and preface by ÍA. P. Al'kor (Koshkin). Khabarovsk, Dal'giz. HRAF RX2 Gilyak, Doc #1.

Sibley, Charles G., and Ahlquist, Jon E. (1984) The phylogeny of the hominoid primates, as indicated by DNA-DNA hybridization. *Journal of Molecular Evolution, 20*: 2–15.

Sibley, Charles G. and Ahlquist, Jon E. (1987) DNA hybridization evidence of hominoid phylogeny: Evidence from an expanded data set. *Journal of Molecular Evolution, 26:* 99–121.

Slater, Elizabeth (1983a) Conclusions on nine psychologicials. June 30. Mt. Rainier Md. Fund for UFO Research.

Slater, Elizabeth (1983b) Addendum to conclusions on nine psychologicials. October 30. Mt. Rainier Md. Fund for UFO Research.

Slemmons, D. B. (1966) Cenozoic volcanism of the central Sierra Nevada, California. *Bulletin of the California Division of Mines and Geology, 190:* 199–208.

Smith, C. H., ed. (1991) *Alfred Russel Wallace: An Anthology of His Shorter Writings.* Oxford, Oxford University Press.

Smith, Theresa S. (1995) *The Island of the Anishnaabeg: Thunderers and Water Monsters in the Traditional Ojibwe Life-World.* Moscow, Idaho, University of Idaho Press.

Southall, J. (1882) Pliocene man in America. *Journal of the Victoria Institute, 15:* 191–201.

Speck, Frank G. (1931) *A Study of the Delaware Indians Big House Ceremony.* Publications of Pennsylvania Historical Commission. Vol. 2. Harrisburg, Pennsylvania Historical Commission, pp. 22–23.

Spehlmann, R. (1981) *EEG Primer.* New York, Elsevier.

Spencer, Walter Baldwin and Gillen, F. J. (1927*) The Arunta: A Study of a Stone Age People.* London, Macmillan. HRAF OI8 Aranda, Doc # 1.

Spraggett, Allen (1970) *Kathryn Kuhlman—The Woman Who Believes in Miracles.* New York, Crowell.

Sproul, Barbara C. (1979) *Primal Myths: Creating the World.* San Francisco, Harper and Row.

Sri Brahma Samhita (1985) Sanskrit text, Roman transliteration, English equivalents; translated with elaborate purports by Bhaktisiddhanta Sarasvati. Los Angeles, Bhaktivedanta Book Trust.

Sri Caitanya-caritamrta of Krsna dasa Kaviraja Gosvami (1996) Sanskrit text, Roman transliteration, synonyms; translated with elaborate purports by Bhaktivedanta Swami Prabhupada. Los Angeles, Bhaktivedanta Book Trust.

Srimad Bhagavatam of Krsna Dvaipayana Vyasa (1985). Sanskrit text, Roman transliteration, English equivalents; translated with elaborate purports by Bhaktivedanta Swami Prabhupada. Los Angeles, Bhaktivedanta Book Trust.

Staiano, Kathryn Vance (1986) Interpreting signs of illness: A case study in medical semiotics. *Approaches to Semiotics, 72.* Berlin, Mouton de Gruyter. HRAF SA12 Garifuna, Doc. # 5.

Stanner, W. E. H. (1956) The Dreaming. In Hungerford, T. A. G., ed. *Australian Signpost.* Melbourne, F. W. Cheshire, pp. 51–65.

Stapp, Henry P. (1994) *A Report on the Gaudiya Vaishnava Vedanta Form of Vedic Ontology.* Berkeley, Bhaktivedanta Institute.

Stark, Sherle (1990) Dr. Jean Mundy, therapeutic breakthroughs. *UFO, 5(4):* 30–33.

Steiger, Brad (1979) *Worlds Before Our Own.* New York, Berkley.

Steinman, Gary and Cole, Marian N. (1967) Synthesis of biologically pertinent peptides under possible primordial conditions. *Proceedings of the National Academy of Sciences USA, 58:* 735–741.

Stern, J. T., Jr. and Susman, R. L. (1983). The locomotor anatomy of *Australopithecus afarensis. American Journal of Physical Anthropology, 60:* 279–318.

Stevens, E. W. (1887) *The Watseka Wonder: A Narrative of Startling Phenomena Occurring in the Case of Mary Lurancy Vennum.* Chicago, Religio-Philosophical Publishing House.

Stevenson, Ian (1974) *Twenty Cases Suggestive of Reincarnation*, 2nd edition. Charlottesville, University Press of Virginia.

Stevenson, Ian (1984) *Unlearned Language: New Studies in Xenoglossy.* Charlottesville, University Press of Virginia.

Stevenson, Ian (1992) A new look at maternal impressions: An analysis of 50 published cases and reports of two recent examples. *Journal of Scientific Exploration, 6(4):* 353–373.

Stevenson, Ian (1993) Birthmarks and birth defects corresponding to wounds on deceased persons. *Journal of Scientific Exploration, 7(4)* (Winter): 403–416.

Stevenson, Ian (1997) *Reincarnation and Biology: A Contribution to the Etiology of Birthmarks and Birth Defects.* 2 Vols. Westport, Connecticut, Praeger Publishers.

Stone, R. W. (1932) *Building Stones of Pennsylvania.* Harrisburg, Pennsylvania Geological Survey.

Stoneking, M., Bhatia, K. and Wilson, A. C. (1986) Rate of sequence divergence estimated from restricted maps of mitochondrial DNAs from Papua New Guinea. *Cold Springs Harbor Symposium on Quantitative Biology, 51:* 433–439.

Stopes, Henry (1881) Traces of man in the Crag. *British Association for the Advancement of Science, Report of the Fifty-first Meeting,* p. 700.

Stuart, M. (1919) Suggestions regarding the origin and history of the rock-salt deposits of the Punjab and Kohat. *Records of the Geological Survey of India, 50:* 57–97.

Sturrock, Peter A. (1977) Report on a survey of the membership of the American Astronomical Society concerning the UFO problem. Report no. 681, January. Stanford University, California, Institute for Plasma Research.

Susman, R. L., Stern, J. T., Jr. and Jungers, W. L. (1984) Arboreality and bipedality in Hadar hominids. *Folia Primatologica, 43:* 113–156.

Swanton, John Reed (1905) *Social Condition, Beliefs, and Linguistic Relationship of the Tlinget Indians.* Bureau of American Ethnology Annual Report 26, 1904–1905, pp. 391–486. HRAF NA12 Tlingit, Doc #10.

Swift, David W. (1990) *Seti Pioneers: Scientists Talk About Their Search for Extraterrestrial Intelligence.* Tucson, University of Arizona Press.

Talayesva, Don C. (1942) *Sun Chief: The Autobiography of a Hopi Indian.* Edited by Leo W. Simmons. New Haven, Yale University Press. HRAF NT9 Hopi, No. 7, pp. 17–18.

Targ, Russell (1996) Remote viewing at Stanford Research Institute in the 1970s: A memoir. *Journal of Scientific Exploration, 10(1):* 77–88.

Targ, Russell and Puthoff, Harold (1974) Information transmission under conditions of sensory shielding. *Nature, 251(5476)* (October 18): 602–607.

Taylor, Douglas MacRae (1951) *The Black Carib of British Honduras. Publications in Anthropology*, Viking Fund, 17. New York, Wenner-Gren Foundation for Anthropological Research, Inc. HRAF SA12 Garifuna, Doc #7.

Taylor, John (1975) *Superminds.* New York, The Viking Press, Inc.

Taylor, John (1980) *Science and the Supernatural.* New York, E. P. Dutton.

Tedder, W. and Monty, M. (1981) Exploration of long-distance PK: A conceptual replication of the influence on a biological system. In Roll, W. G. et al., eds. *Research in Parapsychology 1980.* Metuchen, New Jersey, Scarecrow, pp. 90–93.

Templeton, Alan R. (1992) Human origins and analysis of mitochondrial DNA sequences. *Science, 255:* 737.

Templeton, Alan R. (1993) The 'Eve' hypothesis: A genetic critique and reanalysis. *American Anthropologist, 95(1):* 51–72.

The Mahabharata of Krsna-Dvaipayana Vyasa (1970) Translated into English prose from the original Sanskrit text by Kisari Mohan Ganguli. 3rd improved edition. New Delhi, Munshiram Manoharlal Publishers.

Thomas, Northcote W. (1914) *Anthropological Report on Ibo-Speaking Peoples of Nigeria. Part IV. Law and Custom of the Ibo of the Asaba District, S. Nigeria.* London, Harrison and Sons. HRAF FF26 Igbo, Doc #20.

Thompson, Richard L. (1993) *Alien Identities: Ancient Insights into Modern UFO Phenomena.* San Diego, Govardhan Hill Publishing.

Thomson, K. S. (1988) *Morphogenesis and Evolution.* Oxford, Oxford University Press.

Thorndike, Lynn (1923) *A History of Magic and Experimental Science.* Vols. I–II, *The First Thirteen Centuries in our Era.* New York, The MacMillan Company.

Thorndike, Lynn (1941) *A History of Magic and Experimental Science.* Vols. V–VI, *The Sixteenth Century.* New York, The MacMillan Company.

Thorndike, Lynn (1958) *A History of Magic and Experimental Science.* Vols. VII–VIII, *The Seventeenth Century.* New York, The MacMillan Company.

Thorne, A. G. and Wolpoff, M. H. (1992) The multiregional evolution of humans. *Scientific American, 266(4): 76–83.*

Thurston, Herbert S. J. (1952) *The Physical Phenomena of Mysticism.* London, Burns Oates.

Townshend, Chauncey Hare (1852) Recent clairvoyance of Alexis Didier. *The Zoist, IX* (January): 402–411.

Townshend, Chauncey Hare (1853) Indisputable clairvoyance of M. Adolphe Didier. *The Zoist, XI* (April): 75–78.

Travis, John (2000a) Human, mouse, rat . . . what's next. Scientists lobby for a chimpanzee genome project. *Science News, 158*: 236–239.

Travis, John (2000b) Molecule sparks origin of life debate. *Science News, 157*: 363.

Travis, J. (2000c) Brain wiring depends on multifaceted gene. *Science News, 157*: 406.

Travis, John (2000d) Placental puzzle: Do captured viral genes make human pregnanices possible? *Science News, 157*: 318–319.

Trinkaus, Erik and Shipman, Pat (1994*) The Neandertals: Of Skeletons, Scientists, and Scandal.* 1st Vintage Books edition. New York, Vintage Books.

Tuttle, R. H. (1985) Ape footprints and Laetoli impressions: A response to the SUNY claims. In Tobias, P. V., ed. *Hominid Evolution: Past, Present, and Future.* New York, Alan R. Liss, pp. 129–133.

Tuttle, R. H. (1990) The pitted pattern of Laetoli feet. *Natural History, 99:* 60–65.

Uchendu, Victor Chikenzie (1965) *The Igbo of Southeast Nigeria.* New York, Holt, Rinehart and Winston. HRAF FF26 Igbo, Doc #4.

U. S. Library of Congress. Congressional Research Service (1983) *Research Into 'Psi' Phenomena: Current Status and Trends of Congressional Concern.* Compiled by C. H. Dodge.

Utts, Jessica (1996) An assessment of the evidence for psychic functioning. *Journal of Scientific Exploration, 10:* 3–30.

Valentine, Jerris (1993) *The Garifuna Understanding of Death.* National Printers, Ltd.

Vallee, Jacques (1969a) *Passport to Magonia: From Folklore to Flying Saucers.* Chicago, Henry Regnery Company.

Vallee, Jacques (1969b) The pattern behind UFO landings. In Michel,

Aimé. *The Humanoids*. Charles Bowen, editor. Chicago, Henry Regnery Company.

Vallee, Jacques (1979) *Messengers of Deception*. Berkeley, California, And/Or Press.

Vallee, Jacques (1988) *Dimensions: A Casebook of Alien Contact*. New York, Ballantine Books.

Vecsey, Christopher (1983) *Traditional Ojibwa Religion and Its Historical Changes*. Philadelphia, The American Philosophical Society.

Velasco, Jean-Jacques (1987) Scientific approach and results of studies into the unidentified aerospace phenomena in France. *MUFON 1987 International UFO Symposium Proceedings*. Seguin, Texas, MUFON, Inc., pp. 51–58.

Vigilant, L., Stoneking, M., Harpending, H., Hawkes, K. and Wilson, A. C. (1991) African populations and the evolution of human mitochondrial DNA. *Science, 253*: 1503–1507.

Wade, Jenny (1996) *Changes of Mind: A Holonomic Theory of the Evolution of Consciousness*. Albany, State University of New York Press.

Wagner, M. W. and Monet, M. (1979) Attitudes of college professors toward extrasensory preception. *Zetetic Scholar, (5)*: 7–16.

Walker, J. C. G. (1977) *Evolution of the Atmosphere*. New York, Macmillan.

Wallace, Alfred Russel (1869) Sir Charles Lyell on geological climates and the origin of species. *Quarterly Review, 126:* 359–394. Authorship acknowledged after publication.

Wallace, Alfred Russel (1870) *Contributions to the Theory of Natural Selection. A Series of Essays*. London, Macmillan.

Wallace, Alfred Russel (1874) A defence of modern spiritualism. Parts 1 and 2. *Fortnightly Review, 15 (new series)(89)* (1874): 630–657; *(90)* (1874): 785–807.

Wallace, Alfred Russel (1876) Presidential address to Section D (Biology) of the British Association for the Advancement of Science, delivered in Glasgow, September 6, 1876.

Wallace, Alfred Russel (1885a) Are the phenomena of spiritualism in harmony with science? *The Medium and Daybreak, 16*: 809–810.

Wallace, Alfred Russel (1885b) Harmony of spiritualism and science. *Light, 5*: 352.

Wallace, Alfred Russel (1887) The antiquity of man in North America. *Nineteenth Century, 22*: 667–679.

Wallace, Alfred Russel (1892) Spiritualism. *Chamber's Encyclopaedia.* Vol. 9. London, William and Robert Chambers, Ltd., pp. 645–649.

Wallace, Alfred Russel (1896) *Miracles and Modern Spiritualism.* 3rd ed. London, George Redway.

Wallace, Alfred Russel (1905) *My Life: A Record of Events and Opinions.* 2 vols. London, Chapman & Hall.

Wallace, Bruce (1984) Adaptation, neo-Darwinian tautology and population fitness. A reply. In Hecht, M. H., Wallace, B. and Prance, G. T., eds. *Evolutionary Biology, 17:* 59–71.

Wallace, D. C. (1992) Mitochondrial genetics: A paradigm for aging and degenerative diseases? *Science, 256*: 628–632.

Wallis, C. (1996) Faith and healing: Can prayer, faith and spirituality really improve your physical health? A growing and surprising body of scientific evidence says they can. *Time, 147*: 58.

Walsh, William T. (1947) *Our Lady of Fatima.* New York, Macmillan.

Walton, J. C. (1977) Organization and the origin of life. *Origins, 4:* 16–35.

Wambach, H. (1981) *Life Before Life.* New York, Bantam.

Webb, David (1985) The influence of hypnosis in the investigation of abduction cases. *MUFON 1985 UFO Symposium Proceedings.* Sequin, Texas, MUFON, Inc., pp. 88–95.

Webb, Walter N. (1988) Encounter at Buff Ledge: A UFO case history. *MUFON 1988 International UFO Symposium Proceedings.* Seguin, Texas. MUFON, Inc., pp. 20–36.

Wells, Jonathan (1998) Unseating naturalism: Insights from developmental biology. In Dembski, William A. ed. *Mere Creation: Science, Faith, and Intelligent Design.* Downers Grove, Illinois, Intervarsity Press, pp. 51–68.

Wendt, H. (1972) *From Ape to Adam.* Indianapolis, Bobbs-Merrill.

Whitney, Josiah D. (1880) The auriferous gravels of the Sierra Nevada of California. *Harvard University, Museum of Comparative Zoology Memoir, 6(1).*

Whitrow, G. (1959) *The Structure and Evolution of the Universe.* New York, Harper & Row.

Wilberforce, Samuel (1860) Origin of species. *Quarterly Review, 108:* 225–264.

Winchell, A. (1881) *Sparks from a Geologist's Hammer.* Chicago, S. C. Griggs.

Winslow, C. F. (1873) The President reads extracts from a letter from Dr. C. F. Winslow relating the discovery of human remains in Table Mountain, Cal. (Jan 1). *Proceedings of the Boston Society of Natural History, 15:* 257–259.

Wodak, J. and Oldroyd, D. (1995) 'Vedic creationism': A new twist to the evolution debate. *Social Studies of Science, 28:* 192–213.

Wood, B. A. (1987) Who is the 'real' *Homo habilis? Nature, 327:* 187–188.

Wright, G. F. (1912) *Origin and Antiquity of Man.* Oberlin, Bibliotheca Sacra.

Wynne, A. B. (1875) The Trans-Indus Salt Range in the Kohat District, with an appendix on the Kohat Mines or Quarries, by H. Warth. *Memoirs of the Geological Society of India, 11(2).* Calcutta, Geological Survey of India.

Wynne, A. B. (1878) On the Geology of the Salt Range in the Punjab. *Memoirs of the Geological Survey of India, 14.* Calcutta, Geological Survey of India.

Yeats, R. S., Khan, S. H., and Akhtar, M. (1984) Late Quaternary deformation of the Salt Range of Pakistan. *Geological Society of America Bulletin, 95:* 958–966.

Zuber, Rudolf (1914) Beiträge zur Geologie des Punjab (Ostindien). *Jahrbuch der Geologischen Reichsanstalt, 64: 32–356.*

INDEX

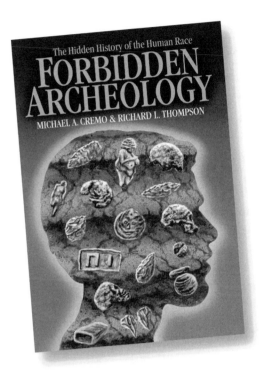

Forbidden Archeology

by Michael A. Cremo &
Richard L. Thompson

Scientific Establishment Found Guilty of Withholding Evidence!

The evolutionists' "knowledge filter," at work over the last 200 years, has left us with a radically altered view of human origins and antiquity.

Since 1993, when the controversial book *Forbidden Archeology* was first published, it has shocked the scientific world with its extensive evidence for extreme human antiquity. It documents hundreds of anomalies in the archeological record that contradict the prevailing theory, and shows how this massive amount of evidence was systematically filtered out!

This book puts all the pieces on the table. You can then judge for yourself how objective the scientific community is in its pursuit of knowledge.

$44.95 ISBN: 978-0-89213-294-2, 6"x 9", hardbound, 952 pages, 25 tables, 141 illustrations

"One of the landmark intellectual achievements of the late twentieth century... Sooner or later, whether we like it or not, our species is going to have to come to terms with the facts that are so impressively documented... and these facts are stunning."

—Graham Hancock, author of *Fingerprints of the Gods*

Order your copies today!

Available from your local bookseller, or just fill out the order form in back and fax it to **559-337-2354,** or call us toll free at **1-800-443-3361**.

Abridged Version

352 pages
Softbound

$15.95

ISBN: 978-0-89213-325-3

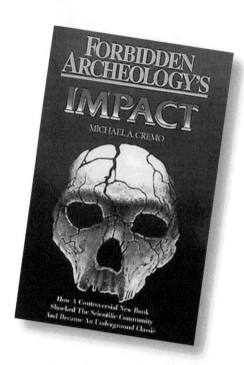

Forbidden Archeology's
IMPACT

*How a Controversial New Book Shocked
the Scientific Community and Became
an Underground Classic*

Compiled by
Michael A. Cremo

How did the scientific community respond
to *Forbidden Archeology*'s cogent challenge to its deeply held beliefs? In this
provocative compilation of reviews, correspondence, and media interviews, readers get a stunning inside look at how the
book itself almost became a victim of the
"knowledge filter."

$35.00 ISBN: 0-89213-283-3
6" x 9", hardbound, 600 pages

Here are some of the varied reactions to *Forbidden Archeology*:

"All the reasons and evidence why modern humans are not rather recent, but
most ancient."
—Cyprian Broodbank, in *Antiquity*, December 1993

"A must for anyone interested in keeping up with goofy, popular anthropology:
it is a veritable cornucopia of dreck."
—Johnathon Marks, *American Journal of Physical
Anthropology*, January 1994

"Your book is pure humbug and does
not deserve to be taken seriously by
anyone but a fool."
—Richard Leakey, anthropologist and author

"A stunning description of some of
the evidence that was once known to
science, but which has disappeared
from view due to the 'knowledge filter'
that protects the ruling paradigm."
—Phillip E. Johnson, School of Law, University of California at Berkeley, author of *Darwin on Trial*

"Cremo and Thompson have thrown
down a perfectly reasonable challenge.
If 'respectable' scientists choose to
ignore it, the rest of us will feel justified
in concluding it is one more argument
for the formidable case against scientific orthodoxy presented in *Forbidden
Archeology*."
—From the Foreword by Colin Wilson

Book Order Form

☎ Telephone orders: Call 1-800-HIDDEN-1 (1-800-443-3361).
   Have your credit card ready.

✳ Fax orders: 559-337-2354

✉ Postal orders: Torchlight Publishing, P. O. Box 52,
   Badger, CA 93603, USA

▲ **World Wide Web: www.torchlight.com**

Please send the following:

☐ *Forbidden Archeology* — The full, unabridged original edition, 952 pages,
   141 illustrations, 25 tables, hardback, $44.95

☐ *Forbidden Archeology's Impact* — 600 pages, hardback, $35.00

☐ *The Hidden History of the Human Race* — The abridged version of *Forbidden
   Archeology,* 352 pages, 120 illustrations, softback, $15.95

☐ *Human Devolution* — 558 pages, hardback, $35.00

☐ **Please send me your catalog and info on other books by Torchlight Publishing.**

Company_____

Name_____

Address_____

City _____ State_____ Zip_____

(I understand that I may return any books for a full refund—no questions asked.)

Payment:

☐ Check / money order enclosed   ☐ VISA   ☐ MasterCard   ☐ AmEx

Card number_____

Name on card_____ Exp. date_____

Signature_____

Shipping and handling (CA residents add 7.75% sales tax):

Forbidden Archeology, Forbidden Archeology's Impact, and Human Devolution —
Book rate: USA $6.00 for first book, $3.00 for each additional book.
The Hidden History of the Human Race — Book rate: USA $4.00 for first book, $3.00 for
each additional book.

Surface shipping may take 3–4 weeks. Foreign orders: please phone, e-mail, or fax for details.